# Sams Teach Yourself Java™ in 21 Days

Rogers Cadenhead

# Sams**Teach Yourself**

# Java

## in **21 Days**

### Eighth Edition

221 F

Hobo

# Sams Teach Yourself Java in 21 Days, Eighth Edition

Copyright © 2020 by Pearson Education, Inc.

ISBN-13: 978-0-672-33795-6
ISBN-10: 0-672-33795-9

Library of Congress Control Number: 2019912868

1 2020

## Trademarks

All terms mentioned in this book that are known to be trademarks or service marks have been appropriately capitalized. Sams Publishing cannot attest to the accuracy of this information. Use of a term in this book should not be regarded as affecting the validity of any trademark or service mark.

Microsoft and/or its respective suppliers make no representations about the suitability of the information contained in the documents and related graphics published as part of the services for any purpose all such documents and related graphics are provided "as is" without warranty of any kind. Microsoft and/or its respective suppliers hereby disclaim all warranties and conditions with regard to this information, including all warranties and conditions of merchantability, whether express, implied or statutory, fitness for a particular purpose, title and non-infringement. In no event shall Microsoft and/or its respective suppliers be liable for any special, indirect or consequential damages or any damages whatsoever resulting from loss of use, data or profits, whether in an action of contract, negligence or other tortious action, arising out of or in connection with the use or performance of information available from the services.

The documents and related graphics contained herein could include technical inaccuracies or typographical errors. Changes are periodically added to the information herein. Microsoft and/or its respective suppliers may make improvements and/or changes in the product(s) and/or the program(s) described herein at any time. Partial screen shots may be viewed in full within the software version specified.

Microsoft® Windows®, and Microsoft Office® are registered trademarks of the Microsoft Corporation in the U.S.A. and other countries. This book is not sponsored or endorsed by or affiliated with the Microsoft Corporation.

## Warning and Disclaimer

Every effort has been made to make this book as complete and as accurate as possible, but no warranty or fitness is implied. The information provided is on an "as is" basis. The author and the publisher shall have neither liability nor responsibility to any person or entity with respect to any loss or damages arising from the information contained in this book.

## Special Sales

For information about buying this title in bulk quantities, or for special sales opportunities (which may include electronic versions; custom cover designs; and content particular to your business, training goals, marketing focus, or branding interests), please contact our corporate sales department at corpsales@pearsoned.com or (800) 382-3419.

For government sales inquiries, please contact governmentsales@pearsoned.com.

For questions about sales outside the U.S., please contact international@pearsoned.com.

**Editor-in-Chief**
Mark Taub

**Acquisitions Editor**
Greg Doench

**Development Editor**
Mark Taber

**Project Editor**
Mandie Frank

**Copy Editor**
Kitty Wilson

**Technical Editor**
Boris Minkin

**Design**
Chuti Prasertsith

**Proofreading**
Donna Mulder

**Indexer**
Cheryl Lenser

**Composition**
codeMantra

# Figure Credits

# Contents at a Glance

# Table of Contents

## LESSON 5: Creating Classes and Methods                                        123

## LESSON 12: Responding to User Input                    333

## LESSON 13: Creating Java2D Graphics                    359

# Dedication

*To my sons, Max, Eli, and Sam Cadenhead, who have flown the coop and earned their places at two great Florida universities. In the decades since I completed my trek through Stephen F. Austin State University, Richland College, the University of Texas at Arlington, and the University of North Texas, I've learned that you bank all of the experience and education from college and draw from it for the rest of your life. I'm extremely proud to see you surpass me academically.*

*—Dad*

# About the Author

**Rogers Cadenhead** is an experienced software developer who has written more than 30 books on programming and web publishing, including *Sams Teach Yourself Java in 24 Hours* and *Absolute Beginner's Guide to Minecraft Mods Programming*. He creates applications on the ServiceNow cloud platform, using Java and JavaScript. He maintains this book's official website, at www.java21days.com, and can be contacted on Twitter at @rcade and on his weblog, at http://workbench.cadenhead.org.

# Acknowledgments

A book of this scope (and heft!) requires the hard work and dedication of numerous people. Most of them are at Pearson, and to them I owe considerable thanks—in particular, to Boris Minkin, Mandie Frank, Kitty Wilson, Greg Doench, and Mark Taber. Most of all, thanks to my wife, Mary, and my sons, Max, Eli, and Sam.

I'd also like to thank readers who have sent helpful comments about corrections, typos, and suggested improvements regarding this book and its prior editions. The list includes the following people: Dave Barton, Patrick Benson, Ian Burton, Lawrence Chang, Jim DeVries, Ryan Esposto, Kim Farr, Sam Fitzpatrick, Bruce Franz, Owen Gailar, Rich Getz, Bob Griesemer, Jenny Guriel, Brenda Henry-Sewell, Ben Hensley, Jon Hereng, Drew Huber, John R. Jackson, Bleu Jaegel, Natalie Kehr, Mark Lehner, Stephen Loscialpo, Brad Kaenel, Chris McGuire, Paul Niedenzu, E.J. O'Brien, Chip Pursell, Pranay Rajgarhia, Peter Riedlberger, Darrell Roberts, Luke Shulenburger, Mike Tomsic, John Walker, Joseph Walsh, Mark Weiss, P.C. Whidden, Chen Yan, Kyu Hwang Yeon, and J-F. Zurcher.

# We Want to Hear from You!

As the reader of this book, *you* are our most important critic and commentator. We value your opinion and want to know what we're doing right, what we could do better, what areas you'd like to see us publish in, and any other words of wisdom you're willing to pass our way.

We welcome your comments. You can email or write to let us know what you did or didn't like about this book—as well as what we can do to make our books better.

*Please note that we cannot help you with technical problems related to the topic of this book.*

When you write, please be sure to include this book's title and author as well as your name and email address. We will carefully review your comments and share them with the author and editors who worked on the book.

Email:   community@informit.com


# Reader Services

Register your copy of *Sams Teach Yourself Java in 21 Days* at informit.com for convenient access to downloads, updates, and corrections as they become available. To start the registration process, go to informit.com/register and log in or create an account.* Enter the product ISBN, 9780672337956, and click Submit. Once the process is complete, you will find any available bonus content under Registered Products.

*Be sure to check the box that you would like to hear from us in order to receive exclusive discounts on future editions of this product.

# Introduction

Some revolutions catch the world by surprise. Slack, Linux, the Popeye's chicken sandwich, and *The Masked Singer* all rose to prominence unexpectedly.

The remarkable success of the Java programming language, on the other hand, caught nobody by surprise. Java has been a source of great expectations since its launch 25 years ago. When Java was introduced in web browsers, a torrent of publicity welcomed the arrival of the new language.

Sun Microsystems cofounder Bill Joy proclaimed, "This represents the end result of nearly 15 years of trying to come up with a better programming language and environment for building simpler and more reliable software."

Sun, which created Java in 1991 and first released it to the public four years later, was acquired by Oracle in 2010. Oracle, which has been committed to Java development since its earliest years, has continued to support the language and produce new versions. There's now an open source implementation as well.

Java has lived up to a considerable amount of its early hype. The language is as strong a part of software development as the beverage of the same name. One kind of Java keeps programmers up nights. The other kind enables programmers to rest easier after they have developed their software.

Java was originally offered as a technology for enhancing websites with programs that run in browsers. Today, it's more likely to be found on servers, driving dynamic cloud applications backed by relational databases on some of the Web's largest sites and on millions of Android cell phones and tablets running popular apps such as Subway Surfers and Instagram.

Each new release of Java strengthens its capabilities as a general-purpose programming language for a wide range of environments. Java is being put to use in desktop applications, Internet servers, mobile devices, and many other environments.

Now in its 13th release—Java 12—the Java language has matured into a full-featured competitor to other general-purpose development languages, such as C++, Python, and JavaScript.

You might be familiar with Java programming tools such as Eclipse, NetBeans, and IntelliJ IDEA. These programs make it possible to develop functional Java programs, and you also can use Oracle's Java Development Kit and the open source OpenJDK. Those two kits, which are available for free on the Web with different licensing terms, offer command-line tools for writing, compiling, and testing Java programs. NetBeans, another free tool offered by Apache, is an integrated development environment for the creation of Java programs. It can be downloaded from https://netbeans.apache.org.

This book introduces you to all aspects of Java software development, using the most current version of the language and the best available techniques in Java Standard Edition, the most widely used version of the language. Programs are prepared and tested using Apache NetBeans, so you can quickly demonstrate the skills you master in each lesson.

Reading this book will help you understand why Java has become the most widely employed programming language on the planet.

# How This Book Is Organized

*Sams Teach Yourself Java in 21 Days* teaches you about the Java language and how to use it to create applications for any computing environment. By the time you have finished the book, you'll have well-rounded knowledge of Java and the Java class libraries. Using your new skills, you will be able to develop your own programs for tasks such as web services, database connectivity, XML processing, and network programming.

You'll learn by doing in this book, creating several programs in each lesson that demonstrate the topics being introduced. The source code for all these programs is available on the book's official website, at www.java21days.com, along with other supplemental material such as answers to reader questions.

This book covers the Java language and its class libraries in 21 lessons, organized into three parts, each covering a broad area of developing Java programs.

In the first part, you learn about the Java language itself:

- Lesson 1 covers the basics—what Java is, why you should learn the language, and how to create software using a powerful style of development called object-oriented programming. In this lesson, you'll create your first Java application.
- In Lesson 2, you'll dive into the fundamental Java building blocks—data types, variables, and expressions.

- Lesson 3 goes into detail about how to deal with objects in Java—how to create them, use their variables, call their methods, and compare them.

- In Lesson 4, you'll give Java programs some brainpower using conditionals, and you'll work with arrays and loops.

- Lesson 5 fully explores creating classes—the basic building blocks of any Java program.

- In Lesson 6, you'll discover more about interfaces and packages, which are useful for grouping classes and organizing a class hierarchy.

- Lesson 7 covers three powerful features of Java: exceptions, the ability to deal with errors; threads, the capability to run different parts of a program simultaneously; and assertions, a technique for making programs more reliable.

Part 2 is dedicated to the most useful classes offered by Oracle for use in your own Java programs:

- Lesson 8 introduces data structures that you can use as an alternative to strings and arrays—array lists, stacks, maps, hash maps, and bit sets. It also describes a special `for` loop that makes them easier to use.

- Lesson 9 begins a five-lesson exploration of visual programming. You'll learn how to create a graphical user interface using Swing classes for interfaces, graphics, and user input.

- Lesson 10 covers more than a dozen interface components you can use in a Java program, including buttons, text fields, sliders, scrolling text areas, and icons.

- Lesson 11 explains how to make a user interface look marvelous by using *layout managers*, a set of classes that determines how components on an interface are arranged.

- Lesson 12 concludes the coverage of Swing with event-handling classes, which enable a program to respond to mouse clicks and other user interactions.

- In Lesson 13, you'll learn about drawing shapes and characters on user interface components.

- Lesson 14 finishes the exploration of Swing with the introduction of a helpful threaded class and a sophisticated layout manager.

Part 3 moves into advanced topics:

- Lesson 15 provides a complete introduction to lambda expressions, also called *closures*. Lambda expressions make it possible to use a new type of Java coding, called *functional programming*, for the first time. Inner classes are explored in greater depth as they relate to closures.

■ Lesson 16 covers input and output using *streams*, a set of classes that enables file access, network access, and other sophisticated data handling.

■ In Lesson 17, you'll extend your knowledge of streams to write programs that communicate on the Internet using HTTP, including socket programming, buffers, channels, and URL handling.

■ Lesson 18 shows you how to connect to relational databases using Java Database Connectivity (JDBC). You'll learn how to exploit the capabilities of Derby, the open source database that's included with Java.

■ Lesson 19 covers how to read and write RSS documents using the XML Object Model (XOM), an open source Java class library. RSS feeds, one of the most popular XML dialects, enable millions of people to follow site updates and other new web content.

■ Lesson 20 explores how to write web services clients with another open source library, Apache XML-RPC.

■ Lesson 21 brings it all together, showing how to create a puzzle game called `Banko`. You'll take a deep dive into the source code of a complete Java application as a trial run on the process you'll undertake when you close the book and create your own full-fledged programs.

## Who Should Read This Book

This book teaches the Java language to three groups:

■ Novices who are relatively new to programming

■ People who have been introduced to earlier versions of Java

■ Experienced developers in other languages, such as Visual C++, JavaScript, and Python

When you're finished with this book, you'll be able to tackle any aspect of the Java language. You'll also be able to tackle your own ambitious programming projects, both on and off the Web.

If you're somewhat new to programming or have never written a program, you might wonder whether this is the right book for you. Because all the concepts in this book are illustrated with working programs, you'll be able to work your way through the subject regardless of your experience level. If you understand what variables and loops are, you'll be able to benefit from this book. You might want to read this book if any of the following are true:

- You had some beginning programming lessons in school, you grasp what programming is, and you've heard that Java is easy to learn, powerful, and cool.
- You've programmed in another language for a few years, you keep hearing great things about Java, and you want to see whether it lives up to its hype.
- You've heard that Java is great for web application and Android programming.

If you've never been introduced to object-oriented programming, which is the style of programming that Java embodies, don't be discouraged. This book assumes that you have no background in object-oriented design. You'll get a chance to learn this development methodology as you're learning Java.

If you're a complete beginner to programming, this book might move a little fast for you. Java is a good language to start with, though, and if you take it slowly and work through all the examples, you can still pick up Java and start creating your own programs.

# Conventions Used in This Book

**NOTE** — A Note presents an interesting, sometimes technical, piece of information related to the discussion.

**TIP** — A Tip offers advice, such as an easier way to do something.

**CAUTION** — A Caution advises you of potential problems and helps you steer clear of disaster.

Text that you type and text that appears onscreen is presented in a `monospace` font:

```
Monospace looks like this. Hi, Mom!
```

This font represents how text looks onscreen. Placeholders for variables and expressions appear in `monospace italic`.

The end of each lesson offers several special features: answers to commonly asked questions about the lesson's subject matter, a quiz to test your knowledge of the material, two exercises that you can try on your own, and a practice question in case you're preparing for Java certification. Solutions to the exercises and the answer to the certification question can be found on the book's official website, at www.java21days.com.

# PART I
# The Java Language

# LESSON 1
# Getting Started with Java

*The thing that Java tries to do and is actually remarkably successful at is spanning a lot of different domains, so you can do app server work, you can do cell phone work, you can do scientific programming, you can write software, do interplanetary navigation, all kinds of stuff...*

—Java language creator James Gosling

When the Java programming language was unleashed on the public over 20 years ago, it was an inventive toy for web browsers that had the potential to be much more.

The word *potential* is a compliment that comes with an expiration date. Sooner or later, potential must be realized, or new words and phrases are used in its place, such as *slacker*, *letdown*, *waste of space*, or *major disappointment to your mother and me*.

As you develop your skills over the course of this book, you'll be in a great position to judge whether the language has lived up to all the early hype.

You'll also become a Java programmer with a lot of potential.

# The Java Language

Since its first public implementation as Java 1.0 in 1996, the Java programming language has lived up to many of the expectations that accompanied its arrival. More than 15 million programmers have learned the language and are using it in places like Google, NASA, IBM, ServiceNow, and Netflix. It's a core part of the academic curriculum in computer science departments around the world. First used to create simple programs on web pages, Java can be found today in the following places (and many more):

- Cloud servers
- Relational databases
- Orbiting telescopes
- Ebook readers
- Cell phones

Although Java remains useful in web applications and servers, its ambitions now extend far beyond the Web. Java has matured into one of the most popular general-purpose programming languages.

## History of the Language

The story of the Java language is well known by this point. James Gosling and a team of developers were working on an interactive TV project at Sun Microsystems in the 1990s when Gosling became frustrated with C++, the programming language being used. C++ is an object-oriented programming language that had been developed a decade earlier as an extension of the C language.

To address things making him irate about C++, Gosling holed up in his office and created a new language that was suitable for his project.

Although that interactive TV project flopped, Gosling's language had unforeseen applicability to a new medium that was becoming popular at the same time: the World Wide Web.

Java was released to the public for the first time as "alpha version 1.0a2" on March 23, 1995. Although most of the language's features were primitive compared with those of C++ (and Java today), it had a killer app: Special Java programs called applets could be run as part of web pages on the most popular web browser at that time, Netscape Navigator.

This functionality—the first interactive programming available on the Web—drew so much attention to the new language that several hundred thousand programmers learned Java in its first six months.

By the time that the novelty of Java programs running on web pages wore off, the overall benefits of the language had become clear and all those programmers stuck around. There are more professional Java programmers today than C++ programmers.

Sun Microsystems controlled the development of the Java language from its inception until 2010, when the company was gobbled up by the database and enterprise software giant Oracle in a $7.4 billion deal. Oracle, a longtime user of the language on its own products, has a strong commitment to supporting Java and continues to increase its capabilities with each new release.

## Introduction to Java

Java is an object-oriented, platform-neutral, secure language designed to be easier to learn and harder to misuse than C++.

*Object-oriented programming* (*OOP*) is a software development methodology in which a program is conceptualized as a group of objects that work together. Objects are created from templates called *classes*, and they contain data and the code required to use that data. Java is extremely object oriented, as you'll see later in this lesson when you create your first class and use it to create objects.

*Platform neutrality* is a program's ability to run without modification in different computing environments. Java programs are transformed into a format called *bytecode* that can be run by any computer or device equipped with a Java Virtual Machine (JVM). You can create a Java program on a Windows 10 machine that runs as the same bytecode on a Linux web server, an Apple Mac using OS 10.14, and a Samsung Galaxy S10 phone. As long as a platform has a JVM, it can run the bytecode.

Although the relative ease of learning one language over another is always a point of ferocious contention among programmers, Java was designed to be easier than C++ primarily in the following ways:

- Java automatically takes care of memory allocation and deallocation, freeing programmers from this error-prone and tedious task.
- Java doesn't include pointers, a powerful feature for experienced programmers that can be easily misused and can open up major security vulnerabilities.
- Java includes only single inheritance of classes in object-oriented programming.
- Java doesn't have to be compiled on each different platform, executing the same bytecode everywhere.

The lack of pointers and the presence of automatic memory management are two key elements of Java security.

## Selecting a Development Tool

Now that you've been introduced to Java as a spectator, it's time to put some of these concepts into play and create your first Java program.

As you code your way through the 21 lessons of this book, you'll become well versed in Java's capabilities, including graphics, XML processing, microservices, and database development. You will write programs that can run on computers, web servers, phones, and other computing environments.

Before you get started, you must have software on your computer that can be used to edit, prepare, and run Java programs that use the most up-to-date versions of the language.

Several popular integrated development environments (IDEs) for Java support version 1213, including the open source Apache NetBeans and Eclipse and the commercial IntelliJ IDEA. Java 13 also may be supported by the time you read this.

If you are learning to use these tools at the same time you are learning Java, it can be a somewhat daunting task. Most IDEs are aimed primarily at experienced programmers who want to be more productive, not new people who are taking their first tentative steps into a new language.

The simplest tool for Java development is the Java Development Kit (JDK), which is free and can be downloaded from the Java SE Downloads page at www.oracle.com/technetwork/java/javase/downloads.

Whenever Oracle releases a new version of Java, it also makes a free JDK available over the Web to support that version. The JDK for the most current version of Java should be the first one on the downloads page, which at the time of this writing is Java SE 12.0.2 Oracle JDK.

The drawback of developing Java programs entirely with the JDK is that it's a set of command-line tools with no graphical user interface for editing programs, preparing them to be run, packaging them for deployment, or testing them. A command line is simply a prompt for typing text commands. It's available in Windows as the program Command Prompt and Macs as Terminal.

As an alternative, there's an excellent, free IDE for Java programmers called Apache NetBeans at https://netbeans.apache.org. Although NetBeans is a sophisticated IDE, it is reasonably easy to learn how to use it for the basics of Java program creation and testing. Because NetBeans is simpler to use for most people than the command-line JDK, it's employed throughout this book.

If you don't have a Java development tool on your computer yet and want to try NetBeans, you can find out how to get started with the software in Appendix A, "Using the

NetBeans Integrated Development Environment." The appendix covers how to download and install the IDE and use it to create a sample Java program to make sure it works.

As soon as you have a Java development tool on your computer that supports the most recent version of Java, you're ready to dive into the language.

If you don't have one on your computer yet, now's the time to set one up.

**TIP**

For information on the other IDEs for Java mentioned in this section, visit the IDEA site, at www.jetbrains.com/idea, and the Eclipse site, at www.eclipse.org.

# Object-Oriented Programming

The biggest challenge for a new Java programmer is learning object-oriented programming while learning the Java language.

Although this might sound daunting if you've never programmed in this style before, think of it as a two-for-one discount for your brain. You will learn object-oriented programming by learning Java. There's no other way to learn the language.

Object-oriented programming is an approach to building computer programs that mimics how objects are assembled in the physical world.

By using this style of development, you can create programs that are more reusable, reliable, and understandable. To get to that point, you first must explore how Java embodies the principles of object-oriented programming (often described by its acronym, OOP).

If you already are familiar with object-oriented programming, much of this lesson will be a review for you. Even if you skim the introductory material, you should create the sample program to get some experience in developing, compiling, and running a Java program.

There are many ways to conceptualize a computer program. One way is to think of a program as a series of instructions carried out in sequence; this is called *procedural programming*. The early programming language BASIC is procedural.

Procedural languages mirror how a computer carries out instructions, so the programs you write are tailored to the computer's manner of doing things. One of the first things a procedural programmer must learn is how to break a problem into a series of simple steps that are followed in order.

Object-oriented programming looks at a computer program from a different angle, focusing on the task the program was created to perform rather than on how a computer handles tasks.

In object-oriented programming, a computer program is conceptualized as a set of objects that work together to accomplish a job. Each object is a separate part of the program, interacting with the other parts in highly controlled ways.

For a real-life example of object-oriented design, consider a home stereo system. Most systems are built by hooking together a bunch of different objects, which are more commonly called *components*. If you came back from a shopping trip with a stereo, you might bring home these different objects:

- Speaker components that play midrange and high-frequency sounds
- A subwoofer component that plays low bass frequency sounds
- A tuner component that receives radio broadcast signals
- A CD player component that reads audio data from CDs
- A turntable component that reads audio data from vinyl records

These components are designed to interact with each other using standard input and output connectors. Even if you bought the speakers, subwoofer, tuner, CD player, and turntable from five different companies, you could combine them to form a stereo system—as long as each component has standard connectors.

Object-oriented programming works under the same principle: You put together a program by creating new objects and connecting them to each other and to existing objects. These objects can be ones that you create or ones provided by Oracle, Google, the Apache Project, or another software developer. Each object is a component in the larger program, and they are combined in a standard way. Each object plays a specific role in the larger program.

An *object* is a self-contained component of a computer program that represents a related group of features and is designed to accomplish specific tasks. A well-designed object does the minimum required to get its job done. If an object has too much to do, that's a sign its job could be divided into two or more objects.

## Objects and Classes

Object-oriented programming is modeled on the observation that in the physical world, objects are made up of many kinds of smaller objects.

The capability to combine objects is only one aspect of object-oriented programming. Another is the use of classes.

A *class* is a template used to create an object. Every object created from the same class has similar features and function.

Classes embody all facets of a set of objects. When you write a program in an object-oriented language, you don't define individual objects. Instead, you define classes and use those classes to create the objects.

If you were writing a computer networking program in Java, you could create a `Router` class that describes the features of all Internet routers. These devices have the following common features:

- They connect to a computer's Ethernet port.
- They send and receive information.
- They communicate with Internet servers.

The `Router` class serves as an abstract model for the concept of such a device. To have something concrete you can manipulate in a program, you need an object. You must use the `Router` class to create a `Router` object. The process of creating an object from a class is called *instantiation*, which is why objects also are called *instances*.

A `Router` class can be used to create different `Router` objects in a program, each with different features such as the following:

- Some function as a high-speed modem, whereas others do not.
- They have a security firewall.
- They support different communications protocols.

Even with these differences, two `Router` objects still have enough in common to be recognizable as closely related objects.

Here's another example: Using Java, you could create a class to represent all command buttons—the clickable boxes that appear on windows and other parts of a graphical user interface.

When the `Button` class is developed, it could define these features:

- The text displayed on the button
- The size of the button
- The behavior when it is clicked
- Aspects of its appearance, such as whether it has a 3D shadow

After you define the `Button` class, you can create instances of that button—in other words, `Button` objects. The objects all take on the basic features of a button, as defined by the class. But each one could have a different appearance and slightly different behavior, depending on what you need that object to do.

By creating a `Button` class, you don't have to keep rewriting code for each button you want to use in your programs. You can reuse the `Button` class to create different kinds of buttons as you need them in any program you are working on.

When you write a Java program, you design and construct a set of classes. When your program runs, objects are created from those classes and used as needed. Your task as a Java programmer is to create the right set of classes to accomplish what your program needs to accomplish.

Fortunately, you don't have to start from scratch. The Java language includes the Java Class Library, more than 4,400 classes that implement most of the functionality you will need. These classes are installed along with a development tool such as NetBeans or the JDK.

When you're talking about programming in the Java language, you're actually talking about using this class library and the standard keywords and operators defined in Java.

The class library handles numerous tasks, such as mathematical functions, text processing, graphics display, user interaction, and networking. Working with these classes is no different from working with Java classes you create.

For complicated Java programs, you might create a set of new classes that form their own class library that you can distribute for use in other programs.

Reuse is one of the fundamental benefits of object-oriented programming.

**NOTE**    In the Java Class Library, one of Java's standard classes, `JButton` in the `javax.swing` package, encompasses all the functionality of this hypothetical `Button` example, along with a lot more. You'll get a chance to create objects from this class in Lesson 9, "Creating a Graphical User Interface."

# Attributes and Behavior

A Java class consists of two types of information: attributes and behavior. Both are present in `MarsRobot`, a project you will implement now as a class. This project, a simple simulation of a planetary exploration vehicle, is inspired by the Mars Exploration Rovers used by NASA's Jet Propulsion Laboratory program to do research on the geology of the planet Mars.

Before you create the program, you need to learn some things about how object-oriented programs are designed in Java. These concepts may be difficult to understand as you're introduced to them, but you'll get plenty of practice with them throughout the book.

# Attributes of a Class of Objects

*Attributes* are the data that differentiate one object from another. They can be used to determine the appearance, state, and other qualities of objects that belong to that class.

A Mars exploration vehicle could have the following attributes:

- **Status:** Exploring, moving, returning home
- **Speed:** Measured in miles per hour
- **Temperature:** Measured in degrees Fahrenheit

In a class, attributes are defined by *variables*—places to store information in a computer program. *Instance variables* are attributes that have values that differ from one object to another.

An instance variable defines an attribute of one particular object. The object's class defines what kind of attribute it is, and each instance stores its own value for that attribute. Instance variables also are called *object variables*.

Each class attribute has a single corresponding variable. You change that attribute of the object by changing the value of the variable.

For example, the `MarsRobot` class defines a `speed` instance variable. It must be an instance variable because each robot travels at its own speed. The value of a robot's `speed` instance variable could be changed to make the robot move more quickly or slowly.

Instance variables can be given a value when an object is created and then stay constant throughout the life of the object. They also can be given different values as the object is used in a running program.

For some variables that don't need to be different in each object, it makes more sense to have one value shared by all objects of that class. These attributes are called *class variables*.

A class variable defines an attribute of an entire class. The variable applies to the class itself and to all its instances, so only one value is stored, no matter how many objects of that class have been created in a program.

An example of a class variable for the `MarsRobot` class would be a `topSpeed` variable that holds the maximum speed at which any robot is capable of traveling. If an instance variable were created to hold the speed, each object could have a different value for this variable. This could cause problems because no robot can exceed it.

Using a class variable prevents this problem because all objects of that class share the same value automatically. Each `MarsRobot` object would have access to that variable.

## Behavior of a Class of Objects

*Behavior* refers to the things that a class of objects can do to themselves and to other objects. Behavior can be used to change an object's attributes, receive information from other objects, and send messages to other objects, asking them to perform tasks.

A Mars robot could have the following behavior:

- Check your current temperature
- Begin a survey of the area
- Accelerate or decelerate your speed
- Report your current location

Behavior for a class of objects is implemented using methods.

A *method* is a group of statements in a class that performs a task. Methods are used to accomplish specific tasks on their own objects and on other objects. They are comparable to functions and subroutines in other programming languages. A well-designed method performs only one task.

Objects communicate with each other using methods. Such a method is like one object giving another object a command. A class or an object might call methods in another object for many reasons, including the following:

- To report a change to another object
- To tell the other object to change something about itself
- To ask another object to do something

For example, two Mars robots could use methods to report their locations to each other and avoid collisions, and one robot could tell another to stop so that it can pass by safely.

Just as there are instance and class variables, there also are instance and class methods. Instance methods, which usually are just called *methods*, are used when you are working with an object of a class. If a method changes an individual object, it must be an instance method. Class methods apply to a class itself.

## Creating a Class

So far you have learned about object-oriented programming in the abstract. To see classes, objects, attributes, and behavior in action, you will now develop a `MarsRobot` class, create objects from that class, and work with them in a running program.

**NOTE**
> The main purpose of this project is to explore object-oriented programming. You'll learn more about Java programming syntax in Lesson 2, "The ABCs of Programming."

Before beginning work on MarsRobot, some prep work is required.

This book uses NetBeans as its primary development tool for creating Java programs. NetBeans organizes Java classes into projects. It will be useful to have a project to hold the classes you'll create throughout the lessons in this book. Run NetBeans, and if you have not done so already, create a project by undertaking these steps:

1. Choose the menu command File, New Project. The New Project dialog appears.

2. In the Categories pane, choose Java with Ant.

3. In the Projects pane, choose Java Application and click Next. The New Java Application dialog opens (if Java SE support has been activated).

4. If you're told that Java SE support must be activated, click Activate. When activation is done, the New Java Application dialog appears.

5. In the Project Name text field, enter the name of the project (such as Java21). The Project Folder field is updated as you type the name. Make a note of this folder; it's where your Java programs can be found on your computer.

6. Deselect the check box Create Main Class.

7. Click Finish.

The new project is created. You can use it throughout the book.

If you have created a project already, it likely will be open in NetBeans. If not, choose the menu command File, Open Recent Project to find and select it.

A new class you create will be added to the current project.

To begin your first class, start by creating a new program:

1. Choose the menu command File, New File. The New File dialog opens.

2. In the Categories pane, choose Java.

3. In the File Types pane, choose Empty Java File and click Next. The Empty Java File dialog opens.

4. In the Class Name text field, enter MarsRobot.

5. In the Package field, enter com.java21days. The file you're creating is shown in the Created File field, and it can't be edited. This file has the name MarsRobot.java.

6. Click Finish.

The NetBeans source code editor opens with nothing in it. Fill it with the code provided in Listing 1.1. When you're done, save the file using the menu command File, Save. The file MarsRobot.java is saved.

**NOTE** _____ | Don't type the numbers at the beginning of each line in the listing. They're not part of the program. They are included so that individual lines can be described for instructive purposes in this book.

**LISTING 1.1**   The Full Text of MarsRobot.java

```
 1: package com.java21days;
 2:
 3: class MarsRobot {
 4:     String status;
 5:     int speed;
 6:     float temperature;
 7:
 8:     void checkTemperature() {
 9:         if (temperature < -80) {
10:             status = "returning home";
11:             speed = 5;
12:         }
13:     }
14:
15:     void showAttributes() {
16:         System.out.println("Status: " + status);
17:         System.out.println("Speed: " + speed);
18:         System.out.println("Temperature: " + temperature);
19:     }
20: }
```

When you save this file, if it has no errors, NetBeans automatically creates a MarsRobot class. This process is called *compiling* the class, and it involves using a tool called a *compiler*. The compiler turns the lines of source code into bytecode that can be run by the JVM.

The package statement in line 1 of Listing 1.1 places the class in a *package*, which provides a way to group related classes together in Java. The package has the name com.java21days.

The `class` statement in line 3 defines and names the `MarsRobot` class. Everything contained between the opening brace ({) on line 3 and the closing brace (}) on line 20 is part of this class.

The `MarsRobot` class contains three instance variables and two instance methods.

The instance variables are defined in lines 4–6:

```
String status;
int speed;
float temperature;
```

The variables are named `status`, `speed`, and `temperature`. Each is used to store a different type of information:

- `status` holds a `String` object—a group of letters, numbers, punctuation, and other characters.
- `speed` holds an `int`, a numeric integer value.
- `temperature` holds a `float`, a floating-point number.

`String` objects are created from the `String` class, which is part of the Java Class Library.

**NOTE** As you might have noticed from the use of `String` in this program, a class can use an object as an instance variable.

The first instance method in the `MarsRobot` class is defined in lines 8–13:

```
void checkTemperature() {
    if (temperature < -80) {
        status = "returning home";
        speed = 5;
    }
}
```

A method is defined in a manner similar to a class. It begins with a statement that names the method, identifies the type of information the method produces, and defines other things.

The `checkTemperature()` method is contained within the opening brace on line 8 of Listing 1.1 and the closing brace on line 13. This method can be called on a `MarsRobot` object to find out its temperature. This method checks to see whether the object's `temperature` instance variable has a value less than −80. If it does, two other instance variables are changed:

- The `status` variable is changed to the text "returning home," indicating that the temperature is too cold, and the robot is heading back to its base.
- The speed is changed to `5`. (Presumably, this is as fast as the robot can boogie.)

The second instance method, `showAttributes()`, is defined in lines 15–19:

```
void showAttributes() {
    System.out.println("Status: " + status);
    System.out.println("Speed: " + speed);
    System.out.println("Temperature: " + temperature);
}
```

This method calls the method `System.out.println()` to display the values of three instance variables, along with some text explaining what each value represents.

If you haven't saved this program yet, choose File, Save. If the file hasn't been changed since the last time you saved it, this command is disabled.

## Running the Program

Even if you typed the `MarsRobot` program in Listing 1.1 correctly and successfully compiled it into a class, you can't do anything with it. The class you've created defines what a `MarsRobot` object is like, but it doesn't actually create one of these objects and make it do anything.

There are two ways to put the `MarsRobot` class to use:

- Write a separate Java program that creates an object belonging to that class.
- Add a special class method called `main()` to the `MarsRobot` class so that it can be run as an application and then create an object of that class in that method.

The first option is chosen for this exercise.

Listing 1.2 contains the source code for `MarsApplication`, a Java class that creates a `MarsRobot` object, sets its instance variables, and calls methods. Following the same steps as before, create a new Java file in NetBeans in the `com.java21days` package and name it `MarsApplication`.

To begin this second class, follow these steps in NetBeans:

**1.** Choose File, New File from the menu. The New File dialog opens.

**2.** In the Categories pane, choose Java.

3. In the File Types pane, choose Empty Java File and click Next. The Empty Java File dialog opens.

4. In the Class Name text field, enter `MarsApplication`.

5. In the Package field, enter `com.java21days` (if it isn't there already). The file you're creating is shown in the Created File field and has the name `MarsApplication.java`.

6. Click Finish.

The new file is created. Enter the code shown in Listing 1.2 into the NetBeans source code editor.

**LISTING 1.2**   The Full Text of `MarsApplication.java`

```
 1: package com.java21days;
 2:
 3: class MarsApplication {
 4:     public static void main(String[] arguments) {
 5:         MarsRobot spirit = new MarsRobot();
 6:         spirit.status = "exploring";
 7:         spirit.speed = 2;
 8:         spirit.temperature = -60;
 9:
10:         spirit.showAttributes();
11:         System.out.println("Increasing speed to 3.");
12:         spirit.speed = 3;
13:         spirit.showAttributes();
14:         System.out.println("Changing temperature to -90.");
15:         spirit.temperature = -90;
16:         spirit.showAttributes();
17:         System.out.println("Checking the temperature.");
18:         spirit.checkTemperature();
19:         spirit.showAttributes();
20:     }
21: }
```

When you choose File, Save to save the file, NetBeans automatically compiles it into the `MarsApplication` class, which contains bytecode for the JVM to run.

**TIP**

If you encounter problems compiling or running any program in this book, you can find a copy of the source code file and other related files on the book's official website, at www.java21days.com.

After you have compiled the application, run the program by choosing the menu command Run, Run File. The output displayed by the MarsApplication class appears in an Output pane in NetBeans, as shown in Figure 1.1.

**FIGURE 1.1**

The output of the MarsApplication class.

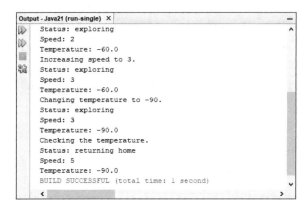

```
Output - Java21 (run-single) ×                                    ―
      Status: exploring                                           ^
      Speed: 2
      Temperature: -60.0
      Increasing speed to 3.
      Status: exploring
      Speed: 3
      Temperature: -60.0
      Changing temperature to -90.
      Status: exploring
      Speed: 3
      Temperature: -90.0
      Checking the temperature.
      Status: returning home
      Speed: 5
      Temperature: -90.0
      BUILD SUCCESSFUL (total time: 1 second)
                                                                  v
   <                                                        >
```

Using Listing 1.2 as a guide, you can see the following things taking place in the main() class method of this application:

- **Line 4:** The main() method is created and named. All main() methods look like this, as you'll see in Lesson 5, "Creating Classes and Methods." For now, the most important thing to note is the static keyword, which indicates that the method is a class method shared by all MarsRobot objects.

- **Line 5:** A new MarsRobot object is created, using the class as a template. The object is given the name spirit.

- **Lines 6–8:** Three instance variables of the spirit object are given values: status is set to the text "exploring", speed is set to 2, and temperature is set to -60.

- **Line 10:** The showAttributes() method of the spirit object is called, and it displays the current values of the instance variables status, speed, and temperature.

- **Line 11:** A call to the System.out.println() method displays the text within parentheses to the screen.

- **Line 12:** The speed instance variable is set to the value 3 before attributes are shown again.

- **Line 15:** The temperature instance variable is set to the value -90 before attributes are shown a third time.

- **Line 18:** The checkTemperature() method of the spirit object is called. This method checks to see whether the temperature instance variable is less than −80. If it is, status and speed are assigned new values.

NOTE
> If for some reason you can't use NetBeans or another IDE to write Java programs and must instead use the Java Development Kit, you can find out how to install it in Appendix D, "Using the Java Development Kit."

# Organizing Classes and Class Behavior

An introduction to object-oriented programming in Java requires a plunge into two more concepts: inheritance and packages. Both inheritance and packages are mechanisms for organizing classes.

## Inheritance

Inheritance, one of the most crucial concepts in object-oriented programming, has a direct impact on how you design and write your own Java classes.

*Inheritance* is a mechanism that enables one class to inherit the behavior and attributes of another class. Through inheritance, a class automatically picks up the functionality of an existing class. The new class only must define how it is different from that existing class.

With inheritance, all classes—including those you create and the ones in the Java Class Library—are arranged in a hierarchy. A class that inherits from another class is called a *subclass*. The class that gives the inheritance is called a *superclass*. A class can have only one superclass, but it can have an unlimited number of subclasses. Subclasses inherit all the attributes and behavior of their superclass.

In practical terms, this means that if the superclass has behavior and attributes your class needs, you don't have to redefine the behavior or copy that code to have the same behavior and attributes. Your class automatically receives these things from its superclass, the superclass gets them from its superclass, and so on, all the way up the hierarchy. Your class becomes a combination of its own features and all the features of the classes above it in the hierarchy.

The situation is comparable to how you inherited traits from your parents, such as your height, hair color, and love of peanut-butter-and-banana sandwiches. They inherited some of these things from their parents, who inherited from theirs, and backward through time.

Figure 1.2 shows how a hierarchy of classes is arranged.

**FIGURE 1.2**
A class hierarchy.

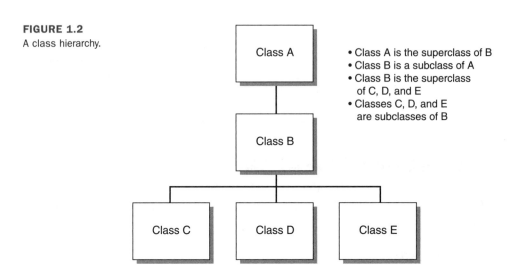

- Class A is the superclass of B
- Class B is a subclass of A
- Class B is the superclass of C, D, and E
- Classes C, D, and E are subclasses of B

At the top of the Java class hierarchy is the class `Object`. It contains the behavior and attributes necessary to be an object in the language.

All classes inherit from this superclass. `Object` is the most general class in the hierarchy. It defines behavior inherited by all the classes in the Java Class Library.

Each class further down the hierarchy becomes more tailored to a specific purpose. A class hierarchy defines abstract concepts at the top of the hierarchy. Those concepts become more concrete further down the line of subclasses.

Often when you create a new class in Java, you want all the functionality of an existing class except for some additions or modifications of your own creation. For example, you might want a new version of `Button` that makes a sound when clicked. This could be called `AudioButton`.

To receive all the `Button` functionality without doing any work to recreate it, you could define your new `AudioButton` class as a subclass of `Button`.

Because of inheritance, your class automatically inherits behavior and attributes defined in `Button` as well as the behavior and attributes defined in the superclasses of `Button`. All you have to worry about are the things that make your new class different from `Button` itself, which is called *subclassing*.

Subclassing is the creation of a new class that inherits from an existing class. The only code needed in the subclass is to indicate the differences in behavior and attributes between the subclass and its superclass.

If your class defines entirely new behavior and isn't a subclass of another class, you can inherit directly from the `Object` class.

If you create a class that doesn't extend a superclass, Java assumes that the new class inherits directly from `Object`. The `MarsRobot` class you created earlier in this lesson did not specify a superclass, so it's a subclass of `Object`.

# Creating a Class Hierarchy

If you're creating a large set of classes, it makes sense for your classes to inherit from the existing class hierarchy and to form a hierarchy themselves. This gives your classes several advantages:

- Functionality common to multiple classes can be put into a superclass, which enables it to be part of all classes below it in the hierarchy.
- Changes to a superclass automatically are reflected in all its subclasses, their subclasses, and so on. There is no need to change or recompile any of the lower classes; they receive the new information through inheritance.

For example, imagine that you have created a Java class to implement all the features of an exploratory robot. (This shouldn't take much imagination.)

The `MarsRobot` class is completed and works successfully. Your boss at NASA asks you to create a Java class called `MercuryRobot`.

These two kinds of robots have similar features. Both are research robots that work in hostile environments and conduct research. Both keep track of their current temperature and speed.

Your first impulse might be to open the `MarsRobot.java` source code file, copy it into a new source file called `MercuryRobot.java`, and then make the necessary changes for the new robot to do its job. This is a bad impulse.

A much better plan is to figure out the common functionality of `MercuryRobot` and `MarsRobot` and organize it into a more general class hierarchy. This might be a lot of work just for the classes `MarsRobot` and `MercuryRobot`, but what if you also expect later to add `MoonRobot`, `UnderseaRobot`, and `DesertRobot`? Factoring common behavior into a reusable superclass significantly reduces the overall amount of work you must do.

To design a class hierarchy that might serve this purpose, start at the top with the class `Object`, the pinnacle of all Java classes.

The most general class to which these robots belong might be called `Robot`. A robot, generally, could be defined as an autonomous exploration device. In the `Robot` class, you define only the behavior that qualifies something to be a device, to be self-controlled, and to be designed for exploration.

There could be two classes below `Robot`: `WalkingRobot` and `DrivingRobot`. The obvious thing that differentiates these classes is that one travels by foot and the other by wheel. The behavior of walking robots might include bending over to pick up something, ducking, running, and the like. Driving robots would behave differently. Figure 1.3 shows what you have so far.

**FIGURE 1.3**
The basic `Robot` hierarchy.

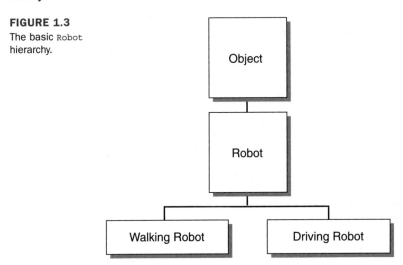

Now, the hierarchy can become even more specific.

With `WalkingRobot`, you might have several classes: `ScienceRobot`, `GuardRobot`, `SearchRobot`, and so on. As an alternative, you could factor out still more functionality and have intermediate classes for `TwoLegged` and `FourLegged` robots, with different behaviors for each (see Figure 1.4).

**FIGURE 1.4**
Two-legged and four-legged walking robots.

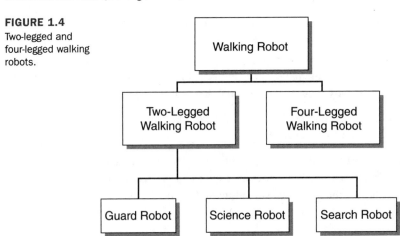

Finally, the hierarchy is done, and you have a place for `MarsRobot`. It can be a subclass of `ScienceRobot`, which is a subclass of `WalkingRobot`, which is a subclass of `Robot`, which is a subclass of `Object`.

Where do attributes such as `status`, `temperature`, and `speed` come in? At the place they fit into the class hierarchy most naturally. Because all robots need to keep track of the temperature of their environment, it makes sense to define `temperature` as an instance variable in `Robot`. All subclasses would have that instance variable as well. Remember that you need to define a behavior or an attribute only once in the hierarchy, and it is inherited automatically by each subclass.

**NOTE**

> Designing an effective class hierarchy involves a lot of planning and revision. As you attempt to put attributes and behavior into a hierarchy, you're likely to find reasons to move some classes to different spots in the hierarchy. The goal is to reduce the number of repetitive features (and redundant code) needed.

## Inheritance in Action

Inheritance in Java works much more simply than it does in the real world. No wills or courts are required when inheriting from a parent.

When you create a new object, Java keeps track of each variable defined for that object and each variable defined for each superclass of the object. In this way, all the classes combine to form a template for the current object, and each object fills in the information appropriate to its situation.

Methods operate similarly. A new object has access to all method names of its class and superclass. This is determined dynamically when a method is used in a running program. If you call a method of an object, the JVM first checks the object's class for that method. If the method isn't found, the JVM looks for it in the superclass of that class, and so on, until the method definition is found. This is illustrated in Figure 1.5.

Things get complicated when a subclass defines a method that matches a method defined in a superclass in name and other aspects. In this case, the method definition found first (starting at the bottom of the hierarchy and working upward) is the one that is used.

Because of this, you can create a method in a subclass that prevents a method in a superclass from being used. To do this, you give the method the same name, return type, and arguments as the method in the superclass. This procedure, shown in Figure 1.6, is called *overriding*.

**FIGURE 1.5**
How methods are located in a class hierarchy.

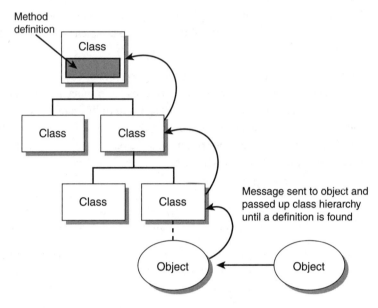

**FIGURE 1.6**
Overriding methods.

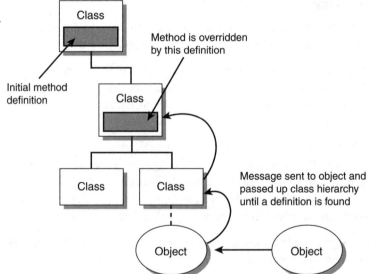

NOTE

> Java's form of inheritance is called *single inheritance* because each Java class can have only one superclass, although any given superclass can have multiple subclasses.
>
> In other object-oriented programming languages, such as C++, classes can have more than one superclass, and they inherit combined variables and methods from all those superclasses. This is called *multiple inheritance*. Java makes inheritance simpler by allowing only single inheritance.

## Packages

The programs you created during this lesson were put in the `com.java21days` package. Packages allow you to group related classes and interfaces. They eliminate potential naming conflicts among classes.

Classes in Java can be referred to by a short name such as `Object` or a full name that includes the package name, such as `java.lang.Object`.

Your Java classes can refer to any class in the `java.lang` package using only its short name. The `java.lang` package provides basic language features such as string handling and mathematical operations. To use classes from any other package, you must refer to them either by explicitly using their full package name or using an `import` command for a particular package. Using `import` tells the Java compiler to look in that package when turning a short name of a class into the full name.

There's a `Color` class in the `java.awt` package in the Java Class Library. If you want to use this class in your own program, you can refer to it by the full name `java.awt.Color`.

You can make things easier by using this `import` statement in the program:

```
import java.awt.Color;
```

This makes it possible to refer to the class simply as `Color`.

An `import` statement can use an asterisk to specify all classes in a package:

```
import java.awt.*;
```

The use of the asterisk as a wildcard causes every class in the package to be checked, so `Color` and all other classes in the `java.awt` package could be referenced by their shorter names.

**CAUTION** ___ | Many Java programmers avoid using the * version of `import` statements, preferring instead to have a series of `import` statements that identify every class used in a program. NetBeans can do this for you. When you write a line of code that first uses a class by its short name, the NetBeans editor flags an error on the left edge of that line. Click the error to see a pop-up menu that includes a command to import the class. If you choose the command, an `import` statement is added.

The package for a class is determined by the `package` statement. Many of the classes you create in this book are put in the `com.java21days` package, like so:

```
package com.java21days;
```

This statement must be the first line of the program. When it is omitted, the class belongs to an unnamed package called the *default package*.

# Summary

If this lesson was your first exposure to object-oriented programming, it probably seemed theoretical and a bit overwhelming. Many others have had the same reaction when first learning the mysterious methodology called OOP.

Because your brain has been stuffed with object-oriented programming concepts and terminology for the first time, you might be worried that no room is left for the rest of the Java language. The British have two handy pieces of advice for situations like this:

- Don't panic.
- Keep calm and carry on.

At this point, you should have a basic understanding of classes, objects, attributes, and behavior. You also should be familiar with instance variables and methods. You'll use these right away in the next lesson.

The other aspects of object-oriented programming, such as inheritance and packages, are covered in much more detail in upcoming lessons.

You'll work with object-oriented programming for the entirety of the book. There's no other way to write programs in Java.

By the time you finish the first seven lessons, you'll have working experience with objects, classes, inheritance, and all other aspects of the methodology.

# Q&A

**Q** **Methods are functions defined inside classes. If they look like functions and act like functions, why aren't they called functions?**

**A** Some object-oriented programming languages do call them functions. (C++ calls them member functions.) Other object-oriented languages differentiate between functions inside and outside the body of a class or object because in those languages, the use of the separate terms is important to understanding how each function works. Because the difference is relevant in other languages and because the term *method* now is in common use in object-oriented terminology, Java used the term as well. Functional programming languages also call them functions.

**Q** **What's the distinction between instance variables and methods and their counterparts, class variables and methods?**

**A** Almost everything you do in a Java program involves instances (also called objects) rather than classes. However, some behavior and attributes make more sense if stored in a class rather than in an object.

For example, the `Math` class in the `java.lang` package includes a class variable called `PI` that holds the approximate value of pi. This value does not change, so there's no reason different objects of that class would need their own individual copy of the `PI` variable. On the other hand, every `String` object contains a method called `length()` that reveals the number of characters in that `String`. This value can be different for each object of that class, so it must be an instance method.

Class variables occupy memory until a Java program is finished running, so they should be used with care. If a class variable references an object, that object will remain in memory as well. This is a common problem that causes a program to take up too much memory and run slowly.

**Q** **When a Java class imports an entire package, does it increase the compiled size of that class?**

**A** No. The use of the term *import* in Java is misleading. The `import` keyword does not add the code of one class or package to the class you are creating. Instead, it makes it easier to refer to classes within another class.

The sole purpose of importing is to shorten the class names when they're used in Java statements. It would be cumbersome to always have to refer to full class names such as `javax.swing.JButton` and `java.util.Random` in your code instead of calling them `JButton` and `Random`.

1

# Quiz

Review this lesson's material by taking this three-question quiz.

## Questions

1. What is another word for a class?

   **A.** Object

   **B.** Template

   **C.** Instance

2. When you create a subclass, what must you define about that class?

   **A.** Nothing. Everything is defined already.

   **B.** Things that are different from its superclass

   **C.** Everything about the class

3. What does an instance method of a class represent?

   **A.** The attributes of that class

   **B.** The behavior of that class

   **C.** The behavior of an object created from that class

## Answers

1. B. A class is an abstract template used to create objects that are similar to each other.

2. B. You define how the subclass is different from its superclass. The things that are similar are already defined for you because of inheritance. Answer A is technically correct, but if everything in the subclass is identical to the superclass, there's no reason to create the subclass.

3. C. Instance methods refer to a specific object's behavior. Class methods refer to the behavior of all objects belonging to that class.

# Certification Practice

The following question is the kind of thing you could expect to be asked on a Java programming certification test. Answer it without looking at this lesson again.

Which of the following statements is true?

    **A.** All objects created from the same class must be identical.

    **B.** All objects created from the same class can have different attributes than each other.

    **C.** An object inherits attributes and behavior from the class used to create it.

    **D.** A class inherits attributes and behavior from its subclass.

The answer is available on the book's website, at www.java21days.com. Visit the Lesson 1 page and click the Certification Practice link.

# Exercises

To extend your knowledge of the subjects covered during this lesson, try the following exercises:

    **1.** In the `main()` method of the `MarsRobot` class, create a second `MarsRobot` robot named `opportunity`, set up its instance variables, and display them.

    **2.** Create an inheritance hierarchy for the pieces of a chess set. Decide where the instance variables `color`, `startingPosition`, `forwardMovement`, and `sideMovement` should be defined in the hierarchy.

Where applicable, exercise solutions are offered on the book's website, at www.java21days.com.

# LESSON 2
# The ABCs of Programming

A Java program is made up of classes and objects, which are made up of methods and variables. Methods are made up of statements and expressions, which are made up of operators.

At this point, you might be worried that Java is like a set of Russian nesting matryoshka dolls. Each doll has a smaller doll inside it, as intricate and detailed as its larger companion, until you reach the smallest one.

This lesson clears away the big dolls to reveal the smallest elements of Java programming. It sets aside classes, objects, and methods and examines the basic things you can do in a single line of Java code. The following subjects are covered:

Statements and expressions

- Variables and primitive data types

- Constants

- Comments

- Literals

- Arithmetic

- Comparisons

- Logical operators

# Statements and Expressions

Any task you want to accomplish in a Java program can be broken down into a series of statements. In a programming language, a *statement* is a simple command that causes something to happen.

A statement represents a single action taken in a Java program. Here are three simple Java statements:

```
int bowlingScore = 225;
System.out.println("Free the bound periodicals!");
song.duration = 230;
```

A statement can convey a value, such as when two numbers are added together or when two variables are compared to find out if they are equal.

A statement that produces a value is called an *expression*. The value can be stored for later use in the program, used immediately in another statement, or disregarded. The value produced by a statement is called its *return value*.

An expression may produce a numeric return value, as when two numbers are added or multiplied. Or it may produce a Boolean value—either `true` or `false`—or even a Java object. Those types of statements are discussed later in this lesson.

Although many Java programs contain one statement per line, a line does not determine where one statement ends and another one begins. Each statement in Java is terminated with a semicolon character (;). A programmer can put more than one statement on a line, and it will compile successfully, as in the following example:

```
spirit.speed = 2; spirit.temperature = 60;
```

To make your program more readable to other programmers (and yourself), you should follow the convention of putting only one statement on each line.

Statements in Java are grouped using an opening brace ({) and a closing brace (}). A group of statements placed between these characters is called a *block* (or block statement). You'll learn more about them in Lesson 4, "Lists, Logic, and Loops."

# Variables and Data Types

In the `MarsRobot` application in Lesson 1, "Getting Started with Java," you used variables to keep track of information. A variable can store information a program is running. The value can be changed at any point in any statement in the program—hence the name *variable*.

To create a variable, you must give it a name and identify the type of information it will store. You also can give a variable an initial value at the same time you create it.

Java has three kinds of variables: instance variables, class variables, and local variables.

Instance variables, as you learned in Lesson 1, define an object's attributes.

Class variables define the attributes of an entire class of objects and apply to all instances of it.

Local variables are used inside method definitions or even smaller blocks of statements within a method. You can use them only while the method or block is being executed by the Java Virtual Machine (JVM). They cease to exist afterward.

Although all three kinds of variables are created in much the same way, class and instance variables are used in a different manner than local variables. You'll learn about local variables in this lesson and explore instance and class variables in Lesson 3, "Working with Objects."

## Creating Variables

Before you can use a variable in a Java program, you must create the variable by declaring its name and the type of information it will store. The type of information is listed first, followed by the name of the variable. The following all are examples of variable declarations:

```
int loanLength;
String message;
boolean gameOver;
```

In these examples, the `int` type represents integers, `string` is an object that holds text, and `boolean` is used for Boolean `true`/`false` values.

Local variables can be declared at any place inside a method, like any other Java statement, but they must be declared before they can be used.

In the following example, three variables are declared at the top of a program's `main()` method:

```
public static void main(String[] arguments) {
    int total;
    String reportTitle;
    boolean active;
}
```

If you are creating several variables of the same type, you can declare all of them in the same statement by separating the variable names with commas. The following statement creates three `String` variables named `street`, `city`, and `state`:

```
String street, city, state;
```

You can assign a value to a variable when you create it by using an equals sign (=) followed by the value. The following statements create new variables and give them initial values:

```
String zipCode = "02134";
int box = 350;
boolean pbs = true;
String name = "Zoom", city = "Boston", state = "MA";
```

As the last statement demonstrates, you can assign values to multiple variables of the same type by using commas to separate them.

You must give values to local variables before you use them in a program, or the program won't compile successfully. For this reason, it is good practice to give initial values to all local variables.

An instance or class variable definition is given an initial value depending on the type of information it holds.

The default value is `0` for numeric variables and `false` for Booleans. For `String` variables and any other objects, the default is `null`, a special value that means "nothing." For characters, the default value is `\u0000`. This is the null character in the standard Unicode character set.

## Naming Variables

Variable names in Java must start with a letter, an underscore character (_), or a dollar sign ($). Variable names cannot start with a number and cannot be an underscore as a single character. After the first character, variable names can include any combination of letters, numbers, underscore characters, or dollar signs.

**NOTE** _____ | In addition, the Java language uses the Unicode character set, which includes thousands of character sets to represent international alphabets. Accented characters and other symbols can be used in variable names if they have Unicode character numbers.

When naming a variable and using it in a program, it's important to remember that Java is case-sensitive: The capitalization of letters must be consistent. Because of this, a program can have a variable named x and another named X (so Rose is not rose is not ROSE).

In programs in these lessons and elsewhere, Java variables are given meaningful names that include several joined words. To make it easier to spot the words, the following general rule is used:

- The first letter of the variable name is lowercase.
- Each successive word in the variable name begins with a capital letter.
- All other letters are lowercase.

The following variable declarations follow the rule:

```
JButton loadFile;
int localAreaCode;
boolean quitGame;
```

This rule is called *camelCase* because the capital letters resemble a camel's humps.

Although underscores are permitted in variable names, they are used commonly in only one situation: When a variable's entire name is capitalized, each word is separated by an underscore, as in this example:

```
static int DAYS_IN_WEEK = 7;
```

You will see why a variable name might be capitalized like this later in this lesson.

Dollar signs never should be used in variable names, even though they're permitted. The official documentation for Java always has discouraged their use, so programmers follow this convention.

## Variable Types

In addition to a name, a variable declaration must include the data type of information being stored. The type can be any of the following:

- One of the primitive data types, such as int or boolean
- The name of a class
- An array

You'll learn how to work with array variables in Lesson 4. This lesson focuses on the other variable types.

## Data Types

Java has eight basic data types that store integers, floating-point numbers, characters, and Boolean values. These often are called *primitive types* because they are built-in parts of the language, instead of classes of objects, to make them easier to use. These data types have the same sizes and characteristics no matter what operating system and platform you're on, unlike some data types in other programming languages.

You can use four data types to store integers, each holding a different range of numbers, as shown in Table 2.1.

**TABLE 2.1**  Integer Types

| Type | Size | Values That Can Be Stored |
|------|------|---------------------------|
| byte | 8 bits | −128 to 127 |
| short | 16 bits | −32,768 to 32,767 |
| int | 32 bits | −2,147,483,648 to 2,147,483,647 |
| long | 64 bits | −9,223,372,036,854,775,808 to 9,223,372,036,854,775,807 |

All these types are *signed*, which means they can hold either positive or negative numbers. The type used for a variable must allow for the entire range of values it might need to hold. None of these integer variables can store a value too large or too small for its designated variable type, so keep that in mind when designating the type.

Another type of number that can be stored is a floating-point number, which has the type float or double. A floating-point number is a number with a decimal point. The float type can handle any number from 1.4e-45 to 3.4e+38, while the double type can be used for more precise numbers ranging from 4.9e-324 to 1.7e+308. Because double has more precision, that type generally is preferred.

The char type is used for individual characters, such as letters, numbers, punctuation, and other symbols.

The last of the eight primitive data types is boolean. As you have learned, this data type holds either true or false.

All these variable types appear in lowercase, and you must use them as such in programs. Some classes have the same names as these data types, but with different capitalization, such as Boolean and Double. These are classes, so they are created and referenced differently in a Java program. In the next lesson you will see how to use these special classes.

> **NOTE** There's actually a ninth primitive data type in Java, `void`, which represents the value "nothing." It's used in methods to indicate that they do not return values.

## Class Types

In addition to the primitive data types, a variable can have a class as its type, as in the following examples:

```
String lastName = "Hopper";
Color hair;
MarsRobot robbie;
```

When a variable has a class as its type, the variable refers to an object of that class or one of its subclasses.

The last statement in the preceding list creates a variable named `robbie` that is reserved for a `MarsRobot` object. The next lesson covers how to associate objects with variables.

## Assigning Values to Variables

After a variable has been declared, a value can be assigned to it with the assignment operator, which is an equal sign (`=`). The following are examples of assignment statements:

```
idCode = 8675309;
accountOverdrawn = false;
```

## Constants

Variables are useful when you need to store information that can be changed as a program runs.

If a value never should change in a program, you can use a *constant*, which is a variable with a value that never changes. (This might seem like an oxymoron, given the meaning of the word *variable*.)

In Java, you can create constants for all kinds of variables: instance, class, and local. To declare a constant, use the `final` keyword before the variable declaration and include an initial value for that variable, as in the following examples:

```
final double PI = 3.141592;
final boolean DEBUG = false;
final int PENALTY = 25;
```

Constants can be handy for naming various states of an object and then testing for those states. Suppose you have a program that takes directional input from the numeric keypad on the keyboard: Press 8 to go up, 4 to go left, 6 to go right, and 2 to go down. You can define those values as constant integers:

```
final int LEFT = 4;
final int RIGHT = 6;
final int UP = 8;
final int DOWN = 2;
```

Constants often make a program easier to understand. To illustrate this point, consider which of the following statements gives a better idea about what it does:

```
guide.direction = 4;
guide.direction = LEFT;
```

**NOTE** In the preceding statements, the names of the constants such as DEBUG and LEFT are capitalized. This is a convention adopted by Java programmers to make it clear that a variable is a constant. Java does not require that constants be capitalized in this manner, but it's a good practice to adopt.

When a constant's variable name is more than one word, putting it in all caps would make the words run together confusingly, as in ESCAPECODE. Separate the words with an underscore character (_), like this:

```
final int ESCAPE_CODE = 27;
```

This lesson's first project is a Java application that creates several variables, assigns them initial values, and displays them as output.

Run NetBeans and create a new Java program by undertaking these steps:

1. Choose the menu command File, New File. The New File dialog box opens.
2. In the Categories pane, choose Java.
3. In the File Types pane, choose Empty Java File and click Next. The Empty Java File dialog box opens.
4. In the Class Name text field, enter Variables, which gives the source code file the name Variables.java.
5. In the Package Name text field, enter org.cadenhead.java21.
6. Click Finish.

Enter the code shown in Listing 2.1 into the editor.

**LISTING 2.1**  The Full Text of `Variables.java`

```
 1: package com.java21days;
 2:
 3: public class Variables {
 4:
 5:     public static void main(String[] arguments) {
 6:         final char UP = 'U';
 7:         byte initialLevel = 12;
 8:         short location = 13250;
 9:         int score = 3500100;
10:         boolean newGame = true;
11:
12:         System.out.println("You have reached level " + initialLevel
13:             + " with a score of " + score + " at location " + location +
                ".");
14:         System.out.println("Press " + UP + " to go up.");
15:         System.out.println("Is this a new game? " + newGame);
16:     }
17: }
```

Save the file by choosing File, Save. NetBeans automatically compiles the application if it contains no errors. Run the program by choosing Run, Run File. This program produces the output shown in Figure 2.1.

**FIGURE 2.1**
Creating and displaying variable values.

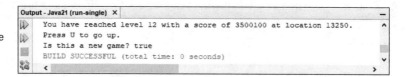

```
Output - Java21 (run-single)  ×                                              _
    You have reached level 12 with a score of 3500100 at location 13250.   ^
    Press U to go up.
    Is this a new game? true
    BUILD SUCCESSFUL (total time: 0 seconds)                               v
    <                                                              >
```

The package name of the class is established by the `package` statement, which must be the first line of a Java program when it is used:

```
package com.java21days;
```

This class uses four local variables and one constant, making use of `System.out.println()` in lines 12–15 to produce output.

`System.out.println()` is a method called to display strings and other information to the screen. This method takes a single argument within its parentheses: a string. To present more than one variable or literal as the argument to `println()`, the + operator combines the elements into a single string.

Java also has a `System.out.print()` method that displays a string without terminating it with a newline character. You can call `print()` instead of `println()` to display several strings on the same line.

# Comments

One of the most effective ways to improve a program's readability is to use *comments*, text in a program that explains what's going on in the code. The Java compiler ignores comments when preparing a bytecode version of a Java source file that can be run as a class by the JVM, so there's no penalty for using them.

You can use three kinds of comments in Java programs.

A single-line comment is preceded by two slash characters (`//`). Everything from the slashes to the end of the line is considered a comment and is disregarded by the compiler, as in the following statement:

```
int creditHours = 3; // set up credit hours for course
```

The compiler ignores everything from the slashes onward. As far as the compiler is concerned, the preceding line is this:

```
int creditHours = 3;
```

A multi-line comment begins with `/*` and ends with `*/`. Everything between these two delimiters is considered a comment, even over multiple lines, as in the following code:

```
/* This program occasionally deletes all files on
your hard drive and renders it unusable
forever when you click the Save button. */
```

A Javadoc comment begins with `/**` and ends with `*/`. Everything between these delimiters is considered to be official documentation on how the class and its methods work.

Javadoc comments are designed to be read by utilities such as `javadoc` in the Java Development Kit (JDK). This tool uses these comments to create web pages that document the functionality of a Java class, show its place in relation to its superclass and subclasses, and describe each of its methods.

2

# Literals

In addition to variables, you can work with values as literals in a Java statement. A *literal* is any number, text, or other information that directly represents a value.

The following assignment statement uses a literal:

```
int year = 2019;
```

The literal 2019 represents the integer value 2019. Numbers, characters, and strings are all examples of literals. Java has types of literals that represent different kinds of numbers, characters, strings, and Boolean values.

## Number Literals

Java has several integer literals. The number 4, for example, is an integer literal of the `int` variable type. It also can be assigned to `byte` and `short` variables because the number is small enough to fit into those integer types. An integer literal larger than an `int` can automatically hold is considered to be of the type `long`. You also can indicate that a literal should be a `long` integer by adding the letter L to the number (either in upper- or lowercase), like this:

```
pennyTotal = pennyTotal + 4L;
```

This statement adds the value 4, formatted as a `long`, to the current value of the `pennyTotal` variable.

To represent a negative number as a literal, precede it with a minus sign (-), as in -45.

Floating-point literals use a period character (.) for the decimal point, as you would expect. The following statement uses a literal to set up a `double` variable:

```
double average = .344;
```

All floating-point literals are considered to be of the `double` variable type instead of `float`. To specify a literal of `float`, add the letter `F` to the literal (in upper- or lowercase):

```
float piValue = 3.1415927F;
```

You can use exponents in floating-point literals by using the letter `e` or `E` followed by the exponent, which can be a negative number. The following statements use exponential notation:

```
double x = 12e22;
double y = 19E-95;
```

A large integer literal can include an underscore character (_) to make it more readable to humans. The underscore serves the same purpose as a comma in a large number, making its value more apparent. Consider these two examples, one of which uses underscores:

```
int jackpot = 3500000;
int jackpot = 3_500_000;
```

Both examples equal 3,500,000, which is easier to see in the second statement. The Java compiler ignores the underscores.

Java also supports numeric literals that use binary, octal, and hexadecimal numbering.

Binary is a base-2 numbering system in which only the values 0 and 1 are used. Values made up of 1s and 0s are the simplest form for a computer and are a fundamental part of computing. Counting up from 0, binary values are 0, 1, 10, 11, 100, 111, and so on. Each digit in the number is called a *bit*. The combination of eight numbers is a byte. A binary literal is specified by preceding it with 0b, as in 0b101 for 101 (5 in decimal) and 0b01111111 (127 in decimal).

Octal is a base-8 numbering system, which means it can represent only the values 0 through 7 as a single digit. The eighth number in octal is 10. Octal literals begin with a 0, so 010 is the decimal value 8, 012 is 9, and 020 is 16.

Hexadecimal is a base-16 numbering system that can represent 16 numbers as a single digit. The letters A through F represent the last six digits, so the first 16 numbers are 0, 1, 2, 3, 4, 5, 6, 7, 8, 9, A, B, C, D, E, and F. Hexadecimal literals begin with 0x, as in 0x12 (decimal 18) and 0xFF (decimal 255).

The octal and hexadecimal systems are better suited for certain tasks in programming than the decimal system. If you ever have chosen a color for an element on a web page, you might have used hexadecimal numbers, such as 0x001100 (green), 0x000011 (blue), or 0xFFCC99 (butterscotch).

## Boolean Literals

The Boolean literals `true` and `false` are the only two values you can use when assigning a value to a `boolean` variable type or using a Boolean in a statement.

The following statement sets a `boolean` variable:

```
boolean chosen = true;
```

> **CAUTION**    If you have programmed in other languages, you might expect that a value of 1 is equivalent to true and 0 is equivalent to false. This isn't the case in Java; you must use the values `true` and `false` to represent Boolean values.

Note that the literal `true` does not have quotation marks around it. If it did, the Java compiler would assume that it is a string of characters instead.

## Character Literals

A character literal is expressed as a single character surrounded by single quotation marks, such as `'a'`, `'#'`, and `'3'`. You might be familiar with the ASCII character set, which contains 128 characters, including letters, numerals, punctuation, and other characters that are useful in computing. Java supports ASCII along with thousands of additional characters through the 16-bit Unicode standard.

Some character literals represent characters that are not readily printable or accessible from a keyboard. Table 2.2 lists the codes that can represent these special characters as well as characters from the Unicode character set.

**TABLE 2.2**   Character Escape Codes

| Escape | Meaning |
| --- | --- |
| \n | Newline |
|  | Tab |
| \b | Backspace |
| \r | Carriage return |
| \f | Formfeed |
| \\ | Backslash |
| \' | Single quotation mark |
| \" | Double quotation mark |

| Escape | Meaning |
|--------|---------|
| \\*d* | Octal |
| \\x*d* | Hexadecimal |
| \\u*d* | Unicode character |

In Table 2.2, the letter d in the octal, hex, and Unicode escape codes represents a number or a hexadecimal digit (a through f or A through F). You already encountered one of these codes during this lesson: \u0000 as the default value of the character data type.

## String Literals

The final literal that you can use in a Java program represents a string of characters. A string in Java is an object rather than a primitive data type. Strings are not stored in arrays as they are in other programming languages (such as C).

Because strings are objects, methods are available to combine strings, modify strings, and determine whether two strings have the same value.

A string literal consists of a series of characters inside double quotation marks, as in the following statements:

```
String quitMsg = "Are you sure you want to quit?";
String password = "drowssap";
```

Strings can include the character escape codes listed in Table 2.2, as shown here:

```
String example = "Socrates asked, \"Hemlock is poison?\"";
System.out.println("Sincerely,\nMillard Fillmore\n");
String title = "Sams Teach Yourself Node in the Commode\u2122";
```

In the last example, the Unicode code sequence \u2122 produces a ™ symbol on devices that have been configured to support Unicode.

**CAUTION**

Although Java supports the transmission of Unicode characters, a computer or mobile device also must support it for the characters to be displayed when the program is run. Unicode support provides a way to encode its characters for systems that support the standard. Java supports the display of any Unicode character that can be represented by a host font.

For more information about Unicode, visit the Unicode Consortium website, at www.unicode.org.

Although string literals are used in a manner like other literals in a program, they are handled differently behind the scenes in the JVM.

With a string literal, Java stores that value as a `string` object. You don't have to explicitly create a new object, as you must when working with other objects, so string literals are as easy to work with as primitive data types. Strings are unusual in this respect: None of the basic types are stored as an object when used. You'll learn more about strings and the `String` class during this lesson.

# Expressions and Operators

2

An *expression* is a statement that can convey a value. The most common expressions are mathematical, as in the following examples:

```
int x = 13;
int y = x;
int z = x * y;
```

All three of these statements are expressions; they convey values that can be assigned to variables. The first assigns the literal `13` to the variable `x`. The second assigns the value of the variable `x` to the variable `y`. In the third expression, the multiplication operator `*` is used to multiply the `x` and `y` integers, and the result is stored in the `z` integer.

An expression can be any combination of variables, literals, and operators. It also can be a method call because a method sends back a value to the object or class that called the method.

The value conveyed by an expression is called a *return value*. This value can be assigned to a variable and used in many other ways in your Java programs.

Most of the expressions in Java use operators such as `*`. *Operators* are special symbols used for mathematical functions, assignment statements, and logical comparisons.

## Arithmetic

Five operators are used to accomplish basic arithmetic in Java, as shown in Table 2.3.

**TABLE 2.3**   Arithmetic Operators

| Operator | Meaning | Example |
|---|---|---|
| + | Addition | `3 + 4` |
| - | Subtraction | `5 - 7` |
| * | Multiplication | `5 * 5` |
| / | Division | `14 / 7` |
| % | Modulus | `20 % 7` |

Each operator takes two operands, one on each side of the operator. The subtraction operator also can be used to negate a single operand, which is equivalent to multiplying that operand by −1.

One thing to be mindful of when performing division is the type of numbers being used. If you store a division operation in an integer, the result is truncated to the next-lower whole number because the `int` data type can't handle floating-point numbers. For example, the expression `31 / 9` results in 3 if stored as an integer.

Modulus division, which uses the % operator, produces the remainder of a division operation. The expression `31 % 9` equals 4 because 31 divided by 9, with the whole number result of 3, leaves a remainder of 4.

It's important to note that many arithmetic operations involving integers produce an `int`, regardless of the original type of the operands. If you're working with other numbers, such as floating-point numbers or `long` integers, you should make sure that the operands have the same type you're hoping to end up with.

The next project is `Weather`, a Java class that demonstrates how to perform simple arithmetic in the language. Create a new empty Java file in NetBeans called `Weather` in the `com.java21days` package and enter the code in Listing 2.2 into the source code editor. Save the file with the menu command File, Save when you're done.

**LISTING 2.2**   The Full Text of `Weather.java`

```
1: package com.java21days;
2:
3: public class Weather {
4:     public static void main(String[] arguments) {
5:         float fah = 86;
6:         System.out.println(fah + " degrees Fahrenheit is ...");
7:         // To convert Fahrenheit into Celsius
8:         // begin by subtracting 32
```

```
 9:             fah = fah - 32;
10:             // Divide the answer by 9
11:             fah = fah / 9;
12:             // Multiply that answer by 5
13:             fah = fah * 5;
14:             System.out.println(fah + " degrees Celsius\n");
15:
16:             float cel = 33;
17:             System.out.println(cel + " degrees Celsius is ...");
18:             // To convert Celsius into Fahrenheit
19:             // begin by multiplying by 9
20:             cel = cel * 9;
21:             // Divide the answer by 5
22:             cel = cel / 5;
23:             // Add 32 to the answer
24:             cel = cel + 32;
25:             System.out.println(cel + " degrees Fahrenheit");
26:     }
27: }
```

2

Run the program by selecting Run, Run File. It produces the output shown in Figure 2.2.

**FIGURE 2.2**
Converting
temperatures with
expressions.

In this Java application, a temperature in Fahrenheit is converted to Celsius using the arithmetic operators:

- **Line 5:** The floating-point variable `fah` is created, with a value of 86.
- **Line 6:** The current value of `fah` is displayed.
- **Line 7:** The first of several comments explains what the program is doing. The Java compiler ignores these comments.
- **Line 9:** `fah` is set to its current value minus 32.
- **Line 11:** `fah` is set to its current value divided by 9.
- **Line 13:** `fah` is set to its current value multiplied by 5.
- **Line 14:** Now that `fah` has been converted to a Celsius value, `fah` is displayed again.

A similar thing happens in lines 16–25, but in the reverse direction: A temperature in Celsius is converted to Fahrenheit.

## More About Assignment

Assigning a value to a variable is an expression because it produces a value. Taking advantage of this language feature, you can combine assignment statements in an unusual way:

```
x = y = z = 7;
```

When this statement is executed, all three variables x, y, and z end up with the value 7.

The right side of an assignment expression always is calculated before the assignment takes place. This makes it possible to use an expression like the following:

```
int x = 5;
x = x + 2;
```

In the expression x = x + 2, the first thing that happens is x + 2 is calculated. The result, 7, is then assigned to x.

Using an expression to assign a value to a variable is a common task in programming. Several operators are used strictly in these situations. Table 2.4 shows these assignment operators and the expressions they are functionally equivalent to.

**TABLE 2.4** Assignment Operators

| Expression | Meaning |
|------------|---------|
| x += y | x = x + y |
| x -= y | x = x − y |
| x *= y | x = x * y |
| x /= y | x = x / y |

These shorthand assignment operators are functionally equivalent to the longer assignment statements for which they substitute. If either side of your assignment statement is part of a complex expression, however, there are cases where the operators are not equivalent.

**CAUTION** _____

> Are you curious about when a shorthand operator produces a different result than its longer form? If x equals 20 and y equals 5, the following two statements do not produce the same value:
>
> ```
> x = x / y + 5;
> x /= y + 5;
> ```
>
> The first statement produces an x value of 9 and the second an x value of 2. When in doubt about what an expression is doing, simplify it by using multiple assignment statements and don't use a shorthand operator.

2

# Incrementing and Decrementing

An extremely common task required in programming is to add or subtract 1 from an integer variable. These expressions have special operators called *increment* and *decrement operators*. Incrementing a variable means adding 1 to its value, and decrementing a variable means subtracting 1.

The increment operator is ++, and the decrement operator is --. These operators are placed immediately after or before a variable name, as in the following code:

```
int x = 7;
x++;
```

In this example, the statement x++ increments the x variable from 7 to 8.

Increment and decrement operators also can be placed before a variable name. The placement affects the value of expressions that involve these operators.

Increment and decrement operators are called *prefix* operators if listed before a variable name and *postfix* operators if listed after.

In a simple expression such as count--;, using a prefix or postfix operator produces the same result, making the operators interchangeable. When increment and decrement operations are part of a larger expression, however, the choice between prefix and postfix operators is important.

Consider the following code:

```
int x, y, z;
x = 42;
y = x++;
z = ++x;
```

The last two expressions in this code yield different results because of the difference between prefix and postfix operations.

When you use postfix operators on a variable in an expression, the variable's value is evaluated in the expression before it is incremented or decremented. So in y = x++, y receives the value of x before it is incremented by 1.

When using prefix operators on a variable in an expression, the variable is incremented or decremented before its value is evaluated in that expression. Therefore, in z = ++x, x is incremented by 1 before the value is assigned to z.

The result of the preceding code example is that y equals 42, z equals 44, and x equals 44.

If you're still having trouble figuring this out, here's the example again, now with comments describing each step:

```
int x, y, z;  // x, y, and z are declared
x = 42;       // x is given the value 42
y = x++;      // y is given x's value before it is incremented (42)
              // and x then is incremented to 43
z = ++x;      // x is incremented to 44, then z is given x's value
```

**CAUTION**

Using increment and decrement operators in complex expressions can produce results you might not expect.

The concept of "assigning x to y before x is incremented" isn't precisely right because Java evaluates everything on the right side of an expression before assigning its value to the left side.

Java stores some values before handling an expression to make postfix work the way it has been described in this section.

If you're not getting the results you expect from a complex expression that includes prefix and postfix operators, try breaking the expression into multiple statements to simplify it.

## Comparisons

Java has several operators for making comparisons between variables, between variables and literals, or between other types of information in a program.

These operators are used in expressions that return the Boolean values true or false, depending on whether the comparison being made is true or not. Table 2.5 shows the comparison operators.

**TABLE 2.5**  Comparison Operators

| Operator | Meaning | Example |
|----------|---------|---------|
| == | Equal to | x == 3 |
| != | Not equal to | x != 3 |
| < | Less than | x < 3 |
| > | Greater than | x > 3 |
| <= | Less than or equal to | x <= 3 |
| >= | Greater than or equal to | x >= 3 |

The following example shows a comparison operator in use:

```
boolean isHip;
int age = 37;
isHip = age < 30;
```

The expression `age < 30` produces a result of either `true` or `false`, depending on the value of the integer `age`. Because `age` is 37 in this example (which is not less than 30), `isHip` is given the Boolean value `false`.

## Logical Operators

Expressions that result in Boolean values, such as comparison operations, can be combined to form more complex expressions. This is handled through logical operators, which are used for the logical combinations AND, OR, XOR, and logical NOT.

For AND combinations, the `&` or `&&` logical operator is used. When two Boolean expressions are linked by one of these operators, the combined expression returns a `true` value only if both Boolean expressions are true.

Consider this example:

```
boolean extraLife = (score > 75000) & (playerLives < 10);
```

This expression combines two comparison expressions: `score > 75000` and `playerLives < 10`. If both expressions are true, the Boolean value `true` is assigned to the variable `extraLife`. In any other circumstance, the value `false` is assigned to the variable.

The difference between the `&` and `&&` operators lies in how much work the JVM does on the combined expression. If `&` is used, the expressions on both sides of the `&` are evaluated no matter what. If `&&` is used and the left side of the `&&` is false, the expression on the right side of the `&&` never is evaluated.

2

The `&&` operator is efficient because no unnecessary work is performed. In the preceding code example, if `score` is not greater than 75,000, there's no need to consider whether `playerLives` is less than 10.

For OR combinations, the `|` or `||` logical operator is used. These combined expressions return a `true` value if either Boolean expression is true.

Consider this example:

```
boolean extralife = (score > 75000) || (playerLevel == 0);
```

This expression combines two comparison expressions: `score > 75000` and `playerLevel == 0`. If either expression is true, the Boolean value `true` is assigned to the variable `extraLife`. The value `false` is assigned only if both of these expressions are false.

Note the use of `||` instead of `|`. Because of this usage, if `score > 75000` is true, `extraLife` is set to `true`, and the second expression never is evaluated.

The XOR combination has one logical operator, `^`. This results in a `true` value only if the Boolean expressions it combines have opposite values. If both are true or both are false, the `^` operator produces a `false` value.

The NOT combination uses the `!` logical operator followed by a single expression. It reverses the value of a Boolean expression in the same way that a minus sign reverses the positive or negative sign on a number. For example, if the expression `age < 30` returns a `true` value, `!(age < 30)` returns a `false` value.

The logical operators may seem illogical when you first encounter them. You will get plenty of opportunities to work with them, especially on Lesson 5, "Creating Classes and Methods."

## Operator Precedence

When more than one operator is used in an expression, Java has a precedence hierarchy to determine the order in which operators are evaluated. In many cases, this precedence determines the expression's overall value.

For example, consider the following expression:

```
y = 6 + 4 / 2;
```

The `y` variable equals 5 or 8, depending on which arithmetic operation is handled first. If the `6 + 4` expression comes first, `y` equals 5. Otherwise, `y` equals 8.

In general, the order of evaluation from first to last is as follows:

**1.** Increment and decrement operations

**2.** Arithmetic operations

**3.** Comparisons

**4.** Logical operations

**5.** Assignment expressions

If two operations have the same precedence, the one on the left in the expression is handled before the one on the right. Table 2.6 shows the specific precedence of the various operators in Java. Operators higher up in the table are evaluated first.

**TABLE 2.6**  Operator Precedence

| Operator | Notes |
| --- | --- |
| . [] () | Parentheses (()) are used to group expressions. A period (.) is used for access to methods and variables within objects and classes. Square brackets ([]) are used for arrays. |
| ++ -- ! ~ instanceof | The instanceof operator returns true or false, based on whether the object is an instance of the named class or any of its subclasses. |
| new (type)expression | The new operator is used to create new instances of classes. The parentheses in this case are for casting a value to another type. |
| * / % | Multiplication, division, modulus |
| + - | Addition and subtraction |
| << >> >>> | Bitwise left and right shift |
| < > <= >= | Relational comparison tests |
| == != | Equality |
| & | AND |
| ^ | XOR |
| \| | OR |
| && | Logical AND |
| \|\| | Logical OR |
| ? : | Ternary operator |
| = += -= *= /= %= ^= | Shorthand assignments |
| &= \|= >>= >>>= | Shorthand assignments |

2

Several of the operators in Table 2.6 are covered in subsequent lessons.

Returning to the expression `y = 6 + 4 / 2`, Table 2.6 shows that division is evaluated before addition, so the value of `y` equals `8`.

To change the order in which expressions are evaluated, place parentheses around the expressions that should be evaluated first. You can nest one set of parentheses inside another to make sure that expressions are evaluated in the desired order; the innermost parenthetic expression is evaluated first.

The following expression results in the value `5`:

```
y = (6 + 4) / 2
```

`5` is the result because `6 + 4` is calculated first, and then the result, 10, is divided by 2.

Parentheses also can improve an expression's readability. If an expression's precedence isn't immediately clear to you, adding parentheses to impose the desired precedence can make the statement easier to understand.

# String Arithmetic

As stated earlier, the `+` operator has a double life outside the world of mathematics. It also can concatenate two or more strings.

The word *concatenate* means "to link two things." For reasons unknown, it is the verb of choice in computer programming when describing the act of combining two strings, winning out over *paste*, *glue*, *affix*, *combine*, *link*, *smush together*, and *conjoin*.

In several code examples, you have seen statements that take a form like this:

```
String brand = "Jif";
System.out.println("Choosy mothers choose " + brand);
```

These two lines result in the display of the following text:

```
Choosy mothers choose Jif
```

The `+` operator combines strings, other objects, and variables to form a single string. In the preceding example, the literal `"Choosy mothers choose "` is concatenated to the value of the `String` object `brand`.

Working with the concatenation operator is made easier in Java by the fact that the operator can handle any variable type and object value as if it were a string. If any part of a concatenation operation is a `String` object or a string literal, all elements of the operation are treated like strings:

```
System.out.println(4 + " score and " + 7 + " years ago");
```

This produces the output text `4 score and 7 years ago`, as if the integer literals 4 and 7 were strings.

There also is a `+=` shorthand operator to append something to the end of a string. For example, consider the following expression:

```
String myName = "Robert Downey";
myName += " Jr.";
```

This expression is equivalent to the following:

```
myName = myName + " Jr.";
```

In this example, `+=` changes the value of `myName`, so `"Robert Downey"` becomes `Robert Downey Jr.`.

To summarize, Table 2.7 lists the operators you have learned about.

**TABLE 2.7**  Operator Summary

| Operator | Meaning |
| --- | --- |
| + | Addition |
| – | Subtraction |
| * | Multiplication |
| / | Division |
| % | Modulus |
| < | Less than |
| > | Greater than |
| <= | Less than or equal to |
| >= | Greater than or equal to |
| == | Equal to |
| != | Not equal to |
| && | Logical AND |

| Operator | Meaning |
|---|---|
| \|\| | Logical OR |
| ! | Logical NOT |
| & | AND |
| \| | OR |
| ^ | XOR |
| = | Assignment |
| ++ | Increment |
| - - | Decrement |
| += | Add and assign |
| -= | Subtract and assign |
| *= | Multiply and assign |
| /= | Divide and assign |
| %= | Modulus and assign |

# Summary

Anyone who pops open a set of matryoshka dolls has to be a bit disappointed upon reaching the smallest doll in the group. In this lesson you reached Java's smallest nesting doll. Using statements and expressions enables you to begin building effective methods, which makes effective objects and classes possible.

You also learned about creating variables and assigning values to them. You used literals to represent numeric, character, and string values and worked with operators. In the next lesson, you'll put these skills to use developing classes.

# Q&A

**Q What happens if I assign an integer value to a variable that is too large for that variable to hold?**

**A** Logically, you might think that the variable is converted to the next-larger type, but this isn't what happens. Instead, an overflow occurs—a situation in which the number wraps around from one size extreme to the other. An example of overflow would be a `byte` variable going from 127 (an acceptable value) to 128 (unacceptable). It would wrap around to the lowest acceptable value, which is −128, and start counting upward from there. Overflow isn't something you can readily detect in a program, so be sure to give your numeric variables plenty of space in the chosen data type.

Small data types like `byte` were more necessary when computers had much less memory than they do today and every byte counted. Now, with plentiful memory and hard disk space measured in terabytes, it is better to use larger data types like `int` to ensure that you have enough space to store all possible values in a particular variable.

**Q Why does Java have all these shorthand operators for arithmetic and assignment? It's really hard to read that way.**

**A** Java's syntax is based on C++, which is based on C (more Russian nesting doll behavior). C is a language that values programming power over readability, and the shorthand operators are one of the legacies of that design priority. Using them in a program isn't required because effective substitutes are available, so you can avoid them in your own programming if you prefer. But as you get more comfortable with Java, you likely will find them as easy to read as the longer alternatives.

**Q If I create a program that does not include a `package` statement, does that mean it isn't in a package?**

**A** Every Java program belongs to a package. When the `package` statement appears in a program, the program is part of the named package. The programs you created during this lesson are all in the `com.java21days` package.

A program that does not have a `package` statement is put into the default package, which does not have a name. Although programs can be created in this unnamed package, it's good practice to always specify a package with each program you create in Java.

# Quiz

Review this lesson's material by taking this three-question quiz.

## Questions

**1.** Which of the following literals is a valid value for a `boolean` variable?

    **A.** `"false"`

    **B.** `false`

    **C.** `10`

2. Which of these is not a convention for naming variables in Java?

   A. After the first word in the variable name, each successive word begins with a capital letter.

   B. The first letter of the variable name is lowercase.

   C. All letters are capitalized.

3. Which of these data types holds numbers from −32,768 to 32,767?

   A. `char`

   B. `byte`

   C. `short`

## Answers

1. B. In Java, a `boolean` only can be `true` or `false`. If you put quotation marks around the value, it is treated like a `String` rather than one of the two `boolean` values.

2. C. Constant names are capitalized to make them stand out from other variables.

3. C. The `short` primitive data type has that range of values.

# Certification Practice

The following question is the kind of thing you could expect to be asked on a Java programming certification test. Answer it without looking at this lesson again.

Which of the following data types can hold the number 3,000,000,000 (that is, 3 billion)?

A. `short, int, long, float`

B. `int, long, float`

C. `long, float`

D. `byte`

The answer is available at www.java21days.com. Visit the Lesson 2 page and click the Certification Practice link.

# Exercises

To extend your knowledge of the subjects covered in this lesson, try the following exercises:

1. Create a program that calculates how much a $14,000 investment would be worth if it increased in value by 40% during the first year, lost $1,500 in value the second year, and increased 12% in the third year.

2. Write a program that displays two numbers and uses the / and % operators to display the result and remainder after they are divided. Use the \t character escape code to separate the result and remainder in your output with a tab character.

Where applicable, exercise solutions are offered at www.java21days.com.

2

# LESSON 3
# Working with Objects

Java is an object-oriented programming language. When you do work in Java, you primarily use objects to get the job done. You create objects, modify them, change their variables, call their methods, and combine them with other objects. You develop classes, create objects out of those classes, and use them with other classes and objects.

In this lesson, you'll work extensively with objects as you undertake these essential tasks:

- Creating objects

- Testing and modifying objects' class and instance variables

- Calling an object's methods

- Converting objects from one class to another

# Creating New Objects

When you write a Java program, you define a set of classes. As you learned during Lesson 1, "Getting Started with Java," a class is a template used to create one or more objects. These objects, which also are called *instances*, are self-contained elements of a program with related features and data. For the most part, you use a class merely to create instances and then work with those instances. In this section, you'll learn how to create a new object from any given class.

When using strings during Lesson 2, "The ABCs of Programming," you learned that a string literal (a series of characters enclosed in double quotation marks) can be used to create a new instance of the class `String` with the value of that string. The `String` class is unusual in that respect. Although it's a class, it can be assigned a value with a literal as if it were a primitive data type. This shortcut is available only for strings and classes that represent primitive data types, such as `Integer` and `Double`. To create instances for all other classes, the `new` operator is used.

> **NOTE**
>
> What about the literals for numbers and characters? Don't they create objects, too? They don't. The primitive data types for numbers and characters create numbers and characters, but for efficiency they aren't objects. In Lesson 5, "Creating Classes and Methods," you'll learn how to use objects to represent primitive values.

## Using `new`

To create a new object, you use the `new` operator with the name of the class that should be used as its template. The name of the class is followed by parentheses, as in these three examples:

```
String name = new String("Kamala Khan");
URL address = new URL("https://www.informit.com");
MarsRobot robbie = new MarsRobot();
```

The parentheses are important and can't be omitted. They can be empty, however, in which case the simplest object of the specified class is created. The parentheses also can contain arguments that determine the values of instance variables or other initial qualities of that object.

Here are two objects being created with arguments:

```
Random seed = new Random(606843071);
Point pt = new Point(0, 0);
```

The number and type of arguments to include inside the parentheses are defined by the class itself, using a special method called a *constructor* (which is introduced later in this lesson). If you try to create a new instance of a class with the wrong number or wrong type of arguments, or if you give it no arguments and it needs them, an error occurs when the program is compiled.

The lesson's first project demonstrates how to create different types of objects with different numbers and types of arguments. The StringTokenizer class in the java.util package divides a string into a series of shorter strings called *tokens*.

You divide a string into tokens by applying a character or characters as a delimiter. For example, the text 02/20/67 could be divided into three tokens—02, 20, and 67—by using the slash character (/) as a delimiter.

The first project in this lesson is a Java application that uses string tokens to examine stock price data. In NetBeans, create a new empty Java file for the class TokenTester in the com.java21days package and enter the code in Listing 3.1 as its source code. This program creates StringTokenizer objects by using new in two different ways and then displays each token the objects contain.

**LISTING 3.1**   The Full Text of TokenTester.java

```
 1: package com.java21days;
 2:
 3: import java.util.StringTokenizer;
 4:
 5: class TokenTester {
 6:
 7:     public static void main(String[] arguments) {
 8:         StringTokenizer st1, st2;
 9:
10:         String quote1 = "TWTR 37.14 7.28";
11:         st1 = new StringTokenizer(quote1);
12:         System.out.println("Token 1: " + st1.nextToken());
13:         System.out.println("Token 2: " + st1.nextToken());
14:         System.out.println("Token 3: " + st1.nextToken());
15:
16:         String quote2 = "RHT@185.98@80";
17:         st2 = new StringTokenizer(quote2, "@");
18:         System.out.println("\nToken 1: " + st2.nextToken());
```

```
19:            System.out.println("Token 2: " + st2.nextToken());
20:            System.out.println("Token 3: " + st2.nextToken());
21:     }
22: }
```

Save this file by choosing File, Save or clicking Save All on the NetBeans toolbar. Run the application by choosing Run, Run File to see the output displayed in Figure 3.1.

**FIGURE 3.1**

Displaying a
StringTokenizer
object's tokens.

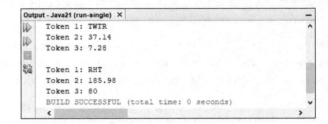

In the application, two StringTokenizer objects are created, using different arguments to the constructor.

The first object is created using new StringTokenizer() with one argument, a String object named quote1 (line 11). This creates a StringTokenizer object that uses the default delimiters, which are blank spaces, tabs, newlines, carriage returns, or formfeed characters.

If any of these characters is contained in the string, it is used to divide the string. Because the quote1 string contains spaces, these are used as delimiters dividing the tokens. Lines 12–14 display the values of all three tokens: TWTR, 37.14, and 7.28.

The second StringTokenizer object in this example has two arguments when it is constructed in line 16—a String object named quote2 and an at-sign character (@). This second argument indicates that the @ character should be used as the delimiter between tokens. The StringTokenizer object created in line 17 contains three tokens: RHT, 185.98, and 80.

## How Objects Are Constructed

Several things happen when you use the new operator. The new instance of the given class is created, memory is allocated for it, and a special method defined in the given class is called. This method is called a *constructor*.

Using a constructor is a way to create a new instance of a class. A constructor initializes the new object and its variables, creates any other objects that the object needs, and performs any additional operations the object requires to initialize itself.

A class can have several different constructors, each with a different number or type of argument. When you use `new`, you can specify different arguments in the argument list, and the correct constructor for those arguments is called.

In the `TokenTester` program, multiple constructor definitions enabled the `StringTokenizer` class to accomplish different things with different uses of the `new` operator. When you create your own classes, you can define as many constructors as you need to implement the behavior of the class.

No two constructors in a class can have the same number and type of arguments because this is the only way constructors are differentiated from each other.

If a class defines no constructors, a constructor with no arguments is called by default when an object of the class is created. The only thing this constructor does is call the same constructor in its superclass.

3

**CAUTION**

> The default constructor only exists in a class that has not defined any constructors. Once you define at least one constructor in a class, you can't count on there being a default constructor with no arguments.

# Memory Management

If you are familiar with other object-oriented programming languages, you might wonder whether the `new` operator has an opposite that destroys an object when it is no longer needed.

Memory management in Java is dynamic and automatic. When you create a new object, Java automatically allocates the proper amount of memory for that object. You don't have to allocate any memory for objects explicitly. The Java Virtual Machine (JVM) does it for you.

Because Java memory management is automatic, you don't need to deallocate the memory an object uses when you're finished using it. Under most circumstances, when you are finished with an object you have created, Java can determine that the object no longer has any live references to it. (In other words, the object isn't assigned to any variables still in use or stored in any arrays.)

As a program runs, the JVM periodically looks for unused objects and reclaims the memory that those objects are using. This process, called *garbage collection*, occurs without any programming on your part. You don't have to explicitly free the memory taken up by an object; you only must make sure that you're not still holding onto an object you want to get rid of.

This feature is one of the most touted advantages of the language over its predecessor C++, where memory leaks caused by programmers who forget to deallocate an object are the most common cause of software crashes.

# Using Class and Instance Variables

At this point, you can create your own object with class and instance variables, but how do you work with those variables? They're used in largely the same manner as the local variables you learned about in the previous lesson. You can put them in expressions, assign values to them in statements, and so on. You just refer to them slightly differently.

## Getting Values

To get to the value of an instance variable, you use *dot notation*, a form of addressing in which an instance or a class variable name has two parts:

- A reference to an object or class on the left side of a dot operator ( . )
- A variable on the right side

You use dot notation to refer to an object's instance variables and methods. For example, if you have an object named `customer` with a variable called `orderTotal`, here's how that variable could be referred to in a statement:

```
float total = customer.orderTotal;
```

This statement assigns the value of the `customer` object's `orderTotal` instance variable to a floating-point variable named `total`.

Accessing variables in dot notation involves an expression (meaning that it returns a value). Both sides of the dot also are expressions. This means that you can chain instance variable access.

Extending the preceding example, suppose the `customer` object is an instance variable of the `store` class. Dot notation can be used twice, as in this statement:

```
float total = store.customer.orderTotal;
```

Dot expressions are evaluated from left to right, so you start with store's instance variable customer, which itself has an instance variable orderTotal. The value of this variable is assigned to the total variable.

One thing to note when chaining objects together in this manner is that the statement will fail with an error if any object in the chain does not have a value yet. If the variable called store has not been assigned an object as its value, the above line of code will fail with an error called a NullPointerException. You'll learn more about errors like these in Lesson 7, "Exceptions and Threads."

## Setting Values

Assigning a value to an instance variable with dot notation employs the = operator, which is also used with variables holding primitive types. This statement uses dot notation:

```
customer.layaway = true;
```

This statement sets the value of a boolean instance variable named layaway to true.

The PointSetter application in Listing 3.2 tests and modifies the instance variables in a Point object. Point, a class in the java.awt package, represents points in a coordinate system with (x, y) values.

Create a new empty Java file in NetBeans with the class name PointSetter and the package name com.java21days; then type the source code shown in Listing 3.2 and save the file.

**LISTING 3.2**  The Full Text of PointSetter.java

```
 1: package com.java21days;
 2:
 3: import java.awt.Point;
 4:
 5: class PointSetter {
 6:
 7:     public static void main(String[] arguments) {
 8:         Point location = new Point(4, 13);
 9:
10:         System.out.println("Starting location:");
11:         System.out.println("X equals " + location.x);
12:         System.out.println("Y equals " + location.y);
13:
14:         System.out.println("\nMoving to (7, 6)");
15:         location.x = 7;
16:         location.y = 6;
17:
```

```
18:          System.out.println("\nEnding location:");
19:          System.out.println("X equals " + location.x);
20:          System.out.println("Y equals " + location.y);
21:      }
22: }
```

When you run this application, the output should match Figure 3.2.

**FIGURE 3.2**
Setting and displaying an object's instance variables.

In this application, you create an instance of Point where x equals 4 and y equals 13 (line 8). These individual values are retrieved using dot notation.

The value of x is changed to 7 and y to 6 (lines 15–16). The values are displayed again to show how they have changed.

## Class Variables

Class variables, as you have learned, are variables defined and stored in a class. Their values apply to the class and all its instances.

With instance variables, each new instance of a class gets a new copy of the instance variables that the class defines. Each instance then can change the values of those instance variables without affecting any other instances. With class variables, only one copy of that variable exists when the class is loaded. Changing the value of that variable changes it for all instances of that class.

You define a class variable by including the static keyword before the variable. For example, consider the following partial class definition:

```
class FamilyMember {
    static String surname = "Mendoza";
    String name;
    int age;
}
```

Each instance of the class `FamilyMember` has its own values for `name` and `age`, but the class variable `surname` has only one value for all family members: Mendoza. If the value of `surname` is changed, all instances of `FamilyMember` are affected.

**NOTE**

> These variables also are called *static variables*, which takes the meaning of the word *static* as "fixed in one place." If a class has a static variable, every object of that class has the same value for that variable.

To access class variables, you use the same dot notation as with instance variables. To retrieve or change the value of the class variable, use either the instance or the name of the class on the left side of the dot operator. Both lines of output in this example display the same value:

```
FamilyMember dad = new FamilyMember();
System.out.println("Family's surname is: " + dad.surname);
System.out.println("Family's surname is: " + FamilyMember.surname);
```

Because you can use an object to change the value of a class variable, it's easy to become confused about class variables and where their values are coming from. Remember that the value of a class variable affects all objects of that class. If the `surname` instance variable of one `FamilyMember` object were set to `"Paciorek"`, all objects of that class would have that new surname.

To reduce confusion when using class variables, it's a good idea to use the name of the class when you refer to a class variable—not an object of that class. This makes the use of a class variable more clear and helps make strange results easier to debug.

# Calling Methods

Methods of an object are called to make it do something.

Calling a method in an object also makes use of dot notation. The object whose method is being called is on the left side of the dot, and the name of the method and its arguments are on the right side:

```
customer.addToCart(itemNumber, price, quantity);
```

Every method call must have parentheses at the end, even when the method takes no arguments, as in this example:

```
customer.cancelOrder();
```

In Listing 3.3, the `StringChecker` application shows an example of calling some methods defined in the `String` class. Strings include methods for string tests and modification. Create this program in NetBeans as an empty Java file with the class name `StringChecker` and package name `org.cadenhead.java21`.

**LISTING 3.3**    The Full Text of `StringChecker.java`

```
 1: package com.java21days;
 2:
 3: class StringChecker {
 4:
 5:     public static void main(String[] arguments) {
 6:         String str = "You know nothing, Jon Snow";
 7:         System.out.println("The string is: " + str);
 8:         System.out.println("Length of this string: "
 9:             + str.length());
10:         System.out.println("The character at position 7: "
11:             + str.charAt(7));
12:         System.out.println("The substring from 9 to 16: "
13:             + str.substring(9, 16));
14:         System.out.println("The index of the first 'w': "
15:             + str.indexOf('w'));
16:         System.out.println("The index of the beginning of the "
17:             + "substring \"Jon\": " + str.indexOf("Jon"));
18:         System.out.println("The string in uppercase: "
19:             + str.toUpperCase());
20:     }
21: }
```

Running the program produces the output shown in Figure 3.3.

**FIGURE 3.3**
Calling `String` methods to learn more about a string.

```
Output - Java21 (run-single)  ×
    run-single:
    The string is: You know nothing, Jon Snow
    Length of this string: 26
    The character at position 7: w
    The substring from 9 to 16: nothing
    The index of the first 'w': 7
    The index of the beginning of the substring "Jon": 18
    The string in uppercase: YOU KNOW NOTHING, JON SNOW
    BUILD SUCCESSFUL (total time: 0 seconds)
```

In line 6, you create a new instance of `String` by using the string literal `"You know nothing, Jon Snow"`. The remainder of the program calls string methods to do different operations on that string:

- Line 7 prints the value of the string.

- Line 9 calls the `length()` method in the new `String` object to find out how many characters it contains.

- Line 11 calls the `charAt()` method, which returns the character at the given position in the string.

- Line 13 calls the `substring()` method, which takes two integers indicating a range and returns the substring with those starting and ending points. The `substring()` method also can be called with only one argument, which returns the substring from that position to the end of the string.

- Line 15 calls the `indexOf()` method, which returns the position of the first instance of the given character. Character literals are surrounded by single quotation marks, so the argument is `'w'` (not `"w"`).

- Line 17 shows a different use of the `indexOf()` method, which takes a string argument and returns the index of the beginning of that string. String literals always are surrounded by double quotation marks.

- Line 19 uses the `toUpperCase()` method to return a copy of the string in all uppercase.

**NOTE**

If you compare the output of the `StringChecker` application to the characters in the string, you might be wondering how `'w'` could be at position 7 when it is the eighth character in the string. All of the methods look like they're off by one (except for `length()`). The reason is that the methods are zero based, which means they begin counting with 0 instead of 1. So `'Y'` is at position 0, `'o'` at position 1, `'u'` at position 2, and so on. This kind of numbering is something you encounter often in Java (and other programming languages).

# Formatting Strings

Numbers with special formats, such as money, need to be displayed in a precise manner. A money amount has only two places after the decimal for the number of cents, a dollar sign ($) preceding the value, and commas separating groups of three numbers—as in $5,848.30 (the amount the U.S. National Debt increases in one second).

This kind of formatting when displaying strings can be accomplished with the `System.out.format()` method. The method takes two arguments: the output format template and the string to display. Here's an example that adds a dollar sign and commas to the display of an integer:

```
int accountBalance = 5005;
System.out.format("Balance: $%,d%n", accountBalance);
```

This code produces the output `Balance: $5,005`.

The formatting string begins with a percent sign (`%`) followed by one or more flags. The `%,d` code displays a decimal with commas dividing each group of three digits. The `%n` code displays a newline character.

The next example displays the value of pi to 11 decimal places:

```
double pi = Math.PI;
System.out.format("%.11f%n", pi);
```

The output is `3.14159265359`.

**TIP**
Oracle's Java site includes a beginner's tutorial for this kind of print output formatting that describes some of the most useful codes; see https://docs.oracle.com/javase/tutorial/java/data/numberformat.html.

# Nesting Method Calls

A method can return a reference to an object, a primitive data type, or no value at all. In the `StringChecker` application, all the methods called on the `String` object returned values that are displayed. The `charAt()` method returned a character at a specified position in the string.

The value returned by a method also can be stored in a variable:

```
String label = "From";
String upper = label.toUpperCase();
```

In this example, the `String` object `upper` contains the value returned by calling `label.toUpperCase()`, which is the text `FROM`.

If the method returns an object, you can call the methods of that object in the same statement. This makes it possible for you to nest methods as you would variables.

Earlier, you saw an example of a method called with no arguments:

```
customer.cancelOrder();
```

If the `cancelOrder()` method returns an object, you can call methods of that returned object in the same statement, as in this example:

```
customer.cancelOrder().fileComplaint();
```

This statement calls the `fileComplaint()` method, which is defined in the object returned by the `cancelOrder()` method of the `customer` object.

You can combine nested method calls and instance variable references as well. In the next example, the `putOnLayaway()` method is defined in the object stored by the `orderTotal` instance variable, which itself is part of the `customer` object:

```
customer.orderTotal.putOnLayaway(itemNumber, price, quantity);
```

This manner of nesting variables and methods is demonstrated in a method you've used frequently in the first three lessons of this book: `System.out.println()`. This method displays strings and other data to the computer's standard output device.

The `System` class, part of the `java.lang` package, describes behavior specific to the computer on which Java is running. `System.out` is a class variable that contains an instance of the class `PrintStream`, representing the system's standard output, which normally is the monitor but can be a printer or a file. `PrintStream` objects have a `println()` method that sends a string to that output stream. The `PrintStream` class is in the `java.io` package.

## Class Methods

Just like class variables, class methods, also called *static methods*, apply to a class as a whole and not to its instances. Class methods commonly are used as general utility methods that might not operate directly on an object of that class but do fit with that class conceptually.

For example, the `String` class contains a class method called `valueOf()` that can take one of many types of arguments (integers, Booleans, objects, and so on). The `valueOf()` method then returns a new instance of `String` that contains the argument's string value. This method doesn't operate directly on an existing instance of `String`, but it makes sense to use the `String` class to define behavior such as getting a string from another object or data type.

Class methods also can be useful for gathering general methods in one place. For example, the `Math` class, defined in the `java.lang` package, contains a large set of mathematical operations as class methods. No objects can be created from the `Math` class, but you still can use its methods with numeric or Boolean arguments.

For example, the class method `Math.max()` takes two arguments and returns the larger of the two. You don't need to create a new instance of `Math`; it can be called anywhere you need it, as in the following example:

```
int firstPrice = 225;
```

```
int secondPrice = 217;
int higherPrice = Math.max(firstPrice, secondPrice);
```

Dot notation is used to call a class method. As with class variables, you can use either an instance of the class or the class itself on the left side of the dot. For the same reasons noted earlier about class variables, using the name of the class makes your code easier to read.

The last two lines in this example both produce strings equal to `"550"`:

```
String s, s2;
s = "potrzebie";
s2 = s.valueOf(550);
s2 = String.valueOf(550);
```

# References to Objects

As you work with objects, it's important to understand references. A *reference* is an address that indicates where an object's variables and methods are stored.

You aren't directly using objects when you assign an object to a variable or pass an object to a method as an argument. You aren't even using copies of the objects. Instead, you're using references to those objects.

To better illustrate what this means, the `RefTester` application in Listing 3.4 shows how references work. Create an empty Java file in NetBeans for the class `RefTester` in the package `com.java21days` and enter Listing 3.4 as the application's source code.

**LISTING 3.4**  The Full Text of `RefTester.java`

```
 1: package com.java21days;
 2:
 3: import java.awt.Point;
 4:
 5: class RefTester {
 6:     public static void main(String[] arguments) {
 7:         Point pt1, pt2;
 8:         pt1 = new Point(100, 190);
 9:         pt2 = pt1;
10:
11:         pt1.x = 200;
12:         pt1.y = 290;
13:         System.out.println("Point1: " + pt1.x + ", " + pt1.y);
14:         System.out.println("Point2: " + pt2.x + ", " + pt2.y);
15:     }
16: }
```

Save and run the application. Figure 3.4 shows the output.

**FIGURE 3.4**
Putting references to a test.

```
Output - Java21 (run-single) ×
  compile-single:
  run-single:
  Point1: 200, 290
  Point2: 200, 290
  BUILD SUCCESSFUL (total time: 0 seconds)
```

The following takes place in the first part of this program:

- **Line 7:** Two `Point` variables are created.
- **Line 8:** A new `Point` object is assigned to pt1.
- **Line 9:** The variable pt1 is assigned to pt2.

Lines 11–14 are the tricky part. The x variable of pt1 is set to 200, the y variable is set to 290, and all variables of pt1 and pt2 are displayed.

You might expect pt1 and pt2 to have different values, but Figure 3.4 shows this not to be the case. The x and y variables of pt2 also have changed even though nothing in the program explicitly changes them. This happens because line 9 creates a reference from pt2 to pt1 instead of creating pt2 as a new object copied from pt1.

The variable pt2 is a reference to the same object as pt1. Either variable can be used to refer to the object or to change its variables.

If you wanted pt1 and pt2 to refer to separate objects, you could use separate `new Point()` statements on lines 8–9 to create separate objects, as shown here:

```
pt1 = new Point(100, 190);
pt2 = new Point(200, 190);
```

References in Java become particularly important when arguments are passed to methods. You'll learn more about this later in the lesson.

**NOTE**

Programmers with experience in the C and C++ languages may be wondering at this point if Java has explicit pointers or pointer arithmetic. It does not. The absence of these features, which can be difficult to implement without error, is a major reason the Java language was created. By using references and Java arrays, you can duplicate most pointer capabilities without many of the drawbacks of pointers.

3

# Casting Objects and Primitive Types

One thing you discover quickly about Java is how finicky it is about the information it will handle. Like Goldilocks, the child who is oddly hard to please about porridge despite being a person who breaks into homes, Java methods and constructors require things to take a specific form and won't accept alternatives.

When you send arguments to methods or use variables in expressions, you must use variables of the correct data types. If a method requires an `int`, the Java compiler responds with an error if you try to send a `float` value to the method. Likewise, if you set up one variable with the value of another, they must be of compatible types: Either the two variables must be the same type or the variable receiving the value must be big enough to hold the value.

**NOTE**

> There is one area where Java's compiler is decidedly flexible: with the `String` object. String handling in `println()` methods, assignment statements, and method arguments is simplified by the + concatenation operator. If any variable in a group of concatenated variables is a string, Java treats the whole thing as a `String`. This makes the following possible:
>
> ```
> float gpa = 3.25F;
> System.out.println("Honest, mom, my GPA is a " +
>    (gpa + 1.5));
> ```
>
> Using the concatenation operator, a single string can hold the text representation of multiple objects and primitive types in Java.

Sometimes you have a value in your Java class that isn't the right type for what you need. It might be the wrong class or the wrong data type, such as a `float` when you need an `int`.

In these situations, you can use a process called *casting* to convert a value from one type to another.

Although casting is reasonably simple, the process is complicated by the fact that Java has both primitive types (such as `int`, `float`, and `boolean`) and object classes (`String`, `Point`, and the like). This section discusses three forms of casts and conversions:

- Casting between primitive types, such as `int` to `float` or `float` to `double`
- Casting from an object of a class to an object of another class, such as from `Object` to `String`
- Casting primitive types to objects and then extracting primitive values from those objects

When discussing casting, it can be easier to think in terms of a source and a destination. The *source* is the variable being cast into another type. The *destination* is the result.

## Casting Primitive Types

Casting between primitive types makes it possible to convert the value of one type to another. This most commonly occurs with the numeric types, but one primitive type never can be used in a cast: Boolean values must be either `true` or `false` and cannot be used in a casting operation.

In many casts between primitive types, the destination can hold larger values than the source, so the value is converted easily. An example would be casting a `byte` into an `int`. Because a `byte` holds values from −128 to 127 and an `int` holds from around −2,100,000 to 2,100,000, there's more than enough room to cast a `byte` into an `int`.

Often you can automatically use a `byte` or `char` as an `int`, an `int` as a `long`, an `int` as a `float`, or anything as a `double`. In most cases, because the larger type provides more precision than the smaller, no loss of information occurs as a result. The exception is casting integers to floating-point values. Casting a `long` to a `float` or a `long` to a `double` can cause some loss of precision.

3

**NOTE**

> A character can be used as an `int` because each character has a corresponding numeric code that represents its position in the character set. If the variable `key` has the value `65`, the cast `(char)` `key` produces the character value `A`. The numeric code associated with a capital A is 65 in the ASCII character set, which Java adopted as part of its character support.

You must use an explicit cast to convert a value in a large type to a smaller type. Explicit casts take the following form:

```
(typename) value
```

Here *typename* is the name of the primitive data type to which you're converting, such as `short`, `int`, or `float`. *Value* is an expression that results in the value of the source type. For example, in the following statement, the value of `x` is divided by the value of `y`, and the result is cast into an `int`:

```
float x = 5.0F;
float y = 2.0F;
int result = (int)(x / y);
```

Note that because the precedence of casting is higher than that of arithmetic, you have to use parentheses here. Otherwise, first the value of x would be cast into an int, and then it would be divided by y, which could produce a different result.

## Casting Objects

Objects of classes also can be cast into objects of other classes when the source and destination classes are related by inheritance and one class is a subclass of the other.

Some objects might not need to be cast explicitly. In particular, because a subclass contains all the information as its superclass, you can use an object of a subclass anywhere a superclass is expected.

For example, consider a method that takes two arguments, one of type Object and another of type Component, in the java.awt package (which has classes for a graphical user interface).

You can pass an instance of any class for the Object argument because all Java classes are subclasses of Object.

For the Component argument, you can pass in its subclasses, such as Button, Container, and Label (all in java.awt).

This is true anywhere in a program, not just inside method calls. If you had a variable defined as class Component, you could assign objects of that class or any of its subclasses to that variable without casting.

This also is true in the reverse, so you can use a superclass when a subclass is expected. There is a catch, however: Because subclasses contain more behavior than their superclasses, a loss of precision occurs in the casting. Those superclass objects might not have all the behavior needed to act in place of a subclass object.

Consider this example: If you have an operation that calls methods in objects of the class Integer, using an object of its superclass Number won't include many methods specified in Integer. Errors occur if you try to call methods that the destination object doesn't have.

To use superclass objects where subclass objects are expected, you must explicitly cast them. You won't lose any information in the cast, but you gain all the methods and variables that the subclass defines.

To cast an object to another class, you use the same operation as for primitive types, which takes this form:

```
(classname) object
```

In this template, *classname* is the name of the destination class, and *object* is a reference to the source object. Casting creates a reference to the old object of the type *classname*; the old object continues to exist as it did before.

The following example casts an instance of the class `VicePresident` to an instance of the class `Employee`. `VicePresident` is a subclass of `Employee` with more information:

```
Employee emp = new Employee();
VicePresident veep = new VicePresident();
emp = veep; // no cast needed for upward use
veep = (VicePresident) emp; // must cast explicitly
```

When you begin working with graphical user interfaces in Lesson 9, "Creating a Graphical User Interface," you will see that casting one object is necessary whenever you use Java2D graphics operations. You must cast a `Graphics` object to a `Graphics2D` object before you can draw onscreen. The following example uses a `Graphics` object called `screen` to create a new `Graphics2D` object called `screen2D`:

```
Graphics2D screen2D = (Graphics2D) screen;
```

`Graphics2D` is a subclass of `Graphics`, and both belong to the `java.awt` package. You'll explore this subject fully in Line 13, "Creating Java2D Graphics."

In addition to casting objects to classes, you can cast objects to interfaces, but only if an object's class or one of its superclasses actually implements the interface. Casting an object to an interface means that you can call one of that interface's methods even if that object's class does not actually implement that interface.

## Converting Primitive Types to Objects and Vice Versa

One thing you can't do is cast from an object to a primitive data type or vice versa.

Primitive types and objects are different things in Java. The `java.lang` package includes classes that correspond to each primitive data type: `Float`, `Boolean`, `Byte`, and so on. Most of these classes have the same names as the data types, except that the class names begin with a capital letter (`Short` instead of `short`, `Double` instead of `double`, and the like). Also, two classes have names that differ from the corresponding data type: `Character` is used for `char` variables, and `Integer` is used for `int` variables.

Using the classes that correspond to each primitive type, you can create an object that holds the same value. The following statement creates an instance of the `Integer` class with the integer value `7801`:

```
Integer dataCount = new Integer(7801);
```

After you have created an object in this manner, you can use it as you would any object (although you cannot change its value). When you want to use that value again as a primitive value, there are methods for that as well. For example, the following statement shows how to get an int value from the dataCount object:

```
int newCount = dataCount.intValue(); // returns 7801
```

A common translation you need in programs is converting a String to a numeric type, such as an integer. When you need an int as the result, this can be done by using the parseInt() class method of the Integer class. The String to convert is the only argument sent to the method, as in the following example:

```
String pennsylvania = "65000";
int penn = Integer.parseInt(pennsylvania);
```

The following classes can be used to work with objects instead of primitive data types: Boolean, Byte, Character, Double, Float, Integer, Long, Short, and Void. These classes are commonly called *object wrappers* because they provide an object representation that contains a primitive value.

**CAUTION**

> If you try to use the preceding example in a program, your program won't compile. The parseInt() method is designed to fail with a NumberFormatException error if the argument to the method is not a valid numeric value. To deal with errors of this kind, you must use special error-handling statements, which are introduced in Lesson 7, "Exceptions and Threads."

Working with primitive types and objects that represent the same values is made easier through an automatic conversion process called *autoboxing* and *unboxing*. Autoboxing automatically converts a primitive type to an object. Unboxing converts in the other direction.

If you write a statement that uses an object where a primitive type is expected or vice versa, the value is converted so that the statement executes successfully.

Here's an example of autoboxing and unboxing:

```
Float f1 = 12.5F;
Float f2 = 27.2F;
System.out.println("Lower number: " + Math.min(f1, f2));
```

The Math.min() method takes two float values as arguments, but the preceding example instead sends the method two Float objects as arguments.

The compiler does not report an error over this discrepancy. Instead, the `Float` objects automatically are unboxed into `float` values before being sent to the `min()` method.

---

**CAUTION**   Unboxing an object works only if the object has a value. If no constructor has been called to set up the object, the Java program will not compile.

---

# Comparing Object Values and Classes

In addition to casting, you often will perform three other common tasks that involve objects:

- Comparing objects
- Finding out the class of any given object
- Testing whether an object is an instance of a given class

## Comparing Objects

In the previous lesson, you learned about operators for comparing values—equal, not equal, less than, and so on. Most of these operators work only on primitive types, not on objects. If you try to use other values as operands, the Java compiler reports an error.

The exceptions to this rule are the `==` operator for equality and the `!=` operator for inequality. When applied to objects, these operators don't do what you might first expect. Instead of checking whether one object has the same value as the other, they determine whether both sides of the operator refer to the same object.

To compare objects of a class and have meaningful results, you must implement special methods in your class and call those methods.

A good example of this is the `String` class. It is possible to have two different `String` objects that represent the same text. If you were to employ the `==` operator to compare these objects, however, they would be considered unequal because they are not entirely equal. Although their contents match, they are not the same object.

To see whether two `String` objects have matching values, an `equals()` method of the class is called. The method tests each character in the string and returns `true` if the two strings have the same value. The `EqualsTester` application shown in Listing 3.5 illustrates this. Create the application with NetBeans in the `com.java21days` package and save the file, either by choosing File, Save or clicking the Save All toolbar button.

**LISTING 3.5**   The Full Text of EqualsTester.java

```
 1: package com.java21days;
 2:
 3: class EqualsTester {
 4:     public static void main(String[] arguments) {
 5:         String str1, str2;
 6:         str1 = "Boy, that escalated quickly.";
 7:         str2 = str1;
 8:
 9:         System.out.println("String1: " + str1);
10:         System.out.println("String2: " + str2);
11:         System.out.println("Same object? " + (str1 == str2));
12:
13:         str2 = new String(str1);
14:
15:         System.out.println("String1: " + str1);
16:         System.out.println("String2: " + str2);
17:         System.out.println("Same object? " + (str1 == str2));
18:         System.out.println("Same value? " + str1.equals(str2));
19:     }
20: }
```

The program's output appears in Figure 3.5.

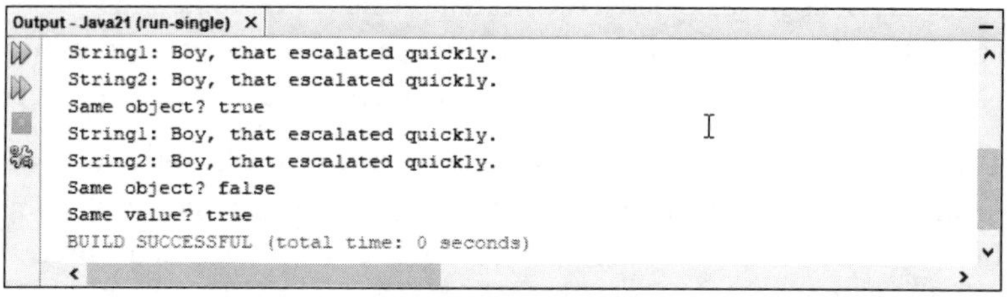

**FIGURE 3.5**
Comparing
the equality of
String objects.

```
Output - Java21 (run-single)  X
    String1: Boy, that escalated quickly.
    String2: Boy, that escalated quickly.
    Same object? true
    String1: Boy, that escalated quickly.
    String2: Boy, that escalated quickly.
    Same object? false
    Same value? true
    BUILD SUCCESSFUL (total time: 0 seconds)
```

The first part of this program declares two variables (str1 and str2), assigns the literal "Boy, that escalated quickly." to str1, and then assigns that value to str2 (lines 5–7). As you learned earlier, str1 and str2 now point to the same object, and the equality test at line 11 proves that.

In the second part of this program, you create a new String object with the same value as str1 and assign str2 to that new String object.

Now you have two different string objects in str1 and str2, both with the same value. Testing them to see whether they're the same object by using the == operator returns the expected answer: false (line 17). They are not the same object in memory. Testing them using the equals() method in line 18 also returns the expected answer, true, which shows that they have the same value.

**NOTE**

> Why can't you just use another literal when you change `str2`, instead of using `new`? String literals are optimized in Java. If you create a string using a literal and then use another literal in another statement with the same characters, Java gives you back the first `String` object. Both strings are the same object; you have to explicitly create two separate objects.

## Determining the Class of an Object

Want to find out the name of an object's class? Here's how for an object assigned to the variable `key`:

```
String name = key.getClass().getName();
```

The `getClass()` method is defined in the `Object` class, so it can be called in all Java objects. The method returns a `Class` object that represents the object's class. That object's `getName()` method returns a string holding the name of the class.

Another useful test is the `instanceof` operator, which has two operands: a reference to an object on the left and a class name on the right. The expression produces a Boolean value: `true` if the object is an instance of the named class or any of that class's subclasses and `false` otherwise, as in these examples:

```
boolean check1 = "Texas" instanceof String; // true

Object obiwan = new Object();
boolean check2 = obiwan instanceof String; // false
```

The `instanceof` operator also can be used for interfaces. If an object implements an interface, the `instanceof` operator returns `true` when this is tested.

Unlike other operators in Java, `instanceof` is not a form of punctuation like * for multiplication or + for addition. Instead, the `instanceof` keyword is the operator.

# Summary

Now that you have spent three lessons exploring how object-oriented programming is implemented in Java, you're in a better position to decide how useful it can be in your programming.

If you are a "glass half empty" kind of person, you may see object-oriented programming (OOP) as a level of abstraction that gets in the way of using a programming language.

You might change your mind as you learn more about why OOP is thoroughly ingrained in Java in the coming lessons.

If you are a "glass half full" kind of person, you may see OOP as beneficial because of its benefits: improved reliability, reusability, and maintenance.

This lesson demonstrates how you can deal with objects—by creating them, reading their values and changing them, and calling their methods. You also learned how to cast objects from one class to another, cast to and from primitive data types and classes, and take advantage of automatic conversions through autoboxing and unboxing.

# Q&A

**Q I'm confused about the differences between objects and the primitive data types, such as `int` and `boolean`.**

**A** The primitive types (`byte`, `short`, `int`, `long`, `float`, `double`, `boolean`, and `char`) are not objects, although in many ways they can be handled like objects. They can be assigned to variables and passed in and out of methods.

Objects are instances of classes and, as such, are much more complex data types than simple numbers and characters. They often contain numbers and characters as instance or class variables.

**Q The `length()` and `charAt()` methods in the `StringChecker` application don't appear to make sense. If `length()` says that a string is 33 characters long, shouldn't the characters be numbered from 1 to 33 when `charAt()` is used to display characters in the string?**

**A** The two methods look at strings differently. The `length()` method counts the characters in the string, with the first character counting as 1, the second as 2, and so on. The `charAt()` method considers the first character in the string to be located at position number 0. This is the same numbering system used with array elements in Java. Consider the string `"Charlie Brown"`. It has 13 characters ranging from position 0 (the letter *C*) to position 12 (the letter *n*).

**Q If Java lacks pointers, how can I do something like use linked lists, where there's a pointer from one node to another so that they can be traversed?**

**A** It's more accurate to state that Java has no *explicit* pointers than to say it has no pointers. Object references are effectively pointers. To create something like a linked list, you could create a class called `Node`, which would have an instance variable also of type `Node`. To link node objects, you assign a node object to the instance variable of the object immediately before it in the list. Because object references are pointers, linked lists set up this way behave as you would expect them to. (You'll work with the Java Class Library's version of linked lists in Lesson 8, "Data Structures.")

# Quiz

Review this lesson's material by taking this three-question quiz.

## Questions

1. What operator do you use to call an object's constructor and create a new object?

    **A.** `+`

    **B.** `new`

    **C.** `instanceof`

2. What kinds of methods apply to all objects of a class rather than an individual object?

    **A.** Universal methods

    **B.** Instance methods

    **C.** Class methods

3. If you have a program with objects named `obj1` and `obj2`, what happens when you use the statement `obj2 = obj1`?

    **A.** The instance variables in `obj2` are given the same values as `obj1`.

    **B.** `obj2` and `obj1` are considered to be the same object.

    **C.** Neither A nor B.

## Answers

1. **B.** The `new` operator is followed by a call to the object's constructor.

2. **C.** Class methods can be called without creating an object of that class.

3. **B.** The `=` operator does not copy values from one object to another. Instead, it makes both variables refer to the same object.

# Certification Practice

The following question is the kind of thing you could expect to be asked on a Java programming certification test. Answer it without looking at this lesson again or using the Java compiler to test the code.

Given:

```java
public class AyeAye {
    int i = 40;
    int j;

    public AyeAye() {
        setValue(i++);
    }

    void setValue(int inputValue) {
        int i = 20;
        j = i + 1;
        System.out.println("j = " + j);
    }
}
```

What is the value of the `j` variable at the time it is displayed inside the `setValue()` method?

    **A.** 42

    **B.** 40

    **C.** 21

    **D.** 20

The answer is available on the book's website, at www.java21days.com. Visit the Lesson 3 page and click the Certification Practice link.

# Exercises

To extend your knowledge of the subjects covered in this lesson, try the following exercises:

1. Create a program that turns a birthday in MM/DD/YYYY format (such as 04/29/2020) into three individual strings.

2. Create a class with instance variables for `height`, `weight`, and `depth`, making each an integer. Create a Java application that uses your new class, sets each of these values in an object, and displays the values.

Where applicable, exercise solutions are offered on the book's website, at www.java21days.com.

# LESSON 4
# Lists, Logic, and Loops

During this lesson, you'll learn about three of the most boring features in the Java language:

- How to organize groups of the same class or data type into lists called arrays

- How to make a program decide whether to do something based on logic

- How to make part of a Java program repeat itself by using loops

If these features don't sound boring to you, that's good. Most of the significant work that you will accomplish with your Java software will use all three.

These topics are boring for computers. They enable software to do one of the things at which it excels: performing repetitive tasks repeatedly.

# Arrays

At this point, you have dealt with only a few variables in each Java program. In some cases, it's manageable to use individual variables to store information, but what if you had 20 items of related information to track? You could create 20 different variables and set up their initial values, which might sound tedious but is achievable. That kind of approach becomes progressively more cumbersome as you deal with larger amounts of information. What if there were 100 items, or even 1,000?

An array allows you to store a list of items that have the same primitive data type, the same class, or a common parent class. Each item on the list goes into its own numbered slot so that you can easily access the information.

An array can contain any type of information that is stored in a variable, but after the array is created, you can use it for that information type only. For example, you can have an array of integers, an array of `String` objects, or an array of arrays, but you can't have an array that contains both `String` objects and primitive type integers.

There is one way around this prohibition: An array can hold a class and any of its subclasses. So an array of the `Object` class could contain any object in Java, including the classes that represent the same values as primitive types.

Java implements arrays differently than other programming languages—as objects treated like other objects.

To create an array in Java, you must do the following:

**1.** Declare a variable to hold the array.

**2.** Create a new array object and assign it to the array variable.

**3.** Store information in that array.

## Declaring Array Variables

The first step in array creation is to declare a variable that will hold the array. An array variable indicates the object or data type that the array will hold and the array's name. To differentiate from regular variable declarations, a pair of empty brackets (`[]`) is added to the object or data type or to the variable name.

The following statements are array variable declarations:

```
String[] requests;
Point[] targets;
float[] donations;
```

You also can declare an array by putting the brackets after the variable name instead of the information type, as in the following statements:

```
String requests[];
Point targets[];
float donations[];
```

The choice of which array-declaration style to use is a matter of personal preference. The sample programs in this book place the brackets after the information type rather than the variable name, which is far more popular among Java programmers.

## Creating Array Objects

After you declare an array variable, the next step is to create an array object and assign it to that variable. To do this:

- Use the new operator.
- Initialize the contents of the array directly.

Because arrays are objects in Java, you can use the new operator to create a new instance of an array, as in the following statement:

```
String[] players = new String[10];
```

This statement creates a new array of strings with 10 slots that can contain String objects. When you create an array object by using new, you must indicate how many slots the array will hold. This statement does not put actual String objects in the slots; you must do that later.

Array objects can contain primitive types, such as integers or Booleans, just as they can contain objects:

```
int[] temps = new int[99];
```

When you create an array object using new, all its slots automatically are given an initial value (0 for numeric arrays, false for Booleans, \0 for character arrays, and null for objects).

4

| NOTE | The Java keyword `null` refers to a `null` object (and can be used for any object reference). It is not equivalent to `0` or `\0`, as is the `NULL` constant in C. |
| --- | --- |

Because each object in an array of objects has a `null` reference when created, you must assign an object to each array element before using it.

The following example creates an array of three `Integer` objects and then assigns each element an object:

```
Integer[] series = new Integer[3];
series[0] = new Integer(10);
series[1] = new Integer(3);
series[2] = new Integer(5);
```

You can create and initialize an array at the same time by enclosing the array's elements inside braces (`{ }`), separated by commas:

```
Point[] markup = { new Point(1,5), new Point(3,3), new Point(2,3) };
```

Each of the elements inside the braces must be the same type as the variable that holds the array. When you create an array with initial values in this manner, the array is the same size as the number of elements you include within the braces. The preceding example creates an array of `Point` objects named `markup` that contains three elements.

Because `String` objects can be created and initialized without the `new` operator, you can do the same when creating an array of strings:

```
String[] titles = { "Mr.", "Mrs.", "Ms.", "Miss", "Dr." };
```

This statement creates a five-element array of `String` objects named `titles`.

Every array has an instance variable named `length` that holds a count of the number of elements in the array. Extending the preceding example, the variable `titles.length` contains the value `5`.

The first element of an array has a subscript of 0 rather than 1, so an array with five elements has array slots accessed using subscripts 0 through 4. In the `titles` array, the string `"Mr."` is at element 0, and `"Dr."` at element 4.

## Accessing Array Elements

After you have an array set up with initial values, you can retrieve, change, and test the values in each slot of that array. The value in a slot is accessed using the array name followed by a subscript enclosed in square brackets. This name and subscript can be put into expressions, as in the following:

```
testScore[40] = 920;
```

This statement sets the 41st element of the `testScore` array to a value of `920`, since element numbering begins with 0. The `testScore` side of this expression is a variable holding an array object, although it also can be an expression that results in an array. The subscript expression specifies the slot to access within the array.

All array subscripts are checked to make sure that they are inside the array's boundaries, as specified when the array was created. In Java, it is impossible to access or assign a value to an array slot outside the array's boundaries. This avoids the problems that result from overrunning the bounds of an array in other languages. Note the following two statements:

```
float[] rating = new float[20];
rating[20] = 3.22F;
```

Typing these statements into NetBeans would produce an error because the `rating` array does not have a slot numbered 20; it has 20 slots that begin at 0 and end at 19. The Java compiler would fail with an `ArrayIndexOutOfBoundsException` error.

4

The Java Virtual Machine (JVM) also notes an error if the array subscript is calculated when the program is running and the subscript is outside the array's boundaries. You'll learn more about errors, which in Java commonly are called *exceptions*, in Lesson 7, "Exceptions and Threads."

One way to avoid accidentally overrunning the end of an array in your programs is to use the `length` instance variable. The following statement displays the number of elements in the `rating` array:

```
System.out.println("Elements: " + rating.length);
```

## Changing Array Elements

As you have seen in previous examples, you can assign a value to a specific slot in an array by putting an assignment statement after the array name and subscript, as in the following:

```
temperature[4] = 85;
day[0] = "Sunday";
manager[2] = manager[0];
```

It's important to remember that an array of objects in Java is an array of references to those objects. When you assign a value to a slot in an object array, you are creating a reference to that object. When you move around values inside arrays, you are reassigning the reference rather than copying a value from one slot to another. Arrays of a primitive data type, such as int and float, do copy the values from one slot to another, as do elements of a String array, even though they are objects.

Arrays are simple to create and modify, and they provide an enormous amount of functionality in Java. The HalfDollars application, shown in Listing 4.1, creates, initializes, and displays elements of three arrays. Create a new empty Java file in NetBeans called HalfDollars in the com.java21days package and enter the listing's source code into the editor.

**LISTING 4.1**  The Full Text of HalfDollars.java

```
 1: package com.java21days;
 2:
 3: class HalfDollars {
 4:     public static void main(String[] arguments) {
 5:         int[] denver = { 2_100_000, 2_900_000, 6_100_000 };
 6:         int[] philadelphia = new int[denver.length];
 7:         int[] total = new int[denver.length];
 8:         int average;
 9:
10:         philadelphia[0] = 2_100_000;
11:         philadelphia[1] = 1_800_000;
12:         philadelphia[2] = 4_800_000;
13:
14:         total[0] = denver[0] + philadelphia[0];
15:         total[1] = denver[1] + philadelphia[1];
16:         total[2] = denver[2] + philadelphia[2];
17:         average = (total[0] + total[1] + total[2]) / 3;
18:
19:         System.out.print("2016 production: ");
20:         System.out.format("%,d%n", total[0]);
21:         System.out.print("2017 production: ");
22:         System.out.format("%,d%n", total[1]);
23:         System.out.print("2018 production: ");
24:         System.out.format("%,d%n", total[2]);
25:         System.out.print("Average production: ");
26:         System.out.format("%,d%n", average);
27:     }
28: }
```

The HalfDollars application uses three integer arrays to store production totals for U.S. half-dollar coins produced at the Denver and Philadelphia mints. When you run the program, it displays the output shown in Figure 4.1.

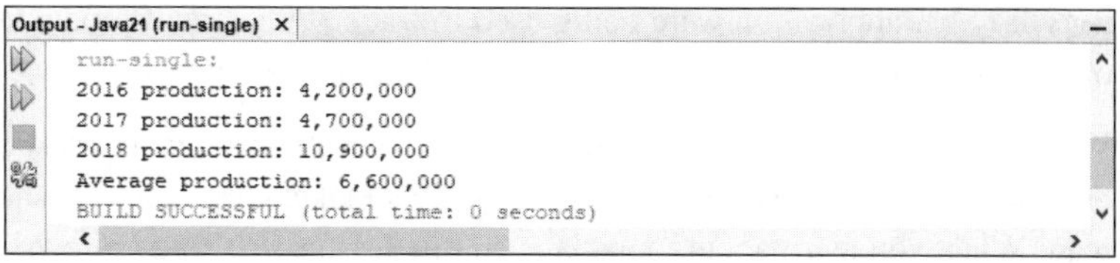

**FIGURE 4.1**
Displaying the
contents of a
String array.

The class created here, `HalfDollars`, has three instance variables that hold arrays of integers.

The first, which is named `denver`, is declared and initialized on line 5 to contain three integers: `2_100_000` in element 0, `2_900_000` in element 1, and `6_100_000` in element 2. These figures are the total half-dollar production at the Denver mint for three years. The integers use an underscore character (_) after every three digits to make the numbers more human readable. The compiler ignores the underscores.

The second and third instance variables, `philadelphia` and `total`, are declared on lines 6 and 7. The `philadelphia` array contains the production totals for the Philadelphia mint, and `total` is used to store the overall production totals.

No initial values are assigned to the slots of the `philadelphia` and `total` arrays in lines 6 and 7. For this reason, each element is given the default value for integers: `0`.

The `denver.length` variable is used to give both of these arrays the same number of slots as the `denver` array. Every array contains a `length` variable that you can use to keep track of the number of elements it contains.

The rest of the `main()` method of this application does the following:

- Line 8 creates an integer variable called `average`.
- Lines 10–12 assign new values to the three elements of the `philadelphia` array.
- Lines 14–16 assign new values to the elements of the `total` array. In line 14, `total` element 0 is given the sum of `denver` element 0 and `philadelphia` element 0. Similar expressions are used in lines 15 and 16.
- Line 17 sets `average` to the average of the three `total` elements. Because `average` and the three `total` elements are integers, the average is expressed as an integer rather than as a floating-point number.
- Lines 19–26 display the values stored in the `total` array and the `average` variable, using the `System.out.format()` method to display the numeric values in a more readable form, using commas.

This application handles arrays inefficiently. The statements are almost identical, except for the subscripts that indicate the array element to which you are referring. If the

`HalfDollars` application were being used to track 100 years of production totals instead of 3, this approach would require a lot of redundant statements.

When dealing with arrays, you can use loops to cycle through an array's elements instead of dealing with each element individually. This makes the code a lot shorter and easier to read. When you learn about loops later in this lesson, you'll see a rewrite of the current example.

## Multidimensional Arrays

Arrays can be multidimensional, containing more than one subscript to store information in multiple dimensions.

A common use of a multidimensional array is to represent the data in an (x, y) grid of array elements.

Java supports this by enabling an array to hold an array as each of its elements. Those arrays also can contain arrays, and so on, for as many dimensions as needed.

For example, consider a program that needs to accomplish the following tasks:

- Record an integer value each day for a year.
- Organize those values by week.

One way to organize this data is to create a 52-element array in which each element contains a 7-element array:

```
int[][] dayValue = new int[53][7];
```

This array of arrays contains a total of 371 integers, enough room for each day of the year (plus a few extra). You could set the value for the first day of the 10th week with the following statement:

```
dayValue[9][0] = 14200;
```

Remember that array indexes start at 0 instead of 1, so the 10th week is at element 9, and the first day is at element 0.

You can use the `length` instance variable with these arrays as you would any other. The following statement contains a three-dimensional array of integers and displays the number of elements in each dimension:

```
int[][][] cen = new int[100][52][7];
System.out.println("Elements in 1st dimension: " + cen.length);
System.out.println("Elements in 2nd dimension: " + cen[0].length);
System.out.println("Elements in 3rd dimension: " + cen[0][0].length);
```

# Block Statements

Statements in Java are grouped into blocks. The beginning and ending boundaries of a block are noted with brace characters—an opening brace ({) for the beginning and a closing brace (}) for the ending.

You have used blocks to hold the variables and methods in a class definition and define statements that belong in a method.

Blocks also are called *block statements* because an entire block can be used anywhere a single statement could be used. Each statement inside the block then is executed from top to bottom.

You can put blocks inside other blocks, just as you do when you put a method inside a class definition.

An important thing to note about using a block is that it creates a scope for the local variables created inside the block. Scope is the part of a program where a variable exists and can be used. If you try to use a variable outside its scope, an error occurs.

In Java, the scope of a variable is the block in which it was created. When you can declare and use local variables inside a block, those variables cease to exist after the block is finished executing. For example, the following method contains a block inside the method:

4

```java
void testBlock() {
    int x = 10;
    { // start of block
        int y = 40;
        y = y + x;
    } // end of block
}
```

Two variables are defined in this method: x and y. The scope of the y variable is the block it's in, which is marked by the comments // start of block and // end of block. The variable can be used only within that block. An error would result if you tried to use the y variable in another part of the method.

The x variable was created inside the method but outside the inner block, so it can be used anywhere in the method. You can modify the value of x anywhere within the method.

Block statements are used in class and method definitions and the logic and looping structures you'll learn about next. The way the preceding example uses the inner block is not common—it's done here for illustrative purposes—but it's valid Java.

# if **Conditionals**

A key aspect of any programming language is how it enables a program to make decisions. This is handled through a type of statement called a *conditional*, a statement executed only if a specific condition is met.

The simplest conditional in Java is if. The if conditional uses a Boolean expression to decide whether a statement should be executed. If the expression produces a true value, the statement is executed.

Here's a simple example that displays the message Not enough arguments only if the value of an instance variable is less than 3:

```
if (arguments.length < 3) {
    System.out.println("Not enough arguments");
    System.exit(-1);
}
```

If you want something else to happen when an if expression is not true, you can use the else keyword. The following example uses both if and else:

```
String server;
int duration;
if (arguments.length < 1) {
    server = "localhost";
} else {
    server = arguments[0];
}
```

The if conditional executes different statements based on the result of a single Boolean test.

> **NOTE**        A difference between if conditionals in Java and those in other languages is that Java conditionals produce only Boolean values (true or false). In C and C++, such a test can return an integer.

Using if, you can include only a single statement as the code to execute if the test expression is true and another statement if the expression is false.

However, as you learned earlier, a block can appear anywhere in Java that a single statement can appear. If you want to do more than one thing as a result of an `if` statement, you can enclose those statements inside a block. Note the following code, which is also used in Lesson 1, "Getting Started with Java":

```
int speed;
String status;
float temperature = -60;

if (temperature < -80) {
    status = "returning home";
    speed = 5;
}
```

The `if` statement in this example contains the test expression `temperature < -80`. If the `temperature` variable contains a value less than −80, the block statement is executed, and two things occur:

- The `status` variable is given the value `returning home`.
- The `speed` variable is set to `5`.

If the `temperature` variable is equal to or greater than −80, the entire block is skipped, and nothing happens.

All `if` and `else` statements use Boolean tests to determine whether statements are executed. You can use a `boolean` variable itself for this test, as in the following:

```
String status;
boolean outOfGas = true;
if (outOfGas) {
    status = "inactive";
}
```

The preceding example uses a `boolean` variable called `outOfGas`. It functions exactly like the following:

```
if (outOfGas == true) {
    status = "inactive";
}
```

# Switch Conditionals

A common programming practice is to test a variable against a value, and if it doesn't match, test it again against a different value, and so on.

This approach can become unwieldy if you're using only `if` statements, depending on how many different values you have to test. For example, you might end up with a set of `if` statements something like the following:

```
if (operation == '+') {
    add(object1, object2);
} else if (operation == '-') {
    subtract(object1, object2);
} else if (operation == '*') {
    multiply(object1, object2);
} else if (operation == '/') {
    divide(object1, object2);
}
```

This use of `if` statements is called a *nested* if *statement* because each `else` statement contains another `if` until all possible tests have been made.

A better way to handle this situation in Java is by grouping conditions with the `switch` statement. The following example demonstrates `switch` usage:

```
char grade = 'D';
switch (grade) {
    case 'A':
        System.out.println("Great job!");
        break;
    case 'B':
        System.out.println("Good job!");
        break;
    case 'C':
        System.out.println("You can do better!");
        break;
    default:
        System.out.println("Ouch!");
}
```

A `switch` statement is built on a test variable. In the preceding example, the variable is the value of the `grade` variable, which holds a `char` value.

The test variable can be the primitive types `byte`, `char`, `short`, or `int` or the class `String`. The following code uses the value of a `String` object named `command` to decide which method to call:

```
String command = "close";
switch (command) {
    case "open":
        openFile();
        break;
```

```
    case "close":
        closeFile();
        break;
    default:
        System.out.println("Invalid command");
    }
}
```

The test variable is compared in turn with each `case` value. If a match is found, the statement or statements after the test are executed.

If no match is found, the `default` statement or statements are executed providing a `default` statement is optional. If it is omitted and there is no match for any of the `case` statements, the `switch` statement might complete without executing anything.

The test cases in a `switch` statement are limited to primitive types that can be cast to an `int`, such as `char` or strings. You cannot use larger primitive types such as `long` or `float` or test for any relationship other than equality.

The following is a revision of the nested `if` example shown previously. It has been rewritten as a `switch` statement:

```
switch (operation) {
    case '+':
        add(object1, object2);
        break;
    case '-':
        subtract(object1, object2);
        break;
    case '*':
        multiply(object1, object2);
        break;
    case '/':
        divide(object1, object2);
        break;
}
```

After each `case`, you can include a single result statement or as many as you need. Unlike `if` statements, multiple statements don't require a block statement.

The `break` statement included with each `case` section determines when to stop executing statements in response to a matching `case`. Suppose a `case` section has no `break` statement. After a match is made, the statements for that match and all the statements further down the `switch` are executed until a `break` or the end of the switch is found.

In some situations, this might be exactly what you want to do. Otherwise, you should include break statements to ensure that only the right code is executed. The break statement, which you'll use again later in this lesson, in the section "Breaking Out of Loops," stops execution at the current point. Then it jumps to the statement after the closing brace that ends the switch statement.

One handy use of falling through without a break occurs when multiple values need to execute the same statements. To accomplish this task, you can use multiple case lines with no result; the switch executes the first statement it finds.

For example, in the following switch statement, the string x is an even number is printed if x has a value of 2, 4, 6, or 8; all other values of x cause the string x is an odd number to be printed:

```
int x = 5;
switch (x) {
    case 2:
    case 4:
    case 6:
    case 8:
        System.out.println("x is an even number");
        break;
    default:
        System.out.println("x is an odd number");
}
```

The next project, the DayCounter application in Listing 4.2, takes a month and a year as arguments and displays the number of days in that month. A switch statement, if statements, and else statements are used. Create this application in NetBeans as an empty Java file in the com.java21days package.

**LISTING 4.2**    The Full Text of DayCounter.java

```
 1: package com.java21days;
 2:
 3: class DayCounter {
 4:     public static void main(String[] arguments) {
 5:         int yearIn = 2020;
 6:         int monthIn = 2;
 7:         if (arguments.length > 0) {
 8:             monthIn = Integer.parseInt(arguments[0]);
 9:         }
10:         if (arguments.length > 1) {
11:             yearIn = Integer.parseInt(arguments[1]);
12:         }
13:         System.out.println(monthIn + "/" + yearIn + " has "
```

```
14:                       + countDays(monthIn, yearIn) + " days.");
15:         }
16:
17:      static int countDays(int month, int year) {
18:           int count = -1;
19:           switch (month) {
20:                case 1:
21:                case 3:
22:                case 5:
23:                case 7:
24:                case 8:
25:                case 10:
26:                case 12:
27:                     count = 31;
28:                     break;
29:                case 4:
30:                case 6:
31:                case 9:
32:                case 11:
33:                     count = 30;
34:                     break;
35:                case 2:
36:                     if (year % 4 == 0) {
37:                          count = 29;
38:                     } else {
39:                          count = 28;
40:                     }
41:                     if ((year % 100 == 0) & (year % 400 != 0)) {
42:                          count = 28;
43:                     }
44:           }
45:           return count;
46:      }
47: }
```

This application uses command-line arguments to specify the month and year to check. The first argument is the month, which should be expressed as a number from 1 to 12. The second argument is the year, which should be expressed as a full four-digit year.

If the application is run without setting the arguments, it uses 2 as the month and 2020 as the year, displaying the output in Figure 4.2.

**FIGURE 4.2**
Using switch and
case to handle numer-
ous conditionals.

To set command-line arguments in NetBeans, choose Run, Set Project Configuration, Customize. The Project Properties dialog opens, as shown in Figure 4.3.

**FIGURE 4.3**
Setting command-line arguments for an application in NetBeans.

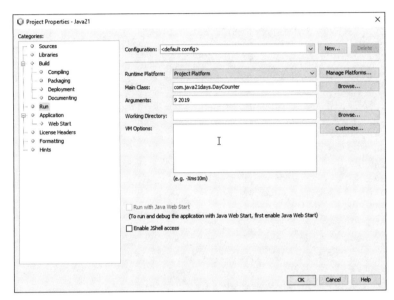

In the Main Class field, enter the name of the class that contains the `main()` method that will be run: `com.java21days.DayCounter`. In the Arguments field, enter the command-line arguments separated by spaces, such as `9 2019`. Click OK to save this configuration.

To run the application with these arguments in NetBeans, choose Run, Run Project (instead of Run, Run File). When run with `9` and `2019` as arguments, the output is as shown in Figure 4.4.

**FIGURE 4.4**
Using `switch` and `case` to handle numerous conditionals.

The `DayCounter` application uses a `switch` statement to count the days in a month. This statement is part of the `countDays()` method that begins on line 17 of Listing 4.2.

The `countDays()` method has two `int` arguments: `month` and `year`. The number of days is stored in the `count` variable, which is given an initial value of `-1` and is replaced by the correct count later.

The switch statement that begins on line 19 uses month as its conditional value.

The number of days in a month is easy to determine for 11 months of the year. January, March, May, July, August, October, and December have 31 days. April, June, September, and November have 30 days.

The count for these 11 months is handled in lines 20–34 of Listing 4.2. Months are numbered from 1 (January) to 12 (December), as you would expect. When one of the case statements has the same value as month, every statement after that is executed until break or the end of the switch statement is reached.

February is more complex and is handled in lines 36–43. Every leap year has 29 days in February, whereas other years have 28. A leap year must meet either of the following conditions:

- The year must be evenly divisible by 4 and not evenly divisible by 100.
- The year must be evenly divisible by 400.

As you learned in Lesson 2, "The ABCs of Programming," the modulus operator (%) returns the remainder of a division operation. This is used with several if-else statements to determine how many days there are in February, depending on what year it is.

The if-else statement in lines 36–40 sets count to 29 when the year is evenly divisible by 4 and sets it to 28 otherwise.

The if statement in lines 41–43 uses the & operator to combine two conditional expressions: year % 100 == 0 and year % 400 != 0. If both these conditions are true, count is set to 28.

The countDays method ends by returning the value of count in line 45.

When you run the DayCounter application, the main() method in lines 4–15 is executed.

In all Java applications, command-line arguments are stored in an array of String objects. This array is called arguments in DayCounter. The first command-line argument is stored in argument[0], the second in argument[1], and upward until all arguments have been stored. If the application is run with no arguments, the array is created with no elements.

Lines 5 and 6 create yearIn and monthIn, two integer variables to store the year and month that should be checked.

The if statement in line 7 uses arguments.length to make sure that the arguments array has at least one element. If it does, line 8 is executed.

4

Line 8 calls `parseInt()`, a class method of the `Integer` class, with `arguments[0]` as an argument. This method takes a `String` object as an argument, and if the string could be a valid integer, it returns that value as an `int`. This converted value is stored in `monthIn`. A similar thing happens in line 11: `parseInt()` is called with `arguments[1]`, and this is used to set `yearIn`.

The program's output is displayed in lines 13–14. As part of the output, the `countDays()` method is called with `monthIn` and `yearIn`, and the value returned by this method is displayed.

**NOTE** _____ | At this point, you might want to know how to collect input from a user in a program rather than using command-line arguments to receive it. There isn't a method comparable to `System.out.println()` that receives input. Instead, you must learn a bit more about Java's input and output classes before you can receive input in a program without a graphical user interface. This topic is covered in Lesson 16, "Working with Input and Output."

# The Ternary Operator

An alternative to using the `if` and `else` keywords in a conditional statement is to use the *ternary operator*, also called the *conditional operator*. This operator is ternary because it has three operands (the word *ternary* refers to having three parts).

This operator is an expression, meaning that it returns a value—unlike the more general `if`, which can result in only a statement or block being executed. The operator is most useful for short or simple conditionals and takes the following form:

```
test ? trueResult : falseResult;
```

test is an expression that returns `true` or `false`, just like the test in the `if` statement. If test is `true`, the conditional operator returns the value of trueResult. If test is `false`, the conditional operator returns the value of falseResult. For example, the following conditional tests the values of `myScore` and `yourScore` and sets the variable `ourBestScore` equal to one of them:

```
int ourBestScore = myScore > yourScore ? myScore : yourScore;
```

In this statement, the larger value of `myScore` and `yourScore` is copied to `ourBestScore`.

This use of the ternary operator is equivalent to the following `if-else` code:

```
int ourBestScore;
if (myScore > yourScore) {
    ourBestScore = myScore;
} else {
    ourBestScore = yourScore;
}
```

The ternary operator has low precedence. Usually it is evaluated only after all its subexpressions have been evaluated. The only operators lower in precedence are the assignment operators. For a refresher on operator precedence, refer to Table 2.6 in Lesson 2.

**NOTE**

> The ternary operator's functionality is duplicated in simpler use of `if-else` statements, so in most cases there's no need to use this operator while you're beginning to learn the language. But the ternary operator comes into its own when you need to return a value, which doesn't happen in Java with an `if` statement.

# for **Loops**

4

A `for` loop is used to repeat a statement until a condition is met. Although `for` loops frequently are used for simple iteration in which a statement is repeated a certain number of times, `for` loops can be used for just about any kind of loop.

The `for` loop in Java has the following structure:

```
for (initialization; test; increment) {
    statement;
}
```

The start of a `for` loop has three parts:

- *initialization* is an expression that initializes the start of the loop. If you have a loop index, this expression might declare and initialize it, such as int i = 0. Variables that you declare in this part of the `for` loop are local to the loop itself. They cease to exist after the loop is finished executing. You can initialize more than one variable in this section by separating the expressions with commas. The statement int i = 0, j = 10 in this section would declare the variables i and j, and both would be local to the loop.

- *test* is the test that occurs before each pass of the loop. The test must be a Boolean expression or a function that returns a `boolean` value, such as `i < 10`. If the test is `true`, the loop executes. When the test is `false`, the loop stops executing.

- *increment* is any expression or method call. Commonly, the increment is used to change the value of the loop index to bring the state of the loop closer to returning `false` and stopping the loop. The increment takes place after each pass of the loop. As with the *initialization* section, you can put more than one expression in this section by separating the expression with commas.

The *statement* part of the `for` loop is the statement that is executed each time the loop iterates. As with `if`, you can include either a single statement or a block statement. The previous example uses a block because that is more common. The following example is a `for` loop that sets all slots of a `String` array to the value `"Mr."`:

```
String[] salutation = new String[10];
int i; // the loop index variable
for (i = 0; i < salutation.length; i++) {
    salutation[i] = "Mr.";
}
```

In this example, the variable `i` serves as a loop index; it counts the number of times the loop has been executed. Before each trip through the loop, the index value is compared with `salutation.length`, the number of elements in the `salutation` array. When the index is equal to or greater than `salutation.length`, the loop is exited.

The final element of the `for` statement is `i++`. This causes the loop index to increment by 1 each time the loop is executed. Without this statement, the loop would never stop.

The statement inside the loop sets an element of the `salutation` array equal to `"Mr."`. The loop index is used to determine which element is modified.

Any part of the `for` loop can be an empty statement; in other words, you can include a semicolon with no expression or statement, and that part of the `for` loop is ignored. Note that if you do use an empty statement in your `for` loop, you might have to initialize or increment any loop variables or loop indexes yourself elsewhere in the program.

You also can have an empty statement as the body of your `for` loop if everything you want to do is in the first line of that loop. For example, the following `for` loop finds the first prime number higher than 4,000. (It assumes the existence of a method called `notPrime()` that returns a Boolean value to indicate when `i` is not prime.)

```
for (i = 4001; notPrime(i); i += 2);
```

The semicolon at the end of the `for` statement indicates that the loop has no statements in its body.

A common mistake in `for` loops is accidentally putting a semicolon at the end of the line that includes the `for` statement:

```
int x = 1;
for (i = 0; i < 10; i++);
    x = x * i; // this line is not inside the loop!
```

In this example, the semicolon outside the parentheses in the `for` statement ends the loop without executing `x = x * i` as part of the loop. The `x = x * i` line is executed only once because it is outside the `for` loop. Be careful not to make this mistake in your Java programs.

The next project you'll undertake is a rewrite of the `HalfDollar` application that uses `for` loops to remove redundant code.

The original application works with an array that is only three elements long. The new version, called `HalfLooper` and shown in Listing 4.3, is shorter and more flexible, and it returns the same output. Create an empty Java file with that class name and the package name `com.java21days` in NetBeans.

4

**LISTING 4.3**   The Full Text of `HalfLooper.java`

```
 1: package com.java21days;
 2:
 3: class HalfLooper {
 4:     public static void main(String[] arguments) {
 5:         int[] denver = { 2_100_000, 2_900_000, 6_100_000 };
 6:         int[] philadelphia = { 2_100_000, 1_800_000, 4_800_000 };
 7:         int[] total = new int[denver.length];
 8:         int sum = 0;
 9:
10:         for (int i = 0; i < denver.length; i++) {
11:             total[i] = denver[i] + philadelphia[i];
12:             System.out.format((i + 2015) + " production: %,d%n",
13:                 total[i]);
14:             sum += total[i];
15:         }
16:
17:         System.out.format("Average production: %,d%n",
18:             (sum / denver.length));
19:     }
20: }
```

The output of `HalfLooper` is the same as for the `HalfDollars` application in Figure 4.1.

Instead of going through the elements of the three arrays one by one, this example uses a `for` loop. The following things take place in the loop, which is contained in lines 10–15:

- **Line 10:** The loop is created with an `int` variable called i as the index. The index increments by 1 for each pass through the loop and stops when i is equal to or greater than `denver.length`, the total number of elements in the `denver` array.
- **Lines 11–12:** The value of one of the `total` elements is set using the loop index and then is displayed with some text identifying the year.
- **Line 14:** The value of a `total` element is added to the `sum` variable, which is used to calculate the average yearly production.

Using a more general-purpose loop to iterate over an array enables you to use the program with arrays of different sizes and still have it assign correct values to the elements of the total array and display those values.

**NOTE**

> Java also includes a `for` loop that can be used to iterate through all the elements of data structures, such as array lists, linked lists, hash maps, and other collections. This loop is covered along with those structures in Lesson 8, "Data Structures."

# `while` **and** do **Loops**

The remaining types of loops are `while` and `do`, which also enable a block of Java code to be executed repeatedly until a specific condition is met.

## `while` **Loops**

A `while` loop repeats a statement for as long as a particular condition remains `true`. Here's an example:

```
while (i < 13) {
    x = x * i++; // the body of the loop
}
```

The condition that accompanies the `while` keyword is a Boolean expression—i < 13 in the preceding example. If the expression returns `true`, the `while` loop executes the body of the loop and then tests the condition again. This process repeats until the condition is `false`.

Although the preceding loop uses opening and closing braces to form a block statement, the braces are unneeded because the loop contains only one statement: x = x * i++. Using the braces does not create any problems, though, and the braces will be required if you add another statement inside the loop later.

The ArrayCopier application in Listing 4.4 uses a while loop to copy the elements of an array of integers (array1) to an array of float variables (array2), casting each element to a float as it goes. The one catch is that if any of the elements in the first array is 1, the loop immediately exits at that point.

Create an empty Java file in NetBeans with the class name ArrayCopier and package com.java21days. Enter Listing 4.4 as the source code.

**LISTING 4.4**    The Full Text of ArrayCopier.java

```
 1: package com.java21days;
 2:
 3: class ArrayCopier {
 4:     public static void main(String[] arguments) {
 5:         int[] array1 = { 7, 4, 8, 1, 4, 1, 4 };
 6:         float[] array2 = new float[array1.length];
 7:
 8:         System.out.print("array1: [ ");
 9:         for (int i = 0; i < array1.length; i++) {
10:             System.out.print(array1[i] + " ");
11:         }
12:         System.out.println("]");
13:
14:         System.out.print("array2: [ ");
15:         int count = 0;
16:         while ( count < array1.length && array1[count] != 1) {
17:             array2[count] = (float) array1[count];
18:             System.out.print(array2[count++] + " ");
19:         }
20:         System.out.println("]");
21:     }
22: }
```

The output is shown in Figure 4.5.

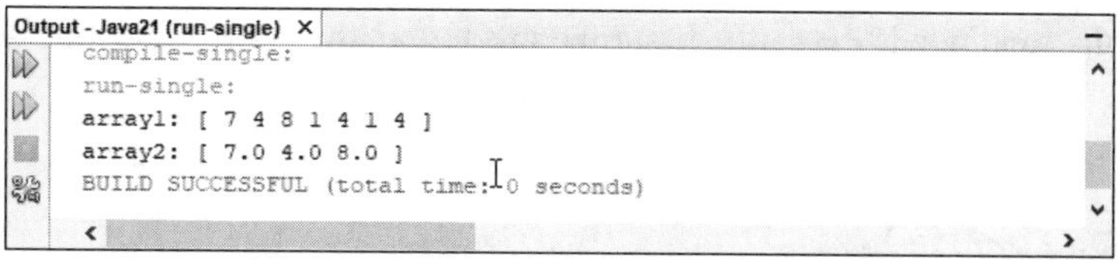

**FIGURE 4.5**

Using a while loop to examine an array.

```
Output - Java21 (run-single)  ×
    compile-single:
    run-single:
    array1: [ 7 4 8 1 4 1 4 ]
    array2: [ 7.0 4.0 8.0 ]
    BUILD SUCCESSFUL (total time: 0 seconds)
```

Here is what's going on in the `main()` method:

- Lines 5 and 6 declare the arrays. `array1` is an array of integers, which are initialized to some suitable numbers. `array2` is an array of floating-point numbers the same length as `array1`.

- Lines 9–11 iterate through `array1` using a `for` loop to print its values.

- Lines 16–19 assign the values of `array2` (converting the numbers to floating-point numbers along the array) and print them. You start with a `count` variable, which keeps track of the array index elements. The test in the `while` loop keeps track of the two conditions for exiting the loop, where those two conditions are running out of elements in `array1` or encountering a 1 in `array1`.

- You can use the logical conditional `&&` operator to keep track of the test; remember that `&&` makes sure that both conditions are `true` before the entire expression is `true`. If either one is `false`, the expression returns `false`, and the loop exits.

The program's output shows that the first four elements in `array1` were copied to `array2`, but a 1 in the middle stopped the loop from going any further. Without the 1, `array2` should end up with all the same elements as `array1`. If the `while` loop's test initially is `false` the first time it is tested (for example, if the first element in that first array is 1), the body of the `while` loop will never be executed. If you need to execute the loop at least once, you can do one of two things:

- Duplicate the body of the loop outside the `while` loop.

- Use a `do` loop (as described in the following section).

The `do` loop is considered the better solution.

## do-while **Loops**

The `do` loop is like a `while` loop, with one major difference—the place in the loop where the condition is tested.

A `while` loop tests the condition before looping, so if the condition is `false` the first time it is tested, the body of the loop never executes.

A `do` loop executes the body of the loop at least once before testing the condition. So if the condition is `false` the first time it is tested, the body of the loop already will have executed once.

The following example uses a do loop to keep doubling the value of a long integer until it is larger than 3 trillion:

```
long i = 1;
do {
    i *= 2;
    System.out.print(i + " ");
} while (i < 3_000_000_000_000L);
```

The body of the loop is executed once before the test condition, i < 3_000_000_000_000L, is evaluated. Then, if the test evaluates as true, the loop runs again. If it is false, the loop exits. Keep in mind that the body of the loop executes at least once with do loops.

The difference between do and while recalls every rebellious teen's favorite saying: "It's better to ask forgiveness than beg permission." The while loop does nothing without the permission of a true test. The do loop does one trip through the loop before checking whether the test is true.

The for, while, and do loops all accomplish the same purpose in slightly different ways. When writing your own code, you may have trouble deciding which one to use. There's often no wrong answer. Whether you use a for, while, or do loop is largely a matter of preference.

4

# Breaking Out of Loops

Any loop ends when a tested condition is met. There might be times when something occurs during execution of a loop, and you want to exit the loop early. In that case, you can use the break and continue keywords.

You already have seen break as part of the switch statement; break stops execution of the switch statement, and the program continues. The break keyword, when used with a loop, does the same thing: It immediately halts execution of the current loop. If you have nested loops within loops, execution picks up with the next outer loop. Otherwise, the program continues executing the next statement after the loop.

For example, recall the while loop from the ArrayCopier application in Listing 4.4. It copies elements from an integer array into an array of floating-point numbers until either the end of the array or a `1` is reached. You can test for the latter case inside the body of the `while` loop and then use `break` to exit the loop:

```
int count = 0;
while (count < array1.length) {
    if (array1[count] == 1) {
        break;
    }
    array2[count] = (float) array2[count++];
}
```

The `continue` keyword starts the loop over at the next iteration. For `do` and `while` loops, this means that the execution of the block statement starts over again; with `for` loops, the increment expression is evaluated, and then the block statement is executed.

The `continue` keyword is useful when you want to make a special case out of elements within a loop. With the previous example of copying one array to another, you could test for whether the current element is equal to `1` and use `continue` to restart the loop after every `1` so that the resulting array never contains `0`. Note that because you're skipping elements in the first array, you now must keep track of two different array counters:

```
int count = 0;
int count2 = 0;
while (count++ <= array1.length) {
    if (array1[count] == 1) {
        continue;
    }
    array2[count2++] = (float) array1[count];
}
```

## Labeled Loops

Both `break` and `continue` can have an optional label that indicates where to resume execution of the program. Without a label, `break` jumps outside the nearest loop to an enclosing loop or to the next statement outside the loop. The `continue` keyword restarts the loop it is enclosed within. Using `break` and `continue` with a label enables you to use `break` to go to a point outside a nested loop or to use `continue` to go to a loop outside the current loop.

To use a labeled loop, add the label before the initial part of the loop with a colon between the label and the loop. Then, when you use `break` or `continue`, add the name of the label after the keyword, as in the following:

```
out: for (int i = 0; i < 10; i++) {
    for (int j = 0; j < 50; j++) {
        if (i * j > 400) {
```

```
            break out;
        }
    }
}
```

In this code snippet, the label `out` labels the outer loop. Then, inside both the `for` loops, when a particular condition is met, a `break` causes the execution to break out of both loops. Without the label `out`, the `break` statement would exit the inner loop and resume execution with the outer loop.

Labeled loops are used infrequently in Java. There's usually another way to accomplish the same thing.

# Summary

Now that you have been introduced to lists, loops, and logic, you can make a computer decide whether to repeatedly display the contents of an array.

You've learned how to declare an array variable, assign an object to it, and access and change elements of the array. With the `if` and `switch` conditional statements, you can branch to different parts of a program based on a Boolean test. You learned about the `for`, `while`, and `do` loops, and you learned that each enables a portion of a program to be repeated until a given condition is met. You'll use all three of these features frequently in your Java programs.

It bears repeating: You'll use all three of these features frequently in your Java programs.

4

# Q&A

**Q I declared a variable inside a block statement for an `if`. When the `if` was done, the definition of that variable vanished. Where did it go?**

**A** In technical terms, block statements form a new lexical scope. This means that if you declare a variable inside a block, it's visible and usable only inside that block. When the block finishes executing, all the variables you declared go away.

It's a good idea to declare most of your variables in the outermost block in which they'll be needed—usually at the top of a block statement. The exception might be simple variables, such as index counters in `for` loops, where declaring them in the first line of the `for` loop is an easy shortcut.

**Q Why can't I use `switch` with strings?**

**A** You can. If it isn't working in NetBeans, you must make sure that you have a current version of Java installed and that your development environment has been set up to use it. The feature was introduced in Java 7.

In NetBeans, to see whether the current project is set up for Java 12 or higher, choose File, Project Properties to open the properties dialog. Choose `Libraries` in the Categories pane and set Java Platform to at least `JDK 12` if it isn't already. Click OK to save the change and exit the dialog.

# Quiz

Review this lesson's material by taking this three-question quiz.

## Questions

**1.** What kind of loop is used to execute the statements in the loop at least once before the conditional expression is evaluated?

    **A.** `do-while`

    **B.** `for`

    **C.** `while`

**2.** Which of the following cannot be used as the test in a `case` statement?

    **A.** Characters

    **B.** Strings

    **C.** Objects

**3.** Which instance variable of an array is used to find out how big the array is?

    **A.** `size`

    **B.** `length`

    **C.** `MAX_VALUE`

## Answers

**1.** A. In a `do-while` loop, the `while` conditional statement appears at the end of the loop. Even if it is initially false, the statements in the loop are executed once.

**2.** C. It used to be true that strings could not be used as the test, but that is no longer the case.

**3.** B. The `length` variable is an integer that returns the array's size.

# Certification Practice

The following question is the kind of thing you could expect to be asked on a Java programming certification test. Answer it without looking again at this lesson or using the Java compiler to test the code.

Given:

```java
public class Cases {
    public static void main(String[] arguments) {
        float x = 9;
        float y = 5;
        int z = (int)(x / y);
        switch (z) {
            case 1:
                x = x + 2;
            case 2:
                x = x + 3;
            default:
                x = x + 1;
        }
        System.out.println("Value of x: " + x);
    }
}
```

What will be the value of x when it is displayed?

**A.** 9.0

**B.** 11.0

**C.** 15.0

**D.** The program will not compile.

The answer is available on the book's website, at www.java21days.com. Visit the Lesson 4 page and click the Certification Practice link.

# Exercises

To extend your knowledge of the subjects covered in this lesson, try the following exercises:

1. Using the `countDays()` method from the `DayCounter` application, create an application that displays every date in a given year in a single list from January 1 to December 31.

2. Create a class that takes words for the first 10 numbers (that is, `one` to `ten`) and converts them into a single `long` integer. Use a `switch` statement for the conversion and command-line arguments for the words.

Where applicable, exercise solutions are offered on the book's website, at www.java21days.com.

# LESSON 5
# Creating Classes and Methods

If you're coming to Java from another programming language, you might be struggling with the meaning of the term *class*. It seems synonymous with the term *program*, but you might be uncertain about the relationship between the two.

In Java, a program is made up of a main class and any other classes needed to support the main class. These support classes include any you might need from the Java Class Library, such as `String`, `Math`, and the like.

In this lesson, the meaning of `class` is clarified as you create classes and methods, which define the behavior of an object or class. You'll learn about each of the following:

- The parts of a class

- The creation and use of instance variables

- The creation and use of methods

- The use of the `main()` method in applications

- The creation of overloaded methods

- The creation of constructors

# Defining Classes

Because you have created classes in each of the previous lessons, you should be familiar with the basics of their creation at this point. A class is defined via the `class` keyword and the name of the class, as in the following example:

```
class Ticker {
    // body of the class
}
```

By default, classes inherit from the `Object` class, the superclass of all classes in the Java class hierarchy.

The `extends` keyword is used to indicate the superclass of a class, as in this example, which is defined as a subclass of `Ticker`:

```
class SportsTicker extends Ticker {
    // body of the class
}
```

Because Java has single inheritance, `extends` only can be used to inherit from one superclass. A class that does not use `extends` to identify its superclass has `Object` as its superclass.

# Creating Instance and Class Variables

Whenever you create a class, you must define behavior that makes the new class different from its superclass.

This behavior is defined by specifying the variables and methods of the new class. In this section, you'll work with three kinds of variables: instance variables, local variables, and class variables. The subsequent section covers methods.

## Defining Instance Variables

In Lesson 2, "The ABCs of Programming," you learned how to declare and initialize local variables, which are variables inside method definitions.

Instance variables are declared and defined in almost the same manner as local variables. The main difference is their location in the class definition.

Variables are considered instance variables if they are declared outside a method definition and are not modified by the `static` keyword. By programming custom, most instance variables are defined right after the first line of the class definition, but they could just as permissibly be defined at the end.

Here's a simple class definition for the class `MarsRobot`, which inherits from the superclass `ScienceRobot`:

```
class MarsRobot extends ScienceRobot {
    String status;
    int speed;
    float temperature;
    int power;
}
```

This class definition contains four variables. Because these variables are not defined inside a method, they are instance variables. The variables are as follows:

- **status:** A string indicating the robot's current activity (for example, `"exploring"` or `"returning home"`)
- **speed:** An integer that indicates the robot's current rate of travel
- **temperature:** A floating-point number that indicates the current temperature of the robot's environment
- **power:** An integer indicating the robot's current battery power

## Class Variables

As you have learned, class variables apply to a class as a whole rather than to a particular object of that class.

Class variables are good for sharing information between different objects of the same class or for keeping track of common information among a set of objects.

The `static` keyword is used in the class declaration to declare a class variable, as in the following example:

```
static int SUM;
static final int MAX_OBJECTS = 10;
```

By convention, many Java programmers capitalize the entire name of a class variable so that it's distinguished in code from other type of variables. This is not a requirement of the language but is a practice that's recommended.

5

# Creating Methods

As you learned in Lesson 3, "Working with Objects," methods define an object's behavior—anything that happens when the object is created as well as the various tasks the object can perform during its lifetime.

This section introduces method definitions and how methods work. Later in this lesson, you'll learn about more sophisticated things you can do with methods.

## Defining Methods

In Java, a method definition has four basic parts:

- The method's name
- A list of parameters
- The type of object or primitive type that the method returns
- The body of the method

The first two parts of the method definition form the method's *signature*.

<table>
<tr>
<td>NOTE</td>
<td>Two optional parts of the method definition have been left out of this section: a modifier, such as <code>public</code> or <code>private</code>, and the <code>throws</code> keyword, which indicates the exceptions a method can throw. You'll learn about these parts of method definition in Lesson 6, "Packages, Interfaces, and Other Class Features," and Lesson 7, "Exceptions and Threads."</td>
</tr>
</table>

In other languages, the name of the method (which might be called a function, subroutine, or procedure) is enough to distinguish it from other methods in the program.

In Java, you can have several methods in the same class with the same name but different signatures. This practice is called *method overloading*, and you'll learn more about it later in this lesson.

Here's what a basic method definition looks like:

```
returnType methodName(type1 arg1, type2 arg2, type3 arg3 ...) {
    // body of method
}
```

*returnType* is the primitive type or class of the value returned by the method (or `void` if the method does not return a value).

The method's parameter list is a set of variable declarations separated by commas and placed inside parentheses. These parameters become local variables in the body of the method, receiving their values when the method is called.

If a method returns an array object, the array brackets can go after either the return type or the closing parenthesis of the parameter list. Because having the brackets after the return type is easier to read, that approach is used in this book. For instance, the following declares a method that returns an integer array:

```
int[] makeRange(int lower, int upper) {
    // body of method
}
```

Inside the body of a method, you can have statements, expressions, method calls on other objects, conditionals, loops, and so on.

Unless a method has been declared with `void` as its return type, the method returns some kind of value when it is completed. This value must be explicitly returned at some exit point inside the method by using the `return` keyword.

Listing 5.1 contains `RangeLister`, a class that defines a `makeRange()` method. This method takes two integers—a lower boundary and an upper boundary—and creates an array that contains all the integers between those two boundaries. The boundaries themselves are included in the array of integers.

Create a new empty Java file in NetBeans for a class called `RangeLister` (in the package `com.java21days`) and enter the code from Listing 5.1 into it.

**LISTING 5.1** The Full Text of `RangeLister.java`

```
1: package com.java21days;
2:
3: class RangeLister {
4:     int[] makeRange(int lower, int upper) {
5:         int[] range = new int[(upper-lower) + 1];
6:
7:         for (int i = 0; i < range.length; i++) {
8:             range[i] = lower++;
9:         }
10:        return range;
11:    }
12:
13:    public static void main(String[] arguments) {
14:        int[] range;
15:        RangeLister lister = new RangeLister();
16:
```

```
17:            range = lister.makeRange(4, 13);
18:            System.out.print("The array: [ ");
19:            for (int i = 0; i < range.length; i++) {
20:                System.out.print(range[i] + " ");
21:            }
22:            System.out.println("]");
23:        }
24: }
```

Run the program by choosing Run, Run File in NetBeans to produce the output shown in Figure 5.1.

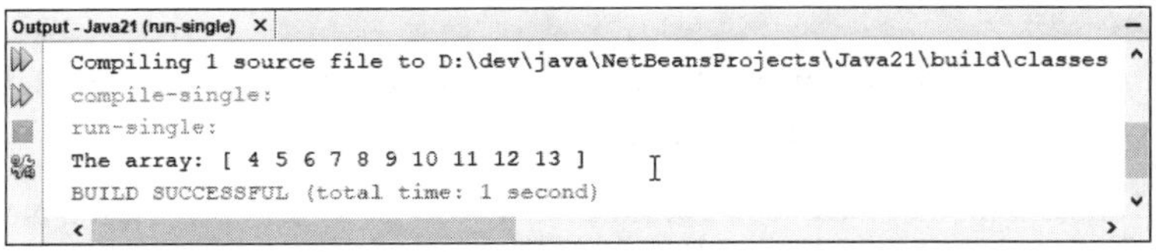

**FIGURE 5.1**

Using a method to make and display an array.

```
Output - Java21 (run-single)  ×
Compiling 1 source file to D:\dev\java\NetBeansProjects\Java21\build\classes
compile-single:
run-single:
The array: [ 4 5 6 7 8 9 10 11 12 13 ]      I
BUILD SUCCESSFUL (total time: 1 second)
```

The `main()` method in this class tests the `makeRange()` method by calling it with the arguments 4 and 13. The method creates an empty integer array and uses a `for` loop to fill the new array with values from 4 through 13 in lines 7–9.

## The `this` Keyword

In the body of a method definition, sometimes you need to refer to the object that contains the method (in other words, the object itself). For example, you might need to access the object's instance variables or pass the current object as an argument to another method.

To refer to the object in its own method, use the `this` keyword where you normally would refer to an object's name.

The `this` keyword refers to the current object, and you can use it anywhere an object might be used: in dot notation, as an argument to a method, as the return value for the current method, and so on. Here are statements that use `this` (with explanatory comments):

```
top = this.x;            // the x instance variable for this object
zed.resetData(this);     // call the resetData method, defined in
                         // the zed class, and pass it the current object

return this;             // return the current object
```

In many cases, you might not need to explicitly use the `this` keyword because it is assumed. For instance, you can refer to both instance variables and method calls defined in the current class simply by name; the `this` is implicit in those references. Therefore, you could write the first example as follows:

```
top = x;            // the x instance variable for this object
```

The viability of omitting the `this` keyword for instance variables depends on whether variables of the same name are declared in the local scope. You'll explore this further in the next section.

Because `this` is a reference to the current instance of a class, you can only use it inside the body of an instance method definition or constructor. Class methods—which are declared with the `static` keyword—cannot use `this`.

## Variable Scope and Method Definitions

One thing you must know about a variable in order to use it is the variable's scope. *Scope* is the part of a program in which a variable exists, making it possible to use the variable in statements and expressions. When the part defining the scope has finished executing, the variable ceases to exist.

When you declare a variable in Java, that variable always has limited scope. A variable with local scope, for example, can be used only inside the block in which it was defined. Instance variables have a scope that extends to the entire class, so they can be used by any of the instance methods within that class.

When you refer to a variable, Java checks for its definition outward, starting with the innermost scope.

The innermost scope could be a block statement, such as the contents of a `while` loop. The second-innermost scope could be the method in which the block is contained.

If the variable hasn't been found in the method, the class itself is checked.

Because of how Java checks for the scope of a given variable, it is possible for you to create a variable in a lower scope that hides (or replaces) the original value of that variable and introduces subtle bugs into your code.

For example, consider the following Java application:

```
class ScopeTest {
    int test = 10;

    void printTest() {
```

5

```
        int test = 20;
        System.out.println("Test: " + test);
    }

    public static void main(String[] arguments) {
        ScopeTest app = new ScopeTest();
        app.printTest();
    }
}
```

This class has two variables with the same name, test. The first, an instance variable, is initialized with the value 10. The second is a local variable with the value 20.

The local variable test within the printTest() method hides the instance variable test in that scope. When the printTest() method is called, it displays that test equals 20, even though there's a test instance variable that equals 10. You could avoid this problem by using this.test to refer to the instance variable and using test to refer to the local variable.

A more insidious example occurs when you redefine a variable in a subclass that already occurs in a superclass. This can create subtle bugs in your code. For example, you might call methods that are intended to change the value of an instance variable, but the wrong variable may be changed. Another bug might occur when you cast an object from one class to another. The value of your instance variable might mysteriously change because the variable was getting that value from the superclass instead of from your class.

The best way to avoid this behavior is to be aware of the variables defined in the superclass of your class and avoid duplicating a variable name used higher in the class hierarchy.

## Passing Arguments to Methods

When you call a method with an object as a parameter, the object is passed into the method's body as a reference to that object. Any change made to the object inside the method persists outside the method.

Keep in mind that this includes arrays and all objects contained in arrays. When you pass an array into a method and modify its contents, the original array is affected. Primitive types and strings, on the other hand, are passed by value. You can't do anything in the method that changes those types.

The Passer class in Listing 5.2 demonstrates how this works. Create this class in NetBeans in the com.java21days package.

**LISTING 5.2**  The Full Text of `Passer.java`

```
 1: package com.java21days;
 2:
 3: class Passer {
 4:
 5:     void toUpperCase(String[] text) {
 6:         for (int i = 0; i < text.length; i++) {
 7:             text[i] = text[i].toUpperCase();
 8:         }
 9:     }
10:
11:     public static void main(String[] arguments) {
12:         Passer passer = new Passer();
13:         passer.toUpperCase(arguments);
14:         for (int i = 0; i < arguments.length; i++) {
15:             System.out.print(arguments[i] + " ");
16:         }
17:         System.out.println();
18:     }
19: }
```

This application takes one or more command-line arguments and displays them in all uppercase letters.

In NetBeans, set the arguments by choosing Run, Set Project Configuration, Customize. The Project Properties dialog appears. Enter `com.java21days.Passer` as the Main Class and `Athos Aramis Porthos` (or words of your choosing) as the Arguments and click OK. Run the application by choosing Run, Run Project.

If you use the suggested arguments, the program produces the output shown in Figure 5.2.

**FIGURE 5.2**
Testing how objects are passed to a method.

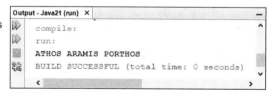

```
Output - Java21 (run)  ×                              _
  compile:                                         ^
  run:
  ATHOS ARAMIS PORTHOS
  BUILD SUCCESSFUL (total time: 0 seconds)          v
  <                                          >
```

The `Passer` application uses command-line arguments stored in the `arguments` array of strings.

The application creates a `Passer` object and calls its `toUpperCase()` method with the `arguments` array as an argument (lines 12–13).

5

Because a reference to the array object is passed to the method, changing the value of each array element in line 7 changes the actual element (rather than a copy of it). Displaying the array with lines 14–16 demonstrates this.

<table>
<tr><td>CAUTION</td><td>If nothing happens when you run the <code>Passer</code> application in NetBeans, you're running it with the command Run, Run File instead of Run, Run Project. The Run File command does not use the arguments set up in the project configuration. The Run Project command does.</td></tr>
</table>

## Class Methods

The relationship between class and instance variables is directly comparable to how class and instance methods work.

Class methods are available to any instance of the class itself and can be made available to other classes. In addition, unlike an instance method, a class does not require an object of the class for its methods to be called.

For example, the Java Class Library includes the `System` class, which defines a set of methods that are useful when displaying text, retrieving configuration information, and accomplishing other tasks. Here are two statements that use its class methods:

```
System.exit(0);
long now = System.currentTimeMillis();
```

The `exit()` method closes an application with an argument that indicates success if it equals `0` or failure if it's any other value. The `currentTimeMillis()` method returns a `long` holding the number of milliseconds since midnight on January 1, 1970. This number is a representation of the current date and time.

To define class methods, use the `static` keyword in front of the method definition, as you would in front of a class variable. For example, the class method `exit()` in the preceding example might have the following signature:

```
static void exit(int argument) {
    // body of method
}
```

The Java Class Library includes wrapper classes such as `Integer` and `Float` for each of the primitive types. By using class methods defined in those classes, you can create objects for primitive types and vice versa. The same value is represented in either form.

For example, the `parseInt()` class method in the `Integer` class can be used with a string argument, and it returns an `int` representation of that string:

```
int count = Integer.parseInt("42");
```

In this statement, `parseInt()` converts the `String` value `"42"` to the integer `42`, which is stored in the `count` variable.

The lack of a `static` keyword in front of a method name makes it an instance method. An instance method operates on one object rather than on a class of objects. In Lesson 1, "Getting Started with Java," you created an instance method called `checkTemperature()` that checked the temperature in the planetary robot's environment.

**TIP**

> Still not clear on the distinction? Methods that affect an object should be defined as instance methods. Methods that provide some general capability but do not directly affect an object of the class should be declared as class methods.

Class methods, unlike instance methods, are not inherited. A class method in a superclass cannot be overridden in a subclass.

# Creating Java Applications

Now that you know how to create classes, objects, class and instance variables, and class and instance methods, you can put them all together in a Java program.

A Java application consists of one or more classes and can be as large or as small as you want it to be. Although all the applications you've created up to this point do nothing visually other than display characters, you also can create Java applications that use windows, graphics, and a graphical user interface.

The only thing you need to make a Java application run is one class that serves as the starting point. That class needs only one thing: a `main()` method. When the application is run, the Java Virtual Machine (JVM) calls this method.

The signature for the `main()` method takes the following form:

```
public static void main(String[] arguments) {
    // body of method
}
```

5

Here's a rundown of the components of the `main()` method:

- `public` means that this method is available to other classes and objects, which is a form of access control. The `main()` method must be declared `public`. You'll learn more about access methods during Lesson 6, "Packages, Interfaces, and Other Class Features."
- `static` means that `main()` is a class method.
- `void` means that the `main()` method doesn't return a value.
- `main()` takes one parameter, which is an array of strings. This argument holds command-line arguments.

The body of the `main()` method contains any code you need to start your application, such as the initialization of variables or the creation of objects.

The `main()` method is a class method. An object of the class that holds `main()` is not created automatically when your application runs. If you want to treat that class as an object, you have to create an instance of it in the `main()` method (as you did in the *Passer* application in Listing 5.2 on line 12).

In a NetBeans project, one class can be designated as the main class of the project. When the project is packaged into a single Java archive (JAR) file, the main class is run if the JAR file is executed.

To set the main class, choose Run, Set Project Configuration, Customize. In the Project Properties dialog, enter the name of this class in the Main Class field.

## Helper Classes

Your Java application may consist of a single class—the one with the `main()` method—or several classes that use each other. (In reality, even a simple tutorial program uses numerous classes in the Java Class Library.) You can create as many classes as you want for your program.

As long as Java can find the class, your program uses it when it runs. Note, however, that only the starting-point class needs a `main()` method. After it is called, the methods inside the various classes and objects used in your program take over. Although you can include `main()` methods in helper classes, they are ignored when the program runs.

# Java Applications and Arguments

Because Java applications are stand-alone programs, it's useful to pass arguments to an application to customize how it operates.

You can use arguments to determine how an application will run or to enable an application to operate on different kinds of input. You can use program arguments for many purposes, such as to turn on debugging input or to indicate a filename to load.

## Passing Arguments to Java Applications

How you pass arguments to a Java application varies depending on the environment in which Java is being run.

To pass arguments to a Java program with the `java` interpreter included with the Java Development Kit (JDK), the arguments would be appended to the command line when the program is run. Consider this example:

```
java Transmitter April 450 -10
```

Here `java` is the name of the interpreter, `Transmitter` is the Java application, and the rest are three arguments passed to a program: `April`, `450`, and `-10`. Note that a space separates each pair of arguments.

To group an argument that has spaces in it, surround the argument with quotation marks. For example, consider the following command line:

```
java Transmitter Wilhelm Niekro Hough "Tim Wakefield" 49
```

Putting quotation marks around `"Tim Wakefield"` causes that text to be treated as a single argument. The application would receive five arguments: `Wilhelm`, `Niekro`, `Hough`, `Tim Wakefield`, and `49`. The quotation marks prevent the space within `Tim Wakefield` from being used to separate arguments. Those spaces are not included as part of the argument when it is sent to the program and received using the `main()` method.

5

**CAUTION**

> One thing quotation marks are not used for is to identify strings. Every argument passed to an application is stored in an array of `String` objects, even if it has a numeric value (such as `450`, `-10`, and `49` in the preceding examples).

Because NetBeans runs the JVM behind the scenes, there's no command line on which to specify arguments. Instead, you can set them in the project configuration with the Run, Set Project Configuration, Customize command, as you did earlier in this lesson to run the `RangeLister` application.

# Handling Arguments in Your Java Application

When an application is run with arguments, Java stores the arguments as an array of strings and passes the array to the application's `main()` method. Take another look at the signature for `main()`:

```
public static void main(String[] arguments) {
    // body of method
}
```

Here, `arguments` is the name of the array of strings that contains the list of arguments. You can call this array anything you want.

Inside the `main()` method, you handle the arguments your program was given by looping through the array. The `Averager` class in Listing 5.3 is a Java application that takes numeric arguments and returns the sum and average of those arguments.

Create a new empty Java file in NetBeans for the `Averager` class in the `com.java21days` package.

**LISTING 5.3**   The Full Text of `Averager.java`

```
 1: package com.java21days;
 2:
 3: class Averager {
 4:     public static void main(String[] arguments) {
 5:         int sum = 0;
 6:
 7:         if (arguments.length > 0) {
 8:             for (int i = 0; i < arguments.length; i++) {
 9:                 sum += Integer.parseInt(arguments[i]);
10:             }
11:             System.out.println("Sum is: " + sum);
12:             System.out.println("Average is: " +
13:                 (float) sum / arguments.length);
14:         }
15:     }
16: }
```

Before running the application in NetBeans, choose two or more numeric arguments in the project configuration, as you did with the `RangeLister` application. They all should be integers.

The `Averager` application makes sure in line 7 that at least one argument is passed to the program. This is handled through `length`, the instance variable that contains the number of elements in the `arguments` array.

You must always do things like this when dealing with command-line arguments. Otherwise, your programs crash with `ArrayIndexOutOfBoundsException` errors whenever the user supplies fewer command-line arguments than you were expecting.

If at least one argument is passed to the application, the `for` loop iterates through all the strings stored in the `arguments` array (lines 8–10).

Because all command-line arguments are passed to a Java application as `String` objects, you must convert them to numeric values before using them in any mathematical expressions. The `parseInt()` class method of the `Integer` class takes a `String` object as input and returns an `int` (line 9).

If `75 1080 95 16` were submitted as your arguments, you would see output matching that in Figure 5.3.

**FIGURE 5.3**
Receiving arguments in an application.

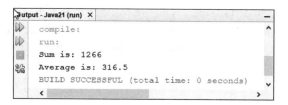

# Creating Methods with the Same Name

When you work with the Java Class Library, you often encounter classes that have numerous methods with the same name.

Two things differentiate these same-named methods from each other:

- The number of arguments they take
- The primitive type or objects of each argument

These two things are part of a method's signature. Using several methods with the same name and different signatures is called *overloading*.

Method overloading can eliminate the need for entirely different methods that do essentially the same thing. Overloading also makes it possible for methods to behave differently based on the arguments they receive.

When you call a method in an object, Java matches the method name and arguments to choose which method definition to execute.

5

To create an overloaded method, you create different method definitions in a class, each with the same name but different argument lists. The difference can be the number, the type of arguments, or both. Java allows method overloading as long as each argument list is unique for the same method name.

**CAUTION**

> Java does not consider the return type when differentiating among overloaded methods. If you attempt to create two methods with the same signature and different return types, the class won't compile. In addition, the variable names that you choose for each argument to the method are irrelevant. The number and the type of arguments are the two things that matter.

The next project you'll undertake creates an overloaded method. It begins with a simple class definition for a class called Box that defines a rectangular shape with four instance variables to define the upper-left and lower-right corners of the rectangle, $(x1, y1)$ and $(x2, y2)$:

```
class Box {
    int x1 = 0;
    int y1 = 0;
    int x2 = 0;
    int y2 = 0;
}
```

When a new instance of the Box class is created, all its instance variables are initialized to 0.

A buildBox() instance method sets the variables to specified values:

```
Box buildBox(int x1, int y1, int x2, int y2) {
    this.x1 = x1;
    this.y1 = y1;
    this.x2 = x2;
    this.y2 = y2;
    return this;
}
```

This method takes four integer arguments and returns a reference to the resulting Box object. Because the arguments have the same names as the instance variables, the keyword this is used inside the method when referring to the instance variables.

This method can be used to create rectangles, but what if you wanted to define a rectangle's dimensions differently? An alternative would be to use Point objects rather than individual coordinates—because a `Point` object contains both an `x` and `y` value as an instance variable.

You can overload `buildBox()` by creating a second version of the method with an argument list that takes two `Point` objects:

```
Box buildBox(Point topLeft, Point bottomRight) {
    x1 = topLeft.x;
    y1 = topLeft.y;
    x2 = bottomRight.x;
    y2 = bottomRight.y;
    return this;
}
```

For this code to work, the full name of the `java.awt.Point` class must be imported so that it can be referred to by the short name `Point`.

Another possible way to define the rectangle is to use a top corner, a height, and a width:

```
Box buildBox(Point topLeft, int w, int h) {
    x1 = topLeft.x;
    y1 = topLeft.y;
    x2 = (x1 + w);
    y2 = (y1 + h);
    return this;
}
```

To finish this example, a `printBox()` method displays the rectangle's coordinates. A `main()` method turns `Box` into an application and tries out everything on a `Box` object.

Listing 5.4 shows the completed class definition. Create this class using NetBeans in the package `com.java21days`.

5

**LISTING 5.4**   The Full Text of `Box.java`

```
 1: package com.java21days;
 2:
 3: import java.awt.Point;
 4:
 5: class Box {
 6:     int x1, y1, x2, y2 = 0;
 7:
 8:     Box buildBox(int x1, int y1, int x2, int y2) {
 9:         this.x1 = x1;
10:         this.y1 = y1;
11:         this.x2 = x2;
12:         this.y2 = y2;
13:         return this;
14:     }
```

```
15:
16:     Box buildBox(Point topLeft, Point bottomRight) {
17:          x1 = topLeft.x;
18:          y1 = topLeft.y;
19:          x2 = bottomRight.x;
20:          y2 = bottomRight.y;
21:          return this;
22:     }
23:
24:     Box buildBox(Point topLeft, int w, int h) {
25:          x1 = topLeft.x;
26:          y1 = topLeft.y;
27:          x2 = (x1 + w);
28:          y2 = (y1 + h);
29:          return this;
30:     }
31:
32:     void printBox(){
33:          System.out.print("Box: <" + x1 + ", " + y1);
34:          System.out.println(", " + x2 + ", " + y2 + ">");
35:     }
36:
37:     public static void main(String[] arguments) {
38:          Box rect = new Box();
39:
40:          System.out.println("Calling buildBox with "
41:               + "coordinates (25,25) and (50,50):");
42:          rect.buildBox(25, 25, 50, 50);
43:          rect.printBox();
44:
45:          System.out.println("\nCalling buildBox with "
46:               + "points (10,10) and (20,20):");
47:          rect.buildBox(new Point(10, 10), new Point(20, 20));
48:          rect.printBox();
49:
50:          System.out.println("\nCalling buildBox with "
51:               + "point (10,10), width 50 and height 50:");
52:
53:          rect.buildBox(new Point(10, 10), 50, 50);
54:          rect.printBox();
55:     }
56: }
```

Run the application to see the output shown in Figure 5.4.

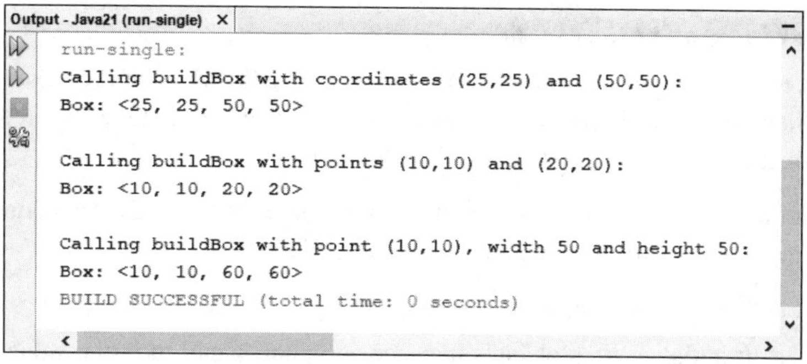

**FIGURE 5.4**
Calling several
similar methods.

```
Output - Java21 (run-single) X
run-single:
Calling buildBox with coordinates (25,25) and (50,50):
Box: <25, 25, 50, 50>

Calling buildBox with points (10,10) and (20,20):
Box: <10, 10, 20, 20>

Calling buildBox with point (10,10), width 50 and height 50:
Box: <10, 10, 60, 60>
BUILD SUCCESSFUL (total time: 0 seconds)
```

You can define as many versions of a method as you need to implement the behavior needed for the class.

When you have several methods that do similar things, consider using one method to call another as a way to simplify the code. For example, the buildBox() method in lines 16–22 of Listing 5.4 can be replaced with this much shorter method:

```
Box buildBox(Point topLeft, Point bottomRight) {
    return buildBox(topLeft.x, topLeft.y,
        bottomRight.x, bottomRight.y);
}
```

The return statement in this method calls the buildBox() method in lines 8–14 with four integer arguments, producing the same result in fewer statements.

This application uses a programming shortcut for working with objects that hasn't been employed up to this point. Look at line 53:

```
rect.buildBox(new Point(10, 10), 50, 50);
```

The new operator is used as an argument to a method. This makes the argument the object created by calling that constructor, which is possible in Java because calling new is an expression whose value is the newly created object.

The preceding statement accomplishes the same thing as these two lines of code:

```
Point rectangle = new Point(10, 10);
rect.buildBox(rectangle, 50, 50);
```

The one-line version is more efficient because it doesn't store an object in a variable that will be used only once and never needs to be accessed in any subsequent code. You will find this kind of shortcut employed often in Java programs.

5

# Constructors

You also can define constructors in your class definition that are called automatically when objects of that class are created. A *constructor* is a method called on an object when it is created—in other words, when it is constructed.

Unlike other methods, a constructor cannot be called directly. Java does three things when `new` is used to create an instance of a class:

- It allocates memory for the object.
- It initializes that object's instance variables, either to initial values or to a default (`0` for numbers, `null` for objects, `false` for Booleans, or `\0` for characters).
- It calls a constructor of the class.

If a class doesn't have any constructors defined, an object still is created when the `new` operator is used in conjunction with the class. However, you might have to set its instance variables or call other methods that the object needs to initialize itself.

When an object is created of a class that has no constructors, a constructor with no arguments is implicitly provided by Java. This constructor is called to create the object. For this reason, a constructor with no arguments can be called with `new` even when no constructors are defined.

By defining constructors in your own classes, you can set initial values of instance variables, call methods based on those variables, call methods on other objects, and set an object's initial properties.

When creating a class, you can overload constructors, as you can do with methods, to create an object that has specific properties based on the arguments you give to `new`.

If a class has a constructor that takes one or more arguments, a constructor with no arguments can be called only if one has been defined in the class.

## Basic Constructors

A constructor looks a lot like a regular method, with three basic differences:

- It always has the same name as the class.
- It doesn't have a return type.
- It cannot return a value in the method by using the `return` statement.

For example, the following class uses a constructor to initialize its instance variables based on arguments for new:

```
class MarsRobot {
    String status;
    int speed;
    int power;

    MarsRobot(String in1, int in2, int in3) {
        status = in1;
        speed = in2;
        power = in3;
    }
}
```

You could create an object of this class with the following statement:

```
MarsRobot curiosity = new MarsRobot("exploring", 5, 200);
```

The status instance variable would be set to "exploring", speed to 5, and power to 200.

## Calling Another Constructor

If you have a constructor that duplicates some behavior of an existing constructor, you can call the first constructor from inside the body of the second. Java provides special syntax for doing this. Use the following code to call a constructor defined in the current class:

```
this(argument1, argument2, argument3);
```

The use of this with a constructor is similar to how this can be used to access a current object's variables. In the preceding statement, the arguments with this() are the arguments for the constructor.

For example, consider a simple class that defines a circle using the (x, y) coordinate of its center and the length of its radius. The class, Circle, could have two constructors: one where the radius is defined and one where the radius is set to a default value of 1. Here's code that does this:

```
class Circle {
    int x, y, radius;

    Circle(int xPoint, int yPoint, int radiusLength) {
        this.x = xPoint;
        this.y = yPoint;
```

5

```
        this.radius = radiusLength;
    }

    Circle(int xPoint, int yPoint) {
        this(xPoint, yPoint, 1);
    }
}
```

The second constructor in `Circle` takes only the (x, y) coordinates of the circle's center. Because no radius is defined, the default value of 1 is used. The first constructor is called with the arguments `xPoint`, `yPoint`, and the integer literal 1.

## Overloading Constructors

Like methods, constructors also can take varying numbers and types of arguments. This enables you to create an object with exactly the properties you want it to have, or alternatively allows the object to calculate properties from different kinds of input.

For example, the `buildBox()` methods defined in the `Box` class earlier in this lesson would make excellent constructors because they are used to initialize an object's instance variables to the appropriate values. So instead of the original `buildBox()` method, which took four arguments for the corners' coordinates, you could create a constructor.

Listing 5.5 shows a new class, `Box2`, that has the same functionality as the original `Box` class but uses overloaded constructors instead of overloaded `buildBox()` methods. Create the `Box2` class in NetBeans and put it in the package `com.java21days`.

**LISTING 5.5** The Full Text of `Box2.java`

```
 1: package com.java21days;
 2:
 3: import java.awt.Point;
 4:
 5: class Box2 {
 6:     int x1, y1, x2, y2 = 0;
 7:
 8:     Box2(int x1, int y1, int x2, int y2) {
 9:         this.x1 = x1;
10:         this.y1 = y1;
11:         this.x2 = x2;
12:         this.y2 = y2;
13:     }
14:
15:     Box2(Point topLeft, Point bottomRight) {
16:         this(topLeft.x, topLeft.y, bottomRight.x,
17:             bottomRight.y);
18:     }
```

```
19:
20:        Box2(Point topLeft, int w, int h) {
21:            this(topLeft.x, topLeft.y, topLeft.x + w,
22:                topLeft.y + h);
23:        }
24:
25:        void printBox() {
26:            System.out.print("Box: <" + x1 + ", " + y1);
27:            System.out.println(", " + x2 + ", " + y2 + ">");
28:        }
29:
30:        public static void main(String[] arguments) {
31:            Box2 rect;
32:
33:            System.out.println("Calling Box2 with coordinates "
34:                + "(13,35) and (10,40):");
35:            rect = new Box2(13, 35, 10, 40);
36:            rect.printBox();
37:
38:            System.out.println("\nCalling Box2 with points "
39:                + "(9,27) and (17,19):");
40:            rect = new Box2(new Point(9, 27), new Point(17, 19));
41:            rect.printBox();
42:
43:            System.out.println("\nCalling Box2 with 1 point "
44:                + "(5,40), width 22 and height 20:");
45:            rect = new Box2(new Point(5, 40), 22, 20);
46:            rect.printBox();
47:
48:        }
49: }
```

Run the application to see the output shown in Figure 5.5.

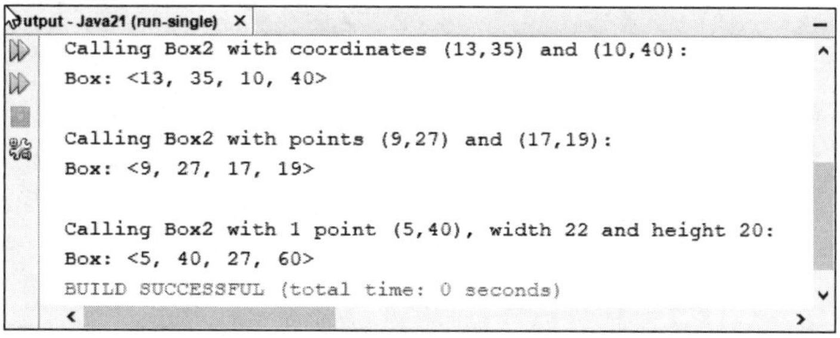

**FIGURE 5.5**
Calling overloaded methods.

```
Output - Java21 (run-single)  X
    Calling Box2 with coordinates (13,35) and (10,40):
    Box: <13, 35, 10, 40>

    Calling Box2 with points (9,27) and (17,19):
    Box: <9, 27, 17, 19>

    Calling Box2 with 1 point (5,40), width 22 and height 20:
    Box: <5, 40, 27, 60>
    BUILD SUCCESSFUL (total time: 0 seconds)
```

In Listing 5.5, the second and third constructors use `this` in lines 16–17 and lines 21–22 to call the first constructor, giving it the task of creating the object with the specified parameters.

# Overriding Methods

When you call an object's method, Java looks for that method definition in the object's class. If it doesn't find it, the method is sought in the object's superclass, then its superclass, and on up the class hierarchy until a method definition is found. Inheritance enables you to define and use methods repeatedly in subclasses without having to duplicate the code.

However, there might be times when you want an object to respond to the same method but have different behavior when that method is called. In such a case, you can override the method. To do this, define a method in a subclass with the same signature (name and argument list) as a method in a superclass. Then, when the method is called, the subclass method is found and executed instead of the one in the superclass. This is called *overriding* a method.

## Creating Methods That Override Existing Methods

To override a method, all you have to do is create a method in your subclass that has the same signature as a method defined by your class's superclass. Because Java executes the first method definition it finds that matches the signature, the new signature hides the original method definition.

Here's a simple example. Listing 5.6 contains two classes. `Printer` contains a method called `printMe()` that displays information about objects of that class. `SubPrinter` is a subclass that adds a `z` instance variable to the class. Create this class and name it `Printer` in NetBeans (in the package `com.java21days`).

**LISTING 5.6**  The Full Text of `Printer.java`

```
 1: package com.java21days;
 2:
 3: class Printer {
 4:     int x = 0;
 5:     int y = 1;
 6:
 7:     void printMe() {
 8:         System.out.println("x is " + x + ", y is " + y);
 9:         System.out.println("I am an instance of the class " +
10:             this.getClass().getName());
11:     }
12: }
13:
14: class SubPrinter extends Printer {
15:     int z = 3;
16:
```

```
17:      public static void main(String[] arguments) {
18:          SubPrinter obj = new SubPrinter();
19:          obj.printMe();
20:      }
21: }
```

When this file is compiled, it results in two class files instead of one. Because the source file defines the `Printer` and `SubPrinter` classes, the compiler produces both. Run `SubPrinter` (by selecting Run, Run File in NetBeans), and you see the output shown in Figure 5.6.

**FIGURE 5.6**
Calling a superclass method in a subclass.

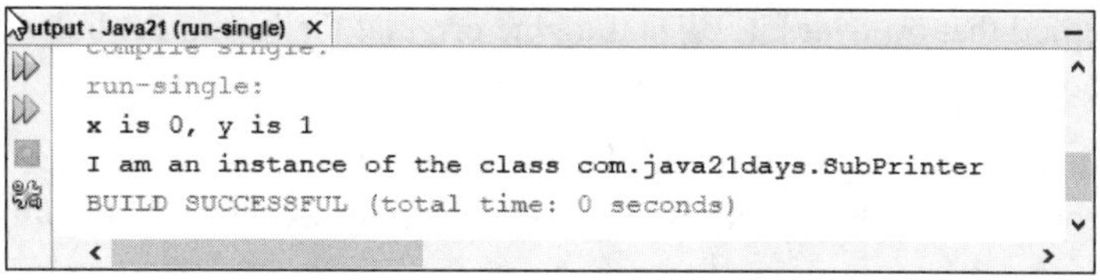

```
Output - Java21 (run-single)  ×
  compile-single:
  run-single:
  x is 0, y is 1
  I am an instance of the class com.java21days.SubPrinter
  BUILD SUCCESSFUL (total time: 0 seconds)
```

**CAUTION**

The `Printer` class does not have a `main()` method, so it cannot be run as an application. So when you choose Run, Run File in NetBeans, it automatically runs the `SubPrinter` application's `main()` method because no other class in the file has such a method. If a source code file contains more than one class with `main()`, NetBeans asks which one should be run.

5

In the application, a `SubPrinter` object was created, and the `printMe()` method was called in the `main()` method of `SubPrinter`. Because `SubPrinter` does not define this method, Java looks for it in the superclasses of `SubPrinter`, starting with `Printer`. `Printer` has a `printMe()` method, so it is executed. Unfortunately, this method does not display the z instance variable, as you can see from the preceding output. The superclass does not define this variable, so it could not display it.

To correct the problem, you can override the `printMe()` method in `SubPrinter` by adding a statement to display the z instance variable:

```
void printMe() {
    System.out.println("x is " + x + ", y is " + y +
        ", z is " + z);
    System.out.println("I am an instance of the class " +
        this.getClass().getName());
}
```

## Calling the Original Method

Usually, there are two reasons you want to override a method that a superclass already has implemented:

- To replace the definition of that original method
- To augment the original method with additional behavior

Overriding a method and giving it a new definition hides the original method definition. However, sometimes behavior should be added to the original definition instead of being replaced, particularly when behavior is duplicated in both the original method and the method that overrides it. By calling the original method in the body of the overriding method, you can add only what you need.

Use the `super` keyword to call the original method from inside a method definition. This keyword passes the method call up the hierarchy, as shown in the following:

```
void doMethod(String a, String b) {
    // do stuff here
    super.doMethod(a, b);
    // do more stuff here
}
```

The `super` keyword, similar to the `this` keyword, is a placeholder for the class's superclass. You can use it anywhere that you use `this`, but `super` refers to the superclass rather than to the current object.

## Overriding Constructors

Technically, constructors cannot be overridden. Because a constructor always has the same name as the current class, new constructors are created instead of being inherited. This system is sufficient much of the time; when your class's constructor is called, the constructor with the same signature for all your superclasses also is called. Therefore, initialization can happen for all parts of a class you inherit.

However, when you are defining constructors for your own class, you might want to change how your object is initialized—not only by initializing new variables added by your class but also by changing the contents of variables that already are there. To do this, explicitly call the constructors of the superclass and change whatever variables need to be changed.

To call a regular method in a superclass, you use `super.methodname(arguments)`. Because a constructor method doesn't have a method name to call, the following form is used:

```
super(argument1, argument2, ...);
```

Java has a rule for the use of super(): It must be the first statement in your constructor definition. If you don't call super() explicitly in that first statement, Java automatically calls super() with no arguments before the first statement in the constructor.

Because a call to a super() method must be the first statement, you can't do something like the following in your overriding constructor:

```
if (condition == true) {
    super(1,2,3); // call one superclass constructor
} else {
    super(1,2); // call a different constructor
}
```

Similar to using this() in a constructor, super() calls the constructor for the immediate superclass (which might, in turn, call the constructor of its superclass, and so on). Note that a constructor with that signature has to exist in the superclass for the call to super() to work. The Java compiler checks this when a class is compiled.

You don't have to call the constructor in your superclass that has the same signature as the constructor in your class; you must call the constructor only for the values you need initialized. In fact, you can create a class that has constructors with entirely different signatures from any of the superclass's constructors.

Listing 5.7 shows a class called NamedPoint, which extends the class Point from the java.awt package. The Point class has only one constructor, which takes an x and a y argument and returns a Point object. NamedPoint has an additional instance variable (a string for the name) and defines a constructor to initialize x, y, and the name. Create this class in NetBeans in the com.java21days package.

5

**LISTING 5.7**   The NamedPoint Class

```
 1: package com.java21days;
 2:
 3: import java.awt.Point;
 4:
 5: class NamedPoint extends Point {
 6:     String name;
 7:
 8:     NamedPoint(int x, int y, String name) {
 9:         super(x, y);
10:         this.name = name;
11:     }
12:
13:     public static void main(String[] arguments) {
14:         NamedPoint np = new NamedPoint(5, 5, "SmallPoint");
15:         System.out.println("x is " + np.x);
```

```
16:                System.out.println("y is " + np.y);
17:                System.out.println("Name is " + np.name);
18:        }
19: }
```

The output is displayed in Figure 5.7.

**FIGURE 5.7**
Extending a super-
class constructor in
a subclass.

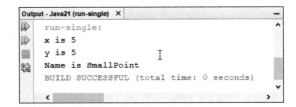

The constructor defined for NamedPoint calls Point's constructor to initialize the
instance variables of Point (5.x and y). Although you can just as easily initialize
x and y yourself, you might not know what other things Point is doing to initialize
itself. Therefore, it is always a good idea to pass constructors up the hierarchy to make
sure that everything is set up correctly.

# Summary

After finishing this lesson, you should have a pretty good idea of the relationship among
classes in Java and programs you create using the language.

Everything you create in Java involves the use of a main class that interacts with other
classes, as needed. It's a different programming mind-set than you might be used to with
other languages.

During this lesson, you put together everything you have learned about creating Java
classes. You learned about these topics:

- Instance and class variables, which hold the attributes of a class and objects created
  from it.

- Instance and class methods, which define the behavior of a class. You learned how
  to define methods, including the parts of a method signature, how to return values
  from a method, how arguments are passed to methods, and how to use the this
  keyword to refer to the current object.

- The main() method of Java applications and how to pass arguments to it.

- Overloaded methods, which reuse method names by giving them different arguments.
- Constructors, which define the initial variables and other starting conditions of objects.

# Q&A

**Q I have a class with an instance variable called `origin`. It also has a local variable called `origin` in a method, which, because of variable scope, gets hidden by the local variable. Is there any way to access the instance variable's value?**

A The easiest way to avoid this problem is to give your local variables different names than your instance variables. If for some reason you prefer to call a local variable `origin` when there's an instance variable of the same name, you can use `this.origin` to refer to the instance variable and `origin` to refer to the local variable.

**Q I created two methods with the following signatures:**

```
int total(int arg1, int arg2, int arg3) { ... }
float total(int arg1, int arg2, int arg3) { ... }
```

**The Java compiler complains when I try to compile the class with these method definitions, even though their signatures are different. What did I do wrong?**

A The error occurs because your methods have the same signature. Method overloading in Java works only if the argument lists are different in either number or type of arguments. Return type is not part of a method signature, so it's not considered when methods have been overloaded. Looking at it from the point at which a method is called, this makes sense: If two methods have exactly the same argument list, how would Java know which one to call?

**Q When I create the `Averager` application in NetBeans, why is there a warning icon over the line number of line 8 with the message `Use enhanced for loop to iterate over the array`?**

A This occurs because NetBeans is encouraging you to write the `for` loop with a better technique, called an enhanced `for` loop. This type of loop is introduced in Lesson 8, "Data Structures," as a simpler way to iterate over the elements of an array or some data-holding classes in Java.

5

NetBeans can convert a normal `for` loop to an enhanced one. Click the warning icon and choose `Use enhanced for loop to iterate over the array`. This converts line 8 from this:

```
for (int i = 0; i < arguments.length; i++) {
```

to this:

```
for (String argument : arguments) {
```

Lines 9–10 work the same either way. To switch back, press Ctrl+Z to undo the change.

**Q I wrote a program to take four arguments, but when I give it too few arguments, it crashes with a runtime error. Why?**

**A** It's up to you to test for the number and type of arguments your program expects; Java won't do it for you. If your program requires four arguments, test in the `main()` method that you have indeed been given four arguments by using the `length` variable of an array, which contains the count of its elements. Return an error message if you haven't and end the program.

# Quiz

Review this lesson's material by taking this three-question quiz.

## Questions

1. If a local variable has the same name as an instance variable, how can you refer to the instance variable in the scope of the local variable?

    **A.** You can't; you should rename one of the variables.

    **B.** Use the keyword `this` before the instance variable name.

    **C.** Use the keyword `super` before the name.

2. Where are instance variables declared in a class?

    **A.** Anywhere in the class

    **B.** Outside all methods in the class

    **C.** After the class declaration and above the first method

3. How can you send to a program an argument that includes a space or spaces?

    **A.** Surround the argument with double quotes.

    **B.** Separate the arguments with commas.

    **C.** Separate the arguments with periods.

## Answers

**1.** B. Answer A is a good idea, but variable name conflicts can be a source of subtle errors in Java programs.

**2.** B. Customarily, instance variables are declared right after the class declaration and before any methods. It's necessary only that they be outside all methods.

**3.** A. The quotation marks are not included in the argument when it is passed to the program.

# Certification Practice

The following question is the kind of thing you could expect to be asked on a Java programming certification test. Answer it without looking again at this lesson or using the Java compiler to test the code.

Given:

```java
public class BigValue {
    float result;

    public BigValue(int a, int b) {
        result = calculateResult(a, b);
    }

    float calculateResult(int a, int b) {
        return (a * 10) + (b * 2);
    }

    public static void main(String[] arguments) {
        BiggerValue bgr = new BiggerValue(2, 3, 4);
        System.out.println("The result is " + bgr.result);
    }
}

class BiggerValue extends BigValue {

    BiggerValue(int a, int b, int c) {
        super(a, b);
        result = calculateResult(a, b, c);
    }

    // answer goes here
        return (c * 3) * result;
    }
}
```

5

What statement should replace `// answer goes here` so that the `result` variable equals 312.0?

**A.** `float calculateResult(int c) {`

**B.** `float calculateResult(int a, int b) {`

**C.** `float calculateResult(int a, int b, int c) {`

**D.** `float calculateResult() {`

The answer is available on the book's website, at www.java21days.com. Visit the Lesson 5 page and click the Certification Practice link.

# Exercises

To extend your knowledge of the subjects covered in this lesson, try the following exercises:

**1.** Modify the `MarsRobot` project from Lesson 1 so that it includes constructors.

**2.** Create a class for four-dimensional points called `FourDPoint` that is a subclass of `Point` from the `java.awt` package.

Where applicable, exercise solutions are offered on the book's website, at www.java21days.com.

# LESSON 6

# Packages, Interfaces, and Other Class Features

Classes, the templates used to create objects that can store data and accomplish tasks, turn up in everything you do with the Java language.

In this lesson, you'll extend your knowledge of classes by learning more about how to create them, use them, organize them, and establish rules for how other classes can use them.

The following subjects are covered:

- Controlling access to methods and variables from outside a class

- Finalizing classes, methods, and variables so that their values or definitions cannot be overridden in subclasses

- Creating abstract classes and methods for factoring common behavior into superclasses

- Grouping classes into packages

- Using interfaces to bridge gaps in a class hierarchy

# Modifiers

In the lessons so far, you have learned how to define classes, methods, and variables in Java. The programming techniques you'll learn in this lesson involve different ways of thinking about how a class is organized. All these techniques use special modifiers in the Java language. *Modifiers* are keywords that you add to those definitions to change their meanings.

The Java language has these modifiers:

- The `public`, `protected`, and `private` modifiers for controlling access to a class, method, or variable
- The `static` modifier for creating class methods and variables
- The `final` modifier for finalizing the implementations of classes, methods, and variables
- The `abstract` modifier for creating abstract classes and methods
- The `synchronized` and `volatile` modifiers, which are used for threads

To add a modifier, you include its keyword in the definition of a class, method, or variable. The modifier precedes the rest of the statement, as in these examples:

```
public class RedButton extends javax.swing.JButton {
    // ...
}

private boolean offline;

static final double WEEKS = 9.5;

protected static final int MEANING_OF_LIFE = 42;

public static void main(String[] arguments) {
    // body of method
}
```

If you're using more than one modifier in a statement, you can place them in any order if all modifiers precede the element they are modifying. Be sure to avoid treating a method's return type—such as `void`—as if it were one of the modifiers. The return type must precede the method name, with no modifiers between them.

Modifiers are optional, as you might have recognized after using some of them in the preceding five lessons. However, there are many good reasons to use them in your programs.

# Access Control for Methods and Variables

The modifiers that you will use most often control access to methods and variables: `public`, `private`, and `protected`. These modifiers determine which variables and methods of a class are visible to other classes.

By using access control, you can dictate how your class is used by other classes. Some variables and methods in a class are of use only within the class itself and should be hidden from other classes. This process is called *encapsulation*: An object controls what the outside world can know about it and how the outside world can interact with it. Encapsulation is the process that prevents class and instance variables from being read or modified by other classes. The only way to use these variables is by calling methods of the class if they are available.

The Java language provides four levels of access control: public, private, protected, and a default level specified by using none of the three access control modifiers.

## Default Access

Variables and methods can be declared without any modifiers, as in the following examples:

```
String version = "0.7a";

boolean processOrder() {
    // ...
    return true;
}
```

A variable or method declared without an access control modifier is available to any other class in the same package. The Java Class Library is organized into packages such as `javax.swing`, a collection of windowing classes for use in graphical user interface programming, and `java.util`, a useful group of utility classes.

Any variable declared without a modifier can be read or changed by any other class in the same package. Any method declared the same way can be called by any other class in the same package. No other classes can access these elements in any way.

This level of access control doesn't control much access, so it's less useful when you begin thinking about how you want a class to be used by other classes.

6

## Private Access

To completely hide a method or variable and keep it from being used by other classes, use the `private` modifier. The only place these methods or variables can be accessed is within their own class.

A private instance variable can be used by methods in its own class but not by objects of any other class. Private methods can be called by other methods in their own class but cannot be called by any others. This restriction also affects inheritance: Neither private variables nor private methods are inherited by subclasses.

A private variable is useful in two circumstances:

- When other classes have no reason to use that variable
- When another class could wreak havoc by changing the variable in an inappropriate way

For example, consider a Java class called `CouponMachine` that generates discounts for an online shopping site. A variable in that class called `salesRatio` could control the size of discounts based on product sales. This variable has a big impact on the business's bottom line. If the variable were changed by other classes, `CouponMachine`'s performance would change significantly. To guard against this scenario, you could declare the `salesRatio` variable as `private`.

The following class uses private access control:

```java
class Logger {
    private String format;

    public String getFormat() {
        return this.format;
    }

    public void setFormat(String fmt) {
        if ( ("common".equals(fmt)) || ("combined".equals(fmt)) ) {
            this.format = fmt;
        }
    }
}
```

In this code, the `format` variable of the `Logger` class is private, so there's no way for other classes to retrieve or set its value directly.

Instead, it's available through two public methods: `getFormat()`, which returns the value of `format`, and `setFormat(String)`, which sets its value.

The latter method contains logic that allows the variable to be set to only `"common"` or `"combined"`. This demonstrates a benefit of using public methods as the only means of accessing instance variables of a class: The methods can give the class control over how the variable is accessed and limit the values it can take.

Using the `private` modifier is the main way in which an object encapsulates itself. You can't limit the ways in which a class is used without using `private` to hide variables and methods. Another class is free to change the variables inside a class and call its methods in many possible ways if you don't control access.

A big advantage of privacy is that it lets the implementation of a class change without affecting the users of that class. If you come up with a better way to accomplish something, you can rewrite the class as long as its public methods take the same arguments and return the same kinds of values.

## Public Access

In some cases, you might want a method or variable in a class to be completely available to any other class that wants to use it. For example, the `Color` class in the `java.awt` package has public variables for common colors such as `black`. This variable is used when any class that displays graphics wants to draw something in the color black, so `black` should have no access control.

Class variables often are declared to be public. An example is a set of variables in a `Football` class that represent the number of points used in scoring. The `TOUCHDOWN` variable could equal `6`, the `FIELD_GOAL` variable could equal `3`, and `SAFETY` could equal `2`. If these variables are public, other classes could use them in statements such as the following:

```
if (yard < 0) {
    System.out.println("Touchdown!");
    score = score + Football.TOUCHDOWN;
}
```

The `public` modifier makes a method or variable completely available to all classes. You have used it in every application you have written so far in their `main()` methods:

```
public static void main(String[] arguments) {
    // ...
}
```

6

The `main()` method of an application must be public. Otherwise, it could not be called by a Java Virtual Machine (JVM) to run the class.

Because of class inheritance, all public methods and variables of a class are inherited by its subclasses.

## Protected Access

The next level of access control is to limit a method and variable to use by the following two groups:

- Subclasses of a class
- Other classes in the same package

You do so by using the `protected` modifier, as in the following statement:

```
protected boolean outOfData = true;
```

**NOTE**

You might be wondering how these two groups differ. After all, aren't subclasses part of the same package as their superclass? Not always. An example is the `java.sql.Date` class, which represents calendar dates in an SQL database. It is a subclass of `java.util.Date`, a more generic date class. Protected access differs from default access in this way: Protected variables are available to subclasses, even if they aren't in the same package.

This level of access control is useful if you want to make it easier for a subclass to be implemented. Your class might use a method or variable to help the class do its job. Because a subclass inherits much of the same behavior and attributes, it might have the same job to do. Protected access gives the subclass a chance to use the helper method or variable while preventing an unrelated class from trying to use it.

Consider the example of a class called `AudioPlayer` that plays audio files. `AudioPlayer` has a method called `openSpeaker()`, which interacts with the hardware to prepare the speaker for playing. `openSpeaker()` isn't important to anyone outside the `AudioPlayer` class, so at first glance you might want to make it private. A snippet of `AudioPlayer` might look something like this:

```
class AudioPlayer {

    private boolean openSpeaker(Speaker sp) {
        // implementation here
    }
}
```

This code works fine if `AudioPlayer` won't be subclassed. But what if later you need a class called `StreamingAudioPlayer` that is a subclass of `AudioPlayer`? That class needs access to the `openSpeaker()` method to override it and provide support for streaming audio devices. You still don't want the method to be generally available to random objects, so it shouldn't be public, but you want any subclasses to have access to it.

## Comparing Levels of Access Control

The differences among the various protection types can be confusing, particularly in the case of protected methods and variables. Table 6.1, which summarizes exactly what is allowed where, helps clarify the differences from the least restrictive (public) to the most restrictive (private) forms of protection.

**TABLE 6.1**    The Different Levels of Access Control

| Visibility | Public | Protected | Default | Private |
| --- | --- | --- | --- | --- |
| From the same class | Yes | Yes | Yes | Yes |
| From any class in the same package | Yes | Yes | Yes | No |
| From any class outside the package | Yes | No | No | No |
| From a subclass in the same package | Yes | Yes | Yes | No |
| From a subclass outside the same package | Yes | Yes | No | No |

## Access Control and Inheritance

One last issue regarding access control for methods involves subclasses. When you create a subclass and override a method, you must consider the access control in place on the original method.

As a rule, you cannot override a method in Java and make the new method more restrictively controlled than the original. You can, however, make it more public. The method in a subclass can't reduce the visibility of the one it overrides. The following rules for inherited methods are enforced:

- Methods declared public in a superclass also must be public in all subclasses.

- Methods declared protected in a superclass must be either protected or public in subclasses; they cannot be private.

- Methods declared without access control (no modifier used) can be declared more private in subclasses.

Methods declared private are not inherited, so the rules don't apply.

6

## Accessor Methods

In many cases, you may have an instance variable in a class that has strict rules for the values it can contain. An example is a `zipCode` variable. A zip code in the United States must be a five-digit number. (There also is a zip+4 format that's nine digits.)

To prevent an external class from setting the `zipCode` variable incorrectly, you can declare it private:

```
private int zipCode;
```

However, what if other classes must be able to set the `zipCode` variable for the class to be useful? In that circumstance, you can give other classes access to a private variable by using an accessor method inside the same class as `zipCode`.

An accessor method provides access to a variable that otherwise would be off-limits. By using a method to provide access to a private variable, you can control how that variable is used. In the zip code example, the class could prevent anyone else from setting `zipCode` to an incorrect value.

Often, separate accessor methods to read and write a variable are available. Reading methods typically have a name beginning with `get`, and writing methods have a name beginning with `set`, as in `getZipCode()` and `setZipCode(int)`.

There's one exception to this convention: If the variable being accessed is a Boolean, the accessor method doesn't begin with `get`. Instead, it starts with `is`, as in `isValid()` for a `boolean` variable named `valid`. Here's an example:

```
private boolean empty;

public boolean isEmpty() {
    return empty;
}
```

Using accessor methods to access instance variables is a common technique in object-oriented programming. This approach makes classes more reusable by guarding against improper use.

# Static Variables and Methods

A modifier that you already have used in programs is `static`, which was described in detail in Lesson 5, "Creating Classes and Methods." The `static` modifier is used to create class methods and variables, as in the following example:

```
public class Circle {
    public static double PI = 3.14159265F;
```

```
    public double radius;

    public double area() {
        return PI * radius * radius;
    }
}
```

Class variables and methods can be accessed using the class name followed by a dot and the name of the variable or method, as in `Color.black` or `Circle.PI`. You also can use the name of an object belonging to the class, but for class variables and methods, using the class name is better. This approach makes it more clear what kind of variable or method you're working with; instance variables and methods never can be referred to by a class name.

The following statements use class variables and methods:

```
double circumference = 2 * Circle.PI * radius;
double randomNumber = Math.random();
```

TIP

> For the same reason as with instance variables, class variables can benefit from being private and having their use limited to accessor methods only.

The first project you'll undertake in this lesson is a class called `InstanceCounter` that uses class and instance variables to keep track of how many objects of that class have been created. In NetBeans, create an empty Java file named `InstanceCounter` in the `com.java21days` package you've been using for most of this book. Enter the code shown in Listing 6.1 in the source code file and save it when you're done.

**LISTING 6.1**   The Full Text of `InstanceCounter.java`                    6

```
 1: package com.java21days;
 2:
 3: public class InstanceCounter {
 4:     private static int numInstances = 0;
 5:
 6:     protected static int getCount() {
 7:         return numInstances;
 8:     }
 9:
10:     private static void addInstance() {
11:         numInstances++;
12:     }
```

```
13:
14:        InstanceCounter() {
15:            InstanceCounter.addInstance();
16:        }
17:
18:        public static void main(String[] arguments) {
19:            System.out.println("Starting with " +
20:                InstanceCounter.getCount() + " objects");
21:            for (int  i = 0; i < 500; ++i) {
22:                new InstanceCounter();
23:            }
24:            System.out.println("Created " +
25:                InstanceCounter.getCount() + " objects");
26:        }
27: }
```

NetBeans attempts to compile a Java class when it is saved or run. If there are no errors, you can run it to see the output shown in Figure 6.1.

**FIGURE 6.1**
Working with class and instance variables.

This application demonstrates several features of the Java language. In line 4, a private class variable is declared to hold the number of objects. It is a class variable (declared static) because the number of objects is relevant to the class as a whole, not to any particular object. It's private so that it can be retrieved with only an accessor method.

Note the initialization of numInstances. Just as an instance variable is initialized when its instance is created, a class variable is initialized when its class is created. This class initialization happens essentially before anything else can happen to that class or its instances, so that the class in the example will work as planned.

In lines 6–8, a get method is defined so that the private instance variable's value can be retrieved. This method also is declared as a class method because it applies directly to the class variable. The getCount() method is declared protected, as opposed to public, because only this class and perhaps its subclasses are interested in that value; other random classes, therefore, are restricted from seeing it.

Note that there is no accessor method to set the value. The value of the variable should be incremented only when a new instance is created; it should not be set to any random value.

Instead of creating an accessor method, a special private method called `addInstance()` is defined in lines 10–12 that increments the value of `numInstances` by 1.

Lines 14–16 create the constructor for this class. Constructors are called when a new object is created, which makes this the most logical place to call `addInstance()` and to increment the variable.

The `main()` method indicates that you can run this as a Java application and test all the other methods. In the `main()` method, 500 objects of the `InstanceCounter` class are created, and then the value of the `numInstances` class variable is displayed.

# Final Classes, Methods, and Variables

The `final` modifier is used with classes, methods, and variables to indicate that they will never be changed. It has different meanings for each thing that can be made final, as follows:

- A `final` class cannot be subclassed.
- A `final` method cannot be overridden by any subclasses.
- A `final` variable cannot change in value.

## Variables

Final variables often are called constants (or constant variables) because they do not change in value at any time.

With variables, the `final` modifier is used with `static` when making a constant a class variable. If the value never changes, you don't have much reason to give each object in the same class its own copy of the value. They all can use the class variable with the same functionality.

The following statements are examples of declaring constants:

```
public static final int TOUCHDOWN = 6;
static final String TITLE = "Captain";
```

6

## Methods

Final methods never can be overridden by a subclass. You declare them using the `final` modifier in the class declaration, as in the following example:

```
public final void getSignature() {
    // body of method
}
```

The most common reason to declare a method final is to make the class run more efficiently. Normally, when the JVM runs a method, first it checks the current class to find the method, then it checks its superclass, and so on up the class hierarchy until the method is found. This process sacrifices some speed in the name of flexibility and ease of development.

If a method is final, the Java compiler can put the method's executable bytecode directly into any program that calls the method; the method will never change because of a subclass overriding it.

When you first develop a class, you don't have much reason to use `final`. However, if you need to make a class execute more quickly, you can change a few methods to final methods to speed up the process. Doing so removes the possibility that the method later will be overridden in a subclass, so consider this change carefully before continuing.

The Java Class Library declares many of the commonly used methods final so that they can be executed more quickly when used in programs that call them.

**NOTE**      Private methods are final without being declared that way because they can't be overridden in a subclass under any circumstance.

## Classes

You make a class impossible to subclass by using the `final` modifier in the class's declaration, as in the following:

```
public final class ChatServer {
    // body of method
}
```

A `final` class cannot appear after `extends` in a class declaration to create a subclass. As with `final` methods, this process introduces some speed benefits to the Java language at the expense of flexibility.

If you're wondering what you lose by using `final` classes, you must not have tried to subclass anything in the Java Class Library. Many of the popular classes are final, such as `java.lang.String`, `java.lang.Math`, and `java.net.URL`. If you want to create a class that behaves like strings but with some new changes, you can't subclass `String` and define only the behavior that is different. You must start from scratch.

All methods in a final class are automatically final themselves, so you don't have to use modifiers in their declarations.

Because classes that can provide behavior and attributes to subclasses are much more useful, you should strongly consider whether the benefit of using `final` on one of your classes is outweighed by the cost.

# Abstract Classes and Methods

In a class hierarchy, the higher the class, the more abstract its definition. A class at the top of a hierarchy of other classes can define only the behavior and attributes common to all the classes. More-specific behavior and attributes fall somewhere lower down the hierarchy.

When you factor out common behavior and attributes during the process of defining a hierarchy of classes, you might at times find yourself with a class that never needs to be instantiated directly. Instead, such a class serves as a place to hold common behavior and attributes shared by their subclasses.

These classes are called *abstract classes*, and they are created using the `abstract` modifier. The following is an example:

```
public abstract class Palette {
    // ...
}
```

An example of an abstract class is `java.awt.Component`, the superclass of graphical user interface components. Because numerous components inherit from this class, it contains methods and variables that are useful to each of them. However, there's no such thing as a generic component that can be added to a user interface, so you would never need to create a `Component` object in a program.

Abstract classes can contain anything a normal class can contain, including constructors, because their subclasses might need to inherit them. Abstract classes also can contain abstract methods, which are method signatures with no implementation. These methods are implemented in subclasses of the abstract class. Abstract methods are declared with the `abstract` modifier. You cannot declare an abstract method in a class that isn't itself abstract. If an abstract class has nothing but abstract methods, you're better off using an interface, as you'll see later in this lesson.

6

# Packages

Using packages is a way of organizing groups of classes. A package contains classes that are related in purpose, in scope, or by inheritance.

If your first programs comprise a limited number of classes, you might find little need to explore packages. But as your efforts become more ambitious, you'll quickly discover the benefit of organizing them into packages.

Packages are useful for several broad reasons:

- They enable you to organize your classes into units. Just as you have folders on your hard drive to organize your files and applications, packages enable you to organize your classes into groups so that you use only what you need for each program.

- Packages reduce problems with conflicts about names. As the number of Java classes grows, so does the likelihood that you'll use the same class name as another developer. This introduces the possibility of naming clashes and error messages if you try to integrate groups of classes into a single program. Packages provide a way to refer specifically to the desired class, even if it shares a name with a class in another package.

- They enable you to protect classes, variables, and methods in larger ways than on a class-by-class basis. You'll learn more about protections with packages later.

- Packages can be used to uniquely identify your work.

Every time you use the `import` command or refer to a class by its full package name (`java.util.StringTokenizer`, for example), you are using packages.

To use a class contained in a package, you can use one of three techniques:

- If the class you want to use is in the package `java.lang` (for example, `System` or `Date`), you can use the class name to refer to that class. The `java.lang` classes automatically are available to you in all your programs.

- If the class you want to use is in some other package, you can refer to that class by its full name, including any package names (for example, `java.awt.Font`).

- For classes from other packages that you use frequently, you can import individual classes or a whole package of classes. After a class or package has been imported, you can refer to that class by its class name.

If you don't declare that your class belongs to a package, it is put into an unnamed default package. You can refer to that class and any other unpackaged class by its class name from anywhere in other classes.

To refer to a class in another package, you can use its full name: the class name preceded by its package. You do not have to import the class or package to use it in this manner:

```
java.awt.Font text = new java.awt.Font();
```

For classes that you use only once or twice in a program, using the full name might make sense. If you use a class multiple times, you can import the class to save yourself some typing. But there's no reason not to use `import`, so you may decide to follow this book's convention of always using it so that class names are short and code is more readable.

## The `import` Declaration

To import classes from a package, use the `import` declaration. You can import an individual class, as in this statement:

```
import java.util.ArrayList;
```

You also can import an entire package of classes by using an asterisk (*) in place of an individual class name:

```
import java.awt.*;
```

In an `import` statement, the asterisk can be used only in place of a class name. It does not make it possible to import multiple packages with similar names.

For example, the Java Class Library includes the `java.util`, `java.util.jar`, and `java.util.prefs` packages. You could not import all three packages with the following statement:

```
import java.util.*;
```

This merely imports the `java.util` package. To make all three available in a class, the following statements are required:

```
import java.util.*;
import java.util.jar.*;
import java.util.prefs.*;
```

Also, you cannot indicate partial class names (such as L* to import all the classes that begin with the letter *L*). Your only options when using an `import` declaration are to identify a single class or use an asterisk to load all the classes in a package.

The `import` declarations in your class definition go at the top of the file, before any class definitions but after the package declaration, as you'll see in the next section.

Using individual `import` declarations or importing packages is mostly a question of your own coding style. Importing a group of classes does not slow down your program or

6

make it any larger; only the classes that you actually use in your code are loaded as they are needed. Importing specific classes makes it easier for readers of your code to figure out what classes are being used in the code.

**NOTE**

> If you're familiar with C or C++, you might expect the `import` declaration to work like `#include` and potentially result in a large executable program because it includes source code from another file. This isn't the case in Java. The only function of the `import` keyword is to tell the Java compiler where to look for the full name of a class when its short name is used. It doesn't actually import code from any classes.

The `import` statement also can be used to refer to constants in a class by name.

Normally, class constants are prefaced with the name of the class, as in `Color.black`, `Math.PI`, and `File.separator`.

An `import static` statement makes the constants in an identified class available in shorter form. The keywords `import static` are followed by the name of an interface or class and an asterisk. For example:

```
import static java.lang.Math.*;
```

This statement makes it possible to refer to the constants in the `Math` class, `E` and `PI`, using only their names. Here's a short example of a class that takes advantage of this feature:

```
import static java.lang.Math.*;

public class ShortConstants {
    public static void main(String[] arguments) {
        System.out.println("PI: " + PI);
        System.out.println("" + (PI * 3));
    }
}
```

## Class Name Conflicts

After you have imported a class or a package of classes, you usually can refer to a class by its name, without the package identifier. However, you must be more explicit when you import two classes from different packages that have the same class name.

One situation where a naming conflict might occur is during database programming, which you'll undertake in Lesson 18, "Accessing Databases with JDBC and Derby." This kind of programming can involve the `java.util` and `java.sql` packages, which both contain a class named `Date`.

If you're working with both packages in a class that reads or writes data in a database, you could import them with these statements:

```
import java.sql.*;
import java.util.*;
```

When both these packages are imported, an error occurs when you refer to the `Date` class without specifying a package name, as in this statement:

```
Date now = new Date();
```

The error occurs because the Java compiler has no way of knowing which `Date` class is being referenced in the statement. The package must be included in the class name, like this:

```
java.util.Date = new java.util.Date();
```

**TIP**

NetBeans makes it easy to import individual classes as you write a program. As you enter statements in the source code editor, NetBeans detects when a class you use hasn't been imported. A warning icon (a lightbulb and red circle) appears at the left edge of the editor on that line. When you click the icon, a pop-up menu appears with a command to import the class. Choose that command, and an `import` statement is added at the top of the class.

6

# Creating Your Own Packages

Creating a package for your classes in Java is easier than creating a class.

## Picking a Package Name

The first step in creating a package is to decide on a name, based on how you will use those classes. Perhaps you'll name your package after yourself, your company, or a part of the Java system you're working on (such as `graphics` or `messaging`). If you intend to distribute your package as an open source or commercial product, use a package name that uniquely identifies its authorship.

Oracle recommends using a domain name that you control as the basis for a unique package name.

To form the name, reverse the elements of the domain so that the last part becomes the first part of the package name, followed by the second-to-last part. I use this convention, and because my personal domain name is cadenhead.org, Java packages I create often begin with the name org.cadenhead, such as org.cadenhead.game and org.cadenhead.xml.

This book's website is at the domain java21days.com, so the package for the classes created in these pages is com.java21days.

This convention provides a reasonable assurance that no other Java developers will offer a package with the same name, as long as they follow the same rule themselves (as most developers do).

By another convention, package names use no capital letters, which distinguishes them from class names. For example, in the full name of the class java.lang.String, you can easily distinguish the package name java.lang from the class name String.

## Creating the Folder Structure

The second step in creating a package is to create a folder structure that matches the package name, which requires a separate folder for each part of the name. The package org.cadenhead.rss requires an org folder, a cadenhead folder inside org, and an rss folder inside cadenhead. The classes in the package then are stored in the rss folder.

In NetBeans, when you put a class in a package, the folders are created automatically, and the source code and class files are stored in the correct subfolder. All you have to worry about is choosing the package name.

To see this, click the Files tab in the Projects pane to bring it to the front (see Figure 6.2). The files and folders of the Java21 project are shown. You have been using the package com.java21days in your programs in this book. Expand the src folder, the com subfolder, then the java21days subfolder. All the Java source files for classes in this package are then listed.

**FIGURE 6.2**
Viewing a project's
package folder hierarchy
in NetBeans.

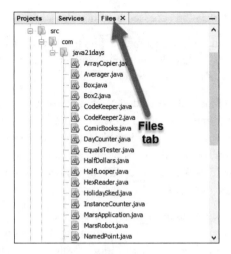

## Adding a Class to a Package

The final step in putting a class inside a package is to add a statement above any `import` declarations and the `class` declaration. The `package` declaration is followed by the full name of the package:

```
package org.cadenhead.rss;
```

The `package` declaration must be the first line of code in your source file, disregarding comments or blank lines.

## Packages and Class Access Control

Earlier in this lesson, you learned about access control modifiers for methods and variables. You also can control access to classes.

Classes have the default access control if no modifier is specified, which means that the class is available to all other classes in the same package but is not visible or available outside that package. The class cannot be imported or referred to by name; classes with package protection are hidden inside the package in which they are contained.

To allow a class to be visible and importable outside your package, you can give it public protection by adding the `public` modifier to its definition:

```
public class Visible {
    // ...
}
```

6

Classes declared as public can be accessed by other classes outside the package.

Note that when you use an `import` statement with an asterisk, you import only the public classes inside that package. Other classes remain hidden and can be used only by the other classes in that package.

Why would you want to hide a class inside a package? For the same reasons that you want to hide variables and methods inside a class: so that you can have utility classes and behavior that are useful only to your implementation, or so that you can limit your program's interface to minimize the effects of larger changes. As you design your classes, consider the whole package, and decide which classes you want to declare public and which you want to be hidden.

Creating a good package consists of defining a small, clean set of public classes and methods for other classes to use and then implementing them by using any number of hidden support classes. You'll see another use for private classes later in this lesson.

# Interfaces

Interfaces, like abstract classes and methods, provide templates of behavior that other classes are expected to implement. They also offer significant advantages in class and object design that complement Java's single-inheritance approach to object-oriented programming.

## The Problem of Single Inheritance

As you begin turning a project into a hierarchy of classes related by inheritance, you might discover that the simplicity of the class organization is restrictive. This is especially true when you have some behavior that needs to be used by classes that do not share a common superclass.

Other object-oriented programming (OOP) languages include the concept of multiple inheritance, which solves this problem by letting a class inherit from more than one superclass, acquiring behavior and attributes from all its superclasses at once.

This concept makes a programming language more challenging to learn and use. Questions of method invocation and how the class hierarchy is organized become far more complicated with multiple inheritance. They also become more open to confusion and ambiguity.

Because one of the goals of Java was to be simpler than languages that inspired its creation, multiple inheritance was rejected in favor of single inheritance.

A Java interface is a collection of abstract behavior that can be adopted by any class without being inherited from a superclass.

An interface contains abstract method definitions and constants. It has no instance variables or method implementations.

Interfaces are implemented and used throughout the Java Class Library when behavior is expected to be implemented by a number of disparate classes. Later in this lesson, you'll use one of the interfaces, `java.lang.Comparable`.

## Interfaces and Classes

Classes and interfaces, despite their different definitions, have a great deal in common. Both are declared in source files and compiled into `.class` files. In most cases, an interface can be used anywhere you can use a class.

You can substitute an interface name for a class name in almost every example in this book. Java programmers often say "class" when they actually mean "class or interface." Interfaces complement and extend the power of classes, and the two can be treated almost the same, but an interface cannot be instantiated: `new` can only create an instance of a non-abstract class.

## Implementing and Using Interfaces

You can do two things with interfaces: use them in your own classes and define your own. For now, start with using them in your own classes.

To use an interface, include the `implements` keyword as part of your class definition:

```
public class AnimatedSign extends Sign
    implements Runnable {
    //...
}
```

In this example, the `Runnable` interface extends the behavior of the `AnimatedSign` class, which is a subclass of `Sign`.

6

When interfaces provide abstract method definitions, you must implement those methods in your own classes, using the same method signatures in the interface.

To implement an interface, you must offer all the methods in that interface; you can't pick and choose the methods you need. By implementing an interface, you're telling users of your class that you support the entire interface.

After your class implements an interface, subclasses of your class inherit those new methods and can override or overload them. If your class inherits from a superclass that implements a given interface, you don't have to include the `implements` keyword in your own class definition.

## Implementing Multiple Interfaces

Unlike with inheritance, where a class can have only one superclass, you can include as many interfaces as you need in a class. Your class must implement the combined behavior of all the included interfaces. To include multiple interfaces in a class, separate their names with commas:

```
public class AnimatedSign extends Sign
    implements Runnable, Observer {

    // ...
}
```

Note that complications might arise from implementing multiple interfaces. What happens if two different interfaces both define the same method? You can solve this problem in three ways:

- If the methods in each interface have identical signatures, you implement one method in your class, and that definition satisfies both interfaces.

- If the methods have different argument lists, it is a simple case of method overloading: You implement both method signatures, and each definition satisfies its respective interface definition.

- If the methods have the same argument lists but different return types, you cannot create a method that satisfies both. (Remember that a method signature does not include the method's return type.) In this case, trying to compile a class that implements both interfaces would produce a compiler error message. Encountering this problem suggests that your interfaces have some design flaws that you might need to reexamine.

## Other Uses of Interfaces

Almost everywhere that you can use a class, you can use an interface instead. For example, you can declare a variable to be of an interface type:

```
Iterator loop;
```

When a variable is declared to be of an interface type, it must be used to hold an object that implements the interface. Any class that implements the `Iterator` interface can be stored in `loop`. In this case, because `loop` is an object of the type `Iterator`, the assumption is that you can call all three of the interface's methods on that object: `hasNext()`, `next()`, and `remove()`.

You can cast objects to an interface, just as you can cast objects to other classes.

# Creating and Extending Interfaces

After you use interfaces for a while, the next step is to define your own interfaces. Interfaces look a lot like classes; they are declared in much the same way and can be arranged into a hierarchy. However, you must follow certain rules for declaring them.

## New Interfaces

To create a new interface, you declare it like this:

```
interface Expandable {
    // ...
}
```

This declaration is, effectively, the same as a class definition, with the word `interface` replacing the word `class`. Inside the interface definition are methods and variables.

The method definitions inside the interface are public and abstract. You can explicitly declare them as such, or they will be turned into public and abstract methods if you do not include those modifiers. You cannot declare a method inside an interface to be either private or protected.

As an example, here's an `Expandable` interface with one method explicitly declared public and abstract and one declared implicitly:

```
public interface Expandable {
    public abstract void expand(); // explicitly public and abstract
    void contract(); // effectively public and abstract
}
```

Both methods are public and abstract.

Like abstract methods in classes, methods inside interfaces do not have bodies. An interface consists of only method signatures; no implementation is involved.

6

In addition to methods, interfaces can have variables, but those variables must be declared `public`, `static`, and `final` (making them constant). As with methods, you can explicitly define a variable with these modifiers, or it is implicitly defined as such if you don't use those modifiers. Here's that same `Expandable` definition with two new variables:

```
public interface Expandable {
    public static final int INCREMENT = 10;
    long CAPACITY = 15000; // becomes public static and final

    public abstract void expand(); // explicitly public and abstract
    void contract(); // effectively public and abstract
}
```

Interfaces, just like classes, must have either public or package protection. Note, however, that interfaces without the `public` modifier do not automatically convert their methods to public and abstract nor their constants to public. A non-public interface also has non-public methods and constants that can be used only by classes and other interfaces in the same package.

Interfaces, like classes, can belong to a package. Interfaces also can import other interfaces and classes from other packages, just as classes can.

## Methods Inside Interfaces

Here's one trick to note about methods inside interfaces: Those methods are supposed to be abstract and apply to any kind of class, but how can you define arguments to those methods? You don't know what class will be using them! The answer lies in the fact that you use an interface name anywhere a class name can be used, as you learned earlier. By defining your method arguments to be interface types, you can create generic arguments that apply to any class that might use this interface.

Consider the interface `Trackable`, which defines methods with no arguments for `track()` and `quitTracking()`. You also might have a method for `beginTracking()`, which has one argument: an object of the `Trackable` class.

What class should that argument be? It should be any object that implements the `Trackable` interface rather than a particular class and its subclasses. The solution is to declare the argument as simply `Trackable` in the interface:

```
public interface Trackable {
    public abstract Trackable beginTracking(Trackable self);
}
```

Then, in an actual implementation for this method in a class, you can cast the generic `Trackable` argument to the appropriate object:

```
public class Monitor implements Trackable {

    public Trackable beginTracking(Trackable self) {
        Monitor mon = (Monitor) self;
        // ...
        return mon;
    }
}
```

# Extending Interfaces

As you can do with classes, you can organize interfaces into a hierarchy. When one interface inherits from another interface, that subinterface acquires all the method definitions and constants that its superinterface declared.

To extend an interface, you use the `extends` keyword just as you do in a class definition:

```
interface PreciselyTrackable extends Trackable {
    // ...
}
```

Note that unlike with classes, the interface hierarchy has no equivalent of the `Object` class: There is no root superinterface from which all interfaces descend; interfaces can either exist entirely on their own or inherit from other interfaces.

Note also that unlike the class hierarchy, the inheritance hierarchy can have multiple inheritance. For example, a single interface can extend as many classes as it needs to (separated by commas in the `extends` part of the definition), and the new interface contains a combination of all its parent's methods and constants.

In interfaces, the rules for managing method name conflicts are the same as for classes that use multiple interfaces; methods that differ only in return type result in compiler error messages.

6

# Creating an Online Storefront

To explore all the topics covered up to this point, the `storefront` application uses packages, access control, interfaces, and encapsulation. This application manages the items in an online storefront, handling two main tasks:

- Calculating the sale price of each item, depending on how much of it is presently in stock
- Sorting items according to sale price

The Storefront application consists of two classes, Storefront and Item. These classes will be organized as a new package called org.cadenhead.ecommerce.

In NetBeans, choose File, New File, indicate that you're creating a new empty Java file, and then click Next. Give it the class name Item and the package name org.cadenhead.ecommerce. Click Finish and then enter the code shown in Listing 6.2.

**LISTING 6.2**    The Full Text of Item.java

```
 1: package org.cadenhead.ecommerce;
 2:
 3: public class Item implements Comparable {
 4:     private final String id;
 5:     private final String name;
 6:     private final double retail;
 7:     private final int quantity;
 8:     private double price;
 9:
10:     Item(String idIn, String nameIn, String retailIn, String qIn) {
11:         id = idIn;
12:         name = nameIn;
13:         retail = Double.parseDouble(retailIn);
14:         quantity = Integer.parseInt(qIn);
15:
16:         if (quantity > 400) {
17:             price = retail * .5D;
18:         } else if (quantity > 200) {
19:             price = retail * .6D;
20:         } else {
21:             price = retail * .7D;
22:         }
23:         price = Math.floor( price * 100 + .5 ) / 100;
24:     }
25:
26:     @Override
27:     public int compareTo(Object obj) {
28:         Item temp = (Item) obj;
29:         if (this.price < temp.price) {
30:             return 1;
31:         } else if (this.price > temp.price) {
32:             return -1;
33:         }
34:         return 0;
35:     }
36:
37:     public String getId() {
38:         return id;
39:     }
40:
```

```
41:        public String getName() {
42:            return name;
43:        }
44:
45:        public double getRetail() {
46:            return retail;
47:        }
48:
49:        public int getQuantity() {
50:            return quantity;
51:        }
52:
53:        public double getPrice() {
54:            return price;
55:        }
56: }
```

When you save this file, look in the Projects pane of NetBeans. The `Item.java` source code file has been put in a different place, as shown in Figure 6.3.

**FIGURE 6.3**
Grouping packages in a NetBeans project.

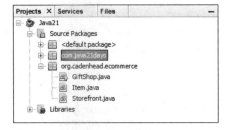

NetBeans puts the source code file in the `org.cadenhead.ecommerce` category.

The `Item` class is a support class that represents a product sold by an online store. It contains private instance variables for the product ID code, name, how many are in stock (`quantity`), and retail and sale prices.

Because all the instance variables of this class are private, no other class can set or retrieve their values. Simple accessor methods are created in lines 37–55 to provide a way for other programs to retrieve these values. Each method begins with `get` followed by the capitalized name of the variable, which is a standard convention in Java programming used throughout the Java Class Library. The `getPrice()` method returns a `double` containing the value of `price`. No methods are provided for setting any of these instance variables. That is handled in the constructor method for this class.

6

Line 1 establishes that the `Item` class is part of the `org.cadenhead.ecommerce` package.

The `Item` class implements the `Comparable` interface (line 3), which makes it easy to sort a class's objects. This interface has only one method, `compareTo(Object)`, which returns an integer.

The `compareTo()` method compares two objects of a class: the current object and another object passed as an argument to the method. The value returned by the method defines the natural sorting order for objects of this class:

- If the current object should be sorted above the other object, return `-1`.
- If the current object should be sorted below the other object, return `1`.
- If the two objects are equal, return `0`.

You determine in the `compareTo()` method which of an object's instance variables to consider when sorting. Lines 27–35 override the `compareTo()` method for the `Item` class, sorting on the basis of the `price` variable. Items are sorted by price from highest to lowest.

After you have implemented the `Comparable` interface for an object, two class methods can be called to sort an array or a class holding those objects. You'll see this later in this section, when the `Storefront` class is created.

The `Item()` constructor in lines 10–24 takes four `String` objects as arguments and uses them to set up the `id`, `name`, `retail`, and `quantity` instance variables. The last two must be converted from strings to numeric values by using the `Double.parseDouble()` and `Integer.parseInt()` class methods, respectively.

The value of the `price` instance variable depends on how much of that item is presently in stock:

- If more than 400 are in stock, `price` is 50% of `retail` (lines 16–17).
- If between 201 and 400 are in stock, `price` is 60% of `retail` (lines 18–19).
- For everything else, `price` is 70% of `retail` (lines 20–22).

Line 23 rounds off `price` so that it contains two or fewer decimal places, turning a value such as $6.92999999999999 into $6.93. The `Math.floor()` method rounds off decimal numbers to the next-lowest integer and returns them as double values.

As the next step in the project, you need a class that represents a storefront for these products. Create an empty Java file with the class name `Storefront` and package name `org.cadenhead.ecommerce` and enter the code shown in Listing 6.3.

**LISTING 6.3**   The Full Text of `Storefront.java`

```
 1: package org.cadenhead.ecommerce;
 2:
 3: import java.util.*;
 4:
 5: public class Storefront {
 6:     private final LinkedList catalog = new LinkedList();
 7:
 8:     public void addItem(String id, String name, String price,
 9:         String quant) {
10:
11:         Item it = new Item(id, name, price, quant);
12:         catalog.add(it);
13:     }
14:
15:     public Item getItem(int i) {
16:         return (Item) catalog.get(i);
17:     }
18:
19:     public int getSize() {
20:         return catalog.size();
21:     }
22:
23:     public void sort() {
24:         Collections.sort(catalog);
25:     }
26: }
```

Because it belongs to the same package as the `Item` class, `Storefront` will be listed with it in the NetBeans Projects pane.

The `Storefront` class is used to manage a collection of products in an online store. Each product is an `Item` object, and these objects are stored together in a `LinkedList` instance variable named `catalog` (line 6).

The `addItem()` method in lines 8–13 creates a new `Item` object based on four arguments sent to the method: `id`, `name`, `price`, and `quant`, for the ID, name, price, and quantity of the item that is in stock. After the item is created, it is added to the `catalog` linked list through a call to its `add(Object)` method, with the `Item` object as an argument.

The `getItem()` and `getSize()` methods provide an interface to the information stored in the private `catalog` variable. The `getSize()` method in lines 19–21 calls the `catalog.size()` method, which returns the number of objects contained in `catalog`.

Because objects in a linked list are numbered like arrays and other data structures, you can retrieve them by using an index number. The `getItem()` method in lines 15–17 calls

6

`catalog.get(int)` with an index number as an argument and returns the object stored at that location in the linked list.

The `sort()` method in lines 23–25 is where you benefit from the implementation of the `Comparable` interface in the `Item` class. The class method `Collections.sort()` sorts a linked list and other data structures based on the natural sort order of the objects they contain, calling the object's `compareTo()` method to determine this order.

To finish this project, the `GiftShop` application is a class that makes use of `Item` and `Storefront` objects. This application also belongs to the `org.cadenhead.ecommerce` package. Create the new Java class `GiftShop` with the source code shown in Listing 6.4.

**LISTING 6.4**   The Full Text of `GiftShop.java`

```
 1: package org.cadenhead.ecommerce;
 2:
 3: public class GiftShop {
 4:     public static void main(String[] arguments) {
 5:         Storefront store = new Storefront();
 6:         store.addItem("C01", "MUG", "9.99", "150");
 7:         store.addItem("C02", "LG MUG", "12.99", "82");
 8:         store.addItem("C03", "MOUSEPAD", "10.49", "800");
 9:         store.addItem("D01", "T SHIRT", "16.99", "90");
10:         store.sort();
11:
12:         for (int i = 0; i < store.getSize(); i++) {
13:             Item show = (Item) store.getItem(i);
14:             System.out.println("\nItem ID: " + show.getId() +
15:                 "\nName: " + show.getName() +
16:                 "\nRetail Price: $" + show.getRetail() +
17:                 "\nPrice: $" + show.getPrice() +
18:                 "\nQuantity: " + show.getQuantity());
19:         }
20:     }
21: }
```

The `GiftShop` class demonstrates each part of the public interface that the `Storefront` and `Item` classes make available. You can do the following:

- Create an online store
- Add items to it
- Sort the items by sale price
- Loop through a list of items to display information about each one

The output is shown in Figure 6.4.

**FIGURE 6.4**
Displaying a gift shop's inventory, sorted by price.

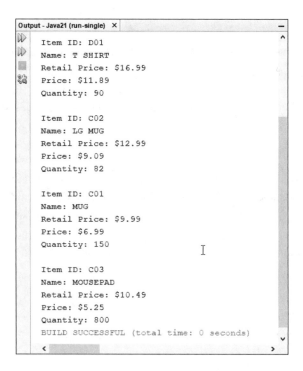

```
Output - Java21 (run-single)  ×

    Item ID: D01
    Name: T SHIRT
    Retail Price: $16.99
    Price: $11.89
    Quantity: 90

    Item ID: C02
    Name: LG MUG
    Retail Price: $12.99
    Price: $9.09
    Quantity: 82

    Item ID: C01
    Name: MUG
    Retail Price: $9.99
    Price: $6.99
    Quantity: 150

    Item ID: C03
    Name: MOUSEPAD
    Retail Price: $10.49
    Price: $5.25
    Quantity: 800
    BUILD SUCCESSFUL (total time: 0 seconds)
```

Many implementation details of these classes are hidden from `GiftShop` and other classes that would use the package. For instance, the programmer who developed `GiftShop` doesn't need to know that `Storefront` uses a linked list to hold all the store's product data. If the developer of `Storefront` later decides to use a different data structure, as long as `getSize()` and `getItem()` return the expected values, `GiftShop` will continue to work correctly.

# Summary

6

In this lesson you learned how to encapsulate an object by using access control modifiers for its variables and methods. You also learned how to use other modifiers, such as `static`, `final`, and `abstract`, to develop Java classes and class hierarchies.

To further the effort of developing and using a set of classes, you learned how to group classes into packages. These groupings better organize your programs and help you share classes with the many other Java programmers making their code publicly available.

Finally, you learned how to implement interfaces and inner classes, an extremely helpful Java language feature that models behavior outside a class hierarchy.

# Q&A

**Q Won't using accessor methods everywhere slow down my Java code?**

**A** Not always. As Java compilers improve and can implement better optimizations, they will be able to make accessor methods fast automatically. But if you're concerned about speed, you can always declare accessor methods to be `final`, and they'll be comparable in speed to direct instance variable accesses under most circumstances.

**Q Based on what I've learned, private abstract methods and final abstract methods and classes don't seem to make sense. Are they legal?**

**A** No. They cause compiler errors, as you have guessed. To be useful, abstract methods must be overridden, and abstract classes must be subclassed, but neither of those operations would be legal if they were also `private` or `final`.

# Quiz

Review this lesson's material by taking this three-question quiz.

## Questions

1. What packages are automatically imported into your Java classes?

   **A.** None

   **B.** The classes stored in the folders of your `Classpath`

   **C.** The classes in the `java.lang` package

2. According to the convention for naming packages, what should be the first part of the name of a package you create?

   **A.** Your name followed by a period

   **B.** Your top-level Internet domain followed by a period

   **C.** The text `java` followed by a period

3. If you create a subclass and override a public method, what access modifiers can you use with that method?

   **A.** `public` only

   **B.** public or protected

   **C.** `public`, `protected`, or default access

## Answers

1. C. All other packages must be imported if you want to use short class names such as `LinkedList` instead of full package and class names such as `java.util.LinkedList`.

2. B. This convention assumes that all Java package developers will own an Internet domain or have access to one so that the package can be made available for download.

3. A. All public methods must remain public in subclasses. Access control in a subclass can be more public or the same as its subclass, but it can't be more private.

# Certification Practice

The following question is the kind of thing you could expect to be asked on a Java programming certification test. Answer it without looking again at this lesson or using the Java compiler to test the code.

Given:

```
package org.cadenhead.bureau;

public class Information {
    public int duration = 12;
    protected float rate = 3.15F;
    float average = 0.5F;
}
```

and:

```
package org.cadenhead.bureau;

public class MoreInformation extends Information {
    public int quantity = 8;
}
```

6

and:

```
package org.cadenhead.bureau.us;

import org.cadenhead.bureau.*;

public class EvenMoreInformation extends MoreInformation {
    public int quantity = 9;
```

```
EvenMoreInformation() {
    super();
    int i1 = duration;
    float i2 = rate;
    float i3 = average;
}
}
```

Which instance variables are visible in the `EvenMoreInformation` class?

    **A.** `quantity`, `duration`, `rate`, and `average`

    **B.** `quantity`, `duration`, and `rate`

    **C.** `quantity`, `duration`, and `average`

    **D.** `quantity`, `rate`, and `average`

The answer is available on the book's website, at www.java21days.com. Visit the Lesson 6 page and click the Certification Practice link.

# Exercises

To extend your knowledge of the subjects covered in this lesson, try the following exercises:

    **1.** Create a modified version of the `Storefront` project that includes a `noDiscount` variable for each item. When this variable is `true`, sell the item at the retail price.

    **2.** Create a `ZipCode` class that uses access control to ensure that its `zipCode` instance variable always has a five-digit value.

Where applicable, exercise solutions are offered on the book's website, at www.java21days.com.

# LESSON 7
# Exceptions and Threads

This lesson dives into two of Java's most useful elements: threads and exceptions. *Threads* enable programs to make efficient use of resources by isolating the computing-intensive parts of a program so that they don't slow down everything else. *Exceptions* enable programs to recognize errors and respond to them. Exceptions even make it possible for programs to correct the conditions and continue running, when possible.

Threads are objects that implement the `Runnable` interface or extend the `Thread` class to indicate that they can run simultaneously with other parts of a Java program. Exceptions are objects that represent errors that may occur as a Java program runs.

Exceptions are covered first in this lesson because they're one of the things you use when working with threads.

# Exceptions

Programmers in any language endeavor to write programs that are bug free, never crash, can handle any circumstance with grace, and always recover from unusual situations.

So much for that idea.

Errors occur because programmers didn't anticipate possible problems or didn't test enough. Or programs encounter situations out of their control, such as bad data from users, corrupt files that don't have the correct data in them, network connections that don't connect, hardware devices that don't respond, sunspots, gremlins, and on and on.

In Java, the strange events that might cause a program to fail are called *exceptions*. Java defines several language features that deal with exceptions:

- How to handle exceptions in your code and recover gracefully from potential problems
- How to tell code that uses your classes that you're expecting a potential exception
- How to create an exception if you detect one
- How your code is limited yet made more robust by exceptions

With most programming languages, handling error conditions requires much more work than handling a program that is running properly. It can require a confusing structure of conditional statements to deal with errors that might occur.

As an example, consider the following code that could be used to load a file from disk. File input and output can be problematic because of disk errors, file-not-found errors, and the like. If a program must have the data from the file to operate properly, it must deal with all these circumstances before continuing.

Here's the structure of one possible solution:

```
int status = loadTextFile();
if (status != 1) {
    // something unusual happened; report it
    switch (status) {
        case 2:
            System.out.println("File not found");
            break;
        case 3:
            System.out.println("Disk error");
            break;
        case 4:
            System.out.println("File corrupted");
            break;
```

```
        default:
            System.out.println("Error");
    }
} else {
    // file loaded OK; continue with program
}
```

This code tries to load a file by calling the method `loadTextFile()`, which presumably has been defined elsewhere in the class. The method returns an integer that indicates whether the file loaded properly (a value of 1) or an error occurred (2, 3, 4, or higher).

The program uses a `switch` statement keyed on that error code to address the problem. The end result is a block of code in which the most common circumstance—a successful file load—can be lost amid the error-handling code. This is the result of handling only one possible error. If other errors take place later in the program, you might end up with more nested `if-else` and `switch-case` blocks.

As you can see, error management would become unmanageable in larger programs, making a Java class difficult to read and maintain.

Dealing with errors in this manner makes it impossible for the compiler to check for consistency the way it can check to make sure that you called a method with the right arguments or set a variable to the right class of object.

Although the previous example uses Java syntax, you never have to deal with errors that way with the Java language. You can use a group of classes called *exceptions* that work much better.

Exceptions include errors that could be fatal to your program and other circumstances that indicate a problem. By managing exceptions, you can manage errors and possibly work around them.

Errors and other conditions in Java programs can be more easily managed through a combination of language features, consistency checking at compile time, and a set of extensible exception classes.

With these features, you can add a whole new dimension to the behavior and design of your classes, your class hierarchy, and your overall system. Your classes and interface describe how your program is supposed to behave under the best circumstances. With exceptions, you can consistently describe how the program will behave when circumstances are not ideal and allow programmers who use your classes to know what to expect in those cases.

7

## Exception Classes

At this point, it's likely that you've run into at least one Java exception. Maybe you tried to run a Java application without providing the command-line arguments that were needed and saw an `ArrayIndexOutOfBoundsException` message.

Chances are, when an exception occurred, the application quit and spewed a bunch of mysterious errors to the screen. Those errors are exceptions. When a program stops without successfully finishing its work, an exception is thrown. Exceptions can be thrown by the Java Virtual Machine (JVM), by classes you use, or intentionally in your own programs.

Just as exceptions are thrown, they also can be caught. Catching an exception involves dealing with the exceptional circumstance so that your program doesn't crash, as you'll learn later in this lesson.

Exceptions in Java are instances of classes that inherit from the `Throwable` class. An instance of a `Throwable` class is created when an exception is thrown.

`Throwable` has two subclasses: `Error` and `Exception`. Instances of `Error` are internal errors involving the JVM. These errors are rare and usually fatal to the program; there's not much you can do about them, other than catch them or throw them yourself. An example of one is `OutOfMemoryError`, which signals the catastrophic condition that the program has no memory left to run in.

The class `Exception` is more relevant to your own programming. Subclasses of `Exception` fall into two general groups:

- Unchecked exceptions (subclasses of the class `RuntimeException`), such as `ArrayIndexOutofBoundsException`, `SecurityException`, and `NullPointerException`
- Checked exceptions, such as `EOFException` and `MalformedURLException`

Unchecked exceptions, also called *runtime exceptions*, usually occur when code isn't very robust. An `ArrayIndexOutOfBoundsException`, for example, should never be thrown if you're properly checking to make sure that your code stays within the bounds of an array. `NullPointerException` happens when you try to use a variable that doesn't refer to an object yet.

| CAUTION | If your program is causing unchecked exceptions, you should fix those problems by improving your code. Don't rely on exception management to handle programming mistakes that can be corrected while you're creating a Java program. |
| --- | --- |

A checked exception indicates that something strange and out of control is happening. An `EOFException`, for example, happens when you're reading a file and the file ends before it was expected to. A `MalformedURLException` happens when a web address (also called a URL) isn't in the right format. This group includes exceptions that you create to signal unusual cases that might occur in your own programs.

Exceptions are arranged in a hierarchy, just as other classes are, where the superclasses are more general kinds of problems, and the subclasses are more specific. This organization becomes more important to you as you deal with exceptions in your own code.

The primary exception classes are part of the `java.lang` package: `Throwable`, `Exception`, and `RuntimeException`. Many of the other packages in the Java Class Library define other exceptions, which are used throughout the library.

The `java.io` package defines a general exception class called `IOException`. It is subclassed not only in the `java.io` package for input and output exceptions (`EOFException` and `FileNotFoundException`) but also in the `java.net` classes for networking exceptions such as `MalformedURLException` and in the `java.util` package with `ZipException`.

# Managing Exceptions

Now that you know what an exception is, how do you deal with one in your own code? In many cases, the Java compiler enforces exception management when you try to use methods that throw exceptions; you need to deal with those exceptions in your own code, or it won't compile, and NetBeans will flag the error. In this section, you'll learn about consistency checking and how to use three new keywords—`try`, `catch`, and `finally`—to deal with exceptions that might occur.

## Exception Consistency Checking

The more you work with the Java Class Library, the more likely you are to run into an exception such as this one:

```
Exception java.lang.InterruptedException
must be caught or it must be declared in the throws clause
of this method.
```

In Java, a method can indicate the kinds of errors it might potentially throw. For example, methods that read from files can throw `IOException` errors, so those methods are declared with a special modifier that indicates potential errors. When you use those methods in your own Java programs, you have to protect your code against the exceptions.

7

This rule is enforced by the compiler itself, in the same way that it checks to make sure that you're using methods with the correct number of arguments and that all your variable types match what you're assigning to them.

Why is this check in place? It makes programs less likely to crash with fatal errors because you know up front the kind of exceptions that can be thrown by the methods a program uses.

If you define your methods so that they indicate the exceptions they can throw, Java can tell your objects' users to handle those errors.

# Protecting Code and Catching Exceptions

Assume that you've been happily coding, and an exception occurs as a class is compiled. According to the error message, you have to either catch the error or declare that your method throws it.

First, you deal with catching potential exceptions, which requires two things:

- Protect the code that contains the method that might throw an exception inside a `try` block.
- Handle an exception inside a `catch` block.

A `try` block tries a block of code to see if it can execute all of it without causing an exception. If it fails and an exception occurs, a `catch` block deals with it.

You've seen `try` and `catch` before. In Lesson 6, "Packages, Interfaces, and Other Class Features," you used the following code to create an integer from a `string` value:

```
public SquareTool(String input) {
    try {
        float in = Float.parseFloat(input);
        // rest of method
    } catch (NumberFormatException nfe) {
        System.out.println(input + " is not a valid number.");
    }
}
```

In this code, the `Float.parseFloat()` class method might throw an exception of the class `NumberFormatException`, which signifies that the string is not in a valid format as a number. (One situation that triggers this exception is if `input` equals `15x`, which is not a number.)

To handle the exception, the call to `parseFloat()` is placed inside a `try` block, and an associated `catch` block has been set up. The `catch` block receives any `NumberFormatException` objects thrown within the `try` block.

The part of the `catch` clause inside the parentheses is similar to a method definition's argument list. It contains the class of exception to be caught and a variable name. You can use the variable to refer to that exception object inside the `catch` block.

An exception object has a `getMessage()` method that displays a detailed error message describing what happened.

The following example is a revised version of the `try-catch` block used in Lesson 6:

```
try {
    float in = Float.parseFloat(input);
} catch (NumberFormatException nfe) {
    System.out.println("Oops: " + nfe.getMessage());
}
```

The examples you have seen thus far catch a specific type of exception. Because exception classes are organized into a hierarchy, and you can use a subclass anywhere that a superclass is expected, you can catch groups of exceptions within the same `catch` statement.

When you write programs that handle input and output from files, Internet servers, and similar places, you deal with several types of `IOException` exceptions (the `IO` stands for input/output). These exceptions include two of its subclasses, `EOFException` and `FileNotFoundException`. By catching `IOException`, you also catch instances of any `IOException` subclass.

To catch several different exceptions that aren't related by inheritance, you can use multiple `catch` blocks for a single `try`, like this:

```
try {
    // code that might generate exceptions
} catch (IOException ioe) {
    System.out.println("Input/output error");
    System.out.println(ioe.getMessage());
} catch (ClassNotFoundException cnfe) {
    System.out.println("Class not found");
    System.out.println(cnfe.getMessage());
} catch (InterruptedException ie) {
    System.out.println("Program interrupted");
    System.out.println(ie.getMessage());
}
```

In a multiple-`catch` block, the first `catch` block that matches is executed, and the rest is ignored.

7

**CAUTION**

> You can run into unexpected problems by using an `Exception` superclass in a `catch` block followed by one or more of its subclasses in their own `catch` blocks. For example, the input/output exception `IOException` is the superclass of the end-of-file exception `EOFException`. If you put an `IOException` block above an `EOFException` block, the subclass never catches any exceptions.

You also can catch more than one class of exceptions in the same `catch` statement. The classes must be separated by a pipe character |. Here's an example:

```
try {
    // code that reads a file from disk
} catch (EOFException | FileNotFoundException exc) {
    System.out.println("File error: " + exc.getMessage());
}
```

This code catches two exceptions, `EOFException` and `FileNotFoundException`, in the same `catch` block. The exception is assigned to the `exc` argument, and its `getMessage()` method is called. The first class in the list that matches the thrown exception will be assigned to the argument.

The exceptions declared as alternatives in the `catch` statement cannot be superclasses or subclasses of each other unless they are in the proper order. The following would not work:

```
try {
    // code that reads a file from disk
} catch (IOException | EOFException | FileNotFoundException exc) {
    System.out.println("File error: " + exc.getMessage());
}
```

This code fails to compile because `IOException` is the superclass of the other two exceptions, and it precedes them in the list. Because a superclass can catch exceptions of its subclasses, the second and third exceptions in that statement never would be caught.

Here's a fixed version that would work:

```
try {
    // code that reads a file from disk
} catch (EOFException | FileNotFoundException exc) {
    System.out.println("File error: " + exc.getMessage());
} catch (IOException ioe) {
    System.out.println("IO error: " + ioe.getMessage());
}
```

CAUTION

> Exceptions have a `printStackTrace()` method that displays the sequence of method calls that led to the statement that generated the exception. If you use this in a program, NetBeans flags it for a warning in the source code editor. The reason is that `printStackTrace()` contains debugging information that for security reasons should not be shared with users after a program has been finished.

A `catch` statement must be needed by the corresponding `try` block. The exception class in `catch` has to be one that could be thrown in that block (or a superclass of one that could be thrown). The compiler will fail with an error otherwise.

For example, if you used `catch` for `FileNotFoundException` in a program that did not read any files, the program would not compile.

## The `finally` Clause

Suppose that there is some action in your code that you absolutely must do, no matter what happens, regardless of whether an exception is thrown. You might need to free some external resource after acquiring it, close a file after opening it, or do something similar.

One example comes up when you are working with databases, as you'll do in Lesson 18, "Accessing Databases with JDBC and Derby." The database connection and objects you create to access the database are closed in a `finally` block to free those resources because they're no longer needed.

Although you could put that action both inside a `catch` block and outside it, you should avoid duplicating the same code in two different places as much as possible. Instead, put that code inside a special optional block of the `try-catch` statement that uses the keyword `finally`:

```
try {
    readTextFile();
} catch (IOException ioe) {
    // deal with IO errors
} finally {
    closeTextFile();
}
```

This lesson's first project shows how a `finally` statement can be used inside a method.

7

The HexReader application in Listing 7.1 reads sequences of two-digit hexadecimal numbers and displays their decimal values. There are three sequences to read:

- 000A110D1D260219

- 78700F1318141E0C

- 6A197D45B0FFFFFF

As you learned in Lesson 2, "The ABCs of Programming," hexadecimal is a base-16 numbering system in which the single-digit numbers range from 00 (decimal 0) to 0F (decimal 15). Double-digit numbers range from 10 (decimal 16) to FF (decimal 255).

Create the HexReader class in NetBeans as an empty Java file in the com.java21days package and enter the source code shown in Listing 7.1.

**LISTING 7.1**   The Full Text of HexReader.java

```
 1: package com.java21days;
 2:
 3: class HexReader {
 4:     String[] input = { "000A110D1D260219 ",
 5:         "78700F1318141E0C ",
 6:         "6A197D45B0FFFFFF " };
 7:
 8:     public static void main(String[] arguments) {
 9:         HexReader hex = new HexReader();
10:         for (int i = 0; i < hex.input.length; i++)
11:             hex.readLine(hex.input[i]);
12:     }
13:
14:     void readLine(String code) {
15:         try {
16:             for (int j = 0; j + 1 < code.length(); j += 2) {
17:                 String sub = code.substring(j, j + 2);
18:                 int num = Integer.parseInt(sub, 16);
19:                 if (num == 255) {
20:                     return;
21:                 }
22:                 System.out.print(num + " ");
23:             }
24:         } finally {
25:             System.out.println("**");
26:         }
27:     }
28: }
```

Figure 7.1 shows the output of this program.

**FIGURE 7.1**

Displaying decimal values converted from hexadecimal.

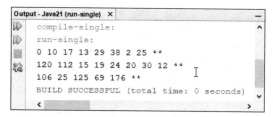

```
Output - Java21 (run-single)  ×
    compile-single:
    run-single:
    0 10 17 13 29 38 2 25 **
    120 112 15 19 24 20 30 12 **
    106 25 125 69 176 **
    BUILD SUCCESSFUL (total time: 0 seconds)
```

Line 17 of the program reads two characters from `code`, the string that was sent to the `readLine()` method, by calling the string's `substring(int, int)` method.

**NOTE**

> In the `substring()` method of the `String` class, you select a substring in a somewhat counterintuitive way. The first argument specifies the index of the first character to include in the substring, but the second argument does not specify the last character. Instead, the second argument indicates the index of the last character plus 1. A call to `substring(2, 5)` for a string would return the characters from index position 2 to index position 4.

The two-character substring contains a hexadecimal number stored as a `String`. The `Integer` class method `parseInt` can be used with a second argument to convert this number into an integer. Use 16 as the argument for a hexadecimal (base-16) conversion, 8 for an octal (base-8) conversion, and so on.

In the `HexReader` application, the hexadecimal FF is used to fill out the end of a sequence and should not be displayed as a decimal value. This is accomplished by using a `try-finally` block in lines 15–26 of Listing 7.1.

The `try-finally` block causes an unusual thing to happen when the end of the method is encountered after line 26. You would expect this to cause the `readLine()` method to be exited immediately.

Because it is within a `try-finally` block, the statement within the `finally` block is executed no matter how the `try` block is exited. The text `**` is displayed at the end of a line of decimal values.

There's a way to ensure that resources are freed properly even when an operation inside a `try` block fails with an exception. The `try-with-resources` feature enables statements that claim resources to be declared inside parentheses in a `try` statement.

7

The following code contains two statements that read data from an Internet server using a networking socket (a type of connection):

```
Socket digit = new Socket(host, 79);
BufferedReader in = new BufferedReader(
    new InputStreamReader(digit.getInputStream()));
```

To ensure that resources are properly released, they can be declared inside the `try` statement:

```
try (Socket digit = new Socket(host, 79);
    BufferedReader in = new BufferedReader(
        new InputStreamReader(digit.getInputStream()));
    ) {

    // code goes here
} catch (IOException e) {
    System.out.println("IO Error:" + e.getMessage());
}
```

No matter how the code in the `try` block exits—whether through success or an exception—the `digit` and `in` resources will be disposed of properly.

NetBeans issues a warning in the source code editor on any statement that ought to be in a `try`-with-resources statement but isn't. Use this technique whenever you can because it eliminates the common error of forgetting to close a resource that is no longer in use.

# Declaring Methods That Might Throw Exceptions

You have learned how to deal with methods that might throw exceptions by protecting code and catching any exceptions that occur. The Java compiler checks to make sure that you've dealt with a method's exceptions. But how does it know which exceptions to tell you about?

The answer is that the original method indicates the exceptions that it might possibly throw as part of its definition. You can use this mechanism in your own methods. In fact, it's good style to do so to make sure that users of your classes are alerted to the errors your methods might experience.

To indicate that a method will possibly throw an exception, you use a special clause in the method definition called `throws`.

## The `throws` Clause

If some code in your method's body might throw an exception, add the `throws` keyword after the method's closing parenthesis, followed by the name or names of the exception that your method throws. Here's an example:

```
public void getPoint(int x, int y) throws NumberFormatException {
    // body of method
}
```

If your method might throw multiple kinds of exceptions, you can declare them all in the `throws` clause, separated by commas:

```
public void storePoint(int x, int y)
    throws NumberFormatException, EOFException {
        // body of method
}
```

As with `catch`, you can use a superclass of an exception to indicate that your method might throw any subclass of that exception. For instance:

```
public void loadPoint() throws IOException {
    // body of method
}
```

Keep in mind that adding a `throws` clause to your method definition simply means that the method might throw an exception if something goes wrong, not that it actually will. The `throws` clause provides extra information in your method definition about potential exceptions and allows Java to make sure that your method is being used correctly by other classes.

Think of a method's overall description as a contract between the designer of that method and the caller of the method. (You can be on either side of that contract, of course.)

Usually the description indicates the types of a method's arguments, what it returns, and the particulars of what it normally does. By using `throws`, you are adding information about the abnormal things the method can do. This new part of the contract helps make explicit all the places where exceptional conditions should be handled in your program.

## Which Exceptions Should You Throw?

7

After you decide to declare that your method might throw an exception, you must decide which exceptions it might throw and actually throw them or call a method that will throw them. (You'll learn about throwing your own exceptions in the next section.)

In many instances, which exceptions might be thrown is apparent from the operation of the method itself. Perhaps you're already creating and throwing your own exceptions, in which case you'll know exactly which exceptions to throw.

You don't have to list all possible exceptions that your method could throw. Unchecked exceptions are handled by the JVM and are so common that you don't have to deal with them.

In particular, exceptions of the `Error` or `RuntimeException` classes or any of their subclasses do not have to be listed in your `throws` clause. They get special treatment because they can occur anywhere within a Java program and are usually conditions that you, as the programmer, did not directly cause.

One good example is `OutOfMemoryError`, which occurs when the JVM has run out of memory, which can happen anywhere, at any time, for any number of reasons.

Unchecked exceptions are subclasses of the `RuntimeException` and `Error` classes and are usually thrown by the JVM. You don't have to declare that your method throws them and usually do not need to deal with them in any other way.

**NOTE** _____    You can choose to list these errors and runtime exceptions in your `throws` clause if you want, but classes that call the method will not be forced to handle them. Only non-runtime exceptions must be handled.

All other exceptions are called *checked exceptions* and are potential candidates for a `throws` clause in your method.

## Passing on Exceptions

There are times when it doesn't make sense for a method to deal with an exception. It might be better for the method that calls the method to deal with that exception. For example, consider the hypothetical example of `WebRetriever`, a class that loads a web page using its web address and stores it in a file. As you'll learn in Lesson 17, "Communicating Over HTTP," you can't work with web addresses without dealing with `MalformedURLException`, the exception thrown when an address is in the wrong format.

To use `WebRetriever`, another class calls its constructor with the address as an argument. If the address specified by the other class is in the wrong format, a

`MalformedURLException` is thrown. Instead of dealing with this, the constructor of the `WebRetriever` class could have the following declaration:

```
public WebRetriever() throws MalformedURLException {
    // body of constructor
}
```

This would force any class that works with `WebRetriever` objects to deal with `MalformedURLException` errors or pass the buck with its own `throws` clause.

One thing is always true: It's better to pass on exceptions to calling methods than to catch them and do nothing in response.

In addition to declaring methods that throw exceptions, there's one other instance in which a method definition may include a `throws` clause: when, within that method, you want to call a method that throws an exception, but you don't want to catch or deal with that exception.

Rather than use the `try` and `catch` clauses in your method's body, you can declare your method with a `throws` clause so that it, too, might possibly throw the appropriate exception. It's then the responsibility of the method that calls your method to deal with that exception. This is the other case that tells the Java compiler that you have done something with a given exception.

Using this technique, you could create a method that deals with a `NumberFormatException` without a `try-catch` block:

```
public void readFloat(String input) throws NumberFormatException {
    float in = Float.parseFloat(input);
}
```

After you declare your method to throw an exception, you can use other methods that also throw those exceptions inside the body of this method, without needing to catch the exception.

**NOTE**

You can, of course, deal with other exceptions by using `try` and `catch` in the body of your method in addition to passing on the exceptions you listed in the `throws` clause. You also can both deal with the exception in some way and then rethrow it so that your method's calling method must deal with it anyhow.

7

## `throws` **and Inheritance**

If your method definition overrides a method in a superclass that includes a `throws` clause, there are special rules for how your overridden method deals with `throws`. Unlike other parts of the method signature that must mimic those of the method it is overriding, your new method does not require the same set of exceptions listed in the `throws` clause.

Because there's a possibility that your new method might deal with an exception instead of throwing it, your method can potentially throw fewer types of exceptions. It could even throw no exceptions. This means that you can have the following two class definitions, and things will work fine:

```
public class RadioPlayer {
    public void startPlaying() throws SoundException {
        // body of method
    }
}
public class StereoPlayer extends RadioPlayer {
    public void startPlaying() {
        // body of method
    }
}
```

The converse of this rule is not true: A subclass method cannot throw more checked exceptions (either exceptions of different types or more general exception classes) than its superclass method.

Any exception thrown by the subclass must be the same as the superclass or a subclass of that exception. Consider this example:

```
void readFields() throws IOException {
    // body of method
}
```

If this method is in a superclass and you override the method, this would not be allowed in the subclass:

```
void readFiles() throws SQLException {
    // body of method
}
```

`SQLException` is not a subclass of `IOException`, so this code will not compile. But the method could throw `FileNotFoundException`, because that's a subclass of `IOException`.

# Creating and Throwing Exceptions

There are two sides to every exception: the side that throws the exception and the side that catches it. An exception can be tossed around a number of times to a number of methods before it's caught, but eventually it will be caught and dealt with.

Many exceptions are thrown by the Java runtime or by methods inside the Java classes themselves. You also can throw any of the standard exceptions that the Java Class Library defines, or you can create and throw your own exceptions.

## Throwing Exceptions

Declaring that a method throws an exception is useful to classes that use the method and to the Java compiler, which checks to make sure that all the exceptions are being handled. The declaration itself doesn't do anything to throw that exception should it occur; you must do that as needed in the body of the method.

You need to create a new object of an exception class to throw an exception. After you have that object, use the `throw` statement to throw it.

Here's an example using a hypothetical `NotInServiceException` class that is a subclass of the `Exception` class:

```
NotInServiceException nise = new NotInServiceException();
throw nise;
```

You only can throw objects that are subclasses of the `Throwable` class.

Depending on the exception class, the exception also may have arguments to its constructor that you can use. The most common of these is a string argument, which enables you to describe the problem in greater detail (which can be useful for debugging purposes). Here's an example:

```
NotInServiceException nise = new
    NotInServiceException("Database Not in Service");
throw nise;
```

After an exception is thrown, the method exits without executing any other code, other than the code inside a `finally` block, if one exists. The method won't return a value, either. If the calling method does not have a `try` or `catch` surrounding the call to your method, the program might exit based on the exception you threw.

7

## Creating Your Own Exceptions

Creating new exceptions is easy. Your new exception should inherit from another exception in the Java class hierarchy. All user-created exceptions should be part of the Exception hierarchy rather than the Error hierarchy, which is reserved for errors involving the JVM. Look for an exception that's close to the one you're creating; for example, an exception for a bad file format would logically fit under IOException. If you can't find a closely related exception for your new exception, consider inheriting from Exception, which sits atop the exception hierarchy for checked exceptions. Unchecked exceptions should inherit from RuntimeException.

Exception classes typically have two constructors: The first takes no arguments, and the second takes a single string as an argument.

Exception classes are like other classes. Here's an extremely simple one::

```
public class SunSpotException extends Exception {
    public SunSpotException() {}

    public SunSpotException(String message) {
        super(message);
    }
}
```

## Combining throws, try, and throw

Say that you want to combine the approaches described thus far: You want to handle incoming exceptions in your method, but you also want the option to pass on the exception to your method's caller. Simply using try and catch doesn't pass on the exception, and adding a throws clause eliminates your chance of dealing with the exception.

If you want to both manage an exception and pass it on to the caller, use all three mechanisms—the throws clause, the try statement, and a throw statement—to explicitly rethrow the exception.

Here's a method that uses this technique:

```
public void readMessage() throws IOException {
    MessageReader mr = new MessageReader();

    try {
        mr.loadHeader();
    } catch (IOException e) {
        // do something to handle the
        // IO exception and then rethrow
        // the exception ...
        throw e;
    }
}
```

This works because exception handlers can be nested. You handle the exception by doing something responsible with it but decide that it is important enough to give the method's caller a chance to handle it as well.

Exceptions can float all the way up the chain of method callers this way (not being handled by most of them), until finally the JVM handles any uncaught exceptions by aborting the program and printing an error message.

If it's possible for you to catch an exception and do something necessary with it, you should.

When you use `throw` in a `catch` block for an exception superclass, it throws that superclass. This represents a potential loss of information because the exception could be a subclass with more information about the error.

Here's a situation where that occurs:

- A `try-catch` statement in a file reader looks for an `IOException`.
- An `EOFException` occurs because the end of the file is reached.
- The exception is caught in the `catch` block because `IOException` is the superclass of `EOFException`.

If `throw` is used with this exception, it throws an `IOException`, not an `EOFException`. Java introduced a technique that enables a more precise exception to be thrown: Use the `final` keyword in the `catch` statement for the object. The following code rewrites the previous example to do this:

```
try {
    mr.loadHeader();
catch (final IOException e) {
    throw e;
}
```

**CAUTION**

NetBeans must be set up to recognize new features in Java, or the IDE will flag them as errors. If you enter the preceding code in NetBeans, and it displays an error message, make sure your project has been set to the current version of the language. Choose File, Project Properties to open the Project Properties dialog, choose the category Libraries, and make sure the Java Platform drop-down is set to JDK 12.

7

# When Not to Use Exceptions

There are several situations in which you should not use exceptions.

First, don't use them in circumstances you could avoid easily in your code. For example, although you can rely on an `ArrayIndexOutofBoundsException` to indicate when you've gone past the end of an array, it's simple to use the array's `length` variable to keep from going beyond the bounds.

Another situation that shouldn't require an exception involves calling an object with the value `null`. This causes a `NullPointerException`, but instead of using a `try-catch` block for that, you should revise your code to check whether an object equals `null` before attempting to call it.

In addition, if your users will enter data that must be an integer, testing to make sure that the data is an integer is a much better idea than throwing an exception and dealing with it somewhere else.

Exceptions take up a lot of processing time. A simple conditional will run much faster than exception handling and will make your program more efficient. Exceptions should be used only for truly exceptional cases that are out of your control.

It's also easy to get carried away with exceptions and to try to make sure that all your methods have been declared to throw all the possible exceptions that they can throw.

| TIP | You create more work for everyone involved when you get carried away with exceptions. Declaring a method to throw either few or many exceptions is a trade-off; the more exceptions your method can throw, the more complex that method is to use. Declare only the exceptions that have a reasonably fair chance of happening and that make sense for the overall design of your classes. |
| --- | --- |

## Bad Style Using Exceptions

When you first start using exceptions, it might be appealing to work around the compiler errors that result when you use a method that declares a `throws` statement. Although it is permissible to add an empty `catch` clause or to add a `throws` statement to your own method (and there are appropriate reasons for doing so), intentionally dropping exceptions without dealing with them subverts the checks that the Java compiler does for you.

Compiler errors regarding exceptions are there to remind you to reflect on these issues. Take the time to deal with the exceptions that might affect your code. This extra care richly rewards you as you reuse your classes in later projects and in larger and larger programs. The Java Class Library has been written with exactly this degree of care, and that's one of the reasons it's robust enough to be used in your Java projects.

# Threads

One thing to consider in Java programming is how system resources are being used. Graphics, complex math computations, and other intensive tasks can take up a lot of processor time.

This is especially true of programs that have a graphical user interface, which is a style of software that you'll explore soon.

If you write a graphical Java program that does something that consumes a lot of the computer's time, you might find that the program's user interface responds slowly—with drop-down lists that take a second or more to appear, button clicks that are recognized slowly, and so on.

To solve this problem, you can segregate the processor-hogging functions in a Java class so that they run separately from the rest of the program. This is possible through the use of threads.

*Threads* are parts of a program that run on their own while the rest of the program does something else. This also is called *multitasking* because the program handles more than one task simultaneously.

Threads are ideal for anything that takes up a lot of processing time and runs continuously.

By putting a program's hardest workload into a thread, you free up the rest of the program to handle other things. You also make the program easier for the JVM because the most intensive work is isolated.

## Writing a Threaded Program

Threads are implemented in Java with the `Thread` class in the `java.lang` package.

The simplest use of threads is to make a program pause in execution and stay idle during that time. To do this, call the `Thread` class method `sleep(long)` with the number of milliseconds to pause as the only argument.

7

The `sleep(long)` method throws an `InterruptedException` when the paused thread has been interrupted for some reason. (One possible reason is a user closing the program while it is sleeping.)

The following statements stop a program in its tracks for three seconds:

```
try {
    Thread.sleep(3000);
} catch (InterruptedException ie) {
    // do nothing
}
```

The `catch` block does nothing, which is typical when you're using `sleep()`.

One way to use threads is to put all the time-consuming behavior in its own class.

A thread can be created in two ways: by subclassing the `Thread` class or implementing the `Runnable` interface in another class. Both `Thread` and `Runnable` belong to the `java.lang` package.

Because the `Thread` class implements `Runnable`, the two techniques result in objects that start and stop threads in the same manner.

To implement the `Runnable` interface, add the keyword `implements` to the class declaration, followed by the name of the interface, as in this example:

```
public class StockTicker implements Runnable {
    public void run() {
        // ...
    }
}
```

The `Runnable` interface contains only one method to implement, `run()`.

The first step in creating a thread is to create a reference to an object of the `Thread` class:

```
Thread runner;
```

This statement creates a reference to a thread, but no `Thread` object has been assigned to it yet. Threads are created by calling the constructor `Thread(Object)` with the threaded object as an argument. You could create a threaded `StockTicker` object with the following statement:

```
StockTicker tix = new StockTicker();
Thread tickerThread = new Thread(tix);
```

Two good places to create threads are in the constructor for an application and in the constructor for a component (such as a panel).

A thread is begun by calling its start() method, as in the following statement:

```
tickerThread.start();
```

The following statements can be used in a thread class to start the thread:

```
Thread runner = null;
if (runner == null) {
    runner = new Thread(this);
    runner.start();
}
```

The this keyword used in the Thread() constructor refers to the object in which these statements are contained. The runner variable has a value of null before any object is assigned to it, so the if statement is used to make sure that the thread is not started more than once.

To run a thread, its start() method is called. Calling a thread's start() method causes another method to be called: the run() method, which must be present in all threaded objects. The run() method is the engine of a threaded class, containing the processor-intensive behavior and calling methods to perform it.

# A Threaded Application

Threaded programming will become more clear when you see it in action.

Listing 7.2 contains PrimeFinder, a class that finds a specific prime number in a sequence, such as the 100th, 1,000th, or 30,000th prime. This can take some time, especially for numbers beyond 100,000, so the search for the right prime takes place in its own thread.

Enter the code shown in Listing 7.2 in NetBeans and save it as the class name PrimeFinder in the package com.java21days.

**LISTING 7.2** The Full Text of PrimeFinder.java

```
1: package com.java21days;
2:
3: public class PrimeFinder implements Runnable {
4:     public long target;
5:     public long prime;
6:     public boolean finished = false;
7:     private Thread runner;
```

```
 8:
 9:        PrimeFinder(long inTarget) {
10:            target = inTarget;
11:            if (runner == null) {
12:                runner = new Thread(this);
13:                runner.start();
14:            }
15:        }
16:
17:        public void run() {
18:            long numPrimes = 0;
19:            long candidate = 2;
20:            while (numPrimes < target) {
21:                if (isPrime(candidate)) {
22:                    numPrimes++;
23:                    prime = candidate;
24:                }
25:                candidate++;
26:            }
27:            finished = true;
28:        }
29:
30:        boolean isPrime(long checkNumber) {
31:            double root = Math.sqrt(checkNumber);
32:            for (int i = 2; i <= root; i++) {
33:                if (checkNumber % i == 0)
34:                    return false;
35:            }
36:            return true;
37:        }
38: }
```

Save the `PrimeFinder` class when you're finished. This class doesn't have a `main()` method, so you can't run it as an application. Next, you'll create a program that uses this class.

The `PrimeFinder` class implements the `Runnable` interface, so it can be run as a thread.

There are three public instance variables:

- `target` is a `long` that indicates when the specified prime in the sequence has been found. If you're looking for the 5,000th prime, `target` equals `5000`.
- `prime` is a `long` that holds the last prime number found by this class.
- `finished` is a Boolean that indicates when the target has been reached.

There's also a private instance variable called `runner` that holds the `Thread` object this class runs in. This object equals `null` before the thread is started.

The `PrimeFinder` constructor method in lines 9–15 sets the `target` instance variable and starts the thread if it hasn't been started. When the thread's `start()` method is called, it in turn calls the `run()` method of the threaded class.

The `run()` method is in lines 17–28. This method does most of the work of the thread. This method uses two new variables: `numPrimes`, the number of primes that have been found, and `candidate`, the number that might possibly be prime. The `candidate` variable begins at the first possible prime number, which is 2.

The `while` loop in lines 20–26 continues until the right number of primes has been found. First, it checks whether the current `candidate` is prime by calling the `isPrime(long)` method, which returns `true` if the number is prime and `false` otherwise. If the `candidate` is prime, `numPrimes` increases by 1, and the `prime` instance variable is set to this prime number. The `candidate` variable is then incremented by 1, and the loop continues.

After the right number of primes has been found, the `while` loop ends, and the `finished` instance variable is set to `true`. This indicates that the `PrimeFinder` object has found the right prime number and is finished searching. The end of the `run()` method is reached in line 28, and the thread no longer does any work.

The `isPrime()` method is contained in lines 30–37. This method determines whether a number is prime by using the `%` operator, which returns the remainder of a division operation. If a number is evenly divisible by 2 or any higher number (leaving a remainder of 0), it is not a prime number.

Listing 7.3 is an application that uses the `PrimeFinder` class. Enter the code shown in Listing 7.3 in NetBeans as a new Java class named `PrimeThreads` in the `com.java21days` package.

**LISTING 7.3**   The Full Text of `PrimeThreads.java`

```
1: package com.java21days;
2:
3: public class PrimeThreads {
4:     public static void main(String[] arguments) {
5:         PrimeThreads pt = new PrimeThreads(arguments);
6:     }
7:
8:     public PrimeThreads(String[] arguments) {
9:         PrimeFinder[] finder = new PrimeFinder[arguments.length];
10:         for (int i = 0; i < arguments.length; i++) {
11:             try {
12:                 long count = Long.parseLong(arguments[i]);
13:                 finder[i] = new PrimeFinder(count);
14:                 System.out.println("Looking for prime " + count);
```

7

```
15:                 } catch (NumberFormatException nfe) {
16:                     System.out.println("Error: " + nfe.getMessage());
17:                 }
18:             }
19:             boolean complete = false;
20:             while (!complete) {
21:                 complete = true;
22:                 for (int j = 0; j < finder.length; j++) {
23:                     if (finder[j] == null) continue;
24:                     if (!finder[j].finished) {
25:                         complete = false;
26:                     } else {
27:                         displayResult(finder[j]);
28:                         finder[j] = null;
29:                     }
30:                 }
31:                 try {
32:                     Thread.sleep(1000);
33:                 } catch (InterruptedException ie) {
34:                     // do nothing
35:                 }
36:             }
37:         }
38:
39:         private void displayResult(PrimeFinder finder) {
40:             System.out.println("Prime " + finder.target
41:                 + " is " + finder.prime);
42:         }
43: }
```

Specify the prime numbers that you're looking for as command-line arguments (using Run, Set Project Configuration, Customize) and include as many as you want.

If this program is run with the command-line arguments 5000 12000 50000 120000, it is likely to produce the output shown in Figure 7.2. Because there's no guarantee of the order in which threads will finish, the report of the prime numbers found may be ordered differently.

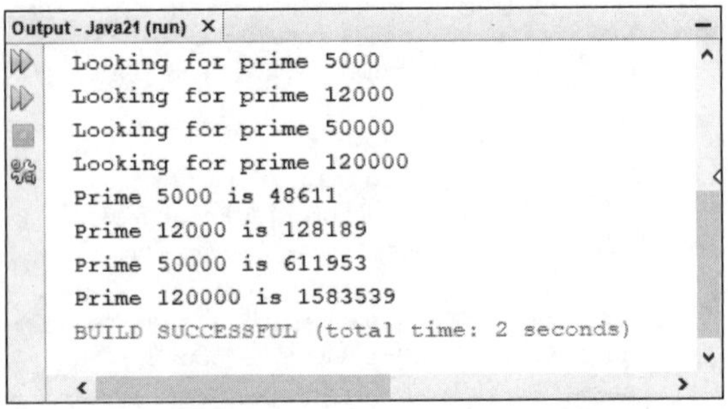

**FIGURE 7.2**
Using threads to find multiple primes in a sequence.

```
Output - Java21 (run) ×

    Looking for prime 5000
    Looking for prime 12000
    Looking for prime 50000
    Looking for prime 120000
    Prime 5000 is 48611
    Prime 12000 is 128189
    Prime 50000 is 611953
    Prime 120000 is 1583539
    BUILD SUCCESSFUL (total time: 2 seconds)
```

The `for` loop in lines 10–18 of the `PrimeThreads` application creates one `PrimeFinder` object for each command-line argument specified when the program is run.

Because arguments are `String` objects, and the `PrimeFinder` constructor requires `long` values, the `Long.parseLong(String)` class method is used to handle the conversion. All the number-parsing methods throw `NumberFormatException` exceptions, so they are enclosed in `try-catch` blocks to deal with arguments that are not numeric.

When a `PrimeFinder` object is created, the object starts running in its own thread (as specified in the `PrimeFinder` constructor).

The `while` loop in lines 20–36 checks to see whether any `PrimeFinder` thread has completed, which is indicated by its `finished` instance variable equaling `true`. When a thread has completed, the `displayResult()` method is called in line 27 to display the prime number that was found. The thread then is set to `null`, freeing the object's resources (and preventing its result from being displayed more than once).

The call to `Thread.sleep(1000)` in line 32 causes the `while` loop to pause for one second during each pass through the loop. A slowdown in loops helps keep the JVM from executing statements at such a furious pace that it becomes bogged down.

## Stopping a Thread

Stopping a thread is a little more complicated than starting one. The best way to stop a thread is to place a loop in the thread's `run()` method that ends when a variable changes in value, as in the following example:

```
public void run() {
    while (okToRun == true) {
        // ...
    }
}
```

The `okToRun` variable could be an instance variable of the thread's class. If it is changed to `false`, the loop inside the `run()` method ends.

Another option you can use to stop a thread is to loop in the `run()` method only while the currently running thread has a variable that references it.

A class method, `Thread.currentThread()`, returns a reference to the current thread (in other words, the thread in which the object is running).

The following `run()` method loops as long as `runner` and `currentThread()` refer to the same object:

```
public void run() {
    Thread thisThread = Thread.currentThread();
    while (runner == thisThread) {
        // body of loop
    }
}
```

If you use a loop like this, you can stop the thread anywhere in the class with the following statement:

```
runner = null;
```

# Summary

Exceptions and threads strengthen the robustness of your programs.

Exceptions enable you to manage potential errors. By using `try`, `catch`, and `finally`, you can protect code that might result in exceptions by handling those exceptions as they occur.

Handling exceptions is only half the battle; the other half is generating and throwing exceptions. A `throws` clause tells a method's users that the method might throw an exception. It also can be used to pass on an exception from a method call in the body of your method.

You learned how to create and throw your own methods by defining new exception classes and by throwing instances of any exception classes using `throw`.

Threads enable you to run the most processor-intensive parts of a Java class separately from the rest of the class. This is especially useful when the class is doing something computing intensive, such as animation, complex math, or looping through a large amount of data quickly. You also can use threads to do several things at once and to start and stop threads externally.

Threads implement the `Runnable` interface, which contains one method: `run()`. When you start a thread by calling its `start()` method, the thread's `run()` method is called automatically.

# Q&A

**Q I'm still not sure I understand the difference between exceptions, errors, and runtime exceptions. Is there another way of looking at them?**

**A** Errors are caused by dynamic linking or JVM problems. Thus, they are too low level for most programs to care about—or to be able to handle even if they did care.

Runtime exceptions are generated by the normal execution of Java code. Although they occasionally reflect a condition you will want to handle explicitly, more often they reflect a coding mistake made by the programmer and thus simply print an error to help flag that mistake.

Non-runtime exceptions (such as `IOException`) are conditions that, because of their nature, should be explicitly handled by any robust and well-thought-out code. The Java Class Library has been written using only a few of these, but those few are important to using the system safely and correctly. The compiler helps you handle these exceptions properly via its `throws` clause checks and restrictions.

**Q Does Java support unit testing to make programs more reliable?**

**A** Unit testing, a technique for ensuring the reliability of software by adding tests, is supported by the open source Java Class Library JUnit. This is the most popular unit-testing framework for Java programmers. Visit www.junit.org to download it.

With JUnit, you write a set of tests, called a suite, that create the Java objects you've developed and call their methods. The values produced by these tests are checked to see whether they're what you expected. All tests must pass for your software to pass.

Although unit testing is only as good as the tests you create, the existence of a test suite is extremely helpful when you make changes to your software. By running the tests again after the changes, you can better assure yourself that your software continues to work correctly.

Some Java programmers believe so strongly in the benefits of unit testing that they write tests before any code.

# Quiz

Review this lesson's material by taking this three-question quiz.

7

## Questions

**1.** What keyword is used to jump out of a `try` block and into a `finally` block?

    **A.** `catch`

    **B.** `return`

    **C.** `while`

**2.** What class should be the superclass of any exceptions you create in Java?

    **A.** `Throwable`

    **B.** `Error`

    **C.** `Exception`

**3.** If a class implements the `Runnable` interface, what methods must the class contain?

    **A.** `start()`, `stop()`, and `run()`

    **B.** `actionPerformed()`

    **C.** `run()`

## Answers

**1.** B. The `return` statement exits the block.

**2.** C. The kinds of errors you'll want to note in your programs generally belong in the `Exception` hierarchy.

**3.** C. The `Runnable` interface requires only the `run()` method.

# Certification Practice

The following question is the kind of thing you could expect to be asked on a Java programming certification test. Answer it without looking again at this lesson or using the Java compiler to test the code.

The `AverageValue` application is supposed to take up to 10 floating-point numbers as command-line arguments and display their average.

Given:

```
public class AverageValue {
    public static void main(String[] arguments) {
        float[] temps = new float[10];
        float sum = 0;
        int count = 0;
        int i;
        for (i = 0; i < arguments.length & i < 10; i++) {
```

```
        try {
            temps[i] = Float.parseFloat(arguments[i]);
            count++;
        } catch (NumberFormatException nfe) {
            System.out.println("Invalid input: " + arguments[i]);
        }
        sum += temps[i];
    }
    System.out.println("Average: " + (sum / i));
}
}
```

Which statement contains an error?

**A.** `for (i = 0; i < arguments.length & i < 10; i++) {`

**B.** `sum += temps[i];`

**C.** `System.out.println("Average: " + (sum / i));`

**D.** None of them; the program is correct.

The answer is available on the book's website, at www.java21days.com. Visit the Lesson 7 page and click the Certification Practice link.

# Exercises

To extend your knowledge of the subjects covered in this lesson, try the following exercises:

1. Modify the `PrimeFinder` class so that it throws a new exception, `NegativeNumberException`, if a negative number is sent to the constructor.

2. Modify the `PrimeThreads` application so that it can handle the new `NegativeNumberException` error.

Where applicable, exercise solutions are offered on the book's website, at www.java21days.com.

7

# PART II
# The Java Class Library

# LESSON 8
# Data Structures

Up to this point, you've learned about the core elements of the Java language: objects, classes, and interfaces, along with the keywords, statements, expressions, and operators they contain.

Now the focus shifts from the classes you create to the ones that have been created for you. The Java Class Library is a set of official packages from Oracle that has more than 4,400 classes you can use in your own Java programs. This lesson focuses on classes that represent data.

The following data structures are covered in this lesson:

- Bit sets, which hold Boolean values
- Array lists, which are arrays that can grow and shrink in size
- Stacks, which are structures stored in last-in, first-out (LIFO) order
- Hash maps, which store items using keys

# Moving Beyond Arrays

The Java Class Library provides a set of data structures in the `java.util` package that give you flexibility in organizing and manipulating data. A solid understanding of data structures and when to employ them will be useful throughout your Java programming efforts.

Many Java programs that you create rely on some means of storing and manipulating data within a class. Up to this point, you have used three structures to store and retrieve data: variables, `String` objects, and arrays.

These are just a few of the data classes available in Java. If you don't understand the full range of data structures, you'll find yourself trying to use arrays or strings when other options would be more efficient or easier to implement.

Outside of primitive types and strings, arrays are the simplest data structure that Java supports. An array is a series of data elements of the same primitive type or class. It's treated as a single object but contains multiple elements that can be accessed independently. Arrays are useful when you need to store and access related information.

A glaring limitation of arrays is that they can't adjust in size to accommodate more or fewer elements. You can't add new elements to an array that's already full. One data structure you'll learn about in this lesson, array lists, does not have this limitation.

**NOTE**  Unlike the data structures provided by the `java.util` package, arrays are considered such a core component of Java that they are implemented in the language itself. Therefore, you can use arrays in Java without using an object to hold their data.

# Java Structures

The data structures provided by the `java.util` package perform a wide range of functions. These data structures consist of the `Iterator` interface, `Map` interface, and classes such as the following:

- `BitSet`
- `ArrayList`
- `Stack`
- `HashMap`

Each of these data structures provides a way to store and retrieve information in a well-defined manner. The `Iterator` interface itself isn't a data structure, but it defines a means to retrieve successive elements from a data structure. For example, `Iterator` defines a method called `next()` that gets the next element in a data structure containing multiple elements.

8

**NOTE**
> `Iterator` is an expanded and improved version of the `Enumeration` interface from early versions of the language. Although `Enumeration` is still supported, `Iterator` should be used instead because it has simpler method names and support for removing items. `Iterator` also has been designed to detect a problem-prone situation with threads: It fails with a `ConcurrentModificationException` when one thread changes an item while another one is looping through the elements.

The `BitSet` class implements a group of bits, or flags, that can be set and cleared individually. This class is useful when you need to keep up with a set of Boolean values; you simply assign a bit to each value and set or clear it, as appropriate. A flag is a Boolean value that represents one of a group of on/off type states in a program.

The `ArrayList` class is similar to an array, except that it can grow as necessary to accommodate new elements, and it also can shrink. As with an array, elements of an `ArrayList` object can be accessed via an index value. The nice thing about using an array list is that you aren't required to give it a specific size upon creation; it shrinks and grows automatically as needed.

The `Stack` class implements a LIFO stack of elements. You can think of a stack as a vertical stack of objects. When you add a new element, it's stacked on top of the others. When you pull an element off the stack, it comes off the top. The capability to remove an item differs from that in a structure like an array, where the elements always are available.

The `HashMap` class implements `Dictionary`, an abstract class that defines a data structure for mapping keys to values. This is useful when you want to access data through a particular key rather than an integer index. Because the `Dictionary` class is abstract, it provides only the framework for a key-mapped data structure rather than a specific implementation. A key is an identifier used to reference, or look up, a value in a data structure.

The `HashMap` class provides an implementation of a key-mapped data structure. `HashMap` organizes data based on a user-defined key structure. For example, in a zip code list stored in a hash map, you could store data using each zip code as a key. The specific meaning of keys in a hash map depends on how the map is used and the data it contains.

The next section looks at these data structures in more detail and shows how they work.

## Iterator

The Iterator interface provides a standard means of progressing through a list of elements in a defined sequence, which is a common task for many data structures.

Even though you can't use the interface outside a particular data structure, understanding how the Iterator interface works helps you understand other Java data structures.

With that in mind, look at three methods defined by the Iterator interface:

```
boolean hasNext();
Object next();
void remove();
```

These methods lack code because interfaces don't have implementations. The class that implements an interface must provide the code to define the methods.

The hasNext() method determines whether the structure contains more elements. You can call this method to see whether you can continue iterating through a structure.

The next() method retrieves the next element in a structure. If there are no more elements, next() throws a NoSuchElementException exception. To avoid this, you can use hasNext() in conjunction with next() to make sure there is another element to retrieve.

The following while loop uses these two methods to iterate through a data structure called users that implements the Iterator interface:

```
while (users.hasNext()) {
    Object ob = users.next();
    System.out.println(ob);
}
```

This sample code displays the contents of each list item by using the hasNext() and next() methods.

The next() method returns an object of the class Object. You can cast this to another class that the structure holds. Here's an example for a data structure that holds String objects:

```
while (users.hasNext()) {
    String ob = (String) users.next();
    System.out.println(ob);
}
```

NOTE

Because `Iterator` is an interface, you never use it directly as a data structure. Instead, you use the methods defined by `Iterator` for structures that implement the interface. This provides a consistent way to work with many of Java's standard data structures, which makes them easier to learn and use.

# Bit Sets

The `BitSet` class is useful when you need to represent a large amount of binary data—bit values that equal either 0 or 1. These also are called on-or-off values (with 1 representing on and 0 representing off) or Boolean values (with 1 meaning `true` and 0 meaning `false`).

With the `BitSet` class, you can use individual bits to store Boolean values without requiring bitwise operations to extract bit values. You simply refer to each bit using an index. Another nice feature of `BitSet` is that it automatically grows to represent the number of bits that a program requires. Figure 8.1 shows the logical organization of a bit set data structure.

**FIGURE 8.1**
The organization of a bit set.

| Index | 0 | 1 | 2 | 3 |
|-------|---|---|---|---|
| Value | Boolean0 | Boolean1 | Boolean2 | Boolean3 |

You can use a `BitSet` object to hold attributes that easily can be modeled by Boolean values. Because the individual bits in a set are accessed via an index, you can define each attribute as a constant index value, as in this class:

```
class ConnectionAttributes {
    public static final int READABLE = 0;
    public static final int WRITABLE = 1;
    public static final int STREAMABLE = 2;
    public static final int FLEXIBLE = 3;
}
```

In this class, the attributes are assigned increasing values, beginning with 0. You can use these values to get and set the appropriate bits in a set. First, you need to create a `BitSet` object:

```
BitSet connex = new BitSet();
```

This constructor creates a set with no specified size. You also can create a set with a specific size:

```
BitSet connex = new BitSet(4);
```

This creates a set containing four Boolean bits. Regardless of the constructor used, all bits in new sets initially are set to `false`. After you have a set, you can set and clear the bits by using `set(int)` and `clear(int)` methods with the bit constants you defined:

```
connex.set(ConnectionAttributes.WRITABLE);
connex.set(ConnectionAttributes.STREAMABLE);
connex.set(ConnectionAttributes.FLEXIBLE);

connex.clear(ConnectionAttributes.WRITABLE);
```

In this code, the `WRITABLE`, `STREAMABLE`, and `FLEXIBLE` attributes are set, and then the `WRITABLE` bit is cleared. The class name is used for each attribute because the constants are class variables in the `ConnectionAttributes` class.

You can get the values of individual bits in a set by using the `get()` method:

```
boolean isWriteable = connex.get(ConnectionAttributes.WRITABLE);
```

You can find out how many bits a set represents with the `size` method:

```
int numBits = connex.size();
```

The `BitSet` class also provides other methods for performing comparisons and bitwise operations on sets, such as AND, OR, and XOR. All these methods take a `BitSet` object as their only argument.

The first project in this lesson is `HolidaySked`, a Java class that uses a set to keep track of which days in a year are holidays.

A set is used here because `HolidaySked` must be able to take any day of the year and answer the same yes/no question: Are you a holiday?

Enter the code shown in Listing 8.1 into an empty Java file in NetBeans named `HolidaySked`, in the `com.java21days` package.

**LISTING 8.1**    The Full Text of `HolidaySked.java`

```
1: package com.java21days;
2:
3: import java.util.*;
4:
```

8

```
5: public class HolidaySked {
6:     BitSet sked;
7:
8:     public HolidaySked() {
9:         sked = new BitSet(365);
10:        int[] holiday = { 1, 15, 50, 148, 185, 246,
11:            281, 316, 326, 359 };
12:        for (int i = 0; i < holiday.length; i++) {
13:            addHoliday(holiday[i]);
14:        }
15:    }
16:
17:    public void addHoliday(int dayToAdd) {
18:        sked.set(dayToAdd);
19:    }
20:
21:    public boolean isHoliday(int dayToCheck) {
22:        boolean result = sked.get(dayToCheck);
23:        return result;
24:    }
25:
26:    public static void main(String[] arguments) {
27:        HolidaySked cal = new HolidaySked();
28:        if (arguments.length > 0) {
29:            try {
30:                int whichDay = Integer.parseInt(arguments[0]);
31:                if (cal.isHoliday(whichDay)) {
32:                    System.out.println("Day number " + whichDay +
33:                        " is a holiday.");
34:                } else {
35:                    System.out.println("Day number " + whichDay +
36:                        " is not a holiday.");
37:                }
38:            } catch (NumberFormatException nfe) {
39:                System.out.println("Error: " + nfe.getMessage());
40:            }
41:        }
42:    }
43: }
```

This application requires one command-line argument: a number from 1 to 365 that represents the day of the year. (These numbers are defined in lines 10–11 and would be different for each year.) Use the command Run, Set Project Configuration, Customize to set the argument.

Test the program with values such as 15 (Martin Luther King Day) or 103 (my birthday). The application should respond that day 15 is a holiday but day 103, sadly, is not.

The output of the application for day 170 is shown in Figure 8.2.

**FIGURE 8.2**

Trying out the BitSet data structure.

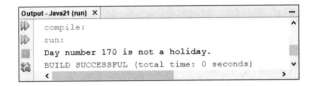

The HolidaySked class contains only one instance variable, sked, a BitSet that holds values for each day in a year.

The constructor of the class creates the sked bit set with 365 positions, with a value of 0 (lines 8–15). All bit sets are filled with 0 values when they are created.

Next, an integer array called holiday is created. This array holds the day number of each work holiday in the year, beginning with 1 (New Year's Day) and ending with 359 (Christmas).

The holiday array is used to add each holiday to the sked bit set. A for loop iterates through the holiday array and calls the method addHoliday(int) with each one (lines 12–14).

The addHoliday(int) method is defined in lines 17–19. The argument represents the day that should be added. The bit set's set(int) method is called to set the bit at the specified position to 1. For example, if set(359) is called, the bit at position 359 is given the value 1.

The HolidaySked class also can determine whether a specified day is a holiday. This is handled by the isHoliday(int) method (lines 21–24). The method calls the bit set's get(int) method, which returns true if the specified position has the value 1 and false otherwise.

This class can be run as an application because of the main() method (lines 26–42). The application takes a single command-line argument: a number from 1 to 365 that represents one of the days of the year. The application displays whether that day is a holiday according to the schedule of the HolidaySked class.

## Array Lists

One of the most popular data structures in Java, the ArrayList class implements an expandable and contractible array of objects, making it more flexible and useful than arrays. Because the ArrayList class is responsible for changing size as necessary, it must decide when and how much to grow or shrink as elements are added and removed.

An array list can be created with a constructor that takes no arguments:

```
ArrayList golfer = new ArrayList();
```

This constructor creates a default array list that contains no elements. All lists are empty upon creation. One of the attributes that determines how a list sizes itself is its initial capacity—the number of elements for which it allocates memory to hold.

The size of an array list is the number of elements currently stored in it. A list's capacity is always greater than or equal to the size.

The following code shows how to create an array list with a specified capacity:

```
ArrayList golfer = new ArrayList(30);
```

This list allocates enough memory to support 30 elements. If the capacity fills up, the list automatically expands by half the initial size. So if a 30th element is put in `golfer`, the list expands to make room for 45 elements.

Because allocating additional space for the list takes time and consumes memory, it's best to create a list with as many elements as you expect to use.

You can't just use square brackets `[]` to access the elements in an array list, as you can in an array. You must use methods of the `ArrayList` class.

Use the `add(Object)` method to add an element to an array list, like this:

```
golfer.add("Park");
golfer.add("Lewis");
golfer.add("Ko");
```

The `lastElement()` method returns an `Object` because the `ArrayList` class supports all classes of objects. You must cast it to the class that was put into the list. Here, because strings were stored in `golfer`, the returned object is cast to a string.

The `get()` method retrieves a list element by using a numeric index, as shown in the following code:

```
String s1 = (String) golfer.get(0);
String s2 = (String) golfer.get(2);
```

Because array list numbering is zero-based, the first call to `get()` retrieves the `"Park"` string, and the second call retrieves the `"Lewis"` string.

Just as you can retrieve an element at a particular index, you also can add and remove elements at an index by using the `add(int, Object)` and `remove(int)` methods:

```
golfer.add(1, "Kim");
golfer.add(0, "Thompson");
golfer.remove(3);
```

The first call to add() inserts an element at index 1, between the "Park" and "Lewis" strings. The "Lewis" and "Ko" strings are moved by an element in the list to accommodate the inserted "Kim" string. The second call to add() inserts an element at index 0, which is the beginning of the list. All existing elements are moved up one space in the list to accommodate the inserted "Thompson" string. At this point, the contents of the list look like this:

**0.** "Thompson"

**1.** "Park"

**2.** "Kim"

**3.** "Lewis"

**4.** "Ko"

The call to remove() removes the element at index 3, which is the "Lewis" string. The resulting list consists of the following strings:

**0.** "Thompson"

**1.** "Park"

**2.** "Kim"

**3.** "Ko"

You can use the set() method to change a specific element:

```
golfer.set(1, "Pressel");
```

This method replaces the "Park" string with the "Pressel" string, resulting in the following list:

**0.** "Thompson"

**1.** "Pressel"

**2.** "Kim"

**3.** "Ko"

If you want to clear out the array list, you can remove all the elements with the clear() method:

```
golfer.clear();
```

The `ArrayList` class also provides some methods for working with elements without using indexes. These methods search through the list for a particular element. The first of these methods is the `contains(Object)` method, which simply checks whether an object is in the list:

```
boolean isThere = golfer.contains("Kerr");
```

Another method for searching is the `indexOf(Object)` method, which finds the index of an element matching an object:

```
int i = golfer.indexOf("Ko");
```

The `indexOf()` method returns the index or `-1` if the object is not in the list. The `remove(Object)` method works similarly, removing an object from the list, as in this statement:

```
golfer.remove("Pressel");
```

The `ArrayList` class offers a few methods for determining and manipulating a list's size. First, the `size` method determines the number of elements in the list:

```
int size = golfer.size();
```

Recall that lists have two attributes related to size: size and capacity. The size is the number of elements in the list, and the capacity is the amount of memory allocated to hold all the elements. The capacity always is greater than or equal to the size. You can force the capacity to exactly match the size by using the `trimToSize()` method:

```
golfer.trimToSize();
```

**CAUTION**

> The Java Class Library also includes `Vector`, a data structure that works a lot like array lists. When you use vectors in NetBeans, a warning is displayed that calls the class an "obsolete collection." This occurs because array lists are considered a superior version of vectors.

# Looping Through Data Structures

If you're interested in working sequentially with all the elements in a list, you can use the `iterator()` method, which returns an `Iterator` that holds a list of the elements you can loop through:

```
Iterator it = golfer.iterator();
```

As you learned earlier in this lesson, you can use an iterator to step through elements sequentially. In this example, you can work with the it list by using the methods defined by the Iterator interface.

The following for loop uses an iterator and its methods to traverse an entire array list:

```
for (Iterator i = golfer.iterator(); i.hasNext(); ) {
    String name = (String) i.next();
    System.out.println(name);
}
```

This lesson's next project demonstrates the care and feeding of array lists. The CodeKeeper class, shown in Listing 8.2, holds a set of text codes, some provided by the class and others provided by users. Because the amount of space needed to hold the codes isn't known until the program is run, an array list is used instead of an array to store the data. Create this class in NetBeans, remembering to put it in the com.java21days package.

**LISTING 8.2** The Full Text of CodeKeeper.java

```
 1: package com.java21days;
 2:
 3: import java.util.*;
 4:
 5: public class CodeKeeper {
 6:     ArrayList list;
 7:     String[] codes = { "alpha", "lambda", "gamma", "delta", "zeta" };
 8:
 9:     public CodeKeeper(String[] userCodes) {
10:         list = new ArrayList();
11:         // load built-in codes
12:         for (int i = 0; i < codes.length; i++) {
13:             addCode(codes[i]);
14:         }
15:         // load user codes
16:         for (int j = 0; j < userCodes.length; j++) {
17:             addCode(userCodes[j]);
18:         }
19:         // display all codes
20:         for (Iterator ite = list.iterator(); ite.hasNext(); ) {
21:             String output = (String) ite.next();
22:             System.out.println(output);
23:         }
24:     }
25:
```

```
26:        private void addCode(String code) {
27:            if (!list.contains(code)) {
28:                list.add(code);
29:            }
30:        }
31:
32:        public static void main(String[] arguments) {
33:            CodeKeeper keeper = new CodeKeeper(arguments);
34:        }
35: }
```

8

NetBeans may display a warning that this class uses "unchecked or unsafe operations." This isn't as severe as it sounds. The code works properly as written and is not unsafe. The warning serves as a strong hint that there's a better way to work with array lists and other data structures. You'll learn about this technique later in this lesson.

The CodeKeeper class uses an ArrayList instance variable named list to hold the text codes.

First, five built-in codes are read from a string array into the list (lines 12–14).

Next, any codes provided by the user as command-line arguments are added (lines 16–18).

Codes are added by calling the addCode() method (lines 26–30). addCode() adds a new text code only if it isn't already present, using the list's contains(Object) method to make this determination.

You add command-line arguments in NetBeans by selecting Project, Set Project Configuration, Customize. The arguments should be a list of codes separated by spaces.

After the codes have been added to the list, its contents are displayed. Running the class with the command-line arguments gamma, beta, and delta produces the output shown in Figure 8.3.

**FIGURE 8.3**
Manipulating and displaying an array list.

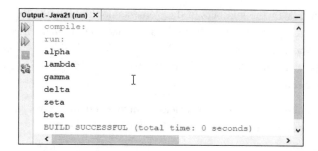

A simpler `for` loop can be used to iterate through a data structure. The loop takes the form `for (variable : structure)`, where `structure` is a data structure that implements the `Iterator` interface. The `variable` section declares an object that holds each element of the structure as the loop progresses.

This `for` loop uses an iterator and its methods to traverse an array list named `golfer`:

```
for (Object name : golfer) {
    System.out.println(name);
}
```

The loop can be used with any data structure that works with `Iterator`.

## Stacks

Stacks are a data structure used to model information accessed in a specific order. The `Stack` class in Java is implemented as a LIFO stack, which means that the last item added to the stack is the first one to be removed. Figure 8.4 shows the logical organization of a stack.

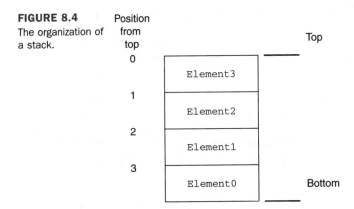

**FIGURE 8.4**
The organization of a stack.

You might wonder why the numbers of the elements don't match their positions from the top of the stack. Keep in mind that elements are added to the top, so `Element0`, which is on the bottom, was the first element added to the stack. Likewise, `Element3`, which is on top, was the last element added. Also, because `Element3` is at the top of the stack, it will be the first to be removed.

The `Stack` class defines only one constructor, which is a default constructor that creates an empty stack. You use this constructor to create a stack like this:

```
Stack s = new Stack();
```

Stacks in Java contain methods to manipulate the stack.

You can add new elements to a stack by using the `push()` method, which pushes an element onto the top of the stack:

```
s.push("One");
s.push("Two");
s.push("Three");
s.push("Four");
s.push("Five");
s.push("Six");
```

This code pushes six strings onto the stack, with the last string (`"Six"`) ending up on top. You remove elements from the stack by using the `pop()` method, which pops them off the top:

```
String s1 = (String) s.pop();
String s2 = (String) s.pop();
```

This code pops the last two strings off the stack, leaving the first four strings. This code results in the `s1` variable containing the `"Six"` string and the `s2` variable containing the `"Five"` string.

If you want to use the top element on the stack without actually popping it off the stack, you can use the `peek()` method:

```
String s3 = (String) s.peek();
```

This call to `peek()` returns the `"Four"` string but leaves the string on the stack. You can search for an element on the stack by using the `search()` method:

```
int i = s.search("Two");
```

The `search()` method returns the distance from the top of the stack to the element if it is found or -1 if not. In this case, the `"Two"` string is the third element from the top, so the `search()` method returns 2.

**NOTE**

> As in all Java data structures that deal with indexes or lists, the `Stack` class reports element positions in a zero-based fashion: The top element in a stack has a location of 0, the fourth element down has a location of 3, and so on.

The last method defined in the `Stack` class is `empty()`, which indicates whether a stack is empty:

```
boolean isEmpty = s.empty();
```

## Map

The `Map` interface defines a framework for implementing a key-mapped data structure, a place to store objects, each referenced by a key. The key serves the same purpose as an element number in an array: It's a unique value used to access the data stored at a position in the data structure.

You can put the key-mapped approach to work by using the `HashMap` class or one of the other classes that implement the `Map` interface. You'll learn about the `HashMap` class in the next section.

The `Map` interface defines a means of storing and retrieving information based on a key. This is similar in some ways to the `ArrayList` class, in which elements are accessed through an index, which is a specific type of key. However, keys in the `Map` interface can be just about anything. You can create your own classes to use as the keys for accessing and manipulating data in a dictionary. Figure 8.5 shows how keys map to data in a dictionary.

**FIGURE 8.5**
The organization of a key-mapped data structure.

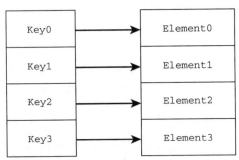

The `Map` interface declares a variety of methods for working with the data stored in a dictionary. Implementing classes have to implement all those methods to be truly useful. The `put(String, Object)` and `get(String, Object)` methods are used to store objects in the dictionary and retrieve them.

Assuming that `look` is an object that implements the `Map` interface, the following code shows how to use the `put()` method to add elements:

```
Rectangle r1 = new Rectangle(0, 0, 5, 5);
look.put("small", r1);
```

```
Rectangle r2 = new Rectangle(0, 0, 15, 15);
look.put("medium", r2);
Rectangle r3 = new Rectangle(0, 0, 25, 25);
look.put("large", r3);
```

This code adds three `Rectangle` objects to the map (from the `java.awt` package), using strings as the keys. To get an element, use the `get()` method and specify the appropriate key:

```
Rectangle r = (Rectangle) look.get("medium");
```

You also can remove an element with a key by using the `remove()` method:

```
look.remove("large");
```

You can find out how many elements are in the structure by using the `size()` method, as in the `ArrayList` class:

```
int size = look.size();
```

You also can check whether the structure is empty by using the `isEmpty()` method:

```
boolean isEmpty = look.isEmpty();
```

## Hash Maps

The `HashMap` class implements the `Map` interface and provides a complete implementation of a key-mapped data structure. Hash maps let you store data based on some type of key and have an efficiency defined by the map's load factor. The load factor is a floating-point number between 0.0 and 1.0 that determines how and when the hash map allocates space for more elements.

Like array lists, hash maps have a capacity, or an amount of allocated memory. Hash maps allocate memory by comparing the map's current size with the product of the capacity and the load factor. If the size of the hash map exceeds this product, the map increases its capacity by rehashing itself.

Load factors closer to 1.0 result in a more efficient use of memory at the expense of a longer lookup time for each element. Similarly, load factors closer to 0.0 result in more efficient lookups but tend to be more wasteful of memory. Determining the load factor for your own hash maps involves considering how you use each map and whether your priority is performance or memory efficiency.

You can create hash maps in one of three ways. The first constructor creates a default hash map with an initial capacity of 16 elements and a load factor of 0.75:

```
HashMap hash = new HashMap();
```

The second constructor creates a hash map with the specified initial capacity and a load factor of 0.75:

```
HashMap hash = new HashMap(20);
```

Finally, the third constructor creates a hash map with the specified initial capacity and load factor:

```
HashMap hash = new HashMap(20, 0.5F);
```

All the abstract methods defined in `Map` are implemented in the `HashMap` class. In addition, the `HashMap` class implements a few other methods that perform functions specific to supporting maps. One of these is the `clear()` method, which clears a map of all its keys and elements:

```
hash.clear();
```

The `containsValue(Object)` method checks whether an object is stored in the hash map:

```
Rectangle box = new Rectangle(0, 0, 5, 5);
boolean isThere = hash.containsValue(box);
```

The `containsKey(String)` method searches a map for a key:

```
boolean isThere = hash.containsKey("Small");
```

The practical use of a hash map comes from its capability to represent data that is too time-consuming to search or reference by value. The data structure comes in handy when you're working with complex data, and it's more efficient to access the data by using a key than by comparing the data objects themselves. This key, which is called a *hash code*, is a computed key that uniquely identifies each element in a hash map.

This technique of computing and using hash codes for object storage and reference is exploited heavily throughout the Java Class Library. The parent of all classes, `Object`, defines a `hashCode()` method that is overridden in most standard Java classes. Any class that defines a `hashCode()` method can be efficiently stored and accessed in a hash map. A class that wants to be hashed also must implement the `equals()` method, which defines a way of telling whether two objects are equal. The `equals()` method usually just performs a straight comparison of all the member variables defined in a class.

The next project you'll undertake in this lesson uses maps for a shopping application.

The `ComicBooks` application prices collectible comic books according to their base value and condition. The condition is described as one of the following: mint, near mint, very fine, fine, good, or poor. Each condition has a specific effect on a comic's value:

- Mint books are worth 3 times their base price.
- Near mint books are worth 2 times their base price.
- Very fine books are worth 1.5 times their base price.
- Fine books are worth their base price.
- Good books are worth 0.5 times their base price.
- Poor books are worth 0.25 times their base price.

To associate text such as "mint" or "very fine" with a numeric value, you put them into a hash map. The keys to the map are the condition descriptions, and the values are floating-point numbers such as 3.0, 1.5, and 0.25.

Enter the code shown in Listing 8.3 in NetBeans as the class `ComicBooks` in the package `com.java21days`.

**LISTING 8.3**    The Full Text of `ComicBooks.java`

```
 1: package com.java21days;
 2:
 3: import java.util.*;
 4:
 5: public class ComicBooks {
 6:
 7:     public ComicBooks() {
 8:     }
 9:
10:     public static void main(String[] arguments) {
11:         // set up hash map
12:         HashMap quality = new HashMap();
13:         float price1 = 3.00F;
14:         quality.put("mint", price1);
15:         float price2 = 2.00F;
16:         quality.put("near mint", price2);
17:         float price3 = 1.50F;
18:         quality.put("very fine", price3);
```

```
19:            float price4 = 1.00F;
20:            quality.put("fine", price4);
21:            float price5 = 0.50F;
22:            quality.put("good", price5);
23:            float price6 = 0.25F;
24:            quality.put("poor", price6);
25:            // set up collection
26:            Comic[] comix = new Comic[3];
27:            comix[0] = new Comic("Amazing Spider-Man", "1A", "very fine",
28:                12_000.00F);
29:            comix[0].setPrice( (Float) quality.get(comix[0].condition) );
30:            comix[1] = new Comic("Incredible Hulk", "181", "near mint",
31:                680.00F);
32:            comix[1].setPrice( (Float) quality.get(comix[1].condition) );
33:            comix[2] = new Comic("Cerebus", "1A", "good", 190.00F);
34:            comix[2].setPrice( (Float) quality.get(comix[2].condition) );
35:            for (int i = 0; i < comix.length; i++) {
36:                System.out.println("Title: " + comix[i].title);
37:                System.out.println("Issue: " + comix[i].issueNumber);
38:                System.out.println("Condition: " + comix[i].condition);
39:                System.out.println("Price: $" + comix[i].price + "\n");
40:            }
41:        }
42: }
43:
44: class Comic {
45:     String title;
46:     String issueNumber;
47:     String condition;
48:     float basePrice;
49:     float price;
50:
51:     Comic(String inTitle, String inIssueNumber, String inCondition,
52:         float inBasePrice) {
53:
54:         title = inTitle;
55:         issueNumber = inIssueNumber;
56:         condition = inCondition;
57:         basePrice = inBasePrice;
58:     }
59:
60:     void setPrice(float factor) {
61:         price = basePrice * factor;
62:     }
63: }
```

When you run the ComicBooks application, it produces the output shown in Figure 8.6.

**FIGURE 8.6**

Storing comic book values in a hash map.

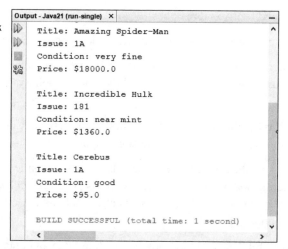

```
Output - Java21 (run-single)  ×                              —

    Title: Amazing Spider-Man
    Issue: 1A
    Condition: very fine
    Price: $18000.0

    Title: Incredible Hulk
    Issue: 181
    Condition: near mint
    Price: $1360.0

    Title: Cerebus
    Issue: 1A
    Condition: good
    Price: $95.0

    BUILD SUCCESSFUL (total time: 1 second)
```

The `ComicBooks` application is implemented as two classes: an application class called `ComicBooks` and a helper class called `Comic`.

In the application, the hash map is created in lines 12–24. First, the map is created in line 12. Next, a `float` called `price1` is created with the value `3.00`. This value is added to the map and associated with the key `"mint"`. (Remember that hash maps, like other data structures, can hold only objects. The float value is automatically converted to a `Float` object through autoboxing.)

The process is repeated for each of the other comic book conditions, from near mint to poor.

After the hash map is set up, an array of `Comic` objects called `comix` is created to hold each comic book currently for sale.

The `Comic` constructor is called with four arguments: the book's title, issue number, condition, and base price. The first three are strings, and the last is a `float`.

After a `Comic` has been created, its `setPrice(float)` method is called to set the book's price based on its condition. Here's an example, from line 29:

```
comix[0].setPrice( (Float) quality.get(comix[0].condition) );
```

The hash map's `get(String)` method is called with the book's condition, a string that is one of the keys in the map. An `Object` is returned that represents the value associated with that key. (In line 29, because `comix[0].condition` is equal to `"very fine"`, `get()` returns the floating-point value `3.00F`.)

Because `get()` returns an `Object`, it must be cast as a `Float`. The `Float` argument is unboxed as a `float` value automatically through unboxing.

This process is repeated for two more books.

Lines 35–40 display information about each comic book in the `comix` array.

The `Comic` class is defined in lines 44–63. It has five instance variables—the `String` object's `title`, `issueNumber`, and `condition`, and the floating-point value's `basePrice` and `price`.

The constructor method of the class, located in lines 51–58, sets the value of four instance variables to the arguments sent to the constructor.

The `setPrice(Float)` method in lines 60–62 sets the price of a comic book. The argument sent to the method is a `float` value. A comic's price is calculated by multiplying this `float` by the comic's base price. Consequently, if a book is worth $1,000, and its multiplier is 2.0, the book is priced at $2,000.

A hash map is a powerful data structure for manipulating large amounts of data. The fact that these maps are so widely supported in the Java Class Library via the `Object` class should give you a clue as to their importance in Java programming.

# Generics

The data structures that you have learned about in this lesson are some of the most essential utility classes in the Java Class Library.

Hash maps, array lists, stacks, and the other structures in the `java.util` package are useful regardless of the kind of programs you want to develop. Almost every software program handles data in some manner.

These data structures are well suited for use in code that applies generically to a wide range of classes of objects. A method written to manipulate array lists could be written to function equally well on strings, string buffers, character arrays, or other objects that represent text. A method in an accounting program could take objects that represent integers, floating-point numbers, and other math classes, using each to calculate a balance.

This flexibility comes at a price: When a data structure works with any kind of object, the Java compiler can't display a warning when the structure is being misused.

For instance, the `ComicBooks` application uses a hash map named `quality` to associate condition descriptions such as `"mint"` and `"good"` with price multipliers. Here's the statement for `"near mint"`:

```
quality.put("near mint", 1.50F);
```

By design, the `quality` map should hold only floating-point values (as `Float` objects). However, the class compiles successfully regardless of the class of the value added to a map. You might goof and unintentionally add a string to the map, as in this revised statement:

```
quality.put("near mint", "1.50");
```

The class compiles successfully, but when it is run, it fails with a `ClassCastException` error in the following statement:

```
comix[1].setPrice( (Float) quality.get(comix[1].condition) );
```

The reason for the error is that the statement tries to cast the map's `"near mint"` value to a `Float`, which fails because it receives the string `"1.50"` instead.

Runtime errors are much more troublesome than compiler errors for programmers. A compiler error stops you in your tracks and must be fixed before you can continue. A runtime error might creep its way into the code, unbeknownst to you, and cause problems for users of your software.

You can specify the class or classes expected in a data structure by using a feature of the language called *generics*. The expected class information is added to statements where the structure is assigned a variable or created with a constructor. The class or classes are placed within < and > characters and follow the name of the class, as in this statement:

```
ArrayList<Integer> zipCodes = new ArrayList<>();
```

This statement creates an array list that will be used to hold `Integer` objects. The compiler uses inference to correctly guess the type of the class the second time the < and > characters appear. The <> after a class name sometimes is called a *diamond operator*. Here's another example:

```
HashMap<String, Float> quality = new HashMap<>();
```

The diamond operator (<>) infers the classes based on what they would have to be for the statement to make sense.

Because the list is declared with a class specified, the following statements cause a compiler error that NetBeans will flag in the source code editor:

```
zipCodes.add("90210");
zipCodes.add("02134");
zipCodes.add("20500");
```

The compiler recognizes that `String` objects do not belong in this array list. The proper way to add elements to the list is to use integer values:

```
zipCodes.add(90210);
zipCodes.add(02134);
zipCodes.add(20500);
```

These integers are converted to `Integer` objects through autoboxing.

Data structures that use multiple classes, such as hash maps, take these class names separated by commas within the `<` and `>` characters.

The `ComicBooks` application can take advantage of generics by changing line 12 of Listing 8.3 to the following:

```
HashMap<String, Float> quality = new HashMap<>();
```

This sets up a map to use `String` objects for keys and `Float` objects for values. With this statement in place, a string no longer can be added as the value for a condition such as near mint. A compiler error flags a problem of this kind.

Generics also make it easier to retrieve objects from a data structure because you don't have to use casting to convert them to the desired class. For example, the `quality` map no longer requires a cast to produce `Float` objects in statements like this one:

```
comix[1].setPrice(quality.get(comix[1].condition));
```

From a stylistic standpoint, the addition of generics in variable declarations and constructor methods is likely to appear intimidating. However, when you become accustomed to working with them (and using autoboxing, unboxing, and the new `for` loops), data structures are significantly easier to work with and less error prone.

The `CodeKeeper2` class, shown in Listing 8.4, is a new version of `CodeKeeper` that has been rewritten to use generics, type inference, and the `for` loop, which can iterate through data structures such as array lists.

**LISTING 8.4**   The Full Text of `CodeKeeper2.java`

```
1: package com.java21days;
2:
3: import java.util.*;
4:
5: public class CodeKeeper2 {
6:     ArrayList<String> list;
7:     String[] codes = { "alpha", "lambda", "gamma", "delta", "zeta" };
8:
```

```
 9:     public CodeKeeper2(String[] userCodes) {
10:         list = new ArrayList<>();
11:         // load built-in codes
12:         for (int i = 0; i < codes.length; i++) {
13:             addCode(codes[i]);
14:         }
15:         // load user codes
16:         for (int j = 0; j < userCodes.length; j++) {
17:             addCode(userCodes[j]);
18:         }
19:         // display all codes
20:         for (String code : list) {
21:             System.out.println(code);
22:         }
23:     }
24:
25:     private void addCode(String code) {
26:         if (!list.contains(code)) {
27:             list.add(code);
28:         }
29:     }
30:
31:     public static void main(String[] arguments) {
32:         CodeKeeper2 keeper = new CodeKeeper2(arguments);
33:     }
34: }
```

The only modifications to the class are in line 6, where the generics declaration for an array list of strings is made; line 10, where type inference figures out the proper generics declaration; and lines 20 and 21, the simpler for loop that displays all the codes.

# Enumerations

A common use of constants in Java is to attach a meaningful label to a series of integers, as you did earlier in this lesson when you worked with bit sets:

```
class ConnectionAttributes {
    public static final int READABLE = 0;
    public static final int WRITABLE = 1;
    public static final int STREAMABLE = 2;
    public static final int FLEXIBLE = 3;
}
```

These constants are useful because of the extra information provided in statements that contain them. Compare these two statements, which do the same thing:

```
setConnectionType(1);
setConnectionType(ConnectionAttributes.WRITABLE);
```

The latter is much easier to understand for a programmer examining the code.

Java has a data type called *enumerations* that serves the same purpose and has advantages over using constants in a class. The enum keyword is used in place of class, and the values are separated by commas.

Here's a simple enumeration called Compass for the eight compass directions:

```
public enum Compass {
    NORTH,
    EAST,
    SOUTH,
    WEST,
    NORTHEAST,
    SOUTHEAST,
    SOUTHWEST,
    NORTHWEST
}
```

Each of these values is implicitly static and final, just like constants. They can appear in statements, method calls, and other code just as if they were class constants. Here's an application that uses the enumeration:

```
public class DirectionSetter {
    Compass current;
    public void setDirection(Compass dir) {
        current = dir;
    }

    public static void main(String[] arguments) {
        DirectionSetter app = new DirectionSetter();
        app.setDirection(Compass.WEST);
        System.out.println(app.current);
    }
}
```

This class sets the current instance variable to WEST from the Compass enumeration and displays the variable, which is output as the text WEST.

An advantage to using enum over class constants is that the compiler can detect errors when an invalid value is used. The only acceptable values that can be sent to the setDirection(Compass) method are the values of the Compass enumeration.

By comparison, a method that took ConnectionAttributes values as an argument could be called with any integer value.

There are other advantages to enumerations, which can function like classes, with methods and variables of their own.

Any time you need a fixed set of constants, you can make them an enumeration.

8

# Summary

In this lesson, you learned about several data structures you can use in your Java programs:

- **Bit sets:** Large sets of Boolean on-or-off values
- **Array lists:** Arrays that can change in size dynamically and that can be shrunken or expanded as needed
- **Stacks:** Structures in which the last item added is the first item removed
- **Hash maps:** Objects stored and retrieved using unique keys

These data structures are part of the `java.util` package, a collection of useful classes for handling data, dates, strings, and other things. The addition of generics and new `for` loops for iteration enhances their capabilities.

You also were introduced to enumerations, a data type for representing a set of related values as constants.

Learning about the ways in which you can organize data in Java has benefits in all aspects of software development. Whether you're learning the language to write servlets, desktop applications, apps, or something else, you need to represent data in numerous ways.

# Q&A

**Q The `HolidaySked` project from this lesson could be implemented as an array of Boolean values. Is one way preferable to the other?**

**A** It depends. One thing you'll find as you work with data structures is that there are often many ways to implement something. A bit set is somewhat preferable to a Boolean array when the size of your program matters, because a bit set is smaller. An array of a primitive type such as Boolean is preferable when the speed of your program matters because arrays are somewhat faster. The `HolidaySked` class, for example, is so small that the difference is negligible, but as you develop your own robust, real-world applications, these kinds of decisions can sometimes make a difference.

**Q** **The Java compiler's warning for data structures that don't use generics is pretty ominous. It doesn't sound like a very good idea to release a class that has "unchecked or unsafe operations." Is there any reason to stick with old code or not use generics with data structures?**

**A** The compiler's warning about safety is a bit overstated. Java programmers have been using array lists, hash maps, and other structures in their classes for years, creating software that runs reliably and safely. The lack of generics meant that more work was necessary to ensure that runtime problems didn't occur because of wrong classes being placed in a structure.

It's more accurate to state that data structures can be made safer through the use of generics than to suggest that previous versions of Java were unsafe. My personal rule is to use generics in new code and old code that's being reorganized or significantly rewritten but leave alone old code that works correctly.

# Quiz

Review this lesson's material by taking this three-question quiz.

## Questions

**1.** Which of the following kinds of data cannot be stored in a hash map?

    **A.** `String`

    **B.** `int`

    **C.** Both can be stored in a map.

**2.** An array list is created, and three strings, `"Tinker"`, `"Evers"`, and `"Chance"`, are added to it. The method `remove("Evers")` is called. Which of the following `ArrayList` methods retrieves the string `"Chance"`?

    **A.** `get(1);`

    **B.** `get(2);`

    **C.** `get("Chance");`

**3.** Which of these classes implements the `Map` interface?

    **A.** `Stack`

    **B.** `HashMap`

    **C.** `BitSet`

## Answers

**1.** C. In past versions of Java, to store primitive types such as `int` in a map, objects had to be used to represent their values (such as `Integer` for integers). This is no longer true. Primitive types are converted automatically to the corresponding object class through a process called *autoboxing*.

**2.** A. The index numbers of the items in an array list can change as items are added or removed. Because `"Chance"` becomes the second item in the list after `"Evers"` is removed, it is retrieved by calling `get(1)`.

**3.** B. `HashMap` implements the interface, as does a similar class called `Hashtable`.

# Certification Practice

The following question is the kind of thing you could expect to be asked on a Java programming certification test. Answer it without looking again at this lesson or using the Java compiler to test the code.

Given:

```java
public class Recursion {
    public int dex = -1;

    public Recursion() {
        dex = getValue(17);
    }

    public int getValue(int dexValue) {
        if (dexValue > 100) {
            return dexValue;
        } else {
            return getValue(dexValue * 2);
        }
    }

    public static void main(String[] arguments) {
        Recursion r = new Recursion();
        System.out.println(r.dex);
    }
}
```

What will be the output of this application?

**A.** `-1`

**B.** `17`

**C.** `34`

**D.** `136`

The answer is available on the book's website, at www.java21days.com. Visit the Lesson 8 page and click the Certification Practice link.

# Exercises

To extend your knowledge of the subjects covered in this lesson, try the following exercises:

1. Add two more conditions to the `ComicBooks` application: pristine mint for books that should sell at 5 times their base price and coverless for books that should sell at 0.1 times their base price.

2. Rewrite the `ComicBooks` application so that the set of possible conditions of a comic is an enumeration.

Where applicable, exercise solutions are offered on the book's website, at www.java21days.com.

# LESSON 9

# Creating a Graphical User Interface

Most computer users today expect software to feature a graphical user interface (GUI) with a variety of widgets such as text boxes, sliders, and scrollbars. The Java Class Library includes Swing, a set of packages that enable Java programs to offer a sophisticated GUI and collect user input with the mouse, keyboard, and other input devices.

In this lesson, you will use Swing to create applications that feature these GUI components:

- **Frames:** Windows with a title bar; menu bar; and Maximize, Minimize, and Close buttons
- **Containers:** Components that hold other components
- **Buttons:** Clickable rectangles with text or graphics indicating their purpose
- **Labels:** Text or graphics that provide information
- **Text fields and text areas:** Windows that accept keyboard input of one line or multiple lines
- **Drop-down lists:** Groups of related items that are selected from drop-down menus or scrolling windows
- **Check boxes and radio buttons:** Small squares or circles that can be selected or deselected
- **Image icons:** Graphics added to buttons, labels, and other components
- **Scrolling panes:** Panels for components too big for a user interface that can be accessed in full by using a scrollbar

Swing is the most extensive set of related classes introduced thus far in the book. Learning to create graphical applications with these packages is good practice for utilizing a class library in Java, which is something you'll do often in your own projects.

# Creating an Application

Swing enables the creation of a Java program with an interface that adopts the style of the native operating system, such as Windows or Linux, or a style that's unique to Java. Each of these styles is called a *look and feel* because it describes both the appearance of the interface and how its components function when they are used.

Java offers a distinctive look and feel called Nimbus that's unique to the language.

Swing components are part of the `javax.swing` package, a standard part of the Java Class Library. To refer to a Swing class using its short name—without referring to the package, in other words—you must make it available with an `import` statement or use a catchall statement such as the following:

```
import javax.swing.*;
```

Two other packages that support GUI programming are `java.awt`, the Abstract Window Toolkit (AWT), and `java.awt.event`, event-handling classes that handle user input.

When you use a Swing component, you work with objects of that component's class. You create the component by calling its constructor and then calling methods of the component as needed for proper setup.

All Swing components are subclasses of the abstract class `JComponent`. It includes methods to set a component's size, change the background color, define the font used for any displayed text, and set up *tooltips*. A tooltip is explanatory text that appears when you hover the mouse over the component for a few seconds.

**CAUTION**

Swing classes inherit from many of the same superclasses as the Abstract Window Toolkit, so it is possible to use Swing and AWT components together in the same interface. However, the two types of components will not be rendered correctly in a container, so it's best to always use Swing components; there's one for every AWT component.

Before components can be displayed in a user interface, they must be added to a *container*, a component that can hold other components. Swing containers are subclasses of `java.awt.Container`. This class includes methods to add and remove components from a container, arrange components using an object called a *layout manager*, and set up borders around the edges of a container. Containers often can be placed in other containers.

# Creating a Graphical User Interface

The first step in creating a Swing application is to create a class that represents the main GUI. An object of this class serves as a container that holds all the other components to be displayed.

In many projects, the main interface object is a frame (the `JFrame` class in the `javax.swing` package). A frame is a window shown whenever you open an application on your computer. A frame has a title bar; Maximize, Minimize, and Close buttons; and other features.

In a graphical environment such as Windows or macOS, users expect to be able to move, resize, and close the windows of programs. One way to create a graphical Java application is to make the interface a subclass of `JFrame`, as in the following class declaration:

```
public class FeedReader extends JFrame {
    // body of class
}
```

The constructor of the class should handle the following tasks:

- Call a superclass constructor with `super()` to give the frame a title and handle other setup procedures.
- Set the size of the frame's window, either by specifying the width and height in pixels or by letting Swing choose the size.
- Decide what to do if a user closes the window.
- Display the frame.

The `JFrame` class has the simple constructors `JFrame()` and `JFrame(String)`. One sets the frame's title bar to the specified text, and the other leaves the title bar empty. You also can set the title by calling the frame's `setTitle(String)` method.

The size of a frame can be established by calling the `setSize(int, int)` method with the width and height as arguments. A frame's size is indicated in pixels, so, for example, calling `setSize(650, 550)` creates a frame 650 pixels wide and 550 pixels tall.

**NOTE**

You also can call the method `setSize(Dimension)` to set up a frame's size. `Dimension` is a class in the `java.awt` package that represents the width and height of a user interface component. Calling the `Dimension(int, int)` constructor creates a `Dimension` object representing the width and height specified as arguments.

Another way to set a frame's size is to fill the frame with the components it will contain and then call the frame's `pack()` method. This resizes the frame based on the preferred size of the components inside it. If the frame is bigger than it needs to be, `pack()` shrinks it to the minimum size required to display the components. If the frame is too small (or the size has not been set), `pack()` expands it to the required size.

Frames are invisible when they are created. You can make them visible by calling the frame's `setVisible(boolean)` method with the literal `true` as an argument.

If you want a frame to be displayed when it is created, call one of these methods in the constructor. You also can leave the frame invisible and require any class that uses the frame to make it visible by calling `setVisible(true)`. As you probably have surmised, calling `setVisible(false)` makes a frame invisible.

When a frame is displayed, the default behavior is for it to be positioned in the upper-left corner of the computer's desktop. You can specify a different location by calling the `setBounds(int, int, int, int)` method. The first two arguments to this method are the (x, y) position of the frame's upper-left corner on the desktop. The last two arguments are the frame's width and height.

Another way to set the bounds is with a `Rectangle` object from the `java.awt` package. Create the rectangle with the `Rectangle(int, int, int, int)` constructor. The first two arguments are the (x, y) position of the upper-left corner. The next two are the width and height. Call `setBounds(Rectangle)` to draw the frame at that spot.

The following class represents a 300×100 frame with "Edit Payroll" in the title bar:

```
public class Payroll extends JFrame {
    public Payroll() {
        super("Edit Payroll");
        setSize(300, 100);
        setVisible(true);
    }
}
```

Every frame has Maximize, Minimize, and Close buttons on the title bar that the user can control—the same controls present in the interface of other software running on your computer.

There's a wrinkle to using frames that you might not expect: The normal behavior when a frame is closed is for the application to keep running. When a frame serves as a program's main GUI, this leaves a user with no way to stop the program.

To change this, you must call a frame's `setDefaultCloseOperation(int)` method with one of four static variables as an argument:

- **EXIT_ON_CLOSE:** Exits the application when the frame is closed
- **DISPOSE_ON_CLOSE:** Closes the frame, removes the frame object from Java Virtual Machine (JVM) memory, and keeps running the application
- **DO_NOTHING_ON_CLOSE:** Keeps the frame open and continues running
- **HIDE_ON_CLOSE:** Closes the frame and continues running

These variables are part of the `JFrame` class because it implements the `WindowConstants` interface. To prevent a user from closing a frame, add the following statement to the frame's constructor method:

```
setDefaultCloseOperation(JFrame.DO_NOTHING_ON_CLOSE);
```

If you are creating a frame to serve as an application's main user interface, the expected behavior is probably `EXIT_ON_CLOSE`, which shuts down the application along with the frame.

As mentioned earlier, you can customize the overall appearance of a user interface in Java by designating a look and feel. The `UIManager` class in the `javax.swing` package manages this aspect of Swing. To set the look and feel, call the class method `setLookAndFeel(String)` with the name of the look and feel's class as the argument. Here's how to choose the Nimbus look and feel:

```
UIManager.setLookAndFeel(
    "javax.swing.plaf.nimbus.NimbusLookAndFeel"
);
```

This method call should be contained within a `try-catch` block because it might generate five different exceptions. Catching the `Exception` class and ignoring it causes the default look and feel to be used in the unlikely circumstance that Nimbus can't be chosen properly.

**CAUTION**

Using `EXIT_ON_CLOSE` shuts down the entire JVM, so it should be used only in the frame for an application's main window. If anything needs to happen after the frame closes, `DISPOSE_ON_CLOSE` or `HIDE_ON_CLOSE` should be used instead.

9

## Developing a Framework

This lesson's first project is an application that displays a frame containing no other interface components. In NetBeans, create a new Java file with the class name SimpleFrame and the package name com.java21days and then enter Listing 9.1 as the source code. This simple application displays a frame 300×100 pixels in size and can serve as a framework—pun unavoidable—for any applications you create that use a GUI.

**LISTING 9.1**  The Full Text of SimpleFrame.java

```
 1: package com.java21days;
 2:
 3: import javax.swing.*;
 4:
 5: public class SimpleFrame extends JFrame {
 6:     public SimpleFrame() {
 7:         super("Frame Title");
 8:         setSize(300, 100);
 9:         setDefaultCloseOperation(JFrame.EXIT_ON_CLOSE);
10:         setVisible(true);
11:     }
12:
13:     private static void setLookAndFeel() {
14:         try {
15:             UIManager.setLookAndFeel(
16:                 "javax.swing.plaf.nimbus.NimbusLookAndFeel"
17:             );
18:         } catch (Exception exc) {
19:             // ignore error
20:         }
21:     }
22:
23:     public static void main(String[] arguments) {
24:         setLookAndFeel();
25:         SimpleFrame sf = new SimpleFrame();
26:     }
27: }
```

When you compile and run the application, you should see the frame displayed in Figure 9.1.

**FIGURE 9.1**
Displaying a frame.

The `SimpleFrame` application isn't much to look at. The GUI contains no components, aside from the standard Minimize, Maximize, and Close (X) buttons on the title bar, as shown in Figure 9.1. You'll add components later in this lesson.

In the application, a `SimpleFrame` object is created in the `main()` method in lines 23–26. If you had not displayed the frame when it was constructed, you could call `sf.setVisible(true)` in the `main()` method to display the frame.

Nimbus is set as the frame's look and feel in lines 15–17.

The work involved in creating the frame's user interface takes place in the `SimpleFrame()` constructor in lines 6–11. Components can be created and added to the frame within this constructor.

9

## Creating a Component

Creating a GUI is a great way to get experience working with objects in Java because each interface component is represented by its own class.

To use an interface component in Java, you create an object of that component's class. You already have worked with the container class `JFrame`.

One of the simplest components to employ is `JButton`, the class that represents clickable buttons.

In any program, buttons trigger actions. You could click Install to begin installing software, click a Run button to begin a new game of Angry Birds, click the Minimize button to prevent your boss from seeing Angry Birds running, and so on.

A Swing button can feature a text label, a graphical icon, or both.

You can use the following constructors for buttons:

- `JButton(String)`: A button labeled with the specified text
- `JButton(Icon)`: A button that displays the specified graphical icon
- `JButton(String, Icon)`: A button with the specified text and graphical icon

The following statements create three buttons with text labels:

```
JButton play = new JButton("Play");
JButton stop = new JButton("Stop");
JButton rewind = new JButton("Rewind");
```

Graphical buttons with icons are covered later in this lesson.

## Adding Components to a Container

Before you can display a user interface component such as a button in a Java program, you must add it to a container and display that container.

To add a component to a container, call the container's add(*Component*) method with the component as the argument. (All user interface components in Swing inherit from java. awt.Component.)

The simplest Swing container is a panel (the JPanel class). The following example creates a button and adds it to a panel:

```
JButton quit = new JButton("Quit");
JPanel panel = new JPanel();
panel.add(quit);
```

Use the same technique to add components to frames and windows.

The ButtonFrame class, shown in Listing 9.2, expands on the application framework created earlier in this lesson. A panel is created, three buttons are added to the panel, and then the panel is added to a frame. Enter the source code of Listing 9.2 into a new Java file called ButtonFrame in NetBeans, making sure to put it in the com.java21days package.

**LISTING 9.2**   The Full Text of ButtonFrame.java

```
 1: package com.java21days;
 2:
 3: import javax.swing.*;
 4:
 5: public class ButtonFrame extends JFrame {
 6:     JButton load = new JButton("Load");
 7:     JButton save = new JButton("Save");
 8:     JButton unsubscribe = new JButton("Unsubscribe");
 9:
10:     public ButtonFrame() {
11:         super("Button Frame");
12:         setSize(340, 170);
13:         setDefaultCloseOperation(JFrame.EXIT_ON_CLOSE);
14:         JPanel pane = new JPanel();
15:         pane.add(load);
16:         pane.add(save);
17:         pane.add(unsubscribe);
18:         add(pane);
19:         setVisible(true);
20:     }
21:
22:     private static void setLookAndFeel() {
23:         .    try {
```

```
24:                UIManager.setLookAndFeel(
25:                    "javax.swing.plaf.nimbus.NimbusLookAndFeel"
26:                );
27:            } catch (Exception exc) {
28:                System.out.println(exc.getMessage());
29:            }
30:        }
31:
32:        public static void main(String[] arguments) {
33:            setLookAndFeel();
34:            ButtonFrame bf = new ButtonFrame();
35:        }
36: }
```

9

When you run the application, a small frame opens that contains the three buttons, as shown in Figure 9.2.

**FIGURE 9.2**
The `ButtonFrame` application.

The `ButtonFrame` class has three instance variables: the `load`, `save`, and `unsubscribe` `JButton` objects.

In lines 14–17 of Listing 9.2, a new `JPanel` object is created, and the three buttons are added to the panel by calls to its `add(Component)` method. When the panel contains all the buttons, the frame's own `add(Component)` method is called in line 18 with the panel as an argument, and the panel is added to the frame.

**NOTE**

If you click the buttons at this point, nothing happens. Doing something in response to a button click is covered in Lesson 12, "Responding to User Input."

# Working with Components

Swing offers more than two dozen user interface components in addition to the buttons and containers you have used so far. You will work with many of these components throughout the rest of this lesson and further in Lesson 10, "Building an Interface."

All Swing components inherit several useful methods from their common superclass, JComponent.

The setEnabled(*boolean*) method determines whether a component can receive user input (the argument true) or is inactive and cannot receive input (false). Components are enabled by default. Many components change in appearance to indicate whether they are presently usable. For instance, a disabled JButton has light gray borders and gray text. If you want to check whether a component is enabled, you can call the isEnabled() method, which returns a boolean value.

The setVisible(*boolean*) method works for all components the way it does for containers. Use true to display a component and false to hide it. There also is a boolean isVisible() method.

The setSize(*int, int*) method resizes the component to the width and height specified as arguments, and setSize(*Dimension*) uses a Dimension object to accomplish the same thing. For most components, you don't need to set a size; the default is usually acceptable. To find out a component's size, call its getSize() method, which returns a Dimension object with the dimensions in height and width instance variables.

As you will see, similar Swing components have other methods in common inherited from superclasses, such as setText() and getText() for text components and setValue() and getValue() for components that store numeric values.

**CAUTION**

> When working with Swing components, a common source of mistakes is to set up aspects of a component after it has been added to a container. Be sure to set up a component fully with all required configuration before placing it in a panel or any other container.

## Image Icons

Swing supports the use of graphical ImageIcon objects on buttons and other components in which a label can be provided. An *icon* is a small graphic that can be placed on a button, a label, or another user interface element to identify it. Examples include a garbage can or recycling bin icon for deleting files and folder icons for opening and storing files.

You can create an ImageIcon object by specifying the filename of a graphic as the only argument to the constructor. The following example loads an icon from the graphics file subscribe.gif and creates a JButton with the icon as its label:

```
ImageIcon subscribe = new ImageIcon("subscribe.gif");
JButton button = new JButton(subscribe);
JPanel pane = new JPanel();
```

```
pane.add(button);
add(pane);
setVisible(true);
```

Listing 9.3 is a Java application that creates four image icons with text labels, adds them to a panel, and then adds the panel to a frame. Create a new empty Java file in NetBeans for a class named `IconFrame` in the package `com.java21days` and enter this listing with the source code editor.

**LISTING 9.3**    The Full Text of `IconFrame.java`

9

```
 1: package com.java21days;
 2:
 3: import javax.swing.*;
 4:
 5: public class IconFrame extends JFrame {
 6:     JButton load, save, subscribe, unsubscribe;
 7:
 8:     public IconFrame() {
 9:         super("Icon Frame");
10:         setDefaultCloseOperation(JFrame.EXIT_ON_CLOSE);
11:         JPanel panel = new JPanel();
12:         // create icons
13:         ImageIcon loadIcon = new ImageIcon("load.gif");
14:         ImageIcon saveIcon = new ImageIcon("save.gif");
15:         ImageIcon subscribeIcon = new ImageIcon("subscribe.gif");
16:         ImageIcon unsubscribeIcon = new ImageIcon("unsubscribe.gif");
17:         // create buttons
18:         load = new JButton("Load", loadIcon);
19:         save = new JButton("Save", saveIcon);
20:         subscribe = new JButton("Subscribe", subscribeIcon);
21:         unsubscribe = new JButton("Unsubscribe", unsubscribeIcon);
22:         // add buttons to panel
23:         panel.add(load);
24:         panel.add(save);
25:         panel.add(subscribe);
26:         panel.add(unsubscribe);
27:         // add the panel to a frame
28:         add(panel);
29:         pack();
30:         setVisible(true);
31:     }
32:
33:     public static void main(String[] arguments) {
34:         IconFrame ike = new IconFrame();
35:     }
36: }
```

Figure 9.3 shows the result.

**FIGURE 9.3**
An interface containing buttons
labeled with icons.

The icons' graphics referred to in lines 13–16 can be found on this book's official
website, at www.java21days.com, on the Lesson 9 page.

In NetBeans, the graphics must be part of the project in order for this application to run
correctly. The graphics need to be stored in the main folder of the Java21 project you've
been using throughout this book to hold the classes you create. Follow these steps:

1. Save the graphics files to a temporary folder on your computer.

2. Click the Files tab to bring that pane to the front. The Files pane opens, as shown in
   Figure 9.4, listing the files in the project.

**FIGURE 9.4**
Dragging files into the
NetBeans Files pane.

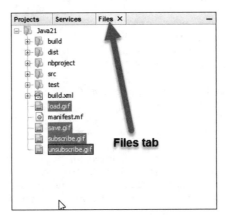

3. Drag and drop the four graphics files into the Java21 folder in this pane.

The IconFrame application does not set the size of the frame in pixels. Instead, the
pack() method is called in line 29 to expand the frame to the minimum size required to
present the four buttons next to each other.

If the frame were set to be tall rather than wide—for instance, by calling setSize(100,
400) in the constructor—the buttons would be stacked vertically.

9

**NOTE**
Some of the project's graphics are from Oracle's Java Look and Feel Graphics Repository, a collection of icons suitable for use in your own programs. If you're looking for icons to experiment with in Swing applications, you can find some at www.oracle.com/technetwork/java/index-138612.html.

# Labels

A *label* is a component that holds text, an icon, or both. Labels, which are created from the JLabel class, identify the purposes of other components on an interface. A user cannot edit them directly.

To create a label, you can use these simple constructors:

- JLabel(*String*): A label with the specified text
- JLabel(*String*, *int*): A label with the specified text and alignment
- JLabel(*String*, *Icon*, *int*): A label with the specified text, icon, and alignment

A label's alignment determines how its text or icon is aligned in relation to the area taken up by the window. Three static class variables of the SwingConstants interface are used to specify alignment: LEFT, CENTER, and RIGHT.

You can set a label's contents with the setText(*String*) or setIcon(*Icon*) methods. You also can retrieve these things with the getText() and getIcon() methods.

The following statements create three labels with left, center, and right alignment, respectively:

```
JLabel feedsLabel = new JLabel("Feeds: ", SwingConstants.LEFT);
JLabel urlLabel = new JLabel("URL: ", SwingConstants.CENTER);
JLabel dateLabel = new JLabel("Date: ", SwingConstants.RIGHT);
```

# Text Fields

A *text field* is a location on an interface where a user can enter and modify text using the keyboard. Text fields are represented by the JTextField class, and each can handle one line of input. The next section describes a text area component that can handle multiple lines.

Constructors for text fields include the following:

- JTextField(): An empty text field
- JTextField(*int*): A text field with the specified width
- JTextField(*String*, *int*): A text field with the specified text and width

A text field's width attribute has relevance only if the interface is organized in a manner that does not resize components. You'll get more experience with this when you work with layout managers in Lesson 11, "Arranging Components on a User Interface."

The following statements create an empty text field that has enough space for roughly 60 characters and a text field of the same size with the starting text "Enter feed URL here":

```
JTextField rssUrl = new JTextField(60);
JTextField rssUrl2 = new JTextField("Enter feed URL here", 60);
```

Text fields and text areas both inherit from the superclass `JTextComponent`, and they share many common methods.

The `setEditable(boolean)` method determines whether a text component can be edited (`true`) or not (`false`). An `isEditable()` method returns a corresponding `boolean` value.

The `setText(String)` method changes the text to the specified string, and the `getText()` method returns the component's current text as a string. Another method retrieves only the text that a user has highlighted in the `getSelectedText()` component.

Password fields are text fields that hide the characters a user types into the field. They are represented by the `JPasswordField` class, a subclass of `JTextField`. The `JPasswordField` constructors take the same arguments as those of the parent class.

After you have created a password field, call its `setEchoChar(char)` method to obscure input by replacing each input character with the specified character.

The following statements create a password field and set its echo character to #:

```
JPasswordField codePhrase = new JPasswordField(20);
codePhrase.setEchoChar('#');
```

## Text Areas

*Text areas*, editable text fields that can handle more than one line of input, are implemented by the `JTextArea` class. It has these constructors:

- `JTextArea(int, int)`: A text area with the specified number of rows and columns
- `JTextArea(String, int, int)`: A text area with the specified text, rows, and columns

You can use the `getText()`, `getSelectedText()`, and `setText(String)` methods with text areas as you would text fields. Also, an `append(String)` method adds the specified text at the end of the current text, and an `insert(String, int)` method inserts the specified text at the indicated position.

The `setLineWrap(boolean)` method determines whether text entered into the component will wrap to the next line when it reaches the right edge. Call `setLineWrap(true)` to cause line wrapping to occur.

The `setWrapStyleWord(boolean)` method determines what wraps to the next line—either the current word (`true`) or the current character (`false`).

The next project you'll create, the `Authenticator` application shown in Listing 9.4, uses several Swing components to collect user input: a text field, a password field, and a text area. Labels also are used to indicate the purpose of each text component. In NetBeans, create an empty Java file called `Authenticator` in the package `com.java21days`.

9

**LISTING 9.4**    The Full Text of `Authenticator.java`

```
 1: package com.java21days;
 2:
 3: import javax.swing.*;
 4:
 5: public class Authenticator extends javax.swing.JFrame {
 6:     JTextField username = new JTextField(15);
 7:     JPasswordField password = new JPasswordField(15);
 8:     JTextArea comments = new JTextArea(4, 15);
 9:     JButton ok = new JButton("OK");
10:     JButton cancel = new JButton("Cancel");
11:
12:     public Authenticator() {
13:         super("Account Information");
14:         setSize(300, 220);
15:         setDefaultCloseOperation(JFrame.EXIT_ON_CLOSE);
16:
17:         JPanel pane = new JPanel();
18:         JLabel usernameLabel = new JLabel("Username: ");
19:         JLabel passwordLabel = new JLabel("Password: ");
20:         JLabel commentsLabel = new JLabel("Comments: ");
21:         comments.setLineWrap(true);
22:         comments.setWrapStyleWord(true);
23:         pane.add(usernameLabel);
24:         pane.add(username);
25:         pane.add(passwordLabel);
26:         pane.add(password);
27:         pane.add(commentsLabel);
28:         pane.add(comments);
29:         pane.add(ok);
30:         pane.add(cancel);
31:         add(pane);
32:         setVisible(true);
33:     }
34:
```

```
35:     private static void setLookAndFeel() {
36:         try {
37:             UIManager.setLookAndFeel(
38:                 "javax.swing.plaf.nimbus.NimbusLookAndFeel"
39:             );
40:         } catch (Exception exc) {
41:             System.out.println(exc.getMessage());
42:         }
43:     }
44:
45:     public static void main(String[] arguments) {
46:         Authenticator.setLookAndFeel();
47:         Authenticator auth = new Authenticator();
48:     }
49: }
```

This application sets up components and adds them to a panel in lines 17–30. Figure 9.5 shows the application in use. The password is obscured with asterisk characters (*), which is the default when no other echo character is designated through a call to the field's `setEchoChar(char)` method.

**FIGURE 9.5**
The Authenticator application.

The text area in this application behaves in a manner that you might not expect. When you reach the bottom of the field and continue entering text, the component grows to make more room for input (and even scrolls below the bottom edge of the frame). The next section describes how to add scrollbars to prevent the area from changing in size.

## Scrolling Panes

Text areas in Swing do not include horizontal or vertical scrollbars, and there's no way to add them using this component alone.

Swing supports scrollbars through a container that can be used to hold any component that can be scrolled: `JScrollPane`.

A scrolling pane is associated with a component in the pane's constructor. You can use the following constructors:

- **JScrollPane(Component):** A scrolling pane that contains the specified component
- **JScrollPane(Component, int, int):** A scrolling pane with the specified component, vertical scrollbar configuration, and horizontal scrollbar configuration

Scrollbars are configured using one of six static class variables of the ScrollPaneConstants interface. There are three for vertical scrollbars:

- VERTICAL_SCROLLBAR_ALWAYS
- VERTICAL_SCROLLBAR_AS_NEEDED
- VERTICAL_SCROLLBAR_NEVER

9

There also are three variables for horizontal scrollbars with the names you'd expect.

After you create a scrolling pane containing a component, you can add the pane to containers in place of that component.

The following example creates a text area with a vertical scrollbar and no horizontal scrollbar and then adds it to a container:

```
JPanel pane = new JPanel();
JTextArea comments = new JTextArea(4, 15);
JScrollPane scroll = new JScrollPane(comments,
    ScrollPaneConstants.VERTICAL_SCROLLBAR_ALWAYS,
    ScrollPaneConstants.HORIZONTAL_SCROLLBAR_NEVER);
pane.add(scroll);
add(pane);
```

**NOTE**

This book's website contains `Authenticator2`, a full application that makes use of this code. Visit www.java21days.com and open the Lesson 9 page to find a link to `Authenticator2.java`.

# Check Boxes and Radio Buttons

Check boxes and radio buttons hold only two possible values: selected or not selected.

Check boxes are used to make simple choices in an interface, such as yes/no or on/off. Radio buttons are grouped so that only one button can be selected at any time.

Check boxes (the `JCheckBox` class) appear as labeled or unlabeled boxes that contain a check mark when they are selected and nothing otherwise. Radio buttons (the `JRadioButton` class) appear as circles that contain a dot when selected and nothing otherwise.

Both the `JCheckBox` and `JRadioButton` classes have several useful methods inherited from `JToggleButton`, their common superclass:

- `setSelected(boolean):` Selects the component if the argument is `true` and deselects it otherwise
- `isSelected():` Returns a Boolean indicating whether the component is currently selected

The following constructors can be used for the `JCheckBox` class:

- `JCheckBox(String):` A check box with the specified text label
- `JCheckBox(String, boolean):` A check box with the specified text label that is selected if the second argument is `true`
- `JCheckBox(Icon):` A check box with the specified graphical icon
- `JCheckBox(Icon, boolean):` A check box with the specified graphical icon that is selected if the second argument is `true`
- `JCheckBox(String, Icon):` A check box with the specified text label and graphical icon
- `JCheckBox(String, Icon, boolean):` A check box with the specified text label and graphical icon that is selected if the third argument is `true`

The `JRadioButton` class has constructors with the same arguments and functionality.

Check boxes and radio buttons by themselves are *nonexclusive*, meaning that if you have five check boxes in a container, all five can be checked or unchecked at the same time. To make them exclusive, as radio buttons should be, you must organize related components into groups.

To organize several radio buttons into a group, allowing only one to be selected at a time, create a `ButtonGroup` class object, as demonstrated in the following statement:

```
ButtonGroup choice = new ButtonGroup();
```

The `ButtonGroup` object keeps track of all radio buttons in its group. Call the group's `add(Component)` method to add the specified component to the group.

The following example creates a group and two radio buttons that belong to it:

```
ButtonGroup saveFormat = new ButtonGroup();
JRadioButton s1 = new JRadioButton("JSON", false);
saveFormat.add(s1);
JRadioButton s2 = new JRadioButton("XML", true);
saveFormat.add(s2);
```

The saveFormat object groups the s1 and s2 radio buttons. The s2 object, which has the label "XML", is selected. Only one member of the group can be selected at a time. If one component is selected, the ButtonGroup object ensures that all others in the group are deselected.

Create a new empty Java file in NetBeans called FormatFrame in the package com.java21days. Enter the source code shown in Listing 9.5 to create an application with four radio buttons in a group.

**LISTING 9.5**  The Full Text of FormatFrame.java

```
 1: package com.java21days;
 2:
 3: import javax.swing.*;
 4:
 5: public class FormatFrame extends JFrame {
 6:     JRadioButton[] teams = new JRadioButton[4];
 7:
 8:     public FormatFrame() {
 9:         super("Choose an Output Format");
10:         setSize(320, 120);
11:         setDefaultCloseOperation(JFrame.EXIT_ON_CLOSE);
12:         teams[0] = new JRadioButton("Atom");
13:         teams[1] = new JRadioButton("RSS 0.92");
14:         teams[2] = new JRadioButton("RSS 1.0");
15:         teams[3] = new JRadioButton("RSS 2.0", true);
16:         JPanel panel = new JPanel();
17:         JLabel chooseLabel = new JLabel(
18:             "Choose an output format for syndicated news items.");
19:         panel.add(chooseLabel);
20:         ButtonGroup group = new ButtonGroup();
21:         for (JRadioButton team : teams) {
22:             group.add(team);
23:             panel.add(team);
24:         }
25:         add(panel);
26:         setVisible(true);
27:     }
28:
29:     private static void setLookAndFeel() {
```

```
30:            try {
31:                UIManager.setLookAndFeel(
32:                    "com.sun.java.swing.plaf.nimbus.NimbusLookAndFeel"
33:                );
34:            } catch (Exception exc) {
35:                System.out.println(exc.getMessage());
36:            }
37:        }
38:
39:        public static void main(String[] arguments) {
40:            FormatFrame.setLookAndFeel();
41:            FormatFrame ff = new FormatFrame();
42:        }
43: }
```

Figure 9.6 shows the application running. The four JRadioButton objects are stored in an array in lines 12–15. In the for loop in lines 21–24, each element is first added to a button group and then is added to a panel. After the loop ends, the panel is added to the frame.

**FIGURE 9.6**
The FormatFrame application.

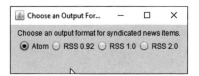

Choosing one of the radio buttons causes the existing choice to be deselected.

## Combo Boxes

The Swing class JComboBox can be used to create combo boxes, components that present a drop-down menu from which a single value can be selected. The menu is hidden when the component is not being used, thus taking up less space in a GUI.

After a combo box is created by calling the JComboBox() constructor with no arguments, the combo box's addItem(Object) method adds items to the list.

Another way to create a combo box is to call JComboBox(Object[]) with an array that contains the items. If the items are text, a String array would be the argument.

In a combo box, users can select only one of the items on the drop-down menu. If the component's setEditable() method is called with true as an argument, it also supports text entry. This feature gives combo boxes their name: A component configured in this manner serves as both a drop-down menu and a text field.

The JComboBox class has several methods you can use to control a drop-down list or combo box:

- **getItemAt(*int*):** Returns the text of the list item at the index position specified by the integer argument. As with arrays, the first item of a choice list is at index position 0, the second is at position 1, and so on.

- **getItemCount():** Returns the number of items in the list.

- **getSelectedIndex():** Returns the index position of the currently selected item in the list.

- **getSelectedItem():** Returns the text of the currently selected item.

- **setSelectedIndex(*int*):** Selects the item at the indicated index position.

- **setSelectedIndex(*Object*):** Selects the specified object in the list.

The FormatFrame2 application, shown in Listing 9.6, rewrites the preceding radio button example. The program uses a noneditable combo box from which a user can choose one of four options.

**LISTING 9.6**    The Full Text of FormatFrame2.java

```
 1: package com.java21days;
 2:
 3: import javax.swing.*;
 4:
 5: public class FormatFrame2 extends JFrame {
 6:     String[] formats = { "Atom", "RSS 0.92", "RSS 1.0", "RSS 2.0" };
 7:     JComboBox<String> formatBox = new JComboBox<>(formats);
 8:
 9:     public FormatFrame2() {
10:         super("Choose a Format");
11:         setSize(220, 150);
12:         setDefaultCloseOperation(JFrame.EXIT_ON_CLOSE);
13:         JPanel pane = new JPanel();
14:         JLabel formatLabel = new JLabel("Output formats:");
15:         pane.add(formatLabel);
16:         pane.add(formatBox);
17:         add(pane);
18:         setVisible(true);
19:     }
20:
21:     private static void setLookAndFeel() {
22:         try {
23:             UIManager.setLookAndFeel(
24:                 "com.sun.java.swing.plaf.nimbus.NimbusLookAndFeel"
25:             );
26:         } catch (Exception exc) {
```

```
27:                    System.out.println(exc.getMessage());
28:            }
29:       }
30:
31:     public static void main(String[] arguments) {
32:            FormatFrame2.setLookAndFeel();
33:            FormatFrame2 ff = new FormatFrame2();
34:       }
35: }
```

A string array is defined in line 6, and then these strings are used in the combo box constructor in line 7 to set its possible values. The JComboBox constructor uses generics to indicate that its values are strings. Figure 9.7 shows the application as the combo box is expanded so that a value can be selected.

**FIGURE 9.7**
The FormatFrame2 application.

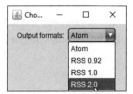

# Lists

The last Swing component to be introduced in this lesson is similar to combo boxes. Lists, which are represented by the JList class, allow you to select one or more values.

You can create and fill lists with the contents of an array or a vector (a data structure similar to array lists). The following constructors are available:

- JList(): Creates an empty list
- JList(*Object []*): Creates a list that contains an array of the specified class (such as String)
- JList(*Vector<Class>*)[: Creates a list that contains the specified java.util. Vector object of the specified class

An empty list can be filled by calling its setListData() method with either an array or a vector as the only argument.

Unlike combo boxes, lists display more than one of their rows when they are presented in a user interface. The default is to display eight items. To change this, call setVisibleRowCount(*int*) with the number of items to display.

The `getSelectedValuesList()` method returns a list of objects containing all the items selected in the list. This list can be cast to an `ArrayList`.

You can use generics with `JList` to indicate the class of the object array the list contains.

The `Subscriptions` application in the `com.java21days` package, shown in Listing 9.7, displays items from an array of strings.

**LISTING 9.7**   The Full Text of `Subscriptions.java`

```
 1: package com.java21days;
 2:
 3: import javax.swing.*;
 4:
 5: public class Subscriptions extends JFrame {
 6:     String[] subs = { "Burningbird", "Freeform Goodness", "Inessential",
 7:         "Manton.org", "Micro Thoughts", "Rasterweb", "Self Made Minds",
 8:         "Whole Lotta Nothing", "Workbench" };
 9:     JList<String> subList = new JList<>(subs);
10:
11:     public Subscriptions() {
12:         super("Subscriptions");
13:         setSize(150, 335);
14:         setDefaultCloseOperation(JFrame.EXIT_ON_CLOSE);
15:         JPanel panel = new JPanel();
16:         JLabel subLabel = new JLabel("RSS Subscriptions:");
17:         panel.add(subLabel);
18:         subList.setVisibleRowCount(8);
19:         JScrollPane scroller = new JScrollPane(subList);
20:         panel.add(scroller);
21:         add(panel);
22:         setVisible(true);
23:     }
24:
25:     private static void setLookAndFeel() {
26:         try {
27:             UIManager.setLookAndFeel(
28:                 "javax.swing.plaf.nimbus.NimbusLookAndFeel"
29:             );
30:         } catch (Exception exc) {
31:             System.out.println(exc.getMessage());
32:         }
33:     }
34:
35:     public static void main(String[] arguments) {
36:         Subscriptions.setLookAndFeel();
37:         Subscriptions app = new Subscriptions();
38:     }
39: }
```

9

The application is shown in Figure 9.8. The `Subscriptions` application has an interface with a label atop a list displaying nine items. A `JScrollPane` is used in lines 19–20 to enable the list to be scrolled to see the list's final item, which wouldn't be visible otherwise. It's a container that causes its contents to have scrollbars so that it doesn't take up too much space in a user interface.

**FIGURE 9.8**
The `Subscriptions` application.

## The Java Class Library

The first part of this book is devoted to the building blocks of the Java language, including statements, expressions, and operators, and the components of object-oriented programming (OOP), such as methods, constructors, classes, and interfaces.

The second part covers how to build things with those blocks by using the Java Class Library. A lot of your work as a programmer is done for you, provided that you know where to look.

The Java Class Library contains more than 4,400 classes. Many of them will be useful in programs that you create.

**NOTE**

There also are Java class libraries produced by other organizations. Apache has more than a dozen Java open source projects, including `HttpComponents`, a set of classes for creating web servers, clients, and crawlers. To see these projects, visit http://projects.apache.org. You can search for useful Java class libraries in the Maven Central Repository at https://search.maven.org.

Oracle offers comprehensive documentation for the Java Class Library on the Web. A page from this documentation is shown in Figure 9.9.

**FIGURE 9.9**
The Java Class
Library's online
documentation.

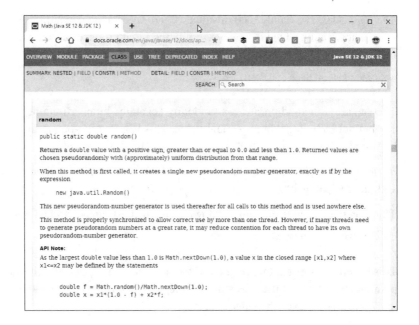

9

The home page is divided into sections. The largest section lists all the packages that compose the library, with a description of each. A package's name describes its purpose, such as the `java.io` package of classes for input and output from files, Internet servers, and other data sources; and `java.time` for time and date classes.

On the home page, the largest section presents a list of packages and a short description of each one. Click the name of a package to load a page listing all of its classes.

Each class in the library has its own page of documentation. To get a taste of how to use this reference, follow these steps:

1. In a web browser, load the page https://docs.oracle.com/en/java/javase/12/docs/api.

2. Click the java.base link.

3. Click the link for the `java.lang` package. That package's page opens.

4. Scroll down to the link for the `Math` class and click it. The page for the class opens.

5. Find the `random()` method link and click it. The page jumps to that section.

The `Math` class page describes the purpose and package for this class. Use a class page to learn how to create an object of the class and what variables and methods it contains.

The `Math` class has handy methods that extend Java's math capabilities and turn up often in Java applications. One is `random()`, a method that produces a random `double` value from 0.0 to 1.0. Here's a statement that uses this method:

```
double d100 = Math.random() * 100;
```

The `random()` method produces a randomly generated number ranging from 0.0 up to 1.0, but not including that maximum value. This is a floating-point number, so it needs to be stored in a `float` or `double`.

Because this random number is multiplied by 100, the number will be anything from 0 to 100 (not including 100).

This statement rounds the number down to the nearest integer and adds 1:

```
d100 = Math.floor(roll) + 1;
```

This statement uses another method of the `Math` class, `floor()`, which rounds a floating-point number down to the closest lower integer. A value of 47.52 would be rounded down to 47. Adding 1 makes the value of `d100` 48.

Without the `Math` class, you'd have to create your own class to produce random numbers, which is a highly complex task.

Poking around the Java Class Library documentation is a good way to find classes that will save you an enormous amount of time.

Because you're new to Java, you likely will find some of the documentation difficult to understand as it's written for experienced programmers. But as you read this book and encounter interesting Java classes, use this reference to find out more about them. A good place to begin is to look up the methods in a class, each of which performs a job, and see what arguments they take and what values they return.

While you are learning about Swing user interface components and classes in the next five lessons, check out their pages in the official documentation. They have more cool methods than this book has time to cover.

# Summary

In this lesson you began working with Swing, the package of classes that enables your Java programs to support a GUI.

You used more than a dozen classes in this lesson, creating interface components such as buttons, labels, and text fields. You put each of these into containers: components that include panels, frames, and windows.

This kind of programming can be complicated. Swing is the largest package of classes that a new Java programmer must deal with in learning the language. However, as you have experienced with components such as text areas and text fields, Swing components have many superclasses in common. This makes it easier to extend your knowledge into new components and containers, along with the other aspects of Swing programming you will explore in the coming lessons.

# Q&A

**Q Is there a way to change the font of text that appears on a button and other components?**

**A** The `JComponent` class includes a `setFont(Font)` method that can be used to set the font for text displayed by that component. You will work with `Font` objects, color, and more graphics in Lesson 13, "Creating Java2D Graphics."

# Quiz

Review this lesson's material by taking this three-question quiz.

## Questions

1. Which of the following user interface components is not a container?

   **A.** `JScrollPane`

   **B.** `JTextArea`

   **C.** `JPanel`

2. Which component can be placed into a Scroll pane?

   **A.** `JTextArea`

   **B.** `JTextField`

   **C.** Any component

3. If you use `setSize()` on an application's main frame, where will it appear on your desktop?

   **A.** In the center of the desktop

   **B.** In the same spot where the last application appeared

   **C.** In the upper-left corner of the desktop

## Answers

**1.** B. `JTextArea` requires a container to support scrolling, but it is not a container itself.

**2.** C. Any component can be added to a Scroll pane, but most are unlikely to need scrolling.

**3.** C. This is a trick question. Calling `setSize()` has nothing to do with a window's position on the desktop. You must call `setBounds()` rather than `setSize()` to choose where a frame will appear.

## Certification Practice

The following question is the kind of thing you could expect to be asked on a Java programming certification test. Answer it without looking again at this lesson or using the Java compiler to test the code.

Given:

```
import javax.swing.*;

public class Display extends JFrame {
    public Display() {
        super("Display");
        // answer goes here
        JLabel hello = new JLabel("Hello");
        JPanel pane = new JPanel();
        add(hello);
        pack();
        setVisible(true);
    }

    public static void main(String[] arguments) {
        Display ds = new Display();
    }
}
```

What statement needs to replace `// answer goes here` to make the application function properly?

**A.** `setSize(300, 200);`

**B.** `setDefaultCloseOperation(JFrame.EXIT_ON_CLOSE);`

**C.** `Display ds = new Display();`

**D.** No statement is needed.

The answer is available on the book's website, at www.java21days.com. Visit the Lesson 9 page and click the Certification Practice link.

# Exercises

To extend your knowledge of the subjects covered in this lesson, try the following exercises:

1. Create an application with a frame that includes several DVR controls as individual components: play, stop/eject, rewind, fast-forward, and pause. Choose a size for the window that enables all the components to be displayed on a single row.

2. Create a frame that opens a smaller frame with fields asking for a username and password.

Where applicable, exercise solutions are offered on the book's website, at www.java21days.com.

9

# LESSON 10
# Building an Interface

Although computers can be operated in a command-line environment such as the Linux shell or Windows command prompt, most computer users expect software to feature a graphical user interface (GUI) and take input from a mouse and keyboard.

Working with GUI software can be one of the more challenging tasks for a novice programmer, but as you learned in the previous lesson, Java has simplified the process with Swing.

Swing offers the following features:

- Common user interface components, including buttons, text fields, text areas, labels, check boxes, radio buttons, scrollbars, lists, menu items, and sliders.

- Containers—interface components that can be used to hold other components (including other containers). Containers include frames, panels, menus, menu bars, and tabbed panes.

# Swing Features

Most components and containers you've learned about so far have been Swing versions of classes that are part of the Abstract Window Toolkit, the original Java package for GUI programming.

Swing offers many additional new components, including keyboard mnemonics, tooltips, and standard dialogs.

## Standard Dialogs

The JOptionPane class offers several methods you can use to create standard dialogs: small windows that ask a question, warn a user, or provide an important message. Figure 10.1 shows an example.

**FIGURE 10.1**
A standard dialog.

You have doubtless seen dialogs like the one shown in Figure 10.1. When your system crashes, a dialog appears to break the bad news. When you delete files, a dialog pops up to make sure that you really want to do so.

Dialogs provide an effective way to communicate with a user without the overhead of creating a new class to represent the window, adding components to it, and writing event-handling methods to receive input. All these tasks are handled automatically when one of the standard dialogs offered by JOptionPane is used.

The four types of standard dialogs are as follows:

- Confirm Dialog: Asks a question, with buttons for Yes, No, and Cancel responses
- Input dialog: Prompts for text input
- Message dialog: Displays a message
- Option dialog: Combines all three of the other dialog types

Each of these dialogs has its own display method in the JOptionPane class.

## Confirm Dialogs

The easiest way to create a Yes/No/Cancel dialog is by calling the showConfirmDialog (Component, Object) method. The Component argument specifies the container that's the parent of the dialog, which determines where the dialog window should be displayed.

If `null` is used instead of a container, or if the container is not a `JFrame` object, the dialog will be centered onscreen.

The second argument, *Object*, can be a string, a component, or an `Icon` object. If it's a string, that text will be displayed in the dialog. If it's a component or an `Icon`, that object will be displayed in place of a text message.

The `showConfirmDialog()` method returns one of five possible integer values, each a class constant of JOptionPane: YES_OPTION, NO_OPTION, CANCEL_OPTION, OK_OPTION, or CLOSED_OPTION.

The following example uses a confirm dialog (refer to Figure 10.1) with a text message and stores the response in the `response` variable:

```
int response = JOptionPane.showConfirmDialog(null,
    "Should I delete all of your irreplaceable personal files?");
```

Another method offers more options for the dialog: showConfirmDialog(*Component*, *Object*, *String*, *int*, *int*). The first two arguments are the same as those in other `showConfirmDialog()` methods. The last three arguments are the following:

- A string that will be displayed in the dialog's title bar.
- An integer that indicates which option buttons will be shown. It should be equal to one of the class constants YES_NO_CANCEL_OPTION or YES_NO_OPTION.
- An integer that describes the kind of dialog it is, using the class constants ERROR_MESSAGE, INFORMATION_MESSAGE, PLAIN_MESSAGE, QUESTION_MESSAGE, or WARNING_MESSAGE. (This argument is used to determine which icon to draw in the dialog along with the message.)

For example:

```
int response = JOptionPane.showConfirmDialog(null,
    "Error reading file. Want to try again?",
    "File Input Error",
    JOptionPane.YES_NO_OPTION,
    JOptionPane.ERROR_MESSAGE);
```

Figure 10.2 shows the resulting dialog.

**FIGURE 10.2**
A confirm dialog with Yes and No buttons.

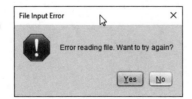

## Input Dialogs

An input dialog asks a question and uses a text field to store the response. Figure 10.3 shows an example.

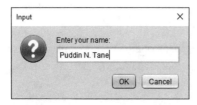

The easiest way to create an input dialog is with a call to the showInputDialog (*Component, Object*) method. The arguments are the parent component and the string, component, or icon to display.

The input dialog method call returns a string that represents the user's response. The following statement creates the input dialog shown in Figure 10.3:

```
String response = JOptionPane.showInputDialog(null,
    "Enter your name:");
```

You also can create an input dialog with the showInputDialog(*Component, Object, String, int*) method. The first two arguments are the same as in the shorter method call, and the last two are the following:

- The title to display in the dialog title bar
- One of five class constants describing the type of dialog: ERROR_MESSAGE, INFORMATION_MESSAGE, PLAIN_MESSAGE, QUESTION_MESSAGE, or WARNING_MESSAGE

The following statement uses this method to create an input dialog:

```
String response = JOptionPane.showInputDialog(null,
    "What is your ZIP code?",
    "Enter ZIP Code",
    JOptionPane.QUESTION_MESSAGE);
```

## Message Dialogs

A message dialog is a simple window that displays information, as shown in Figure 10.4.

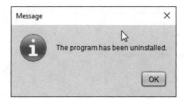

A message dialog can be created with a call to the showMessageDialog (*Component*, *Object*) method. As with other dialogs, the arguments are the parent component and the string, component, or icon to display.

Unlike the other dialogs, message dialogs do not return response values. The following statement creates the message dialog shown in Figure 10.4:

```
JOptionPane.showMessageDialog(null,
    "The program has been uninstalled.");
```

You also can create a message input dialog by calling the showMessageDialog (*Component*, *Object*, *String*, *int*) method. The use is identical to the use of the showInputDialog() method, with the same arguments, except that showMessageDialog() does not return a value.

The following statement creates a message dialog using this method:

```
JOptionPane.showMessageDialog(null,
    "An asteroid has destroyed the Earth.",
    "Asteroid Destruction Alert",
    JOptionPane.WARNING_MESSAGE);
```

**10**

## Option Dialogs

The most complex of the dialogs is the option dialog, which combines the features of all the other dialogs. It can be created with the showOptionDialog (*Component*, *Object*, *String*, *int*, *int*, *Icon*, *Object[]*, *Object*) method.

The arguments to this method are as follows:

- The parent component of the dialog
- The text, icon, or component to display
- A string to display in the title bar
- The type of option dialog, using the class constant YES_NO_OPTION or YES_NO_CANCEL_OPTION, or the value 0 if other buttons will be used instead
- The icon to display, using the class constants ERROR_MESSAGE, INFORMATION_MESSAGE, PLAIN_MESSAGE, QUESTION_MESSAGE, or WARNING_MESSAGE, or the value 0 if none of these should be used
- An Icon object to display instead of one of the icons in the preceding argument
- An array of objects holding the objects that represent the choices in the dialog if YES_NO_OPTION and YES_NO_CANCEL_OPTION are not being used
- The object representing the default selection if YES_NO_OPTION and YES_NO_CANCEL_OPTION are not being used

The final two arguments offer a wide range of possibilities for the dialog. You can create an array of strings that holds the text of each button to display.

The following example creates an option dialog that uses an array of `string` objects for the options in the box and the `osPreference[2]` element as the default selection:

```
String[] osPreference = {
    "Windows",
    "Mac OS",
    "Linux"
};
int response = JOptionPane.showOptionDialog(null,
    "What is your favorite OS?",
    "Operating System",
    0,
    JOptionPane.INFORMATION_MESSAGE,
    null,
    osPreference,
    osPreference[2]);
System.out.println("You chose " + osPreference[response]);
```

Figure 10.5 shows the resulting dialog.

**FIGURE 10.5**
An option dialog.

## Using Dialogs

The next project shows a series of dialogs in a working program. The `FeedInfo` application in the `com.java21days` package uses dialogs to get information from the user; that information is then placed into text fields in the application's main window.

Enter Listing 10.1 and save the result.

**LISTING 10.1**   The Full Text of `FeedInfo.java`

```
 1: package com.java21days;
 2:
 3: import java.awt.GridLayout;
 4: import java.awt.event.*;
 5: import javax.swing.*;
 6:
 7: public class FeedInfo extends JFrame {
 8:     private final JLabel nameLabel = new JLabel("Name: ",
 9:         SwingConstants.RIGHT);
10:     private final JTextField name;
```

```
11:     private final JLabel urlLabel = new JLabel("URL: ",
12:         SwingConstants.RIGHT);
13:     private final JTextField url;
14:     private final JLabel typeLabel = new JLabel("Type: ",
15:         SwingConstants.RIGHT);
16:     private final JTextField type;
17:
18:     public FeedInfo() {
19:         super("Feed Information");
20:         setSize(400, 145);
21:         setDefaultCloseOperation(JFrame.EXIT_ON_CLOSE);
22:         setLookAndFeel();
23:         // Site name
24:         String response1 = JOptionPane.showInputDialog(null,
25:             "Enter the site name:");
26:         name = new JTextField(response1, 20);
27:
28:         // Site address
29:         String response2 = JOptionPane.showInputDialog(null,
30:             "Enter the site address:");
31:         url = new JTextField(response2, 20);
32:
33:         // Site type
34:         String[] choices = { "Personal", "Commercial", "Unknown" };
35:         int response3 = JOptionPane.showOptionDialog(null,
36:             "What type of site is it?",
37:             "Site Type",
38:             0,
39:             JOptionPane.QUESTION_MESSAGE,
40:             null,
41:             choices,
42:             choices[0]);
43:         type = new JTextField(choices[response3], 20);
44:
45:         setLayout(new GridLayout(3, 2));
46:         add(nameLabel);
47:         add(name);
48:         add(urlLabel);
49:         add(url);
50:         add(typeLabel);
51:         add(type);
52:         setLookAndFeel();
53:         setVisible(true);
54:     }
55:
56:     private void setLookAndFeel() {
57:         try {
58:             UIManager.setLookAndFeel(
59:                 "javax.swing.plaf.nimbus.NimbusLookAndFeel"
60:             );
61:             SwingUtilities.updateComponentTreeUI(this);
62:         } catch (Exception e) {
63:             System.err.println("Couldn't use the system "
```

10

```
64:                        + "look and feel: " + e);
65:            }
66:        }
67:
68:        public static void main(String[] arguments) {
69:            FeedInfo frame = new FeedInfo();
70:        }
71: }
```

After you fill in the fields in each dialog, you see the application's main window, which is displayed in Figure 10.6. Three text fields have values supplied by dialogs.

**FIGURE 10.6**
The main window of the `FeedInfo` application.

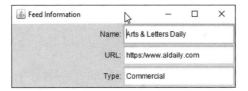

Much of this application is boilerplate code that can be used with any Swing application. The following lines relate to the dialogs:

- In lines 24–26, an input dialog asks the user to enter a site name. This name is used in the constructor for a `JTextField` object, placing it in the text field.

- In lines 29–31, a similar input dialog asks for a site address, which is used in the constructor for another `JTextField` object.

- In line 34, an array of `String` objects called `choices` is created, and three elements are given values.

- In lines 35–42, an option dialog asks for the site type. The `choices` array is the seventh argument, which sets up three buttons on the dialog, labeled with the strings in the array: `"Personal"`, `"Commercial"`, and `"Unknown"`. The last argument, `choices[0]`, designates the first array element as the default selection in the dialog.

- Line 43 contains the response to the option dialog—an integer identifying the array element that was selected. It is stored in a `JTextField` component called `type`.

The look and feel, which is established in the `setLookAndFeel()` method in lines 58–60, is called at the beginning and end of the frame's constructor. Because you're opening several dialogs in the constructor, you must set up the look and feel before opening them.

This class designates a look and feel differently than previous examples in this lesson. The `setLookAndFeel()` method is called within the constructor in line 22. To ensure that all components in the user interface reflect the look and feel, the `SwingUtilities` class method `SwingUtilities.updateComponentTreeUI(Component)` is called with `this` as the argument, which refers to the `FeedInfo` object being created.

# Sliders

Sliders, which are implemented in Swing with the JSlider class, enable the user to set a number by sliding a control within the range of a minimum value and maximum value. In many cases, a slider can be used for numeric input instead of a text field. This has the advantage of restricting input to a range of acceptable values.

Figure 10.7 shows a JSlider component.

Sliders are horizontal by default. You can explicitly set the orientation by using two class constants of the SwingConstants interface: HORIZONTAL or VERTICAL.

**FIGURE 10.7**
A JSlider
component.

You can use the following constructors:

- **JSlider(*int*):** A slider with the specified orientation, a minimum value of 0, maximum value of 100, and starting value of 50
- **JSlider(*int*, *int*):** A slider with the specified minimum value and maximum value
- **JSlider(*int*, *int*, *int*):** A slider with the specified minimum value, maximum value, and starting value
- **JSlider(*int*, *int*, *int*, *int*):** A slider with the specified orientation, minimum value, maximum value, and starting value

Slider components have an optional label that can be used to indicate the minimum value, maximum value, and two different sets of tick marks ranging between the values. The default values are a minimum of 0, maximum of 100, starting value of 50, and horizontal orientation.

The elements of this label are established by calling several methods of JSlider:

- **setMajorTickSpacing (*int*):** Separates major tick marks by the specified distance. The distance is not in pixels but in values between the minimum and maximum values represented by the slider.
- **setMinorTickSpacing (*int*):** Separates minor tick marks by the specified distance. Minor ticks are displayed as half the height of major ticks.
- **setPaintTicks (*boolean*):** Determines whether the tick marks should be displayed (true) or not (false).
- **setPaintLabels (*boolean*):** Determines whether the slider's numeric label should be displayed (true) or not (false).

These methods should be called on the slider before it is added to a container.

10

Listing 10.2 contains the `Slider.java` source code, which creates the application shown in Figure 10.7.

**LISTING 10.2**   The Full Text of `Slider.java`

```
 1: package com.java21days;
 2:
 3: import javax.swing.*;
 4:
 5: public class Slider extends JFrame {
 6:
 7:     public Slider() {
 8:         super("Slider");
 9:         setDefaultCloseOperation(JFrame.EXIT_ON_CLOSE);
10:         setLookAndFeel();
11:         JSlider pick = new JSlider(JSlider.HORIZONTAL, 0, 30, 5);
12:         pick.setMajorTickSpacing(10);
13:         pick.setMinorTickSpacing(1);
14:         pick.setPaintTicks(true);
15:         pick.setPaintLabels(true);
16:         add(pick);
17:         pack();
18:         setVisible(true);
19:     }
20:
21:     private void setLookAndFeel() {
22:         try {
23:             UIManager.setLookAndFeel(
24:                 "com.sun.java.swing.plaf.nimbus.NimbusLookAndFeel"
25:             );
26:             SwingUtilities.updateComponentTreeUI(this);
27:         } catch (Exception e) {
28:             System.err.println("Couldn't use the system "
29:                 + "look and feel: " + e);
30:         }
31:     }
32:
33:     public static void main(String[] arguments) {
34:         Slider frame = new Slider();
35:     }
36: }
```

Lines 12–17 contain the code that's used to create a `JSlider` component, set up its tick marks to be displayed, and add the component to a container. The rest of the program is a basic framework for an application that consists of a main `JFrame` container with no menus.

# Scroll Panes

In early versions of Java, text areas and some other components had a built-in scrollbar. Scrollbars could be used when the text in the component took up more space than the component could display. Scrollbars could be used in either the vertical or horizontal direction to scroll through the text.

One of the most common examples of scrolling is in a web browser, where a scrollbar can be used on any page that is bigger than the browser's display area.

Swing changes the rules for scrollbars to the following:

- For a component to be able to scroll, it must be added to a `JScrollPane` container.
- This `JScrollPane` container is added to a container in place of the scrollable component.

Scroll panes can be created using the `JScrollPane(Object)` constructor, where `Object` represents the component that can be scrolled.

10

The following example creates a text area in a Scroll pane called `scroller` and then adds it to a container called `mainPane`:

```java
JTextArea textBox = new JTextArea(7, 30);
JScrollPane scroller = new JScrollPane(textBox);
mainPane.add(scroller);
```

As you work with a Scroll pane, it can be useful to indicate the size you want it to occupy on the interface. You do so by calling the `setPreferredSize(Dimension)` method of the Scroll pane before adding it to a container. The `Dimension` object represents the width and height of the preferred size, in pixels.

The following code builds on the previous example by setting the preferred size of `scroller`:

```java
Dimension pref = new Dimension(350, 100);
scroller.setPreferredSize(pref);
```

You should set the dimensions before `scroller` is added to a container.

**CAUTION**

This is one of many situations in Swing where you must do something in the proper order for it to work correctly. For most components, the order is as follows: Create the component, set up the component fully, and add the component to a container.

By default, a Scroll pane does not display scrollbars unless they are needed. If the component inside the pane is no larger than the pane itself, the bars won't appear. In the case of components such as text areas, where the component size might increase as the program is used, the scrollbars automatically appear when they're needed and disappear when they're not.

To override this behavior, you can set a policy for a component when you create it, using one of several constants in the `ScrollPaneConstants` interface:

- `HORIZONTAL_SCROLLBAR_ALWAYS`
- `HORIZONTAL_SCROLLBAR_AS_NEEDED`
- `HORIZONTAL_SCROLLBAR_NEVER`
- `VERTICAL_SCROLLBAR_ALWAYS`
- `VERTICAL_SCROLLBAR_AS_NEEDED`
- `VERTICAL_SCROLLBAR_NEVER`

These class constants are used with the `JScrollPane(Object, int, int)` constructor, which specifies the component in the pane, the vertical scrollbar policy, and the horizontal scrollbar policy. Here's an example:

```
JScrollPane scroller = new JScrollPane(textBox,
    VERTICAL_SCROLLBAR_ALWAYS,
    HORIZONTAL_SCROLLBAR_NEVER);
```

## Toolbars

A *toolbar*, created in Swing with the `JToolBar` class, is a container that groups several components into a row or column. These components are most often buttons.

Toolbars are rows or columns of components that group the most commonly used program options. Toolbars often contain buttons and lists and can be used as an alternative to pull-down menus or shortcut keys.

Toolbars are horizontal by default, but the orientation can be set explicitly with the `HORIZONTAL` or `VERTICAL` class variables of the `SwingConstants` interface.

Constructors include the following:

- `JToolBar()`: Creates a new toolbar
- `JToolBar(int)`: Creates a new toolbar with the specified orientation

After you have created a toolbar, you can add components to it with the toolbar's `add(Object)` method, where `Object` represents the component to place on the toolbar.

Many programs that use toolbars enable the user to move the bars. These are called *dockable toolbars* because you can dock them along an edge of the screen, similar to docking a boat. Swing toolbars also can be docked to a new window, separate from the original.

For best results, a dockable JToolBar component should be arranged in a container using the BorderLayout class, which is a user interface class called a *layout manager*. A border layout divides a container into five areas: north, south, east, west, and center. Each of the directional components takes up whatever space it needs, and the rest are allocated to the center.

The toolbar should be placed in one of the directional areas of the border layout. The only other area of the layout that can be filled is the center. (You'll learn about layout managers such as border layout in Lesson 11, "Arranging Components on a User Interface.")

Figure 10.8 shows a dockable toolbar occupying the south area of a border layout. A text area has been placed in the center.

**10**

**FIGURE 10.8**
A dockable toolbar and a text area.

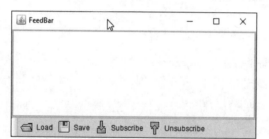

Listing 10.3 shows the source code used to produce this application.

**LISTING 10.3**    The Full Text of FeedBar.java

```
 1: package com.java21days;
 2:
 3: import java.awt.*;
 4: import javax.swing.*;
 5:
 6: public class FeedBar extends JFrame {
 7:
 8:     public FeedBar() {
 9:         super("FeedBar");
10:         setDefaultCloseOperation(JFrame.EXIT_ON_CLOSE);
11:         setLookAndFeel();
12:         // create icons
13:         ImageIcon loadIcon = new ImageIcon("load.gif");
14:         ImageIcon saveIcon = new ImageIcon("save.gif");
```

```
15:        ImageIcon subIcon = new ImageIcon("subscribe.gif");
16:        ImageIcon unsubIcon = new ImageIcon("unsubscribe.gif");
17:        // create buttons
18:        JButton load = new JButton("Load", loadIcon);
19:        JButton save = new JButton("Save", saveIcon);
20:        JButton sub = new JButton("Subscribe", subIcon);
21:        JButton unsub = new JButton("Unsubscribe", unsubIcon);
22:        // add buttons to toolbar
23:        JToolBar bar = new JToolBar();
24:        bar.add(load);
25:        bar.add(save);
26:        bar.add(sub);
27:        bar.add(unsub);
28:        // prepare user interface
29:        JTextArea edit = new JTextArea(8, 40);
30:        JScrollPane scroll = new JScrollPane(edit);
31:        BorderLayout bord = new BorderLayout();
32:        setLayout(bord);
33:        add("North", bar);
34:        add("Center", scroll);
35:        pack();
37:        setVisible(true);
38:    }
39:
40:    private void setLookAndFeel() {
41:        try {
42:            UIManager.setLookAndFeel(
43:                "javax.swing.plaf.nimbus.NimbusLookAndFeel"
44:            );
45:            SwingUtilities.updateComponentTreeUI(this);
46:        } catch (Exception e) {
47:            System.err.println("Couldn't use the system "
48:                + "look and feel: " + e);
49:        }
50:    }
51:
52:    public static void main(String[] arguments) {
53:        FeedBar frame = new FeedBar();
54:    }
55: }
```

This application uses four images to represent the graphics on the buttons—the same graphics used in the IconFrame project from Lesson 9, "Creating a Graphical User Interface." If you haven't downloaded them yet, you can find them on the book's official website, at www.java21days.com, on the Lesson 9 page. You also can use graphics from your own computer.

Four ImageIcon objects are created from the four graphics in lines 13–16, and then they are used to create buttons in lines 18–21. A JToolbar is created in line 23, and the buttons are added to it in lines 24–27.

The toolbar in this application starts at the top edge of the frame, but it can be moved. The component can be grabbed by its handle—the area immediately to the left of the Load button shown in Figure 10.8. If you drag it within the window, you can dock it along different edges of the application window. When you release the toolbar, the application is rearranged using the border layout manager. You also can drag the toolbar outside the application window.

If the toolbar has been dragged to its own window, when the frame is closed, the toolbar also closes.

Although toolbars are most commonly used with graphical buttons, they can contain textual buttons, combo boxes, and other components.

## Progress Bars

Progress bars are components used to show how much time is left before a task is complete.

10

Progress bars are implemented in Swing through the `JProgressBar` class. Figure 10.9 shows a Java application that uses this component.

**FIGURE 10.9**
A progress bar in a frame.

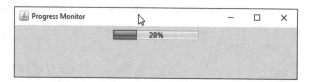

A progress bar is used to track the progress of a task that can be represented numerically. You create one by specifying a minimum value and a maximum value that represent the points at which the task is beginning and ending.

Consider a software program that consists of 335 files when it is installed on a computer. This is a good example of a task that can be numerically quantified. The number of files transferred can be used to monitor the progress of the task. The minimum value is 0, and the maximum value is 335.

Progress bar constructors include the following:

- `JProgressBar()`: Creates a new progress bar
- `JProgressBar(int, int)`: Creates a new progress bar with the specified minimum value and maximum value
- `JProgressBar(int, int, int)`: Creates a new progress bar with the specified orientation, minimum value, and maximum value

The orientation of a progress bar can be established with the SwingConstants.VERTICAL and SwingConstants.HORIZONTAL class constants. Progress bars are horizontal by default. You also can set the minimum and maximum values by calling the progress bar's setMinimum(*int*) and setMaximum (*int*) values with the indicated values.

To update a progress bar, you call its setValue (*int*) method with a value indicating how far along the task is at that moment. This value should be somewhere between the minimum and maximum values established for the bar. The following example tells the install progress bar in the previous example of a software installation how many files have been uploaded thus far:

```
int filesDone = getNumberOfFiles();
install.setValue(filesDone);
```

In this example, the getNumberOfFiles() method represents some code that would be used to keep track of how many files have been copied so far during the installation. When this value is passed to the progress bar by the setValue() method, the bar is immediately updated to represent the percentage of the task that has been completed.

A progress bar may include a text label in addition to the graphic of an empty box filling up. This label displays the percentage of the task that has been completed. You can set it up for a bar by calling the setStringPainted (*boolean*) method with a value of true. A false argument turns off this label.

Listing 10.4 contains ProgressMonitor, the application shown at the beginning of this section, in Figure 10.9.

**LISTING 10.4**   The Full Text of ProgressMonitor.java

```
 1: package com.java21days;
 2:
 3: import java.awt.*;
 4: import javax.swing.*;
 5:
 6: public class ProgressMonitor extends JFrame {
 7:     JProgressBar current;
 8:     JTextArea out;
 9:   JButton find;
10:     int num = 0;
11:
12:     public ProgressMonitor() {
13:         super("Progress Monitor");
14:         setDefaultCloseOperation(JFrame.EXIT_ON_CLOSE);
15:         setSize(500, 125);
16:         setLayout(new FlowLayout());
17:         current = new JProgressBar(0, 2000);
```

```
18:            current.setValue(0);
19:            current.setStringPainted(true);
20:            add(current);
21:        }
22:
23:        public void iterate() {
24:            while (num < 2000) {
25:                current.setValue(num);
26:                try {
27:                    Thread.sleep(1000);
28:                } catch (InterruptedException e) { }
29:                num += 95;
30:            }
31:        }
32:
33:        private static void setLookAndFeel() {
34:            try {
35:                UIManager.setLookAndFeel(
36:                    "javax.swing.plaf.nimbus.NimbusLookAndFeel"
37:                );
38:            } catch (Exception e) {
39:                System.err.println(e);
40:            }
41:        }
42:
43:        public static void main(String[] arguments) {
44:            ProgressMonitor.setLookAndFeel();
45:            ProgressMonitor frame = new ProgressMonitor();
46:            frame.setVisible(true);
47:            frame.iterate();
48:        }
49: }
```

10

The ProgressMonitor application uses a progress bar to track the value of the num variable. The progress bar is created in line 17, with a minimum value of 0 and a maximum value of 2,000.

The iterate() method, which begins on line 23, loops while num is less than 2,000 and increases num by 95 each iteration. The progress bar's setValue() method is called in line 25 of the loop with num as an argument, causing the bar to use that value when charting progress.

Using a progress bar is a way to make a program more user-friendly when it will be busy for more than a few seconds. Software users like progress bars because they estimate how much more time something will take. Progress bars also provide another essential piece of information: proof that the program is still running and has not crashed.

## Menus

One way you can enhance a frame's usability is to give it a menu bar, a series of pull-down menus used to perform tasks. Menus often duplicate the same tasks you could accomplish by using buttons and other user interface components, giving users two ways to get work done.

Menus in Java are supported by three components that work in conjunction with each other:

- `JMenuItem`: An item on a menu
- `JMenu`: A drop-down menu that contains one or more `JMenuItem` components, other interface components, and separators—lines displayed between items
- `JMenuBar`: A container that holds one or more `JMenu` components and displays their names

A `JMenuItem` component is like a button and can be set up using the same constructors as a `JButton` component. Call it with `JMenuItem(String)` for a text item, `JMenuItem(Icon)` for an item that displays a graphics file, or `JMenuItem(String, Icon)` for both.

The following statements create seven menu items:

```
JMenuItem j1 = new JMenuItem("Open");
JMenuItem j2 = new JMenuItem("Save");
JMenuItem j3 = new JMenuItem("Save as Template");
JMenuItem j4 = new JMenuItem("Page Setup");
JMenuItem j5 = new JMenuItem("Print");
JMenuItem j6 = new JMenuItem("Use as Default Message Style");
JMenuItem j7 = new JMenuItem("Close");
```

A `JMenu` container holds all the menu items for a drop-down menu. To create it, call the `JMenu(String)` constructor with the name of the menu as an argument. This name appears on the menu bar.

After you have created a `JMenu` container, call the `add(JMenuItem)` method to add a menu item to it. New items are placed at the end of the menu.

The item you put on a menu doesn't have to be a menu item. Call the `add(Component)` method with a user interface component as the argument. One component that often appears on a menu is a check box (the `JCheckBox` class).

To add a line separator to the end of a menu, call the `addSeparator()` method. Separators often are used to visually group several related items on a menu.

You also can add to a menu text that serves as a label of some kind. Call the `add(String)` method with the text as an argument.

Using the seven menu items from the preceding example, the following statements create a menu and fill it with all those items and three separators:

```
JMenu m1 = new JMenu("File");
m1.add(j1);
m1.add(j2);
m1.add(j3);
m1.addSeparator();
m1.add(j4);
m1.add(j5);
m1.addSeparator();
m1.add(j6);
m1.addSeparator();
m1.add(j7);
```

A `JMenuBar` container holds one or more `JMenu` containers and displays the name of each one. The most common place to see a menu bar is directly below an application's title bar.

To create a menu bar, call the `JMenuBar()` constructor with no arguments. Add menus to the end of a menu bar by calling the `add(JMenu)` method.

After you have created all your menu items, added them to menus, and added the menus to a bar, you're ready to add them to a frame by calling the frame's `setJMenuBar(JMenuBar)` method.

The following statement finishes the current example by creating a menu bar, adding a menu to it, and then placing the bar on a frame called `gui`:

```
JMenuBar bar = new JMenuBar();
bar.add(m1);
gui.setJMenuBar(bar);
```

Although you can now open and close a menu and select items, nothing happens in response. You'll learn how to receive user input for components in Lesson 12, "Responding to User Input."

The following code adds a menu bar to a frame that holds one menu and four individual items:

```
JMenuItem j1 = new JMenuItem("Load");
JMenuItem j2 = new JMenuItem("Save");
JMenuItem j3 = new JMenuItem("Subscribe");
JMenuItem j4 = new JMenuItem("Unsubscribe");
JMenuBar menubar = new JMenuBar();
JMenu menu = new JMenu("Feeds");
menu.add(j1);
```

```
menu.add(j2);
menu.addSeparator();
menu.add(j3);
menu.add(j4);
menubar.add(menu);
setJMenuBar(menubar);
```

## Tabbed Panes

Tabbed panes, a group of stacked panels in which only one panel can be viewed at a time, are implemented in Swing with the JTabbedPane class.

To view a panel, you click the tab that contains its name. Tabs can be arranged horizontally across the top or bottom of the component or vertically along the left side or right side.

Tabbed panes are created with the following three constructors:

- **JTabbedPane()**: Creates a vertical tabbed pane along the top that does not scroll
- **JTabbedPane(*int*)**: Creates a tabbed pane that does not scroll and has the specified placement
- **JTabbedPane(*int, int*)**: Creates a tabbed pane with the specified placement (first argument) and scrolling policy (second argument)

The placement of a tabbed pane is the position where its tabs are displayed in relation to the panels. Use one of four class variables as the argument to the constructor: JTabbedPane.TOP, JTabbedPane.BOTTOM, JTabbedPane.LEFT, or JTabbedPane.RIGHT.

The scrolling policy determines how tabs will be displayed when there are more tabs than the interface can hold. A tabbed pane that does not scroll displays extra tabs, each on its own line, which can be set up using the JTabbedPane.WRAP_TAB_LAYOUT class variable. A tabbed pane that scrolls displays scrolling arrows beside the tabs. This can be set up with JTabbedPane.SCROLL_TAB_LAYOUT.

After you create a tabbed pane, you can add components to it by calling the pane's addTab(*String, Component*) method, where the *String* argument is used as the tab's label. The second argument is the component that will make up one of the tabs on the pane. It's common but not required to use a JPanel object for this purpose.

The TabPanels application in Listing 10.5 displays a pane with five tabs, each holding its own panel.

**LISTING 10.5**   The Full Text of `TabPanels.java`

```
 1: package com.java21days;
 2:
 3: import java.awt.*;
 4: import javax.swing.*;
 5:
 6: public class TabPanels extends JFrame {
 7:
 8:     public TabPanels() {
 9:         super("Tabbed Panes");
10:         setDefaultCloseOperation(JFrame.EXIT_ON_CLOSE);
11:         setLookAndFeel();
12:         setSize(480, 218);
13:         JPanel mainSettings = new JPanel();
14:         JPanel advancedSettings = new JPanel();
15:         JPanel privacySettings = new JPanel();
16:         JPanel emailSettings = new JPanel();
17:         JPanel securitySettings = new JPanel();
18:         JTabbedPane tabs = new JTabbedPane();
19:         tabs.addTab("Main", mainSettings);
20:         tabs.addTab("Advanced", advancedSettings);
21:         tabs.addTab("Privacy", privacySettings);
22:         tabs.addTab("E-mail", emailSettings);
23:         tabs.addTab("Security", securitySettings);
24:         add(tabs);
25:         setVisible(true);
26:     }
27:
28:     private void setLookAndFeel() {
29:         try {
30:             UIManager.setLookAndFeel(
31:                 "com.sun.java.swing.plaf.nimbus.NimbusLookAndFeel"
32:             );
33:             SwingUtilities.updateComponentTreeUI(this);
34:         } catch (Exception e) {
35:             System.err.println("Couldn't use the system "
36:                 + "look and feel: " + e);
37:         }
38:     }
39:
40:     public static void main(String[] arguments) {
41:         TabPanels frame = new TabPanels();
42:     }
43: }
```

Five panels are created in lines 13–17. After a tabbed pane is created, the panels are added to the tabs in lines 19–23. Each panel can hold its own user interface components.

Figure 10.10 shows the application running.

**FIGURE 10.10**
A tabbed pane with five tabs.

# Summary

You now know how to paint a user interface onto a Java application window by using the components of the Swing package.

Swing includes classes for many of the buttons, bars, lists, and fields you would expect to see on a program. It also includes more advanced components, such as sliders, dialogs, progress bars, and menu bars. You implement interface components by creating an instance of their class and adding it to a container such as a frame. You use the container's add() method or a similar method specific to the container, such as the tabbed pane's addTab() method.

In this lesson, you developed components and added them to an interface. In the next two lessons, you will learn about two tasks required to make a graphical interface usable. You will see how to arrange components to form a whole interface and how to receive input from a user through these components.

Swing offers a lot more user interface components in addition to the ones covered up to this point. Visit Oracle's Javadoc site, at https://docs.oracle.com/en/java/javase/12/docs/api, click the java.desktop module link, and click the javax.swing package link to explore these classes further.

# Q&A

**Q Can an application be created without Swing?**

**A** Certainly. Swing is just an expansion on the Abstract Window Toolkit, so you could use only AWT classes to design your interface and receive input from a user. But there's no comparison between Swing's capabilities and those offered by the

AWT. With Swing, you can use many more components, control them in more sophisticated ways, and count on better performance and more reliability.

Java includes an alternative to Swing called JavaFX that had the original design goal of replacing Swing in a future release of the language.

Other user interface libraries also extend or compete with Swing. One of the most popular is the Standard Widget Toolkit (SWT), an open source GUI library created by the Eclipse project. The SWT offers components that appear and behave like the interface components offered by each operating system. For more information, visit www.eclipse.org/swt.

Another interesting Swing rival is GWT, an open source toolkit created by Google for building graphical web applications. Google used it for AdWords, Inbox, and Wallet. Find out more at www.gwtproject.org.

**Q In the `slider` application, what does the `pack()` statement do?**

**A** Every interface component has a preferred size, although this often is disregarded by the layout manager used to arrange the component within a container. Calling a frame or window's `pack()` method causes it to be resized to fit the preferred size of the components it contains. Because the `slider` application does not set a size for the frame, calling `pack()` sets it to an adequate size before the frame is displayed.

**Q When I try to create a tabbed pane, all that appears are the tabs; the panels are not visible. What can I do to correct this?**

**A** Tabbed panes don't work correctly until their contents have been fully set up with components inside them. If a tab's panes are empty, nothing appears below or beside the tabs. Make sure that the panels you are putting into the tabs display all their components.

# Quiz

Review this lesson's material by taking this three-question quiz.

## Questions

**1.** Which user interface component is common in software installation programs?

    **A.** Sliders

    **B.** Progress bars

    **C.** Dialogs

**2.** Which Java package includes a class for clickable buttons?

   **A.** `java.awt` (Abstract Window Toolkit)

   **B.** `javax.swing` (Swing)

   **C.** Both

**3.** Which user interface component can be picked up and moved around?

   **A.** `JSlider`

   **B.** `JToolBar`

   **C.** Both

## Answers

**1.** B. Progress bars are useful when used to display the progress of a file-copying or file-extracting activity.

**2.** C. Swing duplicates all the simple user interface components included in the Abstract Window Toolkit.

**3.** B. The toolbar can be dragged to the top, right, left, or bottom of the interface and also out of the interface.

# Certification Practice

The following question is the kind of thing you could expect to be asked on a Java programming certification test. Answer it without looking again at this lesson or using the Java compiler to test the code.

Given:

```
import java.awt.*;
import javax.swing.*;

public class AskFrame extends JFrame {
    public AskFrame() {
        setDefaultCloseOperation(JFrame.EXIT_ON_CLOSE);
        JSlider value = new JSlider(0, 255, 100);
        add(value);
        setSize(450, 150);
        setVisible(true);
        super();
    }

    public static void main(String[] arguments) {
        AskFrame af = new AskFrame();
    }
}
```

What will happen when you attempt to compile and run this source code?

**A.** It compiles without error and runs correctly.

**B.** It compiles without error but does not display anything in the frame.

**C.** It does not compile because of the `super()` statement.

**D.** It does not compile because of the `add()` statement.

The answer is available on the book's website, at www.java21days.com. Visit the Lesson 10 page and click the Certification Practice link.

# Exercises

To extend your knowledge of the subjects covered in this lesson, try the following exercises:

1. Create an input dialog that can be used to set the title of the frame that loaded the dialog.

2. Create a modified version of the `ProgressMonitor` application that also displays the value of the `num` variable in a text field.

Where applicable, exercise solutions are offered on the book's website, at www.java21days.com.

# LESSON 11
# Arranging Components on a User Interface

If designing a graphical user interface (GUI) were comparable to painting, currently you could produce only one kind of art: abstract expressionism. You can put components on an interface, but you can't control where they go.

To arrange the components of a user interface in Java, you must use a set of classes called *layout managers*. In this lesson, you will learn how to use layout managers to arrange components in an interface. You will learn how to take advantage of the flexibility of Java's graphical user interface capabilities, which were designed to be presentable on the many platforms that support the language.

You also will learn how to put several layout managers to work on the same interface. This approach is for the many times when one layout manager doesn't suit exactly the interface you seek to design.

# Basic Interface Layout

As you've learned, a GUI designed with Swing is a fluid thing. Resizing a window can wreak havoc on your interface because components move to places on a container that you might not have intended.

This fluidity is a necessary part of Java's support for different platforms, where there are subtle differences in how each platform displays things such as buttons, scrollbars, and other parts of a user interface.

With some programming languages, a component's location on a window is precisely defined by its (x, y) coordinates. Some Java development tools allow similar control over an interface through the use of their own windowing classes (and there's a way to do that in Java).

When using Swing, a programmer gains more control over the layout of an interface, thanks to layout managers.

The platform-independent nature of Swing provides flexibility at the cost of somewhat slower performance and a user interface look and feel that doesn't closely match the native look and feel of the operating system.

## Laying Out an Interface

A layout manager determines how components will be arranged when they are added to a container.

The default layout manager for panels is the `FlowLayout` class. This class lets components flow from left to right in the order in which they are added to a container. When there's no more room, a new row of components begins immediately below the first, and the left-to-right order continues.

Java includes a bunch of general-purpose layout managers: `BorderLayout`, `BoxLayout`, `CardLayout`, `FlowLayout`, and `GridLayout`. To create a layout manager for a container, first call its constructor to create an instance of the class, as in this example:

```
FlowLayout flo = new FlowLayout();
```

After you create a layout manager, you designate it as the layout manager for a container by using the container's `setLayout()` method. The layout manager must be set before any components are added to the container. If no layout manager is specified, the container's default layout is used. The default is `FlowLayout` for panels and `BorderLayout` for frames.

The following statements represent the starting point for a frame that uses a layout manager to control the arrangement of all components that will be added to the frame:

```
import java.awt.*;
import javax.swing.*;

public class Starter extends JFrame {

    public Starter() {
        super("Example Frame");
        FlowLayout manager = new FlowLayout();
        setLayout(manager);
        // add components here
    }
}
```

After the layout manager is set, you can start adding components to the container it manages. For some of the layout managers, such as `FlowLayout`, the order in which components are added is significant. You'll see when this is true (and when it isn't) as you work with each of the managers.

## Flow Layout

The `FlowLayout` class in the `java.awt` package is the simplest layout manager. It lays out components in rows in the same way that words are laid out on a page in English—from left to right until there's no more room at the right edge, and then on to the left edge on the next row.

By default, the components in each row are centered when you use the `FlowLayout()` constructor with no arguments. If you want the components to be aligned along the left or right edge of the container, you can use the `FlowLayout.LEFT` or `FlowLayout.RIGHT` class variable as the constructor's only argument, as in the following statement:

```
FlowLayout righty = new FlowLayout(FlowLayout.RIGHT);
```

The `FlowLayout.CENTER` class variable specifies a centered alignment for components.

**NOTE** _____ | If you need to align components for a non-English-speaking audience where left-to-right order does not make sense, you can use the `FlowLayout.LEADING` and `FlowLayout.TRAILING` variables. They set justification to the side of either the first component in a row or the last, respectively.

The `Alphabet` application in Listing 11.1 displays six buttons arranged by the flow layout manager. Because the `FlowLayout.LEFT` class variable is used in the `FlowLayout()`

11

constructor, the components are lined up along the left side of the application window. Create this application in NetBeans in the `com.java21days` package.

**LISTING 11.1**    The Full Text of `Alphabet.java`

```
 1: package com.java21days;
 2:
 3: import java.awt.*;
 4: import javax.swing.*;
 5:
 6: public class Alphabet extends JFrame {
 7:
 8:     public Alphabet() {
 9:         super("Alphabet");
10:         setDefaultCloseOperation(JFrame.EXIT_ON_CLOSE);
11:         setLookAndFeel();
12:         setSize(360, 120);
13:         FlowLayout lm = new FlowLayout(FlowLayout.LEFT);
14:         setLayout(lm);
15:         JButton a = new JButton("Alibi");
16:         JButton b = new JButton("Burglar");
17:         JButton c = new JButton("Corpse");
18:         JButton d = new JButton("Deadbeat");
19:         JButton e = new JButton("Evidence");
20:         JButton f = new JButton("Fugitive");
21:         add(a);
22:         add(b);
23:         add(c);
24:         add(d);
25:         add(e);
26:         add(f);
27:         setVisible(true);
28:     }
29:
30:     private static void setLookAndFeel() {
31:         try {
32:             UIManager.setLookAndFeel(
33:                 "javax.swing.plaf.nimbus.NimbusLookAndFeel"
34:             );
35:         } catch (Exception exc) {
36:             System.err.println(exc);
37:         }
38:     }
39:
40:     public static void main(String[] arguments) {
41:         Alphabet.setLookAndFeel();
42:         Alphabet frame = new Alphabet();
43:     }
44: }
```

Figure 11.1 shows the application running.

**FIGURE 11.1**
Six buttons
arranged by a flow
layout manager.

The `Alphabet` application creates a flow layout manager in line 13 and sets it to manage the frame in line 14. The buttons added to the frame in lines 21–26 are arranged by this manager.

The manager uses the default gap of 5 pixels between components on a row and a gap of 5 pixels between rows. You can change the horizontal and vertical gap between components with some extra arguments to the `FlowLayout()` constructor or by calling flow layout's `setVgap(int)` and `setHgap(int)` methods with the desired vertical or horizontal gap.

The `FlowLayout(int, int, int)` constructor takes the following three arguments, in order:

- The alignment, which must be one of five class variables of `FlowLayout`: `CENTER`, `LEFT`, `RIGHT`, `LEADING`, or `TRAILING`
- The horizontal gap between components, in pixels
- The vertical gap, in pixels

The following constructor creates a flow layout manager with centered components, a horizontal gap of 30 pixels, and a vertical gap of 10 pixels:

```
FlowLayout flo = new FlowLayout(FlowLayout.CENTER, 30, 10);
```

## Box Layout

A box layout manager can be used to stack components from top to bottom or from left to right. Box layout, managed by the `BoxLayout` class in the `javax.swing` package, improves on flow layout by ensuring that components always line up vertically or horizontally, regardless of how their container is resized.

A box layout manager must be created with two arguments to its constructor: the container it will manage and a class variable that sets up vertical or horizontal alignment.

The alignment, specified with class variables of the `BoxLayout` class, can be `X_AXIS` for left-to-right horizontal alignment or `Y_AXIS` for top-to-bottom vertical alignment.

11

The following code sets up a panel to use vertical box layout:

```
JPanel optionPane = new JPanel();
BoxLayout box = new BoxLayout(optionPane, BoxLayout.Y_AXIS);
optionPane.setLayout(box);
```

Components added to the container will line up on the specified axis and will be displayed at their preferred sizes. In horizontal alignment, the box layout manager attempts to give each component the same height. In vertical alignment, the manager attempts to give each one the same width.

The Stacker application, shown in Listing 11.2, contains a panel of buttons arranged with box layout. Create it in NetBeans in the com.java21days package.

**LISTING 11.2**    The Full Text of Stacker.java

```
 1: package com.java21days;
 2:
 3: import java.awt.*;
 4: import javax.swing.*;
 5:
 6: public class Stacker extends JFrame {
 7:     public Stacker() {
 8:         super("Stacker");
 9:         setSize(430, 150);
10:         setDefaultCloseOperation(JFrame.EXIT_ON_CLOSE);
11:         setLookAndFeel();
12:         // create top panel
13:         JPanel commandPane = new JPanel();
14:         BoxLayout horizontal = new BoxLayout(commandPane,
15:             BoxLayout.X_AXIS);
16:         commandPane.setLayout(horizontal);
17:         JButton subscribe = new JButton("Subscribe");
18:         JButton unsubscribe = new JButton("Unsubscribe");
19:         JButton refresh = new JButton("Refresh");
20:         JButton save = new JButton("Save");
21:         commandPane.add(subscribe);
22:         commandPane.add(unsubscribe);
23:         commandPane.add(refresh);
24:         commandPane.add(save);
25:         // create bottom panel
26:         JPanel textPane = new JPanel();
27:         JTextArea text = new JTextArea(4, 70);
28:         JScrollPane scrollPane = new JScrollPane(text);
29:         // put them together
30:         FlowLayout flow = new FlowLayout();
31:         setLayout(flow);
32:         add(commandPane);
```

```
33:            add(scrollPane);
34:            setVisible(true);
35:        }
36:
37:        private static void setLookAndFeel() {
38:            try {
39:                UIManager.setLookAndFeel(
40:                    "javax.swing.plaf.nimbus.NimbusLookAndFeel"
41:                );
42:            } catch (Exception exc) {
43:                System.err.println(exc);
44:            }
45:        }
46:
47:        public static void main(String[] arguments) {
48:            Stacker.setLookAndFeel();
49:            Stacker st = new Stacker();
50:        }
51: }
```

When the class is compiled and run, the output should resemble the dialog in Figure 11.2.

**FIGURE 11.2**
A user interface with buttons arranged with the box layout manager.

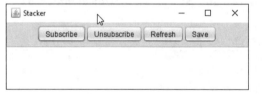

11

This application creates a `JPanel` container named `commandPane` in line 13, creates a box layout manager associated with that pane in lines 13–14, and sets that manager for the panel in line 16.

The panel of buttons along the top edge of the interface is stacked horizontally. If the second argument to the box layout constructor were `BoxLayout.Y_AXIS`, the buttons would be arranged vertically instead.

## Grid Layout

The grid layout manager arranges components into a grid of vertical columns and horizontal rows like the days on a 12-month calendar. Components are added first to the top row of the grid, beginning with the leftmost grid cell and continuing to the right. When all the cells in the top row are full, the next component is added to the leftmost cell in the second row of the grid—if there *is* a second row—and so on.

Grid layout managers are created with the `GridLayout` class, which belongs to the `java.awt` package. Two arguments are sent to the `GridLayout` constructor: the number of rows and the number of columns in the grid.

The following statement creates a grid layout manager with 10 rows and 3 columns:

```
GridLayout gr = new GridLayout(10, 3);
```

As with flow layout, you can specify a vertical and horizontal gap between components with two extra arguments (or by calling the `setHgap()` or `setVgap()` methods). The following statement creates a grid layout with 10 rows and 3 columns, a horizontal gap of 5 pixels, and a vertical gap of 8 pixels:

```
GridLayout gr2 = new GridLayout(10, 3, 5, 8);
```

The default gap between components arranged in grid layout is 0 pixels in both vertical and horizontal directions.

For the next project, create the `Bunch` application in the `com.java21days` package, as shown in Listing 11.3. The program creates a grid with 3 rows, 3 columns, and a 10-pixel gap between components in both the vertical and horizontal directions.

**LISTING 11.3**  The Full Text of `Bunch.java`

```
 1: package com.java21days;
 2:
 3: import java.awt.*;
 4: import javax.swing.*;
 5:
 6: public class Bunch extends JFrame {
 7:
 8:     public Bunch() {
 9:         super("Bunch");
10:         setSize(260, 260);
11:         setDefaultCloseOperation(JFrame.EXIT_ON_CLOSE);
12:         setLookAndFeel();
13:         JPanel pane = new JPanel();
14:         GridLayout family = new GridLayout(3, 3, 10, 10);
15:         pane.setLayout(family);
16:         JButton marcia = new JButton("Marcia");
17:         JButton carol = new JButton("Carol");
18:         JButton greg = new JButton("Greg");
19:         JButton jan = new JButton("Jan");
20:         JButton alice = new JButton("Alice");
21:         JButton peter = new JButton("Peter");
22:         JButton cindy = new JButton("Cindy");
23:         JButton mike = new JButton("Mike");
24:         JButton bobby = new JButton("Bobby");
25:         pane.add(marcia);
```

```
26:            pane.add(carol);
27:            pane.add(greg);
28:            pane.add(jan);
29:            pane.add(alice);
30:            pane.add(peter);
31:            pane.add(cindy);
32:            pane.add(mike);
33:            pane.add(bobby);
34:            add(pane);
35:            setVisible(true);
36:        }
37:
38:        private static void setLookAndFeel() {
39:            try {
40:                UIManager.setLookAndFeel(
41:                    "javax.swing.plaf.nimbus.NimbusLookAndFeel"
42:                );
43:            } catch (Exception exc) {
44:                System.err.println(exc);
45:            }
46:        }
47:
48:        public static void main(String[] arguments) {
49:            Bunch.setLookAndFeel();
50:            Bunch frame = new Bunch();
51:        }
54: }
```

**11**

Figure 11.3 shows this application.

**FIGURE 11.3**
Nine buttons
arranged in a 3×3
grid layout.

The Bunch application displays nine buttons in a grid. The buttons are added to a pane in lines 25–33, and the pane is added to the frame in line 34.

One thing to note about the buttons in Figure 11.3 is that they expanded to fill the space available to them in each cell. This is an important difference between the grid layout manager and some of the other layout managers, which display components at a much smaller size, using the preferred size of those components.

# Border Layout

The layout managers introduced so far have been fairly simple. The next one employs a more complex arrangement called *border layout.*

This layout is created by using the `BorderLayout` class in the `java.awt` package, which divides a container into five sections: north, south, east, west, and center. The five areas in Figure 11.4 show how these sections are arranged.

**FIGURE 11.4**
Components arranged by a border layout manager.

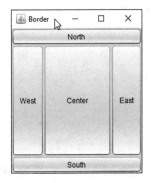

In border layout, the components represented by the four compass points fill their sections, and the center component gets all the space that's left over. Ordinarily, this results in an arrangement with a large central component and four smaller components around it. The layout manager does not use the preferred sizes of the components.

A border layout is created with either the `BorderLayout()` or `BorderLayout(int, int)` constructors. The first constructor creates a border layout with no gap between the components. The second constructor uses arguments to specify the horizontal gap and vertical gap, in that order, and `setVgap()` and `setHgap()` also are available.

After you create a border layout and set it up as a container's layout manager, components are added using a call to the `add()` method that's different from the ones seen previously:

```
add(Component, String)
```

The first argument is the component that should be added to the container. The second argument is a `BorderLayout` class variable that indicates the region of the border layout to which the component should be assigned. The class variables `NORTH`, `SOUTH`, `EAST`, `WEST`, and `CENTER` can be used for this argument.

The following statement adds a button called `quitButton` to the north portion of a border layout:

```
JButton quitButton = new JButton("quit");
add(quitButton, BorderLayout.NORTH);
```

The `Border` application, shown in Listing 11.4, creates the GUI shown earlier in Figure 11.4. Create the `Border` class in the `com.java21days` package.

**LISTING 11.4**   The Full Text of `Border.java`

```
 1: package com.java21days;
 2:
 3: import java.awt.*;
 4: import javax.swing.*;
 5:
 6: public class Border extends JFrame {
 7:
 8:     public Border() {
 9:         super("Border");
10:         setSize(240, 280);
11:         setDefaultCloseOperation(JFrame.EXIT_ON_CLOSE);
12:         setLookAndFeel();
13:         setLayout(new BorderLayout());
14:         JButton nButton = new JButton("North");
15:         JButton sButton = new JButton("South");
16:         JButton eButton = new JButton("East");
17:         JButton wButton = new JButton("West");
18:         JButton cButton = new JButton("Center");
19:         add(nButton, BorderLayout.NORTH);
20:         add(sButton, BorderLayout.SOUTH);
21:         add(eButton, BorderLayout.EAST);
22:         add(wButton, BorderLayout.WEST);
23:         add(cButton, BorderLayout.CENTER);
24:         setVisible(true);
25:     }
26:
27:     private static void setLookAndFeel() {
28:         try {
29:             UIManager.setLookAndFeel(
30:                 "javax.swing.plaf.nimbus.NimbusLookAndFeel"
31:             );
32:         } catch (Exception exc) {
33:             System.err.println(exc);
34:         }
35:     }
36:
37:     public static void main(String[] arguments) {
38:         Border.setLookAndFeel();
39:         Border frame = new Border();
40:     }
41: }
```

11

The `Border` application is a frame that sets its layout manager in a new way in line 13. The call to the `new BorderLayout()` constructor returns a `BorderLayout` object, which then becomes the argument to the `setLayout()` method.

Line 13 is equivalent to the following two statements:

```
BorderLayout bl = new BorderLayout();
setLayout(bl);
```

The advantage of the technique employed in line 13 is that there's no need to create a variable and assign the `BorderLayout` object to it. That object's never needed after the layout manager is designated for the frame.

The application creates the five buttons in lines 14–18 and assigns them to positions in the border layout in lines 19–23.

**TIP**

> When you run the application, increase the application's window size to see how the components respond. Do this for different sizes and note the change to the user interface. As the window becomes larger, the center component grows accordingly. The other components stay the same. This is an advantage of the grid and border layout managers.

# Mixing Layout Managers

At this point, you might be wondering how Java's layout managers can be used on the GUIs you want to design for your own programs. Choosing a layout manager is an experience akin to Goldilocks checking out the home of the three bears: This one is too square! This one is too messy! This one is too strange!

To find the layout that is just right, you often have to combine more than one manager within the same interface. You can do so by putting several containers inside a larger container and giving each of the smaller containers its own layout manager.

The container to use for these smaller containers is the panel, which is created from the `JPanel` class in the `javax.swing` package. Panels are simple containers used to group components. Keep in mind two things when working with panels:

- The panel is filled with components before it is put into a larger container.
- The panel has its own layout manager.

Panels are created with a simple call to the constructor of the `JPanel` class, as shown in the following example:

```
JPanel pane = new JPanel();
```

You set the layout method for a panel by calling the `setLayout()` method on that panel. Here's how to create a layout manager and apply it to a `JPanel` object called `pane`:

```
FlowLayout flo = new FlowLayout();
pane.setLayout(flo);
```

You add components to a panel by calling the panel's `add()` method, which works the same for panels as it does for other containers.

The following statements create a text field and add it to a `JPanel` object called `pane`:

```
JTextField nameField = new JTextField(80);
pane.add(nameField);
```

You'll see several examples of panel use in the rest of the lesson.

As you gain experience with layout managers, you'll get a feel for which ones to use in specific situations. For instance, border layout is good for putting a status line at the bottom and a toolbar at the top, and grid layout is effective for rows and columns of text fields and labels that take the same size.

# Card Layout                                            11

A card layout manager differs from the other layout managers in that it hides some components from view. A card layout is a group of containers or components displayed one at a time, in the same way that a blackjack dealer reveals one card at a time from a deck. Each container in the group is called a *card*.

Anyone who has installed software featuring a wizard has seen card layout. Each step in the installation process has its own card. A Next button advances from one card to the next, and a Back button returns to the previous card.

The most common way to use a card layout is to use a panel container for each card. Components are added to the panels first, and then the panels are added to the container that employs card layout.

A card layout is created from the `CardLayout` class in the `java.awt` package with a simple constructor:

```
CardLayout cc = new CardLayout();
```

The `setLayout()` method makes this the layout manager for the container, as in the following statement:

```
setLayout(cc);
```

After you set a container to use the card layout manager, you must use the `add(Component, String)` method to add components.

The first argument to the `add()` method specifies the container or component that serves as a card. If it is a container, all components must have been added to it before the card is added.

The second argument is a string that names the card. This can be anything you want to call the card, such as `"Card 1"`, `"Card 2"`, `"Card 3"`, or some other naming scheme.

The following statement adds a panel object named `options` to a container and names this card `"Options Card"`:

```
add(options, "Options Card");
```

When a container using card layout is displayed for the first time, the visible card is the first card added to the container.

You can display subsequent cards by calling the `show()` method of the layout manager, which takes two arguments:

- The container holding all the cards
- The name of the card

The following statement calls the `show()` method of a card layout manager called `cc`:

```
cc.show(this, "Fact Card");
```

The `this` keyword would be used in a frame governed by card layout. It refers to the object inside which the `cc.show()` statement appears. In this example, "Fact Card" is the name of the card to reveal, and a card is added to the container that has been given this name.

When a card is shown, the previously displayed card is hidden automatically. Only one card in a card layout can be shown at a time.

In a program that uses the card layout manager, a card change generally is triggered by a user's action. For example, in an installation program, a user could choose a folder where the program should be saved and click the Next button to see the next card.

## Using Card Layout in an Application

The next project demonstrates both card layout and the use of different layout managers within the same GUI.

The `SurveyWizard` class is a panel that implements a wizard interface: a series of simple questions accompanied by a Next button that is used to see the subsequent question. The last question has a Finish button instead, as shown in Figure 11.5.

**FIGURE 11.5**
Using a card layout for a wizard-style interface.

The easiest way to implement a card-based layout is to use panels. This project uses several panels:

- The `SurveyWizard` class is a panel that holds all the cards.
- The `SurveyPanel` helper class is a panel that holds one card.
- Each `SurveyPanel` object contains three panels stacked on top of each other.

The `SurveyWizard` and `SurveyPanel` classes are both panels, the easiest component to use when working with card layout. Each card is created as a panel and is added to a containing panel that will be used to show them in sequence. This takes place in the `SurveyWizard()` constructor, using two instance variables, a card layout manager, and an array of three `SurveyPanel` objects:

```
SurveyPanel[] ask = new SurveyPanel[3];
CardLayout cards = new CardLayout();
```

The constructor sets the class to use the layout manager, creates each `SurveyPanel` object, and then adds it to the class:

```
setLayout(cards);
String question1 = "How would you characterize your diet?";
String[] resp1 = { "healthy", "unhealthy", "not telling" };
ask[0] = new SurveyPanel(question1, resp1, 2);
add(ask[0], "Card 0");
```

Each `SurveyPanel` object is created with three arguments to the constructor: the text of the question, an array of possible responses, and the element number of the default answer.

In the preceding code, the question "How would you characterize your diet?" has the responses "healthy," "unhealthy," and "not telling." The response at position 2, "not telling," is set as the default.

The `SurveyPanel` constructor uses a label component to hold the question and an array of radio buttons to hold the responses:

```
SurveyPanel(String ques, String[] resp, int def) {
    question = new JLabel(ques);
    response = new JRadioButton[resp.length];
    // more to come
}
```

11

The class uses grid layout to arrange its components into a grid with three vertical columns and one horizontal row. Each component placed in the grid is a panel.

First, a panel is created to hold the question label:

```
JPanel sub1 = new JPanel();
JLabel quesLabel = new JLabel(ques);
sub1.add(quesLabel);
```

The default layout for panels, flow layout with centered alignment, determines the placement of the label on the panel.

Next, a panel is created to hold the possible responses. A `for` loop iterates through the string array that holds the text of each response. This text is used to create a radio button. The second argument of the `JRadioButton()` constructor determines whether it is selected. This is implemented with the following code:

```
JPanel sub2 = new JPanel();
for (int i = 0; i < resp.length; i++) {
    if (def == i) {
        response[i] = new JRadioButton(resp[i], true);
    } else {
        response[i] = new JRadioButton(resp[i], false);
    }
    group.add(response[i]);
    sub2.add(response[i]);
}
```

The last panel holds the Next and Finish buttons:

```
JPanel sub3 = new JPanel();
nextButton.setEnabled(true);
sub3.add(nextButton);
finalButton.setEnabled(false);
sub3.add(finalButton);
```

Now that the three panels have been fully set up, they are added to the `SurveyPanel` interface, which completes the work of the constructor:

```
GridLayout grid = new GridLayout(3, 1);
setLayout(grid);
add(sub1);
add(sub2);
add(sub3);
```

There's one extra wrinkle in the SurveyPanel class—a method that enables the Finish button and disables the Next button when the last question has been reached:

```
void setFinalQuestion(boolean finalQuestion) {
    if (finalQuestion) {
        nextButton.setEnabled(false);
        finalButton.setEnabled(true);
    }
}
```

In a user interface that uses card layout, the display of each card usually takes place in response to an action by the user. These actions, called *events*, are covered in Lesson 12, "Responding to User Input."

A brief preview demonstrates how the SurveyPanel class is equipped to handle button clicks. The class implements ActionListener, an interface in the java.awt.event package:

```
public class SurveyWizard extends JPanel implements ActionListener {
    // more to come
}
```

This interface indicates that the class can respond to action events, which represent button clicks, menu choices, and similar user input.

11

Next, each button's addActionListener(Object) method is called:

```
ask[0].nextButton.addActionListener(this);
ask[0].finalButton.addActionListener(this);
```

Listeners are classes that monitor specific kinds of user input. The argument to addActionListener() is the class that's looking for action events. Using this as the argument indicates that the SurveyPanel class handles this job.

The ActionListener interface includes only one method:

```
public void actionPerformed(Action evt) {
    // more to come
}
```

This method is called when a component being listened to generates an action event. In the SurveyPanel class, this happens whenever a button is clicked. In SurveyPanel, this method uses an instance variable that keeps track of which card to display:

```
int currentCard = 0;
```

Every time a button is clicked and the actionPerformed() method is called, this variable is incremented, and the card layout manager's show(Container, String) method is called to display a new card. If the last card has been displayed, the Finish button is disabled.

Listing 11.5 shows the full `SurveyWizard` class with the complete `actionPerformed()` method, which is preceded by an `@Override` annotation to tell the Java compiler that a method of a superclass or interface is being overridden. Create a new empty Java file in NetBeans called `SurveyWizard` and assign it to the `com.java21days` package.

**LISTING 11.5**    The Full Text of `SurveyWizard.java`

```
 1: package com.java21days;
 2:
 3: import java.awt.*;
 4: import java.awt.event.*;
 5: import javax.swing.*;
 6:
 7: public class SurveyWizard extends JPanel implements ActionListener {
 8:     int currentCard = 0;
 9:     CardLayout cards = new CardLayout();
10:     SurveyPanel[] ask = new SurveyPanel[3];
11:
12:     public SurveyWizard() {
13:         super();
14:         setSize(240, 140);
15:         setLayout(cards);
16:         // set up survey
17:         String question1 = "What is your gender?";
18:         String[] resp1 = { "female", "male", "not telling" };
19:         ask[0] = new SurveyPanel(question1, resp1, 2);
20:         String question2 = "What is your age?";
21:         String[] resp2 = { "Under 25", "25-34", "35-54",
22:             "Over 54" };
23:         ask[1] = new SurveyPanel(question2, resp2, 1);
24:         String question3 = "How often do you exercise each week?";
25:         String[] resp3 = { "Never", "1-3 times", "More than 3" };
26:         ask[2] = new SurveyPanel(question3, resp3, 1);
27:         ask[2].setFinalQuestion(true);
28:         addListeners();
29:     }
30:
31:     private void addListeners() {
32:         for (int i = 0; i < ask.length; i++) {
33:             ask[i].nextButton.addActionListener(this);
34:             ask[i].finalButton.addActionListener(this);
35:             add(ask[i], "Card " + i);
36:         }
37:     }
38:
39:     @Override
40:     public void actionPerformed(ActionEvent evt) {
41:         currentCard++;
```

```
42:            if (currentCard >= ask.length) {
43:                System.exit(0);
44:            }
45:            cards.show(this, "Card " + currentCard);
46:        }
47: }
48:
49: class SurveyPanel extends JPanel {
50:     JLabel question;
51:     JRadioButton[] response;
52:     JButton nextButton = new JButton("Next");
53:     JButton finalButton = new JButton("Finish");
54:
55:     SurveyPanel(String ques, String[] resp, int def) {
56:         super();
57:         setSize(160, 110);
58:         question = new JLabel(ques);
59:         response = new JRadioButton[resp.length];
60:         JPanel sub1 = new JPanel();
61:         ButtonGroup group = new ButtonGroup();
62:         JLabel quesLabel = new JLabel(ques);
63:         sub1.add(quesLabel);
64:         JPanel sub2 = new JPanel();
65:         for (int i = 0; i < resp.length; i++) {
66:             if (def == i) {
67:                 response[i] = new JRadioButton(resp[i], true);
68:             } else {
69:                 response[i] = new JRadioButton(resp[i], false);
70:             }
71:             group.add(response[i]);
72:             sub2.add(response[i]);
73:         }
74:         JPanel sub3 = new JPanel();
75:         nextButton.setEnabled(true);
76:         sub3.add(nextButton);
77:         finalButton.setEnabled(false);
78:         sub3.add(finalButton);
79:         GridLayout grid = new GridLayout(3, 1);
80:         setLayout(grid);
81:         add(sub1);
82:         add(sub2);
83:         add(sub3);
84:     }
85:
86:     void setFinalQuestion(boolean finalQuestion) {
87:         if (finalQuestion) {
88:             nextButton.setEnabled(false);
89:             finalButton.setEnabled(true);
90:         }
91:     }
92: }
```

11

The SurveyWizard class is a JPanel component that creates a card layout manager as an instance variable in line 9 and assigns it to the panel in line 15. This class lacks a main() method, so it must be added to another program's user interface to be tested.

The SurveyFrame application, shown in Listing 11.6, contains a frame that displays a survey panel. Create it in NetBeans (in the package com.java21days).

**LISTING 11.6**    The Full Text of SurveyFrame.java

```
 1: package com.java21days;
 2:
 3: import javax.swing.*;
 4:
 5: public class SurveyFrame extends JFrame {
 6:     public SurveyFrame() {
 7:         super("Survey");
 8:         setSize(290, 140);
 9:         setDefaultCloseOperation(JFrame.EXIT_ON_CLOSE);
10:         setLookAndFeel();
11:         SurveyWizard wiz = new SurveyWizard();
12:         add(wiz);
13:         setVisible(true);
14:     }
15:
16:     private static void setLookAndFeel() {
17:         try {
18:             UIManager.setLookAndFeel(
19:                 "javax.swing.plaf.nimbus.NimbusLookAndFeel"
20:             );
21:         } catch (Exception exc) {
22:             System.err.println(exc);
23:         }
24:     }
25:
26:     public static void main(String[] arguments) {
27:         SurveyFrame.setLookAndFeel();
28:         SurveyFrame surv = new SurveyFrame();
29:     }
30: }
```

A SurveyWizard object is created in line 11 and is added to the frame in line 12. The running application is shown earlier, in Figure 11.5.

## Cell Padding and Insets

By default, no components have extra space around them (which is easiest to see in components that fill their cells). The horizontal and vertical gaps that appear when you create a new layout manager are used to determine the amount of space between components in a panel. *Insets*, however, are used to determine the amount of space around a panel. The Insets class includes values for the top, bottom, left, and right insets, which then are used when the panel is drawn.

Insets determine the amount of space between the edges of a panel and the panel's components.

The following statement creates an Insets object that specifies 20 pixels of insets above and below and 13 pixels to the left and right:

```
Insets whitespace = new Insets(20, 13, 20, 13);
```

You can establish insets in any container by overriding its getInsets() method and returning an Insets object, as in this example:

```
public Insets getInsets() {
    return new Insets(10, 30, 10, 30);
}
```

11

# Summary

When it comes to designing a user interface in Java, you've seen that abstract expressionism goes only so far. Getting the desired user interface layout in a Swing application requires the use of layout managers. These managers require some adjustment for people who are used to more precise control over where components appear on an interface.

You now know how to use the five Swing layout managers and panels. As you work with Swing, you'll find that it can approximate any kind of interface through the use of nested containers and different layout managers.

When you master the development of a user interface in Java, your programs can offer an interface that works on multiple platforms without modification.

# Q&A

**Q I really dislike working with layout managers; they're either too simplistic or too complicated. Even with a lot of tinkering, I can never get my user interface to look like I want it to. All I want to do is define the sizes of my components and put them at an (x, y) position on the screen. Can I do this?**

**A** It's possible but problematic. Java was designed in such a way that a program's GUI could run equally well on different platforms and with different screen resolutions, fonts, screen sizes, and the like. Relying on pixel coordinates can cause a program that looks good on one platform to be unusable on others. Layout disasters such as components overlapping each other or getting cut off by the edge of a container may result. By dynamically placing elements on the screen, layout managers get around these problems. Although there might be some differences in the end results on different platforms, they are less likely to be catastrophic.

If none of that is persuasive, here's how to ignore my advice: Set the content pane's layout manager with `null` as the argument. Create a `Rectangle` object (from the `java.awt` package) with the (x, y) position, width, and height of the component as arguments. Finally, call the component's `setBounds(Rectangle)` method with that rectangle as the argument.

The following application displays a 300×300-pixel frame with a Click Me button at the (x, y) position 10, 10 that is 120 pixels wide by 30 pixels tall:

```java
import java.awt.*;
import javax.swing.*;

public class Absolute extends JFrame {
    public Absolute() {
        super("Example");
        setSize(300, 300);
        setLayout(null);
        JButton myButton = new JButton("Click Me");
        myButton.setBounds(new Rectangle(10, 10, 120, 30));
        add(myButton);
        setVisible(true);
    }

    public static void main(String[] arguments) {
        Absolute ex = new Absolute();
    }
}
```

You can find out more about `setBounds()`. You can find the documentation for it, along with the rest of the Java Class Library, at `https://docs.oracle.com/en/java/javase/12/docs/api`.

# Quiz

Review this lesson's material by taking this three-question quiz.

## Questions

1. What is the default layout manager for a panel in Java?

   A. None

   B. BorderLayout

   C. FlowLayout

2. Which layout manager uses a compass direction or a reference to the center when adding a component to a container?

   A. BorderLayout

   B. MapLayout

   C. FlowLayout

3. If you want to create an installation wizard that has multiple steps, what layout manager should you use?

   A. GridLayout

   B. CardLayout

   C. BorderLayout

## Answers

1. C. To keep a panel from using flow layout, you can set its layout manager to null.

2. A. Border layout has class variables NORTH, SOUTH, EAST, WEST, and CENTER.

3. B. Card layout enables components to be stacked like cards and displayed one at a time, making it well suited to implementing a wizard.

# Certification Practice

The following question is the kind of thing you could expect to be asked on a Java programming certification test. Answer it without looking again at this lesson or using the Java compiler to test the code.

Given:

```
import java.awt.*;
import javax.swing.*;

public class ThreeButtons extends JFrame {
```

11

```
    public ThreeButtons() {
        super("Program");
        setSize(350, 225);
        setDefaultCloseOperation(JFrame.EXIT_ON_CLOSE);
        JButton alpha = new JButton("Alpha");
        JButton beta = new JButton("Beta");
        JButton gamma = new JButton("Gamma");
        // answer goes here
        add(alpha);
        add(beta);
        add(gamma);
        pack();
        setVisible(true);
    }

    public static void main(String[] arguments) {
        ThreeButtons b3 = new ThreeButtons();
    }
}
```

Which statement should replace `// answer goes here` to make the frame display all three buttons side by side?

**A.** `content.setLayout(null);`

**B.** `content.setLayout(new FlowLayout());`

**C.** `content.setLayout(new GridLayout(3,1));`

**D.** `content.setLayout(new BorderLayout());`

The answer is available on the book's website, at `www.java21days.com`. Visit the Lesson 11 page and click the Certification Practice link.

# Exercises

To extend your knowledge of the subjects covered in this lesson, try the following exercises:

1. Create a user interface that displays a calendar for a single month, including headings for the seven days of the week and a title for the month across the top.

2. Create an interface that incorporates more than one layout manager.

Where applicable, exercise solutions are offered on the book's website, at www.java21days.com.

# LESSON 12
# Responding to User Input

Designing a Java program with a graphical user interface (GUI) isn't very useful if the user can't do anything to it. To make the program completely functional, you must make the interface receptive to user events.

Swing handles events with a set of interfaces called *event listeners*. You create a listener object and associate it with the user interface component being monitored.

During this lesson, you will learn how to add listeners to your Swing WWprograms to handle action events, mouse events, and other interaction. When you're finished, you will have created full Java applications using the Swing set of classes.

# Event Listeners

If a class wants to respond to a user event in Java, it must implement the interface that deals with that type of event. This interface is not the same thing as a GUI. It's an abstract type that defines a set of methods a class must implement.

Interfaces that handle user events are called *event listeners*.

Each listener handles a specific kind of event.

The `java.awt.event` package contains all the basic event listeners, as well as objects that represent specific events. These listener interfaces are some of the most useful:

- `ActionListener`: *Action events*, which are generated when a user performs an action on a component, such as clicking a button
- `AdjustmentListener`: *Adjustment events*, which are generated when a component is adjusted, such as when a scrollbar is moved
- `FocusListener`: *Keyboard focus events*, which are generated when a component such as a text field gains or loses the focus
- `ItemListener`: *Item events*, which are generated when an item such as a check box is changed
- `KeyListener`: *Keyboard events*, which occur when a user enters text by using the keyboard
- `MouseListener`: *Mouse events*, which are generated by mouse clicks, a mouse entering a component's area, and a mouse leaving a component's area
- `MouseMotionListener`: *Mouse movement events*, which track all movement by a mouse over a component
- `WindowListener`: *Window events*, which are generated when a window is maximized, minimized, moved, or closed

Just as a Java class can implement multiple interfaces, a class that takes user input can implement as many listeners as needed. The `implements` keyword in the class declaration is followed by the name of the interface. If more than one interface has been implemented, their names are separated by commas.

The following class is declared to handle both action and text events:

```
public class Suspense extends JFrame implements ActionListener,
    TextListener {
    // body of class
}
```

To refer to these event listener interfaces in your programs, you can import them individually or use an `import` statement with a wildcard to make the entire package available:

```
import java.awt.event.*;
```

## Setting Up Components

When you make a class an event listener, you have set up a specific type of event to be heard by that class. However, the event won't be heard unless you add a matching listener to the GUI component. That listener generates the events when the component is used.

After a component is created, you can call one (or more) of the following methods on the component to associate a listener with it:

- **addActionListener()**: JButton, JCheckBox, JComboBox, JTextField, JRadioButton, and JMenuItem components
- **addFocusListener()**: All Swing components
- **addItemListener()**: JButton, JCheckBox, JComboBox, and JRadioButton components
- **addKeyListener()**: All Swing components
- **addMouseListener()**: All Swing components
- **addMouseMotionListener()**: All Swing components
- **addTextListener()**: JTextField and JTextArea components
- **addWindowListener()**: JWindow and JFrame components

**CAUTION**

> Modifying a component after adding it to a container is an easy mistake to make in a Java program. You must add listeners to a component and handle any other configuration before the component is added to any containers; otherwise, these settings are disregarded when the program is run.

12

The following example creates a `JButton` object and associates an action event listener with it:

```
JButton zap = new JButton("Zap");
zap.addActionListener(this);
```

All the listener adding methods take one argument: the object that is listening for events of that kind. Using `this` indicates that the current class is the event listener. You could specify a different object, as long as its class implements the right listener interface.

## Event-Handling Methods

When you associate an interface with a class, the class must contain methods that implement every method in the interface.

In the case of event listeners, the windowing system calls each method automatically when the corresponding user event takes place.

The `ActionListener` interface has only one method: `actionPerformed()`. All classes that implement `ActionListener` must have a method with the following structure:

```
public void actionPerformed(ActionEvent event) {
    // handle event here
}
```

If only one component in a program's GUI has a listener for action events, you know that this `actionPerformed()` method is called only in response to an event generated by that component. This makes it simpler to write the `actionPerformed()` method. All the method's code responds to that component's user event.

But when more than one component has an action event listener, you must use the method's `ActionEvent` argument to figure out which component was used and act accordingly in your program. You can use this object to discover details about the component that generated the event. `ActionEvent` and all other event objects are part of the `java.awt.event` package.

Every event-handling method is sent an event object of some kind. You can use the object's `getSource()` method to determine which component sent the event, as in the following example:

```
public void actionPerformed(ActionEvent event) {
    Object source = event.getSource();
}
```

The object returned by the `getSource()` method can be compared to components by using the equality operator (`==`). The following statements extend the preceding example to handle user clicks on buttons named `quitButton` and `sortRecords`:

```
if (source == quitButton) {
    quit();
}
if (source == sortRecords) {
    sort();
}
```

The `quit()` method is called if the `quitButton` object generated the event, and the `sort()` method is called if the `sortRecords` button generated the event.

Many event-handling methods call a different method for each kind of event or component. This makes an event-handling method easier to read. In addition, if a class has more than one event-handling method, each one can call the same methods to get work done.

Java's `instanceof` operator can be used in an event-handling method to determine the class of component that generated the event. The following example can be used in a program with one button and one text field, each of which generates an action event:

```
void actionPerformed(ActionEvent event) {
    Object source = event.getSource();
    if (source instanceof JTextField) {
        calculateScore();
    } else if (source instanceof JButton) {
        quit();
    }
}
```

If the event-generating component belongs to the `JTextField` class, the `calculateScore()` method is called. If the component belongs to `JButton`, the `quit()` method is called instead.

The `TitleBar` application, shown in Listing 12.1, displays a frame with two `JButton` components, which are used to change the text on the frame's title bar. Create a new empty Java file called `TitleBar`, in the package `com.java21days`, and enter the class's source code.

**LISTING 12.1**   The Full Text of `TitleBar.java`

```
 1: package com.java21days;
 2:
 3: import java.awt.event.*;
 4: import javax.swing.*;
 5: import java.awt.*;
 6:
 7: public class TitleBar extends JFrame implements ActionListener {
 8:     JButton b1;
 9:     JButton b2;
10:
11:     public TitleBar() {
12:         super("Title Bar");
13:         setSize(330, 80);
14:         setDefaultCloseOperation(JFrame.EXIT_ON_CLOSE);
15:         b1 = new JButton("Rosencrantz");
16:         b2 = new JButton("Guildenstern");
17:         b1.addActionListener(this);
18:         b2.addActionListener(this);
19:         FlowLayout flow = new FlowLayout();
20:         setLayout(flow);
21:         add(b1);
```

12

```
22:            add(b2);
23:            setVisible(true);
24:        }
25:
26:    @Override
27:    public void actionPerformed(ActionEvent event) {
28:        Object source = event.getSource();
29:        if (source == b1) {
30:            setTitle("Rosencrantz");
31:        } else if (source == b2) {
32:            setTitle("Guildenstern");
33:        }
34:        repaint();
35:    }
36:
37:    private static void setLookAndFeel() {
38:        try {
39:            UIManager.setLookAndFeel(
40:                "javax.swing.plaf.nimbus.NimbusLookAndFeel"
41:            );
42:        } catch (Exception exc) {
43:            System.err.println(exc);
44:        }
45:    }
46:
47:    public static void main(String[] arguments) {
48:        TitleBar.setLookAndFeel();
49:        TitleBar frame = new TitleBar();
50:    }
51: }
```

After you run this application with the Java Virtual Machine (JVM), the program's interface should resemble Figure 12.1. Click the buttons to see what happens.

**FIGURE 12.1**
The `TitleBar` application.

Only 13 lines are needed to respond to action events in this application:

- Line 3 imports the `java.awt.event` package.
- Line 7 indicates that the class implements the `ActionListener` interface.
- Lines 17–18 add action listeners to both `JButton` objects.
- Lines 27–35 respond to action events that occur from the two `JButton` objects. The `event` object's `getSource()` method determines the event's source. If it is equal to the `b1` button, the frame's title is set to `Rosencrantz`; if it is equal to `b2`, the title is set to `Guildenstern`. A call to `repaint()` is needed so that the frame is redrawn after any title change that might have occurred in the method.

# Working with Methods

The following sections detail the structure of each event-handling method and the methods that can be used in these methods.

In addition to the methods described, the `getSource()` method can be used on any event object to determine which object generated the event.

## Action Events

Action events occur when a user completes an action using components such as buttons, check boxes, menu items, text fields, and radio buttons.

A class must implement the `ActionListener` interface to handle these events. In addition, the `addActionListener()` method must be called on each component that should generate an action event—unless you want to ignore that component's action events.

The `actionPerformed(ActionEvent)` method is the only method of the `ActionListener` interface. It takes the following form:

```
public void actionPerformed(ActionEvent event) {
    // ...
}
```

In addition to the `getSource()` method, you can use the `getActionCommand()` method on the `ActionEvent` object to discover more information about the event's source.

By default, the action command is the text associated with the component, such as the label on a button. You also can set a different action command for a component by calling its `setActionCommand(String)` method. The `String` argument should be the action command's desired text.

The following statements create a button and a menu item and give both of them the action command `"Sort Files"`:

```
JButton sort = new JButton("Sort");
JMenuItem menuSort = new JMenuItem("Sort");
sort.setActionCommand("Sort Files");
menuSort.setActionCommand("Sort Files");
```

**12**

**TIP** | Action commands are useful in a program in which more than one component should cause the same thing to happen. By giving both components the same action command, you can handle them with the same code in an event-handling method.

## Focus Events

A focus event occurs when any component gains or loses input focus on a GUI. A component has the *focus* if it is the component that is active for keyboard input. If one of the fields has the focus (in a user interface with several editable text fields), the cursor blinks in the field. Any text entered goes into this component.

Focus applies to all components that can receive input. You can give a component the focus by calling its requestFocus() method with no arguments, as in this example:

```
JButton ok = new JButton("OK");
ok.requestFocus();
```

To handle a focus event, a class must implement the FocusListener interface, which has two methods: focusGained(*FocusEvent*) and focusLost(*FocusEvent*). They take the following forms:

```
public void focusGained(FocusEvent event) {
    // ...
}
public void focusLost(FocusEvent event) {
    // ...
}
```

To determine which object gained or lost the focus, the getSource() method can be called on the FocusEvent object, sent as an argument to the two methods.

Listing 12.2 contains Calculator, a Java application that displays the sum of two numbers. Focus events are used to determine when the sum needs to be recalculated. In NetBeans create a new Java file with the name Calculator and package name com.java21days with the source code of this listing.

**LISTING 12.2**    The Full Text of Calculator.java

```
 1: package com.java21days;
 2:
 3: import java.awt.event.*;
 4: import javax.swing.*;
 5: import java.awt.*;
 6:
 7: public class Calculator extends JFrame implements FocusListener {
 8:     JTextField value1, value2, sum;
 9:     JLabel plus, equals;
10:
11:     public Calculator() {
12:         super("Add Two Numbers");
13:         setSize(350, 90);
14:         setDefaultCloseOperation(JFrame.EXIT_ON_CLOSE);
15:         FlowLayout flow = new FlowLayout(FlowLayout.CENTER);
16:         setLayout(flow);
```

```
17:        // create components
18:        value1 = new JTextField("0", 5);
19:        plus = new JLabel("+");
20:        value2 = new JTextField("0", 5);
21:        equals = new JLabel("=");
22:        sum = new JTextField("0", 5);
23:        // add listeners
24:        value1.addFocusListener(this);
25:        value2.addFocusListener(this);
26:        // set up sum field
27:        sum.setEditable(false);
28:        // add components
29:        add(value1);
30:        add(plus);
31:        add(value2);
32:        add(equals);
33:        add(sum);
34:        setVisible(true);
35:    }
36:
37:    @Override
38:    public void focusGained(FocusEvent event) {
39:        try {
40:            float total = Float.parseFloat(value1.getText()) +
41:                Float.parseFloat(value2.getText());
42:            sum.setText("" + total);
43:        } catch (NumberFormatException nfe) {
44:            value1.setText("0");
45:            value2.setText("0");
46:            sum.setText("0");
47:        }
48:    }
49:
50:    @Override
51:    public void focusLost(FocusEvent event) {
52:        focusGained(event);
53:    }
54:
55:    private static void setLookAndFeel() {
56:        try {
57:            UIManager.setLookAndFeel(
58:                "javax.swing.plaf.nimbus.NimbusLookAndFeel"
59:            );
60:        } catch (Exception exc) {
61:            System.err.println(exc);
62:        }
63:    }
64:
65:    public static void main(String[] arguments) {
66:        Calculator.setLookAndFeel();
67:        Calculator frame = new Calculator();
68:    }
69: }
```

12

Figure 12.2 shows the application.

**FIGURE 12.2**
The `Calculator`
application.

In this application, the class implements the `FocusListener` interface so that focus listeners can be added to the first two text fields, `value1` and `value2`.

The `focusGained()` method is called whenever either of these fields gains the input focus (lines 38–48). In this method, the sum is calculated by adding the values in the other two fields. If either field contains an invalid value, such as a string, a `NumberFormatException` is thrown, and all three fields are reset to 0.

The `focusLost()` method accomplishes the same behavior by calling `focusGained()` with the focus event as an argument.

One thing to note about this application is that event-handling behavior is not required to collect numeric input in a text field. This is taken care of automatically by any component in which text input is received.

## Item Events

Item events occur when an item is selected or deselected on components such as buttons, check boxes, or radio buttons. A class must implement the `ItemListener` interface to handle these events.

The `itemStateChanged(ItemEvent)` method is the only method in the `ItemListener` interface. It takes the following form:

```
void itemStateChanged(ItemEvent event) {
    // ...
}
```

To determine in which item the event occurred, the `getItem()` method can be called on the `ItemEvent` object.

You also can see whether the item was selected or deselected by using the `getStateChange()` method. This method returns an integer that equals either the class variable `ItemEvent.DESELECTED` or `ItemEvent.SELECTED`.

The `FormatChooser` application in Listing 12.3 illustrates the use of item events, displaying information about a selected combo box item in a label. Create it with NetBeans as an empty Java file with the class name `FormatChooser` and package name `com.java21days`.

**LISTING 12.3**  The Full Text of `FormatChooser.java`

```
 1: package com.java21days;
 2:
 3: import java.awt.*;
 4: import java.awt.event.*;
 5: import javax.swing.*;
 6:
 7: public class FormatChooser extends JFrame implements ItemListener {
 8:     String[] formats = { "(choose format)", "Atom", "RSS 0.92",
 9:         "RSS 1.0", "RSS 2.0" };
10:     String[] descriptions = {
11:         "Atom weblog and syndication format",
12:         "RSS syndication format 0.92 (Netscape)",
13:         "RSS/RDF syndication format 1.0 (RSS/RDF)",
14:         "RSS syndication format 2.0 (UserLand)"
15:     };
16:     JComboBox formatBox = new JComboBox();
17:     JLabel descriptionLabel = new JLabel("");
18:
19:     public FormatChooser() {
20:         super("Syndication Format");
21:         setSize(420, 150);
22:         setDefaultCloseOperation(JFrame.EXIT_ON_CLOSE);
23:         setLayout(new BorderLayout());
24:         for (String format : formats) {
25:             formatBox.addItem(format);
26:         }
27:         formatBox.addItemListener(this);
28:         add(BorderLayout.NORTH, formatBox);
29:         add(BorderLayout.CENTER, descriptionLabel);
30:         setVisible(true);
31:     }
32:
33:     @Override
34:     public void itemStateChanged(ItemEvent event) {
35:         int choice = formatBox.getSelectedIndex();
36:         if (choice > 0) {
37:             descriptionLabel.setText(descriptions[choice-1]);
38:         }
39:     }
40:
41:     @Override
42:     public Insets getInsets() {
43:         return new Insets(50, 10, 10, 10);
44:     }
45:
46:     private static void setLookAndFeel() {
47:         try {
48:             UIManager.setLookAndFeel(
```

12

```
49:                        "javax.swing.plaf.nimbus.NimbusLookAndFeel"
50:                    );
51:            } catch (Exception exc) {
52:                System.err.println(exc);
53:            }
54:    }
55:
56:    public static void main(String[] arguments) {
57:        FormatChooser.setLookAndFeel();
58:        FormatChooser frame = new FormatChooser();
59:    }
60: }
```

This application extends the combo box example from Lesson 9, "Creating a Graphical User Interface." Figure 12.3 shows how it looks after a choice has been made.

**FIGURE 12.3**
The output of the `FormatChooser` application.

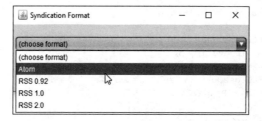

The application creates a combo box from an array of strings and adds an item listener to the component (lines 24–27). Item events are received by the `itemStateChanged(ItemEvent)` method (lines 34–39), which changes a label's text based on the index number of the selected item. Index 1 corresponds with Atom, 2 with RSS 0.92, 3 with RSS 1.0, and 4 with RSS 2.0.

## Key Events

A key event occurs when a keyboard key is pressed. Any component can generate a key event, and a class must implement the `KeyListener` interface to support these events.

The `KeyListener` interface has three methods: `keyPressed(KeyEvent)`, `keyReleased(KeyEvent)`, and `keyTyped(KeyEvent)`. They take the following forms:

```
public void keyPressed(KeyEvent event) {
    // ...
}
public void keyReleased(KeyEvent event) {
    // ...
}
public void keyTyped(KeyEvent event) {
    // ...
}
```

KeyEvent's getKeyChar() method returns the character of the key associated with the event. If no Unicode character can be represented by the key, getKeyChar() returns a character value equal to the class variable KeyEvent.CHAR_UNDEFINED.

For a component to generate key events, it must be able to receive the input focus. Text fields, text areas, and other components that accept keyboard input support this capability automatically. For other components, such as labels and panels, the setFocusable(*boolean*) method should be called with the argument true, as in the following code:

```
JPanel pane = new JPanel();
pane.setFocusable(true);
```

## Mouse Events

A mouse event is generated by a mouse click, a mouse entering a component's area, or a mouse leaving the area. Any component can generate these events, which are implemented by a class through the MouseListener interface, which has five methods:

- mouseClicked(*MouseEvent*)
- mouseEntered(*MouseEvent*)
- mouseExited(*MouseEvent*)
- mousePressed(*MouseEvent*)
- mouseReleased(*MouseEvent*)

Each method has the same basic form as mouseReleased(*MouseEvent*):

```
public void mouseReleased(MouseEvent event) {
    // ...
}
```

12

The following methods can be used on MouseEvent objects:

- **getClickCount()**: Returns, as an integer, the number of times the mouse was clicked
- **getPoint()**: Returns, as a Point object, the (x, y) coordinates within the component where the mouse was clicked
- **getX()**: Returns the x position
- **getY()**: Returns the y position

## Mouse Motion Events

A mouse motion event occurs when the mouse is moved over a component. As with other mouse events, any component can generate mouse motion events. A class must implement the MouseMotionListener interface to support them.

The MouseMotionListener interface has two methods: mouseDragged(*MouseEvent*) and mouseMoved(*MouseEvent*). They take the following forms:

```
public void mouseDragged(MouseEvent event) {
    // ...
}
public void mouseMoved(MouseEvent event) {
    // ...
}
```

Unlike the other event listener interfaces you have dealt with up to this point, MouseMotionListener does not have its own event type. Instead, MouseEvent objects are used. Because of this, you can call the same methods you would call for mouse events: getClick(), getPoint(), getX(), and getY().

The next project you will undertake demonstrates how to detect and respond to mouse events. The MousePrank application, shown in Listing 12.4, consists of two classes, MousePrank and PrankPanel, that implement a user interface button that tries to avoid being clicked.

Create a new empty Java file in NetBeans with the class name MousePrank and package name com.java21days; then enter the code shown in Listing 12.4. The techniques demonstrated in this class are described shortly.

**LISTING 12.4**    The Full Text of MousePrank.java

```
 1: package com.java21days;
 2:
 3: import java.awt.*;
 4: import java.awt.event.*;
 5: import javax.swing.*;
 6:
 7: public class MousePrank extends JFrame implements ActionListener {
 8:     public MousePrank() {
 9:         super("Message");
10:         setDefaultCloseOperation(JFrame.EXIT_ON_CLOSE);
11:         setSize(420, 220);
12:         BorderLayout border = new BorderLayout();
13:         setLayout(border);
14:         JLabel msg = new JLabel("Click OK to close program.");
```

```
15:          add(BorderLayout.NORTH, msg);
16:          PrankPanel prank = new PrankPanel();
17:          prank.ok.addActionListener(this);
18:          add(BorderLayout.CENTER, prank);
19:          setVisible(true);
20:      }
21:
22:      @Override
23:      public void actionPerformed(ActionEvent event) {
24:          System.exit(0);
25:      }
26:
27:      @Override
28:      public Insets getInsets() {
29:          return new Insets(40, 10, 10, 10);
30:      }
31:
32:      private static void setLookAndFeel() {
33:          try {
34:              UIManager.setLookAndFeel(
35:                  "javax.swing.plaf.nimbus.NimbusLookAndFeel"
36:              );
37:          } catch (Exception exc) {
38:              System.err.println(exc);
40:          }
41:      }
42:
43:      public static void main(String[] arguments) {
44:          MousePrank.setLookAndFeel();
45:          new MousePrank();
46:      }
47: }
48:
49: class PrankPanel extends JPanel implements MouseMotionListener {
50:      JButton ok = new JButton("OK");
51:      int buttonX, buttonY, mouseX, mouseY;
52:      int width, height;
53:
54:      PrankPanel() {
55:          super();
56:          setLayout(null);
57:          addMouseMotionListener(this);
58:          buttonX = 110;
59:          buttonY = 110;
60:          ok.setBounds(new Rectangle(buttonX, buttonY,
61:              70, 20));
62:          add(ok);
63:      }
64:
65:      public void mouseMoved(MouseEvent event) {
66:          mouseX = event.getX();
```

12

```
67:              mouseY = event.getY();
68:              width = (int) getSize().getWidth();
69:              height = (int) getSize().getHeight();
70:              if (Math.abs((mouseX + 35) - buttonX) < 50) {
71:                  buttonX = moveButton(mouseX, buttonX, width);
72:                  repaint();
73:              }
74:              if (Math.abs((mouseY + 10) - buttonY) < 50) {
75:                  buttonY = moveButton(mouseY, buttonY, height);
76:                  repaint();
77:              }
78:          }
79:
80:      @Override
81:      public void mouseDragged(MouseEvent event) {
82:          // ignore this event
83:      }
84:
85:      private int moveButton(int mouseAt, int buttonAt, int bord) {
86:          if (buttonAt < mouseAt) {
87:              buttonAt--;
88:          } else {
89:              buttonAt++;
90:          }
91:          if (buttonAt > (bord - 20)) {
92:              buttonAt = 10;
93:          }
94:          if (buttonAt < 0) {
95:              buttonAt = bord - 80;
96:          }
97:          return buttonAt;
98:      }
99:
100:     @Override
101:     public void paintComponent(Graphics comp) {
102:         super.paintComponent(comp);
103:         ok.setBounds(buttonX, buttonY, 70, 20);
104:     }
105: }
```

The MousePrank class is a frame that holds two components arranged with border layout: the label "Click OK to close program" and a panel with an OK button on it. Figure 12.4 shows the user interface for this application.

Because the button does not behave normally, it is implemented with the PrankPanel class, a subclass of JPanel. This panel includes a button that is drawn at a specific position on the panel instead of being placed by a layout manager. This technique is described at the end of Lesson 11, "Arranging Components on a User Interface."

**FIGURE 12.4**
The running
`MousePrank`
application.

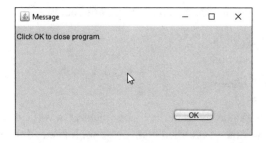

The panel's layout manager is set to `null`, which causes it to stop using flow layout as its default manager:

```
setLayout(null);
```

Next, the button is placed on the panel using `setBounds(Rectangle)`, the same method that determines where a frame or window will appear on a desktop.

A `Rectangle` object is created, and it has four arguments: its x position, y position, width, and height. Here's how `PrankPanel` draws the button:

```
JButton ok = new JButton("OK");
int buttonX = 110;
int buttonY = 110;
ok.setBounds(new Rectangle(buttonX, buttonY, 70, 20));
```

Creating the `Rectangle` object as the argument to `setBounds()` is more efficient than creating an object with a name and using that object as the argument. You don't need to use the object anywhere else in the class, so it doesn't need a name. The following statements accomplish the same thing in two steps:

```
Rectangle box = new Rectangle(buttonX, buttonY, 70, 20);
ok.setBounds(box);
```

The class has instance variables that hold the button's (x, y) position, `buttonX` and `buttonY`. They start out at (110, 110) and change whenever the mouse comes within 50 pixels of the center of the button.

You track mouse movements by implementing the `MouseListener` interface and its two methods, `mouseMoved(MouseEvent)` and `mouseDragged(MouseEvent)`.

The panel uses `mouseMoved()` and ignores `mouseDragged()`.

When the mouse moves, a mouse event object's `getX()` and `getY()` methods return its current (x, y) position, which is stored in the instance variables `mouseX` and `mouseY`.

12

The moveButton(*int*, *int*, *int*) method takes three arguments:

- The button's x or y position
- The mouse's x or y position
- The panel's width or height

This method moves the button away from the mouse in either a vertical or horizontal direction, depending on whether it is called with an x coordinate and the panel height or a y coordinate and the width.

After the button's position has moved, the repaint() method is called, which causes the panel's paintComponent(*Graphics*) method to be called in lines 101–104.

Every component has a paintComponent() method that can be overridden to draw the component. The button's setBounds() method displays it at the current (x, y) position in line 103.

## Window Events

A window event occurs when a user opens or closes a window object, such as a JFrame or JWindow object. Any component can generate these events, and a class must implement the WindowListener interface to support them.

The WindowListener interface has seven methods:

- windowActivated(*WindowEvent*)
- windowClosed(*WindowEvent*)
- windowClosing(*WindowEvent*)
- windowDeactivated(*WindowEvent*)
- windowDeiconified(*WindowEvent*)
- windowIconified(*WindowEvent*)
- windowOpened(*WindowEvent*)

They all have the same form as the windowOpened() method:

```
public void windowOpened(WindowEvent event) {
    // body of method
}
```

The windowClosing() and windowClosed() methods are similar, but one is called as the window is closing, and the other is called after it is closed. In fact, you can take action in a windowClosing() method to stop the window from being closed.

## Using Adapter Classes

A Java class that implements an interface must include all its methods, even if it doesn't plan to do anything in response to some of them.

This requirement can make it necessary to add a lot of empty methods when you're working with an event-handling interface such as WindowListener, which has seven methods.

As a convenience, Java offers *adapters*, which are Java classes that contain empty do-nothing implementations of specific interfaces. By subclassing an adapter class, you can implement only the event-handling methods you need by overriding those methods. The rest inherit those do-nothing methods.

The java.awt.event package includes FocusAdapter, KeyAdapter, MouseAdapter, MouseMotionAdapter, and WindowAdapter. They correspond to the expected listeners for focus, keyboard, mouse, mouse motion, and window events.

Listing 12.5 is a Java application that displays the most recently pressed key and monitors keyboard events through a subclass of KeyAdapter. Enter this source code in a new empty Java class file named KeyChecker in NetBeans in the package com.java21days.

**LISTING 12.5**   The Full Text of KeyChecker.java

```
 1: package com.java21days;
 2:
 3: import java.awt.*;
 4: import java.awt.event.*;
 5: import javax.swing.*;
 6:
 7: public class KeyChecker extends JFrame {
 8:     JLabel keyLabel = new JLabel("Hit any key");
 9:
10:     public KeyChecker() {
11:         super("Hit a Key");
12:         setSize(300, 200);
13:         setDefaultCloseOperation(JFrame.EXIT_ON_CLOSE);
14:         setLayout(new FlowLayout(FlowLayout.CENTER));
15:         KeyMonitor monitor = new KeyMonitor(this);
16:         setFocusable(true);
17:         addKeyListener(monitor);
18:         add(keyLabel);
19:         setVisible(true);
20:     }
21:
22:     private static void setLookAndFeel() {
23:         try {
24:             UIManager.setLookAndFeel(
```

12

```
25:                         "javax.swing.plaf.nimbus.NimbusLookAndFeel"
26:                 );
27:             } catch (Exception exc) {
28:                 System.err.println(exc);
30:             }
31:         }
32:
33:         public static void main(String[] arguments) {
34:             KeyChecker.setLookAndFeel();
35:             new KeyChecker();
36:         }
37: }
38:
39: class KeyMonitor extends KeyAdapter {
40:         KeyChecker display;
41:
42:         KeyMonitor(KeyChecker display) {
43:             this.display = display;
44:         }
45:
46:         @Override
47:         public void keyTyped(KeyEvent event) {
48:             display.keyLabel.setText("" + event.getKeyChar());
49:             display.repaint();
50:         }
51: }
```

The `KeyChecker` application is implemented as a main class of the same name and a `KeyMonitor` helper class.

`KeyMonitor` is a subclass of `KeyAdapter`, an adapter class for keyboard events that implements the `KeyListener` interface. In lines 47–50, the `keyTyped` method overrides the same method in `KeyAdapter`, which does nothing.

When a key is pressed, the key is discovered by calling the `getKeyChar()` method of the user event object. This key becomes the text of the `keyLabel` label in the `KeyChecker` class. This application is shown in Figure 12.5.

**FIGURE 12.5**
The running
`KeyChecker`
application.

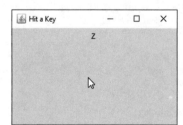

## Using Inner Classes

One of the challenges in taking user input in Java is keeping the code as short and simple as possible. Implementing event listeners and all their methods, even for undesired input, requires a lot of coding.

The `KeyChecker` application (refer to Listing 12.5) uses an adapter class to shorten the amount of programming required to handle key events. A technique to shorten it further would be to use inner classes. An adapter class is created as an inner class in this statement:

```
KeyAdapter monitor = new KeyAdapter() {
    public void keyTyped(KeyEvent event) {
        keyLabel.setText("" + event.getKeyChar());
        repaint();
    }
};
```

The `KeyAdapter` object overrides one method, `keyTyped(KeyEvent)`, to receive keyboard input. The `KeyChecker2` class shown in Listing 12.6 has two advantages over its predecessor. As you create it in NetBeans, see if you can figure out what they are.

**LISTING 12.6**  The Full Text of `KeyChecker2.java`

```
 1: package com.java21days;
 2:
 3: import java.awt.*;
 4: import java.awt.event.*;
 5: import javax.swing.*;
 6:
 7: public class KeyChecker2 extends JFrame {
 8:     JLabel keyLabel = new JLabel("Hit any key");
 9:
10:     public KeyChecker2() {
11:         super("Hit a Key");
12:         setSize(300, 200);
13:         setDefaultCloseOperation(JFrame.EXIT_ON_CLOSE);
14:         setLayout(new FlowLayout(FlowLayout.CENTER));
15:         KeyAdapter monitor = new KeyAdapter() {
16:             public void keyTyped(KeyEvent event) {
17:                 keyLabel.setText("" + event.getKeyChar());
18:                 repaint();
19:             }
20:         };
21:         setFocusable(true);
22:         addKeyListener(monitor);
23:         add(keyLabel);
```

12

```
24:            setVisible(true);
25:        }
26:
27:        private static void setLookAndFeel() {
28:            try {
29:                UIManager.setLookAndFeel(
30:                    "javax.swing.plaf.nimbus.NimbusLookAndFeel"
31:                );
32:            } catch (Exception exc) {
33:                System.err.println(exc);
34:            }
35:        }
36:
37:        public static void main(String[] arguments) {
38:            KeyChecker2.setLookAndFeel();
39:            new KeyChecker2();
40:        }
41: }
```

The `KeyChecker2` application functions identically to the `KeyChecker` version.

The advantages of this version are that it is shorter, not requiring the creation of a separate class, and it does not need to make use of the `this` variable in the inner class to be able to change the label in line 17. The inner class can access the variables and methods of its own class.

Inner classes also can be anonymous, which means they are objects of the class not assigned to variables.

The `TitleBar` application (refer to Listing 12.1), which uses action events to change a frame's title in response to button clicks, could be simplified by using anonymous inner classes. An anonymous inner class becomes the argument to the button's `addActionListener()` method, as you can see here:

```
JButton b1;
b1.addActionListener(new ActionListener() {
    public void actionPerformed(ActionEvent evt) {
        setTitle("Rosencrantz");
    }
});
JButton b2;
b2.addActionListener(new ActionListener() {
    public void actionPerformed(ActionEvent evt) {
        setTitle("Guildenstern");
    }
});
```

The anonymous inner class is an object that implements the `ActionListener` interface. The object's `actionPerformed()` method is overridden to set the frame's title when the corresponding button is clicked. Because each button has its own listener, this is simpler than using one listener for multiple interface components.

Inner classes look more complicated than separate classes, but they can simplify and shorten your Java code.

# Summary

Event handling is added to a GUI in Swing through these fundamental steps:

1. A listener interface is added to the class; it will contain the event-handling methods.
2. A listener is added to each component; it will generate the events to handle.
3. The methods are added, each with an `EventObject` class as the only argument to the method.
4. Methods of that `EventObject` class, such as `getSource()`, are used to learn which component generated the event and what kind of event it was.

When you know these steps, you can work with each of the listener interfaces and event classes. You also can learn about new listeners as they are added to Swing with new components.

# Q&A

**Q Can a program's event-handling behavior be put into its own class instead of being included with the code that creates the interface?**

**A** It can, and many programmers will tell you that this is a good way to design your programs. Separating interface design from your event-handling code allows you to develop the two separately. This makes it easier to maintain the project; related behavior is grouped and isolated from unrelated behavior.

**Q Is there a way to differentiate between the buttons on a `mouseClicked()` event?**

**A** Yes. This feature of mouse events isn't covered in this lesson because right and middle mouse buttons are platform-specific features that are unavailable on some systems where Java programs run.

Every mouse event sends a `MouseEvent` object to its event-handling methods. You can call an object's `getModifiers()` method to receive an integer value that indicates which mouse button generated the event. You can check the value against three class variables. It equals `MouseEvent.BUTTON1_MASK` if the left button was clicked, `MouseEvent.BUTTON2_MASK` if the middle button was clicked, and `MouseEvent.BUTTON3_MASK` if the right button was clicked. See `MouseTest.java` on the Lesson 12 page of the book's website at www.java21days.com for an example that uses this technique.

For more information, see the Java Class Library documentation for the `MouseEvent` class. Visit the web page `https://docs.oracle.com/en/java/javase/12/docs/api`, click the `java.desktop` module link, and click the `java.awt.event` hyperlink to view the classes in that package.

# Quiz

Review this lesson's material by taking this three-question quiz.

## Questions

1. If you use `this` in a method call such as `addActionListener(this)`, what object is being registered as a listener?

   **A.** An adapter class

   **B.** The current class

   **C.** No class

2. What is the benefit of subclassing an adapter class such as `WindowAdapter` (which implements the `WindowListener` interface)?

   **A.** You inherit all the behavior of that class.

   **B.** The subclass automatically becomes a listener.

   **C.** You don't need to implement any `WindowListener` methods you won't be using.

3. What kind of event is generated when you press Tab to leave a text field?

   **A.** `FocusEvent`

   **B.** `WindowEvent`

   **C.** `ActionEvent`

## Answers

1. **B.** The current class must implement the correct listener interface and the required methods.

2. **C.** Because most listener interfaces contain more methods than you need, using an adapter class as a superclass saves the hassle of implementing empty methods just to implement the interface.

3. **A.** A user interface component loses focus when the user stops editing that component and moves to a different part of the interface.

# Certification Practice

The following question is the kind of thing you could expect to be asked on a Java programming certification test. Answer it without looking again at this lesson or using the Java compiler to test the code.

Given:

```
import java.awt.event.*;
import javax.swing.*;
import java.awt.*;

public class Expunger extends JFrame implements ActionListener {
    public boolean deleteFile;

    public Expunger() {
        super("Expunger");
        JLabel commandLabel = new JLabel("Do you want to delete the file?");
        JButton yes = new JButton("Yes");
        JButton no = new JButton("No");
        yes.addActionListener(this);
        no.addActionListener(this);
        setLayout( new BorderLayout() );
        JPanel bottom = new JPanel();
        bottom.add(yes);
        bottom.add(no);
        add("North", commandLabel);
        add("South", bottom);
        pack();
        setVisible(true);
    }

    public void actionPerformed(ActionEvent evt) {
        JButton source = (JButton) evt.getSource();
        // answer goes here
            deleteFile = true;
        else
            deleteFile = false;
    }

    public static void main(String[] arguments) {
        new Expunger();
    }
}
```

12

Which of the following statements should replace `// answer goes here` to make the application function correctly?

**A.** `if (source instanceof JButton)`

**B.** `if (source.getActionCommand().equals("yes"))`

**C.** `if (source.getActionCommand().equals("Yes"))`

**D.** `if source.getActionCommand() == "Yes"`

The answer is available on the book's website, at www.java21days.com. Visit the Lesson 12 page and click the Certification Practice link.

# Exercises

To extend your knowledge of the subjects covered in this lesson, try the following exercises:

1. Create an application that uses `FocusListener` to ensure that a text field's value is multiplied by –1 and is redisplayed whenever a user changes it to a negative value.

2. Create a calculator that adds or subtracts the contents of two text fields whenever the appropriate button is clicked and displays the result as a label.

Where applicable, exercise solutions are offered on the book's website, at www.java21days.com.

# LESSON 13
# Creating Java2D Graphics

In this lesson, you'll work with Java classes that put the graphics in "graphical user interface." Java2D is a set of classes that supports high-quality, scalable, two-dimensional images, color, and text.

Java2D, which includes classes in the `java.awt` and `javax.swing` packages, can be used for all of these visually appealing tasks:

- Drawing text
- Drawing shapes such as circles and polygons
- Using different fonts, colors, and line widths
- Filling shapes with colors and patterns

# **The** Graphics2D **Class**

Everything in Java2D begins with the Graphics2D class in the java.awt package, which represents a *graphics context*—an environment in which something can be drawn. A Graphics2D object can represent a component on a graphical user interface, printer, or another display device. Graphics2D is a subclass of the Graphics class that extends and improves its visual capabilities.

Before you can start using the Graphics2D class, you need a surface on which to draw. Several user interface components can act as a canvas for graphical operations, including panels and windows. As soon as you have a component to use as a canvas, you can draw text, lines, ovals, circles, arcs, rectangles, and other polygons on that object. One component that's suitable for this purpose is JPanel in the javax.swing package. This class represents panels in a graphical user interface that can be empty or that can contain other components.

The following code creates a frame and a panel and then adds the panel to the frame:

```
JFrame main = new JFrame("Welcome Screen");
JPanel pane = new JPanel();
main.add(pane);
```

Like many other user interface components in Java, panels have a paintComponent(*Graphics*) method that is called automatically when the component needs to be redisplayed.

paintComponent() might be called for several reasons:

- The graphical user interface containing the component is displayed for the first time.
- A window that was displayed on top of the component is closed.
- The graphical user interface containing the component is resized.

By creating a subclass of JPanel, you can override the panel's paintComponent() method and put all your drawing operations in this method.

As you might have noticed, a Graphics object—not the Graphics2D object you need—is sent to an interface component's paintComponent() method. To create a Graphics2D object that represents the component's drawing surface, you must use casting to convert it, as in the following example:

```
public void paintComponent(Graphics comp) {
    Graphics2D comp2D = (Graphics2D) comp;
    // body of method
}
```

After a `Graphics2D` object has been cast from the `Graphics` object sent to the method as an argument, all drawing methods use this new object. The `Graphics` object will not be used again.

## The Graphics Coordinate System

Java2D classes use the same (x, y) coordinate system you have used when setting the sizes of frames and other components in your Swing applications.

Java's coordinate system uses pixels as its unit of measure. The origin coordinate (0, 0) is in the upper-left corner of a component.

The value of x coordinates increases to the right of (0, 0), and the value of y coordinates increases downward.

When you set a frame's size by calling its `setSize(int, int)` method, the frame's upper-left corner is at (0, 0), and its lower-right corner is at the two arguments sent to `setSize()`.

The following statement creates a frame 425 pixels wide by 130 pixels tall with its lower-right corner at (425, 130):

```
setSize(425, 130);
```

**CAUTION**      Java2D differs from other drawing systems, in which the (0, 0) origin is at the lower left, and y values increase in an upward direction.

All pixel values are integers; you can't use decimal numbers to display something at a position between two integer values.

Figure 13.1 shows Java's graphical coordinate system visually, with the origin at (0, 0). Two of the points of a rectangle are at (20, 20) and (60, 60).

13

**FIGURE 13.1**
The Java graphics
coordinate system.

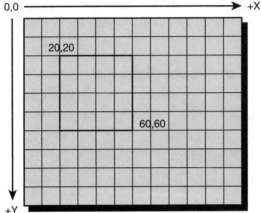

# Drawing Text

Text is the easiest thing to draw in Java2D. To draw text, call a `Graphics2D` object's `drawString(String, int, int)` method with three arguments:

- The string to display
- The x coordinate where it should be displayed
- The y coordinate where it should be displayed

The (x, y) coordinates used in the `drawString()` method represent the pixel at the lower-left corner of the string.

The following `paintComponent()` method draws the string `"Free the bound periodicals"` at the coordinates (22, 100):

```
public void paintComponent(Graphics comp) {
    Graphics2D comp2D = (Graphics2D) comp;
    comp2D.drawString("Free the bound periodicals", 22, 100);
}
```

This example uses a default font. To use a different font, you must create an object of the `Font` class in the `java.awt` package.

A `Font` object represents a font's name, style, and point size. A `Font` object is created by sending three arguments to its constructor:

- The font's name
- The font's style
- The font's point size

A font's name can be its physical name, such as Arial, Courier New, Garamond, or Turman Grotesk. If the font is present on the computer running the application, it is used. If the font is not present, the default font is used.

The name also can be one of five logical fonts: Dialog, DialogInput, Monospaced, SanSerif, or Serif. These fonts can be used to specify the kind of font to use without requiring a specific font. This often is a better choice because some font families might not be present on all Java implementations.

Three Font styles can be selected by using class variables: PLAIN, BOLD, and ITALIC. These constants are integers, and you can add them to combine effects.

The following statement creates a 24-point Dialog font that is bold and italicized:

```
Font f = new Font("Dialog", Font.BOLD + Font.ITALIC, 24);
```

After you have created a font, you can use it by calling the setFont(Font) method of the Graphics2D class with the font as the argument.

The setFont() method sets the current font, which will be used for all subsequent calls to the drawString() method on the same Graphics2D object until another font is set.

The following paintComponent() method creates a new Font object, sets the current font to that object, and draws the string "I'm deeply font of you" in 72-point type at the coordinates (13, 100):

```
public void paintComponent(Graphics comp) {
    Graphics2D comp2D = (Graphics2D) comp;
    Font f = new Font("Arial Narrow", Font.PLAIN, 72);
    comp2D.setFont(f);
    comp2D.drawString("I'm deeply font of you", 13, 100);
}
```

Java applications can ensure that a font is available by including it with the program and loading it from a file. This technique requires the Font class method createFont(int, InputStream), which returns a Font object representing that font.

Input streams, which are covered in Lesson 16, "Working with Input and Output," are objects that can load data from a source such as a disk file or web address. The following statements load a font from a file named Verdana.ttf in the same folder as the class file that uses it:

```
try {
    File ttf = new File("Verdana.ttf");
    FileInputStream fis = new FileInputStream(ttf);
    Font font = Font.createFont(Font.TRUETYPE_FONT, fis);
} catch (IOException|FontFormatException exc) {
    System.out.println("Error: " + exc.getMessage());
}
```

13

The `try-catch` block handles input/output errors, which must be considered when data is loaded from a file. The `File`, `FileInputStream`, and `IOException` classes are part of the `java.io` package (and are discussed in depth in Lesson 16).

When a font is loaded with `createFont()`, the `Font` object is 1 point in size and plain in style. To change the size and style, call the font object's `deriveFont(int, int)` method with two arguments: the desired style and size.

## Improving Fonts and Graphics with Antialiasing

If you displayed text using the skills introduced up to this point, the font's appearance would look crude compared to what you've come to expect from other software. Characters would be rendered with jagged edges, especially on curves and diagonal lines.

Java2D can draw fonts and graphics much more attractively, thanks to its support for *antialiasing*, a rendering technique that smooths out rough edges by altering the color of surrounding pixels. This functionality is off by default. To turn it on, call a `Graphics2D` object's `setRenderingHint()` method with two arguments:

- A `RenderingHint.Key` object that identifies the rendering hint being set
- A `RenderingHint.Key` object that sets the value of that hint

The following code enables antialiasing on a `Graphics2D` object named `comp2D`:

```
comp2D.setRenderingHint(RenderingHints.KEY_ANTIALIASING,
    RenderingHints.VALUE_ANTIALIAS_ON);
```

By calling this method in the `paintComponent()` method of a component, you can cause all subsequent drawing operations to employ antialiasing.

## Finding Information About a Font

To make text look good in a graphical user interface, you often must figure out how much space the text is taking up on an interface component.

The `FontMetrics` class in the `java.awt` package provides methods to determine the size of the characters being displayed with a specified font, and this information can be used for things such as formatting and centering text.

`FontMetrics` can be used to find out detailed information about the current font, such as the width or height of characters it can display. To use this class's methods, you must create a `FontMetrics` object by using the `getFontMetrics()` method. The method takes a single argument: a `Font` object.

Table 13.1 shows some of the information you can find using font metrics. All these methods should be called on a `FontMetrics` object.

**TABLE 13.1** Font Metrics Methods

| Method Name | Description |
|---|---|
| stringWidth(*String*) | Given a string, returns the full width of that string, in pixels |
| charWidth(*char*) | Given a character, returns the width of that character |
| getHeight() | Returns the font's total height |

Listing 13.1 shows how the Font and FontMetrics classes can be used. The TextFrame application displays a string at the center of a frame, using font metrics to measure the string's width in the selected font. Create it in NetBeans in the com.java21days package.

**LISTING 13.1** The Full Text of TextFrame.java

```
 1: package com.java21days;
 2:
 3: import java.awt.*;
 4: import javax.swing.*;
 5:
 6: public class TextFrame extends JFrame {
 7:     public TextFrame(String text, String fontName) {
 8:         super("Show Font");
 9:         setSize(425, 150);
10:         setDefaultCloseOperation(JFrame.EXIT_ON_CLOSE);
11:         TextFramePanel sf = new TextFramePanel(text, fontName);
12:         add(sf);
13:         setVisible(true);
14:     }
15:
16:     public static void main(String[] arguments) {
17:         if (arguments.length < 2) {
18:             System.out.println("Usage: java TextFrame msg font");
19:             System.exit(-1);
20:         }
21:         TextFrame frame = new TextFrame(arguments[0], arguments[1]);
22:     }
23:
24: }
25:
26: class TextFramePanel extends JPanel {
27:     String text;
28:     String fontName;
29:
30:     public TextFramePanel(String text, String fontName) {
31:         super();
32:         this.text = text;
33:         this.fontName = fontName;
34:     }
```

13

```
35:
36:        @Override
37:        public void paintComponent(Graphics comp) {
38:            super.paintComponent(comp);
39:            Graphics2D comp2D = (Graphics2D) comp;
40:            comp2D.setRenderingHint(RenderingHints.KEY_ANTIALIASING,
41:                RenderingHints.VALUE_ANTIALIAS_ON);
42:            Font font = new Font(fontName, Font.BOLD, 18);
43:            FontMetrics metrics = getFontMetrics(font);
44:            comp2D.setFont(font);
45:            int x = (getSize().width - metrics.stringWidth(text)) / 2;
46:            int y = getSize().height / 2;
47:            comp2D.drawString(text, x, y);
48:        }
49: }
```

The `TextFrame` application takes two command-line arguments, which you can set in NetBeans by choosing Project, Set Project Configuration, Customize. For example, set the Arguments field to `com.java21days.TextFrame Howdy "Courier New"`. To run the application with this configuration, choose Run, Run Project.

Figure 13.2 shows how the application looks with a text message displayed in the font Arial Black. After you run the application, resize the frame window to see how the text moves so that it always remains centered.

**FIGURE 13.2**
Displaying centered text with font metrics.

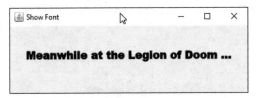

The `TextFrame` application consists of two classes: a frame and a panel subclass called `TextFramePanel`. The text is drawn on the panel by overriding the `paintComponent(Graphics)` method and calling drawing methods of the `Graphics2D` class inside the method.

The `getSize()` method calls in lines 45 and 46 use the panel's width and height to determine where the text should be displayed. When the application is resized, the panel also is resized, and `paintComponent()` is called automatically.

# Color

The `Color` class (in the `java.awt` package) and `ColorSpace` class (in `java.awt.color`) can be used to make a graphical user interface more, well, colorful. With these classes, you can set the color for use in drawing operations, as well as the background color of an interface component and other windows. You also can translate a color from one color system into another.

By default, Java uses colors according to the sRGB color system, which describes each shade by the amounts of red, green, and blue it contains (R, G, and B). Each of the three components can be represented as an integer between 0 and 255. Black is 0, 0, 0—the absence of any red, green, or blue. White is 255, 255, 255—the maximum amount of all three colors. You also can represent sRGB values using three floating-point numbers ranging from 0 to 1.0. Java can represent millions of colors between the two extremes using sRGB.

A color system is called a *color space*, and sRGB is only one such space. There also is XYZ, which was created by an international conference in 1931. Java supports the use of any color space desired, as long as a `ColorSpace` object is available that defines the description system. You also can convert from any color space to sRGB and vice versa.

Java's internal representation of colors using sRGB is just one color space used in a program. An output device such as a monitor or printer also has its own color space.

When you display or print something of a designated color, the output device might not support the designated color. In this circumstance, a different color is substituted or a dithering pattern is used to approximate the unavailable color.

The practical reality of color management is that the color you designate with sRGB will not be available on all output devices. If you need more precise control of the color, you can use `ColorSpace` and other classes in the `java.awt.color` package.

For most needs, the built-in use of sRGB to define colors should be sufficient.

## Using `Color` **Objects**

Colors are represented by `Color` objects, which can be created with a constructor or by specifying one of the small number of standard colors available by name in the `Color` class.

You can call the `Color()` constructor to create a color with three integers that represent the sRGB value of the desired color (or three floating-point numbers that serve the same purpose):

```
Color c1 = new Color(0.807F, 1F, 0F);
Color c2 = new Color(255, 204, 102);
```

The `c1` object describes a neon green color, and `c2` is butterscotch.

13

**NOTE**

> It's easy to confuse floating-point literals such as 0F and 1F with hexadecimal numbers, discussed in Lesson 2, "The ABCs of Programming." Colors often are expressed in hexadecimal, such as when a background color is set on a web page using Cascading Style Sheets. The Java classes and methods you work with don't take hexadecimal arguments, so when you see a literal such as 1F or 0F, you're dealing with floating-point numbers.

## Testing and Setting the Current Colors

The current color for drawing is designated by using the `setColor()` method of the `Graphics2D` class. This method must be called on the `Graphics2D` object that represents the area on which something is being drawn.

Several of the most common colors are available as class variables in the `Color` class. These colors use the following `Color` variables (with corresponding sRGB values in parentheses):

black (0, 0, 0)

blue (0, 0, 255)

cyan (0, 255, 255)

darkGray (64, 64, 64)

gray (128, 128, 128)

green (0, 255, 0)

lightGray (192, 192, 192)

magenta (255, 0, 255)

orange (255, 200, 0)

pink (255, 175, 175)

red (255, 0, 0)

white (255, 255, 255)

yellow (255, 255, 0)

The following statement sets the color for a `Graphics2D` object named `comp2D` by using one of the standard class variables:

```
comp2D.setColor(Color.pink);
```

If you have created a `Color` object, it can be set in a similar fashion:

```
Color brush = new Color(255, 204, 102);
comp2D.setColor(brush);
```

After you set the current color, subsequent methods to draw strings and other graphics use that color.

You can set the background color for a component, such as a panel or frame, by calling the component's `setBackground(Color)` method.

The `setBackground()` method sets the component's background color, as in this example:

```
setBackground(Color.white);
```

If you want to find out what the current color is, use the `getColor()` method on a `Graphics2D` object or the `getBackground()` method on the component.

The following statement sets the current color of `comp2D`—a `Graphics2D` object—to the same color as a component's background:

```
comp2D.setColor(getBackground());
```

# Drawing Lines and Polygons

All the basic drawing commands covered in this lesson are `Graphics2D` methods called within a component's `paintComponent()` method. This is an ideal place for all drawing operations because `paintComponent()` is automatically called any time the component needs to be redisplayed.

If another program's window overlaps the component and it needs to be redrawn, putting all the drawing operations in `paintComponent()` ensures that no part of the drawing is left out.

Java2D features include the following:

- The capability to draw empty polygons and polygons filled with a solid color
- Special fill patterns, such as gradients and patterns
- Strokes that define the width and style of a drawing stroke
- Antialiasing to smooth edges of drawn objects

## User and Device Coordinate Spaces

One concept introduced with Java2D is the difference between an output device's coordinate space and the coordinate space you refer to when drawing an object. Coordinate space is any 2D area that can be described using (x, y) coordinates.

For all drawing operations prior to Java2D, the only coordinate space used was the device coordinate space. You specified the (x, y) coordinates of an output surface, such as a panel, and those coordinates were used to draw text and other elements.

13

Java2D requires a second coordinate space that you refer to when creating an object and actually drawing it. This is called the *user coordinate space*.

Before any 2D drawing has occurred in a program, the device space and user space have the (0, 0) coordinates in the same place—the upper-left corner of the drawing area.

The user space's (0, 0) coordinates can move as a result of the 2D drawing operations being conducted. The x- and y-axes even can shift because of a 2D rotation. You'll learn more about the two coordinate systems as you work with Java2D.

## Specifying the Rendering Attributes

The next step in 2D drawing is to specify how a drawn object is rendered. Java2D offers a wide range of attributes for designating color, including line width, fill patterns, transparency, and many other features.

### Fill Patterns

Fill patterns control how a drawn object will be filled in. With Java2D, you can use a solid color, gradient fill, texture, or pattern of your own devising.

A fill pattern is defined by using the setPaint(Paint) method of Graphics2D with a Paint object as its only argument. Any class that can be a fill pattern, including GradientPaint, TexturePaint, and Color, can implement the Paint interface. Using a Color object with setPaint() is the same as using a solid color as the pattern.

A *gradient fill* is a gradual shift from one color at one coordinate point to another color at a different coordinate point. The shift can occur once between the points—which is called an *acyclic gradient*—or it can happen repeatedly—which is a *cyclic gradient*.

Figure 13.3 shows examples of acyclic and cyclic gradients between white and a darker color. The arrows indicate the points between which the colors shift.

**FIGURE 13.3**
Acyclic and cyclic
gradient shifts.

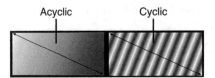

The coordinate points in a gradient do not refer directly to points on the Graphics2D object being drawn onto. Instead, they refer to user space and even can be outside the object being filled with a gradient. Figure 13.4 illustrates this. Both rectangles are filled using the same GradientPaint object as a guide. One way to think of a gradient pattern is as a piece of fabric that has been spread over a flat surface. The shapes being filled with a gradient are the patterns cut from the fabric, and more than one pattern can be cut from the same piece of cloth.

**FIGURE 13.4**
Two rectangles
using the same
GradientPaint.

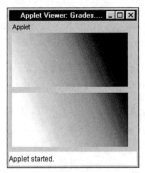

A call to the GradientPaint constructor method takes the following format:

```
GradientPaint gp = new GradientPaint(
    x1, y1, color1, x2, y2, color2);
```

The point (x1, y1) is where the color represented by color1 begins, and (x2, y2) is where the shift ends at color2.

If you want to use a cyclic gradient shift, an extra argument is added at the end:

```
GradientPaint gp = new GradientPaint(
    x1, y1, color1, x2, y2, color2, true);
```

The last argument is a Boolean value that is true for a cyclic shift. A false argument can be used for acyclic shifts, or you can omit this argument; acyclic shifts are the default.

After you have created a GradientPaint object, set it as the current paint attribute by using the setPaint() method. The following statements create and select a gradient:

```
GradientPaint pat = new GradientPaint(0F, 0F, Color.white,
    100F, 45F, Color.blue);
comp2D.setPaint(pat);
```

All subsequent drawing operations to the comp2D object use this fill pattern until another one is chosen.

## Setting a Drawing Stroke

Java2D allows you to vary the width of drawn lines by using the setStroke() method with BasicStroke.

A simple BasicStroke constructor takes three arguments:

- A float value representing the line width, with 1.0 as the norm
- An int value determining the style of cap decoration drawn at the end of a line
- An int value determining the style of juncture between two line segments

13

The endcap- and juncture-style arguments use BasicStroke class variables. Endcap styles apply to the ends of lines that do not connect to other lines. Juncture styles apply to the ends of lines that join other lines.

Possible endcap styles are CAP_BUTT for no endpoints, CAP_ROUND for circles around each endpoint, and CAP_SQUARE for squares. Figure 13.5 shows the endcap styles. As you can see, the only visible difference between the CAP_BUTT and CAP_SQUARE styles is that CAP_SQUARE is longer because of the added square endcap.

**FIGURE 13.5**
Endpoint cap styles.

CAP_BUTT   CAP_ROUND   CAP_SQUARE

Possible juncture styles include JOIN_MITER, which joins segments by extending their outer edges, JOIN_ROUND, which rounds off a corner between two segments, and JOIN_BEVEL, which joins segments with a straight line. Figure 13.6 shows examples of the juncture styles.

**FIGURE 13.6**
Endpoint juncture
styles.

JOIN_MITER   JOIN_ROUND   JOIN_BEVEL

The following statements create a BasicStroke object and make it the current stroke:

```
BasicStroke pen = new BasicStroke(2.0F,
    BasicStroke.CAP_BUTT,
    BasicStroke.JOIN_ROUND);
comp2D.setStroke(pen);
```

The stroke has a width of 2 pixels, plain endpoints, and rounded segment corners.

## Creating Objects to Draw

After you have created a Graphics2D object and specified the rendering attributes, the final steps are to create the object and draw it.

You create a drawn object in Java2D by defining it as a geometric shape using a class in the java.awt.geom package. You can draw lines, rectangles, ellipses, arcs, and polygons.

The Graphics2D class does not have a different method for each shape you can draw. Instead, you define the shape and use it as an argument to the draw() or fill() methods.

### Lines

Lines are created using the Line2D.Float class. This class takes four arguments: the x and y coordinates of one endpoint followed by the x and y coordinates of the other. Here's an example:

```
Line2D.Float ln = new Line2D.Float(60F, 5F, 13F, 28F);
```

This statement creates a line between (60, 5) and (13, 28). Note that an `F` is used with the literals sent as arguments. Otherwise, the Java compiler would assume that the values were integers.

## Rectangles

Rectangles are created by using the `Rectangle2D.Float` class or `Rectangle2D.Double` class. The difference between the two is that one takes `float` arguments, and the other takes `double` arguments.

`Rectangle2D.Float` takes four arguments: x coordinate, y coordinate, width, and height. The following is an example:

```
Rectangle2D.Float rc = new Rectangle2D.Float(10F, 13F, 40F, 20F);
```

This creates a rectangle at (10, 13) that is 40 pixels wide by 20 pixels tall.

## Ellipses

Ellipses can be created with the `Ellipse2D.Float` class. It takes four arguments: x coordinate, y coordinate, width, and height.

The following statement creates an ellipse at (113, 25) with a width of 22 pixels and a height of 40 pixels:

```
Ellipse2D.Float ee = new Ellipse2D.Float(113, 25, 22, 40);
```

## Arcs

Of all the shapes you can draw in Java2D, arcs are the most complex to construct.

Arcs are created with the `Arc2D.Float` class, which takes seven arguments:

- The x and y coordinates of an invisible ellipse that would include the arc if it were drawn (as the first two arguments)
- The width and height of the ellipse (as the third and fourth arguments)
- The starting degree of the arc
- The number of degrees the arc travels on the ellipse
- An integer describing how the arc is closed

13

The number of degrees the arc travels is specified in a counterclockwise direction by using negative numbers.

Figure 13.7 shows where degree values are located when determining an arc's starting degree. The arc's starting angle ranges from 0 to 359 degrees counterclockwise. On a circular ellipse, 0 degrees is at the 3 o'clock position, 90 degrees is at 12 o'clock, 180 degrees is at 9 o'clock, and 270 degrees is at 6 o'clock.

**FIGURE 13.7**
Determining the
starting degree of
an arc.

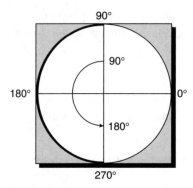

The last argument to the `Arc2D.Float` constructor uses one of three class variables:
`Arc2D.OPEN` for an unclosed arc, `Arc2D.CHORD` to connect the arc's endpoints with a
straight line, and `Arc2D.PIE` to connect the arc to the center of the ellipses like a pie
slice. Figure 13.8 shows each of these styles.

**FIGURE 13.8**
Arc closure styles.

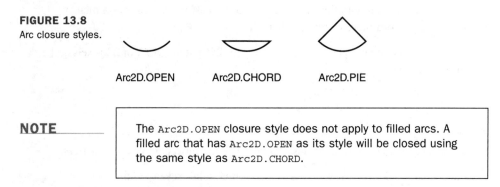

NOTE

> The `Arc2D.OPEN` closure style does not apply to filled arcs. A
> filled arc that has `Arc2D.OPEN` as its style will be closed using
> the same style as `Arc2D.CHORD`.

The following statement creates an `Arc2D.Float` object:

```
Arc2D.Float arc = new Arc2D.Float(
    27F, 22F, 42F, 30F, 33F, 90F, Arc2D.PIE);
```

This creates an arc for an oval at (27, 22) that is 42 pixels wide by 30 pixels tall. The arc
begins at 33 degrees, extends 90 degrees clockwise, and is closed like a pie slice.

## Polygons

You create polygons in Java2D by defining each movement from one point on the
polygon to another. A polygon can be formed from straight lines, quadratic curves, or
Bézier curves.

The movements to create a polygon are defined as a GeneralPath object, which also is part of the java.awt.geom package. A GeneralPath object can be created without any arguments, as shown here:

```
GeneralPath polly = new GeneralPath();
```

The moveTo() method of GeneralPath is used to create the first point on the polygon. The following statement would be used if you wanted to start polly at the coordinate (5, 0):

```
polly.moveTo(5F, 0F);
```

After creating the first point, the lineTo() method is used to create lines that end at a new point. This method takes two arguments: the x and y coordinates of the new point.

The following statements add three lines to the polly object:

```
polly.lineTo(205F, 0F);
polly.lineTo(205F, 90F);
polly.lineTo(5F, 90F);
```

The lineTo() and moveTo() methods require float arguments to specify coordinate points.

If you want to close a polygon, the closePath() method is used without any arguments, as shown here:

```
polly.closePath();
```

This method closes a polygon by connecting the current point with the point specified by the most recent moveTo() method. You can close a polygon without this method by using a lineTo() method that connects to the original point.

After you have created an open or closed polygon, you can draw it like any other shape by using the draw() and fill() methods. The polly object is a rectangle with points at (5, 0), (205, 0), (205, 90), and (5, 90).

## Drawing Objects

After you have defined the rendering attributes, such as color and line width, and have created the object to be drawn, you're ready to draw something in all its 2D glory.

All drawn objects use the same Graphics2D class's methods: draw() for outlines and fill() for filled objects. These methods take an object as the only argument.

13

## Drawing a Map

The next project you will create is an application that draws a simple map using 2D drawing techniques. Create the Map class in the com.java21days package in NetBeans and fill it with the code in Listing 13.2.

**LISTING 13.2** The Full Text of Map.java

```
 1: package com.java21days;
 2:
 3: import java.awt.*;
 4: import java.awt.geom.*;
 5: import javax.swing.*;
 6:
 7: public class Map extends JFrame {
 8:     public Map() {
 9:         super("Map");
10:         setSize(360, 350);
11:         setDefaultCloseOperation(JFrame.EXIT_ON_CLOSE);
12:         MapPane map = new MapPane();
13:         add(map);
14:         setVisible(true);
15:     }
16:
17:     public static void main(String[] arguments) {
18:         Map frame = new Map();
19:     }
20:
21: }
22:
23: class MapPane extends JPanel {
24:     @Override
25:     public void paintComponent(Graphics comp) {
26:         Graphics2D comp2D = (Graphics2D) comp;
27:         comp2D.setColor(Color.blue);
28:         comp2D.setRenderingHint(RenderingHints.KEY_ANTIALIASING,
29:             RenderingHints.VALUE_ANTIALIAS_ON);
30:         Rectangle2D.Float background = new Rectangle2D.Float(
31:             0F, 0F, getSize().width, getSize().height);
32:         comp2D.fill(background);
33:         // draw waves
34:         comp2D.setColor(Color.white);
35:         BasicStroke pen = new BasicStroke(2F,
36:             BasicStroke.CAP_BUTT, BasicStroke.JOIN_ROUND);
37:         comp2D.setStroke(pen);
38:         for (int ax = 0; ax < 340; ax += 10) {
39:             for (int ay = 0; ay < 340 ; ay += 10) {
40:                 Arc2D.Float wave = new Arc2D.Float(ax, ay,
41:                     10, 10, 0, -180, Arc2D.OPEN);
42:                 comp2D.draw(wave);
```

```
43:            }
44:        }
45:        // draw Florida
46:        GradientPaint gp = new GradientPaint(0F, 0F, Color.green,
47:            350F,350F, Color.orange, true);
48:        comp2D.setPaint(gp);
49:        GeneralPath fl = new GeneralPath();
50:        fl.moveTo(10F, 12F);
51:        fl.lineTo(234F, 15F);
52:        fl.lineTo(253F, 25F);
53:        fl.lineTo(261F, 71F);
54:        fl.lineTo(344F, 209F);
55:        fl.lineTo(336F, 278F);
56:        fl.lineTo(295F, 310F);
57:        fl.lineTo(259F, 274F);
58:        fl.lineTo(205F, 188F);
59:        fl.lineTo(211F, 171F);
60:        fl.lineTo(195F, 174F);
61:        fl.lineTo(191F, 118F);
62:        fl.lineTo(120F, 56F);
63:        fl.lineTo(94F, 68F);
64:        fl.lineTo(81F, 49F);
65:        fl.lineTo(12F, 37F);
66:        fl.closePath();
67:        comp2D.fill(fl);
68:        // draw ovals
69:        comp2D.setColor(Color.black);
70:        BasicStroke pen2 = new BasicStroke();
71:        comp2D.setStroke(pen2);
72:        Ellipse2D.Float e1 = new Ellipse2D.Float(235, 140, 15, 15);
73:        Ellipse2D.Float e2 = new Ellipse2D.Float(225, 130, 15, 15);
74:        Ellipse2D.Float e3 = new Ellipse2D.Float(245, 130, 15, 15);
75:        comp2D.fill(e1);
76:        comp2D.fill(e2);
77:        comp2D.fill(e3);
78:    }
79: }
```

In the Map application, line 4 imports the classes in the java.awt.geom package. This statement is required because import java.awt.*; in line 1 handles only classes, not packages, available under java.awt.

Line 26 creates the comp2D object used for all 2D drawing operations. It's a cast of the Graphics object that represents the panel's visible surface.

Lines 35–37 create a BasicStroke object that represents a line width of 2 pixels and then makes this the current stroke with the setStroke() method of Graphics2D.

Lines 38–44 use two nested for loops to create waves from individual arcs.

13

Lines 46–47 create a gradient fill pattern from the color green at (0, 0) to orange at (50, 50). The last argument to the constructor, `true`, causes the fill pattern to repeat as many times as needed to fill an object.

Line 48 sets the current gradient fill pattern using the `setPaint()` method and the `gp` object just created.

Lines 49–67 create the polygon shaped like the author's home state and draw it. This polygon is filled with a green-to-orange gradient pattern.

Line 69 sets the current color to black. This replaces the gradient fill pattern for the next drawing operation because colors are also fill patterns.

Line 70 creates a new `BasicStroke()` object with no arguments, which defaults to a 1-pixel line width.

Line 71 sets the current line width to the new `BasicStroke` object `pen2`.

Lines 72–74 create three ellipses at (235, 140), (225, 130), and (245, 130). Each is 15 pixels wide by 15 pixels tall, making them circles.

Figure 13.9 shows the application running.

**FIGURE 13.9**
The `Map` application.

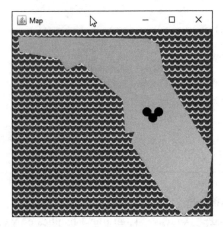

# Summary

You now have some tools to improve the looks of a Java program. You can draw with lines, rectangles, ellipses, polygons, fonts, colors, and patterns onto a frame, a panel, and other user interface components using Java2D.

Java2D uses the same two methods for each drawing operation: `draw()` and `fill()`. Different objects are created using classes of the `java.awt.geom` package, and these are used as arguments for the drawing methods of `Graphics2D`.

# Q&A

**Q** **What does the uppercase** `F` **refer to in source code? It is added to coordinates, as in the method** `polly.moveTo(5F, 0F)`**. Why is** `F` **used for these coordinates and not others, and why is a lowercase** `f` **used elsewhere?**

**A** The `F` or `f` indicates that a number is a floating-point number rather than an integer, and uppercase and lowercase can be used interchangeably. If you don't use one of them, the Java compiler assumes that the number is an `int` value. Many methods and constructors in Java require floating-point arguments but can handle integers because an integer can be converted to floating-point without changing its value. For this reason, constructors such as `Arc2D.Float()` can use arguments such as `10` and `180` instead of `10F` and `180F`.

**Q** **The section "Improving Fonts and Graphics with Antialiasing" mentions a class called** `RenderingHint.Key`**. Why does this class have two names separated by a period? What does this signify?**

**A** The use of two names to identify a class indicates that it is an inner class. The first class name is the enclosing class, followed by a period and the name of the inner class. In this case, the `Key` class is an inner class within the `RenderingHint` class.

# Quiz

Review this lesson's material by taking this three-question quiz.

## Questions

**1.** What object is required before you can draw something in Java using Swing?

    **A.** `Graphics2D`

    **B.** `WindowListener`

    **C.** `JFrame`

**2.** Which of the following is not a valid Java statement to create a `Color` object?

    **A.** `Color c1 = new Color(0F, 0F, 0F);`

    **B.** `Color c2 = new Color(0, 0, 0);`

    **C.** Both are valid.

**3.** What does `getSize().width` refer to?

    **A.** The width of the interface component's window

    **B.** The width of the frame's window

    **C.** The width of any graphical user interface component in Java

13

## Answers

**1.** A. The `Graphics2D` object is cast from a `Graphics` object and represents a graphics context for a graphical user interface component.

**2.** C. Both are valid ways to create the object. You also can use hexadecimal values to create a `Color` object, as in this example:

```
Color c3 = new Color(0xFF, 0xCC, 0x66);
```

**3.** C. You can call `getSize().width` and `getSize().height` on any user interface component.

# Certification Practice

The following question is the kind of thing you could expect to be asked on a Java programming certification test. Answer it without looking again at this lesson or using the Java compiler to test the code.

Given:

```java
import java.awt.*;
import javax.swing.*;
public class Result extends JFrame {

    public Result() {
        super("Result");
        JLabel width = new JLabel("This frame is " +
            getSize().width + " pixels wide.");
        add("North", width);
        setSize(220, 120);
    }

    public static void main(String[] arguments) {
        Result r = new Result();
        r.setVisible(true);
    }
}
```

What will be the reported width of the frame, in pixels, when the application runs?

**A.** 0 pixels

**B.** 120 pixels

**C.** 220 pixels

**D.** The width of the user's monitor

The answer is available on the book's website, at www.java21days.com. Visit the Lesson 13 page and click the Certification Practice link.

# Exercises

To extend your knowledge of the subjects covered in this lesson, try the following exercises:

**1.** Create an application that draws a circle, with its radius, (x, y) coordinates, and color all determined by arguments.

**2.** Create an application that draws a pie graph.

Where applicable, exercise solutions are offered on the book's website, at www.java21days.com.

13

# LESSON 14
# Developing Swing Applications

Designing a graphical user interface with Swing has a lot in common with creating a web page. Components are placed on the interface in a manner that makes them move around depending on the size of the space they've been given to occupy.

You could see this in the Swing interfaces created thus far by resizing the frame as they were running.

This fluidity is a necessary part of the Web because it's presented on so many different devices, screen widths, and resolutions.

In Java, it helps ensure that a user interface will still display reasonably well and function properly on all the platforms where a Java Virtual Machine (JVM) has been installed.

This final lesson on Swing provides some additional features that enhance its capabilities as a canvas for effective GUI design.

In this lesson, you'll extend your knowledge of Swing into the following topics:

- How Swing applications can run into performance slowdowns on time-consuming tasks
- How to address these problems using `SwingWorker`, a class that performs Swing work in its own thread
- How to create a graphical user interface as a grid of cells of different sizes
- How to make a layout cell stretch into other cells
- How to make cells have different heights and widths relative to each other

# Improving Performance with `SwingWorker`

The responsiveness of a Swing application depends largely on how well the software handles time-consuming tasks in response to user input.

An application ordinarily executes tasks in one thread. So if something takes a long time to accomplish, such as loading a large file or parsing data from an XML document, the user might notice a lag in performance while this is taking place.

Swing programs also require all user interface components to be running within the same thread.

The best way to take care of both requirements is to use `SwingWorker`, a class in the `javax.swing` package that's designed to run time-consuming tasks in their own worker thread and report the results.

`SwingWorker` is an abstract class that must be subclassed by applications that require a worker:

```
public class DiceWorker extends SwingWorker {
    // body of class
}
```

The `doInBackground()` method should be overridden in the new class to perform the task.

The next project is a Swing application that rolls three six-sided dice a user-selected number of times and tabulates the results. Sixteen text fields represent the possible values, which range from 3 to 18.

The application is developed as two classes: the `DiceRoller` frame, which holds the graphical user interface, and the `DiceWorker` Swing worker, which handles the dice rolls.

Because the application allows the user to roll the dice thousands or even millions of times, putting this task in a worker keeps the Swing interface responsive to user input.

Listing 14.1 contains the worker class, `DiceWorker`. Create this as an empty Java file in NetBeans with that class name and the package `com.java21days`. In the New File dialog, be sure the project selected is `Java21`, not `PageData`.

**LISTING 14.1**    The Full Text of `DiceWorker.java`

```
1: package com.java21days;
2:
3: import javax.swing.*;
4:
```

```
 5: public class DiceWorker extends SwingWorker {
 6:     int timesToRoll;
 7:
 8:     // set up the Swing worker
 9:     public DiceWorker(int timesToRoll) {
10:         super();
11:         this.timesToRoll = timesToRoll;
12:     }
13:
14:     // define the task the worker performs
15:     @Override
16:     protected int[] doInBackground() {
17:         int[] result = new int[16];
18:         for (int i = 0; i < this.timesToRoll; i++) {
19:             int sum = 0;
20:             for (int j = 0; j < 3; j++) {
21:                 sum += Math.floor(Math.random() * 6);
22:             }
23:             result[sum] = result[sum] + 1;
24:         }
25:         // transmit the result
26:         return result;
27:     }
28: }
```

There's no way to do anything with this class until you create the next one, DiceRoller.

A Swing worker needs only one method, doInBackground(), which performs the task in the background. The method must use the protected level of access control and return a value produced by the work. DiceWorker creates a 16-element integer array that contains dice roll results.

Another class can use this worker in three steps:

1. Call the worker's DiceWorker(int) constructor with the number of rolls as the argument.

2. Call the worker's addPropertyChangeListener(Object) method to add a listener that will be notified when the task is complete.

3. Call the worker's execute() method to begin the work.

The execute() method causes the worker's doInBackground() method to be called.

A property change listener is an event listener from java.beans, the JavaBeans package that establishes ways in which components on a user interface can interact with each other.

14

In this case, a Swing worker wants to announce that its work is finished, which could take place long after the worker began its work. Using listeners is the best way to handle notifications of this kind because they free the graphical user interface to handle other things.

The `propertyChange` listener interface has one method:

```
public void propertyChange(PropertyChangeEvent event) {
    // ...
}
```

The `DiceRoller` class in the `com.java21days` package, shown in Listing 14.2, presents a graphical user interface that can display dice roll results and begin a set of rolls.

**LISTING 14.2**    The Full Text of `DiceRoller.java`

```
 1: package com.java21days;
 2:
 3: import java.awt.*;
 4: import java.awt.event.*;
 5: import java.beans.*;
 6: import javax.swing.*;
 7:
 8: public class DiceRoller extends JFrame implements ActionListener,
 9:     PropertyChangeListener {
10:
11:     // the table for dice-roll results
12:     JTextField[] total = new JTextField[16];
13:     // the "Roll" button
14:     JButton roll;
15:     // the number of times to roll
16:     JTextField quantity;
17:     // the Swing worker
18:     DiceWorker worker;
19:
20:     public DiceRoller() {
21:         super("Dice Roller");
22:         setDefaultCloseOperation(JFrame.EXIT_ON_CLOSE);
23:         setSize(850, 145);
24:
25:         // set up top row
26:         JPanel topPane = new JPanel();
27:         GridLayout paneGrid = new GridLayout(1, 16);
28:         topPane.setLayout(paneGrid);
29:         for (int i = 0; i < 16; i++) {
30:             // create a textfield and label
31:             total[i] = new JTextField("0", 4);
32:             JLabel label = new JLabel((i + 3) + ": ");
33:             // create this cell in the grid
34:             JPanel cell = new JPanel();
```

```
35:                    cell.add(label);
36:                    cell.add(total[i]);
37:                    // add the cell to the top row
38:                    topPane.add(cell);
39:                }
40:
41:                // set up bottom row
42:                JPanel bottomPane = new JPanel();
43:                JLabel quantityLabel = new JLabel("Times to Roll: ");
44:                quantity = new JTextField("0", 5);
45:                roll = new JButton("Roll");
46:                roll.addActionListener(this);
47:                bottomPane.add(quantityLabel);
48:                bottomPane.add(quantity);
49:                bottomPane.add(roll);
50:
51:                // set up frame
52:                GridLayout frameGrid = new GridLayout(2, 1);
53:                setLayout(frameGrid);
54:                add(topPane);
55:                add(bottomPane);
56:
57:                setVisible(true);
58:        }
59:
60:        // respond when the "Roll" button is clicked
61:        @Override
62:        public void actionPerformed(ActionEvent event) {
63:                int timesToRoll;
64:                try {
65:                        // turn off the button
66:                        timesToRoll = Integer.parseInt(quantity.getText());
67:                        roll.setEnabled(false);
68:                        // set up the worker that will roll the dice
69:                        worker = new DiceWorker(timesToRoll);
70:                        // add a listener that monitors the worker
71:                        worker.addPropertyChangeListener(this);
72:                        // start the worker
73:                        worker.execute();
74:                } catch (NumberFormatException exc) {
75:                        System.out.println(exc.getMessage());
76:                }
77:        }
78:
79:        // respond when the worker's task is complete
80:        @Override
81:        public void propertyChange(PropertyChangeEvent event) {
82:                try {
83:                        // get the worker's dice-roll results
84:                        int[] result = (int[]) worker.get();
```

14

```
85:                 // store the results in text fields
86:                 for (int i = 0; i < result.length; i++) {
87:                     total[i].setText("" + result[i]);
88:                 }
89:             } catch (Exception exc) {
90:                 System.out.println(exc.getMessage());
91:             }
92:         }
93:
94:         private static void setLookAndFeel() {
95:             try {
96:                 UIManager.setLookAndFeel(
97:                     "com.sun.java.swing.plaf.nimbus.NimbusLookAndFeel"
98:                 );
99:             } catch (Exception exc) {
100:                 // ignore error
101:             }
102:         }
103:
104:         public static void main(String[] arguments) {
105:             DiceRoller.setLookAndFeel();
106:             DiceRoller app = new DiceRoller();
107:         }
108: }
```

This class can be run as an application. Choose Run, Run File in NetBeans.

Most of `DiceRoller` creates and lays out the user-interface components: 16 text fields, a Times to Roll text field, and a Roll button.

The `actionPerformed()` method responds to a click of the Roll button by creating a Swing worker that will roll the dice, adding a property change listener and starting work.

Calling `worker.execute()` in line 73 causes the worker's `doInBackground()` method to be called.

When the worker is finished rolling the dice, the `propertyChange()` method of `DiceRoller` receives a property change event. This method receives the result of `doInBackground()` by calling the worker's `get()` method (line 84), which must be cast to an integer array:

```
int[] result = (int[] worker.get();
```

The application is shown in Figure 14.1.

**FIGURE 14.1**
Tabulating dice roll results prepared by SwingWorker.

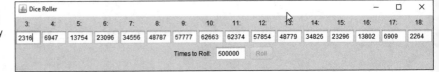

# Grid Bag Layout

During Lesson 11, "Arranging Components on a User Interface," you learned about the layout manager classes `FlowLayout`, `BoxLayout`, `GridLayout`, `BorderLayout`, and `CardLayout`.

There's another layout manager in Java that's not as commonly used but can come in handy in certain situations. Grid bag layout, a sophisticated extension of the grid layout manager, arranges components into rows and columns of individual cells. A grid bag layout differs from grid layout in these ways:

- A component can take up more than one cell in the grid.
- The proportions between different rows and columns do not have to be equal.
- A component does not have to fill the entire cell (or cells) it occupies.
- A component can be aligned along any edge of a cell.

A grid bag layout requires the `GridBagLayout` and `GridBagConstraints` classes, which belong to the `java.awt` package. `GridBagLayout` is the layout manager, and `GridBagConstraints` defines the placement of components in the grid.

The constructor for the grid bag layout manager takes no arguments and can be applied to a container like any other manager. The following statements could be used in a frame's constructor to use grid bag layout in that container:

```
GridBagLayout bag = new GridBagLayout();
setLayout(bag);
```

In a grid bag layout, each component uses a `GridBagConstraints` object to dictate the cell or cells it occupies in the grid, its size, and other aspects of its presentation.

A `GridBagConstraints` object has 11 instance variables that determine component placement:

- `gridx`—The x position of the cell that holds the component (or, if it spans several cells, the x position of the upper-left portion of the component)
- `gridy`—The y position of the cell or its upper-left portion
- `gridwidth`—The number of cells the component occupies in a horizontal direction
- `gridheight`—The number of cells the component occupies in a vertical direction
- `weightx`—A value that indicates the component's size relative to other components on the same row of the grid

14

- weighty—A value that indicates the component's size relative to other components on the same column of the grid

- anchor—A value that determines where the component is displayed within its cell (if it doesn't fill the entire cell)

- fill—A value that determines whether the component expands horizontally or vertically to fill its cell

- insets—An Insets object that sets the white space around the component inside its cell

- ipadx—The amount by which to expand the component's width beyond its minimum size

- ipady—The amount by which to expand the component's height

With the exception of insets, all of these variables can hold integer values.

The easiest way to use this layout manager is to create a constraint with no arguments and set its variables individually. Variables not explicitly set use their default values.

The following code creates a grid bag layout and a constraint used to place components in the grid:

```
GridBagLayout gridbag = new GridBagLayout();
GridBagConstraints constraint = new GridBagConstraints();
setLayout(gridbag);
```

The constraint can be configured with a set of assignment statements:

```
constraint.gridx = 0;
constraint.gridy = 0;
constraint.gridwidth = 2;
constraint.gridheight = 1;
constraint.weightx = 100;
constraint.weighty = 100;
constraint.fill = GridBagConstraints.NONE;
constraint.anchor = GridBagConstraints.CENTER;
```

This code sets up a constraint that can be used to put a component at grid position (0,0) that is two cells wide and one cell tall.

The component's size within its cell and position are set with class variables of GridBagConstraints. The component is centered in its cell (an anchor value of CENTER) and does not expand to fill the entire cell (a fill value of NONE).

The weightx and weighty values make sense only in relation to the same values for other components, as described in detail later in this section.

A component is added to a grid bag layout in two steps:

1. **The** layout manager's `setConstraints(Component, GridBagConstraints)` method is called with the component and constraint as arguments.

2. The component is added to a container that uses that manager.

The following statements continue the preceding example, adding a button to the layout:

```
JButton okButton = new JButton("OK");
gridbag.setConstraints(okButton, constraint);
pane.add(okButton);
```

A constraint must be set before each component in the grid is placed.

## Designing the Grid

Because grid bag layout is more complex than the other layout managers, it helps to do some preparatory work before using it. You can sketch the desired user interface on graph paper or take notes in some other form.

Figure 14.2 shows a rough sketch on graph paper for the layout of a panel in an email program's user interface.

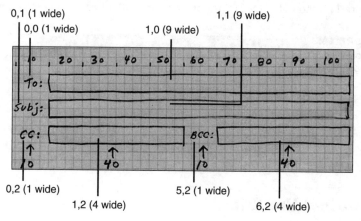

**FIGURE 14.2**
Designing a user interface on a grid.

The panel shown in Figure 14.2 contains a group of labels and text fields that will be filled out when a message is sent.

A grid bag layout suits this interface because it contains components of different widths. All the labels have the same width, but the "To" and "Subject" text fields are larger than the "CC" and "BCC" fields. In grid bag layout, each component must have its own cell and cannot share it with any other components. A component can take up more than one cell.

14

The sketch shown in Figure 14.2 does not indicate individual cells, but it does mark off values from 0 to 100 to indicate the width of components. These are intended as percentage values rather than exact sizes, which is a convenient way to calculate `weightx` and `weighty` values.

> **NOTE**
>
> At this point, you might be wondering why percentage values from 0 to 100 aren't running vertically alongside the sketch. The email interface doesn't need them. All the components have the same height (and, thus, the same `weighty` value).

After the user interface has been sketched to show the relative sizes of components, the cell position and size of each component can be determined.

The width of each component in the email interface was set to multiples of 10, making it easy to use a grid with 10 columns.

Like grid layout, cells begin with (0, 0) as the upper-left corner. The x-coordinate is the column and the y-coordinate is the row. They increase as you move to the left and downward, respectively.

Figure 14.3 shows the (x, y) position and the width of each component, in cells.

**FIGURE 14.3**
Choosing cells for components in the grid.

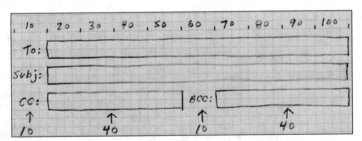

## Creating the Grid

After making a sketch on graph paper, you can write the code necessary to implement the sketch as a Java graphical user interface.

The following statements in the email panel's constructor set it to use grid bag layout and add a "To" label and text field to the panel:

```
// add the label
JLabel toLabel = new JLabel("To: ");
GridBagConstraints constraint = new GridBagConstraints();
```

```
constraint.gridx = 0;
constraint.gridy = 0;
constraint.gridwidth = 1;
constraint.gridheight = 1;
constraint.weightx = 10;
constraint.weighty = 100;
constraint.fill = GridBagConstraints.NONE;
constraint.anchor = GridBagConstraints.EAST;
gridbag.setConstraints(toLabel, constraint);
add(toLabel);
// add the text field
JTextField to = new JTextField();
constraint = new GridBagConstraints();
constraint.gridx = 1;
constraint.gridy = 0;
constraint.gridwidth = 9;
constraint.gridheight = 1;
constraint.weightx = 90;
constraint.weighty = 100;
constraint.fill = GridBagConstraints.HORIZONTAL;
constraint.anchor = GridBagConstraints.WEST;
gridbag.setConstraints(to, constraint);
add(to);
```

The label and text fields each use their own constraint (reusing the constraint variable). Their gridx and gridy values put the label at position (0, 0) and the text field at position (0, 1). The gridwidth values make the label one cell wide and the text field nine cells wide.

The fields use the fill value differently. The label has NONE, so it does not expand in either direction, and the text field has HORIZONTAL, so it expands horizontally only. (The other possible values are VERTICAL and BOTH.)

The fields also use anchor differently. The label is aligned along the right edge of the cell through the EAST class variable. The text field aligns to the left edge through WEST.

Each of the compass directions and CENTER can be used: NORTH, NORTHEAST, EAST, SOUTHEAST, SOUTH, SOUTHWEST, WEST, and NORTHWEST.

The most complex aspect of grid bag constraints are the weightx and weighty values. These variables hold arbitrary integer (or double) values that indicate how big components should be in relation to each other.

The "To" label has a weightx of 10, and the adjacent text field has a weightx of 90, using the same scale as the sketch shown in Figure 14.2. These values make the text field nine times as large as the label. The values are arbitrary: If the label were 3 and the text field were 27, the field would still be nine times as large.

14

When you don't need to give components different weights, use the same value through-out a row or column. For instance, the "To" label and field both have `weighty` values of `100`, so they have the same height as any other components below them in the same column.

Setting up grid bag constraints requires a lot of repetitive code. To save you some typing, the email panel's class has a method to set a component's constraint and add it to the panel:

```
private void addComponent(Component component, int gridx, int gridy,
    int gridwidth, int gridheight, int weightx, int weighty, int fill,
    int anchor) {

    GridBagConstraints constraint = new GridBagConstraints();
    constraint.gridx = gridx;
    constraint.gridy = gridy;
    constraint.gridwidth = gridwidth;
    constraint.gridheight = gridheight;
    constraint.weightx = weightx;
    constraint.weighty = weighty;
    constraint.fill = fill;
    constraint.anchor = anchor;
    gridbag.setConstraints(component, constraint);
    add(component);
}
```

This method doesn't use the `insets`, `ipadx`, and `ipady` variables of the `GridBagConstraints` class, so they retain their default values.

The following statements call this `addComponent()` method to add a "Subject" label and text field to the panel:

```
JLabel subjectLabel = new JLabel("Subject: ");
addComponent(subjectLabel, 0, 1, 1, 1, 10, 100, GridBagConstraints.NONE,
    GridBagConstraints.EAST);
JTextField subject = new JTextField();
addComponent(subject, 1, 1, 9, 1, 90, 100, GridBagConstraints.HORIZONTAL,
    GridBagConstraints.WEST);
```

The panel is completed with statements to add "CC" and "BCC" labels and fields:

```
// add a CC label at (0,2) 1 cell wide
JLabel ccLabel = new JLabel("CC: ");
addComponent(ccLabel, 0, 2, 1, 1, 10, 100, GridBagConstraints.NONE,
    GridBagConstraints.EAST);
// add a CC text field at (1,2) 4 cells wide
JTextField cc = new JTextField();
addComponent(cc, 1, 2, 4, 1, 40, 100, GridBagConstraints.HORIZONTAL,
    GridBagConstraints.WEST);
```

```
// add a BCC label at (5,2) 4 cells wide
JLabel bccLabel = new JLabel("BCC: ");
addComponent(bccLabel, 5, 2, 1, 1, 10, 100, GridBagConstraints.NONE,
    GridBagConstraints.EAST);
// add a BCC text field at (6,2) 4 cells wide
JTextField bcc = new JTextField();
addComponent(bcc, 6, 2, 4, 1, 40, 100, GridBagConstraints.HORIZONTAL,
    GridBagConstraints.WEST);
```

These four components share the same row, which makes their weightx values important. The labels are set to 10 each, and the text fields are set to 40 each, as noted in the initial sketch.

The MessagePanel class, shown in Listing 14.3, contains the source code of the email panel. Create it in NetBeans in the com.java21days package.

**LISTING 14.3** The Full Text of MessagePanel.java

```
 1: package com.java21days;
 2:
 3: import java.awt.*;
 4: import javax.swing.*;
 5:
 6: public class MessagePanel extends JPanel {
 7:     GridBagLayout gridbag = new GridBagLayout();
 8:
 9:     public MessagePanel() {
10:         super();
11:         GridBagConstraints constraints;
12:         setLayout(gridbag);
13:
14:         JLabel toLabel = new JLabel("To: ");
15:         JTextField to = new JTextField();
16:         JLabel subjectLabel = new JLabel("Subject: ");
17:         JTextField subject = new JTextField();
18:         JLabel ccLabel = new JLabel("CC: ");
19:         JTextField cc = new JTextField();
20:         JLabel bccLabel = new JLabel("BCC: ");
21:         JTextField bcc = new JTextField();
22:
23:         addComponent(toLabel, 0, 0, 1, 1, 10, 100,
24:             GridBagConstraints.NONE, GridBagConstraints.EAST);
25:         addComponent(to, 1, 0, 9, 1, 90, 100,
26:             GridBagConstraints.HORIZONTAL, GridBagConstraints.WEST);
27:         addComponent(subjectLabel, 0, 1, 1, 1, 10, 100,
28:             GridBagConstraints.NONE, GridBagConstraints.EAST);
29:         addComponent(subject, 1, 1, 9, 1, 90, 100,
30:             GridBagConstraints.HORIZONTAL, GridBagConstraints.WEST);
31:         addComponent(ccLabel, 0, 2, 1, 1, 10, 100,
```

14

```
32:                  GridBagConstraints.NONE, GridBagConstraints.EAST);
33:          addComponent(cc, 1, 2, 4, 1, 40, 100,
34:              GridBagConstraints.HORIZONTAL, GridBagConstraints.WEST);
35:          addComponent(bccLabel, 5, 2, 1, 1, 10, 100,
36:              GridBagConstraints.NONE, GridBagConstraints.EAST);
37:          addComponent(bcc, 6, 2, 4, 1, 40, 100,
38:              GridBagConstraints.HORIZONTAL, GridBagConstraints.WEST);
39:      }
40:
41:      private void addComponent(Component component, int gridx, int gridy,
42:          int gridwidth, int gridheight, int weightx, int weighty, int fill,
43:          int anchor) {
44:
45:          GridBagConstraints constraints = new GridBagConstraints();
46:          constraints.gridx = gridx;
47:          constraints.gridy = gridy;
48:          constraints.gridwidth = gridwidth;
49:          constraints.gridheight = gridheight;
50:          constraints.weightx = weightx;
51:          constraints.weighty = weighty;
52:          constraints.fill = fill;
53:          constraints.anchor = anchor;
54:          gridbag.setConstraints(component, constraints);
55:          add(component);
56:      }
57: }
```

This class isn't an application, so it can't be run. After the panel has been compiled, it can be used in any GUI. (Presumably this panel would be incorporated into an email program's interface for writing messages.)

To show it in action, the `MessageFrame` class in Listing 14.4 is a simple application that displays a frame with a `MessagePanel` added to it. It also belongs to the `com.java21days` package.

**LISTING 14.4**   The Full Text of `MessageFrame.java`

```
1: package com.java21days;
2:
3: import javax.swing.*;
4:
5: public class MessageFrame extends JFrame {
6:     public MessageFrame() {
7:         super("Message");
8:         setSize(380, 120);
9:         setDefaultCloseOperation(JFrame.EXIT_ON_CLOSE);
10:        MessagePanel mPanel = new MessagePanel();
11:        add(mPanel);
```

```
12:            setVisible(true);
13:        }
14:
15:        private static void setLookAndFeel() {
16:            try {
17:                UIManager.setLookAndFeel(
18:                    "javax.swing.plaf.nimbus.NimbusLookAndFeel"
19:                );
20:            } catch (Exception exc) {
21:                System.out.println("Look and feel error: " + exc.getMessage());
22:            }
23:        }
24:
25:        public static void main(String[] arguments) {
26:            MessageFrame.setLookAndFeel();
27:            MessageFrame frame = new MessageFrame();
28:        }
29:    }
```

The panel is created in line 10 and added to the frame in line 11. This application is shown in Figure 14.4.

**FIGURE 14.4**
Viewing the panel in an application's user interface.

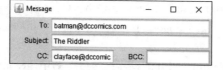

Because the panel does not stipulate its own size, the frame's dimensions determine the panel's height and width. This demonstrates how Swing's grid and grid bag layouts give components the flexibility to adapt to the space available to them in an interface.

If you didn't want the panel to assume the size of its container, its layout manager could be set to null:

```
setLayout(null);
```

As this project illustrates, grid bag layout is much more complex than the other layout managers in Java. If you can design the same interface by mixing other managers, that approach is likely to be easier to maintain in the future, especially when you aren't the only programmer working on the code.

14

# Summary

This lesson describes capabilities that enhance Java's capabilities for application development, including Swing performance improvements through the use of threads.

The `SwingWorker` class improves the performance of Swing applications by putting a time-consuming task in its own thread. The class handles all the work required to start and stop the thread behind the scenes.

When you create a subclass of `SwingWorker`, you can focus on the task that must be performed.

With GridBagLayout added to the others, you now have a set of layout managers for designing sophisticated user interfaces with Swing for your Java programs.

# Q&A

**Q How can I make sure that a `SwingWorker` object has finished working?**

**A** Call the worker's `isDone()` method, which returns `true` when the task has finished executing. Note that this method returns `true` no matter how the task completes. So if it is canceled or interrupted or fails in some other manner, it returns `true`.

The `isCancelled()` method can be used to check whether the task was canceled.

**Q I'm designing an application with `GridBagLayout`. Why are all my components arranged in the center of their part of the user interface?**

**A** The default behavior in grid bag layout is for components to be horizontally centered within their cell. You must change this using the GridBagConstraints object to set new constraints—in particular `anchor` and `fill`.

# Quiz

Review this lesson's material by taking this three-question quiz.

## Questions

**1.** What interface must be implemented for you to be notified when a `SwingWorker` object has finished executing?

    **A.** `ActionListener`

    **B.** `PropertyChangeListener`

    **C.** `SwingListener`

2. If you want a grid layout in which a component can take up more than one cell of the grid, which layout should you use?

   **A.** `GridLayout`

   **B.** `GridBagLayout`

   **C.** None; it isn't possible to do that.

3. What variable of GridBagConstraints sets the width in cells of a component?

   **A.** `ipadx`

   **B.** `weightx`

   **C.** `gridwidth`

## Answers

**1.** B. `PropertyChangeListener` in the `java.beans` package receives a `propertyChange()` event when the worker finishes.

**2.** B. `GridBagLayout` enables a component to take up multiple grid cells.

**3.** C. `gridwidth` determines the width.

# Certification Practice

The following question is the kind of thing you could expect to be asked on a Java programming certification test. Answer it without looking again at this lesson or using the Java compiler to test the code.

Given:

```
import java.awt.*;
import javax.swing.*;

public class SliderFrame extends JFrame {
    public SliderFrame() {
        super();
        setDefaultCloseOperation(JFrame.EXIT_ON_CLOSE);
        JSlider value = new JSlider(0, 255, 100);
        setSize(325, 150);
        setVisible(true);
    }

    public static void main(String[] arguments) {
        new SliderFrame();
    }
}
```

14

What will happen when you attempt to compile and run this source code?

    **A.** It compiles without error and runs correctly.

    **B.** It compiles without error but does not display anything in the frame.

    **C.** It does not compile because the content pane is empty.

    **D.** It does not compile because of the `new SliderFrame()` statement.

The answer is available on the book's website, at www.java21days.com. Visit the Lesson 14 page and click the Certification Practice link.

# Exercises

To extend your knowledge of the subjects covered in this lesson, try the following exercises:

    **1.** Add a text area to the MessagePanel class with a "Message" label and make it support scrolling.

    **2.** Create a simple graphical user interface that uses SwingWorker to load the first 10,000 prime numbers into a text area.

Where applicable, exercise solutions are offered on the book's website, at www.java21days.com.

# PART III
# Java Programming

# LESSON 15
# Using Inner Classes and Lambda Expressions

Each new version of the Java language takes it further from its humble origins in 1995. When it was first released, Java had only 250 classes in the Java Class Library and was primarily used to put interactive programs on web pages. This brought something new to the Web and inspired several hundred thousand programmers to learn the new language.

Because the language was well designed and offered some features that made it a worthy rival to C++ and other choices for software development, Java quickly outgrew its original focus to become a general-purpose programming language. Today it is the most widely implemented and popular language in the world.

There are millions of Java coders putting its classes on several billion devices as the language nears its 25th birthday. Each new release embraces new capabilities that bring to Java sophisticated new methodologies that are eagerly anticipated by programmers.

One of the most-requested features to be added to Java is *lambda expressions*, also called *closures*. They make it possible in Java to employ a methodology called *functional programming*.

In this lesson you will learn about lambda expressions after an introduction to two parts of the language that are prerequisites to their use: inner classes and anonymous inner classes.

# Inner Classes

When you create a class in Java, you must define its attributes and behavior. The attributes are the class and instance variables that hold its data, and the behavior is the methods that use that data to perform tasks.

A class also can contain a third element that combines both attributes and behavior: an inner class.

Inner classes are like helper classes, but they are defined inside the class they were created to help. Because a Java program can have as many classes as you think are necessary, you might be questioning the point of inner classes. A Scheduler class that manages work schedules at your restaurant could have an Employee helper class for each worker and a Day helper class for each weekday the business is open.

Although some of the purpose of an inner class can be accomplished with a helper class, as you learn more about inner classes, you will encounter situations where they're better suited to a particular project. Java includes inner classes for several reasons.

If a class is used by only one other class, it's a good idea to define it inside that class. That keeps the code in one place and makes clear the relationship between the classes.

An inner class can access private methods and variables of its enclosing class that a helper class could not access. This is possible for the same reason that a method in a class can access private variables of that class.

**NOTE**

> Rules governing the scope of an inner class closely match those governing variables. An inner class's name is not visible outside its scope, except in a fully qualified name (the enclosing class name followed by a period and the inner class name). This helps in structuring classes within a package. The code for an inner class can use simple names from enclosing scopes, including class and member variables of enclosing classes, as well as local variables of enclosing blocks.

To create an inner class, use the class keyword and a class declaration, as with any other class, but place it inside the containing class. An inner class usually is put in the same place that class and instance variables are defined.

Here's an inner class called InnerHello in a class called Hello:

```
public class Hello {

    class InnerHello {
```

```
    InnerHello() {
        System.out.println(
            "The method call is coming from inside the class!"
        );
    }
}

public Hello() {
    // empty constructor
}

public static void main(String[] arguments) {
    Hello program = new Hello();
    Hello.InnerHello inner = program.new InnerHello();
}
}
```

The inner class is defined just like any other class, except for its position: It is placed within the { and } brackets of another class.

Creating an object of an inner class requires an object of the outer class. The `new` operator is called on the object, as in this statement from the preceding example:

```
Hello.InnerHello inner = program.new InnerHello();
```

Look at both halves of this assignment statement to learn how the object of the inner class is created.

On the left, the name of the inner class consists of the name of the outer class, a period character (.), and the inner class name—so `Hello.InnerHello` is the name.

On the right, `program` refers to the `Hello` object. The reference to `program` is followed by a period, the `new` operator, and the inner class constructor `InnerHello()`.

The lesson's first project rewrites the `ComicBook` application from Lesson 8, "Data Structures," to use an inner class. That project managed a comic book collection with a main class called `ComicBooks` and a helper class called `Comic` for each comic in a collection. Both were defined in the same source code file but as separate classes. The compiler turned them into the bytecode files `ComicBooks.class` and `Comic.class`.

This time around, there's a `ComicBox` class for the collection and a `InnerComic` inner class.

The `ComicBox` application is shown in Listing 15.1. Create a new empty Java file called `ComicBox.java` for this project in the `com.java21days` package.

**LISTING 15.1**   The Full Text of `ComicBox.java`

```
 1: package com.java21days;
 2:
 3: import java.util.*;
 4:
 5: public class ComicBox {
 6:     class InnerComic {
 7:         String title;
 8:         String issueNumber;
 9:         String condition;
10:         float basePrice;
11:         float price;
12:
13:         InnerComic(String inTitle, String inIssueNumber,
14:             String inCondition, float inBasePrice) {
15:
16:             title = inTitle;
17:             issueNumber = inIssueNumber;
18:             condition = inCondition;
19:             basePrice = inBasePrice;
20:         }
21:
22:         void setPrice(float factor) {
23:             price = basePrice * factor;
24:         }
25:     }
26:
27:     public ComicBox() {
28:         HashMap<String, Float> quality = new HashMap<>();
29:         float price1 = 3.00F;
30:         quality.put("mint", price1);
31:         float price2 = 2.00F;
32:         quality.put("near mint", price2);
33:         float price3 = 1.50F;
34:         quality.put("very fine", price3);
35:         float price4 = 1.00F;
36:         quality.put("fine", price4);
37:         float price5 = 0.50F;
38:         quality.put("good", price5);
39:         float price6 = 0.25F;
40:         quality.put("poor", price6);
41:         InnerComic[] comix = new InnerComic[3];
42:         comix[0] = new InnerComic("Amazing Spider-Man", "1A",
43:             "very fine", 12_000.00F);
44:         comix[0].setPrice(quality.get(comix[0].condition));
45:         comix[1] = new InnerComic("Incredible Hulk", "181",
46:             "near mint", 680.00F);
47:         comix[1].setPrice(quality.get(comix[1].condition));
48:         comix[2] = new InnerComic("Cerebus", "1A", "good", 190.00F);
49:         comix[2].setPrice(quality.get(comix[2].condition));
```

```
50:          for (InnerComic comix1 : comix) {
51:              System.out.println("Title: " + comix1.title);
52:              System.out.println("Issue: " + comix1.issueNumber);
53:              System.out.println("Condition: " + comix1.condition);
54:              System.out.println("Price: $" + comix1.price + "\n");
55:          }
56:      }
57:
58:      public static void main(String[] arguments) {
59:          new ComicBox();
60:      }
61: }
```

The inner class, which is defined in lines 6–25, has a constructor that creates a comic book using the title, issue number, condition, and base price. There's also a setPrice() method in lines 22–24.

The ComicBox class uses this inner class in line 41, creating an array that holds three InnerComic objects. The inner class is referred to as InnerComic, the same as if it were a helper class.

You also could have referred to the inner class using its full name, which includes the name of its enclosing class:

```
ComicBox.InnerComic[] comix = new ComicBox.InnerComic[3];
```

Figure 15.1 shows the output of the application.

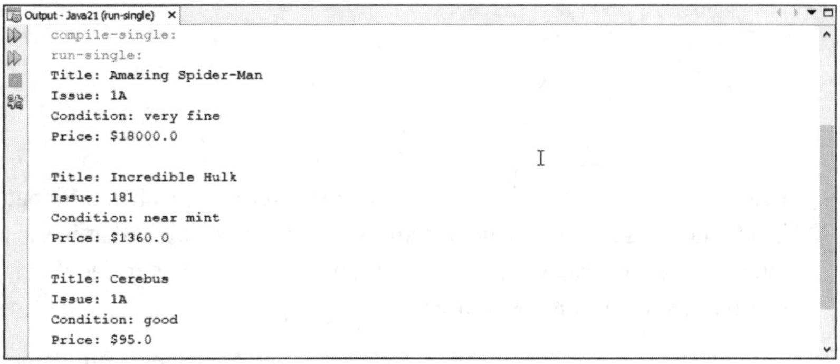

**FIGURE 15.1**
Using inner classes to collect comic books.

```
compile-single:
run-single:
Title: Amazing Spider-Man
Issue: 1A
Condition: very fine
Price: $18000.0

Title: Incredible Hulk
Issue: 181
Condition: near mint
Price: $1360.0

Title: Cerebus
Issue: 1A
Condition: good
Price: $95.0
```

# Anonymous Inner Classes

Often in Java programming you need to create an object in one statement that never will be referred to again. A special type of inner class is well suited to this purpose: an anonymous inner class. This is a class that has no name and is declared and created in the same statement.

To use an anonymous inner class, you replace a reference to an object's variable with the `new` keyword, a call to a constructor, and the class definition inside { and } characters. (This will make more sense when you see it in code.)

The following code creates a thread and starts it without using anonymous inner classes:

```
ThreadClass task = new ThreadClass();
Thread runner = new Thread(task);
runner.start();
```

For this example, assume that the `task` object implements the `Runnable` interface to be run as a thread. Assume as well that the code in `ThreadClass` is simple, and the class needs to be used only once.

In this situation, it's efficient to get rid of `ThreadClass` and put its code inside an anonymous inner class. This code rewrite does exactly this:

```
Thread runner = new Thread(new Runnable()  {
    public void run() {
        // thread does its work here
    }
});
runner.start();
```

The anonymous inner class has replaced the reference to `task` with the following code:

```
new Runnable()  {
    public void run() {
        // thread does its work here
    }
)
```

In Java, the `new` operator is an expression that returns an object. So putting this code inside the `Thread()` constructor returns an unnamed object that implements the `Runnable` interface and overrides the `run()` method. The statements inside that method do the work that has been put in its own thread.

For a deeper look at this concept, the next project provides a full demonstration of how anonymous inner classes are created and why they're so useful.

In Lesson 12, "Responding to User Input," you learned about how to monitor user input in a `Swing` application by using interfaces called *event listeners*. When an application must monitor a particular type of input, such as a user clicking a button, moving a mouse, or typing keys on the keyboard, it must have a class that implements the listener interface for that input. These classes are in the package `java.awt.event`. User clicks are monitored by `KeyListener`, for instance.

One event listener that was not covered in Lesson 12 is `WindowListener`, which tracks the different ways a user can interact with a window. There are methods in the `WindowListener` interface for when a window has been opened and closed, as well as for when it has become the focus or lost the focus.

A class that implements the interface must implement a number of methods: `windowActivated()`, `windowClosed()`, `windowClosing()`, `windowDeactivated()`, `windowDeiconified()`, `windowIconified()`, and `windowOpened()`. That's a lot of methods to implement, especially if you have only one or two possible window interactions that your class is interested in. A frame that only monitors when a window opened would have code that looks something like this:

```
public void windowOpened(WindowEvent event) {
    Window pane = event.getWindow();
    pane.setBackground(Color.CYAN);
}

public void windowClosed(WindowEvent event) {
    // do nothing
}

public void windowActivated(WindowEvent event) {
    // do nothing
}

public void windowDeactivated(WindowEvent event) {
    // do nothing
}
```

This is just part of the window event code required. There are several other do-nothing methods that must be present in a class that implements the `WindowListener` interface.

After all the methods are implemented in a frame, the frame can add a listener to monitor window events:

```
addWindowListener(this);
```

There's a better way to create the listener and add it to the frame: Use a subclass of the `WindowAdapter` class.

The `WindowAdapter` class implements the `WindowListener` interface as a number of methods that each do nothing. There are several adapter classes in `java.awt.event` that simplify the process of listening to a particular event. You can create a subclass of the adapter class that overrides the method (or methods) only where something needs to happen.

Here's code for a window listener that uses `WindowAdapter` and only monitors the `windowClosing()` event:

```
public class WindowCloseListener extends WindowAdapter {
    JFrame frame;
    boolean done;

    public WindowCloseListener(JFrame inFrame) {
        this.frame = inFrame;
    }

    public void windowClosing(WindowEvent event) {
        // user has tried to close window
        if (done) {
            // allow it
            frame.dispose();
            System.exit(0);
        }
    }
}
```

Calling a window's `dispose()` method closes it. This code waits for a user to close a frame and does it only when the Boolean variable `done` equals `true`. That variable is an instance variable of a frame in another class (the one that created the listener). In that frame, the frame's default behavior must be set to ignore attempts to close the window:

```
setDefaultCloseOperation(JFrame.DO_NOTHING_ON_CLOSE);
```

Also, the frame creates the listener object and makes a listener:

```
WindowCloseListener closer = new WindowCloseListener();
addWindowListener(closer);
```

An object of the helper class `WindowCloseListener` is assigned to a variable and set to monitor window events.

This approach to monitoring one window event requires four steps:

1. Create a subclass of `WindowAdapter`.

2. Implement the window-closing method in that class.

3. Create a constructor in that class with the frame that needs the class as an argument.

4. Store that frame in an instance variable.

The constructor and instance variable are needed to link the two classes. The adapter must be able to access the frame's `done` variable.

A simpler approach can be accomplished in the frame's class through the use of an anonymous inner class:

```
setDefaultCloseOperation(WindowConstants.DO_NOTHING_ON_CLOSE);
addWindowListener(new WindowAdapter() {
    // user has tried to close window
    if (done) {
        // allow it
        frame.dispose();
        System.exit(0);
    }
});
```

The listener is created anonymously by calling `new WindowAdapter()` with a definition of the class. The class overrides the `windowClosing()` method so that when a user closes a window, an action can be taken.

This anonymous inner class can do something that a separate helper class could not do: access the `frame` instance variable. Inner classes are able to access the methods and variables of their enclosing class, just like instance variables and methods.

> **NOTE**
> Other adapter classes in the `java.awt.event` packages make it convenient to implement other listeners. The `KeyAdapter` class has empty methods for keyboard events, `MouseAdapter` for mouse events, and `FocusAdapter` for keyboard focus events.

In Lesson 10, "Building an Interface," you created a `ProgressMonitor` application that used a slider as a progress bar. The next project will enhance that code to prevent the program's main window from being closed if the progress bar has not reached 100%.

In NetBeans, create a new empty Java file named `ProgressMonitor2` in the class `com.java21days` and then enter the text of Listing 15.2 into that file. Save your work when you're done.

**LISTING 15.2** The Full Text of `ProgressMonitor2.java`

```
1: package com.java21days;
2:
3: import java.awt.*;
4: import java.awt.event.*;
5: import javax.swing.*;
6:
7: public class ProgressMonitor2 extends JFrame {
8:     JProgressBar current;
```

```
 9:        int num = 0;
10:        boolean done = false;
11:
12:        public ProgressMonitor2() {
13:            super("Progress Monitor 2");
14:            setDefaultCloseOperation(JFrame.DO_NOTHING_ON_CLOSE);
15:            addWindowListener(new WindowAdapter() {
16:                @Override
17:                public void windowClosing(WindowEvent event) {
18:                    // user has tried to close window
19:                    if (done) {
20:                        // allow it
21:                        dispose();
22:                        System.exit(0);
23:                    }
24:                }
25:            });
26:            setSize(400, 100);
27:            setLayout(new FlowLayout());
28:            current = new JProgressBar(0, 2000);
29:            current.setValue(0);
30:            current.setStringPainted(true);
31:            current.setPreferredSize(new Dimension(360, 48));
32:            add(current);
33:            setVisible(true);
34:            iterate();
35:        }
36:
37:        public final void iterate() {
38:            while (num < 2000) {
39:                current.setValue(num);
40:                try {
41:                    Thread.sleep(1000);
42:                } catch (InterruptedException e) { }
43:                num += 95;
44:            }
45:            done = true;
46:        }
47:
48:        private static void setLookAndFeel() {
49:            try {
50:                UIManager.setLookAndFeel(
51:                    "javax.swing.plaf.nimbus.NimbusLookAndFeel"
52:                );
53:            } catch (Exception exc) {
54:                System.err.println(exc);
55:            }
56:        }
57:
58:        public static void main(String[] arguments) {
59:            ProgressMonitor2.setLookAndFeel();
```

```
60:          new ProgressMonitor2();
61:     }
62: }
```

The anonymous inner class is created and used in lines 15–25. It monitors window input using `windowClosing()`, the only method in the `WindowListener` interface the application needs to check, and makes sure the `done` instance variable equals `true` before closing the window.

See Figure 15.2 for the program's output.

**FIGURE 15.2**
Stopping a program from closing until its work is done.

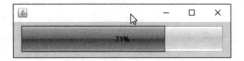

An anonymous inner class cannot have a constructor, which means anonymous inner classes are more limited than other inner classes and helper classes.

Anonymous inner classes are a bit more complex than other aspects of the Java language. They look odd in the source code of a program, and getting the punctuation right can be tricky. When you've added them to your skill set, however, you will find that using them is a powerful, flexible, and concise way to get things done.

# Lambda Expressions

*Lambda expressions*, also called *closures*, enable an object from a class with only a single method to be created with an `->` operator, provided that other conditions are met. This statement is an example:

```
Runnable runner = () -> { System.out.println("Eureka!"); };
```

This code creates an object that implements the `Runnable` interface with a `run()` method equivalent to the following code:

```
public void run() {
    System.out.println("Eureka!");
}
```

In a lambda expression, the statement to the right of the `->` arrow operator defines the method that implements the interface. This is possible only when the interface has a single method to implement, as `Runnable` does with only the `run()` method. When an interface in Java has one method, it's called a *functional interface*.

As you might have spotted, a lambda expression also has something unusual to the left of the arrow operator. In the `Runnable` example, it's an empty set of parentheses.

This part of the expression holds the arguments to send the method of the functional interface. The `run()` method takes no arguments in the `Runnable` interface, so no arguments are required in that expression.

Take a look at another example of a lambda expression that does have something inside the parentheses on the left side of the expression:

```
ActionListener listen = (ActionEvent act) -> {
    System.out.println(act.getSource());
};
```

This expression provides an implementation of the only method in the `ActionListener` interface, `actionPerformed()`. That method takes one argument: an `ActionEvent` object. `ActionListener` is in the `java.awt.event` package. Here's the old way to implement the same functionality:

```
public void actionPerformed(ActionEvent act) {
    System.out.println(act.getSource());
}
```

The `ActionListener` interface handles action events such as a user's button click or menu item selection. The only method in the functional interface is `actionPerformed(ActionEvent)`. The argument contains the user action that triggered the event.

The right half of the lambda expression defines the `actionPerformed()` method as a statement that displays information about the interface component where the event happened. The left half makes an `ActionEvent` object the argument to the method. This object, `act`, is used inside the body of the method. In the expression, the left-half reference to `act` appears to be outside the scope of the right-half method implementation. Lambda expressions allow code to refer to variables of another method outside the scope of those variables.

Like anonymous inner classes, lambda expressions have the effect of making code shorter. A single expression creates an object and implements an interface. Lambda expressions can make code even shorter through Java's support for target typing.

In a lambda expression, it's possible to infer the class of the argument (or arguments) sent to the method. In the `ActionListener` example, the functional interface has a method with an `ActionEvent` object as its only argument. For this reason, the name of the class can be omitted.

Here's a simplified version of the expression, taking this into account:

```
ActionListener listen = (act) -> {
    System.out.println(act.getSource());
}
```

This lesson's final two programs illustrate the difference that lambda expressions bring to Java.

The `CursorMayhem` application in Listing 15.3 is a Swing program that displays three buttons in a panel that change the program's cursor.

Cursors have not been covered up to this point, but they're simple to use. They're represented by the `Cursor` class in the `java.awt` package and can be changed by calling a container's `setCursor(Cursor)` method.

The type of cursor is determined by class variables of the class. The following statements create a panel and set its cursor to the one used in text boxes:

```
JPanel panel = new JPanel();
panel.setCursor(new Cursor(Cursor.TEXT_CURSOR));
```

This statement sets the cursor back to the default:

```
panel.setCursor(new Cursor(Cursor.DEFAULT_CURSOR));
```

This application will be implemented two different ways. The first version uses an anonymous inner class, not a lambda expression, to monitor user clicks on the three buttons. Create a new program in NetBeans with the name `CursorMayhem` in the package `com.java21days` and enter the code shown in Listing 15.3.

**LISTING 15.3**   The Full Text of `CursorMayhem.java`

```
 1: package com.java21days;
 2:
 3: import java.awt.*;
 4: import java.awt.event.*;
 5: import javax.swing.*;
 6:
 7: public class CursorMayhem extends JFrame {
 8:     JButton harry, wade, hansel;
 9:
10:     public CursorMayhem() {
11:         super("Choose a Cursor");
13:         setSize(400, 80);
14:         setDefaultCloseOperation(JFrame.EXIT_ON_CLOSE);
15:         setLayout(new FlowLayout());
```

```
16:           harry = new JButton("Crosshair");
17:           add(harry);
18:           wade = new JButton("Wait");
19:           add(wade);
20:           hansel = new JButton("Hand");
21:           add(hansel);
22:           // begin anonymous inner class
23:           ActionListener act = new ActionListener() {
24:               public void actionPerformed(ActionEvent event) {
25:                   if (event.getSource() == harry) {
26:                       setCursor(new Cursor(Cursor.CROSSHAIR_CURSOR));
27:                   }
28:                   if (event.getSource() == wade) {
29:                       setCursor(new Cursor(Cursor.WAIT_CURSOR));
30:                   }
31:                   if (event.getSource() == hansel) {
32:                       setCursor(new Cursor(Cursor.HAND_CURSOR));
33:                   }
34:               }
35:           };
36:           // end anonymous inner class
37:           harry.addActionListener(act);
38:           wade.addActionListener(act);
39:           hansel.addActionListener(act);
40:           setVisible(true);
41:       }
42:
43:       private static void setLookAndFeel() {
44:           try {
45:               UIManager.setLookAndFeel(
46:                   "javax.swing.plaf.nimbus.NimbusLookAndFeel"
47:               );
48:           } catch (Exception exc) {
49:               System.err.println("Look and feel error: " + exc);
50:           }
51:       }
52:
53:       public static void main(String[] arguments) {
54:           CursorMayhem.setLookAndFeel();
55:           CursorMayhem app = new CursorMayhem();
56:       }
57: }
```

Figure 15.3 shows this program running.

**FIGURE 15.3**
Monitoring action events with an anonymous inner class.

Lines 23–35 of the application define an event listener for the `CursorMayhem` class, using an anonymous inner class. This nameless object contains an implementation of the only method in the `ActionListener` interface: `actionPerformed(ActionEvent)`.

In the method, the frame's cursor is changed by calling its `setCursor()` method. Anonymous inner classes have access to the methods and instance variables of their enclosing class. A separate helper class would lack that access.

As you are running the app, move your cursor over the title bar that reads "Choose a Cursor." It changes from the current cursor to the default. Move it back over the pane, and it again becomes the cursor that you selected.

Now take a look at the `ClosureMayhem` application in Listing 15.4.

**LISTING 15.4** The Full Text of `ClosureMayhem.java`

```
 1: package com.java21days;
 2:
 3: import java.awt.*;
 4: import java.awt.event.*;
 5: import javax.swing.*;
 6:
 7: public class ClosureMayhem extends JFrame {
 8:     JButton harry, wade, hansel;
 9:
10:     public ClosureMayhem() {
11:         super("Choose a Cursor");
12:         setSize(400, 80);
13:         setDefaultCloseOperation(JFrame.EXIT_ON_CLOSE);
14:         setLayout(new FlowLayout());
15:         harry = new JButton("Crosshair");
16:         add(harry);
17:         wade = new JButton("Wait");
18:         add(wade);
19:         hansel = new JButton("Hand");
20:         add(hansel);
21:         // begin closure
22:         ActionListener act = (event) -> {
23:             if (event.getSource() == harry) {
24:                 setCursor(new Cursor(Cursor.CROSSHAIR_CURSOR));
25:             }
26:             if (event.getSource() == wade) {
27:                 setCursor(new Cursor(Cursor.WAIT_CURSOR));
28:             }
29:             if (event.getSource() == hansel) {
30:                 setCursor(new Cursor(Cursor.HAND_CURSOR));
31:             }
32:         };
33:         // end closure
```

```
34:             harry.addActionListener(act);
35:             wade.addActionListener(act);
36:             hansel.addActionListener(act);
37:             setVisible(true);
38:         }
39:
40:     private static void setLookAndFeel() {
41:         try {
42:             UIManager.setLookAndFeel(
43:                 "javax.swing.plaf.nimbus.NimbusLookAndFeel"
44:             );
45:         } catch (Exception exc) {
46:             System.err.println("Look and feel error: " + exc);
47:         }
48:     }
49:
50:     public static void main(String[] arguments) {
51:         ClosureMayhem.setLookAndFeel();
52:         ClosureMayhem app = new ClosureMayhem();
53:     }
54: }
```

The `ClosureMayhem` application implements the action listener in lines 22–32. Everything else is the same as in `CursorMayhem`, except for the lines that refer to the class name.

In `ClosureMayhem`, you don't need to know the name of the method in the `ActionListener` interface to use it in the program. You also don't need to specify the class of the `ActionEvent` that is the method's only argument.

Lambda expressions support functional programming, a methodology for software design that was previously unavailable in the Java language.

With the basic syntax of lambda expressions and two common ways they can be employed in programs, you can begin to exploit this feature. At this point, you should be able to recognize lambda expressions, write statements involving the arrow operator ("=>"), and use this operator to create an object for any single-method interface. These single-method interfaces also are called *functional interfaces*.

# Variable Type Inference

Programmers who prefer other languages often criticize Java for its long-windedness. Composing statements and expressions, declaring variables, calling methods, and referencing objects require a lot of typing.

A recently introduced language feature—local variable type inference—simplifies the language in a powerful way. It's now possible in Java to use the keyword `var` in place of the name of a primitive data type or class in some situations. Here's an example:

```
var marco = "Polo";
```

15

This statement creates a String variable called `marco` with the literal value `"Polo"`. `var` tells the Java compiler to infer the data type based on the information stored in it. Because `"Polo"` is a string literal, the variable `marco` obviously must be a string. The statement using `var` is equivalent to this one, which spells out the class:

```
String marco = "Polo";
```

Variable inference with `var` can be used in several situations:

- As a local variable
- As the variable in a `for` loop
- As the value returned by a method

In all these cases, the variable must be given an initial value. Otherwise, `var` can't infer a primitive type or class because it doesn't know what's being stored in the variable.

There are some situations in which `var` cannot be used:

- As the argument to a method
- As the return type in a method declaration
- As a class or instance variable

Even when a class or an instance variable is declared and set to an initial value, `var` cannot be used. Those statements still must declare their primitive type or class.

# Summary

Like generics, inner classes, anonymous inner classes, and lambda expressions are among the most sophisticated aspects of Java. Before you reach a point where you are comfortable writing lambda expressions, you ought to be able to benefit from inner classes and anonymous inner classes.

A non-anonymous inner class takes the form of a helper class, situated inside a class instead of on its own. The class is defined with the instance variables, class variables, instance methods, and class methods that make up the behavior and attributes of the enclosing class. Because it's defined inside that class, the inner class can read and write its private variables and methods of the class.

An anonymous inner class is created without needing a variable, which makes sense for an object that will be used only once in a program. These classes often are used when a Swing user interface component needs an event listener to monitor user input.

Lambda expressions are deceptively similar in appearance, and they are created with only the -> arrow operator but offer an enormous enhancement to a Java programmer's capabilities.

# Q&A

**Q Is it necessary to use anonymous inner classes?**

**A** Whenever you can get something done without a feature of the Java language, you don't have to use that feature. Programmers generally can accomplish a task in a program in a bunch of different ways. Although any sophisticated new technique is likely to work in fewer lines of code or offer other advantages, there's no penalty in Java for doing something in more statements.

Generally, what matters is that your program works, not how many lines it took to make that happen. With that disclaimer, you should become conversant in features such as anonymous inner classes anyway. They are something you are going to find in Java code. Experienced programmers use inner classes, anonymous inner classes, and lambda expressions. Knowing what they are will help you understand what someone else's code is doing.

**Q What's the origin of the term *lambda expression*?**

**A** The term *lambda* comes from the system of math logic called *lambda calculus*, where the Greek letter lambda represents an anonymous function. The choice of this letter was arbitrary.

Lambda calculus has proven to be extremely useful in math, computation theory, and computer programming. Lambda expressions are available in many programming languages today in addition to Java. They include JavaScript, Python, C#, Scala, Smalltalk, Kotlin, Groovy, and Haskell.

# Quiz

Review this lesson's material by taking this three-question quiz.

## Questions

**1.** What can an inner class access that a separate helper class could not?

    **A.** Anonymous inner classes

    **B.** `private final` variables of another class

    **C.** Threads

**2.** What makes a Java interface qualified to be called a functional interface?

    **A.** The number of methods in that interface

    **B.** The arrow operator

    **C.** Any interface can be functional.

**3.** What does an adapter class make easier?

    **A.** Using lambda expressions

    **B.** Arranging Swing user interface components

    **C.** Implementing an event listener

15

## Answers

**1.** B. An inner class can access the `private` variables and methods of its enclosing class.

**2.** A. An interface that defines only one method is a functional interface.

**3.** C. An adapter implements all the methods in an event listener interface so you can subclass the adapter and override only the method or methods that are useful.

# Certification Practice

The following question is the kind of thing you could expect to be asked on a Java programming certification test. Answer it without looking again at this lesson or using the Java compiler to test the code.

Given:

```java
public class ClassType {
    public static void main(String[] arguments) {
        Class c = String.class;
        try {
            Object o = c.newInstance();
            if (o instanceof String) {
                System.out.println("True");
            } else {
                System.out.println("False");
            }
        } catch (Exception e) {
```

```
                System.out.println("Error");
            }
        }
    }
```

What will be the output of this application?

**A.** `true`

**B.** `false`

**C.** An error

**D.** The program will not compile.

The answer is available on the book's website, at www.java21days.com. Visit the Lesson 15 page and click the Certification Practice link.

# Exercises

To extend your knowledge of the subjects covered in this lesson, try the following exercises:

1. Create a new version of the `DiceRoller` program from Lesson 14, "Developing Swing Applications," that makes `DiceWorker` an inner class.

2. Extend your new `DiceRoller` program to monitor action events with lambda expressions.

Where applicable, exercise solutions are offered on the book's website, at www.java21days.com.

# LESSON 16
# Working with Input and Output

Many of the programs you create with Java need to interact with some kind of data source. Information can be stored on a computer in many ways, including files on a hard drive, pages on a website, and bytes in the computer's memory.

You might expect to need a different technique to handle each different storage device. Fortunately, that isn't the case.

In Java, information can be stored and retrieved using a communications system called *streams*, which are implemented in the `java.io` package and are enhanced by the `java.nio.file` package.

In this lesson, you'll learn how to create input streams to read information and output streams to store information. You'll work with the following:

- Byte streams, which are used to handle bytes, integers, and other simple data types
- Character streams, which handle text files and other text sources

You can deal with all data in the same way when you know how to work with an input stream, whether the information is coming from a disk, the Internet, or another program. The same is true of using output streams to transmit data.

# Introduction to Streams

In Java, all data can be written and read using streams. Streams, like the bodies of water that share the same name, carry something from one place to another.

A stream is a path traveled by data in a program. An input stream sends data from a source into a program, and an output stream sends data from a program to a destination.

You will deal with two types of streams in this lesson: byte streams and character streams. *Byte streams* carry integers with values from 0 to 255. A diverse assortment of data can be expressed in byte format, including numeric data, executable programs, Internet communications, and bytecode—the class files run by a Java Virtual Machine (JVM).

In fact, every kind of data imaginable can be expressed using either individual bytes or a series of bytes combined.

Character streams are a specialized type of byte stream that handles only textual data. They're distinguished from byte streams in that Java's character set supports Unicode, a standard that includes many more characters than could be expressed easily using bytes.

Any kind of data that involves text should use character streams, including text files, web pages, and other common types of text.

## Using a Stream

The procedure for using either a byte stream or character stream in Java is largely the same. Before you start working with the specifics of the `java.io` and `java.nio.file` classes, it's useful to walk through the process of creating and using streams.

For an input stream, the first step is to create an object associated with the data source. For example, if the source is a file on your hard drive, a `FileInputStream` object could be associated with this file.

After you have a stream object, you can read information from that stream by using one of the object's methods. `FileInputStream` includes a `read()` method that returns a byte read from the file.

When you're finished reading information from the stream, you call the `close()` method to indicate that you're finished using the stream.

For an output stream, you begin by creating an object associated with the data's destination. One such object can be created from the `BufferedWriter` class, which is an efficient way to create text files.

Using the `write()` method is the simplest way to send information to the output stream's destination. For instance, a `BufferedWriter` class `write()` method can send individual characters to an output stream.

As with input streams, you call the `close()` method on an output stream when you have no more information to send.

## Filtering a Stream

The simplest way to use a stream is to create it and then call its methods to send or receive data, depending on whether it's an output stream or an input stream.

Many of the classes you will work with in this lesson achieve more sophisticated results when a filter is associated with a stream before reading or writing any data.

A *filter* is a type of stream that modifies how an existing stream is handled. Think of a dam on a mountain stream. The dam regulates the flow of water from the points upstream to the points downstream. The dam is a type of filter. Remove it, and the water flows in a less-controlled fashion.

16

The procedure for using a filter on a stream is as follows:

1. Create a stream associated with a data source or data destination.
2. Associate a filter with that stream.
3. Read data from or write data to the filter rather than to the original stream.

The methods you call on a filter are the same as the methods you call on a stream. There are `read()` and `write()` methods, just as there would be on an unfiltered stream.

You even can associate a filter with another filter, so the following path for information is possible: An input stream associated with a text file is filtered through a Spanish-to-English translation filter, which is then filtered through a no-profanity filter. Finally, it is sent to its destination—a human being who wants to read it.

This may be confusing in the abstract, but you will have opportunities to see the process in practice in the following sections.

## Handling Exceptions

Several exceptions in the `java.io` package might occur when you're working with files and streams. Two common ones are `FileNotFoundException` and `EOFException`:

- **`FileNotFoundException`:** Occurs when you try to create a stream or file object using a file that couldn't be located
- **`EOFException`:** Indicates that the end of a file has been reached unexpectedly as data was being read from the file through an input stream

These exceptions are subclasses of `IOException`. One way to deal with them is to enclose all input and output statements in a `try-catch` block that catches `IOException` objects.

Another is to use a multi-`catch` statement. Call the exception's `toString()` or `getMessage()` methods in a `catch` block to find out more about the problem.

# Byte Streams

All byte streams are a subclass of either `InputStream` or `OutputStream`. These classes are abstract, so you cannot create a stream by creating objects of these classes directly. Instead, you create streams through one of their subclasses, such as the following:

- `FileInputStream` and `FileOutputStream`: Byte streams stored in files on disk, CD, or other storage devices

- `DataInputStream` and `DataOutputStream`: Filtered byte streams from which data such as integers and floating-point numbers can be read

`InputStream` is the superclass of all input streams.

## File Streams

The byte streams you'll work with most often are likely to be file streams. They are used to exchange data with files on your disk drives, DVDs, or other storage devices you can refer to by using a folder path and filename.

You can send bytes to a file output stream and receive bytes from a file input stream.

### File Input Streams

A file input stream can be created with the `FileInputStream(String)` constructor. The *String* argument should be the filename. You can include a path reference with the filename, which enables the file to be in a different folder from the class loading it. The following statement creates a file input stream from the file `scores.dat`:

```
FileInputStream fis = new FileInputStream("scores.dat");
```

Path references can be indicated in a manner specific to a platform, such as this example to read a file on a Windows system:

```
FileInputStream f1 = new FileInputStream("C:\\data\\calendar.txt");
```

**NOTE** _____    Because Java uses backslash characters in escape codes, in path references in Windows and MacOS, the code \\ must be used in place of \ characters.

Here's a Linux example:

```
FileInputStream f2 = new FileInputStream("/data/calendar.txt");
```

A better way to refer to paths is to use the class variable `separator` in the `File` class, which works on any operating system:

```
char sep = File.separator;
FileInputStream f2 = new FileInputStream(sep + "data"
    + sep + "calendar.txt");
```

After you create a file input stream, you can read bytes from the stream by calling its `read()` method. This method returns an integer containing the next byte in the stream. The method returns –1, which is not a possible byte value, when the end of the file stream has been reached.

To read more than one byte of data from the stream, call its `read(byte[], int, int)` method. The arguments to this method are as follows:

- A byte array where the data will be stored
- The element inside the array where the data's first byte should be stored
- The number of bytes to read

Unlike the other `read()` method, this does not return data from the stream. Instead, it returns either an integer that represents the number of bytes read or –1 if no bytes were read before the end of the stream was reached.

The following code uses a `while` loop to read the data in a `FileInputStream` object called `diskfile`:

```
int newByte = 0;
while (newByte != -1) {
    newByte = diskfile.read();
    System.out.print(newByte + " ");
}
```

The loop reads the entire file referenced by `diskfile` one byte at a time and displays each byte, followed by a space character. It also displays –1 when the end of the file is reached; you could guard against this easily with an `if` statement.

The `ByteReader` application, shown in in Listing 16.1, uses a similar technique to read a file input stream. The input stream's `close()` method is used to close the stream after the last byte in the file is read. Always close streams when you no longer need them to free system resources. For this project, create the `ByteReader` class in the `com.java21days` package as an empty Java file in NetBeans.

**LISTING 16.1**    The Full Text of `ByteReader.java`

```
 1: package com.java21days;
 2:
 3: import java.io.*;
 4:
 5: public class ByteReader {
 6:     public static void main(String[] arguments) {
 7:         try (
 8:             FileInputStream file = new
 9:                 FileInputStream("save.gif")
10:             ) {
11:
12:             boolean eof = false;
13:             int count = 0;
14:             while (!eof) {
15:                 int input = file.read();
16:                 System.out.print(input + " ");
17:                 if (input == -1)
18:                     eof = true;
19:                 else
20:                     count++;
21:             }
22:             System.out.println("\nBytes read: " + count);
23:         } catch (IOException e) {
24:             System.out.println("Error -- " + e.toString());
25:         }
26:     }
27: }
```

This application reads the byte data from the `save.gif` file in the main folder of the `Java21` project. That file was used in Lesson 9, "Creating a Graphical User Interface."

When you run the program, each byte in `save.gif` is displayed, followed by a count of the total number of bytes. Figure 16.1 shows the output.

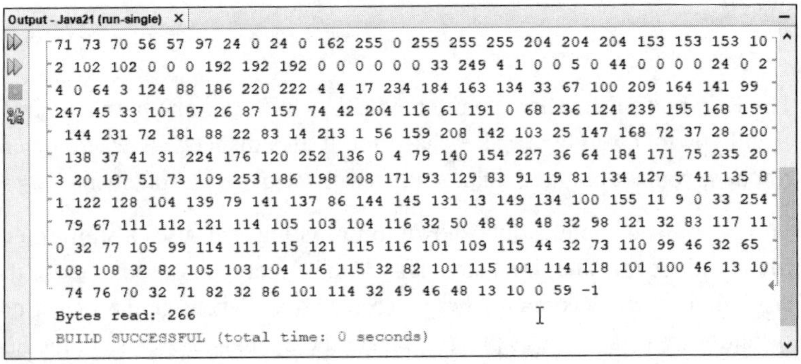

**FIGURE 16.1**
Reading byte data from a file.

```
Output - Java21 (run-single)  ×
 71 73 70 56 57 97 24 0 24 0 162 255 0 255 255 255 204 204 204 153 153 153 10
 2 102 102 0 0 0 192 192 192 0 0 0 0 0 33 249 4 1 0 0 5 0 44 0 0 0 0 24 0 2
 4 0 64 3 124 88 186 220 222 4 4 17 234 184 163 134 33 67 100 209 164 141 99
 247 45 33 101 97 26 87 157 74 42 204 116 61 191 0 68 236 124 239 195 168 159
 144 231 72 181 88 22 83 14 213 1 56 159 208 142 103 25 147 168 72 37 28 200
 138 37 41 31 224 176 120 252 136 0 4 79 140 154 227 36 64 184 171 75 235 20
 3 20 197 51 73 109 253 186 198 208 171 93 129 83 91 19 81 134 127 5 41 135 8
 1 122 128 104 139 79 141 137 86 144 145 131 13 149 134 100 155 11 9 0 33 254
 79 67 111 112 121 114 105 103 104 116 32 50 48 48 48 32 98 121 32 83 117 11
 0 32 77 105 99 114 111 115 121 115 116 101 109 115 44 32 73 110 99 46 32 65
 108 108 32 82 105 103 104 116 115 32 82 101 115 101 114 118 101 100 46 13 10
 74 76 70 32 71 82 32 86 101 114 32 49 46 48 13 10 0 59 -1
Bytes read: 266
BUILD SUCCESSFUL (total time: 0 seconds)
```

The output shown in Figure 16.1 wraps around the right margin. If you don't see wrapped text when you run this application in NetBeans, right-click anywhere in the Output pane and choose Wrap Text from the pop-up menu.

You might be wondering why there's no `file.close()` statement in the program to close the file input stream. That's normally a good practice, but because try-with-`resources` is used to open the stream in lines 7–10, close() is unnecessary.

## File Output Streams

A file output stream can be created with the `FileOutputStream(String)` constructor. The usage is the same as with the `FileInputStream(String)` constructor, so you can specify a path along with a filename.

You have to be careful when specifying the file associated with an output stream. If it's the same as an existing file, the original is wiped out when you start writing data to the stream.

You can create a file output stream that appends data after the end of an existing file with the `FileOutputStream (String, boolean)` constructor. The string specifies the file, and the Boolean argument should equal `true` to append data instead of overwriting existing data.

The file output stream's `write(int)` method is used to write bytes to the stream. After the last byte has been written to the file, the stream's `close()` method closes the stream.

To write more than one byte, use the `write(byte[], int, int)` method. This works in a manner similar to the `read(byte[], int, int)` method described previously. The arguments to this method are the byte array containing the bytes to output, the starting point in the array, and the number of bytes to write.

The `ByteWriter` application, shown in Listing 16.2, writes an integer array to a file output stream. Create it in NetBeans in the `com.java21days` package.

**LISTING 16.2** The Full Text of `ByteWriter.java`

```
1: package com.java21days;
2:
3: import java.io.*;
4:
5: public class ByteWriter {
6:     public static void main(String[] arguments) {
7:         int[] data = { 71, 73, 70, 56, 57, 97, 13, 0, 12, 0, 145,
8:             0, 0, 255, 255, 255, 255, 255, 0, 0, 0, 0, 0, 0, 0, 44,
9:             0, 0, 0, 0, 13, 0, 12, 0, 0, 2, 38, 132, 45, 121, 11,
10:            25, 175, 150, 120, 20, 162, 132, 51, 110, 106, 239, 22,
```

```
11:                    8, 160, 56, 137, 96, 72, 77, 33, 130, 86, 37, 219, 182,
12:                    230, 137, 89, 82, 181, 50, 220, 103, 20, 0, 59 };
13:        try (FileOutputStream file = new
14:            FileOutputStream("pic.gif")) {
15:
16:            for (int i = 0; i < data.length; i++) {
17:                file.write(data[i]);
18:            }
19:        } catch (IOException e) {
20:            System.out.println("Error -- " + e.toString());
21:        }
22:    }
23: }
```

The following things take place in this program:

- Lines 7–12 create an integer array called `data` and fill it with elements.

- Lines 13–14 create a file output stream with the filename `pic.gif` in the main project folder in NetBeans.

- Lines 16–18 use a `for` loop to cycle through the `data` array and write each element to the file stream.

- Line 19 closes the file output stream because the `try` block ends.

The `FileOutputStream` object is created inside the parentheses of the `try` statement to make sure its resources are freed up when the block finishes executing, even if an error occurs.

After you run this program, you can display the `pic.gif` file in any web browser or graphics-editing tool. You also can switch to the Files pane in NetBeans and double-click the file to view it. It's a small image file in GIF format, as shown in Figure 16.2.

**FIGURE 16.2**
The `pic.gif` file
(enlarged).

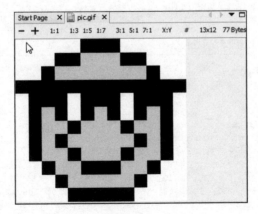

# Filtering a Stream

Filtered streams are streams that modify the information sent through an existing stream. They are created using the subclasses `FilterInputStream` and `FilterOutputStream`.

These classes do not handle any filtering operations themselves. Instead, they have subclasses, such as `BufferInputStream` and `DataOutputStream`, which handle specific types of filtering.

## Byte Filters

Information is delivered more quickly if it can be sent in large chunks, even if those chunks are received faster than they can be handled.

For example, consider which of the following book-reading techniques is faster:

- A friend lends you a book, and you read it.
- A friend lends you a book one page at a time and doesn't give you a new page until you have finished the previous one.

Obviously, the first technique is faster and more efficient. The same benefits are true of buffered streams in Java.

A *buffer* is a storage place where data can be kept before it is needed by a program that reads or writes that data. By using a buffer, you can get data without constantly going back to the original source of the data.

Buffers are essential when reading extremely large files. Without them, the data from a file could take up all of a Java Virtual Machine's memory.

### Buffered Streams

A buffered input stream fills a buffer with data that hasn't been handled yet. When a program needs this data, it looks to the buffer before going to the original stream source.

Buffered byte streams use the `BufferedInputStream` and `BufferedOutputStream` classes.

A buffered input stream is created using one of the following constructors:

- `BufferedInputStream(InputStream)`: Creates a buffered input stream for the specified `InputStream` object
- `BufferedInputStream(InputStream, int)`: Creates the specified `InputStream` buffered stream with a buffer of size `int`

16

The simplest way to read data from a buffered input stream is to call its `read()` method with no arguments. This action normally returns an integer from 0 to 255 representing the next byte in the stream. If the end of the stream has been reached and no byte is available, –1 is returned.

You also can use the `read(byte[], int, int)` method available for other input streams, which loads stream data into a byte array.

A buffered output stream is created using one of these two constructors:

- `BufferedOutputStream(OutputStream)`: Creates a buffered output stream for the specified `OutputStream` object

- `BufferedOutputStream(OutputStream, int)`: Creates the specified `OutputStream` buffered stream with a buffer of size `int`

The output stream's `write(int)` method can be used to send a single byte to the stream, and the `write(byte[], int, int)` method writes multiple bytes from the specified byte array. The arguments to this method are the byte array, array starting point, and number of bytes to write.

**NOTE** _____ Although the `write()` method takes an integer as input, the value should be from 0 to 255. If you specify a number higher than 255, it is stored as the remainder of the number divided by 256. You can test this when running a project you will create later in this lesson.

When data is directed to a buffered stream, it is not output to its destination until the stream fills or the buffered stream's `flush()` method is called.

The next project, the `BufferDemo` application, writes a series of bytes to a buffered output stream associated with a text file. The first and last integers in the series are specified as two arguments.

After writing to the text file, `BufferDemo` creates a buffered input stream from the file and reads the bytes back in. Listing 16.3 contains the source code. Put this class in the `com.java21days` package when creating it in NetBeans.

**LISTING 16.3**  The Full Text of `BufferDemo.java`

```
 1: package com.java21days;
 2:
 3: import java.io.*;
 4:
 5: public class BufferDemo {
 6:     public static void main(String[] arguments) {
 7:         int start = 0;
 8:         int finish = 255;
 9:         if (arguments.length > 1) {
10:             start = Integer.parseInt(arguments[0]);
11:             finish = Integer.parseInt(arguments[1]);
12:         } else if (arguments.length > 0) {
13:             start = Integer.parseInt(arguments[0]);
14:         }
15:         ArgStream as = new ArgStream(start, finish);
16:         System.out.println("\nWriting: ");
17:         boolean success = as.writeStream();
18:         System.out.println("\nReading: ");
19:         boolean readSuccess = as.readStream();
20:     }
21: }
22:
23: class ArgStream {
24:     int start = 0;
25:     int finish = 255;
26:
27:     ArgStream(int st, int fin) {
28:         start = st;
29:         finish = fin;
30:     }
31:
32:     boolean writeStream() {
33:         try (FileOutputStream file = new
34:                 FileOutputStream("numbers.dat");
35:             BufferedOutputStream buff = new
36:                 BufferedOutputStream(file)) {
37:
38:             for (int out = start; out <= finish; out++) {
39:                 buff.write(out);
40:                 System.out.print(" " + out);
41:             }
42:             return true;
43:         } catch (IOException e) {
44:             System.out.println("Exception: " + e.getMessage());
45:             return false;
46:         }
47:     }
48:
```

16

```
49:    boolean readStream() {
50:        try (FileInputStream file = new
51:                FileInputStream("numbers.dat");
52:            BufferedInputStream buff = new
53:                BufferedInputStream(file)) {
54:
55:            int in;
56:            do {
57:                in = buff.read();
58:                if (in != -1) {
59:                    System.out.print(" " + in);
60:                }
61:            } while (in != -1);
62:            System.out.println();
63:            return true;
64:        } catch (IOException e) {
65:            System.out.println("Exception: " + e.getMessage());
66:            return false;
67:        }
68:    }
69: }
```

This program's output depends on the two arguments specified when it was run. If you use 3 and 19, for example, the output in Figure 16.3 is shown.

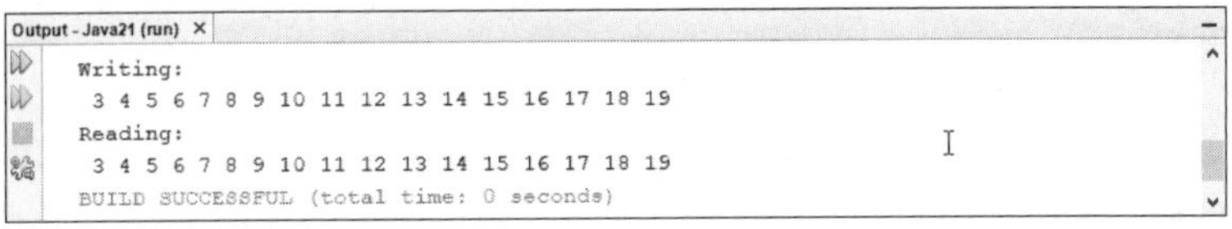

**FIGURE 16.3**
Reading and writing buffered streams.

```
Output - Java21 (run)  ×
    Writing:
    3 4 5 6 7 8 9 10 11 12 13 14 15 16 17 18 19
    Reading:                                        I
    3 4 5 6 7 8 9 10 11 12 13 14 15 16 17 18 19
    BUILD SUCCESSFUL (total time: 0 seconds)
```

It also can be run without arguments, causing it to use 1 and 255 as default values.

This application consists of two classes: BufferDemo and a helper class called ArgStream. BufferDemo gets the two arguments' values, if they are provided, and uses them in the ArgStream() constructor.

The writeStream() method of ArgStream is called in line 17 to write the series of bytes to a buffered output stream, and the readStream() method is called in line 19 to read back those bytes.

Even though they are moving data in two directions, the writeStream() and readStream() methods are substantially the same. They have the following format:

- The filename, numbers.dat, is used to create a file input or output stream.
- The file stream is used to create a buffered input or output stream.

- The buffered stream's `write()` method is used to send data, or the `read()` method is used to receive data.

- The buffered stream is closed.

Because file streams and buffered streams throw `IOException` objects if an error occurs, all operations involving the streams are enclosed in a `try-catch` block for this exception.

> **TIP**
>
> The Boolean return values in `writeStream()` and `readStream()` indicate whether the stream operation was completed successfully. They aren't used in this program, but it's good practice to let callers of these methods know if something goes wrong. When the value is `false`, the operation could be attempted again.

**16**

### Console Input Streams

One of the things many experienced programmers miss when they begin learning Java is the ability to read textual or numeric input from the console while running an application. No input method is comparable to the output methods `System.out.print()` and `System.out.println()`.

Now that you can work with buffered input streams, you can put them to use receiving console input.

The `System` class, part of the `java.lang` package, has a class variable called `in` that is an `InputStream` object. This object receives input from the keyboard through the stream.

You can work with this stream as you would any other input stream. The following statement creates a new buffered input stream associated with the `System.in` input stream:

```
BufferedInputStream command = new BufferedInputStream(System.in);
```

The next project, the `ConsoleInput` class, contains a class method you can use to receive console input in any of your Java applications. Enter the code shown in Listing 16.4 in NetBeans, making sure to put it in the package `com.java21days`.

**LISTING 16.4**  The Full Text of `ConsoleInput.java`

```
1: package com.java21days;
2:
3: import java.io.*;
4:
5: public class ConsoleInput {
6:     public static String readLine() {
7:         StringBuilder response = new StringBuilder();
```

```
 8:            try (BufferedInputStream buff = new
 9:                 BufferedInputStream(System.in)) {
10:
11:                int in;
12:                char inChar;
13:                do {
14:                    in = buff.read();
15:                    inChar = (char) in;
16:                    if ((in != -1) & (in != '\n') & (in != '\r')) {
17:                        response.append(inChar);
18:                    }
19:                } while ((in != -1) & (inChar != '\n') & (in != '\r'));
20:                return response.toString();
21:            } catch (IOException e) {
22:                System.out.println("Exception: " + e.getMessage());
23:                return null;
24:            }
25:        }
26:
27:        public static void main(String[] arguments) {
28:            System.out.print("\nWhat is your name? ");
29:            String input = ConsoleInput.readLine();
30:            System.out.println("\nHello, " + input);
31:        }
32: }
```

The ConsoleInput class includes a main() method that demonstrates how it can be used. When you compile and run it as an application, the output should resemble Figure 16.4.

**FIGURE 16.4**
Reading keyboard input from the console window.

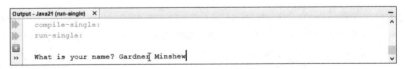

ConsoleInput reads user input through a buffered input stream using the stream's read() method, which returns -1 when the end of input has been reached. This occurs when the user presses the Enter key, a carriage return (character '\r'), or a newline (character '\n').

## Data Streams

If you need to work with data that isn't represented as bytes or characters, you can use data input and data output streams. These streams filter an existing byte stream so that each of the following primitive types can be directly read from or written to the stream: boolean, byte, double, float, int, long, and short.

A data input stream is created with the `DataInputStream(InputStream)` constructor. The argument should be an existing input stream, such as a buffered input stream or a file input stream.

A data output stream requires the `DataOutputStream(OutputStream)` constructor, which indicates the associated output stream.

The following read and write methods apply to data input and output streams, respectively:

- `readBoolean()`, `writeBoolean(boolean)`
- `readByte()`, `writeByte(integer)`
- `readDouble()`, `writeDouble(double)`
- `readFloat()`, `writeFloat(float)`
- `readInt()`, `writeInt(int)`
- `readLong()`, `writeLong(long)`
- `readShort()`, `writeShort(int)`

**16**

Each input method returns the primitive data type indicated by the method's name. For example, the `readFloat()` method returns a `float` value.

There also are `readUnsignedByte()` and `readUnsignedShort()` methods that read in unsigned `byte` and `short` values. Java doesn't support these data types, and they are returned as `int` values.

**NOTE**

Unsigned bytes have values ranging from 0 to 255. This differs from Java's `byte` variable type, which ranges from –128 to 127. Along the same lines, an unsigned `short` value ranges from 0 to 65,535 instead of the –32,768 to 32,767 range supported by Java's `short` type.

A data input stream's different read methods do not all return values that can be used to indicate that the end of the stream has been reached. As an alternative, you can wait for an `EOFException` (end-of-file exception) to be thrown when a read method reaches the end of a stream. The loop that reads the data can be enclosed in a `try` block, and the associated `catch` statement should handle only `EOFException` objects. You can call `close()` on the stream and take care of other cleanup tasks inside the `catch` block. This is demonstrated in the next project.

Listings 16.5 and 16.6 contain two programs that use data streams. The `PrimeWriter` application writes the first 400 prime numbers as integers to a file called `400primes.dat`.

The `PrimeReader` application reads the integers from this file and displays them. Create both classes in the `com.java21days` package.

**LISTING 16.5**    The Full Text of `PrimeWriter.java`

```
 1: package com.java21days;
 2:
 3: import java.io.*;
 4:
 5: public class PrimeWriter {
 6:     public static void main(String[] arguments) {
 7:         int[] primes = new int[400];
 8:         int numPrimes = 0;
 9:         // candidate: the number that might be prime
10:         int candidate = 2;
11:         while (numPrimes < 400) {
12:             if (isPrime(candidate)) {
13:                 primes[numPrimes] = candidate;
14:                 numPrimes++;
15:             }
16:             candidate++;
17:         }
18:
19:         try (
20:             // Write output to disk
21:             FileOutputStream file = new
22:                 FileOutputStream("400primes.dat");
23:             BufferedOutputStream buff = new
24:                 BufferedOutputStream(file);
25:             DataOutputStream data = new
26:                 DataOutputStream(buff);
27:         ) {
28:
29:             for (int i = 0; i < 400; i++)
30:                 data.writeInt(primes[i]);
31:         } catch (IOException e) {
32:             System.out.println("Error -- " + e.toString());
33:         }
34:     }
35:
36:     public static boolean isPrime(int checkNumber) {
37:         double root = Math.sqrt(checkNumber);
38:         for (int i = 2; i <= root; i++) {
39:             if (checkNumber % i == 0)
40:                 return false;
41:         }
42:         return true;
43:     }
44: }
```

**LISTING 16.6**   The Full Text of `PrimeReader.java`

```
 1: package com.java21days;
 2:
 3: import java.io.*;
 4:
 5: public class PrimeReader {
 6:     public static void main(String[] arguments) {
 7:         try (FileInputStream file = new
 8:                 FileInputStream("400primes.dat");
 9:             BufferedInputStream buff = new
10:                 BufferedInputStream(file);
11:             DataInputStream data = new
12:                 DataInputStream(buff)) {
13:
14:             try {
15:                 while (true) {
16:                     int in = data.readInt();
17:                     System.out.print(in + " ");
18:                 }
19:             } catch (EOFException eof) {
20:                 buff.close();
21:             }
22:         } catch (IOException e) {
23:             System.out.println("Error -- " + e.toString());
24:         }
25:     }
26: }
```

Most of the `PrimeWriter` application is the logic to find the first 400 prime numbers. When it has an integer array containing the first 400 primes, it is written to a data output stream in Listing 16.5 in lines 21–30.

This application is an example of using more than one filter on a stream. The stream is developed in a three-step process:

**1.** A file output stream associated with a file called `400primes.dat` is created.

**2.** A new buffered output stream is associated with the file stream.

**3.** A new data output stream is associated with the buffered stream.

The `writeInt()` method of the data stream is used to write the primes to the file.

The `PrimeReader` application is simpler because it doesn't need to do anything regarding prime numbers. It just reads integers from a file using a data input stream.

Lines 7–12 of `PrimeReader` are nearly identical to statements in the `PrimeWriter` application, except that input classes are used instead of output classes.

The `try-catch` block that handles `EOFException` objects is in lines 14–24 of Listing 16.6. The work of loading the data takes place inside the `try`-with-resources block (introduced in Lesson 7, "Exceptions and Threads"). This approach ensures that the input stream objects will be closed properly when no longer needed.

The `while(true)` statement creates an endless loop. This isn't a problem; an `EOFException` automatically occurs when the end of the stream is encountered at some point as the data stream is being read. The `readInt()` method in line 16 of Listing 16.6 reads integers from the stream.

The last several lines of the `PrimeReader` application's output are shown in Figure 16.5.

**FIGURE 16.5**
Reading prime numbers written to a file as integers.

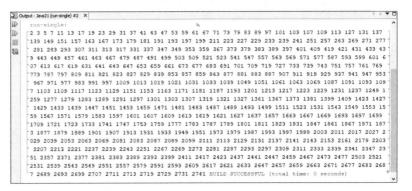

# Character Streams

When you know how to handle byte streams, you have most of the skills needed to handle character streams as well. Character streams are used to work with any text represented by the ASCII character set or Unicode, an international character set that includes ASCII.

Examples of files that you can work with through a character stream are plain-text files, web pages, and Java source files.

The classes used to read and write these streams are all subclasses of `Reader` and `Writer`. You should use these classes for all text input instead of dealing directly with byte streams.

## Reading Text Files

`FileReader` is the main class used when reading character streams from a file. This class inherits from `InputStreamReader`, which reads a byte stream and converts the bytes into integer values that represent Unicode characters.

A character input stream is associated with a file using the FileReader(*String*) constructor. The string indicates the file, and it can contain path folder references in addition to a filename.

The following statement creates a new FileReader object called look and associates it with a text file called index.txt:

```
FileReader look = new FileReader("index.txt");
```

When you have a FileReader object, you can call the following methods on it to read characters from the file:

16

- **read()**: Returns the next character on the stream as an integer
- **read(*char[], int, int*)**: Reads characters into the specified character array with the indicated starting point and number of characters read

The second method works like similar methods for the byte input stream classes. Instead of returning the next character, it returns either the number of characters that were read or -1 if no characters were read before the end of the stream was reached.

The following method loads a text file using the FileReader object text and displays its characters:

```
FileReader text = new FileReader("readme.txt");
int inByte;
do {
    inByte = text.read();
    if (inByte != -1) {
        System.out.print( (char) inByte );
    }
} while (inByte != -1);
System.out.println("");
text.close();
```

Because a character stream's read() method returns an integer, you must cast this to a character before displaying it, storing it in an array, or using it to form a string. Every character has a numeric code that represents its position in the Unicode character set. The integer read from the stream is this numeric code.

If you want to read an entire line of text at a time instead of reading a file character by character, you can use the BufferedReader class in conjunction with a FileReader object.

The `BufferedReader` class reads a character input stream and buffers it for better efficiency. You must have an existing `Reader` object of some kind to create a buffered version. The following constructors can be used to create a `BufferedReader` object:

- **`BufferedReader(Reader)`:** Creates a buffered character stream associated with the specified `Reader` object, such as `FileReader`
- **`BufferedReader(Reader, int)`:** Creates a buffered character stream associated with the specified `Reader` object and with a buffer of size `int`

A buffered character stream can be read using the `read()` and `read(char[], int, int)` methods described for `FileReader`. You can read a line of text by using the `readLine()` method.

The `readLine()` method returns a `String` object that contains the next line of text on the stream, not including the character or characters that represent the end of a line. If the end of the stream is reached, the value of the string returned equals `null`.

An end-of-line is indicated by any of the following:

- A newline character (`'\n'`)
- A carriage return character (`'\r'`)
- A carriage return followed by a newline (`"\n\r"`)

The project contained in Listing 16.7 is a Java application, `SourceReader`, that reads its own source file through a buffered character stream. Create it in the `com.java21days` package.

**LISTING 16.7**    The Full Text of `SourceReader.java`

```
 1: package com.java21days;
 2:
 3: import java.io.*;
 4:
 5: public class SourceReader {
 6:     public static void main(String[] arguments) {
 7:         try (
 8:             FileReader file = new
 9:                 FileReader("SourceReader.java");
10:             BufferedReader buff = new
11:                 BufferedReader(file)) {
12:
13:             boolean eof = false;
14:             while (!eof) {
15:                 String line = buff.readLine();
16:                 if (line == null) {
```

```
17:                        eof = true;
18:                    } else {
19:                        System.out.println(line);
20:                    }
21:                }
22:                buff.close();
23:            } catch (IOException e) {
24:                System.out.println("Error -- " + e.toString());
25:            }
26:        }
27: }
```

Much of this program is comparable to projects created earlier in this lesson:

- **Lines 8–9:** An input source is created: the `FileReader` object associated with the file `SourceReader.java`.

- **Lines 10–11:** A buffering filter is associated with that input source: the `BufferedReader` object `buff`.

- **Lines 13–21:** A `readLine()` method is used inside a `while` loop to read the text file one line at a time. The loop ends when the method returns the value `null`.

Before you run the program, make a copy of `SourceReader.java` in the `Java21` project's root folder. To do this, follow these steps:

**1.** In the Projects pane, right-click `SourceReader.java` and choose Copy. The file is copied to the Clipboard.

**2.** Click the Files pane to bring it to the front.

**3.** Right-click Java21 at the top of the Files pane and then choose Paste.

A copy appears in that folder. Run the program to see the `SourceReader` application's output—the text file `SourceReader.java`.

## Writing Text Files

The `FileWriter` class is used to write a character stream to a file. It's a subclass of `OutputStreamWriter`, which can convert Unicode character codes to bytes.

There are two `FileWriter` constructors: `FileWriter(String)` and `FileWriter(String, boolean)`. The `String` indicates the name of the file that the character stream will be directed into, which can include a folder path. The optional `boolean` argument should equal `true` if the file is to be appended to an existing text file. As with other stream-writing classes, you must be careful not to accidentally overwrite an existing file when you're appending data.

Three methods of `FileWriter` can be used to write data to a stream:

- `write(int):` Writes a character
- `write(char[], int, int):` Writes characters from the specified character array with the indicated starting point and number of characters written
- `write(String, int, int):` Writes characters from the specified string with the indicated starting point and number of characters written

The following example writes a character stream to a file using the `FileWriter` class and the `write(int)` method:

```
FileWriter letters = new FileWriter("alphabet.txt");
for (int i = 65; i < 91; i++)
    letters.write( (char) i );
letters.close();
```

The `close()` method is used to close the stream after all characters have been sent to the destination file. The following is the `alphabet.txt` file produced by this code:

ABCDEFGHIJKLMNOPQRSTUVWXYZ

The `BufferedWriter` class can be used to write a buffered character stream. This class's objects are created with the `BufferedWriter(Writer)` or `BufferedWriter(Writer, int)` constructors. The `Writer` argument can be any of the character output stream classes, such as `FileWriter`. The optional second argument is an integer indicating the size of the buffer to use.

`BufferedWriter` has the same three output methods as `FileWriter`: `write(int)`, `write(char[], int, int)`, and `write(String, int, int)`.

Another useful output method is `newLine()`, which sends the preferred end-of-line character (or characters) for the platform being used to run the program.

---

**TIP**

The different end-of-line markers can create conversion hassles when files are transferred from one operating system to another, such as when a Windows user uploads a file to a web server that's running the Linux operating system. Using `newLine()` instead of a literal (such as `'\n'`) makes your program more user-friendly across different platforms.

---

The `close()` method is called to close the buffered character stream and make sure that all buffered data is sent to the stream's destination.

# Files and Paths

In all the examples thus far, a string has been used to refer to the file that's involved in a stream operation. This often is sufficient for a program that uses files and streams, but if you want to copy or rename files or handle other tasks, you can use a `Path` object from the `java.nio.file` package.

`Path` represents a file or folder reference. It is an improvement on the `File` class in the `java.io` package. The following statement gets a path matching the specified string:

```
Path source = FileSystems.getDefault().getPath("essay.txt");
```

**16**

This is a two-step process. First, a class method of the `FileSystems` class is called. The `getDefault()` method returns a `FileSystem` object that represents the computer's way of storing files. Both of these classes also are in the `java.nio.file` package.

As soon as you have that `FileSystem` object, its `getPath(String)` method returns a `Path` object matching that specified file or folder reference.

A `File` object can be created from a `Path` by calling the `toFile()` method of the latter class, as in this statement:

```
File sourceFile = source.toFile();
```

A `Path` object can be created from a `File` object with a call to its `toPath()` method.

You can call several class methods of the `Files` class in the `java.nio.file` package when working with files:

- **`move (Path, Path)`:** Renames a file from the first path argument to the second
- **`delete(Path)`:** Deletes the file

As with any other file-handling operations, you need to handle these methods with care to avoid deleting the wrong files and folders or wiping out data. These methods throw a `SecurityException` if the program does not have the security to perform the file operation in question, a `NoSuchFileException` if the paths do not exist, and an `IOException` for other I/O errors. If you try to delete a folder that is not empty, a `NoSuchFileException` exception occurs. Therefore, these exceptions need to be dealt with through a `try-catch` block or a `throws` clause in a method declaration.

The `AllCapsDemo` application shown in Listing 16.8 converts all the text in a file to upper-case characters. The file is pulled in using a buffered input stream, and one character is read at a time. After a character is converted to uppercase, it is sent to a temporary file using a buffered output stream. `File` objects are used instead of strings to indicate the files involved, which makes it possible to rename and delete files as needed. In NetBeans, create an empty Java file called `AllCapsDemo` in the `com.java21days` package and add the code from Listing 16.8.

**LISTING 16.8**   The Full Text of `AllCapsDemo.java`

```
1:  package com.java21days;
2:
3:  import java.io.*;
4:  import java.nio.file.*;
5:
6:  public class AllCapsDemo {
7:      public static void main(String[] arguments) {
8:          if (arguments.length < 1) {
9:              System.out.println("You must specify a filename");
10:             System.exit(-1);
11:         }
12:         AllCaps cap = new AllCaps(arguments[0]);
13:         cap.convert();
14:     }
15: }
16:
17: class AllCaps {
18:     String sourceName;
19:
20:     AllCaps(String sourceArg) {
21:         sourceName = sourceArg;
22:     }
23:
24:     void convert() {
25:         try {
26:             // Create file objects
27:             FileSystem fs = FileSystems.getDefault();
28:             Path source = fs.getPath(sourceName);
29:             Path temp = fs.getPath("tmp_" + sourceName);
30:
31:             // Create input stream
32:             FileReader fr = new FileReader(source.toFile());
33:             BufferedReader in = new BufferedReader(fr);
34:
35:             // Create output stream
36:             FileWriter fw = new FileWriter(temp.toFile());
37:             BufferedWriter out = new
38:                 BufferedWriter(fw);
39:
40:             boolean eof = false;
41:             int inChar;
42:             do {
43:                 inChar = in.read();
```

```
44:                    if (inChar != -1) {
45:                        char outChar = Character.toUpperCase(
46:                            (char) inChar);
47:                        out.write(outChar);
48:                    } else
49:                        eof = true;
50:                } while (!eof);
51:                in.close();
52:                out.close();
53:
54:                Files.delete(source);
55:                Files.move(temp, source);
56:            } catch (IOException|SecurityException se) {
57:                System.out.println("Error -- " + se.toString());
58:            }
59:        }
60: }
```

Before running the program, you need a text file that can be converted to all capital letters. One option is to make a copy of AllCapsDemo.java and give it a name like TempFile. java. This file should be stored in the root project folder in NetBeans and specified as a command-line argument (using Run, Set Project Configuration, Customize).

This program does not produce any output. Load the converted file into a text editor to see the results of the application.

# Summary

In this lesson you learned how to work with streams in two directions: pulling data into a program over an input stream and sending data from a program using an output stream.

You used character streams to handle text and byte streams for any other kind of data. Filters were associated with streams to alter how information was delivered through a stream or to alter the information itself.

In addition to these classes, java.io offers other types of streams you might want to explore. Piped streams are useful when communicating data among different threads, and byte array streams can connect programs to a computer's memory.

Because the stream classes in Java are so closely coordinated, you already possess most of the knowledge you need to use these other types of streams. The constructors, read methods, and write methods are largely identical.

Using streams is a powerful way to extend the functionality of your Java programs because streams offer a connection to any kind of data you might want to work with.

# Q&A

**Q The C program that I use creates a file of integers and other data. Can I read this using a Java program?**

**A** You can, but one thing you have to consider is whether your C program represents integers in the same manner that a Java program represents them. As you might recall, all data can be represented as individual bytes or a series of bytes. An integer is represented in Java using 4 bytes arranged in what is called *big-endian order*. You can determine the integer value by combining the bytes from left to right. A C program implemented on an Intel PC is likely to represent integers in little-endian order, which means that the bytes must be arranged from right to left to determine the result. You might have to learn about advanced techniques such as bit shifting to use a data file created with a programming language other than Java.

**Q Can relative paths be used when specifying the name of a file in Java?**

**A** Relative paths are determined according to the current user folder, which is stored in the system properties `user.dir` folder. You can find out the full path to this folder by using the `System` class in the main `java.lang` package, which does not need to be imported.

Call the `System` class `getProperty(String)` method with the name of the property to retrieve, as in this example:

```
String userFolder = System.getProperty("user.dir");
```

The method returns the path as a string.

**Q The `FileWriter` class has a `write(int)` method that's used to send a character to a file. Shouldn't this be `write(char)`?**

**A** The `char` and `int` data types are interchangeable in many ways; you can use an `int` in a method that expects a `char` and vice versa. This is possible because each character is represented by a numeric code that is an integer value. When you call the `write()` method with an `int`, it outputs the character associated with that integer value. When calling the `write()` method, you can cast an `int` value to a `char` to ensure that it's being used as you intended.

# Quiz

Review this lesson's material by taking this three-question quiz.

## Questions

1. What happens when you create a `FileOutputStream` object using a reference to an existing file?

   **A.** An exception is thrown.

   **B.** The data you write to the stream is appended to the existing file.

   **C.** The existing file is replaced with the data you write to the stream.

2. What two primitive types are interchangeable when you're working with streams?

   **A.** `byte` and `boolean`

   **B.** `char` and `int`

   **C.** `byte` and `char`

3. In Java, what is the maximum value of a `byte` variable, and what is the maximum value of an unsigned byte in a stream?

   **A.** Both are 255.

   **B.** Both are 127.

   **C.** 127 for a `byte` variable and 255 for an unsigned byte

## Answers

1. C. That's one of the things to look out for when using output streams: You can easily wipe out existing files. Constructors can use a Boolean value to append data to a file instead of replacing the entire thing.

2. B. Because Java represents a `char` internally as an integer value, you often can use `char` and `int` interchangeably in method calls and other statements.

3. C. The `byte` primitive data type has values ranging from –128 to 127, whereas an unsigned byte can range from 0 to 255.

# Certification Practice

The following question is the kind of thing you could expect to be asked on a Java programming certification test. Answer it without looking again at this lesson or using the Java compiler to test the code.

Given:

```java
import java.io.*;

public class Unknown {
    public static void main(String[] arguments) {
```

```
        String command = "";
        BufferedReader br = new BufferedReader(new
            InputStreamReader(System.in));
        try {
            command = br.readLine();
        }
        catch (IOException e) { }
    }
}
```

Will this program successfully store a line of console input in the `String` object named `command`?

**A.** Yes.

**B.** No, because a buffered input stream is required to read console input.

**C.** No, because it won't compile successfully.

**D.** No, because it reads more than one line of console input.

The answer is available on the book's website, at www.java21days.com. Visit the Lesson 16 page and click the Certification Practice link.

# Exercises

To extend your knowledge of the subjects covered in this lesson, try the following exercises:

**1.** Write a modified version of the `HexReader` program from Lesson 7, "Exceptions and Threads," that reads two-digit hexadecimal sequences from a text file and displays their decimal equivalents.

**2.** Write a program that reads a file to determine the number of bytes it contains and then overwrites all those bytes with 0s. (For obvious reasons, you shouldn't test this program on any file you intend to keep because the file's data will be wiped out.)

Where applicable, exercise solutions are offered on the book's website, at www.java21days.com.

# LESSON 17
# Communicating Over HTTP

Java was initially developed as a language to control a network of interactive consumer devices. Connecting machines was one of the main purposes of the language when it was designed—and that is still one of the purposes of Java today.

The `java.net` package makes it possible to communicate over a network, providing cross-platform abstractions to make connections, transfer files using common web protocols, and create sockets.

When the `java.net` package is used in conjunction with input and output streams, reading and writing files over the network becomes as easy as reading or writing files on disk.

The `java.nio` package expands Java's input and output classes.

In this lesson you'll write networking Java programs that do each of the following:

- Load a document over the Web
- Mimic a popular Internet service
- Serve information to clients

# Networking in Java

Networking allows different computers to make connections with each other and exchange information. In Java, basic networking is supported by classes in the `java.net` package, including support for connecting and retrieving files through Hypertext Transfer Protocol (HTTP) and File Transfer Protocol (FTP), as well as working at a lower level with sockets.

You can communicate with systems on the Internet in three simple ways:

- Load a web page and any other resource with a uniform resource locator (URL).
- Use the socket classes, `Socket` and `ServerSocket`, which open standard socket connections to hosts and read to and write from those connections.
- Call `getInputStream()`, a method that opens a connection to a URL and can extract data from that connection.

## Opening a Stream over the Net

As you learned in Lesson 16, "Working with Input and Output," you can pull information through a stream into your Java programs in several ways. The classes and methods you choose depend on the format of the information and what you want to do with it.

One of the resources you can reach from your Java programs is a text document on the Web, whether it's an HTML file, an XML file, or some other kind of plain-text document.

You can use a four-step process to load a text document from the Web and read it line by line:

1. Create a `URL` object that represents the resource's web address.
2. Create an `HttpURLConnection` object that can load the URL and make a connection to the site hosting it.
3. Use the `getContent()` method of that `HttpURLConnection` object to create an `InputStreamReader` object that can read a stream of data from the URL.
4. Use that `InputStreamReader` object to create a `BufferedReader` object that can efficiently read characters from an input stream.

Much interaction occurs between the web document and your Java program. The URL is used to set up a URL connection, which is used to set up an input stream reader, which is used to set up a buffered input stream reader. The need to deal with any exceptions that occur along the way adds more complexity to the process.

Before you can load anything, you must create a new instance of the class `URL` that represents the address of the resource you want to load. URL is an acronym for *uniform resource locator*, and it refers to the unique address of any document or other resource accessible on the Internet.

`URL` is part of the `java.net` package, so you must import the package or refer to the class by its full name in your programs.

To create a new `URL` object, use one of four constructors:

- `URL(String)`: Creates a `URL` object from a full web address, such as `"http://www.java21days.com"` or `"ftp://ftp.freebsd.org"`

- `URL(URL, String)`: Creates a `URL` object with a base address provided by the specified `URL` and a relative path provided by the `String`

- `URL(String, String, int, String)`: Creates a new `URL` object from a protocol (such as `"http"` or `"ftp"`), hostname (such as `"www.cnn.com"` or `"web.archive.org"`), port number (80 for HTTP), and filename or pathname

- `URL(String, String, String)`: The same as the previous constructor minus the port number

When you use the `URL(String)` constructor, you must deal with `MalformedURLException` exceptions, which are thrown if the string does not appear to be a valid URL. These objects can be handled in a `try-catch` block:

```
try {
    URL load = new URL("http://www.samspublishing.com");
} catch (MalformedURLException e) {
    System.out.println("Malformed URL");
}
```

The `WebReader` application, shown in Listing 17.1, uses the four-step technique to open a connection to a website and read a text document from it. When the document is fully loaded, it is displayed in a text area. Create this class in NetBeans in the `com.java21days` package.

**LISTING 17.1**  The Full Text of `WebReader.java`

```
1: package com.java21days;
2:
3: import javax.swing.*;
4: import java.net.*;
5: import java.io.*;
6:
```

```
 7: public class WebReader extends JFrame {
 8:     JTextArea box = new JTextArea("Getting data ...");
 9:
10:     public WebReader() {
11:         super("Get File Application");
12:         setDefaultCloseOperation(JFrame.EXIT_ON_CLOSE);
13:         setSize(600, 300);
14:         JScrollPane pane = new JScrollPane(box);
15:         add(pane);
16:         setVisible(true);
17:     }
18:
19:     void getData(String address) throws MalformedURLException {
20:         setTitle(address);
21:         URL page = new URL(address);
22:         StringBuilder text = new StringBuilder();
23:         try {
24:             HttpURLConnection conn = (HttpURLConnection)
25:                 page.openConnection();
26:             conn.connect();
27:             InputStreamReader in = new InputStreamReader(
28:                 (InputStream) conn.getContent());
29:             BufferedReader buff = new BufferedReader(in);
30:             box.setText("Getting data ...");
31:             String line;
32:             do {
33:                 line = buff.readLine();
34:                 text.append(line);
35:                 text.append("\n");
36:             } while (line != null);
37:             box.setText(text.toString());
38:         } catch (IOException ioe) {
39:             System.out.println("IO Error:" + ioe.getMessage());
40:         }
41:     }
42:
43:     public static void main(String[] arguments) {
44:         if (arguments.length < 1) {
45:             System.out.println("Usage: java WebReader url");
46:             System.exit(1);
47:         }
48:         try {
49:             WebReader app = new WebReader();
50:             app.getData(arguments[0]);
51:         } catch (MalformedURLException mue) {
52:             System.out.println("Bad URL: " + arguments[0]);
53:         }
54:     }
55: }
```

The `WebReader` application requires one command-line argument—a web address—that you can set in NetBeans in the project configuration (by selecting Run, Set Project Configuration, Customize).

You can choose any URL. Try http://api.icndb.com/jokes/random?limitTo=nerdy to request a nerdy Chuck Norris joke as JSON-formatted data (see Figure 17.1).

**FIGURE 17.1**
Running the
`WebReader`
application.

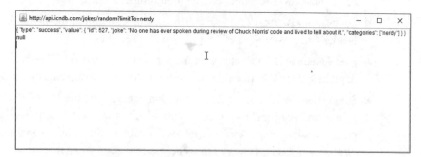

17

Two-thirds of the `WebReader` class is devoted to running the application, creating the user interface, and creating a valid `URL` object. The web document is loaded over a stream and is displayed in a text area in the `getData()` method.

Four objects are used: `URL`, `HttpURLConnection`, `InputStreamReader`, and `BufferedReader`. These objects work together to pull the data from the Internet to the Java application. In addition, two objects are created to hold the data when it arrives: `String` and `StringBuilder` objects.

Lines 24–26 open an HTTP URL connection, which is necessary to get an input stream from that connection. Lines 27–28 use the connection's `getContent()` method to create a new input stream reader. The method returns an input stream representing the connection to the URL. Line 29 uses that input stream reader to create a new buffered input stream reader—a `BufferedReader` object called `buff`.

When you have the `BufferedReader` object, you can use its `readLine()` method to read a line of text from the input stream. The object puts characters in a buffer as they arrive and pulls them out of the buffer when requested.

The `do-while` loop in lines 32–36 reads the web document line by line, appending each line to the `StringBuilder` object created to hold the page's text.

After all the data has been read, line 37 converts the string builder into a string with the `toString()` method. Then it puts that result in the program's text area by calling the component's `setText(String)` method.

The HttpUrlConnection class includes several methods that affect the HTTP request or provide more information:

- **getHeaderField(*int*):** Returns a string containing an HTTP header, such as "Server" (the web server hosting the document) or "Last-Modified" (the date the document was last changed). Headers are numbered from 0 upward. When the end of the headers is reached, this method returns null.

- **getHeaderFieldKey(*int*):** Returns a string containing the name of the numbered header (such as "Server" or "Last-Modified") or null.

- **getResponseCode():** Returns an integer containing the HTTP response code for the request, such as 200 (for valid requests) or 404 (for documents that could not be found).

- **getResponseMessage():** Returns a string containing the HTTP response code and an explanatory message (such as "HTTP/1.0 200 OK"). The HttpUrlConnection class contains integer class variables for each of the valid response codes, including "HTTP_OK", "HTTP_NOT_FOUND", and "HTTP_MOVED_PERM".

- **getContentType():** Returns a string containing the MIME type of the web document; some possible types are "text/html" for web pages and "text/xml" for XML files.

- **setFollowRedirects(*boolean*):** Determines whether URL redirection requests should be followed (true) or ignored (false). When redirection is supported, a URL request can be forwarded by a web server from an obsolete URL to its correct address.

The following code could be added to WebReader's getData() method after line 26 to display headers along with the text of a document:

```java
String key;
String header;
int i = 0;
do {
    key = conn.getHeaderFieldKey(i);
    header = conn.getHeaderField(i);
    if (key == null) {
        key = "";
    } else {
        key = key + ": ";
    }
    if (header != null) {
        text.append(key);
        text.append(header);
        text.append("\n");
    }
    i++;
} while (header != null);
text.append("\n");
```

# Sockets

For networking applications beyond what the `URL` and `URLConnection` classes offer (for example, for other protocols or for more general networking applications), Java provides the `Socket` and `ServerSocket` classes as an abstraction of standard Transmission Control Protocol (TCP) socket programming techniques.

The `Socket` class provides a client-side socket interface similar to standard UNIX sockets. Create a new instance of `Socket` to open a connection, where *hostName* is the host to connect to and *portNumber* is the port number:

```
Socket connection = new Socket(hostName, portNumber);
```

After you create a socket, set its timeout value to determine how long the application waits for data to arrive. This is handled by calling the socket's `setSoTimeOut(int)` method with the number of milliseconds to wait as the only argument:

```
connection.setSoTimeOut(50000);
```

When you use this method, any effort to read data from the socket represented by `connection` waits only 50,000 milliseconds (50 seconds). If the timeout is reached, an `InterruptedIOException` is thrown, which gives you an opportunity in a `try-catch` block to either close the socket or try to read from it again.

If you don't set a timeout in a program that uses sockets, it might hang indefinitely, waiting for data.

**TIP**

> The timeout problem is usually avoided by putting network operations in their own thread and running them separately from the rest of the program, as discussed in Lesson 7, "Exceptions and Threads."

When the socket is open, you can use input and output streams to read from and write to that socket:

```
BufferedInputStream bis = new
    BufferedInputStream(connection.getInputStream());
DataInputStream in = new DataInputStream(bis);

BufferedOutputStream bos = new
    BufferedOutputStream(connection.getOutputStream());
DataOutputStream out = new DataOutputStream(bos);
```

17

You don't need names for all these objects; they are used only to create a stream or stream reader. For an efficient shortcut, combine several statements, as in this example using a `Socket` object named `sock`:

```
DataInputStream in = new DataInputStream(
    new BufferedInputStream(
        sock.getInputStream()));
```

In this statement, the call to `sock.getInputStream()` returns an input stream associated with that socket. This stream is used to create a `BufferedInputStream` object, and the buffered input stream is used to create a `DataInputStream` object.

The only variables you are left with are `sock` and `in`, the two objects needed as you receive data from the connection and close it afterward. The intermediate objects—a `BufferedInputStream` object and an `InputStream` object—are needed only once.

When you're finished with a socket, don't forget to close it by calling the `close()` method. This also closes all the input and output streams you might have set up for that socket. For example:

```
connection.close();
```

Socket programming can be used for many services delivered using TCP/IP networking, including Telnet, Simple Mail Transfer Protocol (SMTP) for incoming mail, WHOIS protocol for requesting domain name records, and Finger.

The last of these, Finger, is a protocol for asking a system about one of its users. By setting up a Finger server, a system administrator enables an Internet-connected machine to answer requests for user information. Users can provide information about themselves by creating `.plan` files, which are sent to anyone who uses Finger to find out more about them.

Although Finger has fallen into disuse because of security concerns, before blogs and social media, using Finger was a popular way for Internet users to share facts about themselves and their activities. You could use Finger on a friend's account at another college or company to see whether that person was online and read the person's current `.plan` file.

As an exercise in socket programming, the Finger application is a rudimentary Finger client. Enter Listing 17.2 as a new class named `Finger` in NetBeans.

**LISTING 17.2**    The Full Text of `Finger.java`

```
1: package com.java21days;
2:
3: import java.io.*;
4: import java.net.*;
5: import java.util.*;
```

```
 6:
 7: public class Finger {
 8:     public static void main(String[] args) {
 9:         String user;
10:         String host;
11:         if ((args.length == 1) && (args[0].contains("@"))) {
12:             StringTokenizer split = new StringTokenizer(args[0],
13:                 "@");
14:             user = split.nextToken();
15:             host = split.nextToken();
16:         } else {
17:             System.out.println("Usage: java Finger user@host");
18:             return;
19:         }
20:         try (Socket digit = new Socket(host, 79);
21:             BufferedReader in = new BufferedReader(
22:                 new InputStreamReader(digit.getInputStream()));
23:             ) {
24:
25:             digit.setSoTimeout(20000);
26:             PrintStream out = new PrintStream(
27:                 digit.getOutputStream());
28:             out.print(user + "\015\012");
29:
30:             boolean eof = false;
31:             while (!eof) {
32:                 String line = in.readLine();
33:                 if (line != null) {
34:                     System.out.println(line);
35:                 } else {
36:                     eof = true;
37:                 }
38:             }
39:             digit.close();
40:         } catch (IOException e) {
41:             System.out.println("IO Error:" + e.getMessage());
42:         }
43:     }
44: }
```

17

When making a Finger request, specify a username followed by an at sign (@) and a hostname, the same format as an email address. One of the last examples that still works is icculus@icculus.org, the Finger address of game developer Ryan Gordon. You can request his .plan file by running the Finger application with that address as the only command-line argument. The output of this request is shown in Figure 17.2.

If icculus has an account on the icculus.org Finger server, running the Finger application displays his `.plan` file and perhaps other information. The server also lets you know when a user can't be found.

**FIGURE 17.2**
Making a Finger request using a socket.

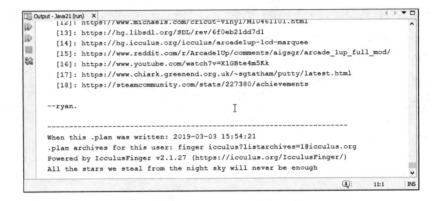

```
[12]: https://www.michaels.com/cricut-vinyl/M10461101.html
[13]: https://hg.libsdl.org/SDL/rev/6f0eb21dd7d1
[14]: https://hg.icculus.org/icculus/arcade1up-lcd-marquee
[15]: https://www.reddit.com/r/Arcade1Up/comments/aigsgr/arcade_1up_full_mod/
[16]: https://www.youtube.com/watch?v=X1GBte4m5Kk
[17]: https://www.chiark.greenend.org.uk/~sgtatham/putty/latest.html
[18]: https://steamcommunity.com/stats/227380/achievements


--ryan.

--------------------------------------------------------------------
When this .plan was written: 2019-03-03 15:54:21
.plan archives for this user: finger icculus?listarchives=1@icculus.org
Powered by IcculusFinger v2.1.27 (https://icculus.org/IcculusFinger/)
All the stars we steal from the night sky will never be enough
```

The Finger application uses the `StringTokenizer` class to convert an address in *user@host* format into two `String` objects: *user* and *host* (lines 11–15).

The following socket activities are taking place:

- **Line 20:** A new `Socket` is created using the hostname and port 79, the port traditionally reserved for Finger services.

- **Lines 21–23:** The socket is used to create an `InputStream` object, which in turn is used to create a `BufferedReader` object.

- **Line 25:** A timeout of 20 seconds is set for the socket.

- **Lines 26–27:** The socket is used to get an `OutputStream` object, which feeds into a new `PrintStream` object.

- **Line 28:** The Finger protocol requires that the username be sent through the socket, followed by a carriage return (`\015`) and linefeed (`\012`). This is handled by calling the `print()` method of the new print stream.

- **Lines 31–38:** The program loops as lines are read from the buffered reader. The end of output from the server causes `in.readLine()` to return `null`, ending the loop.

The same techniques used to communicate with a Finger server through a socket can be used to connect to other popular Internet services. You could turn it into a Telnet or web-reading client with a port change in line 20 and little other modification.

**NOTE**

> The Finger application makes use of the try-with-resources capability of Java in lines 20–23 of Listing 17.2. Declaring the socket and reader within the try statement's parentheses ensures that both of these resources will be closed even when the connection fails with an exception. This makes the explicit call to close the socket in line 39 unnecessary.

# Socket Servers

Server-side sockets work similarly to client sockets, with the exception of the accept() method. A server socket listens on a TCP port for a connection from a client; when a client connects to that port, the accept() method accepts a connection from that client. By using both client and server sockets, you can create applications that communicate with each other over the network.

To create a server socket and bind it to a port, create a new instance of ServerSocket with a port number as an argument to the constructor, as in the following example:

```
ServerSocket servo = new ServerSocket(8888);
```

Use the accept() method to listen on that port (and to accept a connection from any clients, if one is made):

```
servo.accept();
```

After the socket connection is made, you can use input and output streams to read from and write to the client.

To extend the behavior of the socket classes—for example, to allow network connections to work across a firewall or proxy—you can use the abstract class SocketImpl and the interface SocketImplFactory to create a new transport-layer socket implementation. This approach allows those classes to be portable to other systems with different transport mechanisms. The problem with this mechanism is that although it works for simple cases, it prevents you from adding other protocols on top of TCP and from having multiple socket implementations for each Java runtime.

Because the Socket and ServerSocket classes are not final, you can create subclasses of these classes that use either the default socket implementation or your own implementation. This allows much more flexible network capabilities.

## Designing a Server Application

This section provides an example of a Java program that uses the `Socket` classes to implement a simple network-based server application. The `TimeServer` application makes a connection to any client that connects to port 4415, displays the current time, and then closes the connection.

For an application to act as a server, it must monitor at least one port on the host machine for client connections. Port 4415 was chosen arbitrarily for this project, but it could be any number from 1024 to 65,535.

**NOTE**

The Internet Assigned Numbers Authority controls the usage of ports 0 to 1023, but claims are staked to the higher ports on an informal basis. When choosing port numbers for your own client/server applications, it's a good idea to do research on what ports others are using. Search the Web for references to the port you want to use and then search for the phrases "registered port numbers" and "well-known port numbers" to find lists of in-use ports. A good guide to port usage is available at www.sockets.com/services.htm.

When a client is detected, the server creates a `Date` object that represents the current date and time and then sends it to the client as a string.

In this exchange of information between the server and client, the server does almost all the work. The client's only responsibility is to establish a connection to the server and display messages received from the server.

Although you could develop a simple client for a project like this, you also can use any Telnet application to act as the client, as long as it can connect to a port you designate. (Windows includes a command-line application called Telnet that you can use for this purpose.)

Listing 17.3 contains the full source code for the server application, a class called `TimeServer`.

**LISTING 17.3**  The Full Text of `TimeServer.java`

```
1: package com.java21days;
2:
3: import java.io.*;
4: import java.net.*;
5: import java.util.*;
```

```
 6:
 7: public class TimeServer extends Thread {
 8:     private ServerSocket sock;
 9:
10:     public TimeServer() {
11:         super();
12:         try {
13:             sock = new ServerSocket(4415);
14:             System.out.println("TimeServer running ...");
15:         } catch (IOException e) {
16:             System.out.println("Error: couldn't create socket.");
17:             System.exit(1);
18:         }
19:     }
20:
21:     @Override
22:     public void run() {
23:         Socket client;
24:
25:         while (true) {
26:             if (sock == null)
27:                 return;
28:             try {
29:                 client = sock.accept();
30:                 BufferedOutputStream bb = new BufferedOutputStream(
31:                     client.getOutputStream());
32:                 PrintWriter os = new PrintWriter(bb, false);
33:                 String outLine;
34:
35:                 Date now = new Date();
36:                 os.println(now);
37:                 os.flush();
38:
39:                 os.close();
40:                 client.close();
41:             } catch (IOException e) {
42:                 System.out.println("Error: couldn't connect.");
43:                 System.exit(1);
44:             }
45:         }
46:     }
47:
48:     public static void main(String[] arguments) {
49:         TimeServer server = new TimeServer();
50:         server.start();
51:     }
52:
53: }
```

17

The `TimeServer` application creates a server socket on port 4415. When a client connects, a `PrintWriter` object is constructed from a buffered output stream so that a string—the current time—can be sent to the client.

After the string has been sent, the writer's `flush()` and `close()` methods end the data exchange and close the socket to await new connections.

## Testing the Server

The `TimeServer` application must be running for a client to be able to connect to it. The server displays only one line of output if the application is running successfully, as shown in Figure 17.3.

**FIGURE 17.3**
Launching an Internet server in a `ServerSocket` instance.

With the server running, you can connect to the server on port 4415 of your computer by using a Telnet program.

To run Telnet on Windows, choose Start, choose the Search icon, and search for `telnet`. Click the `telnet` item to run it.

**CAUTION**

The Telnet program may be disabled by default on Windows. To enable it, open the Control Panel, choose Programs and Features, and click Turn Windows Features On or Off. The Windows Features dialog opens. Select the Telnet Client check box and click OK.

The hostname `localhost` represents your own computer—the system running the application. You can use it to test server applications before deploying them permanently on the Internet.

Type this command in Telnet on Windows: open localhost 4415. On MacOS, it's `telnet localhost 4415`.

Depending on how Internet connections have been configured on your system, you might need to log on to the Internet before a successful socket connection can be made between a Telnet client and the `TimeServer` application.

If the server is on another computer connected to the Internet, you specify that computer's hostname or IP address rather than `localhost`.

When you use Telnet to make a connection with the `TimeServer` application, it displays the server's current time and closes the connection. The output of the Telnet program should resemble the output in Figure 17.4.

**FIGURE 17.4**
Making a Telnet connection to your `TimeServer` object.

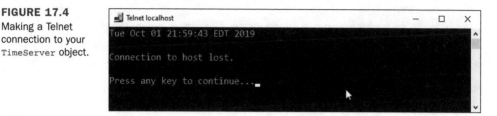

## The `java.nio` **Package**

The `java.nio` package expands Java's networking capabilities with classes that are useful for reading and writing data; working with files, sockets, and memory; and handling text.

Two related packages also are used often when you are working with the new input/output features: `java.nio.channels` and `java.nio.charset`.

### Buffers

The `java.nio` package includes support for buffers—objects that represent data streams stored in memory.

Buffers often are used to improve the performance of programs that read input or write output. They enable a program to put a lot of data in memory, where it can be read, written, and modified more quickly.

A buffer corresponds with the primitive data types in Java:

- `ByteBuffer`
- `CharBuffer`
- `DoubleBuffer`
- `FloatBuffer`
- `IntBuffer`
- `LongBuffer`
- `ShortBuffer`

Each of these classes has a static method called `wrap()` that can be used to create a buffer from an array of the corresponding data type. The only argument to the method should be the array. For example, the following statements create an array of integers and an `IntBuffer` object that holds the integers in memory as a buffer:

```
int[] temperatures = { 90, 85, 87, 78, 80, 75, 70, 79, 85, 92 };
IntBuffer tempBuffer = IntBuffer.wrap(temperatures);
```

A buffer keeps track of how it is used, storing the position where the next item will be read or written. After the buffer is created, its `get()` method reads the data at the current position in the buffer. The following statements extend the previous example and display everything in the integer buffer:

```
for (int i = 0; tempBuffer.remaining() > 0; i++)
    System.out.println(tempBuffer.get());
```

Another way to create a buffer is to set up an empty buffer and then put data in it. To create the buffer, call the static method `allocate(int)` of the desired buffer class with the size of the buffer as an argument.

You can use five `put()` methods to store data in a buffer (or replace the data that is already there). The arguments used with these methods depend on the kind of buffer you're working with. These methods are used with an integer buffer:

- `put(int)`: Stores the integer at the current position in the buffer and then increments the position.

- `put(int, int)`: Stores an integer (the second argument) at a specific position in the buffer (the first argument).

- `put(int[])`: Stores all the elements of the integer array in the buffer, beginning at the first position in the buffer.

- `put(int[], int, int)`: Stores all or a portion of an integer array in the buffer. The second argument specifies the position in the buffer where the first integer in the array should be stored. The third argument specifies the number of elements from the array to store in the buffer.

- `put(IntBuffer)`: Stores the contents of an integer buffer in another buffer, beginning at the first position in the buffer.

As you put data in a buffer, you often must keep track of the current position so that you know where the next data will be stored.

To find out the current position, call the buffer's `position()` method. An integer is returned that represents the position. If this value is `0`, you're at the start of the buffer.

Call the `position(int)` method to change the position to the argument specified as an integer.

Another important position to track when using buffers is the limit—the last place in the buffer that contains data.

It isn't necessary to figure out the limit when the buffer is always full; in that case, you know the buffer's last position has something in it.

However, if there's a chance your buffer might contain less data than you have allocated, you should call the buffer's `flip()` method after reading data into the buffer. This sets the current position to the start of the data you just read and sets the limit to the end.

If the buffer is 1,024 bytes in size and the page contains 1,500 bytes, the first attempt to read data loads the buffer with 1,024 bytes, filling it.

The second attempt to read data loads the buffer with only 476 bytes, leaving the rest empty. If you call `flip()` afterward, the current position is set to the beginning of the buffer, and the limit is set to 476.

The following code creates an array of Fahrenheit temperatures, converts them to Celsius, and then stores the Celsius values in a buffer:

```
int[] temps = { 90, 85, 87, 78, 80, 75, 70, 79, 85, 92, 99 };
IntBuffer tempBuffer = IntBuffer.allocate(temps.length);
for (int i = 0; i < temps.length; i++) {
    float celsius = ( (float) temps[i] - 32 ) / 9 * 5;
    tempBuffer.put( (int) celsius );
}
tempBuffer.position(0);
for (int i = 0; tempBuffer.remaining() > 0; i++) {
    System.out.println(tempBuffer.get());
}
```

After the buffer's position is set back to the start, the buffer's contents are displayed.

## Byte Buffers

You can use the buffer methods introduced so far with byte buffers, but byte buffers also offer additional useful methods.

For starters, byte buffers have methods to store and retrieve data that isn't a byte:

- **`putChar(char)`:** Stores 2 bytes in the buffer that represent the specified `char` value.
- **`putDouble(double)`:** Stores 8 bytes in the buffer that represent a `double` value.
- **`putFloat(float)`:** Stores 4 bytes in the buffer that represent a `float` value.
- **`putInt(int)`:** Stores 4 bytes in the buffer that represent an `int` value.

- **putLong(long):** Stores 8 bytes in the buffer that represent a long value.

- **putShort(short):** Stores 2 bytes in the buffer that represent a short value.

Each of these methods puts more than 1 byte in the buffer and moves the current position forward by the same number of bytes.

There also are methods to retrieve nonbytes from a byte buffer: getChar(), getDouble(), getFloat(), getInt(), getLong(), and getShort().

## Character Sets

Character sets, which are offered in the java.nio.charset package, are a set of classes used to convert data between byte buffers and character buffers.

The three main classes are as follows:

- **Charset:** A Unicode character set with a different byte value for each different character in the set

- **CharsetDecoder:** A class that transforms a series of bytes into a series of characters

- **CharsetEncoder:** A class that transforms a series of characters into a series of bytes

Before you can perform any transformations between byte and character buffers, you must create a Charset object that maps characters to their corresponding byte values.

To create a character set, call the forName(String) static method of the Charset class, specifying the name of the set's character encoding.

Java supports six character encodings:

- **US-ASCII:** The 128-character ASCII set that makes up the Basic Latin block of Unicode (also called ISO 646-US)

- **ISO-8859-1:** The 256-character ISO Latin Alphabet No. 1 character set (also called ISO LATIN-1)

- **UTF-8:** A character set that includes U.S. ASCII and the Universal Character Set (also called Unicode), a set composed of thousands of characters used in the world's languages

- **UTF-16BE:** The Universal Character Set represented as 16-bit characters with bytes stored in big-endian byte order

- **UTF-16LE:** The Universal Character Set represented as 16-bit characters with bytes stored in little-endian byte order

- **UTF-16:** The Universal Character Set represented as 16-bit characters with the order of bytes indicated by an optional byte-order mark

The following statement creates a `Charset` object for the ISO 8859-1 character set:

```
Charset isoset = Charset.forName("ISO-8859-1");
```

When you have a character set object, you can use it to create encoders and decoders. Call the object's `newDecoder()` method to create a `CharsetDecoder` and the `newEncoder()` method to create a `CharsetEncoder`.

To transform a byte buffer into a character buffer, call the decoder's `decode(ByteBuffer)` method, which returns a `CharBuffer` containing the bytes transformed into characters.

To transform a character buffer into a byte buffer, call the encoder's `encode(CharBuffer)` method. A `ByteBuffer` is returned, and it contains the characters' byte values.

The following statements convert a byte buffer called `netBuffer` into a character buffer using the ISO 8859-1 character set:

```
ByteBuffer netBuffer = ByteBuffer.allocate(20480);
// code to fill byte buffer would be here
Charset set = Charset.forName("ISO-8859-1");
CharsetDecoder decoder = set.newDecoder();
netBuffer.position(0);
CharBuffer netText = decoder.decode(netBuffer);
```

17

**CAUTION**

> Before the decoder is used to create the character buffer, the call to `position(0)` resets the current position of `netBuffer` to the start. When you're working with buffers for the first time, it's easy to overlook this, and you may end up with a buffer with much less data than you expected.

## Channels

A common use for a buffer is to associate it with an input stream or an output stream. You can fill a buffer with data from an input stream or write a buffer to an output stream. To do this, you must use a channel—an object that connects a buffer to the stream. Channels are part of the `java.nio.channels` package.

You can associate channels with a stream by calling the `getChannel()` method, which is available in some of the stream classes in the `java.io` package.

The `FileInputStream` and `FileOutputStream` classes have `getChannel()` methods that return a `FileChannel` object. This file channel can be used to read, write, and modify the data in the file.

The following statements create a file input stream and a channel associated with that file:

```
try {
    String source = "prices.dat";
    FileInputStream inSource = new FileInputStream(source);
    FileChannel inChannel = inSource.getChannel();
} catch (FileNotFoundException fne) {
    System.out.println(fne.getMessage());
}
```

After you have created the file channel, you can find out how many bytes the file contains by calling its `size()` method. This is necessary if you want to create a byte buffer to hold the file's contents.

Bytes are read from a channel into a `ByteBuffer` with the `read(ByteBuffer, long)` method. The first argument is the buffer. The second argument is the current position in the buffer, which determines where the file's contents will begin to be stored.

The following statements extend the last example by reading a file into a byte buffer using the `inChannel` file channel:

```
long inSize = inChannel.size();
ByteBuffer data = ByteBuffer.allocate( (int) inSize );
inChannel.read(data, 0);
data.position(0);
for (int i = 0; data.remaining() > 0; i++) {
    System.out.print(data.get() + " ");
}
```

The attempt to read from the channel generates an `IOException` error if a problem occurs. Although the byte buffer is the same size as the file, this isn't a requirement. If you are reading the file into the buffer so that you can modify it, you can allocate a larger buffer.

The next project incorporates the new input/output features you have learned about so far: buffers, character sets, and channels. The `BufferConverter` application reads a small file into a byte buffer, displays the contents of the buffer, converts it to a character buffer, and then displays the characters.

Enter the code shown in Listing 17.4 as the new Java class `BufferConverter` in the `com.java21days` package.

**LISTING 17.4** The Full Text of `BufferConverter.java`

```
 1: package com.java21days;
 2:
 3: import java.nio.*;
 4: import java.nio.channels.*;
 5: import java.nio.charset.*;
 6: import java.io.*;
 7:
 8: public class BufferConverter {
 9:     public static void main(String[] arguments) {
10:         try {
11:             // read byte data into a byte buffer
12:             String data = "friends.dat";
13:             FileInputStream inData = new FileInputStream(data);
14:             FileChannel inChannel = inData.getChannel();
15:             long inSize = inChannel.size();
16:             ByteBuffer source = ByteBuffer.allocate((int) inSize);
17:             inChannel.read(source, 0);
18:             source.position(0);
19:             System.out.println("Original byte data:");
20:             for (int i = 0; source.remaining() > 0; i++) {
21:                 System.out.print(source.get() + " ");
22:             }
23:             // convert byte data into character data
24:             source.position(0);
25:             Charset ascii = Charset.forName("US-ASCII");
26:             CharsetDecoder toAscii = ascii.newDecoder();
27:             CharBuffer destination = toAscii.decode(source);
28:             destination.position(0);
29:             System.out.println("\n\nNew character data:");
30:             for (int i = 0; destination.remaining() > 0; i++) {
31:                 System.out.print(destination.get());
32:             }
33:             System.out.println();
34:         } catch (FileNotFoundException fne) {
35:             System.out.println(fne.getMessage());
36:         } catch (IOException ioe) {
37:             System.out.println(ioe.getMessage());
38:         }
39:     }
40: }
```

17

Before you run the file, you need a copy of `friends.dat`, the small file of byte data used in the application. To download it from the book's website, at www.java21days.com, open the Lesson 17 page, right-click the `friends.dat` hyperlink, and save the file in a folder on your computer. To copy that file into the same place as the application, follow these steps in NetBeans:

1. In the folder where you downloaded `friends.dat`, right-click the file and choose Copy.

2. In NetBeans, click the Files pane to bring it to the front.

3. Right-click Java21 (the top folder in the pane) and choose Paste.

The file is stored in the project's main folder.

**TIP**   You also can create your own file. In NetBeans, choose File, New File. In the New File dialog, choose the category Other and the file type Empty File. Give it the filename `friends.dat`. In the source code editor, type a sentence or two in the document and save the file.

If you use the copy of `friends.dat` from the book's website, your output from the `BufferConverter` application should look as shown in Figure 17.5.

**FIGURE 17.5**
Reading character data from a buffer.

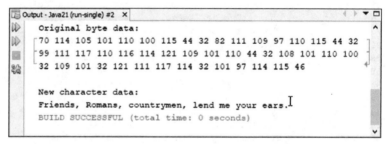

The `BufferConverter` application uses the techniques introduced in this lesson to read data and represent it as bytes and characters, but you could accomplish the same thing with the original input/output package, `java.io`. So why is it worth learning the new package at all? One reason is that buffers enable you to manipulate large amounts of data much more quickly. You'll learn about another reason in the next section.

## Network Channels

A popular feature of the `java.nio` package is its support for nonblocking input and output over a networking connection.

In Java, *blocking* refers to a statement that must complete execution before anything else happens in the program. All the socket programming you have done up to this point has used blocking methods exclusively. For example, in the `TimeServer` application, when the server socket's `accept()` method is called, nothing else happens in the program until a client makes a connection.

As you can imagine, it's problematic for a networking program to wait until a particular statement is executed because numerous things can go wrong. Connections can be broken. A server could go offline. A socket connection could appear to be stalled because a blocked statement is waiting for something to happen.

For example, a client application that reads and buffers data over HTTP might be waiting for a buffer to be filled even though no more data remains to be sent. The program will appear to have halted because the blocked statement never finishes executing.

With the `java.nio` package, you can create networking connections and read to and write from them by using nonblocking methods. Here's how it works:

1. Associate a socket channel with an input stream or an output stream.

2. Configure the channel to recognize the kind of networking events you want to monitor, such as new connections, attempts to read data over the channel, and attempts to write data.

3. Call a method to open the channel. Because the method is nonblocking, the program continues executing so that you can handle other tasks. If one of the networking events you are monitoring takes place, your program is notified; that is, a method associated with the event is called.

This is comparable to how user interface components are programmed in Swing. An interface component is associated with one or more event listeners and is placed in a container. If the interface component receives input being monitored by a listener, an event-handling method is called. Until that happens, the program can handle other tasks.

To use nonblocking input and output, you must work with channels instead of streams.

Nonblocking Socket Clients and Servers

The first step in developing a nonblocking client or server is creating an object that represents the Internet address to which you are connecting. This task is handled by the `InetSocketAddress` class in the `java.net` package.

If the server is identified by a hostname, call `InetSocketAddress(String, int)` with two arguments: the server's name and port number.

If the server is identified by its IP address, use the `InetAddress` class in `java.net` to identify the host. Call the static method `InetAddress.getByName(String)` with the host's IP address as the argument. The method returns an `InetAddress` object representing the address, which you can use in calling `InetSocketAddress(InetAddress, int)`. The second argument is the server's port number.

Nonblocking connections require a socket channel, another of the classes in the `java.nio` package. Call the `open()` static method of the `SocketChannel` class to create the channel.

A socket channel can be configured for blocking or nonblocking communication. To set up a nonblocking channel, call the channel's `configureBlocking(boolean)` method with the argument `false`. Calling it with `true` makes it a blocking channel.

After the channel is configured, call its `connect(InetSocketAddress)` method to connect the socket.

On a blocking channel, the `connect()` method attempts to establish a connection to the server and waits until it is complete; it returns the value `true` to indicate success.

On a nonblocking channel, the `connect()` method returns immediately with the value `false`. To figure out what's going on over the channel and respond to events, you must use a channel-listening object called a selector. A `Selector` object keeps track of things that happen to a socket channel (or another channel in the package that is a subclass of `SelectableChannel`).

To create a `Selector` object, call the `open()` method, as in the following statement:

```
Selector monitor = Selector.open();
```

When you use a `Selector` object, you must indicate the events you want to monitor. You do so by calling a channel's `register(Selector, int, Object)` method. The three arguments to `register()` are as follows:

- The `Selector` object you have created to monitor the channel
- An `int` value that represents the events being monitored (also called selection keys)
- An `Object` that can be delivered along with the key, or `null` otherwise

Instead of using an integer value as the second argument, it's easier to use one or more class variables from the `SelectionKey` class: `SelectionKey.OP_CONNECT` to monitor connections, `SelectionKey.OP_READ` to monitor attempts to read data, and `SelectionKey.OP_WRITE` to monitor attempts to write data.

The following statements create a `Selector` to monitor a socket channel called `wire` for reading data:

```
Selector spy = Selector.open();
channel.register(spy, SelectionKey.OP_READ, null);
```

To monitor more than one kind of key, add together the `SelectionKey` class variables. For example:

```
Selector spy = Selector.open();
channel.register(spy, SelectionKey.OP_READ + SelectionKey.OP_WRITE,
    null);
```

After the channel and selector have been set up, you can wait for events by calling the selector's `select()` or `select(long)` methods.

The `select()` method is a blocking method that waits until something has happened on the channel.

The `select(long)` method is a blocking method that waits until something has happened or the specified number of milliseconds has passed, whichever comes first.

Both `select()` methods return the number of events that have taken place, or `0` if nothing has happened. You can use a `while` loop with a call to the `select()` method as a way to loop until something happens on the channel.

After an event has taken place, you can find out more about it by calling the selector's `selectedKeys()` method, which returns a `Set` object containing details on each of the events.

Use this `Set` object as you would any other set, creating an `Iterator` to move through the set by using its `hasNext()` and `next()` methods.

The call to the set's `next()` method returns an object that should be cast to a `SelectionKey` object. This object represents an event that took place on the channel.

Three methods in the `SelectionKey` class can be used to identify the key in a client program: `isReadable()`, `isWritable()`, and `isConnectible()`. Each returns a `boolean` value. (A fourth method, `isAcceptable()`, is used when you're writing a server.)

After you retrieve a key from the set, call the key's `remove()` method to indicate that you will do something with it.

The last thing to find out about the event is the channel on which it took place. Call the key's `channel()` method, which returns the associated `SocketChannel` object.

17

If one of the events identifies a connection, you must make sure that the connection has been completed before using the channel. Call the key's isConnectionPending() method, which returns true if the connection is still in progress and false if it is complete.

To deal with a connection that is still in progress, you can call the socket's finishConnect() method, which attempts to complete the connection.

Using a nonblocking socket channel involves the interaction of numerous new classes from the java.nio and java.net packages.

To give you a more complete picture of how these classes work together, this lesson's final project is FingerServer, a web application that uses a nonblocking socket channel to handle Finger requests.

Enter the code shown in Listing 17.5 as the class FingerServer in the package com.java21days and save the application.

**LISTING 17.5**   The Full Text of FingerServer.java

```
 1: package com.java21days;
 2:
 3: import java.io.*;
 4: import java.net.*;
 5: import java.nio.channels.*;
 6: import java.util.*;
 7:
 8: public class FingerServer {
 9:
10:     public FingerServer() {
11:         try {
12:             // Create a non-blocking server socket channel
13:             ServerSocketChannel sock = ServerSocketChannel.open();
14:             sock.configureBlocking(false);
15:
16:             // Set the host and port to monitor
17:             InetSocketAddress server = new InetSocketAddress(
18:                 "localhost", 79);
19:             ServerSocket socket = sock.socket();
20:             socket.bind(server);
21:
22:             // Create the selector and register it on the channel
23:             Selector selector = Selector.open();
24:             sock.register(selector, SelectionKey.OP_ACCEPT);
25:
26:             // Loop forever, looking for client connections
27:             while (true) {
28:                 // Wait for a connection
29:                 selector.select();
```

```
30:
31:                    // Get list of selection keys with pending events
32:                    Set keys = selector.selectedKeys();
33:                    Iterator it = keys.iterator();
34:
35:                    // Handle each key
36:                    while (it.hasNext()) {
37:
38:                        // Get the key and remove it from the iteration
39:                        SelectionKey sKey = (SelectionKey) it.next();
40:
41:                        it.remove();
42:                        if (sKey.isAcceptable()) {
43:
44:                            // Create a socket connection with client
45:                            ServerSocketChannel selChannel =
46:                                (ServerSocketChannel) sKey.channel();
47:                            ServerSocket sSock = selChannel.socket();
48:                            Socket connection = sSock.accept();
49:
50:                            // Handle the Finger request
51:                            handleRequest(connection);
52:                            connection.close();
53:                        }
54:                    }
55:                }
56:            } catch (IOException ioe) {
57:                System.out.println(ioe.getMessage());
58:            }
59:        }
60:
61:    private void handleRequest(Socket connection)
62:        throws IOException {
63:
64:        // Set up input and output
65:        InputStreamReader isr = new InputStreamReader (
66:            connection.getInputStream());
67:        BufferedReader is = new BufferedReader(isr);
68:        PrintWriter pw = new PrintWriter(new
69:            BufferedOutputStream(connection.getOutputStream()),
70:            false);
71:
72:        // Output server greeting
73:        pw.println("Nio Finger Server");
74:        pw.flush();
74:
75:        // Handle user input
76:        String outLine = null;
77:        String inLine = is.readLine();
78:
```

17

```
79:            if (inLine.length() > 0) {
80:                outLine = inLine;
81:            }
82:            readPlan(outLine, pw);
83:
84:            // Clean up
85:            pw.flush();
86:            pw.close();
87:            is.close();
88:        }
89:
90:        private void readPlan(String userName, PrintWriter pw) {
91:            try {
92:                FileReader file = new FileReader(userName + ".plan");
93:                BufferedReader buff = new BufferedReader(file);
94:                boolean eof = false;
95:
96:                pw.println("\nUser name: " + userName + "\n");
97:
98:                while (!eof) {
99:                    String line = buff.readLine();
100:
101:                    if (line == null) {
102:                        eof = true;
103:                    } else {
104:                        pw.println(line);
105:                    }
106:                }
107:
108:                buff.close();
109:            } catch (IOException e) {
110:                pw.println("User " + userName + " not found.");
111:            }
112:        }
113:
114:        public static void main(String[] arguments) {
115:            FingerServer nio = new FingerServer();
116:        }
117: }
```

The Finger server requires one or more user .plan files stored in text files. These files should have names that take the form *username*.plan—for example, linus.plan, lucy.plan, and franklin.plan. Before running the server, create one or more .plan files in the root folder of the Java21 project.

When you're done, run the Finger server. The application waits for incoming Finger requests, creating a nonblocking server socket channel and registering one kind of key for a selector to look for: connection events.

Inside a while loop that begins on line 27, the server calls the Selector object's select() method to see whether the selector has received any keys, which would occur when a Finger client makes a connection. When it has, `select()` returns the number of keys, and the statements inside the loop are executed.

After the connection is made, a buffered reader is created to hold a request for a `.plan` file. The syntax for the command is the username of the `.plan` file being requested.

While the Finger server is running, you can test this application with the Finger client. Create a custom project configuration in NetBeans to set the command-line argument of the Finger user:

1. Choose Run, Set Project Configuration, Customize. The Project Properties dialog opens.

2. In the Main Class text field, enter `Finger`.

3. In the Arguments text field, enter `franklin@localhost` and click OK.

4. Run the application by choosing Run, Run Project.

Figure 17.6 shows the output you receive when you request the user `franklin` on the computer `localhost`.

**FIGURE 17.6**
Making a Finger request from your Finger server.

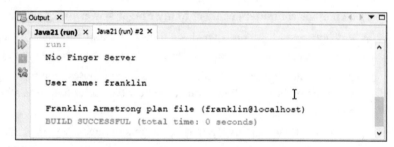

Run the application again with `lucy@localhost` to see Lucy's `.plan` file and then with `linus@localhost` to look for Linus.

When you're done with the Finger server, click the Stop button on the left edge of the Output pane to shut it down.

**CAUTION**

The `.plan` files must be in the root folder of the `Java21` project for the `FingerServer` application to find them. If they were saved somewhere else, you can move them by dragging and dropping in NetBeans. Click the Files tab in the Projects pane to see a list of the project's files. Find the plan files and drag them to the same folder that holds `friends.dat`.

# Summary

In this lesson you have learned how to use URLs, URL connections, and input streams in combination to pull data from the Web into a program.

Networking can be extremely useful. The `WebReader` project is a rudimentary web browser. It can load a web page or RSS file into a Java program and display it. However, it doesn't do anything to make sense of the markup tags; it just presents the raw text delivered by a web server.

In this lesson you created a socket application that implements the basics of the Finger protocol, a method for retrieving user information on the Internet.

You have also learned how client and server programs are written in Java, using the nonblocking techniques in the `java.nio` package. To use nonblocking techniques, you learned about the fundamental classes of Java's new networking package: buffers, character encoders and decoders, socket channels, and selectors.

# Q&A

**Q Can other computers connect to my Finger server over the Internet?**

**A** Probably not. Most computers have firewall settings and router security settings that do not accept incoming requests on port 79, the one used by the Finger protocol.

If you create a server that isn't just for testing purposes, you must figure out how to configure the firewall and router to allow the server to access all the ports that it requires.

Because Internet servers are frequent targets of attack, you must make sure your server can handle malformed client requests and other hacking attempts. You also should run the server with a user account that only has access to the files and system resources it needs and no others. This prevents a hacker from compromising the server and using it to read confidential data, infect the computer with viruses, and launch other harmful exploits.

# Quiz

Review this lesson's material by taking this three-question quiz.

## Questions

1. Which of the following is not an advantage of the `java.nio` package and its related packages?

    A. Large amounts of data can be manipulated quickly with buffers.

    B. Networking connections can be nonblocking for more reliable use in your applications.

    C. Streams are not necessary for reading and writing data over a network.

2. In the Finger protocol, which program makes a request for information about a user?

    A. The client

    B. The server

    C. Both can make that request.

3. Which method is preferred for loading the data from a web page into your Java application?

    A. Creating a socket and an input stream from that socket

    B. Creating a `URL` and an `HttpURLConnection` from that object

    C. Loading the page using the method `toString()`

## Answers

1. C. The `java.nio` classes work in conjunction with streams. They don't replace them.

2. A. The client requests information, and the server sends back something in response. This is traditionally how client/server applications function, although a program may be able to act as both client and server.

3. B. Sockets are good for low-level connections, such as when you are implementing a new protocol. For existing protocols such as HTTP, some classes are better suited to that protocol—such as `URL` and `HttpURLConnection`.

# Certification Practice

The following question is the kind of thing you could expect to be asked on a Java programming certification test. Answer it without looking again at this lesson or using the Java compiler to test the code.

Given:

```java
import java.nio.*;

public class ReadTemps {
    public ReadTemps() {
        int[] temperatures = { 78, 80, 75, 70, 79, 85, 92, 99, 90 };
        IntBuffer tempBuffer = IntBuffer.wrap(temperatures);
        int[] moreTemperatures = { 65, 44, 71 };
        tempBuffer.put(moreTemperatures);
        System.out.println("First int: " + tempBuffer.get());
    }
}
```

What will be the output when this application is run?

**A.** First int: 78

**B.** First int: 71

**C.** First int: 70

**D.** None of the above

The answer is available on the book's website, at www.java21days.com. Visit the Lesson 17 page and click the Certification Practice link.

# Exercises

To extend your knowledge of the subjects covered in this lesson, try the following exercises:

**1.** Write an application that stores some of your favorite web pages on your computer so that you can read them while you are not connected to the Internet.

**2.** Modify the `FingerServer` application to use the `try`-with-resources improvement to `try-catch` blocks in Java.

Where applicable, exercise solutions are offered on the book's website, at www.java21days.com.

# LESSON 18
# Accessing Databases with JDBC and Derby

Almost all Java programs deal with data in some way. So far you have used primitive types, objects, arrays, hash maps, and other data structures.

During this lesson, you'll work with data in a more sophisticated way, exploring Java Database Connectivity (JDBC), a set of classes that connects Java programs to relational databases.

Java includes Java DB, a compact relational database that makes it easy to incorporate a database into your applications. Java DB is Oracle's name for Apache Derby, an open source database maintained by the Apache Software Foundation.

In this lesson you will explore JDBC in the following ways:

- Using JDBC drivers to work with different relational databases
- Accessing a database with Structured Query Language (SQL)
- Reading records from a database using SQL and JDBC
- Adding records to a database using SQL and JDBC
- Creating a new Java DB database and reading its records

# Java Database Connectivity

Java Database Connectivity (JDBC) is a set of classes that can be used to develop client/server applications that work with databases developed by Microsoft, Sybase, Oracle, IBM, and others. It's a standard interface between Java programs and relational databases.

With JDBC, you can use the same methods and classes in Java programs to read and write records and perform other kinds of database access. A class called a *driver* acts as a bridge to the database source. There are drivers for each of the popular databases.

One of the biggest obstacles faced by database programmers is the wide variety of database formats in use, each with its own proprietary method of accessing data.

To simplify using relational database programs, a standard language called Structured Query Language (SQL) was developed. This language supplants the need to learn different database-querying languages for each database format. Java DB supports SQL.

In database programming, a request for records in a database is called a *query*. Using SQL, you can send complex queries to a database and get the records you're looking for in any order you specify.

Consider the example of a database programmer at a student loan company who has been asked to prepare a report on the most delinquent loan recipients. The programmer could use SQL to query a database for all records in which the last payment was more than 180 days ago and the amount due is more than $0.00. SQL also can be used to control the order in which records are returned, so the programmer can get the records in the order of Social Security number, recipient name, amount owed, or another field in the loan database. All this is possible with SQL. The programmer doesn't need any of the proprietary languages associated with popular database formats.

| CAUTION | SQL is supported by many database tools, so, in theory, you should be able to use the same SQL commands for each database tool that supports the language. However, you still need to learn the idiosyncrasies of a specific database tool when accessing it through SQL. |
|---|---|

Using SQL is the industry-standard approach to accessing relational databases. JDBC supports SQL, enabling developers to use a wide range of database formats without knowing the specifics of the underlying database. JDBC also supports the use of database queries specific to a database format.

The JDBC class library's approach to accessing databases with SQL is comparable to existing database-development techniques, so interacting with an SQL database by using JDBC isn't much different from using traditional database tools. Java programmers who already have some database experience can hit the ground running with JDBC.

The JDBC library includes classes for each of the tasks commonly associated with database usage:

- Making a connection to a database
- Creating a statement using SQL
- Executing that SQL query in the database
- Viewing the resulting records

These JDBC classes are all part of the `java.sql` package.

# Database Drivers

Java programs that use JDBC classes can follow the familiar programming model of issuing SQL statements and processing the resulting data. The format of the database and the platform it was prepared on don't matter.

This platform and database independence is made possible by a driver manager. The classes of the JDBC library are largely dependent on driver managers, which keep track of the drivers required to access database records. You need a different driver for each database format that's used in a program, and sometimes you might need several drivers for versions of the same format. Java DB includes its own driver.

18

JDBC also includes a driver that bridges JDBC and another database-connectivity standard, ODBC.

# Examining a Database

NetBeans has extensive support for database programming. Before you begin writing code, you can use it to connect to a database, learn about the tables it contains, and see the data in those tables.

To connect to a Java DB database, first you must start the database server.

In the Projects pane, click the Services tab to bring it to the front, as shown in Figure 18.1. The Databases item includes a Java DB item. Right-click Java DB and choose Start Server.

**FIGURE 18.1**
Starting the Java DB
database server.

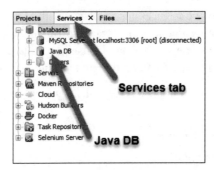

The first time you start a Java DB server in NetBeans, it might fail with a security error. In that circumstance, NetBeans displays a balloon dialog reporting a Security Manager problem (see Figure 18.2).

**FIGURE 18.2**
Dealing with
a Security
Manager error.

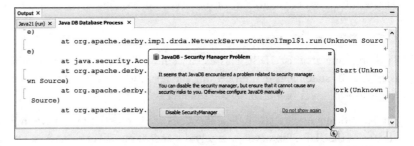

There are no significant security risks when running Java DB to develop and test JDBC applications in this chapter, so click the Disable Security Manager button and then start Java DB again in the Services tab of the Projects pane. Right-click Java DB and choose Start Server.

When Java DB launches after any security issues are resolved, it launches and displays a few lines of text to indicate what it's doing (see Figure 18.3).

This database server calls itself the Apache Derby Network Server, a reflection of the fact that Oracle's Java DB is an implementation of Derby.

**FIGURE 18.3**
Launching a
Java DB server
with NetBeans.

```
Output - Java DB Database Process  ×                              ◄ ► ▼ ☐
Wed Sep 11 20:10:31 EDT 2019 : Security manager installed using the Basic server security policy.
Wed Sep 11 20:10:41 EDT 2019 : Apache Derby Network Server - 10.11.1.2 - (1629631) started and ready
to accept connections on port 1527
```

The server's output indicates that the server is running on port 1527 and is ready to take connections. Keep this window open so that you can monitor the server while it runs.

In the Services pane under Java DB is a sample database named `sample`. Connect to this database by right-clicking `sample` and choosing Connect.

An item in the Services pane changes from a broken icon into an unbroken one: `jdbc:derby://localhost:1527/sample`. This is an active connection to the database. Expand this item and then expand APP, Tables, and CUSTOMER. A list of fields in the CUSTOMER table appears, as shown in Figure 18.4.

**FIGURE 18.4**
Examining tables in a Java DB database.

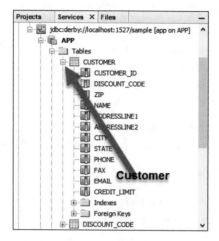

You can view the records in this table by right-clicking CUSTOMER and choosing View Data. Two things appear in other panes on NetBeans. First, an SQL command appears where the source code editor normally appears:

```
select * from APP.CUSTOMER
```

This command, which is called an *SQL query*, selects all fields from APP.CUSTOMER. The asterisk character (*) could be replaced with the name of one or more fields, separated by commas.

Second, you see another pane that displays the result of this command: all the data in this table, organized into rows and columns. Each column is a field, and each row is a record in the table.

Figure 18.5 shows the contents of the CUSTOMER table. This is the table you'll be writing Java code to access.

**FIGURE 18.5**
Displaying database records in a table.

| SELECT * FROM APP.CUSTOME... × | | | | | | |
|---|---|---|---|---|---|---|
| # | CUSTOMER_ID | DISCOUNT_CODE | ZIP | NAME | ADDRESSLINE1 | ADDRESSLINE2 |
| 1 | 1 | N | 95117 | Jumbo Eagle Corp | 111 E. Las Olivas Blvd | Suite 51 |
| 2 | 2 | M | 95035 | New Enterprises | 9754 Main Street | P.O. Box 567 |
| 3 | 25 | M | 85638 | Wren Computers | 8989 Red Albatross Drive | Suite 9897 |
| 4 | 3 | L | 12347 | Small Bill Company | 8585 South Upper Murray Drive | P.O. Box 456 |
| 5 | 36 | H | 94401 | Bob Hosting Corp. | 65653 Lake Road | Suite 2323 |
| 6 | 106 | L | 95035 | Early Central Comp | 829 E Flex Drive | Suite 853 |

## Reading Records from a Database

Your first project in this lesson is a Java application that connects to a sample Java DB database included with NetBeans that reads records from a table.

Working with a database in a Java program is relatively easy if you are conversant with SQL.

The first task in a JDBC program is to load the driver (or drivers) that will be used to connect to a data source. A driver is loaded with the `Class.forName(String)` method. `Class`, part of the `java.lang` package, can be used to load classes into the Java Virtual Machine (JVM). The `forName(String)` method loads the class named by the specified string. This method can throw a `ClassNotFoundException`.

Programs that use Java DB can use `org.apache.derby.jdbc.ClientDriver`, a driver included with the database. Loading this class into the JVM requires the following statement:

```
Class.forName("org.apache.derby.jdbc.ClientDriver");
```

After the driver has been loaded, you can establish a connection to the data source by using the `DriverManager` class in the `java.sql` package.

The `getConnection(String, String, String)` method of `DriverManager` can be used to set up the connection. It returns a reference to a `Connection` object representing an active data connection. This method has three arguments:

- A string identifying the data source and the type of database connectivity used to reach it
- A username
- A password

The last two items are needed only if the data source is secured with a username and password. If it isn't, these arguments can be null strings (`""`).

Here's the string to use when connecting to the `sample` database:

```
jdbc:derby://localhost:1527/sample
```

You've already seen this string in the Services tab of the Projects pane, where it is an item that represents a database connection.

This string identifies the type of database (`jdbc:derby:`), the host and port of the database server (`localhost:1527`), and the name of the database (`sample`). Note the two slash characters (`//`) after the database type and the one slash after the host and port.

The second and third arguments to use are `app` and `APP`, capitalized as shown. They're the username and password.

The following statement could be used to connect to a database called `payroll` with the username `doc` and the password `1rover1`:

```
Connection payday = DriverManager.getConnection(
    "jdbc:derby://localhost:1527/payroll",
    "doc", "1rover1");
```

After you have made a connection, you can reuse it each time you want to retrieve information from or store information to that connection's data source.

The `getConnection()` method and all other methods called on a data source throw `SQLException` errors if something goes wrong as the data source is being used. SQL has its own error messages, and they are passed along as part of `SQLException` objects.

**TIP**

> NetBeans shows the information required to connect to a database, including the driver class, database connection string, username, and password. Right-click the database connection, such as `jdbc:derby://localhost:1527/sample`, and choose Properties from the pop-up menu. A dialog containing the class and other information about the connection appears.

18

An SQL statement is represented in Java by a `Statement` object. `Statement` is an interface, so it can't be instantiated directly. However, an object that implements the interface is returned by the `createStatement()` method of a `Connection` object, as in the following example:

```
Statement lookSee = payday.createStatement();
```

After you have a `Statement` object, you can use it to conduct an SQL query by calling the object's `executeQuery(String)` method. The `String` argument should be an SQL query that follows the syntax of that language.

**CAUTION**

> It's beyond the scope of this lesson to teach SQL, a rich data-retrieval and storage language that has its own book from this publisher: *Sams Teach Yourself SQL in 24 Hours*, 6th edition, by Ryan Stephens, Arie D. Jones, and Ron Plew (ISBN: 0-672-33759-2). Although you need to learn SQL to do extensive work with it, much of the language is easy to pick up from any examples you can find, such as those you are working with here.

The following is an example of an SQL query that could be used on the `sample` database:

```
select NAME, CITY from APP.CUSTOMER where (STATE = 'FL')
    order by CITY;
```

This SQL query retrieves several fields for each record in the database for which the STATE field equals FL. The records returned are sorted according to their CITY field. The lowercase parts of the command are SQL keywords. The uppercase parts are aspects of the table.

The following Java statement executes that query on a `Statement` object named `looksee`:

```
ResultSet set = looksee.executeQuery(
    "select NAME, CITY from APP.CUSTOMER "
    + " where (STATE = 'FL') order by CITY";
);
```

Although SQL queries end with a semicolon character (`;`), one is not needed in the argument to `executeQuery()`.

If the SQL query has been phrased correctly, the `executeQuery()` method returns a `ResultSet` object holding all the records that have been retrieved from the data source.

> **NOTE**
> To add records to a database instead of retrieving them, you should call the statement's `executeUpdate()` method. You'll work with this method later.

When a `ResultSet` object is returned from `executeQuery()`, it is positioned at the first record that has been retrieved. The following methods of `ResultSet` can be used to pull information from the current record:

- **getDate(*String*):** Returns the `Date` value stored in the specified field name (using the `Date` class in the `java.sql` package, not `java.util.Date`)
- **getDouble(*String*):** Returns the `double` value stored in the specified field name
- **getFloat(*String*):** Returns the `float` value stored in the specified field
- **getInt(*String*):** Returns the `int` value in the field
- **getLong(*String*):** Returns the `long` value in the field
- **getString(*String*):** Returns the `String` in the field

These are just the simplest methods available in the `ResultSet` interface. What methods you should use depend on the form that the field data takes in the database. Methods such as `getString()` and `getInt()` can be more flexible in the information they retrieve from a record.

You also can use an integer as the argument to any of these methods, such as `getString(5)`, instead of a string. The integer indicates which field to retrieve (1 for the first field, 2 for the second field, and so on).

An `SQLException` is thrown if a database error occurs as you try to retrieve information from a resultset. You can call this exception's `getSQLState()` and `getErrorCode()` methods to learn more about the error.

After you have pulled the information you need from a record, you can move to the next record by calling the `next()` method of the `ResultSet` object. This method returns a `false` Boolean value when it tries to move past the end of a resultset.

Normally, you can move through a resultset once from start to finish, after which you can't retrieve its contents again.

When you're finished using a connection to a data source, you can close it by calling the connection's `close()` method with no arguments.

Listing 18.1 presents the `CustomerReporter` application, which uses the Java DB driver and an SQL statement to retrieve records from a table in the `sample` database. Four fields are retrieved from each record indicated by the SQL statement: `TABLEID`, `TABLENAME`, `TABLETYPE`, and `SCHEMAID`. The resultset is sorted according to the `TABLENAME` field, and these fields are displayed.

Before creating this application, you must add the `JavaDB` library to the project in NetBeans:

1. Click the Projects tab in the Projects pane to bring it to the front.
2. Scroll down to the bottom of the pane and right-click the `Libraries` folder.
3. Click Add Library from the pop-up menu that appears. The Add Library dialog opens.
4. Choose `Java DB Driver` (or `JavaDB`) under Available Libraries and click Add Library.

The library now appears in the `Libraries` folder. Three new JAR files appear in the Libraries item in the Projects pane: `derby.jar`, `derbyclient.jar`, and `derbynet.jar`. The driver necessary to access the sample database on the Java DB server will be available to the `CustomerReporter` application.

Create the `CustomerReporter` class in the `com.java21days` package in NetBeans with the source code shown in Listing 18.1.

**LISTING 18.1**    The Full Text of `CustomerReporter.java`

```
 1: package com.java21days;
 2:
 3: import java.sql.*;
 4:
 5: public class CustomerReporter {
 6:     public static void main(String[] arguments) {
 7:         String data = "jdbc:derby://localhost:1527/sample";
 8:         try (
 9:             Connection conn = DriverManager.getConnection(
10:                 data, "app", "app");
11:             Statement st = conn.createStatement()) {
12:
13:             Class.forName("org.apache.derby.jdbc.ClientDriver");
14:
15:             ResultSet rec = st.executeQuery(
16:                 "select CUSTOMER_ID, NAME, CITY, STATE " +
17:                 "from APP.CUSTOMER " +
18:                 "order by CUSTOMER_ID");
19:             while (rec.next()) {
20:                 System.out.println("CUSTOMER_ID: "
21:                     + rec.getString(1));
22:                 System.out.println("NAME: " + rec.getString(2));
23:                 System.out.println("CITY: " + rec.getString(3));
24:                 System.out.println("STATE: " + rec.getString(4));
25:                 System.out.println();
26:             }
27:             rec.close();
28:         } catch (SQLException s) {
29:             System.out.println("SQL Error: " + s.toString() + " "
30:                 + s.getErrorCode() + " " + s.getSQLState());
31:         } catch (Exception e) {
32:             System.out.println("Error: " + e.toString()
33:                 + e.getMessage());
34:         }
35:     }
36: }
```

When this program is run with the starting data from the `sample` database, it provides output like that shown in Figure 18.6.

**FIGURE 18.6**
Reading records
from a Java
DB database.

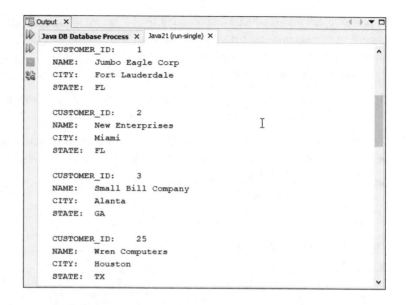

```
CUSTOMER_ID:     1
NAME:    Jumbo Eagle Corp
CITY:    Fort Lauderdale
STATE:   FL


CUSTOMER_ID:     2
NAME:    New Enterprises
CITY:    Miami
STATE:   FL


CUSTOMER_ID:     3
NAME:    Small Bill Company
CITY:    Alanta
STATE:   GA


CUSTOMER_ID:     25
NAME:    Wren Computers
CITY:    Houston
STATE:   TX
```

**CAUTION**

If you run this application and it fails with an SQL error stating "Connection authentication failure occurred. Reason: Userid or password invalid," it may be due to a bug in NetBeans. Change the password used as the final argument to the `getConnection()` method in lines 9–10 from APP to app and run the program again to see if it resolves the problem.

18

## Writing Records to a Database

In the `CustomerReporter` application, you retrieved data from a database by using an SQL statement prepared as a string:

```
select CUSTOMER_ID, NAME, CITY, STATE from APP.CUSTOMER
    order by CUSTOMER_ID;
```

This is a common way to use SQL. You could write a program that asks a user to enter an SQL query and then displays the result. (However, that would be a terrible idea because SQL queries can be used to delete records, tables, and even entire databases.)

The `java.sql` package also supports another way to create an SQL statement: a prepared statement.

A prepared statement, which is represented by the `PreparedStatement` class, is an SQL statement that is compiled before it is executed. This enables the statement to return data more quickly and is a better choice if you are executing an SQL statement repeatedly in the same program or doing multiple inserts or updates.

To create a prepared statement, call a connection's `prepareStatement(String)` method with a string that indicates the structure of the SQL statement.

To indicate the structure, you write an SQL statement in which parameters have been replaced with question marks. Here's an example for a connection object called `cc`:

```
PreparedStatement ps = cc.prepareStatement(
    "select * from APP.CUSTOMER where (ZIP=?) "
    + "order by NAME");
```

Here's another example with more than one question mark:

```
PreparedStatement ps = cc.prepareStatement(
    "insert into APP.CUSTOMER " +
    "VALUES(?, ?, ?, ?, ?, ?, ?, ?, ?, ?, ?, ?, ?)");
```

The question marks in these SQL statements are placeholders for data. Before you can execute the statement, you must put data in each of these places using one of the methods of the `PreparedStatement` class.

To put data into a prepared statement, you must call a method with the position of the placeholder followed by the data to insert. For example, to put the string `"Acme Corp."` in the fifth field of the prepared statement, call the `setString(int, String)` method:

```
ps.setString(5, "Acme Corp.");
```

The first argument indicates the placeholder's position, numbered from left to right. The first question mark is 1, the second is 2, and so on. The second argument is the data to put in the statement at that position.

The following methods are available:

- **`setAsciiStream(int, InputStream, int)`:** At the position indicated by the first argument, inserts the specified `InputStream`, which represents a stream of ASCII characters. The third argument indicates how many bytes from the input stream to insert.

- **`setBinaryStream(int, InputStream, int)`:** At the position indicated by the first argument, inserts the specified `InputStream`, which represents a stream of bytes. The third argument indicates how many bytes to insert from the stream.

- **setCharacterStream(*int*, *Reader*, *int*)**: At the position indicated by the first argument, inserts the specified *Reader*, which represents a character stream. The third argument indicates how many characters to insert from the stream.
- **setBoolean(*int*, *boolean*)**: Inserts a Boolean value at the position indicated by the integer.
- **setByte(*int*, *byte*)**: Inserts a byte value at the indicated position.
- **setBytes(*int*, *byte*[])**: Inserts an array of bytes at the indicated position.
- **setDate(*int*, *Date*)**: Inserts a Date object (from the java.sql package) at the indicated position.
- **setDouble(*int*, *double*)**: Inserts a double value at the indicated position.
- **setFloat(*int*, *float*)**: Inserts a float value at the indicated position.
- **setInt(*int*, *int*)**: Inserts an int value at the indicated position.
- **setLong(*int*, *long*)**: Inserts a long value at the indicated position.
- **setShort(*int*, *short*)**: Inserts a short value at the indicated position.
- **setString(*int*, *String*)**: Inserts a String value at the indicated position.

There's also a setNull(*int*, *int*) method that stores SQL's version of a null (empty) value at the position indicated by the first argument.

The second argument to setNull() should be a class variable from the Types class in java.sql to indicate what kind of SQL value belongs in that position.

There are class variables for each of the SQL data types. The following are some of the most commonly used variables: BIGINT, BIT, CHAR, DATE, DECIMAL, DOUBLE, FLOAT, INTEGER, SMALLINT, TINYINT, and VARCHAR. (Note that this list is not complete.)

The following code puts a null CHAR value at the fifth position in a prepared statement called ps:

```
ps.setNull(5, Types.CHAR);
```

The next project demonstrates the use of a prepared statement to add stock quote data to a database. Quotes are collected from the *Wall Street Journal.*

As a service to people who follow the stock market, the Wall Street Journal offers a way to request stock quote data via a URL such as http://quotes.wsj.com/fb/historical-prices/download?num_rows=1.

The "fb" in this URL is the ticker symbol FB (Facebook). You can change it to request a different company's stock data.

18

You can go to this URL to open the file or save it to a folder on your system. The file, which is only two lines long, contains the stock's price and volume data saved at the last market close. Here's an example of what Facebook's data looked like on September 11, 2019:

```
Date, Open, High, Low, Close, Volume
09/11/19, 186.46, 189.44, 186.08, 188.49, 11538300
```

The first line identifies the fields, which are, in order, the date, opening price, high, low, closing price, and volume. The `QuoteData` application uses each of these fields.

The following takes place in the program:

- A stock's ticker symbol is used as a command-line argument.
- A `QuoteData` object is created with the ticker symbol as an instance variable called `ticker`.
- The object's `retrieveQuote()` method is called to download the stock data and return it as a `String`.
- The object's `storeQuote()` method is called with that `String` as an argument. It saves the stock data to a database using a JDBC-ODBC connection.

Before you can run the application, you must have a database table designed to hold these stock quotes. You can create a new table for this purpose in the `sample` database in NetBeans by following these steps:

1. In the Services tab of the Projects pane, open the APP item under the `jdbc:derby://localhost:1527/sample` item.

2. Right-click this item's Tables folder and choose Create Table from the pop-up menu. The Create Table dialog opens, as shown in Figure 18.7.

**FIGURE 18.7**
Creating a new database table in NetBeans.

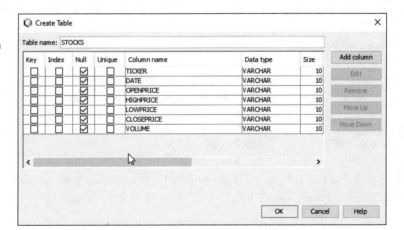

| Key | Index | Null | Unique | Column name | Data type | Size |
|-----|-------|------|--------|-------------|-----------|------|
| ☐ | ☐ | ☑ | ☐ | TICKER | VARCHAR | 10 |
| ☐ | ☐ | ☑ | ☐ | DATE | VARCHAR | 10 |
| ☐ | ☐ | ☑ | ☐ | OPENPRICE | VARCHAR | 10 |
| ☐ | ☐ | ☑ | ☐ | HIGHPRICE | VARCHAR | 10 |
| ☐ | ☐ | ☑ | ☐ | LOWPRICE | VARCHAR | 10 |
| ☐ | ☐ | ☑ | ☐ | CLOSEPRICE | VARCHAR | 10 |
| ☐ | ☐ | ☑ | ☐ | VOLUME | VARCHAR | 10 |

**3.** In the Table Name field, enter STOCKS.

**4.** Click Add Column. The Add Column dialog opens.

**5.** In the Name field, enter TICKER.

**6.** In the Type field, choose VARCHAR.

**7.** In the Size field, enter 10.

**8.** Click OK. The new field appears in the dialog.

**9.** Repeat steps 4–8 for fields named DATE, OPENPRICE, HIGHPRICE, LOWPRICE, CLOSEPRICE, and VOLUME. The type and size are always VARCHAR and 10, respectively.

**10.** Click OK. The STOCKS table appears in the Tables folder.

Now that you have a database table, you can create the QuoteData application, shown in Listing 18.2, to store stock data in a new record of that table. Create the class QuoteData in the com.java21days package in NetBeans and enter the source code shown in the listing.

**LISTING 18.2**   The Full Text of QuoteData.java

```
 1: package com.java21days;
 2:
 3: import java.io.*;
 4: import java.net.*;
 5: import java.sql.*;
 6: import java.util.*;
 7:
 8: public class QuoteData {
 9:     private final String ticker;
10:
11:     public QuoteData(String inTicker) {
12:         ticker = inTicker;
13:     }
14:
15:     private String retrieveQuote() {
16:         StringBuilder builder = new StringBuilder();
17:         try {
18:             URL page = new URL(
19:                 "https://quote.wsj.com/" + ticker
20:                     + "/historical-prices/download?"
21:                     + "num_rows=1");
22:             String line;
23:             URLConnection conn = page.openConnection();
24:             conn.connect();
25:             InputStreamReader in = new InputStreamReader(
26:                 conn.getInputStream());
27:             BufferedReader data = new BufferedReader(in);
```

18

```
28:                while ((line = data.readLine()) != null) {
29:                    if (line.contains("Date")) continue;
30:                    builder.append(line);
31:                    builder.append("\n");
32:                }
33:            } catch (MalformedURLException mue) {
34:                System.out.println("Bad URL: " + mue.getMessage());
35:            } catch (IOException ioe) {
36:                System.out.println("IO Error:" + ioe.getMessage());
37:            }
38:            return builder.toString();
39:        }
40:
41:        private void storeQuote(String data) {
42:            StringTokenizer tokens = new StringTokenizer(data, ",");
43:            String[] fields = new String[6];
44:            for (int i = 0; i < fields.length; i++) {
45:                fields[i] = stripQuotes(tokens.nextToken());
46:            }
47:            String datasource = "jdbc:derby://localhost:1527/sample";
48:            try (
49:                Connection conn = DriverManager.getConnection(
50:                    datasource, "app", "app")
51:                ) {
52:
53:                Class.forName("org.apache.derby.jdbc.ClientDriver");
54:                PreparedStatement prep2 = conn.prepareStatement(
55:                    "insert into " +
56:                    "APP.STOCKS(TICKER, DATE, OPENPRICE, HIGHPRICE, " +
57:                    "LOWPRICE, CLOSEPRICE, VOLUME) " +
58:                    "values(?, ?, ?, ?, ?, ?, ?)");
59:                prep2.setString(1, ticker);
60:                prep2.setString(2, fields[0]);
61:                prep2.setString(3, fields[1]);
62:                prep2.setString(4, fields[2]);
63:                prep2.setString(5, fields[3]);
64:                prep2.setString(6, fields[4]);
65:                prep2.setString(7, fields[5]);
66:                prep2.executeUpdate();
67:                prep2.close();
68:                conn.close();
69:            } catch (SQLException sqe) {
70:                System.out.println("SQL Error: " + sqe.getMessage());
71:            } catch (ClassNotFoundException cnfe) {
72:                System.out.println(cnfe.getMessage());
73:            }
74:        }
75:
76:        private String stripQuotes(String input) {
77:            StringBuilder output = new StringBuilder();
78:            for (int i = 0; i < input.length(); i++) {
79:                if (input.charAt(i) != '\"') {
```

```
80:                    output.append(input.charAt(i));
81:                }
82:            }
83:            return output.toString();
84:        }
85:
86:        public static void main(String[] arguments) {
87:            if (arguments.length < 1) {
88:                System.out.println("Usage: java QuoteData ticker");
89:                System.exit(0);
90:            }
91:            QuoteData qd = new QuoteData(arguments[0]);
92:            String data = qd.retrieveQuote();
93:            qd.storeQuote(data);
94:        }
95: }
```

Before you run the application, you must set a command-line argument. Choose Run, Set Project Configuration, Customize and then enter the main class com.java21days. QuoteData and the argument of a valid ticker symbol, such as FB (Facebook), GOOG (Google), or PSO (Pearson PLC).

The application stores the stock data but does not display any output.

To see that it worked, right-click the STOCKS table in the Services tab and choose View Data. The table records are displayed; they should include at least one day's data for the requested stock ticker symbol, as shown in Figure 18.8.

**FIGURE 18.8**
Records in the
STOCKS table.

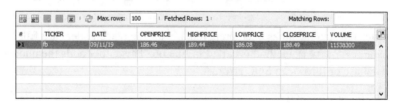

The retrieveQuote() method (lines 15–39) downloads the quote data from *Wall Street Journal* and saves it as a string. (The techniques used here were covered in Lesson 17, "Communicating Over HTTP.")

The storeQuote() method (lines 41–74) uses the SQL techniques covered in this section. The method begins by using the StringTokenizer class to split the quote data into a set of tokens, using the comma character (,) as the delimiter between tokens. The tokens are stored in a String array with nine elements. The array contains the same fields as the *Wall Street Journal* data and in the same order.

Next, a data connection to the QuoteData data source is created, using the Java DB database driver (lines 47–51).

18

This connection then is used to create a prepared statement (lines 54–58). This statement uses the `insert into` SQL statement, which causes data to be stored in a database. In this case, the database is `sample`, and the `insert into` statement refers to the APP. STOCKS table in that database. The prepared statement has six placeholders.

A series of `setString()` methods puts the elements of the `String` array into the prepared statement, in the same order in which the fields exist in the database: date, opening price, high price, low price, closing price, and volume (lines 60–65).

Because some fields in the data are dates, floating-point numbers, and integers, you might think that it would be better to use `setDate()`, `setFloat()`, and `setInt()` for that data. This application stores all the stock data as strings because that's more likely to work, regardless of the database software being used.

> **CAUTION**
>
> Some databases you could use in Java programs, including Microsoft Access, do not support some of these methods when you are using SQL to work with the database, even though they exist in Java. If you try to use an unsupported method, such as `setFloat()`, a SQLException error occurs.
>
> It's easier to send database strings and let the database program automatically convert them into the correct format. This is likely to be true when you are working with other databases; the level of SQL support varies depending on the product and driver involved.

After the statement has been prepared and all the placeholders are filled, the statement's `executeUpdate()` method is called in line 66. This either adds the quote data to the database or throws an SQL error.

The private method `stripQuotes()` is used to remove quotation marks from the *Wall Street Journal's* stock data. This method is called in line 45 to take care of three fields that contain extraneous quotes: the ticker symbol, date, and time.

## Moving Through Resultsets

The default behavior of resultsets permits one trip through the set using its `next()` method to retrieve each record.

By changing how statements and prepared statements are created, you can produce resultsets that support these additional methods:

- `afterLast()`: Moves to a place immediately after the last record in the set
- `beforeFirst()`: Moves to a place immediately before the first record in the set

- **first()**: Moves to the first record in the set
- **last()**: Moves to the last record in the set
- **previous()**: Moves to the previous record in the set

These actions are possible when the resultset's policies have been specified as arguments to a database connection's createStatement() and prepareStatement() methods.

Normally, createStatement() takes no arguments, as in this example:

```
Connection payday = DriverManager.getConnection(
    " jdbc:derby://localhost:1527/sample", "Doc", "1rover1");
Statement lookSee = payday.CreateStatement();
```

For a more flexible resultset, call createStatement() with three integer arguments that set up how it can be used. Here's a rewrite of the preceding statement:

```
Statement lookSee = payday.createStatement(
    ResultSet.TYPE_SCROLL_INSENSITIVE,
    ResultSet.CONCUR_READ_ONLY,
    ResultSet.CLOSE_CURSORS_AT_COMMIT);
```

The same three arguments can be used in the prepareStatement(*String*, *int*, *int*, *int*) method after the text of the statement.

The ResultSet class includes other class variables that offer more options for how sets can be read and modified.

**18**

# Summary

In this lesson you learned to read and write database records using classes that work with any of the popular relational databases. The techniques used to work with Java DB can be used with Microsoft Access, MySQL, and other programs. The only thing that needs to be changed is the database driver class and the strings used to create a connection.

Using Java Database Connectivity (JDBC), you can incorporate existing data-storage solutions into your Java programs.

You can connect to several different relational databases in your Java programs by using JDBC and Structured Query Language (SQL), a standard language for reading, writing, and managing a database.

# Q&A

**Q What's the difference between Java DB and more well-known databases such as Access and MySQL? Which should I use?**

**A** Java DB is intended for database applications that have simpler needs than Access and comparable databases. The entire application takes up under 4MB of space, making it easy to bundle with Java applications that require database connectivity.

Oracle employs Java DB in several parts of the Java Enterprise Edition, which demonstrates that it can deliver strong, reliable performance on important tasks.

# Quiz

Review this lesson's material by taking this three-question quiz.

## Questions

1. What does a `Statement` object represent in a database program?

    **A.** A connection to a database

    **B.** A database query written in Structured Query Language

    **C.** A data source

2. Which Java class represents SQL statements that are compiled before they are executed?

    **A.** `Statement`

    **B.** `PreparedStatement`

    **C.** `ResultSet`

3. What does the `Class.forName(String)` method accomplish?

    **A.** It provides the name of a class.

    **B.** It loads a database driver that can be used to access a database.

    **C.** It deletes an object.

## Answers

1. B. The class, part of the `java.sql` package, represents an SQL statement.

2. B. Because it is compiled, `PreparedStatement` is a better choice when you need to execute the same SQL query numerous times.

3. B. This static method loads a database driver.

# Certification Practice

The following question is the kind of thing you could expect to be asked on a Java programming certification test. Answer it without looking again at this lesson or using the Java compiler to test the code.

Given:

```java
public class ArrayClass {

    public static ArrayClass newInstance() {
        count++;
        return new ArrayClass();
    }

    public static void main(String arguments[]) {
        new ArrayClass();
    }

    int count = -1;
}
```

Which line in this program prevents it from compiling successfully?

**A.** `count++;`

**B.** `return new ArrayClass();`

**C.** `public static void main(String arguments[]) {`

**D.** `int count = -1;`

18

The answer is available on the book's website, at www.java21days.com. Visit the Lesson 18 page and click the Certification Practice link.

# Exercises

To extend your knowledge of the subjects covered in this lesson, try the following exercises:

**1.** Modify the `CustomerReporter` application to pull fields from another table in APP.

**2.** Write an application that reads and displays records from the *Wall Street Journal* stock quote database.

Where applicable, exercise solutions are offered on the book's website, at www.java21days.com.

# LESSON 19
# Reading and Writing RSS Feeds

During this lesson, you'll work with XML (Extensible Markup Language), a popular and widely implemented formatting standard that enables data to be portable.

XML is a form of text markup that will look pretty familiar to anyone who has created web pages with HTML. It enables data to be represented in a structured way in text files. Java can be used to read and write files that are formatted under the rules of XML.

In this lesson, you'll explore XML in the following ways:

- Representing data as XML
- Discovering why using XML is a useful way to store data
- Using XML to publish web content
- Reading and writing XML data

The XML format employed throughout this lesson is Really Simple Syndication (RSS), which enables you to publish web content and share information on site updates. RSS has been adopted by millions of sites.

# Using XML

One of Java's main selling points is that the language produces programs that can run on different operating systems without modification. The portability of software is a big convenience in today's computing world, where Windows, Linux, macOS, iOS, Android, Chrome OS, and other operating systems are in wide use, and many people work with multiple systems.

XML is a format for storing and organizing data that is independent of any software program that works with the data. Data that is compliant with XML is easier to reuse for several reasons.

First, the data is structured in a standard way, making it possible for software that supports XML to read and write the data. If you create an XML file that represents your company's employee database, several dozen XML parsers can read the file and make sense of its contents. This is true no matter what kind of information you collect about each employee. If your database contains only the employee's name, ID number, and salary, XML parsers can read it. If it contains 25 items, including birthday, blood type, and hair color, parsers can read that, too.

Second, the data is self-documenting, making it easier for people to understand a file's purpose by looking at it in a text editor. Anyone who opens your XML employee database should be able to figure out the structure and content of each employee record without any assistance from you. This is evident in Listing 19.1, which contains an RSS file. Because RSS is an XML dialect, it is structured under the rules of XML. Enter this code in NetBeans (category Other, type Empty File) and save it as `workbench.rss`. (You also can download a copy of it from the book's website, at www.java21days.com, on the Lesson 19 page.)

**LISTING 19.1**    The Full Text of `workbench.rss`

```
 1: <?xml version="1.0" encoding="utf-8"?>
 2: <rss version="2.0">
 3:   <channel>
 4:     <title>Workbench</title>
 5:     <link>http://workbench.cadenhead.org/</link>
 6:     <description>Programming, publishing, and popes</description>
 7:     <docs>http://www.rssboard.org/rss-specification</docs>
 8:     <item>
 9:       <title>His Majesty's Dragon by Naomi Novik</title>
10:       <link>http://workbench.cadenhead.org/news/739</link>
11:       <pubDate>Sat, 12 Oct 2019 13:12:45 -0400 </pubDate>
12:       <guid isPermaLink="false">tag:cadenhead.org,2019:w.3787</guid>
13:       <enclosure length="2498623" type="audio/mpeg"
```

```
14:                url="http://mp3.cadenhead.org/3787.mp3" />
15:       </item>
16:       <item>
17:         <title>Enter the TV Deadpool Contest </title>
18:         <link>http://workbench.cadenhead.org/news/737</link>
19:         <pubDate>Sat, 14 Sep 2019 17:17:38 -0400</pubDate>
20:         <guid isPermaLink="false">tag:cadenhead.org,2019:w.3786</guid>
21:       </item>
22:       <item>
23:         <title>I'm a ServiceNow Certified Application Developer</title>
24:         <link>http://workbench.cadenhead.org/news/736</link>
25:         <pubDate>Mon, 05 Aug 2019 19:21:25 -0400</pubDate>
26:         <guid isPermaLink="false">tag:cadenhead.org,2019:w.3785</guid>
27:       </item>
28:     </channel>
29:   </rss>
```

Can you tell what the data represents? The `?xml` tag at the top might be indecipherable, but the rest is clearly a website database of some kind.

The `?xml` tag in the first line of the file has a `version` attribute with a value of `"1.0"` and an `encoding` attribute of `"utf-8"`. This establishes that the file follows the rules of XML 1.0 and is encoded with the UTF-8 character set.

Data in XML is surrounded by tag elements that describe the data. An opening tag begins with a `<` character followed by the name of the tag and a `>` character. A closing tag begins with the `</` characters followed by a name and a `>` character. In Listing 19.1, for example, `<item>` on line 8 is an opening tag, and `</item>` on line 15 is a closing tag. Everything within those tags is considered to be the value of that element.

Elements can be nested within other elements, creating a hierarchy of XML data that establishes relationships within that data. In Listing 19.1, everything in lines 9–14 is related; each element defines something about the same website item.

Elements also can include attributes, which are made up of data that supplements the rest of the data associated with the element. Attributes are defined within an opening tag element. The name of an attribute is followed by an equal sign and text within quotation marks.

In line 12 of Listing 19.1, the `guid` element includes an `isPermaLink` attribute with the value `"false"`. This indicates that the element's value, `tag:cadenhead. org,2019:w.3787`, is not a permalink, the URL at which the item can be loaded in a browser.

XML also supports elements defined by a single tag rather than a pair of tags. The tag begins with a `<` character followed by the name of the tag and ends with the `/>` characters. The RSS file includes an `enclosure` element in lines 13–14 that describes an MP3 audio file associated with the item.

19

XML encourages the creation of data that's understandable and usable even if the user doesn't have the program that created it and cannot find any documentation that describes it.

For the most part, you can understand the purpose of the RSS file shown in Listing 19.1 simply by looking at it. Each item represents a web page that has been updated recently.

<br>

| TIP | Publishing new site content with RSS and a similar format, Atom has become one of the best ways to build readership on the Web. Thousands of people subscribe to RSS files, which are called *feeds*, using reader software such as Feedly and My Yahoo!. |
|-----|---|
|     | Rogers Cadenhead, the author of this book, is the chair of the RSS Advisory Board, the group that publishes the RSS 2.0 specification. For more information on the format, visit the board's website, at www.rssboard.org, or subscribe to its RSS feed, at www.rssboard.org/rss-feed. |
|     | There's also another version of RSS, RDF Site Summary, that's used on some sites for its feeds. Find out more at http://web.resource.org/rss/1.0. |

<br>

Data that follows XML's formatting rules is said to be *well formed*. Any software that can work with XML reads and writes well-formed XML data.

By insisting on well-formed markup, XML simplifies the task of writing programs that work with the data. RSS makes website updates available in a form that software can easily process. The RSS feed for Workbench at http://feeds.cadenhead.org/workbench has two distinct audiences: humans reading the blog through their preferred RSS reader and computers that do something with this data. Feedly, GoodReads, and many other sites can pull data from an RSS feed and present it to users.

# Designing an XML Dialect

Although XML is described as a language and is compared to Hypertext Markup Language (HTML), it's actually much larger in scope. XML is a markup language that defines how to define a markup language. That's an odd distinction to make, and it probably sounds like something you'd encounter in a philosophy textbook. This concept is important to understand because it explains how XML can be used to define data as varied as health-care claims, genealogical records, newspaper articles, and molecules.

The *X* in XML stands for *Extensible*, and it refers to organizing data for your own purposes. Data that's organized using the rules of XML can represent anything you want:

- A programmer at a telemarketing company can use XML to store data on each outgoing call, saving the time of the call, the number, the operator who made the call, and the result.

- A hobbyist can use XML to keep track of the annoying telemarketing calls she receives, noting the time of the call, the company, and the product being peddled.

- A programmer at a government agency can use XML to track complaints about telemarketers, saving the name of the marketing firm and the number of complaints.

Each of these examples uses XML to define a new language that suits a specific purpose. Although you could call them *XML languages*, they're more commonly described as *XML dialects* or *XML document types*.

An XML dialect can be designed using a Document Type Definition (DTD) that indicates the potential elements and attributes it covers.

A special !DOCTYPE declaration can be placed in XML data, right after the initial ?xml tag, to identify its DTD. Here's an example:

```
<!DOCTYPE Library SYSTEM "librml.dtd">
```

The !DOCTYPE declaration is used to identify the DTD that applies to the data. When a DTD is present, many XML tools can read XML created for that DTD and determine whether the data follows all the rules. If it doesn't, it is rejected with a reference to the line that caused the error. This process is called *validating the XML*.

19

One thing you'll run into as you work with XML is data that has been structured as XML but that wasn't defined using a DTD. Most versions of RSS files do not require a DTD. This data can be parsed (as long as it's well formed), so you can read it into a program and do something with it, but you can't check its validity to make sure that it's organized correctly according to the rules of its dialect.

**TIP**

To give you an idea of what kinds of XML dialects have been created, Cover Pages offers a list at http://xml.coverpages.org/xmlApplications.html.

# Processing XML with Java

Java supports XML through the Java API for XML Processing, a set of packages for reading, writing, and manipulating XML data.

The `javax.xml.parsers` package is the entry point to the other packages. These classes can be used to parse and validate XML data using two techniques: the Simple API for XML (SAX) and the Document Object Model (DOM). However, they can be difficult to implement, and other groups have been inspired to offer their own class libraries to work with XML. You'll spend the remainder of the lesson working with one of these alternatives: the XML Object Model (XOM) library, an open source Java class library that makes it extremely easy to read, write, and transform XML data.

# Processing XML with XOM

One of the most important skills you can develop as a Java programmer is the ability to find suitable packages and classes that can be employed in your own projects. For obvious reasons, using a well-designed class library is much easier than developing one on your own.

Although the Java Class Library contains thousands of well-designed classes that cover a comprehensive range of development needs, Oracle isn't the only supplier of classes that may prove useful to your efforts.

Other companies, groups, and individuals offer dozens of Java packages under a variety of commercial and open source licenses. Some of the most notable of them are from the Apache Software Foundation, whose Java projects include the web application framework Wicket, the Java servlet container Tomcat, and the Log4J logging class library.

Another terrific open source Java class library is the XOM library. This tree-based package for XML processing strives to be simple to learn, easy to use, and uncompromising in its adherence to well-formed XML. The XOM library was developed by the programmer and computer book author Elliotte Rusty Harold, based on his experience with XML processing in Java.

XOM originally was envisioned as a fork of JDOM, a popular tree-based model for representing an XML document. Harold contributed code to that open source project and participated in its development. But instead of forking the JDOM code, Harold decided to start from scratch and adopt some of its core design principles in XOM. The XOM library embodies the following principles:

- XML documents are modeled as a tree, with Java classes representing nodes on the tree such as elements, comments, processing instructions, and document type definitions. A programmer can add and remove nodes to manipulate the document in memory, a simple approach that can be implemented gracefully in Java.

- All XML data produced by XOM is well formed and has a well-formed namespace.

- Each element of an XML document is represented as a class with constructors.

- Object serialization is not supported. Instead, programmers are encouraged to use XML as the format for serialized data, enabling it to be readily exchanged with any software that reads XML, regardless of the programming language in which it was developed.

- The library relies on another XML parser to read XML documents and fill trees. XOM uses a SAX parser that must be downloaded and installed separately. Apache Xerces 2.6.1 and later versions should work.

XOM is available for download from www.xom.nu. The current version is 1.3.2, which includes Xerces 2.8 in its distribution.

**CAUTION**

> XOM is released under the open source GNU Lesser General Public License (LGPL), which grants permission to distribute the library without modification with Java programs that use it.
>
> You also can make changes to the XOM class library as long as you offer them under the LGPL. The full license is published online at www.xom.nu/license.xhtml.

You can download XOM as a ZIP or TAR.GZ archive. Download the library and extract the files on a folder on your computer and then follow these steps to add it to NetBeans:

1. Choose Tools, Libraries. The Ant Library Manager opens.

2. Click New Library. The New Library dialog appears.

3. Enter XOM 1.3.2 as the library name and click OK.

4. Back in the Ant Library Manager, click Add JAR/Folder.

5. Browse to the folder where you extracted the XOM archive and open it.

6. In that folder, choose the file xom-1.3.2.jar.

7. Click Add JAR/Folder.

8. In the Ant Library Manager, click OK.

19

After you have added the library to NetBeans, you need to add it to the current project so that you can use XOM classes in your programs:

1. In the Projects pane, scroll down past the `.java` files until you see a folder named Libraries.
2. Right-click this folder and choose Add Library. The Add Library dialog appears.
3. Choose XOM 1.3.2 and click OK.

An item for XOM appears under Libraries in the Projects pane.

## Creating an XML Document

The first application you'll develop in this lesson, `RssWriter`, creates an XML document that contains the start of an RSS feed. The document is shown in Listing 19.2. (You don't have to type in this listing.)

**LISTING 19.2**    The Full Text of `feed.rss`

```
1: <?xml version="1.0"?>
2: <rss version="2.0">
3:    <channel>
4:        <title>Workbench</title>
5:        <link>http://workbench.cadenhead.org/</link>
6:    </channel>
7: </rss>
```

The base `nu.xom` package contains classes for a complete XML document (`Document`) and the nodes a document can contain (`Attribute`, `Comment`, `DocType`, `Element`, `ProcessingInstruction`, and `Text`). The `RssStarter` application uses several of these classes. First, an `Element` object is created by specifying the element's name as an argument:

```
Element rss = new Element("rss");
```

This statement creates an object for the root element of the document, `rss`. `Element`'s one-argument constructor can be used because the document does not employ a feature of XML called namespaces; if it did, a second argument would be necessary: the element's namespace uniform resource identifier (URI). The other classes in the XOM library support namespaces in a similar manner.

In the XML document in line 2 of Listing 19.2, the `rss` element includes an attribute named `version` with the value `"2.0"`. You create an attribute by specifying its name and value in consecutive arguments:

```
Attribute version = new Attribute("version", "2.0");
```

You add attributes to an element by calling its `addAttribute()` method with the attribute as the only argument:

```
rss.addAttribute(version);
```

The text contained within an element is represented by the `Text` class, which is constructed by specifying the text as a `String` argument:

```
Text titleText = new Text("Workbench");
```

When an XML document is composed, all its elements end up inside a root element that is used to create a `Document` object; a `Document` constructor is called with the root element as an argument. In the `RssStarter` application, this element is called `rss`. Any `Element` object can be the root of a document:

```
Document doc = new Document(rss);
```

In XOM's tree structure, the classes representing an XML document and its constituent parts are organized into a hierarchy below the generic superclass `nu.xom.Node`. This class has three subclasses in the same package: `Attribute`, `LeafNode`, and `ParentNode`.

To add a child to a parent node, call the parent's `appendChild()` method with the node to add as the only argument. The following code creates two elements—a parent called `channel` and one child element, `link`:

```
Element channel = new Element("channel");
Element link = new Element("link");
Text linkText = new Text("http://workbench.cadenhead.org/");
link.appendChild(linkText);
channel.appendChild(link);
```

The `appendChild()` method appends a new child below all other children of that parent. The preceding statements produce this XML fragment:

```
<channel>
    <link>http://workbench.cadenhead.org/</link>
</channel>
```

19

The `appendChild()` method also can be called with a `String` argument instead of a node. A `Text` object representing the string is created and added to the element:

```
link.appendChild("http://workbench.cadenhead.org/");
```

After a tree has been created and filled with nodes, it can be displayed by calling the `Document` method `toXML()`, which returns the complete and well-formed XML document as a `String`.

Listing 19.3 shows the complete application. Create the `RssStarter` class in the `com.java21days` package in NetBeans with this listing as the source.

**LISTING 19.3**    The Full Text of `RssStarter.java`

```
 1: package com.java21days;
 2:
 3: import java.io.*;
 4: import nu.xom.*;
 5:
 6: public class RssStarter {
 7:     public static void main(String[] arguments) {
 8:         // create an <rss> element to serve as the document's root
 9:         Element rss = new Element("rss");
10:
11:         // add a version attribute to the element
12:         Attribute version = new Attribute("version", "2.0");
13:         rss.addAttribute(version);
14:         // create a <channel> element and make it a child of <rss>
15:         Element channel = new Element("channel");
16:         rss.appendChild(channel);
17:         // create the channel's <title>
18:         Element title = new Element("title");
19:         Text titleText = new Text("Workbench");
20:         title.appendChild(titleText);
21:         channel.appendChild(title);
22:         // create the channel's <link>
23:         Element link = new Element("link");
24:         Text lText = new Text("http://workbench.cadenhead.org/");
25:         link.appendChild(lText);
26:         channel.appendChild(link);
27:
28:         // create a new document with <rss> as the root element
29:         Document doc = new Document(rss);
30:
31:         // Save the XML document
32:         try (
33:             FileWriter fw = new FileWriter("feed.rss");
34:             BufferedWriter out = new BufferedWriter(fw);
35:         ) {
```

```
36:                  out.write(doc.toXML());
37:              } catch (IOException ioe) {
38:                  System.out.println(ioe.getMessage());
39:              }
40:              System.out.println(doc.toXML());
41:          }
42:  }
```

The `RssStarter` application displays the XML document it creates on standard output and saves it to a file called `feed.rss`. The output is shown in Figure 19.1.

**FIGURE 19.1**
Creating an XML document with XOM.

XOM automatically precedes a document with an XML declaration.

As you can see in Figure 19.1, the XML produced by this application contains no indentation; elements are stacked on the same line.

> **CAUTION**
>
> XOM preserves significant whitespace only when representing XML data. The spaces between elements in the RSS feed contained in Listing 19.2 are strictly for presentation purposes and are not produced automatically when XOM creates an XML document. A subsequent example demonstrates how to control indentation.

**19**

## Modifying an XML Document

The next project, the `DomainEditor` application, makes several changes to the XML document `feed.rss` that was just produced by the `RssStarter` application. The text enclosed by the `link` element is changed, and a new `item` element is added:

```
<item>
  <title>Free the Bound Periodicals</title>
</item>
```

Using the `nu.xom` package, XML documents can be loaded into a tree from several sources: `File`, `InputStream`, or `Reader` objects or a URL (which is specified as a `String` instead of a `java.net.URL` object).

The `Builder` class represents a SAX parser that can load an XML document into a `Document` object. Constructors can be used to specify a particular parser or to let XOM use the first available parser from this list: Xerces 2, Crimson, Piccolo, GNU Aelfred, Oracle, XP, Saxon Aelfred, or Dom4J Aelfred. If none of these is found, the parser specified by the system property `org.xml.sax.driver` is used. Constructors also determine whether the parser is validating or nonvalidating.

The `Builder()` and `Builder(true)` constructors both use the default parser—most likely a version of Xerces. The presence of the Boolean argument `true` in the second constructor configures the parser to be validating. It would be nonvalidating otherwise. A validating parser throws a `nu.xom.ValidityException` if the XML document doesn't validate according to the rules of its document type definition.

The `Builder` object's `build()` method loads an XML document from a source and returns a `Document` object:

```
Builder builder = new Builder();
File xmlFile = new File("feed.rss");
Document doc = builder.build(xmlFile);
```

These statements load an XML document from the file `feed.rss`, barring one of two problems: A `nu.xom.ParseException` is thrown if the file does not contain well-formed XML, and a `java.io.IOException` is thrown if the input operation fails.

Retrieve elements from the tree by calling a method of their parent node. A `Document` object's `getRootElement()` method returns the document's root element:

```
Element root = doc.getRootElement();
```

In the XML document `feed.rss`, the root element is `domains`.

Elements with names can be retrieved by calling their parent node's `getFirstChildElement()` method with the name as a `String` argument:

```
Element channel = root.getFirstChildElement("channel");
```

This statement retrieves the `channel` element contained in the `rss` element (or `null` if that element could not be found). Like other examples, this is simplified by the lack of a namespace in the document; there also are methods where a name and namespace are arguments.

When several elements within a parent have the same name, the parent node's `getChildElements()` method can be used instead:

```
Elements children = channel.getChildElements();
```

The `getChildElements()` method returns an `Elements` object containing each of the elements. This object is a read-only list and does not change automatically if the parent node's contents change after `getChildElements()` is called.

`Elements` has a `size()` method that contains an integer count of the elements it holds. This can be used in a loop to cycle through each element in turn, beginning with the one at position 0. There's a `get()` method to retrieve each element; call it with the integer position of the element to be retrieved:

```
for (int i = 0; i < children.size(); i++) {
    Element link = children.get(i);
}
```

This `for` loop cycles through each `child` element of the `channel` element.

Elements without names can be retrieved by calling their parent node's `getChild()` method with one argument: an integer indicating the element's position within the parent node:

```
Text linkText = (Text) link.getChild(0);
```

This statement creates the `Text` object for the text `"http://workbench.cadenhead.org/"` found within the `link` element. `Text` elements always are at position 0 within their enclosing parent.

To work with this text as a string, call the `Text` object's `getValue()` method, as in this statement:

```
if (linkText.getValue().equals("http://workbench.cadenhead.org/"))
    // ...
}
```

The `DomainEditor` application only modifies a `link` element enclosing the text `"http://workbench.cadenhead.org/"`. The application makes the following changes: The text of the `link` element is deleted, the new text `"http://www.cadenhead.org/"` is added in its place, and then a new `item` element is added.

19

A parent node has two `removeChild()` methods to delete a child node from the document. Calling the method with an integer deletes the child at that position:

```
Element channel = domain.getFirstChildElement("channel");
Element link = dns.getFirstChildElement("link");
link.removeChild(0);
```

These statements would delete the `Text` object contained within the channel's first `link` element.

Calling the `removeChild()` method with a node as an argument deletes that particular node. Extending the previous example, the `link` element could be deleted with this statement:

```
channel.removeChild(link);
```

Listing 19.4 shows the source code of the `DomainEditor` application. Create this class in NetBeans in the `com.java21days` package.

**LISTING 19.4**    The Full Text of `DomainEditor.java`

```
 1: package com.java21days;
 2:
 3: import java.io.*;
 4: import nu.xom.*;
 5:
 6: public class DomainEditor {
 7:     public static void main(String[] args) throws IOException {
 8:         try {
 9:             // create a tree from the XML document feed.rss
10:             Builder builder = new Builder();
11:             File xmlFile = new File("feed.rss");
12:             Document doc = builder.build(xmlFile);
13:
14:             // get the root element <rss>
15:             Element root = doc.getRootElement();
16:
17:             // get its <channel> element
18:             Element channel = root.getFirstChildElement("channel");
19:
20:             // get its <link> elements
21:             Elements children = channel.getChildElements();
22:             for (int i = 0; i < children.size(); i++) {
23:
24:                 // get a <link> element
25:                 Element link = children.get(i);
26:
27:                 // get its text
28:                 Text linkText = (Text) link.getChild(0);
29:
```

```
30:                    // update any link matching a URL
31:                    if (linkText.getValue().equals(
32:                        "http://workbench.cadenhead.org/")) {
33:
34:                        // update the link's text
35:                        link.removeChild(0);
36:                        link.appendChild("http://www.cadenhead.org/");
37:                    }
38:                }
39:
40:            // create new elements and attributes to add
41:            Element item = new Element("item");
42:            Element itemTitle = new Element("title");
43:
44:            // add them to the <channel> element
45:            itemTitle.appendChild(
46:                "Free the Bound Periodicals"
47:            );
48:            item.appendChild(itemTitle);
49:            channel.appendChild(item);
50:
51:            // Save the XML document
52:            try (
53:                FileWriter fw = new FileWriter("feed2.rss");
54:                BufferedWriter out = new BufferedWriter(fw);
55:            ) {
56:                out.write(doc.toXML());
57:            } catch (IOException ioe) {
58:                System.out.println(ioe.getMessage());
59:            }
60:            System.out.println(doc.toXML());
61:        } catch (ParsingException pe) {
62:            System.out.println("Parse error: " + pe.getMessage());
63:            System.exit(-1);
64:        }
65:    }
66: }
```

The DomainEditor application displays the modified XML document to standard output and saves it to a file named feeds2.rss. You can see the program's output in Figure 19.2.

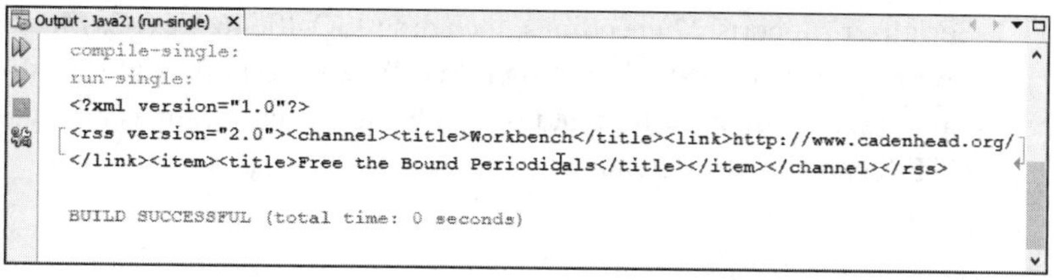

**FIGURE 19.2**
Loading and modifying an XML document.

## Formatting an XML Document

As described earlier, XOM does not retain insignificant whitespace when representing XML documents. This is in keeping with one of XOM's design goals: to disregard anything that has no syntactic significance in XML. (Another example of this is how text is treated identically whether it is created using character entities, CDATA sections, or regular characters.)

The next project is the DomainWriter application. This program adds a comment to the beginning of the XML document feed2.rss and serializes it with indented lines, producing the version shown in Listing 19.5.

**LISTING 19.5** The Full Text of feed2.rss

```
 1: <?xml version="1.0" encoding="ISO-8859-1"?>
 2: <!--File created Sat Oct 12 19:22:00 EDT 2019-->
 3: <rss version="2.0">
 4:    <channel>
 5:      <title>Workbench</title>
 6:      <link>http://www.cadenhead.org/</link>
 7:      <item>
 8:        <title>Free the Bound Periodicals</title>
 9:      </item>
10:    </channel>
11: </rss>
```

The Serializer class in nu.xom offers control over how an XML document is formatted when it is displayed or stored serially. Indentation, character encoding, line breaks, and other formatting are established by objects of this class.

You can create a Serializer object by specifying an output stream and character encoding as arguments to the constructor:

```
FileOutputStream fos = new FileOutputStream("feed3.rss");
Serializer output = new Serializer(fos, "ISO-8859-1");
```

These statements serialize a file using the ISO-8859-1 character encoding.

Serializer supports 22 encodings, including ISO-10646-UCS-2, ISO-8859-1 through ISO-8859-10, ISO-8859-13 through ISO-8859-16, UTF-8, and UTF-16. There's also a Serializer() constructor that takes only an output stream as an argument; this uses the UTF-8 encoding by default.

You set indentation by calling the serializer's `setIndentation()` method with an integer argument specifying the number of spaces:

```
output.setIndentation(2);
```

You can write an entire XML document to the serializer destination by calling the serializer's `write()` method with the document as an argument:

```
output.write(doc);
```

The `DomainWriter` application inserts a comment atop the XML document instead of appending it at the end of a parent node's children. This requires another method of the parent node, `insertChild()`, which is called with two arguments—the element to add and the integer position of the insertion:

```
Builder builder = new Builder();
Document doc = builder.build(arguments[0]);
Comment timestamp = new Comment("File created " +
    new java.util.Date());
doc.insertChild(timestamp, 0);
```

The comment is placed at position 0 atop the document, moving the `domains` tag down one line but remaining below the XML declaration.

Listing 19.6 is the application's source code.

**LISTING 19.6**  The Full Text of `DomainWriter.java`

```
 1: package com.java21days;
 2:
 3: import java.io.*;
 4: import nu.xom.*;
 5:
 6: public class DomainWriter {
 7:     public static void main(String[] args) throws IOException {
 8:         try {
 9:             // Create a tree from an XML document
10:             // specified as a command-line argument
11:             Builder builder = new Builder();
12:             File xmlFile = new File("feed2.rss");
13:             Document doc = builder.build(xmlFile);
14:
15:             // Create a comment with the current time and date
16:             Comment timestamp = new Comment("File created "
17:                 + new java.util.Date());
18:
19:             // Add the comment above everything else in the
```

19

```
20:                    // document
21:                    doc.insertChild(timestamp, 0);
22:
23:                    // Create a file output stream to a new file
24:                    FileOutputStream f = new FileOutputStream("feed3.rss");
25:
26:                    // Using a serializer with indention set to 2 spaces,
27:                    // write the XML document to the file
28:                    Serializer output = new Serializer(f, "ISO-8859-1");
29:                    output.setIndent(2);
30:                    output.write(doc);
31:            } catch (ParsingException pe) {
32:                    System.out.println("Parsing error: " + pe.getMessage());
33:                    System.exit(-1);
34:            }
35:      }
36: }
```

The `DomainWriter` application reads the file `feed2.rss` as input and creates a new modified version called `feed3.rss`.

## Evaluating XOM

The applications you've created so far in this lesson cover the core features of the main XOM package and are representative of its straightforward approach to XML processing.

There also are smaller `nu.xom.canonical`, `nu.xom.converters`, `nu.xom.xinclude`, and `nu.xom.xslt` packages to support XInclude, Extensible Stylesheet Language Transformations (XSLT), canonical XML serialization, and conversions between the XOM model for XML and the one used by DOM and SAX.

Listing 19.7 is an application that works with XML from a dynamic source: RSS feeds of recently updated web content from the feed's producer. The `RssFilter` application searches the feed for specified text in headlines and produces a new XML document that contains only the matching items and shorter indentation. It also modifies the feed's title and adds an RSS 0.91 document type declaration if one is needed in an RSS 0.91 format feed.

Create the `RssFilter` application in the `com.java21days` package in NetBeans.

**LISTING 19.7**    The Full Text of `RssFilter.java`

```
1: package com.java21days;
2:
3: import nu.xom.*;
4:
5: public class RssFilter {
```

```
 6:     public static void main(String[] arguments) {
 7:
 8:         if (arguments.length < 2) {
 9:             System.out.println("Usage: java RssFilter file term");
10:             System.exit(-1);
11:         }
12:
13:         // Save the RSS location and search term
14:         String rssFile = arguments[0];
15:         String term = arguments[1];
16:
17:         try {
18:             // Fill a tree with an RSS file's XML data
19:             // The file can be local or something on the
20:             // Web accessible via a URL.
21:             Builder bob = new Builder();
22:             Document doc = bob.build(rssFile);
23:
24:             // Get the file's root element (<rss>)
25:             Element rss = doc.getRootElement();
26:
27:             // Get the element's version attribute
28:             Attribute rssVersion = rss.getAttribute("version");
29:             String version = rssVersion.getValue();
30:
31:             // Add the DTD for RSS 0.91 feeds, if needed
32:             if ( (version.equals("0.91")) &
33:                 (doc.getDocType() == null) ) {
34:
35:                 DocType rssDtd = new DocType("rss",
36:                     "http://my.netscape.com/publish/formats/rss-0.91.
                         dtd");
37:                 doc.insertChild(rssDtd, 0);
38:             }
39:
40:             // Get the first (and only) <channel> element
41:             Element channel = rss.getFirstChildElement("channel");
42:
43:             // Get its <title> element
44:             Element title = channel.getFirstChildElement("title");
45:             Text titleText = (Text) title.getChild(0);
46:
47:             // Change the title to reflect the search term
48:             titleText.setValue(titleText.getValue() +
49:                 ": Search for " + term + " articles");
50:
51:             // Get all of the <item> elements and loop through them
52:             Elements items = channel.getChildElements("item");
53:             for (int i = 0; i < items.size(); i++) {
54:                 // Get an <item> element
55:                 Element item = items.get(i);
```

19

```
56:
57:                    // Look for a <title> element inside it
58:                    Element iTitle = item.getFirstChildElement("title");
59:
60:                    // If found, look for its contents
61:                    if (iTitle != null) {
62:                        Text iTitleText = (Text) iTitle.getChild(0);
63:
64:                        // If the search text is not found in the item,
65:                        // delete it from the tree
66:                        if (!iTitleText.toString().contains(term)) {
67:                            channel.removeChild(item);
68:                        }
69:                    }
70:                }
71:
72:                // Display the results with a serializer
73:                Serializer output = new Serializer(System.out);
74:                output.setIndent(2);
75:                output.write(doc);
76:            } catch (Exception exc) {
77:                System.out.println("Error: " + exc.getMessage());
78:            }
79:        }
80: }
```

Run the application after setting the command-line arguments by selecting Run, Set Project Configuration, Customize. The first argument is the feed to check, and the second is the word to search for in its titles. One feed that can be used to test the application is https://news.ycombinator.com/rss from the Hacker News weblog. Check it for a word such as Microsoft, JavaScript, or Linux.

Partial output from using `RssFilter` to look for `framework` in this RSS feed is displayed in Figure 19.3.

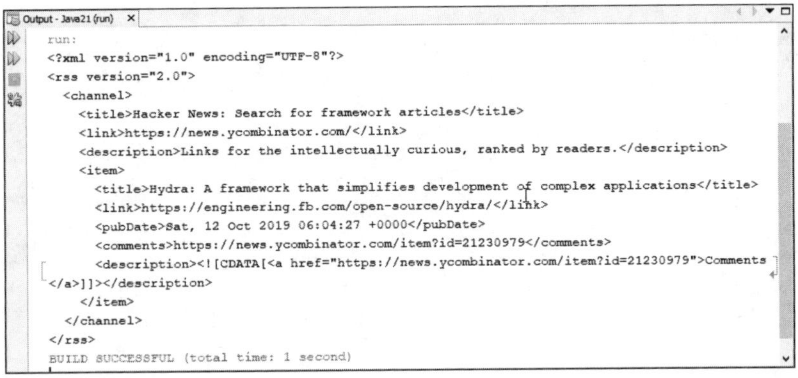

**FIGURE 19.3**
Reading XML data from a website's RSS feed.

Comments in the application's source code describe its functionality.

XOM's design is strongly informed by one overriding principle: enforced simplicity. On the website for the class library, Elliotte Rusty Harold states that XOM "should help inexperienced developers do the right thing and keep them from doing the wrong thing. The learning curve needs to be really shallow, and that includes not relying on best practices that are known in the community but are not obvious at first glance."

The XOM class library is useful for Java programmers whose programs require a steady diet of XML.

# Summary

In this lesson you have learned the basics of another popular format for data representation, XML (Extensible Markup Language), by exploring one of the most popular uses of XML: RSS feeds.

In some ways, XML is the data equivalent of the Java language. It liberates data from the software used to create it and the operating system the software runs on, just as Java can liberate software from a particular operating system.

By using a class library such as the open source XML Object Model (XOM) library, you can easily create and retrieve data from an XML file.

A big advantage of representing data using XML is that you can always get that data back. If you decide to move the data into a relational database or some other form, you can easily retrieve the information. The data being produced as RSS feeds can be mined by software in countless ways, today and in the future.

19

You also can transform XML into other forms, such as HTML, through a variety of technology, both in Java and through tools developed in other languages.

# Q&A

**Q What's the difference between RSS 1.0, RSS 2.0, and Atom?**

**A** RSS 1.0 is a syndication format that employs the Resource Description Framework (RDF) to describe items in the feed. RSS 2.0 shares a common origin with RSS 1.0 but does not make use of RDF. Atom is another syndication format that was created after RSS 1.0 and RSS 2.0. The Internet Engineering Task Force (IETF) has adopted Atom as an Internet standard.

All three formats are suitable for offering web content in XML that can be read with a reader such as Feedly or My Yahoo! or that can be read by software and stored, manipulated, or transformed.

**Q Why is Extensible Markup Language called XML instead of EML?**

**A** None of the founders of the language appears to have documented the reason for choosing XML as the acronym. The general consensus in the XML community is that it was chosen because it "sounds cooler" than EML. Before you snicker at that explanation, the creator of the language you are learning chose the name Java for its programming language using the same criteria, turning down more technical-sounding alternatives such as DNA and WRL. (The name Ruby also was considered and rejected but later was chosen for another language.)

It's possible that the founders of XML were trying to avoid confusion with a programming language called EML (Extended Machine Language), which predates XML.

# Quiz

Review this lesson's material by taking this three-question quiz.

## Questions

1. What does RSS stand for?

    **A.** Really Simple Syndication

    **B.** RDF Site Summary

    **C.** Both

2. What method *cannot* be used to add text to an XML element using XOM?

    **A.** `addAttribute(String, String)`

    **B.** `appendChild(Text)`

    **C.** `appendChild(String)`

3. When all the opening element tags, closing element tags, and other markup are applied consistently in a document, what adjective describes the document?

    **A.** Validating

    **B.** Parsable

    **C.** Well formed

## Answers

1. C. One version, RSS 2.0, claims Really Simple Syndication as its name. The other, RSS 1.0, claims RDF Site Summary.

2. A. Answers B and C both work. One adds the contents of a `Text` element as the element's character data, and the other adds the string.

3. C. For data to be considered XML, it must be well formed.

# Certification Practice

The following question is the kind of thing you could expect to be asked on a Java programming certification test. Answer it without looking again at this lesson or using the Java compiler to test the code.

Given:

```java
public class NameDirectory {
    String[] names;
    int nameCount;

    public NameDirectory() {
        names = new String[20];
        nameCount = 0;
    }

    public void addName(String newName) {
        if (nameCount < 20) {
            // answer goes here
        }
    }
}
```

19

The `NameDirectory` class must be able to hold 20 different names. What statement should replace `// answer goes here` for the class to function correctly?

**A.** `names[nameCount] = newName;`

**B.** `names[nameCount] == newName;`

**C.** `names[nameCount++] = newName;`

**D.** `names[++nameCount] = newName;`

The answer is available on the book's website, at www.java21days.com. Visit the Lesson 19 page and click the Certification Practice link.

# Exercises

To extend your knowledge of the subjects covered in this lesson, try the following exercises:

1. Create a simple XML format to represent a book collection with 10 books and a Java application that searches for books with Naomi Novik as the author, displaying any that it finds.

2. Create two applications: one that retrieves records from a database and produces an XML file that contains the same information, and a second application that reads data from that XML file and displays it.

Where applicable, exercise solutions are offered on the book's website, at www.java21days.com.

# LESSON 20
# Making Web Service Requests

Over the years, much effort has been put into creating a protocol for remote procedure calls (RPCs), which enable one computer program to call a procedure in another program over the Internet or another network. Often, these protocols are language agnostic. A client program written in a language such as C++ can call a remote database server written in Java or something else without either side knowing (or caring) about its partner's implementation language.

Web services—networking programs that use the Web to offer data in a form easily digested by other software—are used to share account authentication between sites, facilitate e-commerce transactions between stores, provide business-to-business information exchange, and provide other innovative offerings.

A simple, useful example of this idea is XML-RPC, a protocol for using Hypertext Transfer Protocol (HTTP) and Extensible Markup Language (XML) for remote procedure calls. In this lesson, you'll learn how to implement it in Java, as the following topics are covered:

- How to communicate with another computer using XML-RPC
- How to structure an XML-RPC request and an XML-RPC response
- How to use XML-RPC in Java programs
- How to send an XML-RPC request
- How to receive an XML-RPC response

# Introduction to XML-RPC

Java supports one well-established technique for remote procedure calling: remote method invocation (RMI). RMI is designed to be a complex, robust solution to a large variety of remote computing tasks. This sophistication has been one of the hindrances to the adoption of RPC. The complexity required to implement some of these solutions can be more than a programmer wants to take on simply to exchange information over a network.

A much simpler alternative, XML-RPC, has been adopted for web services.

Client/server implementations of XML-RPC are available for most platforms and programming languages that are in widespread use.

XML-RPC exchanges information using a combination of HTTP, the protocol of the Web, and XML.

XML-RPC supports the following data types:

- **array:** A data structure that holds multiple elements of any of the other data types, including arrays
- **base64:** Binary data in base-64 format
- **boolean:** True/false values that are either 1 (true) or 0 (false)
- **dateTime.iso8601:** A string containing the date and time in ISO 8601 format, such as `20190927T12:01:15` for 12:01 a.m. (and 15 seconds) on September 27, 2019.
- **double:** 8-byte signed floating-point numbers
- **int (also called i4):** Signed integers ranging in value from –2,147,483,648 to 2,147,483,647, the same size as `int` values in Java
- **string:** Text
- **struct:** Name/value pairs of associated data where the name is a string, and the value can be any of the other data types (comparable to the `HashMap` class in Java)

One thing that is noticeably absent from XML-RPC is a way to represent data as an object. The protocol wasn't designed with object-oriented programming in mind, but you can represent reasonably complex objects with the `array` and `struct` types.

By design, XML-RPC is a simple protocol for programming across a network. The protocol has been implemented on web services running on Windows, Mac, and Linux systems.

> **NOTE**
>
> The full XML-RPC specification is available on XML-RPC.com at http://xmlrpc.info.

After the release of XML-RPC, the specification was extended to create another RPC protocol called Simple Object Access Protocol (SOAP).

SOAP shares design goals of XML-RPC and has been expanded to better support objects, user-defined data types, and other advanced features, resulting in a significantly more complex protocol. SOAP also has become widely popular for web services and other decentralized network programming.

> **NOTE**
>
> Because SOAP is an extension of XML-RPC, it raises the question of why the earlier protocol is still in use. When SOAP came out and was considerably more complex than XML-RPC, some programmers chose to stick with the simpler protocol.
>
> To find out more about SOAP and public servers that can be used with SOAP clients, visit the website www.w3.org/TR/soap.

# Communicating with XML-RPC

XML-RPC is a protocol transmitted via HTTP, the standard for data exchange between web servers and web browsers. The information it transmits is not web pages. Instead, it is XML data encoded in a specific way.

Two kinds of data exchanges are conducted using XML-RPC: client requests and server responses.

20

## Sending a Request

An XML-RPC request is XML data sent to a web server as part of an HTTP post request.

A post request normally is used to transmit data from a web browser to a web server. Java servlets, CGI programs, and other software collect the data from a post request and send back HTML in response. When you submit an email from a web page or vote in an online poll, you're using either post or a similar HTTP request called get.

XML-RPC simply uses HTTP as a convenient protocol for communicating with a server and receiving a response. The request consists of two parts: the HTTP headers required by the `post` transmission and the XML-RPC request, which is expressed as XML.

Listing 20.1 is an example of an XML-RPC request.

**LISTING 20.1**   An XML-RPC Request

```
 1: POST / HTTP/1.0
 2: Host: ping.blo.gs
 3: Connection: Close
 4: Content-Type: text/xml
 5: Content-Length: 151
 6: User-Agent: OSE/XML-RPC
 7:
 8: <?xml version="1.0"?>
 9: <methodCall>
10:     <methodName>weblogUpdates.ping</methodName>
11:     <params>
12:        <param>
13:           <value>
14:              <string>Cadenhead.org</string>
15:           </value>
16:        </param>
17:        <param>
18:           <value>
19:              <string>http://cadenhead.org/</string>
20:           </value>
21:        <param>
22:     </params>
23: </methodCall>
```

In Listing 20.1, lines 1–6 are the HTTP headers, and lines 8–23 are the XML-RPC request. This listing tells you the following:

- The XML-RPC server is at http://ping.blo.gs/ (lines 1 and 2).
- The remote method being called is `weblogUpdates.ping` (line 10).
- The method is being called with two arguments, a string with the value `Cadenhead.org` (line 14) and another string with the value `http://cadenhead.org/` (line 19).

Unlike their counterparts in Java, method names in an XML-RPC request do not include parentheses. A method name in an XML-RPC request consists of the name of an object followed by a period and the name of the method, or simply the name of the method, depending on the XML-RPC server.

CAUTION    XML-RPC, which has been implemented in numerous computer programming languages, has differences in terminology from Java. In XML-RPC, *methods* are called *procedures*, and *method arguments* are called *parameters*. The Java terms are used often during this lesson when Java programming techniques are discussed.

# Responding to a Request

An XML-RPC response is XML data that is sent back from a web server like any other HTTP response. Again, XML-RPC piggybacks on an established process—a web server sending data via HTTP to a web browser—and uses it in a new way.

The response also consists of HTTP headers and an XML-RPC response in XML format.

Listing 20.2 is an example of an XML-RPC response.

**LISTING 20.2**   An XML-RPC Response

```
 1: HTTP/1.0 200 OK
 2: Date: Sun, 15 Sep 2019 22:20:13 GMT
 3: Server: nginx
 4: Content-Type: text/xml
 5:
 6: <?xml version="1.0"?>
 7: <methodResponse>
 8:   <params>
 9:     <param>
10:       <value>
11:         <struct>
12:           <member>
13:               <name>flerror</name>
14:               <value>
15:                   <boolean>0</boolean>
16:               </value>
17:           </member>
18:           <member>
19:               <name>message</name>
20:               <value>
21:                   <string>Succeeded.</string>
22:               </value>
23:           </member>
24:         </struct>
25:       </value>
```

20

```
26:     </param>
27:   </params>
28: </methodResponse>
```

In Listing 20.2, lines 1–4 are the HTTP headers, and lines 6–28 are the XML-RPC response. You can learn the following things from this listing:

- The response is in XML format (line 4).
- The value returned by the remote method is a `struct` that defines a field named `flerror` with a Boolean value of `0` (`false`) and a field named `message` with the string value `Succeeded`. (lines 11–24).

An XML-RPC response contains only one argument, contrary to what you might expect from the `params` tag in line 8. If the remote method does not return a value—for example, it might be a Java method that returns `void`—an XML-RPC server still returns something.

This return value can be primitive data, strings, arrays of varying dimensions, and more sophisticated data structures, such as key/value pairs (the kind of thing you could implement in Java by using `HashMap`).

**NOTE**

> The XML-RPC request and response examples were generated by a server run by WordPress developer Automattic Inc. at the site Blo.gs. You can find out more about the XML-RPC server at http://blo.gs/ping-example.php.
>
> Several XML-RPC debuggers on the Web can be used to call remote methods, which makes it much easier to determine whether a client or server is working correctly. One is available at https://xmlrpc.devzing.com.

# Choosing an XML-RPC Implementation

Although you can work with XML-RPC by creating your own classes to read and write XML and exchange data over the Internet, an easier route is to use a preexisting Java Class Library that supports XML-RPC.

One of the most popular is Apache XML-RPC, an open source project managed by the developers of the Apache web server, Tomcat Java servlet engine, and other popular open source software.

The Apache XML-RPC project, which consists of the `org.apache.xmlrpc` package and three related packages, contains classes that can be used to implement an XML-RPC client and server with a small amount of your own code.

The project has a home page at http://xml.apache.org/xmlrpc (or, alternatively, http://archive.apache.org/dist/ws/xmlrpc). This lesson's projects employ release 3.1.3. To use this project, you must download and install it.

Apache XML-RPC can be downloaded as either a `.zip` archive or `tar.gz` archive.

**CAUTION**
> If you have trouble downloading Apache XML-RPC from the Apache website, you can get it from the book's website. Visit www.java21days.com, go to the page for Lesson 20, and click the Apache XML-RPC Library Version 3.1.3 link. This is a `.zip` archive containing all the project's files. The software is open source and can be shared under the Apache license.

Download the library and extract the files on a folder on your computer. When that's done, follow these steps to add Apache XML-RPC to NetBeans:

1. Choose Tools, Libraries. The Ant Library Manager opens.
2. Click New Library. The New Library dialog appears.
3. Enter `Apache XML-RPC 3.1.3` as the library name and click OK.
4. In the Library Manager, click Add JAR/Folder.
5. Browse to the folder where you extracted the archive and open it.
6. Open the lib subfolder and choose all five JAR files it contains: `commons-logging-1.1.jar`, `ws-commons-util-1.0.2.jar`, `xmlrpc-client-3.1.3.jar`, `xmlrpc-common-3.1.3.jar`, and `xmlrpc-server-3.1.3.jar`. (To select multiple files, hold down the Shift key and click each file.)
7. Click Add JAR/Folder.
8. In the Library Manager, click OK.

After you have added the library to NetBeans, you need to add it to the current project so that you can use the Apache XML-RPC classes:

1. In the Projects pane, look for the folder named Libraries below the `.java` files for the classes you have created.

20

**2.** Right-click the Libraries folder and choose Add Library. The Add Library dialog appears.

**3.** Choose Apache XML-RPC 3.1.3 and click OK.

The five JAR files composing this class library appear under Libraries in the pane.

After the library is set up, an `import` statement makes it easy to refer to the classes in a package, as in this example:

```
import org.apache.xmlrpc.*;
```

This makes it possible to refer to the classes in the main package, `org.apache.xmlrpc`, without using the full package name. You'll work with this package in the next two sections.

# Using an XML-RPC Web Service

An XML-RPC client is a program that connects to a server, calls a method on a program on that server, and stores the result.

Using Apache XML-RPC, the process is comparable to calling any other method in Java. You don't have to create an XML request, parse an XML response, or connect to the server using one of Java's networking classes.

In the `org.apache.xmlrpc.client` package, the `XmlRpcClient` class represents a client. The client is set up with the `XmlRpcClientConfigImpl` class, which holds the configuration settings for the client.

The server is set by calling the configuration object's `setServerURL (URL)` method with a `URL` object that contains the server's address and port number.

When the configuration is complete, the client's `setConfig()` method is called with that configuration as the only argument.

The following statements create a client to an XML-RPC client on the host `cadenhead.org` at port 4413:

```
XmlRpcClientConfigImpl config = new XmlRpcClientConfigImpl();
URL server = new URL("http://cadenhead.org:4413/");
config.setServerURL(server);
XmlRpcClient client = new XmlRpcClient();
client.setConfig(config);
```

If you are calling a remote method with any arguments, they should be stored in an `ArrayList` object, a data structure that holds objects of different classes.

> **NOTE** Array lists are covered in Lesson 8, "Data Structures." They are part of the `java.util` package.

To work with array lists, call the `ArrayList()` constructor with no arguments and call its `add(Object)` method with each object that should be added to the list. Objects can be of any class and must be added to the list in the order in which they are called in the remote method.

The following data types can be arguments to a remote method:

- `byte[]` arrays for `base64` data
- `Boolean` objects for `boolean` values
- `Date` objects for `dateTime.iso8601` values
- `Double` objects for `double` values
- `Integer` objects for `int` values
- `String` objects for `string` values
- `HashMap` objects for `struct` values
- `ArrayList` objects for arrays

The `Date`, `HashMap`, and `ArrayList` classes are in the `java.util` package.

For example, if an XML-RPC server has a method that takes `String` and `Double` arguments, the following code creates an array list that holds each argument:

```
String code = "conical";
Double xValue = 175;
ArrayList parameters = new ArrayList();
parameters.add(code);
parameters.add(xValue);
```

To call the remote method on the XML-RPC server, call the `XmlRpcClient` object's `execute()` method with two arguments:

- The name of the method
- The array list that holds the method's arguments

The name of the method should be specified without any parentheses or arguments. An XML-RPC server usually documents the methods that it makes available to the public.

20

The `execute()` method returns an object that contains the response. This object should be cast to one of the data types sent to a method as arguments: `Boolean`, `byte[]`, `Date`, `Double`, `Integer`, `String`, `HashMap`, or `ArrayList`.

Like other networking methods in Java, `execute()` throws an `XmlRpcException` if the server reports an XML-RPC error.

Objects returned by the `execute()` method have the following data types: `Boolean` for boolean XML-RPC values, `byte[]` for `base64` data, `Date` for `dateTime.iso8601` data, `Double` for `double` values, `Integer` for `int` (or `i4`) values, `String` for strings, `HashMap` for `struct` values, and `ArrayList` for arrays.

To see all this in a working program, enter the code shown in Listing 20.3 into the NetBeans editor as the class `SiteClient` in the package `com.java21days`.

**LISTING 20.3**   The Full Text of `SiteClient.java`

```
 1: package com.java21days;
 2:
 3: import java.io.*;
 4: import java.net.*;
 5: import java.util.*;
 6: import org.apache.xmlrpc.*;
 7: import org.apache.xmlrpc.client.*;
 8:
 9: public class SiteClient {
10:     public static void main(String arguments[]) {
11:         SiteClient client = new SiteClient();
12:         try {
13:             HashMap<String, String> resp = client.getRandomSite();
14:             // Report the results
15:             if (resp.size() > 0) {
16:                 System.out.println("URL: " + resp.get("url")
17:                     + "\nTitle: " + resp.get("title")
18:                     + "\nDescription: " + resp.get("description"));
19:             }
20:         } catch (IOException | XmlRpcException ioe) {
21:             System.out.println("Exception: " + ioe.getMessage());
22:         }
23:     }
24:
25:     public HashMap getRandomSite()
26:         throws IOException, XmlRpcException {
27:
28:         // Create the client
29:         XmlRpcClientConfigImpl config = new
30:             XmlRpcClientConfigImpl();
31:         URL server = new URL("http://localhost:4413/");
```

```
32:                config.setServerURL(server);
33:                XmlRpcClient client = new XmlRpcClient();
34:                client.setConfig(config);
35:                // Create the parameters for the request
36:                ArrayList params = new ArrayList();
37:                // Send the request and get the response
38:                HashMap result = (HashMap) client.execute(
30:                    "curlie.getRandomSite", params);
40:                return result;
41:        }
42: }
```

The `SiteClient` application connects to the XML-RPC server and calls the `curlie.getRandomSite()` method on the server with no arguments. When it works, this method returns a `HashMap` object that contains the site's URL, title, and description in strings with the keys `"url"`, `"title"`, and `"description"`.

The application can be run, but it won't work because the XML-RPC server hasn't been implemented yet.

# Creating an XML-RPC Web Service

An XML-RPC server is a program that receives a request from a client, calls a method in response to that request, and returns the result. The server maintains a list of methods that it allows clients to call; these are different Java classes called *handlers*.

Apache XML-RPC handles all the XML and networking, enabling you to focus on the task you want a remote method to accomplish.

There are several ways to serve methods remotely. The simplest is to use the `WebServer` class in the `org.apache.xmlrpc.webserver` package, which represents a simple HTTP web server that responds to only XML-RPC requests. This class has two constructors:

- `WebServer(int)`: Creates a web server that listens on the specified port number.
- `WebServer(int, InetAddress)`: Creates a web server at the specified port and IP address. The second argument is an object of the `java.net.InetAddress` class.

Both constructors throw `IOException` exceptions if an input/output problem occurs with creating and starting the server.

The web server has an `XmlRpcServer` object associated with it that handles tasks related to the protocol. This class is in another package, `org.apache.xmlrpc.server`. Call the web server's `getXmlRpcServer()` method with no arguments to retrieve it.

20

The following statements create a web server on port 4413 and an object for its XML-RPC server:

```
WebServer server = new WebServer(4413);
XmlRpcServer xmlRpcServer = server.getXmlRpcServer();
```

The web server does not contain the remote methods that clients call via XML-RPC. These reside in handlers. Handlers are set up by another class in the `org.apache.xmlrpc.server` package, `PropertyHandlerMapping`. This class contains configuration settings for an XML-RPC server, which can be set with a properties file or by calling its methods. It can be created with no arguments to the constructor:

```
PropertyHandlerMapping phm = new PropertyHandlerMapping();
```

To add a handler, call the mapping object's `addHandler(String, Object)` method with two arguments.

The first argument to `addHandler()` is a name to give the handler, which can be anything you choose. Naming an XML-RPC method is comparable to naming a variable. Clients use this name when calling remote methods.

The `SiteClient` application created earlier in this lesson calls the remote method `curlie.getRandomSite()`. The first part of this call—the text preceding the period— refers to a handler given the name `curlie`. The second argument to `addHandler()` is a `Class` object for the handler's class.

These statements add a handler named `curlie` to the XML-RPC server's property mapping and then set the server to use that configuration:

```
phm.addHandler("curlie", CurlieHandlerImpl.class);
xmlRpcServer.setHandlerMapping(phm);
```

`CurlieHandlerImpl` is the class that implements the `getRandomSite()` method and any other methods that can be called remotely over XML-RPC. You'll create this class in a moment.

A class that handles remote method calls can be any Java class that contains `public` methods that return values, as long as the methods take arguments that correspond with data types supported by Apache XML-RPC: `boolean`, `byte[]`, `Date`, `double`, `HashMap`, `int`, `String`, and `ArrayList`.

You can put existing Java classes to use as XML-RPC handlers without modification as long as they do not contain `public` methods that should not be called and as long as each `public` method returns a suitable value.

| CAUTION | The suitability of return values relates to the Apache XML-RPC implementation rather than XML-RPC itself. Other implementations of the protocol are likely to have some differences in the data types of the arguments they take in remote method calls and the values they return. |
| --- | --- |

Using Apache XML-RPC, the web server allows any public method in the handler to be called, so you should use access control to keep prying clients out of methods that should remain off limits.

As the first step toward creating an XML-RPC service, the code in Listing 20.4 creates a simple web server that takes XML-RPC requests. In NetBeans, use this listing to create the `CurlieServer` application.

**LISTING 20.4**  The Full Text of `CurlieServer.java`

```
 1: package com.java21days;
 2:
 3: import java.io.*;
 4: import org.apache.xmlrpc.*;
 5: import org.apache.xmlrpc.server.*;
 6: import org.apache.xmlrpc.webserver.*;
 7:
 8: public class CurlieServer {
 9:     public static void main(String[] arguments) {
10:         try {
11:             startServer();
12:         } catch (IOException ioe) {
13:             System.out.println("Server error: " +
14:                 ioe.getMessage());
15:         } catch (XmlRpcException xre) {
16:             System.out.println("XML-RPC error: " +
17:                 xre.getMessage());
18:         }
19:     }
20:
21:     public static void startServer() throws IOException,
22:         XmlRpcException {
23:
24:         // Create the server
25:         System.out.println("Starting Curlie server ...");
26:         WebServer server = new WebServer(4413);
27:         XmlRpcServer xmlRpcServer = server.getXmlRpcServer();
28:         PropertyHandlerMapping phm = new PropertyHandlerMapping();
```

20

```
29:
30:            // Register the handler
31:            phm.addHandler("curlie", CurlieHandlerImpl.class);
32:            xmlRpcServer.setHandlerMapping(phm);
33:
34:            // Start the server
35:            server.start();
36:            System.out.println("Accepting requests ...");
37:        }
38: }
```

This class can't be compiled successfully until you have created the handler class
CurlieHandlerImpl and a CurlieHandler interface that it implements.

The CurlieServer application creates a web server at port 4413 and an associated
XML-RPC server in lines 25–26.

Using the server's property mapping, a handler is added to the server: a
CurlieHandlerImpl object given the name curlie. The server's start() method is
called to begin listening for requests.

That's all the code required to implement a functional XML-RPC server. Most of the
work is in the remote methods you want a client to call. These methods don't require any
special techniques as long as they are public and return suitable values.

To give you a complete example you can test and modify to suit your own needs, the
CurlieHandler interface and CurlieHandlerImpl class are provided in the next two
listings.

The CurlieHandler interface defines the public methods that can be called remotely over
XML-RPC. Create a new empty Java file of this class name and fill it with Listing 20.5.

**LISTING 20.5**    The Full Text of CurlieHandler.java

```
1: package com.java21days;
2:
3: import java.util.*;
4:
5: public interface CurlieHandler {
6:     HashMap getRandomSite();
7: }
```

This interface contains one method, getRandomSite(), which returns a HashMap object.
No other methods can be called.

The CurlieHandlerImpl class is an implementation of the CurlieHandler interface.

The techniques employed in this class are covered in Lesson 18, "Accessing Databases with JDBC and Derby." These techniques are a good review of how to use JDBC to retrieve records from a database—in this example, a database called `cool`.

Enter the code shown in Listing 20.6 in NetBeans as the class `CurlieHandlerImpl`.

**LISTING 20.6**   The Full Text of `CurlieHandlerImpl.java`

```
 1: package com.java21days;
 2:
 3: import java.sql.*;
 4: import java.util.*;
 5:
 6: public class CurlieHandlerImpl implements  CurlieHandler {
 7:
 8:     @Override
 9:     public HashMap getRandomSite() {
10:         Connection conn = getMySqlConnection();
11:         HashMap<String, String> response = new HashMap<>();
12:         try {
13:             Statement st = conn.createStatement();
14:             ResultSet rec = st.executeQuery(
15:                 "SELECT * FROM cooldata ORDER BY RAND() LIMIT 1");
16:             if (rec.next()) {
17:                 response.put("url", rec.getString("url"));
18:                 response.put("title", rec.getString("title"));
19:                 response.put("description",
20:                     rec.getString("description"));
21:             } else {
22:                 response.put("error", "no database record found");
23:             }
24:             st.close();
25:             rec.close();
26:             conn.close();
27:         } catch (SQLException sqe) {
28:             response.put("error", sqe.getMessage());
29:         }
30:         return response;
31:     }
32:
33:     private Connection getMySqlConnection() {
34:         Connection conn = null;
35:         String data = "jdbc:mysql://localhost/cool";
36:         try {
37:             Class.forName("com.mysql.jdbc.Driver");
38:             conn = DriverManager.getConnection(
39:                 data, "cool", "mrfreeze");
40:         } catch (SQLException s) {
41:             System.out.println("SQL Error: " + s.toString() + " "
42:                 + s.getErrorCode() + " " + s.getSQLState());
```

20

```
43:            } catch (ClassNotFoundException e) {
44:                System.out.println("Error: " + e.toString()
45:                    + e.getMessage());
46:            }
47:        return conn;
48:    }
49: }
```

Lines 35–39 of the `CurlieHandlerImpl` application should be changed to reflect your own database, username, and password. In this class, a MySQL database named `cool` is accessed on the local computer with the username `cool` and the password `mrfreeze`. You also might need to change the rest of the string used to connect to the database, depending on your driver.

When the server is up and running, you can run `SiteClient` to see the data from a randomly selected website, as shown in Figure 20.1.

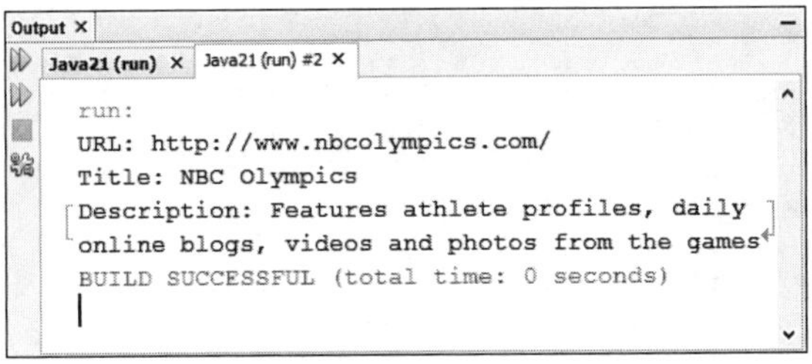

**FIGURE 20.1**

Receiving Curlie website data over XML-RPC.

```
run:
URL: http://www.nbcolympics.com/
Title: NBC Olympics
Description: Features athlete profiles, daily
online blogs, videos and photos from the games
BUILD SUCCESSFUL (total time: 0 seconds)
```

**NOTE**

Running this particular XML-RPC server also requires a database. To download a MySQL database containing information on 1,000 websites from the Open Directory Project, visit this book's website, at www.java21days.com, and open the Lesson 20 page. The database, in a file named `curliedata.dat`, is a text file of SQL commands that can be used to create the database on a MySQL server.

These random sites were culled from the database of the Open Directory Project, a directory of more than 5 million sites that was originally hosted at www.dmoz.org. The directory has relaunched as Curlie at www.curlie.org. The project's data is available for redistribution by others at no cost under the terms of the Open Directory License. For more information, visit https://curlie.org/docs/en/rdf.html.

# Summary

XML-RPC has been described as the "lowest common denominator" of remote procedure call protocols, but its originators don't consider this to be an insult. Most attempts to facilitate software communication over a network have been sophisticated and have scared off developers who have simpler needs.

The XML-RPC protocol can be used to exchange information with any software that supports HTTP, the *lingua franca* of the Web, and XML, a highly popular, structured format for data.

By looking at XML-RPC requests and responses, you should be able to figure out how to use the protocol even without reading the protocol specification. However, as implementations such as Apache XML-RPC become more extensive, you can begin using it quickly without ever looking at the protocol.

# Q&A

**Q When I try to return a `String` array from a remote method, Apache XML-RPC responds with an `XmlRpcException` that states that the object is not supported. Which objects does it support?**

A Apache XML-RPC returns the following data types: `Boolean` for `boolean` XML-RPC values, `byte[]` for `base64` data, `Date` for `dateTime.iso8601` data, `Double` for `double` values, `Integer` for `int` (or `i4`) values, `String` for strings, `HashMap` for `struct` values, and `ArrayList` for arrays. These are specific to Apache XML-RPC. Other class libraries that support this format may work with different data types and classes in Java. Consult the documentation for those libraries.

**Q I'm writing an XML-RPC client to call a method that returns binary data (`base64`, in other words). The `execute()` method of `XmlRpcClient` returns an object instead of an array of bytes. How do I convert this?**

A Arrays are objects in Java, so you can use casting to convert the object returned by `execute()` to an array of bytes (assuming that the object really is an array). The following statement accomplishes this on an object named `fromServer` that contains a byte array:

```
byte[] data = (byte []) fromServer;
```

20

# Quiz

Review this lesson's material by taking this three-question quiz.

## Questions

1. Which popular Internet protocol does XML-RPC not require?

    A. HTML

    B. HTTP

    C. XML

2. Which XML-RPC data type would be best suited to hold the number 8.67?

    A. `boolean`

    B. `double`

    C. `int`

3. Which XML tag indicates that the data is an XML-RPC request?

    A. `methodCall`

    B. `methodResponse`

    C. `params`

## Answers

1. A. XML-RPC uses HTTP (Hypertext Transfer Protocol) to transport data that is formatted as XML (Extensible Markup Language). HTML (Hypertext Markup Language) is not used.

2. B. All floating-point numbers, such as 8.67, are represented by the `double` type in XML-RPC. There are not two different floating-point types, as there are in Java (`float` and `double`).

3. A. The `methodCall` tag is used only in requests, `methodResponse` is used only in responses, and `params` is used in both.

# Certification Practice

The following question is the kind of thing you could expect to be asked on a Java programming certification test. Answer it without looking again at this lesson or using the Java compiler to test the code.

Given:

```
public class Operation {
    public static void main(String[] arguments) {
        int x = 1;
        int y = 3;
        if ((x != 1) && (y++ == 3)) {
            y = y + 2;
        }
    }
}
```

What is the final value of y?

**A.** 3

**B.** 4

**C.** 5

**D.** 6

The answer is available on the book's website, at www.java21days.com. Visit the Lesson 20 page and click the Certification Practice link.

# Exercises

To extend your knowledge of the subjects covered in this lesson, try the following exercises:

**1.** WordPress offers an extensive XML-RPC interface at https://wordpress.com/xmlrpc. php. Write an application that calls the method "system.listMethods" with an empty ArrayList as arguments, gets back a response, and displays the name of each method supported by the XML-RPC interface.

**2.** The XML-RPC interface for the weblog update service blo.gs is at http://blo.gs/ ping.php. Write a client and server that can send and receive the weblogUpdates. ping method.

20

Where applicable, exercise solutions are offered on the book's website, at www.java21days.com.

# LESSON 21
# Writing a Game with Java

Reading the source of a well-written program can be an educational experience. Software developers express themselves through the code they write. Aspiring programmers can learn a lot by reading between the lines.

This final lesson is built on the premise that programming subjects can be taught with the source code of functional, useful programs as the starting point. Read the code; read the story of how it was written; write your own. That's the opposite order from the rest of this book and most others that teach programming languages. The typical approach is to introduce a subject, describe a few short examples, and then put it all together in a program that demonstrates the feature. Taking a code-first approach mimics how programmers often learn new languages and technologies.

The application you'll create in this lesson is a game called `Banko`. The following new techniques are introduced in this lesson:

- Creating a custom button
- Examining adjacent buttons with recursion
- Monitoring button clicks with an action event listener
- Generating random numbers
- Setting values with the ternary operator
- Using constants instead of literals to make class design more flexible
- Making objects work together to form a whole program

# Playing a Game

Figure 21.1 shows a `Banko` game in progress.

**FIGURE 21.1**
Playing the `Banko` puzzle game.

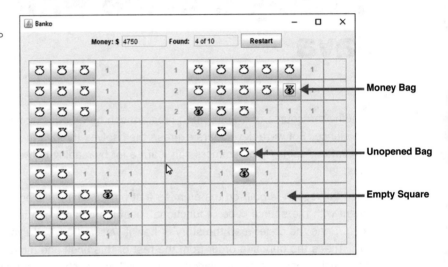

In the game, a player hunts for 10 bags containing money on a 9-by-14 grid that begins with 126 unopened bags.

The rules are simple:

1. Open an empty bag and pay $250.
2. Open a money bag and receive $1,000.

Empty bags disappear when they are opened. The empty squares may provide a clue that helps the player find a money bag—a count of money bags adjacent to that square. (Sometimes it's more than a clue: In Figure 21.1, the circled bag definitely contains money.)

An empty square that isn't close to money is left blank, and any similar squares that touch it are revealed at the same time.

The goal is to find all 10 money bags while spending as little money as possible.

`Banko` consists of a frame class called `Banko`, which loads a game board class `Board`, which in turn loads a game piece class called `Button`.

Two additional files are required: the GIF graphics money_bag.gif and unopened_bag.gif. These files are available for download on the book's website at www.java21days.com on the Lesson 21 page.

The classes of the com.java21days.banko package relate to each other as follows:

- The Button class represents a custom button that holds an unopened bag, a money bag, or a clear square.

- The Board class places all the buttons on the game board, hides money bags, and tells clear squares how close they are to money.

- The Banko class presents the game board on a frame, loads graphics, takes user input, and keeps track of how well a player is doing.

# Part 1: Creating a Custom Button

In this lesson, you will build the Banko project outward, beginning with the buttons on the game board. These buttons, which represent money bags, unopened bags, and empty squares, are objects in the Button class (see Listing 21.1). This class shows how to create a custom button, change a button's icon and label as the class runs, store a button's attributes and behavior in the button, and use recursion to examine adjacent buttons in a grid.

Start the project in NetBeans with Button as its first class.

**LISTING 21.1**   The Full Text of Button.java

```
1: package com.java21days.banko;
2:
3: import javax.swing.ImageIcon;
4: import javax.swing.JButton;
5:
6: public class Button extends JButton {
7:     // the button's position
8:     public int row;
9:     public int column;
10:    // the button's state (-2 money, -1 cleared, 0 uncleared)
11:    public int state;
12:    // the number of adjacent money bags
13:    public int near;
14:    // true if this is a money bag that has been found
15:    public boolean found;
16:    // the game board
17:    private final Board board;
18:    // the two bag graphics
19:    private static ImageIcon unknownBag;
```

21

```
20:        private static ImageIcon moneyBag;
21:
22:
23:        // create a new button
24:        Button(Board board, int row, int column) {
25:            super("");
26:            // store the board that contains this button
27:            this.board = board;
28:            // store the button's position
29:            this.row = row;
30:            this.column = column;
31:            // set up button graphics (if necessary)
32:            if (unknownBag == null) {
33:                unknownBag = board.app.getImageIcon("unknown_bag.gif");
34:                moneyBag = board.app.getImageIcon("money_bag.gif");
35:            }
36:            // set up the button
37:            setup();
38:        }
39:
40:        // set up the button for gameplay
41:        public final void setup() {
42:            fill();
43:            state = 0;
44:            near = 0;
45:            found = false;
46:            // remove the background color (from a previous game)
47:            setBackground(null);
48:        }
49:
50:        // reveal an unopened bag in the square
51:        public void fill() {
52:            // give this button the unopened bag icon
53:            setIcon(unknownBag);
54:            // remove the label
55:            setText("");
56:            // enable the button
57:            setEnabled(true);
58:        }
59:
60:        // reveal an empty square and count adjacent money bags
61:        public void clear(boolean clicked) {
62:            if (clicked) {
63:                /* this square was manually cleared by the user, so tell
64:                   the frame to charge the player */
65:                board.app.spendMoney();
66:            }
67:            // remove the icon
68:            setIcon(null);
69:            // tell the button it is clear and disable it
70:            state = -1;
```

```
 71:                setEnabled(false);
 72:            if (near > 0) {
 73:                // reveal that one or more money bags are nearby
 74:                setText("" + near);
 75:            } else {
 76:                /* inspect the buttons above, below, left, and right
 77:                    of this one */
 78:                Button above = above();
 79:                Button below = below();
 80:                Button left = left();
 81:                Button right = right();
 82:                /* if any of these buttons is clear and has no money bags
 83:                    nearby, clear it -- using recursion to fan out around
 84:                    the board */
 85:                if ((above != null) && (above.state == 0)) {
 86:                    // clear the button above
 87:                    above.clear(false);
 88:                }
 89:                if ((below != null) && (below.state == 0)) {
 90:                    // clear the button below
 91:                    below.clear(false);
 92:                }
 93:                if ((left != null) && (left.state == 0)) {
 94:                    // clear the button to the left
 95:                    left.clear(false);
 96:                }
 97:                if ((right != null) && (right.state == 0)) {
 98:                    // clear the button to the right
 99:                    right.clear(false);
100:                }
101:            }
102:        }
103:
104:        // reveal a money bag
105:        public void revealMoney() {
106:            // give this button the money bag icon
107:            setIcon(moneyBag);
108:            // remove the label
109:            setText("");
110:            if (!found) {
111:                /* this bag has never been found, so tell the frame
112:                    to award money to the player */
113:                board.app.earnMoney();
114:                // tell this bag it has been found
115:                found = true;
116:            }
117:        }
118:
119:        /* these four directional methods inspect four buttons adjacent
120:            to this one, returning null on the edges of the game board */
```

**21**

```
121:        public Button above() {
122:            if (row > 0) {
123:                // return the adjacent button
124:                return board.square[row - 1][column];
125:            }
126:            // return null to indicate a board edge has been passed
127:            return null;
128:        }
129:
130:        public Button below() {
131:            if (row < board.rows - 1) {
132:                return board.square[row + 1][column];
133:            }
134:            return null;
135:        }
136:
137:        public Button left() {
138:            if (column > 0) {
139:                return board.square[row][column - 1];
140:            }
141:            return null;
142:        }
143:
144:        public Button right() {
145:            if (column < board.columns - 1) {
146:                return board.square[row][column + 1];
147:            }
148:            return null;
149:        }
150: }
```

You can't compile this class until you create the `Board` class in the next phase.

The new techniques employed by `Button` are described in the next several sections.

## Designing a Custom Button in Swing

The buttons that fill the `Banko` game board change in appearance as the game is played. A custom subclass of `javax.swing.JButton` provides the means to define this behavior while building on the behavior and attributes of `JButton`.

Game buttons take one of three states:

- A bag that hasn't been opened yet (icon `unknownBag.gif` and no text label)
- A money bag (icon `moneyBag.gif` and no text label)
- An empty square (no icon and a text label if one or more money bags are adjacent to the square)

The state of a button changes within a game. The `Banko` application also reuses buttons, filling them with unopened bags at the start of a new game.

Image icons, which belong to the `javax.swing.ImageIcon` class in Swing, hold GIF graphics of unopened bags and money bags:

```
private static ImageIcon unknownBag;
private static ImageIcon moneyBag;
```

These are class variables, as declared by the `static` keyword, because there's no need for each button to have its own instance of the icons.

The `Button()` constructor loads these icons, calling a method of the `Banko` frame class that will be defined in Part 3:

```
if (unknownBag == null) {
    unknownBag = board.app.getImageIcon("unknown_bag.gif");
    moneyBag = board.app.getImageIcon("money_bag.gif");
}
```

As a subclass of `javax.swing.JButton`, `Button` inherits a constructor to define an image icon and text label when the button is created:

```
Button button = new Button("", unknownBag);
```

The changing states of the button are supported by setting the icon and label through calls to `setIcon(ImageIcon)` and `setText(String)` methods inherited from `JButton`:

```
setIcon(unknownBag);
setText("" + near);
```

When a button's image icon is set, it is reflected immediately in the graphical user interface. Calling `setIcon(null)` removes an icon. Setting the label works similarly, and an empty string causes no label to be displayed.

When a button represents an empty square, the `setEnabled(false)` method prevents it from receiving user input, and `setEnabled(true)` restores it:

```
setEnabled(true);
```

## Creating a Button's Behavior and Attributes

A button holds its position, its current state, the number of adjacent money bags, and whether it has been found (if it's a money bag):

**21**

```
public int row;
public int column;
public int state;
public int near;
public boolean found;
```

The button also contains knowledge of the board on which it has been placed:

```
private Board board;
```

The next phase describes the `Board` class. The button's position and game board are established in its constructor:

```
Button(Board board, int row, int column) {
    this.board = board;
    this.row = row;
    this.column = column;
}
```

The other instance variables are set as three methods are called, either internally within the `Button` class or in other classes.

1. The `fill()` method draws an unopened bag on the button, removes the text label, and enables the button to take input.

2. The `setup()` method prepares the button for play, setting the state to 0 (unopened bag) and other starting values for a new game, and then calls `fill()`.

3. The `revealMoney()` method reveals a money bag, removes the text label, and if the bag is newly discovered, tells the frame to reward the player with money.

## Clearing Empty Squares with Recursion

The meatiest part of the `Button` class, from the perspective of the programming techniques required in the implementation, is the `clear(boolean)` method. This method reveals an empty bag, either in response to a user click (the argument `true`) or for another reason (`false`).

When `clear()` is called, the frame is asked to charge the player money for the action, the button's icon is removed, and its state changes from 0 to -1 (cleared):

```
setIcon(null);
state = -1;
setEnabled(false);
```

If the square is adjacent to at least one money bag, `clear()` sets this count as the button's label, and the method ends:

```
setText("" + near);
```

If the square isn't adjacent to a money bag, things get more interesting. Additional squares are automatically cleared if two things are true:

- The two squares share a side.
- The adjacent square isn't near any money bags.

These rules apply to each successive square that is cleared, and one click can reveal a large number of empty squares as Banko is played.

Button defines methods that identify the buttons above, below, left, and right of the current button:

```
public Button above() {
    if (row > 0) {
        return board.square[row - 1][column];
    }
    return null;
}
```

Each method ensures that there really is a button in that direction; if the current button is on the topmost row (0), above() returns null. Otherwise, the game board's square array holds all buttons on the board separated into a grid of rows and columns, and one can be retrieved by its position:

```
return square[row - 1][column];
```

After the adjacent buttons (if any) have been retrieved, they can be checked to see if any should be cleared:

```
if ((above != null) && (above.state == 0)) {
    above.clear(false);
}
```

The call to clear() is recursive, creating a logical loop that fans around the game board, looking for buttons to see if they should be cleared.

The false argument indicates that the player didn't initiate the action, which prevents money from being deducted.

The check of the button's argument indicates that the player didn't initiate the action, which prevents money from being deducted.

21

The check of the button's state prevents the method from recursively calling itself without termination because the clear() method sets state to -1 when a square has been cleared.

The recursive calls fan out around the board, not stopping until they hit an empty bag that's near one or more money bags.

Because it was created as a subclass of JButton, the Button class takes care of itself by containing its own behavior and attributes. This encapsulation lets the button be self-sufficient. When another class needs a button to reveal its contents or a count of nearby money bags, its revealMoney() and clear() methods can be called.

When a click on an empty square prompts an inspection of adjacent squares, Button looks at those squares through directional methods like left() and right() and then calls their clear() methods.

# Part 2: Displaying the Game Board

The next class created for the com.java21days.banko game provides a place for the buttons: a game board. The board holds all the buttons in a rectangular grid arranged into columns and rows of equal size.

The Board class in Listing 21.2 illustrates how to lay out such a grid in a Swing graphical user interface, generate random numbers, set values with the ternary operator, and assign an event listener to monitor a player's mouse clicks on the board.

**LISTING 21.2**    The Full Text of Board.java

```
 1: package com.java21days.banko;
 2:
 3: import java.awt.Insets;
 4: import java.awt.GridLayout;
 5: import javax.swing.JPanel;
 6:
 7: public class Board extends JPanel {
 8:     // the board's rows, columns, and total money bags
 9:     protected int rows;
10:     protected int columns;
11:     protected int money_bags;
12:     // the buttons on the board
13:     public Button[][] square;
14:     // the game frame
15:     public Banko app;
16:
17:     public Board(Banko app, int rows, int columns, int money_bags) {
18:         // store the frame
19:         this.app = app;
20:         // store the rows, columns, and money bags on the board
21:         this.rows = rows;
22:         this.columns = columns;
23:         this.money_bags = money_bags;
```

```
24:          // create the board and set its layout
25:          square = new Button[rows][columns];
26:          GridLayout grid = new GridLayout(rows, columns);
27:          setLayout(grid);
28:          // set up each button
29:          for (int row = 0; row < rows; row++) {
30:              for (int column = 0; column < columns; column++) {
31:                  // create the button
32:                  Button button = new Button(this, row, column);
33:                  // add it to the board
34:                  square[row][column] = button;
35:                  // assign the frame to monitor button clicks
36:                  button.addActionListener(app);
37:                  // add the button to the user interface
38:                  add(button);
39:              }
40:          }
41:          setup();
42:      }
43:
44:      // set up the board for gameplay
45:      public final void setup() {
46:          // set up each button for gameplay
47:          for (int row = 0; row < rows; row++) {
48:              for (int column = 0; column < columns; column++) {
49:                  square[row][column].setup();
50:              }
51:          }
52:          // count the number of money bags hidden so far
53:          int hidden = 0;
54:          while (hidden < money_bags) {
55:              // choose a random position for the money bag
56:              int row = (int)Math.floor(Math.random() * rows);
57:              int column = (int)Math.floor(Math.random() * columns);
58:              if (square[row][column].state == -2) {
59:                  // there's already a money bag in that square
60:                  continue;
61:              }
62:              // hide a money bag and increment the count
63:              square[row][column].state = -2;
64:              hidden++;
65:          }
66:          // count the number of bags in adjacent squares
67:          for (int row = 0; row < rows; row++) {
68:              for (int column = 0; column < columns; column++) {
69:                  if (square[row][column].state == 0) {
70:                      // count the bags adjacent to this square
71:                      square[row][column].near = getBagCount(row, column);
72:                  }
73:              }
74:          }
```

21

```
 75:      }
 76:
 77:      // determine the money bags adjacent to a square
 78:      private int getBagCount(int row, int column) {
 79:          // start counting
 80:          int count = 0;
 81:          /* set the lower and upper boundaries of the search area around
 82:             a square, making sure not to go outside the game board */
 83:          int above = (row > 0) ? row - 1 : row;
 84:          int below = (row < rows - 1) ? row + 1 : row;
 85:          int left = (column > 0) ? column - 1 : column;
 86:          int right = (column < columns - 1) ? column + 1 : column;
 87:          for (int i = above; i <= below; i++) {
 88:              for (int j = left; j <= right; j++) {
 89:                  if (square[i][j].state == -2) {
 90:                      /* a money bag is nearby, so increment the count
 91:                         for this square */
 92:                      count++;
 93:                  }
 94:              }
 95:          }
 96:          return count;
 97:      }
 98:
 99:      // set the margins of the game board to 15 pixels
100:      @Override
101:      public Insets getInsets() {
102:          // set the top, left, bottom and right inset margins
103:          return new Insets(15, 15, 15, 15);
104:      }
105: }
```

This class cannot be compiled without the final class of the project, the game frame `Banko`, described in the next phase.

The following sections describe the `Board` class.

## Arranging Components as a Grid

The `Board` class holds the game board—the grid of buttons arranged into rows and columns. The buttons are stored in a two-dimensional array of `Button` objects and displayed with the `java.awt.GridLayout` manager:

```
square = new Button[rows][columns];
GridLayout grid = new GridLayout(rows, columns);
setLayout(grid);
```

The grid layout manager establishes a container of individual cells with the specified number of rows and columns. Each component added to the container takes one cell, and the order is the same as for the words on this page: left to right and then down a line when there's no more room.

The Board object is flexible enough to support other sizes, but Banko sets it up with 9 rows, 14 columns, and 126 total cells.

Each button is created, added to the Button array, and added to the container:

```
Button button = new Button(this, row, column);
square[row][column] = button;
add(button);
```

The add(component) call adds the button to the container, which in Board is a panel. The grid layout manager already in place for the container determines the placement.

Each button also has a listener added to it—the frame that contains the board:

```
button.addActionListener(app);
```

Listeners are objects that monitor events caused by a user's interaction with a graphical user interface. Action events are generated by button clicks.

By adding the frame as an action listener to a button, Board assigns the frame the task of responding to mouse clicks on that button.

There's no behavior in Board that causes anything to happen when buttons are clicked.

## Generating Random Numbers

The setup() method sets up the board for play, first by setting up each button on the board:

```
for (int row = 0; row < rows; row++) {
    for (int column = 0; column < columns; column++) {
        square[row][column].setup();
    }
}
```

Next, money bags are hidden at randomly selected positions on the board:

```
int row = (int)Math.floor(Math.random() * rows);
int column = (int)Math.floor(Math.random() * columns);
```

21

Two class methods of the Math class, part of the standard java.lang package, choose a random row and column for a money bag.

The `Math.random()` function produces a double value from 0.0 to 1.0 that's randomly generated (or, more accurately, random enough for the purposes of this game).

The value is multiplied by the total number of rows or columns, producing a double that is rounded down to an integer by the `Math.floor` method.

The end result is a random number from 0 to one less than the number of rows or columns.

If there isn't already a money bag at that position, the button's state is set to -2, which hides a money bag there:

```
square[row][column].state = -2;
```

**NOTE**

> Since I was a teen writing programs in BASIC on a Commodore 64, every introduction of random number generators I've read has warned that the numbers are only "pseudo-random," a cautionary bit of advice that suggests impending disaster.
>
> Random number generators like the one employed by `Math`—the `java.util.Random` class—aren't truly random. They generate extremely large sequences of numbers that do not change.
>
> A seeded value determines where in the sequence to begin taking random numbers. Use the same seed to create two generators, and you'll get the same numbers from both—and in the same order. This doesn't matter in a game like `Banko`. The `random()` function picks a different spot in the sequence each time it's called, producing a good enough approximation of randomness for most Java classes. Where it does matter is with security applications. A predictable random sequence makes software vulnerable to exploits such as one that enabled hackers to obtain the private key used by Sony to digitally sign software on the PlayStation 3.

## Using the Ternary Operator

The setup process for the `Board` class includes a call to `getBagCount(int, int)`, a method that counts the number of money bags adjacent to a button (with `state` equal to -2):

```java
int count = 0;
for (int i = above; i <= below; i++) {
    for (int j = left; j <= right; j++) {
        if (square[i][j].state == -2) {
            count++;
        }
    }
}
```

All eight adjacent buttons are examined in search of money bags, except when a button is on an edge and has only three or five neighbors.

Attempting to access a button that isn't within the boundaries of the `square` array results in an exception. The range of buttons to search is calculated to ensure that this doesn't happen.

The following statements set the leftmost and rightmost columns to include in a search:

```
int left = (column > 0) ? column - 1 : column;
int right = (column < columns - 1) ? column + 1 : column;
```

These statements employ the ternary operator (?) to set a value based on the result of an expression. Ternary expressions take the form `(expression) ? valueIfTrue : valueIfFalse`.

The first ternary expression sets the value of the `left` integer based on the expression `column > 0`. If it's true, `left` is set to `column - 1`. If it's false, `left` equals `column`.

When a button is in column 0 of the game board, the search ranges from column 0 to column 1. Otherwise, the search begins one column to the button's left and ends one column to its right.

The `Banko` game now has individual buttons that display bags of money (or a whole lotta nothing) and a board that contains them.

The `Board` class inherits from the superclass `javax.swing.JPanel`, a convenient container for dividing a graphical user interface into different segments that may have their own layout arrangement.

The board will be added to the frame's main graphical user interface, which appears when the latter class is run.

# Part 3: Presenting a Game Frame

The `Banko` frame ties together all the classes in the `com.java21days.banko` package, presenting a money-grubbing puzzle game that can be run on the desktop.

The `Banko` class establishes the graphical user interface for the application, takes care of user input, and enforces the rules of the game. The `Banko` class, detailed in Listing 21.3, shows how to arrange a graphical user interface by using the border layout manager, receive button clicks as action events, load graphics into a frame, and administer the game as it is played.

21

**LISTING 21.3**   The Full Text of `Banko.java`

```
 1: package com.java21days.banko;
 2:
 3: import java.awt.BorderLayout;
 4: import java.awt.Color;
 5: import java.awt.event.ActionListener;
 6: import java.awt.event.ActionEvent;
 7: import javax.swing.ImageIcon;
 8: import javax.swing.JButton;
 9: import javax.swing.JFrame;
10: import javax.swing.JLabel;
11: import javax.swing.JPanel;
12: import javax.swing.JTextField;
13:
14: public class Banko extends JFrame implements ActionListener {
15:     // the money inside a money bag
16:     public static int REWARD = 1000;
17:     // the cost of opening an empty bag
18:     public static int COST = 250;
19:     // the size of the game board and total number of money bags
20:     public static int ROW_COUNT = 9;
21:     public static int COLUMN_COUNT = 14;
22:     public static int BAG_COUNT = 10;
23:     // the fields that report how a player's doing
24:     private final JTextField moneyField;
25:     private final JTextField foundField;
26:     // the restart button
27:     public JButton restart;
28:     // a player's money and the number of money bags found
29:     public int money;
30:     public int found;
31:     // the game board
32:     private final Board board;
33:
34:     // create the frame
35:     public Banko() {
36:         // call the superclass and give the frame a title
37:         super("Banko");
38:         // set its layout manager
39:         BorderLayout border = new BorderLayout();
40:         setLayout(border);
41:
42:         // create the top panel
43:         JPanel top = new JPanel();
44:         // create the "Money:" label and text field
45:         JLabel moneyLabel = new JLabel("Money: $");
46:         moneyField = new JTextField("", 8);
47:         // prevent it from being edited
48:         moneyField.setEditable(false);
49:         // create the "Found:" label and text field
```

```
 50:            JLabel foundLabel = new JLabel("Found: ");
 51:            foundField = new JTextField("", 8);
 52:            foundField.setEditable(false);
 53:            // create the Restart button
 54:            restart = new JButton("Restart");
 55:            // assign the frame to monitor clicks of this button
 56:            restart.addActionListener(this);
 57:            // add the components to the top panel
 58:            top.add(moneyLabel);
 59:            top.add(moneyField);
 60:            top.add(foundLabel);
 61:            top.add(foundField);
 62:            top.add(restart);
 63:            // add the panel to the border's topmost position
 64:            add(top, BorderLayout.NORTH);
 65:
 66:            // create the game board
 67:            board = new Board(this, ROW_COUNT, COLUMN_COUNT, BAG_COUNT);
 68:            // add the board to the border's center position
 69:            add(board, BorderLayout.CENTER);
 70:            // set up the game
 71:            setup();
 72:            // set the size of the frame
 73:            setSize(650, 450);
 74:            // make the application end when the frame is closed
 75:            setDefaultCloseOperation(EXIT_ON_CLOSE);
 76:            // display the user interface
 77:            setVisible(true);
 78:        }
 79:
 80:        // set up the frame for gameplay
 81:        public final void setup() {
 82:            found = -1;
 83:            money = 0;
 84:            // give the player starting money
 85:            earnMoney();
 86:        }
 87:
 88:        // take money from the player for opening an empty bag
 89:        public void spendMoney() {
 90:            // deduct funds and display the new total
 91:            money = money - COST;
 92:            moneyField.setText("" + money);
 93:            if (money <= 0) {
 94:                // the player's broke, so end the game
 95:                revealBoard();
 96:            }
 97:        }
 98:
 99:        // award money to the player for finding a money bag
100:        public void earnMoney() {
```

21

```
101:          // add funds and display the total
102:          money = money + REWARD;
103:          moneyField.setText("" + money);
104:          // count the newly found bag
105:          found++;
106:          foundField.setText("" + found + " of " + BAG_COUNT);
107:          if (found >= BAG_COUNT) {
108:              // the player's found all bags, so end the game
109:              revealBoard();
110:          }
111:      }
112:
113:    // reveal the entire board at game's end
114:    public void revealBoard() {
115:          // inspect every square on the board
116:          for (int row = 0; row < ROW_COUNT; row++) {
117:              for (int column = 0; column < COLUMN_COUNT; column++) {
118:                  // get the current button
119:                  Button button = board.square[row][column];
120:                  if (button.state == -2) {
121:                      // display this money bag
122:                      button.found = true;
123:                      button.revealMoney();
124:                  } else {
125:                      // set up happy and sad colors
126:                      Color green = new Color(204, 255, 204);
127:                      Color red = new Color(255, 204, 204);
128:                      if (money > 0) {
129:                          // the player won, so make this empty square
                                 green
130:                          button.setBackground(green);
131:                      } else {
132:                          // the player lost, so make this empty square
                                 red
133:                          button.setBackground(red);
134:                      }
135:                  }
136:                  if (button.state == 0) {
137:                      // this square has never been cleared, so do so
                             now
138:                      button.clear(false);
139:                  }
140:              }
141:          }
142:      }
143:
144:    // load a button graphic using its filename
145:    public ImageIcon getImageIcon(String filename) {
146:          // load an image icon
147:          ImageIcon icon = new ImageIcon(filename);
148:          return icon;
```

```
149:        }
150:
151:        // monitor button clicks on the game board and restart button
152:        @Override
153:        public void actionPerformed(ActionEvent event) {
154:            // determine the button the player clicked
155:            Object source = event.getSource();
156:            if (source instanceof Button) {
157:                // the button's on the game board
158:                Button button = (Button) event.getSource();
159:                if (button.state == -2) {
160:                    // it contains a money bag, so reveal it
161:                    button.revealMoney();
162:                } else {
163:                    // it doesn't contain a money bag, so clear it
164:                    button.clear(true);
165:                }
166:            } else {
167:                // the restart button was clicked
168:                // set up the frame anew
169:                setup();
170:                // set up the board too
171:                board.setup();
172:            }
173:        }
174:
175:        public static void main(String[] arguments) {
176:            // start the application
177:            new Banko();
178:        }
179: }
```

The `Banko` class ties together the `com.java21days.banko` project, employing the other two classes in the package to present the game in a frame.

When `Banko` is compiled, the `Board` and `Button` classes are compiled if necessary.

The following sections detail the development and deployment of the `Banko` application.

## Drawing a Graphical User Interface

Swing applications like `Banko` inherit from `javax.swing.JFrame`, inheriting the behavior necessary to run within the context of a browser.

The application's constructor is called as it is first loaded by the browser. `Banko` uses it to set the frame's layout manager:

21

```
BorderLayout border = new BorderLayout();
setLayout(border);
```

BorderLayout subdivides a container into five regions: north, south, east, west, and center. The center region takes up most of the space, and the layout facilitates an interface with one major component surrounded by 1–4 smaller components around it.

Banko uses BorderLayout to place the game board in the center and a scoring panel above it to display a player's money and the number of money bags discovered.

The scoring panel is a JPanel object:

```
JPanel top = new JPanel();
JLabel moneyLabel = new JLabel("Money: $");
JTextField moneyField = new JTextField("", 8);
JLabel foundLabel = new JLabel("Found: ");
JTextField foundField = new JTextField("", 8);
```

The components are added to the scoring panel before they are added to the frame's interface:

```
top.add(moneyLabel);
top.add(moneyField);
top.add(foundLabel);
top.add(foundField);
```

Because the panel has not defined a layout manager, the default for panel containers is employed: java.awt.FlowLayout. Flow layout arranges components like words on a page: left to right on each line while there's room and then on to the left margin of the next line to begin again.

You add the panel to the frame by specifying the component and its placement in BorderLayout:

```
add(top, BorderLayout.NORTH);
```

BorderLayout class variables provide the second argument: NORTH, SOUTH, EAST, WEST, or CENTER.

You add the game board by calling the Board(Banko, int, int, int) constructor:

```
board = new Board(this, ROW_COUNT, COLUMN_COUNT, BAG_COUNT);
add(board, BorderLayout.CENTER);
```

## Running the Banko **Game**

The rules of the Banko game are established primarily through the class variables of the frame:

```
public static int REWARD = 1000;
public static int COST = 250;
public static int ROW_COUNT = 9;
public static int COLUMN_COUNT = 14;
public static int BAG_COUNT = 10;
```

These variables are used instead of literals to make the design of the game more flexible.

A puzzle game like Banko requires some tinkering to find the right combination of money bags, reward, and penalties to result in the most playable games.

Early testing revealed that 16 money bags was too many on a 9-by-14 grid. Reducing the bags from 16 to 10 required only one change—altering the value of the class variable BAG_COUNT.

The frame's spendMoney() and earnMoney() methods enforce the rules of the game. The spendMoney() method deducts the cost of opening an empty bag ($250) from the player's total, setting the moneyField text field to the new value. The earnMoney() method increases the player's funds by $1,000 for the discovery of a money bag and checks to see if all 10 bags have been discovered. These two changes are reflected on the scoring panel.

If either spendMoney() or earnMoney() determines that the game has ended—either because a player is flat broke or finds the last bag—it calls the frame's revealBoard() method.

This method inspects every square on the board:

```
Button button = board.square[row][column];
```

If the square contains a money bag, it's displayed without adding to the player's total:

```
button.found = true;
button.revealMoney();
```

Otherwise, the square's background color becomes either light red or light green, depending on whether the player won:

```
Color green = new Color(204, 255, 204);
Color red = new Color(255, 204, 204);
if (money > 0) {
    button.setBackground(green);
```

21

```
} else {
    button.setBackground(red);
}
```

All that's left is to reveal unopened bags:

```
if (button.state == 0) {
    button.clear(false);
}
```

Calling the button's `clear()` method with a `false` argument prevents the player from losing money for opening an empty bag.

## Receiving Button Clicks in a User Interface

Button clicks and other user input events are ignored in Java unless an event listener has been assigned to monitor them.

A class can handle its own events or delegate the responsibility to another class.

The `Board` class added an action listener to all buttons on the board through the component's `addActionListener(Object)` method:

```
Button button = new Button(this, row, column);
square[row][column] = button;
button.addActionListener(app);
```

The `app` object refers to the frame, and the game board assigns the frame the task of handling button clicks.

The `Banko` class gives itself the responsibility of receiving clicks on the Restart button:

```
JButtonrestart = new JButton("Restart");
restart.addActionListener(this);
```

A class that serves as an event listener must implement the interface that corresponds to the events being monitored. Action events are received by classes that implement the `java.awt.event.ActionListener` interface, which contains a single `actionPerformed(ActionEvent)` method:

```
public void actionPerformed(ActionEvent event) {
    // take action in response to event
}
```

The `ActionEvent` object reveals the source of the event—the button that was clicked:

```
Object source = event.getSource();
```

This listener tracks clicks from two kinds of buttons—game buttons (the `Button` class) and the restart button (`JButton`).

The `instanceof` operator checks the class to indicate which kind of object was clicked:

```
if (source instanceof Button) {
    // game button clicked
} else {
    // restart button clicked
}
```

A click of the Restart button causes the frame and game board to be set up for a new game:

```
setup();
board.setup();
```

Setting up the board causes every game button's `setup()` method to be called as well, so this resets all three classes that comprise the `com.java21days.banko` package.

If the clicked object is an instance of the `Button` class, more work must be done to determine which button was clicked:

```
Button button = (Button) event.getSource();
```

An event's `getSource()` method returns the clicked object, which must be cast to the proper class. This button can be treated like any other. Its `state` variable reveals whether the button contains a money bag (value equal to `-2`):

```
if (button.state == -2) {
    button.revealMoney();
} else {
    button.clear(true);
}
```

The frame tells the button to either reveal a money bag or clear the square; the latter recursively clears adjacent squares.

21

# Summary

This lesson's `Banko` game shows that a playable puzzle game can be implemented in Java using fewer than 500 lines of code. Many of the lines in `Banko` are comments. Although it's good programming practice to use comments to explain your code, they are employed in this lesson to an exaggerated degree so that the program can teach itself.

The game consists of three classes that have well-defined jobs that make conceptual sense: a game contains a board that's made up of buttons. The jobs are performed with methods in the objects. Need to show the money under a button? Call its `revealMoney()` method. Want to configure the game board at the start of play? Call its `setup()` method.

Learning by reading code is an enjoyable way to gain experience in a programming language after completing a book or an online course.

The programming management site GitHub has more than 500 puzzle games implemented in Java, and the source code is available for examination. To see these games, visit https://github.com/search?q=java+puzzle+game.

# Q&A

**Q On the subject of object-oriented programming, why does the `Button` class have methods to examine the buttons adjacent to it? Wouldn't that behavior make more sense in the `Board` class?**

**A** On a conceptual level, it does make sense for each button to only know about itself and for the board to track the buttons collectively and in relation to each other. But as the `Banko` game was developed, it became advantageous to give buttons the ability to examine their neighbors. This design enabled recursion to be employed so that examining one button's neighbors on its four borders caused them to examine their neighbors if they were empty, and so on until a large part of the board could be cleared with a single click by a player.

In object-oriented programming, you should always challenge your initial assumptions. If you can accomplish a task more efficiently and effectively by shifting behavior from one class to another, you should do that.

**Q Why did the `Banko` project have a lot of `import` statements adding individual classes instead of using a wildcard statement such as `import javax.swing.*` to make available all classes in that package?**

**A** Most Java programmers avoid wildcards when using `import` for two reasons. The first is that it reduces the likelihood that class names will collide with each other because two packages have classes of the same name. There's a class in the `java.awt` package called `Button` and a class in the `com.java21days.banko` package called `Button`. If you used `import java.awt.*` in the `Board` class and wrote a statement referencing `Button`, a Java IDE such as NetBeans would flag it as an error because it would be impossible to know which `Button` class you were trying to use. The full class name with its package would be necessary, as in this rewrite of line 32 from Listing 21.2:

```
com.java21days.banko.Button button = new Button(this, row, column);
```

The second reason programmers use `import` on individual classes is that IDEs make it so easy. When you write a statement that references a class by its short name in NetBeans and that class, a red icon may appear to the left of that line. If you click it, an Add Import command appears in the context menu. Click the command to add the `import` statement for that class.

In NetBeans I never write `import` statements before using a class. I reference the class in a statement and let NetBeans offer to add an `import` for me.

# Quiz

Review this lesson's material by taking this three-question quiz.

## Questions

1. What can you do to clear a background color from a Swing user interface component?

    **A.** Call `setColor()` with no arguments.

    **B.** Call `setBackground()` with no arguments.

    **C.** Call `setBackground(null)`.

2. What annotation indicates that a method overrides the same method in a superclass?

    **A.** `@Super`

    **B.** `@Override`

    **C.** `@Inherited`

21

3. What color does the NetBeans source code editor give to the instance variables in a class?

  **A.** Green

  **B.** Blue

  **C.** Brown

## Answers

**1.** C. Calling `setBackground()` with the `null` value clears out the color, which in `Banko` is used to make a button stop being red or green and go back to the default color. Calling `setColor()` in a Swing component sets the foreground color, not the background.

**2.** B. The `@Override` annotation on the line above a method tells the Java compiler it overrides a method. Without the annotation, the compiler would have no way to check this and ensure that the method signature is correct.

**3.** A. Instance variables are green; keywords such as `class`, `void`, and `true` are blue; string literals are brown; and comments are gray.

# Certification Practice

The following question is the kind of thing you could expect to be asked on a Java programming certification test. Answer it without looking again at this lesson or using the Java compiler to test the code.

Given:

```java
public class CharCase {
    public static void main(String[] arguments) {
        float x = 9;
        float y = 5;
        char c = '1';
        switch (c) {
            case 1:
                x = x + 2;
            case 2:
                x = x + 3;
            default:
                x = x + 1;
        }
        System.out.println("Value of x: " + x);
    }
}
```

What will be the value of x when it is displayed?

**A.** `9.0`

**B.** `10.0`

**C.** `11.0`

**D.** The program will not compile.

The answer is available on the book's website, at www.java21days.com. Visit the Lesson 21 page and click the Certification Practice link.

# Exercises

To extend your knowledge of the subjects covered in this lesson, try the following exercises:

**1.** Add a class that saves the top 10 scores achieved in `Banko` and opens a dialog to take a player's name when a player makes the list. Have the class save the player name in the same file as the scores.

**2.** Add a Difficult? check box to the frame that doubles the number of buttons on the board to 18 rows and 28 columns the next time the user restarts the game.

Where applicable, exercise solutions are offered on the book's website, at www.java21days.com.

21

# PART IV

# Appendixes

# APPENDIX A
# Using the NetBeans Integrated Development Environment

Although it's possible to create Java programs with nothing more than the Java Development Kit (JDK) and any text editor, the experience is considerably more pleasant when you use an integrated development environment (IDE).

Most of this book employs Apache NetBeans, a free IDE for Java programmers that Oracle has transferred to the open source Apache Software Foundation. NetBeans is a program that makes it easier to organize, write, compile, and debug Java software. It includes a project and file manager, a graphical user interface designer, and many other tools. One killer feature is a code editor that automatically detects Java syntax errors as you type.

Now in version 11, NetBeans has matured into an excellent IDE, offering functionality and performance for free that used to be available only in commercial development tools for a hefty price. NetBeans also is one of the easiest IDEs for Java novices to use.

In this appendix, you'll install NetBeans and learn how to use it on projects created in this book.

# Installing NetBeans

From inauspicious beginnings, NetBeans has become one of the strongest programming tools for Java developers. James Gosling, creator of the Java language, wrote in the book *NetBeans Field Guide*, "I use NetBeans for all my Java development." After trying most of the IDEs available for the language over the years, I've become a convert as well.

NetBeans supports all facets of Java programming, including web application development, web services, Swing, JavaFX, and microservices.

You can download NetBeans, available for Windows, macOS, and Linux, from https://netbeans.apache.org. Click the Downloads link in the navigation menu to find the right installer file to download for your operating system.

If you have trouble finding the right version of NetBeans used in this book, visit the book's website, at www.java21days.com. There is a Download NetBeans link on the book's home page that steers you to the proper file.

When you have downloaded the NetBeans installer, run it to use an installation wizard that sets up the software.

**TIP**

> After you have installed NetBeans, you can use the IDE to get the latest version of the software when new versions are available. Choose the menu command Help, Check for Updates. (On Windows, you might need to run NetBeans as an administrator. To do this, right-click the NetBeans icon and choose Run as Administrator.)

# Creating a New Project

NetBeans is downloaded as an installation wizard that sets up the software on your system. You can install the software in any folder and menu group you like, but it's best to stick with the default setup options unless you have a good reason to do otherwise.

When you run NetBeans for the first time after installation, you see a start page that displays links to demos and programming tutorials (see Figure A.1). You can read them within the IDE by using NetBeans's built-in web browser.

**FIGURE A.1**
The NetBeans user interface.

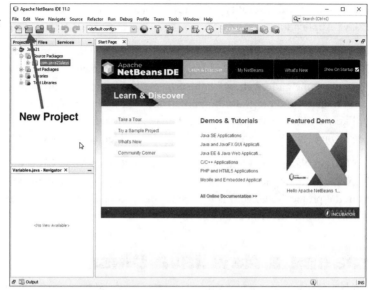

A NetBeans project consists of a set of related Java classes, files used by those classes, and Java class libraries. Each project has its own folder. You can explore and modify the files in the folder outside NetBeans by using text editors and other programming tools, as you can with any other Java source code you create outside NetBeans.

To begin a new project, click the New Project button shown in Figure A.1 or select the File, New Project menu command. The New Project Wizard opens, as shown in Figure A.2.

**FIGURE A.2**
The New Project Wizard.

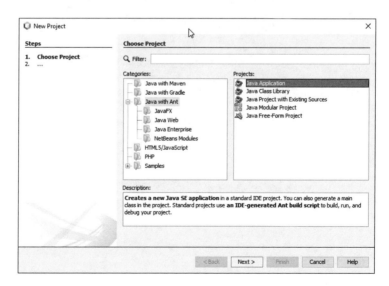

NetBeans can create several types of Java projects, but in this book you can focus on just one: Java Application.

For your first project (and most of the projects in this book), choose the category Java with Ant and the project type Java Application and then click Next. The wizard asks you to choose a name and location for the project. The Project Location text field identifies the root folder of the programming projects you create with NetBeans. In Windows, this most likely will be a subfolder of your Documents folder called NetBeansProjects. All projects you create are stored inside the project folder, each in its own subfolder.

In the Project Name text field, enter Java21. The Create Main Class text box changes in response to the input, recommending java21.Java21 as the name of the main Java class in the project. Change this to Spartacus, accept all the defaults, and click Finish. NetBeans creates the project and its first class.

## Creating a New Java Class

When NetBeans creates a new project, it sets up all the necessary files and folders and creates starting code for the main class. Figure A.3 shows the first class in your project, Spartacus.java, open in the source editor.

**FIGURE A.3**
The NetBeans source editor.

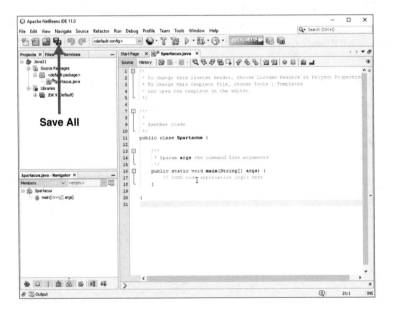

`Spartacus.java` is a bare-bones Java class that consists of only a `main()` method. All the light gray lines of code in the class are comments that explain the purpose and function of the class. Comments are ignored when the class is run.

To make the new class do something, add the following line of code on a new line right below the comment `// TODO code application logic here`:

```
System.out.println("I am Spartacus!");
```

The method `System.out.println()` displays a string of text—in this case, the sentence `I am Spartacus!`.

Be sure to enter this code exactly as it appears. After you ensure that you typed the line correctly and ended it with a semicolon, click the Save All toolbar button shown in Figure A.3 (or select the menu command File, Save All) to save the class.

**NOTE**
As you type, the source editor figures out what you're doing and pops up helpful information related to the `System` class, the `out` instance variable, and the `println()` method. You'll love this helpfulness later, but for now, try your best to ignore it.

Java classes must be compiled into an executable form called *bytecode* before you can run them. This bytecode will be run by an interpreter called the Java Virtual Machine (JVM). NetBeans tries to compile classes automatically. You also can manually compile this class in two ways:

- Choose the menu command Run, Compile File.
- Right-click `Spartacus.java` in the Projects pane to open a pop-up menu and then choose Compile File.

If NetBeans doesn't allow you to choose either option, it already has compiled the class automatically.

If the class does not compile successfully, a white exclamation point in a red circle appears next to the filename `Spartacus.java` in the Projects pane. To fix the error, compare what you've typed in the text editor to the full source code of `Spartacus.java`, shown in Listing A.1, and resave the file. The line numbers in Listing A.1 should not appear in your program; they're used in this book when describing how the code works. (Also, line 9 should have your own username in place of the word `User`.)

**LISTING A.1**    The Full Text of `Spartacus.java`

```
 1: /*
 2:  * To change this license header, choose License Headers in Project
       Properties.
 3:  * To change this template, choose Tools | Templates
 4:  * and open the template in the editor.
 5:  */
 6:
 7: /**
 8:  *
 9:  * @author User
10:  */
11: public class Spartacus {
12:
13:     /**
14:      * @param args the command line arguments
15:      */
16:     public static void main(String[] args) {
17:         // TODO code application logic here
18:         System.out.println("I am Spartacus!");
19:     }
20:
21: }
```

The class is defined in lines 11–21. Everything above lines 11 is a comment included by NetBeans in every new class when you choose Java Application as the project type. Comments help explain things about the program to humans reading the source code. The compiler ignores them.

# Running the Application

After you've created the Java application `Spartacus` and compiled it successfully, you can run it in the JVM within NetBeans in two ways:

- Choose Run, Run File.
- Right-click `Spartacus.java` in the Projects pane and choose Run File.

When you run a Java class, the `main()` method is called by the JVM. In the `Spartacus` class, the string `I am Spartacus!` appears in the Output pane, as shown in Figure A.4.

**FIGURE A.4**

Viewing program output in the NetBeans Output pane.

A Java class must have a `main()` method to be run. If you attempt to run a class that lacks a `main()` method, NetBeans responds with an error.

When you're finished reviewing the program's output, close the Output pane by clicking the X on the pane (in its upper-right corner). This makes the source editor larger so that more lines are displayed, which comes in handy when you are creating a program.

# Fixing Errors

Now that the `Spartacus` application has been written, compiled, and run, it's time to break something to get some experience with how NetBeans responds when things go terribly wrong. Like any other Java programmer, you'll soon get plenty of practice messing up things on your own, but pay attention here anyway.

Return to `Spartacus.java` in the source editor and remove the semicolon from the end of the line that calls `System.out.println()` (line 18 in Listing A.1). Even before you save the file, NetBeans spots the error and displays a red alert icon to the left of the line, as shown in Figure A.5.

Hover over the alert icon to see a dialog appear that describes the error NetBeans thinks it has spotted. In this situation, the error message is simple: `';' expected`.

The NetBeans source editor can identify many common programming errors and typos it detects as you write a Java program. The detection of an error stops the file from being compiled until the error has been fixed.

Put the semicolon back at the end of the line. The error icon disappears, and you can save and run the class again.

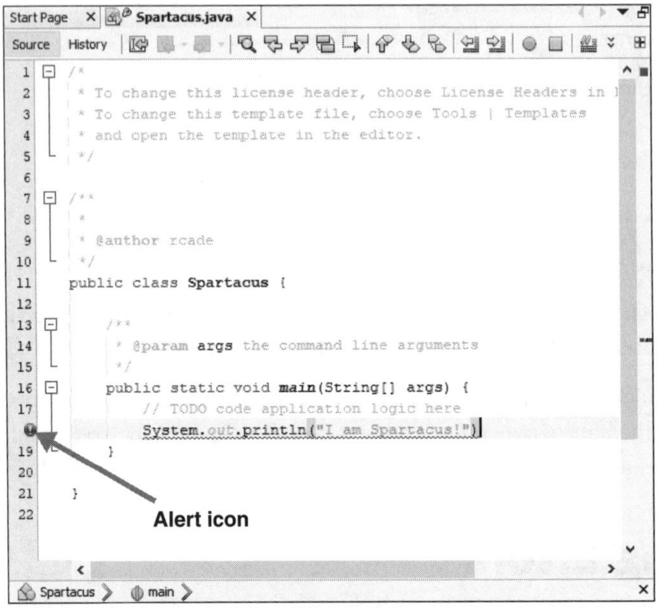

**FIGURE A.5**
Flagging errors in the source editor.

**Alert icon**

# Expanding and Shrinking a Pane

As you use NetBeans, several panes usually will be open at the same time, including the source editor, Projects pane, and Output pane. They all compete for a limited amount of space on the program's user interface.

You can make one pane take up the entire NetBeans interface by double-clicking the pane's tab.

To see this in action, double-click the tab `Spartacus.java` atop the source editor. The editor expands, giving you more room to view the source code and make changes, as shown in Figure A.6.

The other panes close and are listed vertically along the left edge of the pane. Figure A.6 lists four panes: Projects, Services, Files, and Navigator.

To shrink the source editor and go back to the normal appearance of NetBeans, double-click the tab `Spartacus.java` again.

**FIGURE A.6**
Editing source code
in a larger window.

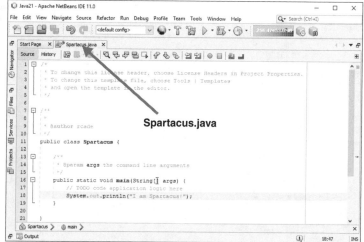

Spartacus.java

As you use NetBeans, it's common to accidentally expand a pane to fill the entire inter-face. You always can shrink it by double-clicking the pane's tab. There's also a Window drop-down in the main menu of NetBeans with commands to open and close each of the panes.

# Exploring NetBeans

The basic features of NetBeans described in this appendix are all you need to create and compile the Java programs in this book.

NetBeans is capable of a lot more than these basic features, but you should focus on learning Java before diving too deeply into the IDE. Use NetBeans as if it were just a simple programming project manager and text editor. Write classes, flag errors, and make sure you can compile and run each project successfully.

When you're ready to learn more about NetBeans, the Start page offers resources to learn how to use it. Oracle offers training and documentation resources at https://netbeans. apache.org/kb.

# APPENDIX B
# Fixing Package Not Visible Errors in NetBeans

Since Java 9, a new feature called *modules* enables Java programs to indicate which parts of the Java Class Library they require and what class packages they export.

Modules also can be used to access Java packages in the class library that aren't normally available. In Lesson 17, "Communicating Over HTTP," the experimental support for the new HTTP client was not usable in a programming project until the module `jdk.incubator.httpclient` was added to that project. This appendix covers what to do when a Java project in NetBeans experiences an error because a module is not available.

# Adding Module Info

The Java Class Library includes hundreds of packages. A small number of them are usable only when their module has been added to a project.

If you try to import a class or group of classes that are in a module that is not yet available, the `import` statement causes an error that is flagged in the NetBeans source code editor.

Here's an example of such a statement:

```
import jdk.incubator.http.*;
```

If this causes an error flagged by a red stop sign icon along the left edge of the source editor, hover over the icon to see the error message:

## Output ▼

```
Package jdk.incubator.http is not visible
(package jdk.incubator.http is declared in module
jdk.incubator.httpclient, which is not in the module
graph)
```

This error message reveals the name of the module that must be added to the project to resolve the problem. In this example, it's `jdk.incubator.http`.

Modules are set in a Java class called `module-info` in the default package (in other words, a class with no `package` statement at all).

Follow these steps to add a module to the `Java21` project in NetBeans:

**1.** Choose File, New File and then choose Java in the Categories pane.

**2.** In the File Types pane, choose Java Module Info.

**3.** Choose Java Module Info and then click Next.

**4.** The dialog displays the class name `module-info` and does not allow you to choose a package name. Click Finish.

The file `module-info.java` opens for editing in the source code editor. It only needs three statements of this form:

```
module Java21 {
    requires jdk.incubator.httpclient;
}
```

The `module` keyword is followed by `Java21` because that's the project's name. If you were adding a module to a different project, the statement would need to be revised accordingly.

Inside the `module` block within the { and } squiggly brackets, the `requires` keyword is followed by the module name `jdk.incubator.httpclient`. If your project requires a different module, edit this statement to reflect that.

A project can have more than one `requires` statement.

When the `module-info`.java file has been saved, the classes in the module (or modules) can be used by any Java program in the project. The `import` statements that add packages in that module will have no error, and the program can be compiled and run.

B

# APPENDIX C
# This Book's Website

As much as I'd like to think otherwise, there are undoubtedly things you're unclear about after completing the 21 lessons of this book. Programming is a specialized, technical field that throws strange concepts and jargon at new learners, such as "instantiation," "ternary operators," and "big- and little-endian byte order."

If you have a question about any topic covered in the book, visit the book's website, at www.java21days.com, for assistance. Click the cover matching this edition of the book to visit its site.

The book's website offers the following:

- **Error corrections and clarifications:** When errors are brought to my attention, they are described on the site with the corrected text and any other material that will help.

- **Answers to reader questions:** If readers have questions that aren't covered in this book's Q&A sections, they may be presented on the site.

- **Sample files:** The source code and class files for all the programs you create during the book are available.

- **Sample Java programs:** Working versions of the programs featured in this book are available.

- **End-of-chapter features:** Solutions, including source code, for activities suggested at the end of each lesson and the answers to each lesson's certification practice question are available.

- **Updated links to the sites mentioned in this book:** If sites mentioned in the book have moved to a new address, the new links are provided.

You also can email me by visiting the book's website. Click the Feedback link to go to a page where you can send email directly from the site. I also can be reached on Twitter at @rcade, where I can be contacted to talk about the book, Java programming, and a wide variety of other topics—including Minecraft, the Jacksonville Jaguars, Sheffield Wednesday, science fiction, and popes.

—Rogers Cadenhead

# APPENDIX D

# Using the Java Development Kit

Oracle offers the Java Development Kit (JDK), a free set of command-line programs that are used to create, compile, and run Java programs. Every new release of Java is accompanied by a new release of the development kit. The current version is JDK version 12.

Although NetBeans and other integrated development environments (IDEs) such as IntelliJ IDEA and Eclipse are more sophisticated, some programmers continue to use the Java Development Kit. This appendix covers how to download and install the JDK, set it up on your computer, and use it to create, compile, and run a simple Java program.

It also describes how to fix a common configuration problem faced by JDK users.

# Choosing a Java Development Tool

If you're using a Microsoft Windows or Apple macOS system, you may have a Java Virtual Machine (JVM) installed on your computer that can run Java programs.

To develop Java programs, you need more than a JVM. You also need a compiler and other tools that are used to create, run, and test programs.

The Java Development Kit includes a compiler, a JVM, a debugger, a file archiving program, and several other programs.

The JDK is simpler than other development tools. It does not offer a graphical user interface, text editor, or other features that many programmers rely on.

To use the kit, you type commands at a text prompt. MS-DOS, Linux, and UNIX users will be familiar with this prompt, which also is called a *command line*.

Here's an example of a command you might type while using the Java Development Kit:

```
javac MailRetriever.java
```

This command tells the `javac` program—the Java compiler included with the JDK—to read a source code file called `MailRetriever.java` and create one or more class files. These files contain compiled bytecode that the JVM can execute.

When `MailRetriever.java` is compiled, one of the files is named `MailRetriever.class`. If the class file was set up to function as an application, the JVM can run it.

People who are comfortable with command-line environments will be at home using the Java Development Kit. Everyone else must become accustomed to the lack of a graphical point-and-click environment as they develop programs.

If you have NetBeans or another Java development tool that is compatible with current versions of Java, you don't need to use the JDK. Many different development tools can be used to create the tutorial programs in this book.

## Installing the Java Development Kit

You can download the Java Development Kit from Oracle's Java website, at www.oracle.com/technetwork/java/javase.

The page's Downloads tab offers links to several versions of the Java Development Kit. It also offers the NetBeans development environment and other products related to the language. The product you should download is in the Java Standard Edition (Java SE) and is called JDK SE 12.0.

The kit is available for Windows, macOS, Linux, and Solaris SPARC systems.

When you're looking for this product, you might find that the Java Development Kit's version number has a number after 12, such as "JDK SE 12.0.1." To fix bugs and address security problems, Oracle periodically issues new releases of the kit and numbers them with a period and digit after the main version number. Choose the most current version of JDK 12 that's offered, whether it's numbered 12.0, 12.1, 12.2, or higher.

CAUTION

Take care not to download two similarly named products from Oracle by mistake: the Java Runtime Environment (JRE) 12.0 or the Java Standard Edition 12.0 Source Release.

To set up the kit, you must download and run an installation program. On the Oracle Java website, after you choose the version of the JDK that's designed for your operating system, you can download it as a single file.

Once you have downloaded the file, you are ready to set up the JDK.

## Windows Installation

To set up the program on a Windows system, double-click the installation file or use Search from the Windows Start menu to find and run the file.

·D

The installation wizard guides you through the process of installing the software. If you accept the terms and conditions for using the JDK, you'll be asked what parts of the kit to install. By default, the wizard installs all components of the JDK:

- **Development tools:** The executable programs needed to create Java software
- **Source code:** The source code for the thousands of classes that make up the Java Class Library
- **Public JRE:** A JVM you can distribute with the programs you create (also called a Java Runtime Environment)

You can save disk space by omitting everything except the program files. However, the source code and Java Runtime Environment can be useful, so it's a good idea to install them.

To prevent a component from being installed, click the hard drive icon next to its name and then choose the This Feature Will Not Be Available option.

After you choose the components to install, click the Next button to continue. You may be asked whether to set up the JRE. The wizard suggests a folder where the kit should be installed. To choose a different folder, click the Change button. Either select or create a new folder and click OK. The wizard returns to the Custom Setup options.

> **TIP**
>
> Before continuing, make note of the folder you have chosen. You'll need it later to configure the JDK and fix any configuration problems that may occur.

After you complete the configuration, the wizard installs the JDK on your system.

### macOS Installation

To set up the program on a macOS system, click the installation file, then click the package (.pkg) file that it opens.

The installation wizard guides you through the process of installing the software, asking a series of questions. Click Continue after answering each question.

When you complete these questions, the wizard installs the JDK on your system. You will be asked whether to move the installer file to the trash. It's OK to say yes since you won't need the wizard again.

# Configuring the Java Development Kit

After the wizard installs the JDK, you must edit your computer's environment variables to include references to the kit.

Experienced MS-DOS users can finish setting up the kit by adjusting one variable. Edit the computer's PATH variable and add a reference to the kit's bin folder (which is C:\ Program Files\Java\jdk-12.0.1\bin if you installed the kit into the C:\Program Files\Java\jdk-12.0.1 folder).

For Windows users unfamiliar with MS-DOS, later sections provide details on how to set the PATH variable on a Windows system.

On macOS there's no need to configure a Path variable. The installation wizard takes care of this.

Users of other operating systems should follow the instructions provided by Oracle on its JDK download page.

## Using a Command-Line Interface

The JDK requires the use of a command line to compile Java programs, run them, and handle other tasks.

A command line provides a way to operate a computer entirely by typing commands using the keyboard rather than by using the mouse. Very few programs designed for Windows or macOS users require the command line today.

To get to a command line in Windows, do the following:

- Type Command Prompt in the Search box.

- Choose Start, find the Search box, enter Command Prompt in the Search box, and click the Command Prompt icon.

- Choose Start, All Programs, Accessories, Command Prompt.

On macOS, the command line is called the Terminal. To find this program, click the Search icon—a magnifying glass—in the upper right corner next to the time. Search for Terminal.

When you open a command line in Windows, a new window opens, in which you can type commands, as shown in Figure D.1.

**FIGURE D.1**
Using a command-line window.

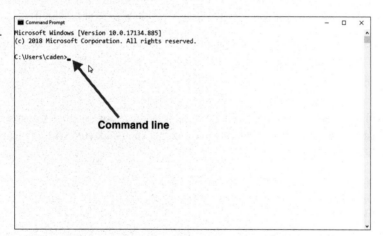

Command line

The command line in Windows uses commands adopted from MS-DOS, the Microsoft operating system that preceded Windows. MS-DOS supports many of the same functions as Windows—copying, moving, and deleting files and folders; running programs; scanning and repairing a hard drive; formatting a drive; and so on.

In the window, a cursor blinks on the command line whenever you can type in a new command. In Figure D.1, C:\Users\caden> is the command line.

Because MS-DOS can be used to delete files and even format your hard drive, you should learn something about the operating system before experimenting with its commands.

---

**NOTE**

If you'd like to learn a lot about MS-DOS, a good book is *Special Edition Using MS-DOS 6.22*, 3rd Edition (ISBN 978-0-78972-573-8), published by Que. The emphasis is on the words *a lot* because this book is 1,056 pages long.

---

However, you need to know only a few things about MS-DOS to use the JDK: how to create a folder, how to open a folder, and how to run a program.

## Opening Folders in MS-DOS

When you are using MS-DOS on a Windows system, you have access to all the folders you normally use in Windows. For example, if you have a `Users` folder on your C: hard drive, the same folder is accessible as `C:\Users` from a command line.

To open a folder in MS-DOS, type the command `cd`, followed by the name of the folder, and press Enter. Here's an example:

```
cd C:\Temp
```

When you enter this command, the `Temp` folder on your system's C: drive is opened, if it exists. After you open a folder, the command line is updated with the name of that folder, as shown in Figure D.2.

**FIGURE D.2**
Opening a folder in a command-line window.

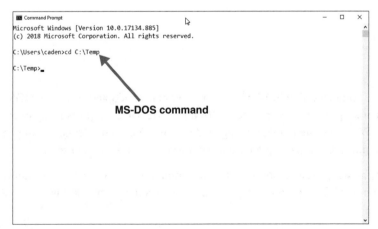

MS-DOS command

You also can use the CD command in other ways:

- Type CD \ to open the root folder on the current hard drive.
- Type CD *foldername* to open a subfolder matching the name you've used in place of *foldername*, if that subfolder exists.
- Type CD .. to open the folder that contains the current folder. For example, if you are in C:\Windows\Fonts, and you use the CD .. command, C:\Windows is opened.

It's helpful to create a folder for the projects you create in this book, such as one named J21work. If you already have done this, you can switch to that folder by using the following commands:

```
cd \
cd J21work
```

If you haven't created that folder yet, you can do so by using an MS-DOS command.

## Creating Folders in MS-DOS

To create a folder from a command line, type the command MD followed by the folder's name and press Enter, as in the following example:

```
md C:\Stuff
```

The Stuff folder is created in the root folder of the system's C: drive. To open a newly created folder, use the cd command followed by that folder's name, as shown in Figure D.3.

**FIGURE D.3**
Creating a new folder in a command-line window.

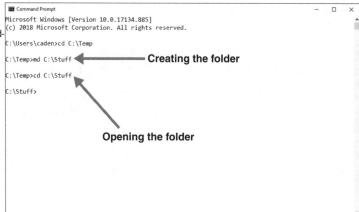

If you haven't already created a J21work folder, you can do so from a command line:

**1.** Change to the root folder (using the cd \ command).

**2.** Type the command md J21work and press Enter.

After J21work has been created, you can go to it at any time from a command line by using this command:

```
cd \J21work
```

The last thing you need to learn about MS-DOS to use the JDK is how to run programs.

## Running Programs in MS-DOS

The simplest way to run a program at the command line is to type its name and press Enter. For example, type dir and press Enter to see a list of files and subfolders in the current folder.

You also can run a program by typing its name followed by a space and some options that control how the program runs. These options are called *arguments*.

To see an example of this, change to the root folder (using cd \) and type dir J21work. You see a list of files and subfclsolders contained in the J21work folder, if it contains any.

After you have installed the JDK, run the JVM to see that it works. Type the following command at a command line:

```
java -version
```

java is the name of the JVM, and -version is an argument that tells it to display its version number.

You can see an example of this in Figure D.4, but your version number might be different, depending on what version of the kit you have installed.

If java -version works and you see a version number, it should begin with 12. Oracle sometimes tacks on a second number and maybe even third number, but as long as the version number begins with 12, you are using the correct version of the JDK.

If you see an incorrect version number or a "Bad command or filename" error after running java -version, you need to make some changes to how the JDK is configured on your system.

**FIGURE D.4**

Running the Java
Virtual Machine in
a command-line
window.

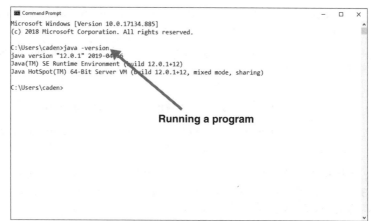

**Running a program**

# Correcting Configuration Errors

When you are writing Java programs for the first time, the most likely source of problems is not typos, syntax errors, or other programming mistakes. Most errors result from a misconfigured JDK.

If you type `java -version` at a command line, and your system can't find the folder that contains `java.exe`, you see one of the following error messages or something similar (depending on your operating system):

- `"Bad command or file name"`

- `"'java' is not recognized as an internal or external command, operable program, or batch file"`

To correct this, you must configure your system's `Path` variable.

## Setting the `Path` Variable on Most Windows Versions

On most versions of Windows, you configure the `Path` variable using the Environment Variables dialog, one of the features of the system's Control Panel.

To open this dialog on Windows, follow these steps:

**1.** Look for the Search box.

**2.** Type `Environment Variables` in the search box.

D

3. Click the search result Edit the System Environment Variables. The System Properties dialog opens, with the Advanced tab in front.

4. Click the Environment Variables button. The Environment Variables dialog opens, as shown in Figure D.5.

To open this dialog in other versions of Windows, follow these steps:

1. Right-click the Computer icon on your desktop or the Start menu and choose Properties. The System Properties dialog opens.

2. Click the Advanced tab or the Advanced System Settings link.

3. Click the Environment Variables button. The Environment Variables dialog opens, as shown in Figure D.5.

**FIGURE D.5**
Setting environment variables in Windows.

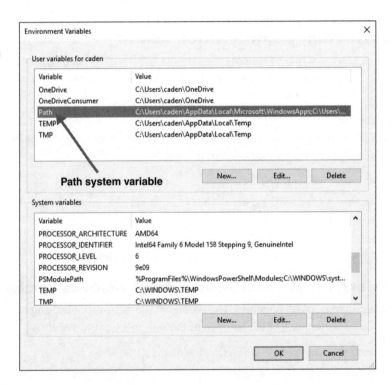

You can edit two kinds of environment variables: system variables, which apply to all users on your computer, and user variables, which apply only to you.

`Path` is a system variable that helps MS-DOS find programs when you run them at a command line. It contains a list of folders separated by semicolons.

To set up the JDK correctly, the folder that contains the Java Virtual Machine must be included in the path. The virtual machine has the filename `java.exe`. If you installed the JDK in the `C:\Program Files\Java\jdk-12.0.1` folder on your system, `java.exe` is in `C:\Program Files\Java\jdk-12.0.1\bin`.

If you can't remember where you installed the JDK, you can look for `java.exe` by using the Search box and typing the filename. You might find several copies in different folders. To see which one is correct, open a command-line window and do the following for each copy you have found:

**1.** Use the `cd` command to open a folder that contains `java.exe`.

**2.** Run the command `java -version` in that folder.

When you know the correct folder, return to the Environment Variables dialog, select `Path` in the User Variables list, and click Edit. The Edit Environment Variable dialog opens, with `Path` in the Variable Name field and a list of folders in the Variable Value field, as shown in Figure D.6.

**FIGURE D.6**
Changing your
system's `Path`
variable.

D

To add a folder to the `Path`, click an empty cell after the last variable in the table.

For example, if `C:\Program Files\Java\jdk-12.0.1\bin` is the correct folder, add the following text in the empty cell:

```
C:\Program Files\Java\jdk-12.0.1\bin
```

After making the change, click OK three times: once to close the Edit Environment Variable dialog, again to close the Environment Variables dialog, and a final time to close System Properties.

Try out the changed path: Open a command-line window and type the command `java -version`. If it displays the correct version of the JDK, your system is probably configured correctly, although you won't know for sure until you try to use the JDK later in this appendix.

# Using a Text Editor

Unlike more sophisticated Java development tools such as NetBeans, the Java Development Kit does not include a text editor to use when you create source files.

For an editor to work with the JDK, it must be able to save text files with no formatting.

This feature has different names in different editors. Look for a format option such as one of the following when you save a document or set the properties for a document:

- Plain text
- DOS text
- Text-only

On Windows, several editors are included with the operating system.

Windows Notepad is a no-frills text editor that works only with plain-text files. It can handle only one document at a time. On Windows, use the Search box and enter `Notepad`, then click the search result Notepad. On earlier versions of Windows, choose Start, Programs, Accessories, Notepad.

Windows WordPad is a step above Notepad. It can handle more than one document at a time and can handle both plain-text and Microsoft Word formats. It also remembers the last several documents it has worked on and makes them available from the File menu. It can be found or run like Notepad.

Linux and UNIX users can author programs with emacs, pico, and vi; Mac users have SimpleText or any of the previously mentioned UNIX tools available for Java source file creation.

One disadvantage of using simple text editors such as Notepad or WordPad is that they do not display line numbers as you edit.

Seeing the line number helps in Java programming because many compilers indicate the line number where an error occurred. Look at the following error generated by the JDK compiler:

```
Palindrome.java:21: Class Font not found in type declaration.
```

The number 21 after the name of the Java source file indicates the line that triggered the compiler error. With a text editor that supports numbering, you can go directly to that line and start looking for the error.

There are better ways to debug a program with a Java IDE environment such as NetBeans. But JDK users must search for compiler-generated errors using the line number indicated by the `javac` tool. This is one of the best reasons to move on to an advanced Java development program after learning the language with the JDK.

**TIP**

> Another alternative is to use the JDK with a programmer's text editor that offers line numbering and other features. One of the most popular for Java is jEdit, a free editor available for Windows, Linux, and other systems; see www.jedit.org.
>
> I use Brackets, an excellent open source text editor for programming and web design. To find out more and download the software, visit http://brackets.io.

D

# Creating a Sample Program

Now that you have installed and set up the JDK, you're ready to create a sample Java program to make sure it works.

Java programs begin as source code—a series of statements created using a text editor and saved as a text file. You can use any program you like to create these files, as long as it can save a file as plain, unformatted text.

The JDK does not include a text editor, but most other Java development tools include a built-in editor for creating source code files.

Load your editor of choice and enter the Java program shown in Listing D.1. Be sure to correctly enter all the parentheses, braces, brackets, and quotation marks in the listing, and capitalize everything in the program exactly as shown. If your editor requires a filename before you start entering anything, call it `HelloUser.java`.

**LISTING D.1**   Source Code of `HelloUser.java`

```
1: public class HelloUser {
2:     public static void main(String[] arguments) {
3:         String username = System.getProperty("user.name");
4:         System.out.println("Hello " + username);
5:     }
6: }
```

The line numbers and colons at the beginning of each line are not part of the program. They're included so that I can refer to specific lines by number in each program as you read this book. If you're ever unsure about the source code of a program in this book, you can compare it to a copy on the book's official website, at www.java21days.com.

After you finish typing in the program, save the file somewhere on your hard drive with the name `HelloUser.java`. Java source files must be saved with the extension `.java`.

> **TIP**
>
> If you have created a folder called `J21work`, you can save `HelloUser.java` in that folder. This makes it easier to find the file while using a command-line window.

If you're using Windows, a text editor might add an extra `.txt` file extension to the filename of any Java source files you save. For example, `HelloUser.java` could be saved as `HelloUser.java.txt`. As a workaround to avoid this problem, place quotation marks around the filename when saving a source file.

The purpose of this project is to test the JDK. None of the Java programming concepts used in the six-line `HelloUser` program are described in this appendix.

You learn the basics of the language during the first several lessons of the book. If you have figured out anything about Java simply by typing in Listing D.1 and making inferences from the code, it's your own fault.

## Compiling and Running the Program in Windows

Now you're ready to compile the source file with the JDK's Java compiler, a program called `javac`. The compiler reads a `.java` source file and creates one or more `.class` files that can be run by the JVM.

Open a command-line window and then open the folder where you saved `HelloUser.java`. If you saved the file in the `J21work` folder inside the root folder on your main hard drive, the following MS-DOS command opens the folder:

```
cd \J21work
```

When you are in the correct folder, you can compile `HelloUser.java` by entering the following at a command prompt:

```
javac HelloUser.java
```

Figure D.7 shows the MS-DOS commands used to switch to the `\J21work` folder and compile `HelloUser.java`.

**FIGURE D.7**

Compiling a Java program in a command-line window.

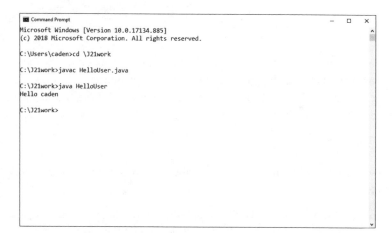

```
Command Prompt                                            —  □  ×
Microsoft Windows [Version 10.0.17134.885]
(c) 2018 Microsoft Corporation. All rights reserved.

C:\Users\caden>cd \J21work

C:\J21work>javac HelloUser.java

C:\J21work>java HelloUser
Hello caden

C:\J21work>
```

D

The JDK's compiler does not display a message if the program compiles successfully. If there are problems, the compiler tells you by displaying a message explaining each error along with the number of the line that triggered the error.

If the program compiles without any errors, a file called `HelloUser.class` is created in the same folder that contains `HelloUser.java`.

The class file contains the Java bytecode that the JVM will execute. If you get any errors, go back to your original source file and make sure that you typed it in exactly as it appears in Listing D.1.

When you have a class file, you can run that file by using the JVM. The kit's JVM is called `java`, and it also is run from the command line.

Run the `HelloUser` program by switching to the folder containing `HelloUser.class` and entering the following:

```
java HelloUser
```

You see the text `"Hello"` followed by a space and your username.

> **CAUTION**
>
> When running a Java class with the kit's JVM, don't specify the `.class` file extension after the class's name. If you do, you'll see an error such as the following:
>
> ```
> Exception in thread "main" java.lang.
> NoClassDefFoundError: HelloUser/class
> ```

This program was created and compiled using the normal process you can employ throughout the book. Java 11 introduced a simpler shortcut for single-file Java programs like `HelloUser.java`. You can skip the compilation and run the source code file directly, like this:

```
java HelloUser.java
```

The source code automatically is compiled into bytecode in memory and executed by the JVM.

Figure D.7 shows the successful output of the `HelloUser` application, along with the commands used to get to that point. If you can compile the program and run it successfully, your JDK is working, and you are ready to start Lesson 1, "Getting Started with Java."

If you cannot get the program to compile successfully even though you have typed it in exactly as it appears in the book, there's one last thing to try. Uninstall all versions of the JDK from your computer, reboot, and install the JDK again.

# APPENDIX E

# Programming with the Java Development Kit

Although the NetBeans IDE is easier for most new programmers learning Java, the Java Development Kit (JDK) also can be used throughout this book to create, compile, and run programs in the language.

The tools that make up the JDK contain numerous features that many programmers don't explore. Some of the tools themselves might be new to you. This appendix covers features of the kit that you can use to create and test Java programs.

# Overview of the JDK

Although you can use numerous IDEs to create Java programs, the most widely used may still be the JDK from Oracle, the set of command-line tools to develop software with the Java language.

There are two big reasons for the kit's popularity:

- It's free for development use. You can download a copy at no cost from the official Java website, at www.oracle.com/technetwork/java/javase.
- It's first. Whenever a new version of the language is released, the first tools that support the new version are in the kit.

The kit uses the command line. This also is called the MS-DOS prompt, command prompt, or console under Windows and the shell prompt under UNIX. You enter commands using the keyboard, as in this example:

```
javac VideoDB.java
```

This command compiles a Java program called `VideoDB.java` using the kit's compiler. The command has two elements: the name of the compiler, `javac`, and the name of the program to compile, `VideoDB.java`. A space separates the two elements.

Each kit command follows the same format: the name of the tool to use, followed by one or more elements indicating what the tool should do. These elements are called *arguments*.

The following illustrates the use of command-line arguments:

```
java VideoDB add DVD "Catch Me If You Can"
```

This command tells the Java Virtual Machine (JVM) to run a class file called `VideoDB` with three command-line arguments: the strings `add`, `DVD`, and `"Catch Me If You Can"`.

**NOTE**

> You might think there are more than three command-line arguments because of the spaces in the string `"Catch Me If You Can"`. The quotation marks around that string cause it to be considered one command-line argument, which makes it possible to include spaces in the argument.

Some arguments used with the JDK modify how a tool functions. These arguments are preceded by a hyphen character and are called *options*.

The following command shows the use of an option:

```
java -version
```

This command tells the JVM to display its version number rather than try to run a class file. It's a way to find out whether the kit is correctly configured to run Java programs on your system. Here's an example of the output run on a system equipped with Java 12:

## Output ▼

```
java version "12.0.1" 2019-04-16
Java(TM) SE Runtime Environment (build 12.0.1+12)
Java HotSpot(TM) 64-Bit Server VM (build 12.0.1+12, mixed mode, sharing)
```

In some instances, you can combine options with other arguments. For example, if you compile a Java class that uses deprecated methods, you can see more information on these methods by compiling the class with a `-deprecation` option, as in the following:

```
javac -deprecation OldVideoDB.java
```

# java, the Java Virtual Machine

The Java Virtual Machine, `java`, is used to run Java applications from the command line. It takes as an argument the name of a class file to run, as in the following example:

```
java BidMonitor
```

E

Although Java class files end with the `.class` extension, this extension is not specified when the JVM is used. The JVM also is called the *Java interpreter*.

The class loaded by the JVM must contain a class method called `main()` that takes the following form:

```
public static void main(String[] arguments) {
    // method here
}
```

A simple Java program might consist of only one class—the one containing the `main()` method. In more complex programs that use other classes, the JVM automatically loads any other classes that are needed.

The JVM runs bytecode, which is compiled instructions that the machine executes. After a Java program is saved in bytecode as a `.class` file, it can be run by different JVMs without modification. If you have compiled a Java program, it will be compatible with any JVM that fully supports Java.

As of Java 11, a single-file Java program can be run without being compiled into a class first. If `BidMonitor.java` is implemented entirely in that file, it can be run with this command:

```
java BidMonitor.java
```

**NOTE**    Interestingly, Java is not the only language that you can use to create Java bytecode. Closure, Groovy, Scala, Kotlin, JRuby, JPython, and other languages compile into `.class` files of executable bytecode through the use of compilers specific to those languages. Robert Tolksdorf maintains a list of these languages at http://vmlanguages.is-research.de.

You can specify the class file that the JVM will run in two different ways. If the class is not part of any package, you can run it by specifying the class's name, as in the preceding `java BidMonitor` example. If the class is part of a package, you must specify the class by using its full package and class name.

For example, consider an `ItemSeller` class that is part of the `org.cadenhead.auction` package. To run this application, you would use the following command:

```
java org.cadenhead.auction.ItemSeller
```

Each element of the package name corresponds to its own subfolder. The JVM looks for the `ItemSeller.class` file in several different places:

- The `org\cadenhead\auction` subfolder of the folder where the `java` command was entered (If the command was entered from the `c:\J21work` folder, for example, the `ItemSeller.class` file can be run successfully if it is in the `c:\J21work\org\cadenhead\auction` folder.)
- The `org\cadenhead\auction` subfolder of any folder in your `Classpath` setting

If you're creating your own packages, one way to manage them is to add a folder to your `Classpath` that's the root folder for any packages you create, such as `C:\javapackages` or something similar. After creating subfolders that correspond to the name of a package, place the package's class files in the correct subfolder.

You can specify a `Classpath` when running a Java application with the command line option `-cp`. Here's an example:

```
java -cp . org.cadenhead.auction.ItemSeller
```

This command sets the `Classpath` to `.`, which represents the current folder.

# The `javac` Compiler

The Java compiler, `javac`, converts Java source code into one or more class files of bytecode that a JVM can run.

Java source code is stored in a file with the `.java` file extension. This file can be created with any text editor that can save a document without any special formatting. The terminology varies depending on the text-editing software being used, but these files are often called plain text, ASCII text, or something similar.

A Java source code file can contain more than one class, but only one of the classes can be declared to be public. A class also can contain no public classes at all.

If a source code file contains a class that has been declared to be public, the filename must match the name of that class. For example, the source code for a public class called `ItemBuyer` must be stored in a file called `ItemBuyer.java`.

E

To compile a file, you run the `javac` tool with the name of the source code file as an argument, as in the following:

```
javac ItemBuyer.java
```

You can compile more than one source file by including each separate filename as a command-line argument, such as this command:

```
javac ItemBuyer.java ItemSeller.java
```

You also can use wildcard characters such as (`*`) and (`?`). Use the following command to compile all `.java` files in a folder:

```
javac *.java
```

When you compile one or more Java source code files, a separate .class file is created for each Java class that compiles successfully. One .class file is created for each class defined in the source file.

Another useful option when running the compiler is -deprecation, which causes the compiler to describe any deprecated methods that are being used in a Java program.

A deprecated method is one that has been replaced with a better alternative, either in the same class or in a different class. Although the deprecated method works, at some point Oracle may decide to remove it from the class. The deprecation warning is a strong suggestion to stop using that method as soon as you can.

Normally, the compiler issues a single warning if it finds any deprecated methods in a program. The -deprecation option causes the compiler to list each method that has been deprecated, as in the following command:

```
javac -deprecation ItemSeller.java
```

If you're more concerned with the speed of a Java program than the size of its class files, you can compile its source code with the -o option. This creates class files that have been optimized for faster performance. Methods that are static, final, or private might be compiled inline, a technique that makes the class file larger but causes the methods to be executed more quickly.

If you plan to use a debugger to look for bugs in a Java class, compile the source with the -g option to put all debugging information in the class file, including references to line numbers, local variables, and source code. (To keep all this out of a class, compile with the -g:none option.)

Normally, the Java compiler doesn't provide a lot of information as it creates class files. In fact, if the source code compiles successfully and no deprecated methods are used, you won't see any output from the compiler. No news is good news in this case.

If you want to see more information on what the javac tool is doing as it compiles source code, use the -verbose option. The verbose compiler describes how long it takes to complete different functions, the classes that are being loaded, and the overall time required.

# The javac **Documentation Tool**

The Java documentation creator, javadoc, takes a .java source code file or package name as input and generates detailed documentation in HTML format.

For `javadoc` to create full documentation for a program, a special type of comment statement must be used in the program's source code. Tutorial programs in this book use `//`, `/*`, and `*/` in source code to create *comments*—information for humans who are trying to make sense of the program.

Java also has a more structured type of comment that the `javadoc` tool can read. This comment is used to describe program elements such as classes, variables, objects, and methods. It takes the following format:

```
/** A descriptive sentence or paragraph.
 * @tag1 Description of this tag.
 * @tag2 Description of this tag.
 */
```

A Java documentation comment should be placed immediately above the program element it is documenting and should succinctly explain what the program element is. For example, if the comment precedes a `class` statement, it describes the class's purpose.

In addition to the descriptive text, different items can be used to document the program element further. These items, called *tags*, are preceded by an at sign (@) and are followed by a space and a descriptive sentence or paragraph.

Listing E.1 contains a documented version of the `QuoteData` application from Lesson 18, "Accessing Databases with JDBC and Derby." The following tags are used in this program:

- **`@author`:** This is the program's author. This tag can be used only when a class is documented. It is ignored unless the `-author` option is used when `javadoc` is run.

- **`@version text`:** This is the program's version number. This also is restricted to class documentation. It requires the `-version` option when you're running `javadoc`, or the tag will be ignored.

- **`@return text`:** This is the variable or object returned by the method being documented.

- **`@param name text`:** This is the variable name and description of an argument to a method.

E

**LISTING E.1**   The Full Text of `QuoteData.java`

```
 1: package com.java21days;
 2:
 3: import java.io.*;
 4: import java.net.*;
 5: import java.sql.*;
 6: import java.util.*;
 7:
 8: /**
 9:  * This class retrieves stock quote data from Yahoo Finance. The
        ticker
10:  * symbol of the stock to check is specified as a command-line
        argument
11:  * when the application is run.
12:  * @author <a href="http://www.java21days.com/">Rogers Cadenhead</a>
13:  * @version 1.0
14:  */
15: public class QuoteData {
16:     private final String ticker;
17:
18:     /**
19:      * Create a QuoteData object for the specified stock.
20:      * @param ticker The ticker symbol of the stock
21:      */
22:     public QuoteData(String ticker) {
23:         this.ticker = ticker;
24:     }
25:
26:     /**
27:      * Retrieve data from Yahoo for the stock.
28:      * @return The stock data as a string in CSV format.
29:      */
30:     private String retrieveQuote() {
31:         StringBuilder builder = new StringBuilder();
32:         try {
33:             URL page = new URL("http://quote.yahoo.com/d/quotes.csv?s=" +
34:                 ticker + "&f=sl1d1t1c1ohgv&e=.csv");
35:             String line;
36:             URLConnection conn = page.openConnection();
37:             conn.connect();
38:             InputStreamReader in = new InputStreamReader(
39:                 conn.getInputStream());
40:             BufferedReader data = new BufferedReader(in);
41:             while ((line = data.readLine()) != null) {
42:                 builder.append(line);
43:                 builder.append("\n");
44:             }
45:         } catch (MalformedURLException mue) {
46:             System.out.println("Bad URL: " + mue.getMessage());
47:         } catch (IOException ioe) {
```

```
48:                    System.out.println("IO Error:" + ioe.getMessage());
49:            }
50:            return builder.toString();
51:    }
52:
53:    /**
54:     * Store the stock's quote data in a Derby database.
55:     * @param data The CSV stock data to split into database fields.
56:     */
57:    private void storeQuote(String data) {
58:        StringTokenizer tokens = new StringTokenizer(data, ",");
59:        String[] fields = new String[9];
60:        for (int i = 0; i < fields.length; i++) {
61:            fields[i] = stripQuotes(tokens.nextToken());
62:        }
63:        String datasource = "jdbc:derby://localhost:1527/sample";
64:        try (
65:            Connection conn = DriverManager.getConnection(
66:                datasource, "app", "app");
67:            PreparedStatement prep2 = conn.prepareStatement("INSERT INTO " +
68:                "app.stocks(ticker, price, date, change, low, " +
69:                "high, priceopen, volume) " +
70:                "VALUES(?, ?, ?, ?, ?, ?, ?, ?)");
71:        ) {
72:            Class.forName("org.apache.derby.jdbc.ClientDriver");
73:            prep2.setString(1, fields[0]);
74:            prep2.setString(2, fields[1]);
75:            prep2.setString(3, fields[2]);
76:            prep2.setString(4, fields[4]);
77:            prep2.setString(5, fields[5]);
78:            prep2.setString(6, fields[6]);
79:            prep2.setString(7, fields[7]);
80:            prep2.setString(8, fields[8]);
81:            prep2.executeUpdate();
82:        } catch (SQLException | ClassNotFoundException oops) {
83:            System.out.println("Error: " + oops.getMessage());
84:        }
85:    }
86:
87:    /**
88:     * Remove quote marks from a string
89:     * @param input The input string.
90:     * @return The modified string.
91:     */
92:    private String stripQuotes(String input) {
93:        StringBuilder output = new StringBuilder();
94:        for (int i = 0; i < input.length(); i++) {
95:            if (input.charAt(i) != '\"') {
96:                output.append(input.charAt(i));
97:            }
98:        }
```

E

```
 99:            return output.toString();
100:        }
101:
102:        /**
103:         * The application's main method.
104:         * @param arguments An array with one element, a ticker symbol to
                 check.
105:         */
106:        public static void main(String[] arguments) {
107:            if (arguments.length < 1) {
108:                System.out.println("Usage: java QuoteData ticker");
109:                System.exit(0);
110:            }
111:            QuoteData app = new QuoteData(arguments[0]);
112:            String data = app.retrieveQuote();
113:            app.storeQuote(data);
114:        }
115: }
```

The following command creates HTML documentation from the source code file
QuoteData.java:

```
javadoc -author -version QuoteData.java
```

The Java documentation tool creates several different web pages in the same folder
as QuoteData.java. These pages document the program in the same manner used in
Oracle's official documentation for the Java Class Library.

| TIP | To see the official documentation for the Java Class Library version 12, visit https://docs.oracle.com/en/java/javase/12/docs. |
|---|---|

To see the documentation that javadoc has created for QuoteData, load the newly
created web page index.html on your web browser. Figure E.1 shows this page loaded
with Google Chrome.

**FIGURE E.1**
Java documentation for the `QuoteData` program.

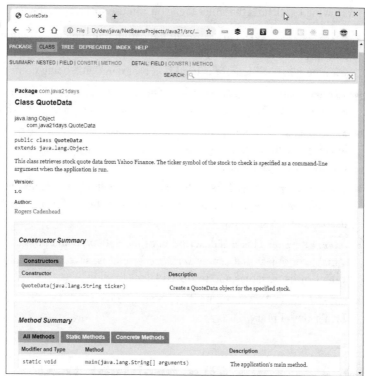

The `javadoc` tool produces extensively hyperlinked web pages. Navigate through the pages to see where the information in your documentation comments and tags shows up.

If you're familiar with HTML markup, you can use HTML tags such as `a`, `b`, and `i` within your documentation comments. Line 12 of the `QuoteData` program uses an `a` tag to turn the text `Rogers Cadenhead` into a hyperlink to this book's website.

The `javadoc` tool also can be used to document an entire package by specifying the package name as a command-line argument. HTML files are created for each `.java` file in the package, along with an HTML file indexing the package.

If you want the Java documentation to be produced in a different folder than the default, use the `-d` option followed by a space and the folder name. The following command creates Java documentation for `QuoteData` in a folder called `C:\JavaDocs\`:

```
javadoc -author -version -d C:\JavaDocs\ QuoteData.java
```

E

The following list details the other tags you can use in Java documentation comments:

- **@deprecated** *text*: This is a note indicating that the class, method, object, or variable has been deprecated. This causes the `javac` compiler to issue a deprecation warning when the feature is used in a program that's being compiled.

- **@exception** *class description*: This is a tag used with methods that throw exceptions. This tag documents the exception's class name and description.

- **@see** *class*: This is the name of another class, which will be turned into a hyperlink to the Java documentation for that class. This can be used without restriction in comments.

- **@see** *class#method*: This is the name of a method of another class, which will be used for a hyperlink directly to the documentation for that method. This can be used without restriction.

- **@serial** *text*: This is a description of the data type and possible values for a variable or object that can be *serialized*—that is, saved to disk along with the values of its variables and retrieved later.

- **@since** *text*: This is a note describing when a method or feature was added to Java's class library.

# The `jar` Java File Archival Tool

When you deploy a Java program, keeping track of all the class files and other files required by the program can be cumbersome.

To make this easier, the JDK includes a tool called `jar` that can pack all a program's files into a Java archive—also called a JAR file. The `jar` tool also can be used to unpack the files in one of these archives.

JAR files can be compressed using the Zip format or packed without using compression.

To use the tool, type the command `jar` followed by command-line options and a series of filenames, folder names, or wildcards.

The following command packs all of a folder's class and GIF image files into a single Java archive called `Animator.jar`:

```
jar cf Animator.jar *.class *.gif
```

The argument `cf` specifies two command-line options that can be used when running the `jar` program. The `c` option indicates that a Java archive file should be created, and `f` indicates that the name of the archive file will follow as one of the next arguments.

You also can add specific files to a Java archive with a command such as the following:

```
jar cf MusicLoop.jar MusicLoop.class muskratLove.mp3 shopAround.mp3
```

This creates a `MusicLoop.jar` archive containing three files: `MusicLoop.class`, `muskratLove.mp3`, and `shopAround.mp3`.

Run `jar` without any arguments to see a list of options that can be used with the tool.

# The jdb Debugger

`jdb`, the Java debugger, is a sophisticated tool that helps you find and fix bugs in Java programs. You also can use it to better understand what is taking place behind the scenes in the JVM as a program is running. It has many features, including some that might be beyond the expertise of a Java programmer who is new to the language.

You don't need to use the debugger to debug Java programs. This is obvious, especially if you've been creating your own Java programs as you read this book. After the Java compiler generates an error, the most common response is to load the source code into an editor, find the line cited in the error message, and try to spot the problem. You repeat this dreaded compile–curse–find–fix cycle until the program compiles without complaint.

After using this debugging method for a while, you might think that the debugger is unnecessary to the programming process because it's such a complicated tool to master. This reasoning makes sense when you're fixing problems that cause compiler errors. Many of these problems are simple things such as a misplaced semicolon, unmatched { and } braces, or the use of the wrong type of data as a method argument. However, when you start looking for logic errors—more subtle bugs that don't stop the program from compiling and running—a debugger is a valuable tool.

The Java debugger has two features that are useful when you're searching for a bug that can't be found by other means: single-step execution and breakpoints. Single-step execution pauses a Java program after every line of code is executed. Breakpoints are points where execution of the program pauses. Using the Java debugger, these breakpoints can be triggered by specific lines of code, method calls, or caught exceptions.

The Java debugger works by running a program using a version of the JVM over which it has complete control.

Before you use the Java debugger with a program, you compile the program with the `-g` option, which causes extra information to be included in the class file. This information

E

greatly aids in debugging. Also, you shouldn't use the -o option because its optimization techniques might produce a class file that does not directly correspond with the program's source code.

# Debugging Applications

If you're debugging an application, you can run the jdb tool with a Java class as an argument. This is shown in the following:

```
jdb Calculator
```

This example runs the debugger with Calculator.class, an application from Lesson 12, "Responding to User Input." Save copies of the files Calculator.class and Calculator. java in a folder (such as C:\Temp on Windows), open a command line, switch to that folder, and run jdb on the Calculator class with the preceding command.

Calculator is a Swing application that adds two numbers. The debugger loads this program but does not begin running it. It displays the following output:

## Output ▼

```
Initializing jdb...
>
```

You control the debugger by typing commands at the > prompt.

To set a breakpoint in a program, you use the stop in or stop at commands. The stop in command sets a breakpoint at the first line of a specific method in a class. You specify the class and method name as an argument to the command, as in the following example:

```
stop in Calculator.setLookAndFeel()
```

This command sets a breakpoint at the first line of the setLookAndFeel() method. Note that no arguments or parentheses are needed after the method name.

The stop at command sets a breakpoint at a specific line number within a class. You specify the class and number as an argument to the command, as in the following example:

```
stop at Calculator:23
```

If you're trying this with the `Calculator` class, you see the following output after entering this command:

## Output ▼

```
Deferring breakpoint Calculator:23
It will be set after the class is loaded.
```

You can set as many breakpoints as you want within a class. To see the breakpoints that are currently set, use the `clear` command without any arguments. The `clear` command lists all current breakpoints by line number rather than method name, even if they were set using the `stop in` command.

By using `clear` with a class name and line number as an argument, you can remove a breakpoint set on that line. Using `clear` with a class name and method name removes a breakpoint on that method. Here's an example of clearing a line breakpoint:

```
clear Calculator:23
```

Within the debugger, you can begin executing a program with the `run` command. The following output shows what the debugger displays after you begin running the `Calculator` class:

## Output ▼

```
run Calculator
VM Started: Set deferred breakpoint Calculator:23

Breakpoint hit: "thread=main", Calculator.main(), line=23 bci=413
23                  value1 = new JTextField("0", 5);
```

After you have reached a breakpoint in the `Calculator` class, experiment with the following commands:

- **list:** At the point where execution stopped, this command displays the source code of the line and several lines around it. This requires access to the `.java` file of the class where the breakpoint has been hit, so you must have `Calculator.java` either in the current folder or in one of the folders in your `Classpath`.
- **locals:** This command lists the values for local variables that are currently in use or will soon be defined.

E

- **print** *text*: This command displays the value of the variable, object, or array element specified by *text*.
- **step**: This command executes the next line and stops again.
- **cont**: This command continues running the program at the point where it was halted.
- **!!**: This command repeats the previous debugger command.

After trying out these commands within the application, you can resume running the program by clearing the breakpoint and using the **cont** command. Use the **exit** command to end the debugging session.

The **Calculator** application opens a graphical user interface. You can verify that this program ran successfully by using it to add two numbers to produce a result.

After you have finished debugging a program and you're satisfied that it works correctly, recompile it without the **-g** option.

## Advanced Debugging Commands

With the features you have learned about so far, you can use the debugger to stop execution of a program and learn more about what's taking place. This might be sufficient for many of your debugging tasks, but the debugger also offers many other commands, including the following:

- **up**: Moves up the stack frame so that you can use **locals** and **print** to examine the program at the point before the current method was called
- **down**: Moves down the stack frame so that you can examine the program after the method call

A Java program often has places where a chain of methods is called. One method calls another method, which calls another method, and so on. At each point where a method is being called, Java keeps track of all the objects and variables within that scope by grouping them. This grouping is called a *stack*, as if you were stacking these objects like a deck of cards. The various stacks in existence as a program runs are called the *stack frame*.

By using **up** and **down** along with commands such as **locals**, you can better understand how the code that calls a method interacts with that method.

You also can use the following commands within a debugging session:

- **classes**: This command lists the classes currently loaded into memory.
- **methods**: This command lists the methods of a class.

- **memory:** This command shows the total amount of memory and the amount that isn't currently in use.
- **threads:** This command lists the threads that are executing.

The `threads` command numbers all the threads. This enables you to use the `suspend` command followed by a number to pause that thread, as in `suspend 1`. You can resume a thread by using the `resume` command followed by the thread's number.

Another convenient way to set a breakpoint in a Java program is to use the `catch` *text* command, which pauses execution when the `Exception` class named by *text* is caught.

You also can cause an exception to be ignored by using the `ignore` *text* command with the `Exception` class named by *text*.

# Using System Properties

One handy feature of the JDK is that the command-line option `-D` can modify the performance of the Java Class Library.

If you have used other programming languages before learning Java, you might be familiar with environment variables, which provide information about the operating system in which a program is running. An example is the `Classpath` setting, which indicates the folders where the JVM should look for a class file.

Because different operating systems have different names for their environment variables, a Java program cannot read them directly. Instead, Java includes several different system properties that are available on any platform with a Java implementation.

E

Some properties are used only to get information. The following system properties are among those that should be available on any Java implementation:

- **java.version:** This is the version number of the JVM.
- **java.vendor:** This is a string identifying the vendor associated with the JVM.
- **os.name:** This is the operating system in use.
- **os.version:** This is the version number of that operating system.
- **file.separator:** This is the character that separates levels of a folder hierarchy in a filename on the operating system. It is \, /, or :, depending on whether you're using Windows, Linux and UNIX, or macOS.

Other properties can affect how the Java Class Library performs when being used inside a Java program. An example is the `java.io.tmpdir` property, which defines the folder that Java's input and output classes use as a temporary workspace.

You can set a property at the command line by using the `-D` option followed by the property name, an equals sign, and the property's new value, as in this command:

```
java -Duser.timezone=Asia/Jakarta Auctioneer
```

The use of the system property in this example sets the default time zone to Asia/Jakarta before running the `Auctioneer` class. This affects any `Date` objects in a Java program that do not set their own zone.

These property changes are not permanent; they apply only to that particular execution of the class and any classes it uses.

**TIP**

In the `java.util` package, the `TimeZone` class includes a class method called `getProperties()` that returns a string array containing all the time zone identifiers that Java supports. The following code displays these identifiers:

```
String[] ids = java.util.TimeZone.getAvailableIDs();

for (int i = 0; i < ids.length; i++) {

    System.out.println(ids[i]);

}
```

You also can create your own properties and read them by using the `getProperty()` method of the `System` class, which is part of the `java.lang` package.

Listing E.2 contains the source code of `ItemProp`, a simple program that displays the value of a user-created property.

**LISTING E.2**    The Full Text of `ItemProp.java`

```
1: class ItemProp {
2:     public static void main(String[] arguments) {
3:         String n = System.getProperty("item.name");
4:         System.out.println("The item is named " + n);
5:     }
6: }
```

If you run this program without setting the `item.name` property on the command line, the output is the following:

## Output ▼

### The item is named null

You can set the `item.name` property by using the `-D` option, as in this command:

```
java -Ditem.name="Microsoft Bob" ItemProp
```

The output is the following:

## Output ▼

```
The item is named Microsoft Bob
```

The `-D` option is used with the JVM.

# Writing Java Statements in a Shell

As you're learning Java for the first time or using a new class from the Java Class Library, you might want to try a few lines of code to better understand how something works. Perhaps you want to call a class method with different arguments, create an object and call one of its methods, or run a loop on a data structure.

The usual way to do these experiments for most of Java's existence was cumbersome. You had to create a simple single-file Java class for temporary purposes—I always call mine `Temp.java`—and put a few lines of code in it to compile and execute. My computer is littered with these little classes that I forget to delete when they're no longer needed.

Since Java 9, the JDK now includes JShell, a tool that lets you write Java code and view its output instantly. To see it in action, type this at a command line:

```
jshell
```

JShell runs, displaying its version number and a line of help text:

## Output ▼

```
Welcome to JShell -  version 12.0.1
For an introduction type: /help intro
jshell>
```

E

The last line is a command prompt that blinks for user input. You can type any valid Java statement and see the output that it produces. For example, type in the statement `Math.random();` and you get the following output with a different floating-point value:

```
jshell> Math.random();
$1 ==> 0.26142932910043104
```

The `random()` method of the `java.lang.Math` class returns a random floating-point number from 0.0 to 1.0. (It's more accurately described as pseudo-random for reasons that aren't necessary to cover here.) The output is preceded by a line that has a dollar sign ($) in front of a number.

You can use `Math.random()` as part of some Java code to generate a random roll of dice, but it takes a little practice the first time you try out the class. JShell is a convenient place to work this out.

In the real world, every die has a specified number of faces, such as 4, 6, 8, 12, or 20. Here, let's make it a six-sided die and multiply the random number by 6 in the shell:

```
jshell> Math.random() * 6;
$2 ==> 1.6161030592507815;
```

The dollar-sign numbering continues, this time incrementing to 2.

The output is now higher than 1, which shows that the number is no longer from 0.0 to 1.0, but it's not a value that's possible on a six-sided die because of all those numbers after the decimal point.

There's another `Math` method called `floor()` that rounds a number down to the closest integer. Let's try it and add 1 to the result:

```
jshell> Math.floor(Math.random() * 6) + 1;
$3 ==> 5.0;
```

Now this is a number that looks like a six-sided die roll. The 1 is added because `floor()` rounds down to 0 for any number lower than 1.0.

Use JShell to run the same code two more times:

```
jshell> Math.floor(Math.random() * 6) + 1;
$4 ==> 1.0;
jshell> Math.floor(Math.random() * 6) + 1;
$5 ==> 3.0;
```

A 1.0 and a 3.0 also are valid values on the die roll. But the numbers are integer values with a decimal digit. You can employ casting to get rid of the unnecessary decimal by converting the method's return value to an `int`:

```
jshell> (int) Math.floor(Math.random() * 6) + 1;
$6 ==> 4;
```

JShell makes it easy to kick the tires on some code to get the syntax and usage right interactively instead of waiting to see a compiled Java program run before learning if you are writing some new code correctly.

This tool is called a REPL, which stands for Read–Evaluate–Print–Loop. A REPL is something that programmers in other languages got so accustomed to having around that it became a part of the JDK.

There's a lot more you can do in JShell. Oracle offers full documentation at `https://docs.oracle.com/javase/9/jshell/introduction-jshell.htm`.

To exit the shell, type this command:

```
jshell> /exit
```

E

# Index

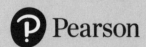